College Reading & Study Skills

TENTH EDITION

Kathleen T. McWhorter
Niagara County Community College

PEARSON
Longman

New York   San Francisco   Boston
London   Toronto   Sydney   Tokyo   Singapore   Madrid
Mexico City   Munich   Paris   Cape Town   Hong Kong   Montreal

Acquisitions Editor: Melanie Craig
Development Editor: Gillian Cook
Senior Supplements Editor: Donna Campion
Media Supplements Editor: Jenna Egan
Marketing Manager: Thomas DeMarco
Project Coordination, Text Design, and Electronic Page Makeup: Thompson Steele, Inc.
Cover Design Manager/Cover Designer: John Callahan
Cover Photo: Top left, top right, and bottom right: Images courtesy of istockphoto.
        Bottom left image: Courtesy of Getty Images, Inc.
Photo Researcher: Jody Potter
Manufacturing Buyer: Roy L. Pickering, Jr.
Printer and Binder: Quebecor World Dubuque
Cover Printer: Phoenix Color Corporation

For permission to use copyrighted material, grateful acknowledgment is made to the copyright holders on pp. 533–537 , which are hereby made part of this copyright page.

Visit us at www.ablongman.com

ISBN 0-321-36478-3

12345678910—QWD—09 08 07 06

BRIEF CONTENTS

DETAILED CONTENTS

PREFACE

Beginning college students require a foundation in reading and study skills that will enable them to handle college-level work. *College Reading and Study Skills,* Tenth Edition, presents the basic techniques for college success, including time management, analysis of learning style, active reading, and note taking. The text offers strategies for strengthening literal and critical comprehension, improving vocabulary skills, and developing reading flexibility. Students also discover methods for reading and learning from textbook assignments, including outlining and summarizing, and for taking exams. The reading and study skills I have chosen to present are those most vital to students' success in college. Each unit teaches skills that are immediately usable—all have clear and direct application to students' course work.

More than 30 years of teaching reading and study courses in two- and four-year colleges have demonstrated to me the need for a text that covers both reading and study skills and provides for both instruction and application. This book was written to meet those needs.

Reading and study skills are inseparable. A student must develop skill in each area in order to handle college work successfully. With this goal in mind, I have tried to provide complete coverage of both skills throughout and to show their relationship and interdependency. In doing so, my emphasis has been on direct instruction. My central aim is to teach reading and study through a how-to approach.

Because I believe that critical thinking and reading skills are essential to college success, these skills are emphasized in the text. I introduce students to critical thinking skills by explaining Bloom's hierarchy of cognitive skills early and then showing their academic application throughout the text. *College Reading and Study Skills* offers direct skill instruction on critical reading and includes key topics such as making inferences, asking critical questions, analyzing arguments, and evaluating Internet sources.

CONTENT OVERVIEW

The units of the text are interchangeable, which enables the instructor to adapt the material to a variety of instructional sequences.

Success Workshops Appearing at the beginning of the text, the Success Workshops use a fun, lively, and accessible format to provide students with skills that will directly and immediately contribute to their college success. Topics include acclimation to the college environment, textbook parts and learning aids, academic image, class participation, concentration, collaborative learning, stress management, learning from feedback, academic integrity, and a vocabulary learning system.

Part One: Building a Foundation for College Success This section provides an introduction to the college experience and presents skills, habits, and attitudes that contribute to college success. Topics include time management and goal setting, learning style, teaching style, active learning, levels of thinking, and the demands and expectations of college. Chapter 3 in this section establishes the theoretical framework of the text by discussing the learning and memory processes and the principles on which many of the skills presented throughout the text are based. Because lecture note taking is integral to college success, it is included in this section, as well.

Part Two: Reading Textbooks and Assignments This section focuses on the development of reading skills for textbook usage. Topics include monitoring concentration, prereading and predicting, defining purposes for reading, and comprehension assessment. Paragraph structure is explained and recognition of thought patterns introduced. Strategies for reading graphics and technical material are presented.

Reading and evaluating electronic sources, including how to adapt reading strategies for online sources and how to avoid cyberplagiarism, are discussed in depth.

Part Three: Critical Reading and Thinking Critical thinking and reading skills are emphasized. Chapter 10 guides students in evaluating an author's message. Topics include making inferences, distinguishing between fact and opinion, recognizing tone, and analyzing arguments. Chapter 11 focuses on evaluating an author's techniques including connotative and figurative language, generalizations, assumptions, and manipulative language.

Part Four: Developing Your Vocabulary This section teaches students how to expand their vocabulary and use reference sources, including the dictionary and the thesaurus. Students are shown methods of learning specialized vocabulary and discover systems for vocabulary learning. Vocabulary skills include contextual aids and structural analysis.

Part Five: Studying Textbooks These chapters teach skills that enable students to learn from text: how to highlight and mark a textbook; how to organize a system of study for various academic disciplines; and how to organize information using outlining, summarizing, and mapping. Methods of learning through writing—paraphrasing, self-testing, and keeping a learning journal—are described.

Part Six: Studying for Exams The purpose of this section is to help students prepare for and take exams. Organizing for study and review, identifying what to study, and methods for review are emphasized. Students learn specific strategies for taking objective tests, standardized tests, and essay exams, as well as for controlling test anxiety.

Part Seven: Reading Flexibility Rate improvement is the focus of this section. Students learn to adjust their rate to suit their purpose, the desired level of comprehension, and the nature of the material they are reading. Specifically, students learn methods for skimming and scanning.

Part Eight: Thematic Readings This section contains 12 readings, grouped according to four themes: body adornment (sociology/cultural anthropology), men's and women's communication (communication), controversies in science (biology/environmental science), and civil liberties (government/political science). These readings, which represent readings that may be assigned in academic courses, provide students with an opportunity to apply skills taught throughout the text. Two activities at the end of each theme, Making Connections and World Wide Web Activity, encourage students to synthesize ideas and develop Internet search skills.

Part Nine: Sample Textbook Chapter A sample textbook chapter, taken from an interpersonal communication college text, titled "Culture and Interpersonal Communication," comprises Part Nine. This chapter allows students to work with actual textbook material to apply skills taught throughout the text.

SPECIAL FEATURES

The following features enhance the text's effectiveness and directly contribute to students' success:

- **Visual Appeal** The text recognizes that many students are visual learners and presents material visually, using maps, charts, tables, and diagrams.
- **Learning Style** The text emphasizes individual student learning styles and encourages students to adapt their reading and study techniques to suit their learning characteristics, as well as the characteristics of the learning task.
- **Reading as a Process** This text emphasizes reading as a cognitive process. Applying the findings from the research areas of metacognition and prose structure analysis, students are encouraged to approach reading as an active mental process of selecting, processing, and organizing information to be learned.

- **Metacognition** Students are encouraged to establish their concentration, activate prior knowledge, define their purposes, and select appropriate reading strategies prior to reading. They are also shown how to strengthen their comprehension, monitor that comprehension, select what to learn, and organize information. They learn to assess the effectiveness of their learning, revise and modify their learning strategies as needed, and apply and integrate course content.
- **Skill Application** Students learn to problem-solve and explore applications through case studies of academic situations included at the end of each chapter. The exercises are labeled "Academic Applications." Students also apply chapter skills when completing the "Collaborative Learning" exercise included at the end of each chapter.
- **Internet-based Activities** The text recognizes the growing importance of the Internet as a learning and research tool. Chapter 9 focuses on locating and evaluating Internet sources. Activities are included at the end of each chapter, as part of the Multimedia Activities page, that encourage students to explore the Internet as an information source. Web activities are also provided for each set of thematic readings.
- **Learning Experiments/Learning Principles** Each chapter begins with an interactive learning experiment designed to engage the student immediately in an activity that demonstrates a principle of learning that will help students learn the chapter content. The student begins the chapter by doing, not simply by beginning to read. For example, Chapter 5, "Active Reading Strategies," begins by asking students to draw the face of a one-dollar bill. Most students quickly discover their recall is poor. The learning principle of *intent to remember* is then introduced and related to textbook learning. Students discover that in order to learn textbook material they must establish an intent to remember, and they are encouraged to use the skills presented in the chapter to do so.
- **Chapter Focus and Purpose Questions** Each chapter opens with a question that models the question students commonly ask before beginning an assigned chapter: Why should I learn this? Following each question are several answers that establish the importance and relevance of the skills taught in the chapter.
- **Interactive Assignments** The Success Workshops, the learning experiments at the beginning of each chapter, and the new multimedia activities at the end of each chapter all engage the student and function as interactive learning opportunities.
- **Writing to Learn** The text emphasizes writing as a means of learning. Writing-to-learn strategies include paraphrasing, self-testing, outlining, summarizing, mapping, and keeping a learning journal.
- **Realistic Reading Assignments** Exercises often include excerpts from a wide range of college texts, providing realistic examples of college textbook reading.
- **Thematic Readings** Twelve readings, grouped according to four themes, are contained in Part Eight. These readings provide realistic materials on which to apply skills taught in the text. They also provide students with an essential link between in-chapter practice exercises and independent application of new techniques in their own textbooks, and valuable practice in synthesizing and evaluating ideas.
- **Multimedia Activities** Each chapter concludes with a group of multimedia activities intended to enhance and extend chapter content. The activities are engaging and interactive, and they demonstrate practical uses of the chapter content. For example, the multimedia activities in Chapter 10, "Evaluating the Author's Message," give students the opportunity to sharpen their critical thinking skills on a brain teasers and puzzles Web site, try an online tutorial on critical reasoning at the Metropolitan Community College of Nebraska, evaluate a television program or movie for evidence of characters using critical thinking skills, or work collaboratively with a classmate to structure an argument.
- **Chapter Summaries** The chapter summaries use an interactive question-answer format that encourages students to become more active learners.

- **Quick Quizzes**   A ten-item multiple choice quick quiz is included at the end of each chapter. Each quiz assesses mastery of chapter content, provides students with feedback on their learning, and prepares students for further evaluation conducted by their instructor.

NEW TO THE TENTH EDITION

The tenth edition of this text includes changes and additions that reflect the changes in student needs, skill levels, and interests. It also takes into account current emphases and directions in research on adult learning processes. The primary purposes of the revision are to increase the coverage of critical reading and thinking skills, and to address the importance of students applying the skills they learn to all their academic courses. Specific changes include the following:

- **Revised, Expanded Coverage of Learning and Memory Techniques**   Chapter 3 has been revised and updated to focus more exclusively on memory strategies and the practical application of skills.
- New **Part Three: Critical Reading and Thinking**   A second critical reading and thinking chapter has been added to the text, creating a new part and providing additional coverage of the crucial skills needed for critical reading and thinking. The existing Chapter 10, now titled "Evaluating the Author's Message," covers skills that enable students to evaluate an author's message: making inferences, evaluating sources, assessing an author's qualifications, distinguishing between fact and opinion, identifying an author's purpose, recognizing bias, analyzing tone, evaluating data and evidence, and analyzing arguments.
- New **Chapter 11: "Evaluating the Author's Techniques"**   This new chapter focuses on the skills writers use to convey their message. Topics covered include understanding connotative language, examining figurative language, watching for omissions, understanding generalizations, examining a writer's assumptions, and identifying manipulative language.
- New **Section on Word Mapping**   A new section on word mapping has been added to Chapter 13, "Expanding Your Vocabulary." Word mapping encourages intensive word study and provides a visual approach to vocabulary development.
- New **Sample Textbook Chapter**   A sample textbook chapter, titled "Culture and Interpersonal Communication," taken from an interpersonal communication college text, makes up Part Nine of the text. This representative but accessible chapter can be used at the instructor's discretion for practice and application of skills. It is also designed for use with the new Textbook Application Exercises that appear in most chapters.
- New **Textbook Application Exercises**   A new exercise, "Applying Your Skills: Sample Textbook Chapter," has been added to most chapters. This exercise directs students to apply skills taught in the chapter to the sample textbook chapter in Part Nine.
- **Revised Thematic Readings**   Part Eight of the book contains 12 readings, grouped according to four themes. One theme has been replaced with a new one—controversies in science. The readings in it address global warming, stem-cell therapy, and depletion of the earth's natural resources. The civil liberties theme has two new readings that reflect current concerns and issues. One reading examines workplace discrimination based on personal appearance. The other considers the issue of personal privacy as it relates to the proliferation of surveillance technology.
- **Revised Quick Quizzes**   The Quiz Quizzes that provide a review of chapter content have been revised. Questions 1–5 now focus on factual content, and Questions 6–10 focus on application of skills.

- **Open-ended Discussion Questions**   In each chapter, the Quick Quizzes are preceded by several discussion questions related to chapter content. These questions stimulate thought and provoke critical thinking and application of skills.
- **Updated Multimedia Activities**   The Multimedia Activities at the end of each chapter have been updated and new Web sites and activities have been added.

THE TEACHING AND LEARNING PACKAGE

Book-Specific Ancillary Materials

- **Assessment Package/Test Bank**   An assessment package/test bank accompanies the text. It contains both content-based chapter quizzes and newly developed self-scoring mastery tests that enable students to apply skills taught in each chapter. The ten-item multiple choice quizzes provide a measure of students' knowledge of chapter content, and the mastery tests provide an assessment of students' ability to apply concepts, principles, and techniques taught in the chapter. The mastery tests simulate actual academic situations, assignments, and course materials and are designed to be self-scoring, if the instructor so desires. ISBN 0-321-10453-6
- **Instructor's Manual**   An instructor's manual gives the instructor a detailed description of the text and offers specific suggestions for classroom use. It includes a complete answer key, strategies for approaching individual chapters, a set of overhead projection materials, and suggestions for integrating the many available Longman ancillaries (including electronic ancillaries) into the classroom. ISBN 0-321-10452-8
- **Companion Website**   A dedicated Website to accompany the McWhorter reading and study skills series is available to instructors and students. This Website, prepared by Gretchen Starks-Martin, includes study tips, electronically scored quizzes and tests, Internet activities and links, a bulletin board, and more. Please visit the site at http://www.ablongman.com/mcwhorter.
- *Vocabulary Simplified*   Instructors may choose to shrink-wrap *College Reading and Study Skills* with a copy of *Vocabulary Simplified*. This book, written by Kathleen McWhorter, works well as a supplemental text providing additional instruction and practice in vocabulary. Students can work through the book independently, or units may be incorporated into weekly lesson plans. Topics covered include methods of vocabulary learning, contextual aids, word parts, connotative meanings, idioms, euphemisms, and many more interesting and fun topics. The book concludes with vocabulary lists and exercises representative of eleven academic disciplines. To preview this book, contact your Longman sales consultant for an examination copy.

In addition to these book-specific supplements, many other skills-based supplements and testing packages are available for both instructors and students. All these supplements are available either at no additional cost or at greatly reduced prices.

THE LONGMAN DEVELOPMENTAL ENGLISH PACKAGE

Longman is pleased to offer a variety of support materials to help make teaching reading easier on teachers and to help students excel in their coursework. Contact your local Longman sales representative for more information on pricing and how to create a package with *College Reading and Study Skills,* Tenth Edition.

Support Materials for Reading and Study Skills Instructors

Printed Test Bank for Developmental Reading (Instructor / ISBN 0-321-08596-5)
Offers more than 3,000 questions in all areas of reading, including vocabulary, main idea,

supporting details, patterns of organization, critical thinking, analytical reasoning, inference, point of view, visual aids, and textbook reading.

Electronic Test Bank for Developmental Reading (Instructor / CD ISBN 0-321-08179-X)
Offers more than 3,000 questions in all areas of reading, including vocabulary, main idea, supporting details, patterns of organization, critical thinking, analytical reasoning, inference, point of view, visual aids, and textbook reading. Instructors simply choose questions, then print out the completed test for distribution or offer the test online.

The Longman Guide to Classroom Management (Instructor / ISBN 0-321-09246-5)
This guide is designed as a helpful resource for instructors who have classroom management problems. It includes helpful strategies for dealing with disruptive students in the classroom and the do's and don'ts of discipline.

The Longman Guide to Community Service-Learning in the English Classroom and Beyond (Instructor / ISBN 0-321-12749-8)
Written by Elizabeth Rodriguez Kessler of California State University–Northridge, this monograph provides a definition and history of service-learning, as well as an overview of how service-learning can be integrated effectively into the college classroom.

The Longman Instructor's Planner (Instructor / ISBN 0-321-09247-3)
This planner includes weekly and monthly calendars, student attendance and grading rosters, space for contact information, Web references, an almanac, and blank pages for notes.

For Students

Vocabulary Skills Study Card (Student / ISBN 0-321-31802-1)
Colorful, affordable, and packed with useful information, Longman's Vocabulary Study Card is a concise, eight-page reference guide to developing key vocabulary skills, such as learning to recognize context clues, reading a dictionary entry, and recognizing key root words, suffixes, and prefixes. This Study Card is laminated for durability, so students can keep it for years to come and pull it out whenever they need a quick review.

Reading Skills Study Card (Student / ISBN 0-321-33833-2)
Colorful, affordable, and packed with useful information, Longman's Reading Skills Study Card is a concise, eight-page reference guide to help students develop basic reading skills, such as concept skills, structural skills, language skills, and reasoning skills. This Study Card is laminated for durability, so students can keep it for years to come and pull it out whenever they need a quick review.

The Longman Textbook Reader, Revised Edition (with answers Student / ISBN 0-321-11895-2 or without answers Student / ISBN 0-321-12223-2)
Offers five complete chapters from our textbooks: computer science, biology, psychology, communications, and business. Each chapter includes additional comprehension quizzes, critical thinking questions, and group activities.

The Longman Reader's Portfolio and Student Planner (Student / ISBN 0-321-29610-9)
This unique supplement provides students with a space to plan, think about, and present their work. The portfolio includes a diagnostic area (including a learning-style questionnaire), a working area (including calendars, vocabulary logs, reading response sheets, book club tips, and other valuable materials), and a display area (including a progress chart, a final table of contents, and a final assessment), as well as a daily planner for students including daily, weekly, and monthly calendars.

***The Longman Reader's Journal*, by Kathleen McWhorter (Student / ISBN 0-321-08843-3)**
The first journal for readers, *The Longman Reader's Journal* offers a place for students to record their reactions to and questions about any reading.

The Longman Planner (Student / ISBN 0-321-04573-4)
Ideal for organizing a busy college life! Included are hour-by-hour schedules, monthly and weekly calendars, an address book, and an almanac of tips and useful information.

10 Practices of Highly Effective Students (Student / ISBN 0-205-30769-8)
This study skills supplement includes topics such as time management, test taking, reading critically, stress, and motivation.

***Newsweek* Discount Subscription Coupon (12 weeks) (Student / ISBN 0-321-08895-6)**
Newsweek gets students reading, writing, and thinking about what's going on in the world around them. The price of the discounted subscription is added to the cost of the book. Instructors receive weekly lesson plans, quizzes, and curriculum guides, as well as a complimentary *Newsweek* subscription.

Interactive Guide to *Newsweek* (Student / ISBN 0-321-05528-4)
Available with the 12-week subscription to *Newsweek,* this guide serves as a workbook for students who are using the magazine.

Research Navigator Guide for English, H. Eric Branscomb & Doug Gotthoffer (Student / ISBN 0-321-20277-5)
Designed to teach students how to conduct high-quality online research and to document it properly, Research Navigator guides provide discipline-specific academic resources in addition to helpful tips on the writing process, online research, and finding and citing valid sources. Research Navigator guides include an access code to Research Navigator™, providing access to thousands of academic journals and periodicals, the New York Times Search by Subject Archive, Link Library, Library Guides, and more.

Penguin Discount Novel Program
In cooperation with Penguin Putnam, Inc., Longman is proud to offer a variety of Penguin paperbacks at a significant discount when packaged with any Longman title. Excellent additions to any developmental reading course, Penguin titles give students the opportunity to explore contemporary and classical fiction and drama. The available titles include works by authors as diverse as Toni Morrison, Julia Alvarez, Mary Shelley, and Shakespeare. To review the complete list of titles available, visit the Longman-Penguin-Putnam Website: http://www.ablongman.com/penguin.

***Oxford American College Dictionary* (Student / ISBN 0-399-14415-3)**
Drawing on Oxford's unparalleled language resources, including a 200-million-word database, this college dictionary contains more than 175,000 entries and more than 1000 illustrations, including line drawings, photographs, and maps.

***The New American Webster Handy College Dictionary* (Student / ISBN 0-451-18166-2)**
A paperback reference text with more than 100,000 entries.

Multimedia Offerings

MyReadingLab (www.myreadinglab.com)
This exciting new Website houses all the media tools any developmental English student will need to improve their reading and study skills, and all in one easy-to-use place. Resources for reading and study skills include:

- **Reading Roadtrip 5.0 Website.** The best-selling reading software available, Reading Roadtrip takes students on a tour of 16 cities and landmarks throughout the United States, with each of the 16 modules corresponding to a reading or study skill. New version 5.0 includes a brand-new design, a new Pioneer Level (fourth to sixth grade level), and new readings.
- **Longman Vocabulary Website.** The Longman Vocabulary Website features hundreds of exercises in ten topic areas to strengthen vocabulary skills. Students also

benefit from "100 Words That All High School Graduates Should Know," a useful resource that provides definitions, vocabulary flashcards, and audio clips.

- **Longman Study Skills Website.** This site offers hundreds of review strategies for college success, time and stress management skills, study strategies, and more.
- **Research Navigator.** In addition to providing valuable help to any college student on how to conduct high-quality online research and to document it properly, Research Navigator provides access to thousands of academic journals and periodicals.

STATE-SPECIFIC SUPPLEMENTS

For Florida Adopters

Thinking Through the Test: A Study Guide for the Florida College Basic Skills Exit Test, by D. J. Henry
This workbook helps students strengthen their reading skills in preparation for the Florida College Basic Skills Exit Test. It features both diagnostic tests to help assess areas that may need improvement and exit tests to help test skill mastery. Detailed explanatory answers have been provided for almost all of the questions. *Package item only—not available for sale.*

Available Versions:	
Thinking Through the Test A Study Guide for the Florida College Basic Skills Exit Tests: Reading and Writing, with Answer Key, 3/e	0-321-38739-2
Thinking Through the Test A Study Guide for the Florida College Basic Skills Exit Tests: Reading and Writing (without Answer Key), 3/e	0-321-38740-6
Thinking Through the Test A Study Guide for the Florida College Basic Skills Exit Tests: Reading, with Answer Key, 3/e	0-321-38737-6
Thinking Through the Test A Study Guide for the Florida College Basic Skills Exit Tests: Reading (without Answer Key), 3/e	0-321-38738-4

Reading Skills Summary for the Florida State Exit Exam, by D. J. Henry (Student / ISBN 0-321-08478-0)
An excellent study tool for students preparing to take Florida College Basic Skills Exit Test for Reading, this laminated reading grid summarizes all the skills tested on the Exit Exam.

CLAST Test Package, Fourth Edition (Instructor / Print ISBN 0-321-01950-4)
These two, 40-item objective tests evaluate students' readiness for the Florida CLAST exams. Strategies for teaching CLAST preparedness are included.

For Texas Adopters

The Longman THEA Study Guide, by Jeannette Harris (Student / ISBN 0-321-27240-0)
Created specifically for students in Texas, this study guide includes straightforward explanations and numerous practice exercises to help students prepare for the reading and writing sections of the THEA Test.

TASP Test Package, Third Edition (Instructor / Print ISBN 0-321-01959-8)
These 12 practice pre-tests and post-tests assess the same reading and writing skills covered in the Texas TASP examination.

For New York/CUNY Adopters

Preparing for the CUNY-ACT Reading and Writing Test, edited by Patricia Licklider (Student / ISBN 0-321-19608-2)
This booklet, prepared by reading and writing faculty from across the CUNY system, is designed to help students prepare for the CUNY-ACT exit test. It includes test-taking tips, reading passages, typical exam questions, and sample writing prompts to help students become familiar with each portion of the test.

ACKNOWLEDGMENTS

In preparing this edition, I appreciate the excellent ideas, suggestions, and advice provided by reviewers: Sheila Allen, Hartford Community College; Christine Arieta, Landmark College; Karen Becker, Youngstown State University; Shirley Blow-Brockman, Old Dominion University; Larry Browning, Baylor University; Jessica Stephens Bryant, Eastern Kentucky University; Judy Colson, West Valley College; Rosann M. Cook, Purdue University, Calumet; Jan Cutshall, Sussex County College; Marvin Epstein, Montgomery County Community College; Blanche Feero, Naugatuck Valley Community–Technical College; Gwendolyn Gray, Eastern Kentucky University; Linda M. Gubbe, University of Toledo; Phyllis Guthrie, Tarleton State University; Carol Hochman, California University of Pennsylvania; Peter Incarderone, New Jersey City University; Ron Kyhos, U.S. Naval Academy; Kathy L. Martin, Lewis and Clark State College; Karen S. McGinney, Georgia Perimeter College; Dorothy Minkoff, The College of New Jersey; Eileen Mullahy, Philadelphia University; Jody Orthey, Normandale Community College; Dianne Shames, Delaware County Community College; Jandy Sharpe, Patrick Henry Community College; Sharon Smallwood, Saint Petersburg Junior College; Laura B. Soldner, Northern Michigan University; Jerry Stevens, Kent State University, Trumbull; Betty Thomas, Missouri State University; Walteen Grady Truly, Pennsylvania State University, Wilkes-Barre; Joann Walker, Central Missouri State University; Suzanne Weisar, San Jacinto College; Barbara Wilan, Northern Virginia Community College, Annandale; Barbara Willig, Miami-Dade Community College.

I am particularly indebted to Gillian Cook, my development editor, for her creative energy, valuable advice, and guidance throughout the project and to Melanie Craig, Acquisitions Editor, for her active role in and enthusiastic support of the revision.

KATHLEEN T. MCWHORTER

SUCCESS WORKSHOPS

To the student: *College Reading and Study Skills* includes nine quick workshops to help you succeed in college. To help get your semester off to a strong start, check out each one. May success be yours!

1 Learn Everything You Can in the First Week

Your first week of classes and your first week on campus are some of the most important days you will ever spend.

DISCOVERING . . .
What Your Courses Require

When you accept a new job, your manager spends time explaining your job and its responsibilities. These first few days are important because you learn what is expected and what you must do to earn your paycheck. The first few days of a college course are equally important. You learn what your instructor expects and what you must do to earn a grade and receive credit for the course. Often, much of this information is contained in a course syllabus—a handout distributed on the first day or in the first week of class. Look and listen for the answers to the following questions.

Course objectives: What are you expected to learn in the course? (Pay particular attention to these; exams measure your ability to achieve these objectives.)

Course organization: How is the course structured? What portions will be lecture, conferences, discussion, small group work, and so forth?

Exams, quizzes, and assignments: When are exams scheduled, and what assignments are due? (Record dates for each in a pocket calendar.) What are the penalties for late assignments? Are make-up exams offered?

Grading system: How will your grade be determined? How much does each test or assignment count?

Class participation and attendance: What are your instructor's policies regarding attendance? Is class participation part of your grade?

Office hours: Where is your instructor's office, and what hours is he or she available?

If any of this information is not provided during the first week of class, be sure to ask your instructor.

ANALYZING . . .
Your Course Syllabi

Examine the syllabus for each of your courses. Identify the course objectives and course organization. Highlight or underline the schedule for assignments, quizzes, and exams. Then immediately transfer these dates into your pocket calendar. After your first week of classes, go through your pocket calendar, noting the due dates for the next month. Begin now to plan how you will schedule your time to meet your due dates.

LEARNING . . .
How Your Campus Is Organized

College is a completely new environment. There is a wealth of programs, services, clubs, and activities available. During your first week you need to learn as much as you can about the college's programs and services and their physical locations. Here's how to find information quickly:

- Read the college catalog and check the college's Web site.
- Read the student newspaper.
- Attend student orientation sessions.
- Get a map of the college and take your own tour.
- Get to know students in your classes and share information.
- Take a guided tour of the library or attend a library orientation workshop.
- Discover what you already know and what you need to know about your college by visiting the book's Web site at
  http://www.ablongman.com/mcwhorter
  and taking the Campus Resources and Rules test.

2 Get the Most Out of Your Textbooks

Have you ever wondered?

Question: How do textbooks differ from other information sources, such as dictionaries, reference books, and most nonfiction books?

Answer: Textbooks contain numerous features to help you learn. Most are not just page after page of print. They contain charts, tables, diagrams, and photographs, each of which is designed to help you learn.

Question: Who writes college textbooks?

Answer: Textbooks are almost always written by college teachers. (Check the title page of your textbooks; you will see the author's name and the name of his or her college or university.) College teachers know what you are likely to need help understanding. They know when you need, for example, a diagram to help you visualize a concept. Consequently, when they write textbooks, they build helpful features into each chapter.

ANALYZING . . .
The Features of Your Textbooks

Using a textbook for one of your other courses, check which of the following features it contains. Place a check mark in front of each item that you find (not all texts will have all features). Then decide how you can use each feature to help you learn.

Feature	Value
❏ Chapter Objectives	_____
❏ Chapter Outline	_____
❏ Marginal Definitions of Key Vocabulary	_____
❏ Problems or Exercises	_____
❏ Discussion Questions	_____
❏ Review Questions	_____
❏ List of Key Terminology	_____
❏ Chapter Summary	_____
❏ Suggested Readings	_____
❏ Glossary	_____
❏ Appendix	_____

GETTING AN OVERVIEW . . .
The Preface or "To the Student"

The preface is the introduction to the book; it describes its organization and use.

■ Read the preface or "To the Student" in one of your other textbooks.

■ Write a list of information you learned about your textbook from reading the preface or "To the Student." Look for the answers to these questions:
  How is the book organized?
  What topics does the book cover?
  What makes the book unique?
  What learning features are included?

■ Of all the information in the preface or "To the Student," what strikes you as most interesting? Why?

Fifteenth Amendment

The constitutional amendment adopted in 1870 to extend **suffrage** to African Americans.

The **Fifteenth Amendment**, adopted in 1870, guaranteed African Americans the right to vote—at least in principle. It said, "The right of citizens to vote shall not be abridged by the United States or by any state on account of race, color, or previous condition of servitude." The gap between these words and their implementation, however, remained wide for a full century. States seemed to outdo one another in developing ingenious methods of circumventing the Fifteenth Amendment.

Many states required potential voters to complete literacy tests before registering to vote. These tests typically required prospective voters to read, write, and understand their state constitution or the U.S. Constitution. In practice, however, the literacy test was rarely administered to Whites, yet the standard of literacy required of Blacks was so high that few were ever able to pass the test. In addition, Oklahoma and other Southern states used a *grandfather clause* that exempted persons whose grandfathers were eligible to vote in 1860 from taking these tests. This exemption did not apply, of course, to the grandchildren of slaves, but did allow illiterate Whites to vote. The law was blatantly unfair; it was also unconstitutional, said the Supreme Court in the 1915 decision *Guinn v. United States*.

poll taxes

Small taxes levied on the right to vote that often fell due at a time of year when poor African-American sharecroppers had the least cash on hand. This method was used by most Southern states to exclude African Americans from voting. Poll taxes were declared void by the **Twenty-fourth Amendment** in 1964.

To exclude African Americans from registering to vote, most Southern states also relied on **poll taxes**, which were small taxes levied on the right to vote that often fell due at a time of year when poor sharecroppers had the least cash on hand. To render African-American votes ineffective, most Southern states also used the **White primary**, a device that permitted political parties in the heavily Democratic South to exclude African Americans from voting in primary elections, thus depriving them of a voice in the most important contests and letting them vote only when it mattered least. The Supreme Court declared White primaries unconstitutional in 1944 in *Smith v. Allwright*.

The civil rights movement put suffrage high on its political agenda; one by one, the barriers to African-American voting fell during the 1960s. Poll taxes in federal elections were prohibited by the **Twenty-fourth Amendment**, which was ratified in 1964. Two years later, the Supreme Court voided poll taxes in state elections in *Harper v. Virginia State Board of Elections*.

White primary

One of the means used to discourage African-American voting that permitted political parties in the heavily Democratic South to exclude African American from primary elections, thus depriving them of a voice in the real contests. The Supreme Court declared White primaries unconstitutional in 1944.

Many areas in the South employed fraudulent or sham voter registration tests—requiring literacy or an understanding of the Constitution, for example—in a discriminatory fashion. Voting registrars would declare literate African Americans to be illiterate and thus ineligible to register to vote, while allowing illiterate Whites to register. The **Voting Rights Act of 1965** prohibited any government from using voting procedures that denied a person the vote on the basis of race or color and abolished the use of literacy requirements for anyone who had completed the sixth grade. Federal election registrars were sent to areas with long histories of discrimination, and these same areas had to submit all proposed changes in their voting laws or practices to a federal official for approval. As a result of these provisions, hundreds of thousands of African Americans registered to vote in Southern states.

Twenty-fourth Amendment

The constitutional amendment passed in 1964 that declared **poll taxes** void in federal elections.

Voting Rights Act of 1965

A law designed to help end formal and informal barriers to African-American suffrage. Under the law, hundreds of thousands of African Americans were registered and the number of African-American elected officials increased dramatically.

The effects of these efforts were swift and certain, as the civil rights movement turned from protest to politics.[5] When the Voting Rights Act passed in 1965, only 70 African Americans held public office in the 11 Southern states. By the early 1980s, more than 2,500 African Americans held elected offices in those states, and the number has continued to grow. There are currently more than 9,000 African-American elected officials in the United States.[6]

The Voting Rights Act of 1965 not only secured the right to vote for African Americans but also ensured that their votes would not be diluted through racial gerrymandering (drawing district boundaries to advantage a specific group). For example, White-majority districts frequently elected members of a city council in at-large seats (in which council members were elected from the entire city) and prevented a geographically concentrated minority from electing a minority council member. When Congress amended the Voting Rights Act in 1982, it further insisted that minorities be

The Voting Rights Act of 1965 produced a major increase in the number of African Americans registered to vote in Southern states. The ability to vote gave African Americans more political clout: In the 20 years following enactment of the law, more than 2,500 African Americans were elected to state and local offices in that region.

able to "elect representatives of their choice" when their numbers and configuration permitted. Thus, redrawing district boundaries was to avoid discriminatory *results* and not just discriminatory *intent*. In 1986, the Supreme Court upheld this principle in *Thornburg v. Gingles*.

Officials in the Justice Department, which was responsible for enforcing the Voting Rights Act, and state legislatures that drew new district lines interpreted these actions as a mandate to create minority-majority districts. Consequently, when congressional district boundaries were redrawn following the 1990 census, several states, including Florida, North Carolina, Texas, Illinois, New York, and Louisiana, created odd-shaped districts that were designed to give minority-group voters a numerical majority. Fourteen new U.S. House districts were drawn specifically to help elect African Americans to Congress, and six districts were drawn to elect new Hispanic members (these efforts worked, as we will see in Chapter 12).

However, in 1993, the Supreme Court heard a challenge to a North Carolina congressional district that in some places was cut no wider than a superhighway to create an African-American majority winding snakelike for 160 miles. In its decision in *Shaw v. Reno*, the Court decried the creation of districts based solely on racial composition, as well as the district drawers' abandonment of traditional redistricting standards such as compactness and contiguity. Thus, the Court gave legal standing to challenges to any congressional map with an oddly shaped minority-majority district that may not be defensible on grounds other than race (such as shared community interest or geographical compactness). The next year, in *Johnson v. DeGrandy*, the Court ruled that a state legislative redistricting plan does not violate the Voting Rights Act if it does not create the greatest possible number of districts in which minority-group votes would make up a majority.

In 1995 in *Miller v. Johnson*, the Court rejected the efforts of the Justice Department to achieve the maximum possible number of minority districts. It held that the use of race as a "predominant factor" in drawing district lines should be presumed to be unconstitutional. The next year, in *Bush v. Vera* and *Shaw v. Hunt*, the Supreme Court voided

Why It Matters

The Voting Rights Act
In passing the Voting Rights Act of 1965, Congress enacted an extraordinarily strong law to protect the rights of minorities to vote. There is little question that officials pay more attention to minorities when they can vote. And many more members of minority groups are now elected to high public office.

Textbooks have features designed to help you learn.

EXAMINING AN OUTLINE . . .
The Table of Contents

The preface or "To the Student" usually gives a summary of the book's organization and content. The table of contents provides you with a more detailed outline of the book's topics. The chapter titles are the main divisions of the book, and the titles within each chapter indicate the smaller subdivisions of the topics.

■ Look at the table of contents of one of your textbooks for another course. Choose one chapter that you will have to read soon.

■ Examine the titles and subtitles for that one chapter. What is the main topic of the chapter? What are the major divisions of that main topic?

■ Think about what you already know about this topic from talking to other people, watching the news, reading, or listening to the radio.

■ What do you expect to learn from reading this chapter?

3 Polish Your Academic Image

Why?

Imagine that you are a teacher meeting a class of students for the first time. Look at the students in the photos below from the **teacher's point of view**. Next to each photo, write your first impressions of how each student will approach his or her course work. For example:

- Who do you think will participate in class?

- Who will turn in careful, neatly organized work?

- Who will be early, on time, or late for class?

- Who will come to your office to ask questions when they don't understand an assignment? Who will you never see there?

- Who will tell you the dog ate his or her homework?

Be prepared to discuss your reasoning.

5

DISCOVERING
How Do You Rate Your Academic Image?

	Always	Sometimes	Never
1. I ask and answer questions in class.	❏	❏	❏
2. I make eye contact with my instructor during class.	❏	❏	❏
3. I speak to my instructors when I see them on campus.	❏	❏	❏
4. I turn in neat, carefully done assignments.	❏	❏	❏
5. I make myself known to instructors by speaking to them before or after class.	❏	❏	❏
6. I attend all classes and explain any necessary lengthy absences to my instructors.	❏	❏	❏
7. I avoid talking with classmates while the instructor is talking.	❏	❏	❏
8. I come to class before the instructor and stay until class is dismissed.	❏	❏	❏
9. I try to stay alert to show that I am interested.	❏	❏	❏
10. I sit in class with other students who demonstrate a positive academic image.	❏	❏	❏

If you answered "Sometimes" or "Never" to more than one or two questions, you should improve your academic image.

Think About It!

When you meet someone new, how do you figure out what they are like? You can't read their minds to know what they are thinking, so, normally, you try to understand others by the way they act—their behavior. Your instructors do the same.

How can your instructor tell that you are interested in the course material? She can watch for behaviors that usually go along with interest—asking questions when you want to know more or don't understand something, answering questions that the instructor poses, paying attention to what she says, and taking notes. She can also see if you ever visit her office for help or if you seem to need extra help.

Suppose you were introduced to a new person, but she only glanced at you and mumbled a quick "hi" while continuing her conversation with someone else. You might think that she didn't want to get to know you or that she was rude. If you talk to your classmates instead of paying attention to your instructor, she will likely make the same judgment about you.

On the other hand, if you meet someone who looks you in the eye, repeats your name, shakes your hand, and spends a few minutes talking with you, you'll have quite a different impression. Which classroom behaviors from the questionnaire above are similar to this example?

You can also tell a lot about people from the pride they take in their work. If you took your car to a mechanic to fix the brakes, and the brakes worked again but made a terrible screeching noise, what judgment would you make about the mechanic's pride of work? What is a similar situation in college classes that can affect your academic image?

Think about it.

CHANGING
Planning a More Successful Academic Image

For each response of "Sometimes" or "Never" you gave in the questionnaire on page 6, write a new statement about how you can change your everyday behavior in class and on campus to improve your academic image. What will help your instructors think of you as a serious, hard-working, responsible student? (Remember what things look like from the front of the room!)

1. I will _____

   _____

2. I will _____

   _____

3. I will _____

   _____

4. I will _____

   _____

5. I will _____

   _____

6. I will _____

   _____

7. I will _____

   _____

REFLECTING
Every Week or Two, Check Again

■ Am I communicating with my instructors?

  • Do I talk to instructors before or after class?

  • Do I take advantage of my instructor's office hours?

  • Have I explained any problems to my instructor?

■ Am I participating in my classes?

  • Am I making eye contact with my instructor?

  • Do I ask and answer questions in class?

  • Do I show my interest and motivation in class?

■ Am I turning in good work?

  • Do I submit neat and complete assignments?

  • Do I always include my name and the date, course title, and section number on my assignments?

  • Do I type or word process all my papers?

■ Am I projecting a successful academic image?

INTEREST

MOTIVATION

ATTENTION

GOOD WORK

ENERGY

4 Participate in Class

Why?

- You will learn more in class if you are actively involved rather than merely observing the other students interacting with the instructor.

- You will find it easier to concentrate and stay interested in the class if you participate.

- Many instructors include class participation as part of your grade.

BRAINSTORMING . . .
What Are Your Options?

What are the different ways students can participate in class? List three to five activities.

1. _____
2. _____
3. _____
4. _____
5. _____

DISCOVERING . . .
How Involved Are You?

	Yes	Sometimes	No
1. As I read assigned material, I record my ideas, impressions, and reactions in the margin in preparation for class.	❏	❏	❏
2. I ask questions in class.	❏	❏	❏
3. I answer questions asked by the instructor.	❏	❏	❏
4. I comment on ideas expressed by other students.	❏	❏	❏
5. Before class begins, I skim through the reading assignment to refresh my memory.	❏	❏	❏

REFLECTING . . .
What Stops You?

Below are two columns. In the left column are reasons students sometimes give for not participating in class. Talk the problem over with a few classmates, and then write a piece of advice in the right column for the student.

My Problem Is . . .	**Our Advice to You Is . . .**
I'm afraid I don't know very much about this subject.	_____
I'm afraid I will not be able to say what I really mean.	_____
I wonder if the other students will laugh at my ideas.	_____
I'm not sure I should say anything if the instructor hasn't asked a specific question.	_____
I'm not as smart as the students who usually participate in class.	_____

Eight Tips for Participating in Class

1. *Say something early*. Even if you are reluctant to speak before a group, try to say something early in the discussion; the longer you wait, the more difficult it becomes. Also, the longer you wait, the greater the chance that someone else will say what you were planning to say.

2. *Make your comments brief.* Make your comments brief and to the point. If your instructor feels you should say more, he or she will probably ask you to explain or elaborate further.

3. *Speak to the group.* Try to avoid getting involved in direct exchanges or disagreements with other class members. Always speak to the group, not to individuals, and be sure that your comments are related to issues of interest to the entire class.

4. *Prepare your listeners.* When you feel it is appropriate to introduce a new idea, clue your listeners that you are changing topics or introducing a new idea. You might say something like "On a related question . . ." or "Another point to consider is . . ."

5. *Jot down ideas.* When you think of comments or ideas that you want to share during the discussion, jot them down. Then, when you get a chance to speak, you will have your notes to refer to. Notes help you organize and present your ideas in a clear and organized fashion.

6. *Be fair.* Keep an open mind. Leave personal dislikes, attitudes toward other members of the group, and your own biases and prejudices aside.

7. *Organize your remarks.* First, connect what you plan to say with what has already been said. Then state your ideas as clearly as possible. Next, develop or explain your idea.

8. *Watch for reactions.* Watch both your instructor and the other students as you speak. Their responses will show whether they understand you or need further information, whether they agree or disagree, and whether they are interested. Based on their responses, you can then decide whether you made your point effectively or whether you need to explain or defend your argument more carefully.

5 Strengthen Your Concentration

Why?

Strengthening your concentration is important. No matter how intelligent you are, or what skills and talents you possess, if you can't keep your mind on the task at hand, studying will be difficult and frustrating. But it doesn't have to be.

What Is Wrong with This Picture?

Why is this student having trouble concentrating? List as many reasons as you can think of below.

_____

_____

_____

Have You Ever Made Comments Like These?

"I just can't seem to concentrate!"

"I've got so much reading to do; I'll never be able to catch up!"

"I try to study, but nothing happens."

"I waste a lot of time just trying to get started."

If you have, consider the following suggestions for improving your study surroundings and focusing your attention.

LEARNING . . .
Improve Your Surroundings

Make sure you create a workable study environment.

- Choose a place with minimal distractions.

- Establish a study area with a table or desk that is yours alone for study.

- Control noise levels. Determine how much background noise, if any, you can tolerate, and choose a place best suited to you.

- Eliminate distracting clutter. Get rid of photos, stacks of bills, mementos, and so forth.

- Have necessary supplies at your fingertips: for example, dictionaries, pens, calculator, calendar, clock.

CHANGING . . .
Plan a Better Study Area

Put a check mark next to each suggestion above that you could use to improve your surroundings. Plan how you will improve each area, assigning one task to do on each of the next three days. (Change the days of the week if you need to.)

On Monday, I will

_____

_____

On Tuesday, I will

_____

_____

On Wednesday, I will

_____

_____

LEARNING . . .
Focus Your Attention

Once your study area is set up, use these ideas to focus your attention.

- Establish goals and time limits for each assignment. Deadlines will keep you motivated and create a sense of urgency in which you are less likely to daydream or become distracted.

- Reward yourself. Use rewards such as phoning a friend or ordering a pizza when you complete an evening of study.

- Use writing to keep mentally and physically active. Highlighting, outlining, or note taking will force you to keep your mind on the material you are reading.

- Vary your activities. Alternate between writing, reading, reviewing, and solving math problems.

- Keep a distractions list. As distracting thoughts enter your mind, jot them on a notepad. You

may, for example, think of your mother's upcoming birthday as you're reading psychology. Writing it down will help you remember it and will eliminate the distraction.

CHANGING . . .
Plan Ways to Focus Your Attention

How many of the ideas above would help you focus your attention while studying? Make a plan here for trying out each idea for a week to see which you find most helpful.

This week, I will _____

_____

_____

In week 2, I will _____

_____

_____

In week 3, I will _____

_____

_____

In week 4, I will _____

_____

_____

In week 5, I will _____

_____

_____

REFLECTING . . .
What Worked, and What Didn't?

In order to learn from what you do, you need to keep track of what worked and what did not. Of the various ideas you have tried, which were the most helpful? Which weren't as helpful? For the ideas that didn't seem to work as well, can you think of different ways to put them into action that might work better for you? Keep experimenting until you think you have made full use of all suggestions.

REMEMBER . . .
Focus

- Figure out how to make your study area work for you.
- Organize your assignments to vary your activities.
- Concentrate on one task at a time.
- Use writing to stay actively engaged in study.
- Set goals and time limits for each assignment.
- Textbooks have features designed to help you learn.

6 Stay Healthy and Relaxed

Why?

Learning to handle the many demands of college life can be stressful, especially if you are trying to raise a family or work a job at the same time. If you stay healthy and learn to manage stress, you will find that your life becomes more enjoyable and fun.

DISCOVERING . . .
Think About Your General Health

1. How much sleep do you usually get each night?
2. How much time do you spend exercising each week?
3. How often do you eat regular, healthy meals?
4. Do you smoke or drink alcohol? If so, how much?

Think About Your Stress Level

5. Do you spend most of your time either studying or worrying about not studying?
6. Have you ever noticed that you get sick when you can least afford it?
7. Do you have a tendency to skip meals, eat junk food, stay up late, or skip exercise when you are over-worked?
8. Do you often feel impatient or irritable without knowing why?
9. Do you feel stressed-out?

Focus on the elements of this workshop that will help you the most in moving toward a healthier, more relaxed lifestyle.

REFLECTING . . .
Do Your Habits Work for You?

Regardless of how busy you are, be sure to:

Get enough sleep. The amount of sleep a person needs is highly individual. Discover how much you need by noticing patterns. For several weeks, analyze how well your day went and consider how much sleep you had the night before. Then adjust your schedule to make sure you get the right amount of sleep for you each night.

Exercise regularly. Exercising three times a week for about 15 minutes each time is a good way to get started on a regular fitness program. Whenever you find yourself getting tense, for example when your shoulders or neck start tensing, take a few minutes immediately to stretch or go for a brief walk.

Eat regular, healthy meals. Give yourself time to eat three meals a day. For snacks in between, eat fruit or vegetables. Avoid a diet heavy in fats, and try to eat balanced meals rather than junk food.

Reduce or eliminate smoking and drinking alcohol. Check with a counselor at the student health center for a program that will help you.

Learn to say "No" to unreasonable requests from friends and family. Explain your schedule to your family, and make sure they understand your academic goals. Then when you need to turn down unreasonable requests, they will understand why.

Take breaks. Constantly pushing yourself compounds stress. Slow down and do nothing for a brief period, even if just for five minutes. If you practice deep breathing on your breaks, you will relax even more. Breathe in through your nose; then breathe out completely through your mouth.

PLANNING . . .
How Can You Improve Your Habits?

Examine your weekly schedule of classes, study, work, and family activities. Look for short time periods that you could use for exercise, better meals, and breaks. Look for ways to increase the amount of sleep you're getting, if that's an issue. Make a plan for improving your health and relaxation by writing the necessary changes into your schedule.

CHANGING . . .
Does Your Thinking Help You?

When you feel as if you don't have enough time in your day to get everything done, don't think negatively—"I'll never be able to get all this done!" This leads to unnecessary stress. Instead think positively—"It's going to feel great to accomplish this!"

- Visualize success. Imagine yourself getting everything done in an orderly, systematic way.
- Focus on the benefits of completing each task. How will completing each task help you or others?

- Develop a plan or schedule that will allow you to get everything done (refer to Chapter 1 for tips on time management).

DISCOVERING . . .
Using Your Senses for Success

Success follows from working productively. Keeping your senses trained on the world around you, rather than on your personal thoughts, can help you focus on the task at hand and increase your productivity. Use this brief exercise to refocus your senses when you take a break from your work.

Stand up and move around your study area for three to five minutes. Look closely at the colors, shapes, and images in the room. As you are looking, listen carefully for all the sounds that you can hear: traffic sounds, music playing, appliances humming, people talking. While looking and listening, notice what you can feel around you: touch different objects, notice the air temperature, feel the floor under your feet. Examine what you are seeing, hearing, and feeling as if the sights, sounds, and sensations are all new to you.

When you return to your work, you will find that you are more able to put aside unrelated thoughts and complete your task more efficiently. During long study periods, repeat this exercise every 50 minutes and notice how much more you can accomplish!

REFLECTING . . .
Every Week or Two, Check Again

- Am I getting enough sleep?
- Am I exercising regularly?
- Am I eating regular, healthy meals?
- Am I taking brief breaks when I start to feel stressed?
- Am I focusing my senses on success?
- Am I focusing on the benefits of completing each task?
- Is my schedule allowing me to get everything done?

7 *Work with Your Classmates*

Why?

You can learn from other students. By discovering how other students approach a task or solve a problem, you sharpen your own thinking.

- ■ It may be required. Instructors may assign group projects or require you to participate in group activities.

- ■ It can be fun. You'll meet new people and form new friendships.

- ■ It is good practice. You will have to work cooperatively with coworkers on the job, so begin polishing your collaborative skills now.

REFLECTING . . .
Your Experiences as a Group Member

Most students have had some experience in working with a group, whether at school or at work. Share one of your experiences with a few other classmates. Figure out what made the group successful or unsuccessful in completing its task. What could you have done to help the group work together more effectively? Reflect on this question again once you have read this workshop.

THINKING AHEAD . . .
How to Make It Work

1. Select alert, energetic classmates if you are permitted to choose group members.

2. Be an active, responsible participant. Accept your share of the work and expect others to do the same. Approach the activity with a serious attitude, rather than joking or complaining about the assignment. This will establish a serious tone and cut down on wasted time.

3. Because organization and direction are essential for productivity, every group needs a leader. Unless some other competent group member immediately assumes leadership, take a leadership role. Leadership may require more work, but you will be in control. (Remember, too, that leadership roles are valuable experiences for your career.) As the group's leader, you will need to direct the group in analyzing the assignment, organizing a plan of action, distributing work assignments, planning, and (in long-term projects) establishing deadlines.

4. Suggest that specific tasks be assigned to each group member and that the group agree upon task deadlines.

5. Take advantage of individual strengths and weaknesses. For instance, a person who seems indifferent or is easily distracted should not be assigned the task of recording the group's findings. The most organized, outgoing member might be assigned the task of making an oral report to the class.

PROBLEM SOLVING . . .
What to Do if It Doesn't Work

If a Group Member . . .	You May Want to Say . . .
hasn't begun to do the work she's been assigned	"You've been given a difficult part of the project. How can we help you get started?"
complains about the workload	"We all seem to have different amounts of work to do. Is there some way we might lessen your workload?"
has missed meetings	"To ensure that we all meet regularly, would it be helpful if I called everyone the night before to confirm the day and time?"
is uncommunicative and doesn't share information	"Since we are all working from different angles, let's each make an outline of what we've done so far, so we can plan how to proceed from here."

In This Case You Could . . .

seems to be making you or other members do all the work	Make up a chart with each member's responsibilities before the meeting. Give each member a copy and ask,
	"Is there any part of your assignment that you have questions or concerns about? Would anyone like to change his or her completion date?" Be sure to get an answer from each member.

8 Establish Your Academic Integrity

Did you know?

Ideas are considered a person's property, just as books or cars are considered personal possessions.

Did you know?

It is wrong to use or borrow ideas or exact wording from an author or speaker without giving the writer or speaker credit.

Even borrowing a unique three- or four-word phrase from someone is considered to be dishonest. Using another person's ideas without giving that person credit is called plagiarism. Plagiarism carries stiff academic penalties. If you take information from a reference book without crediting the source, you can receive a failing grade for the paper or even for the course. In fact, at some institutions, you can even be dismissed from the college. It does not matter whether your plagiarism is accidental or intentional; either way it is considered dishonest.

Tips for Avoiding Plagiarism

- Always place quotation marks around anything you copy out of a source. That way you will always know when you have used an author's exact wording.

SOURCE	USING QUOTATION FROM SOURCE
Anger is one of the eight basic emotions identified in Plutchik's model. It's also an emotion that can create considerable problems if not managed properly. Anger varies from mild annoyance to intense rage; increases in pulse rate and blood pressure usually accompany these feelings. Anger doesn't just happen; you make it happen by your interpretation of events. Yet life events contribute mightily.	Anger management is an important life skill and can make a difference in both personal and career relationships. As DeVito emphasizes in *Messages*, "anger doesn't just happen; you make it happen by your interperation of events"(155). Therefore, people should think before they react, and examine the alternative ways a potentially explosive situation can be interpreted. For example, . . .

■ Keep track of all sources you use. As you take notes from a reference source, make sure you record the source at the top of the page or in the margin.

MacNeil, Robert and William Cran. Do You Speak
American? New York: Doubleday, 2005.

Pages 108-110

Spanglish—combination of half English, half
Spanish

   • Speaker may switch between languages within
   a single sentence

   • It is a hybrid language occurring as a result of
   cultures mixing together

Chicano English—an English dialect

   • One of the languages used on the street in
   Latino sections of Los Angeles

   • It is incorrectly thought of as a language of
   those just learning to speak English

Chicano Spanish—Spanish with some words borrowed
from English

■ Learn how to use citations to credit sources from which you take information. For more information, obtain a handbook for writing research papers or ask a college librarian.

Finding Out

Visit your college library or go online to locate a source that explains how to document sources, write citations, and prepare a list of sources used in an academic paper.

Write the name of your source here: _____

9 Keep a Vocabulary Log

Just as every sport has its own special language (home runs, touchdowns, line drives, and hook shots), each academic discipline also has its own language. Each course you will take has a set of new terminology that you have to master in order to read textbooks, write papers, participate in class, and take exams. In psychology, for example, you may need to learn terms such as intraspecific aggression, modulation, and simulation. In a marketing course, you will need to use terms such as price subsidies, diffusion, and co-branding. How do you learn all this new terminology? Try creating a vocabulary log for each course. A sample log is shown below.

How to Create a Log

1. Use the back pages of your course notebook, create a computer file, or use a stack of index cards.

2. When you find a new term you need to learn, record both the word and its meaning. You might also include its pronunciation and a textbook or notebook page reference.

3. Be creative. You may color code your list by chapter or topic, or include columns to check off when you have learned the word, for instance.

4. In addition to definitions, include pronunciations, examples, and so on. Include anything that will help you remember the term.

5. Study your list or file frequently.

How to Study Your Log

Study your log using the following suggestions.

- Review your log several times a week. Review previously entered words as well as new entries.

- Test yourself. You will never be sure whether you have learned the words in your log by simply rereading them. Instead, test yourself, or work with a classmate and quiz each other.

- For troublesome words, try writing them and their definitions.

Sample Log for American Government

Word	Meaning	Page
Censorship	Government regulation of media content	39
Affirmative action	A policy that gives special treatment to members of a previously disadvantaged group	99
Laissez-faire	The idea that government should not interfere with the economy	107
Consumer price index (CPI)	A measure of inflation that considers price increases over time	116

1 Setting Goals and Managing Your Time

Why Learn to Set Goals and Manage Your Time?

- Setting goals can keep you on track, motivate you to work, and help you measure your progress.
- Managing your time allows you to finish your course work and still have time for a social life.
- Managing your time allows you to make steady progress on long-term projects instead of being surprised at the last minute by rapidly approaching due dates.

Learning Experiment

Form two groups, Group 1 and Group 2. Each group should follow the directions given below for their group.

Directions for Group 1

Study the following photograph for one minute at the beginning of class and one minute at the end of class. Focus on the details of the photograph.

Directions for Group 2

Study the following photograph for two consecutive minutes at the beginning of class.

Both Groups

The members of each group should meet, separate from the other group. The group should write down as many details from the photograph as they can remember. Group members may want to do this partly in the form of a diagram or sketch of the photograph, so they can indicate the placement of the various details.

Each group should then appoint someone to speak for them. The speaker from each group will tell the whole class what his or her group remembered about the photograph. Then the class will compare each group's details with the actual photograph to find out how much they remembered.

The Results

Which group remembered more details, more accurately? Why? Most classes find that the group that studied two separate minutes (Group 1) recalled more items than the group that studied for one two-minute block of time. Group 1 also had a goal in mind as they studied, whereas Group 2 did not.

Learning Principle (What This Means to You)

Several short periods of study are more effective than one large period of study. Having a goal (purpose) for studying also improves recall. This chapter will show you how to set goals and how to plan and manage your time. As you create a semester or weekly study plan, be sure to spread out your study; include three or four short periods of study and review for each of your courses.

ESTABLISHING YOUR GOALS AND PRIORITIES

One of the first steps in getting organized and succeeding in college is to set your priorities—to decide what is and what is not important to you. For most college students, finding enough time to do everything they *should* do and everything they *want* to do is nearly impossible. They face a series of conflicts over the use of their time and are forced to choose among a variety of activities. Here are a few examples:

Want to do:		Should do:
1. Watch late movie	*vs.*	Get good night's sleep
2. Go to hockey game	*vs.*	Work on term paper
3. Go out with friends	*vs.*	Finish psychology reading assignment

These day-to-day choices can be frustrating and can use up valuable time as you weigh the alternatives and make decisions. Often, these choices can be narrowed down to wanting to take part in an enjoyable activity even though you know you should be studying, reading, or writing a paper. At other times, there may be a conflict between two things you need to do, one for your studies and another for something else important in your life.

One of the best ways to handle these frequent conflicts is to identify your goals. Ask yourself, "What is most important to me? What activities can I afford to give up? What is least important to me when I am pressured for time?" For many students, studying is their first priority. For others with family responsibilities, caring for a child is their first priority, and attending college is next in importance.

How to Discover What Is Important

1. **Make a list of the ten most joyous moments in your life.** A phrase or single sentence of description is all that is needed.
2. **Ask yourself, "What do most or all of these moments have in common?"**
3. **Try to write answers to the question above by describing why the moments were important to you—what you got out of them.** (Sample answers: helping others, competing or winning, creating something worthwhile, proving your self-worth, connecting with nature, and so forth.)
4. **Your answers should provide a starting point for defining life goals.**

Defining Goals

In defining your goals, be specific and detailed. Use the following suggestions:

- **Your goals should be positive (what you want) rather than negative (what you want to avoid).** Don't say "I won't ever have to worry about credit card balances and bill collectors." Instead, say "I will have enough money to live comfortably."
- **Your goals should be realistic.** Unless you have strong evidence to believe you can do so, don't say you want to win an Olympic gold medal in swimming. Instead, say you want to become a strong, competitive swimmer.

- **Your goals should be achievable.** Don't say you want to earn a million dollars a year; most people don't. Set more achievable, specific goals, such as "I want to buy my own house by the time I am 30."
- **Your goals should be worth what it takes to achieve them.** Becoming an astronaut or a brain surgeon takes years of training. Are you willing to spend that amount of time?
- **Your goals should include a time frame.** The goal "to earn a bachelor's degree in accounting" should include a date, for example.
- **Don't hesitate to change your goals as your life changes.** The birth of a child or the loss of a loved one may cause you to refocus your life.

You will find that clearly establishing and pursuing your goals eliminates much worry and guilt. You'll know what is important and feel that you are on target, working steadily toward the goals you have established.

EXERCISE 1

DIRECTIONS   Write a list of five to ten goals.

_____

_____

_____

_____

_____

How a College Education Contributes to Your Goals

College can help you achieve many of your life goals. College can provide you with the self-awareness, self-confidence, knowledge, skills, practice facilities, degrees, friendships, business contacts, and so forth that can help you achieve your life goals.

Try to make the connection between college and life goals clear and explicit. College demands hard work and a stick-with-it attitude. You will be more motivated to work hard if you can see directly how that hard work will pay off in helping you fulfill your life goals.

EXERCISE 2

DIRECTIONS   For each of your life goals, explain how attending college will help you achieve that goal.

_____

_____

_____

_____

_____

ANALYZING YOUR TIME COMMITMENTS

Once you've established your priorities, the next step is to analyze your time commitments. They should reflect your priorities. For example, if playing on the volleyball team has high priority, then you must reserve time for practice and games. You can reserve enough time to study for an exam in psychology, do library research, and read biology assignments. To do this, though, you must determine how much time is available and then decide how you will use it.

Let's begin by making some rough estimates. That way, you'll see where your time goes each week. Fill in the chart shown in Figure 1-1, making reasonable estimates. After you've completed the chart, total your hours per week and write the answer in the space marked "Total committed time per week." Next, fill in that total below and complete the subtraction.

$$168 \text{ hours in one week}$$
$$- \underline{\hspace{2cm}} \text{ total committed time}$$
$$\underline{\hspace{2cm}} \text{ hours available}$$

Are you surprised to see how many hours per week you have left? Now answer this question: Do you have enough time available for reading and studying? As a rule of thumb, most instructors expect you to spend two hours studying for every hour spent in class. Complete the following multiplication:

$$\underline{\hspace{2cm}} \text{ hours spent in class} \times 2 = \underline{\hspace{2cm}} \text{ study hours needed}$$

Do you have this much time available each week? If your answer to the question is no, then you are overcommitted. If you are overcommitted, ask yourself the following question: Can I drop any activity or do it in less time? Can I reduce the number of hours I work, or can another family member split some time-consuming responsibilities with me? If you are unable to reduce your committed time, talk with your advisor about taking fewer courses.

If you are overcommitted or feel you want to use your time more efficiently, now is the time to develop a weekly schedule that will help you use your available time more effectively. You are probably concerned at this point, however, that your time analysis did not take into account social and leisure activities. That omission was deliberate up to this point.

Figure 1-1
Weekly Time
Commitments

	Hours per Day	Hours per Week
Sleep	_____	_____
Breakfast	_____	_____
Lunch	_____	_____
Dinner	_____	_____
Part- or full-time job	_____	_____
Time spent in class	_____	_____
Transportation time	_____	_____
Personal care (dressing, shaving, etc.)	_____	_____
Household/family responsibilities (cooking dinner, driving mother to work, etc.)	_____	_____
Sports	_____	_____
Other priorities	_____	_____
Total committed time per week		_____

Although leisure time is essential to everyone's well-being, it should not take precedence over college work. Most students who develop and follow a time schedule for accomplishing their course work are able to devote reasonable amounts of time to leisure and social activities. They also find time to become involved with campus groups and activities—an important aspect of college life.

BUILDING A TERM PLAN

A term plan lists all your unchanging commitments. These may include class hours, transportation to and from school and work, family commitments, religious obligations, part-time job hours (if they are the same each week), sleep, meals, and sports. A sample term plan is shown in Figure 1-2. You should prepare

Figure 1-2
Sample Term Plan

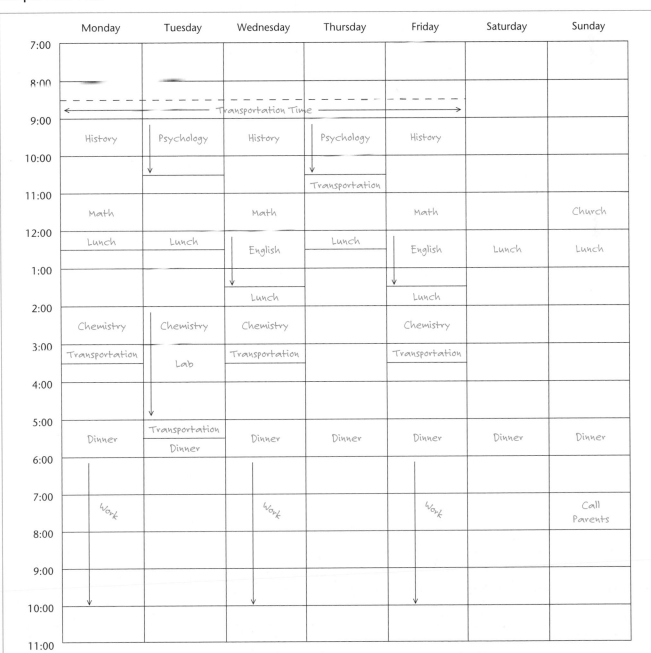

this plan only once a term. Then make enough photocopies of this plan for each week in the term. You'll use your term plan to build weekly time schedules.

EXERCISE 3   DIRECTIONS   Using the form shown in Figure 1-3, build your own term plan.

BUILDING YOUR WEEKLY SCHEDULE

A weekly schedule is a plan of when and what you will study. It includes specific times for studying particular subjects as well as specific times for writing

Figure 1-3
Term Plan

	Monday	Tuesday	Wednesday	Thursday	Friday	Saturday	Sunday
7:00							
8:00							
9:00							
10:00							
11:00							
12:00							
1:00							
2:00							
3:00							
4:00							
5:00							
6:00							
7:00							
8:00							
9:00							
10:00							
11:00							

papers, conducting library research, and completing homework assignments for each course.

At the beginning of each week, decide what you need to accomplish that week. Consider upcoming quizzes, exams, and papers. A schedule will eliminate the need to make frustrating last-minute choices between "should" and "want to" activities. The sample weekly time schedule in Figure 1-4 was developed by a first-year student. Read it carefully, noticing how the student reserved times for studying for each of her courses.

**Figure 1-4
Sample Weekly Time
Schedule**

	Monday	Tuesday	Wednesday	Thursday	Friday	Saturday	Sunday
7:00							
8:00							
9:00			Transportation Time				
	History Class	Psychology Class	History Class	Psychology Class	History Class		
10:00	review History notes; read assignment	study	review History notes; read assignment	Transportation	review History notes	type Chemistry Lab report	revise English paper
11:00	Math Class	Psychology	Math Class	study Psychology	Math Class	(other typing)	Church
12:00	Lunch	Lunch	English Composition	Lunch	English Composition	Lunch	Lunch
1:00	Math homework	review lab procedures	class	Math homework	class	draft English paper	Review History assignment
2:00	Chemistry Class		Chemistry class	read Chemistry	Chemistry class	read Psychology chapter	Math homework
3:00	Transportation	Chemistry Lab			Transportation		read and
4:00						review Psychology notes	study Chemistry
5:00	Dinner	Transportation Dinner	Dinner	Dinner	Dinner	Dinner	Dinner
6:00	WORK		WORK		WORK		
7:00		Write lab report; start reading new chemistry		read English assignment			Call Parents
8:00		chapter; type English Composition		revise returned Composition			plan next week's Schedule
9:00							
10:00							
11:00							

Your Own Weekly Schedule

Now that you have seen a sample weekly schedule, you can begin to build your own. Fill in the blank schedule shown in Figure 1-5 on page 29, using the following suggestions:

1. **Before the week begins, assess the upcoming week's workload.** Reserve a specific time for this activity. Sunday evening works well for many students. Check your assignment notebook or calendar for upcoming quizzes, exams, papers, and assignments.

2. **Write in any appointments, such as with the doctor or dentist or for a haircut.** Add in new commitments such as baby-sitting your niece on Saturday afternoon or helping a friend repair his car.

3. **Estimate the amount of time you will need for each course.** Add extra time if you have an important exam or if the amount of reading is particularly heavy.

4. **Plan ahead.** If there's a paper due next week that requires library research, allow time this week to begin your research.

5. **Block out reasonable amounts of time, especially on weekends, for having fun and relaxing.** For example, mark off the time when your favorite television show is on, or allocate time for going to see a movie.

6. **Study difficult subjects first.** It's tempting to get easy things and short assignments out of the way first, but don't give in to this approach. When you start studying, your mind is fresh and alert and you are at your peak of concentration. This is when you are best equipped to handle difficult subjects. Thinking through complicated problems or studying complex ideas requires maximum brain power, and you have the most at the beginning of a study session.

7. **Leave the routine and more mechanical tasks for later in the evening.** Activities such as recopying papers or alphabetizing a bibliography for a research paper do not require a high degree of concentration and can be left until you are tired.

8. **Schedule study for a particular course close to the time when you attend class.** Plan to study the evening before the class meets or soon after the class meeting. If a class meets on Tuesday morning, plan to study Monday evening or Tuesday afternoon or evening.

9. **Build into your schedule a short break before you begin studying each new subject.** Your mind needs time to refocus—to switch from one set of facts, problems, and issues to another.

10. **Include short breaks when you are working on just one assignment for a long period of time.** A 10-minute break after 50 to 60 minutes of study is reasonable.

11. **When reading or studying a particular subject, try to schedule two or three short, separate blocks of time for that course rather than one long, continuous block.**

12. **Schedule study sessions at times when you know you are usually alert and feel like studying.** Do not schedule a study time early on Saturday morning if you are a person who does not really wake up until noon on weekends, and try not to schedule study time late in the evening if you are usually tired by that time.

13. **Plan to study at times when your physical surroundings are quiet.** If the dinner hour is a rushed and confusing time, don't attempt to study then if there are alternative times available.

14. **Set aside a specific time each week for developing next week's plan and reviewing your prior week's performance.**

EXERCISE 4

DIRECTIONS   Using the form given in Figure 1-5 or a photocopy of the term plan you wrote in Exercise 3, write a plan for next week.

Using your weekly schedule will be a challenge because it will mean saying no in a number of different situations. When friends call or stop by and ask you to join them at a time when you planned to study, you will have to refuse, but you could let them know when you will be free and offer to join them then. When a friend or family member asks you to do a favor—such as driving her or him somewhere—you will have to refuse, but you can suggest some alternative times when you will be free. You will find that your friends and family will accept your restraints and may even respect you for being conscientious. Don't

Figure 1-5
Weekly Time Schedule

	Monday	Tuesday	Wednesday	Thursday	Friday	Saturday	Sunday
7:00							
8:00							
9:00							
10:00							
11:00							
12:00							
1:00							
2:00							
3:00							
4:00							
5:00							
6:00							
7:00							
8:00							
9:00							
10:00							
11:00							

you respect someone who gets a great deal done and is successful in whatever he or she attempts?

Electronic Time Management

There are many computer programs available that provide an electronic calendar that enables you to keep track of important tests and quizzes, paper due dates, and appointments, as well as to plan study time. If you do not have an electronic calendar, you can use a word processor or spreadsheet program to create a weekly calendar like the one in Figure 1-4 by using the commands you would use to create a table. Each week, then, you can easily adjust the calendar to suit upcoming study demands.

TIME-SAVING TIPS FOR STUDENTS WITH BUSY SCHEDULES

Here are a few suggestions that will help you to make the best use of your time. If you are an older student with family responsibilities who is returning to college, or if you are trying both to work and to attend college, you will find these suggestions particularly valuable.

1. **Use the telephone.** When you need information or must make an appointment, phone rather than visit the office. To find out whether a book you've requested at the library has come in, for example, phone the circulation desk.

2. **Use a word processor to write papers.** Computers are time savers. They enable you to make changes to papers easily and quickly without retyping or recopying your work.

3. **Set priorities.** There may be days or weeks when you cannot complete every assignment. Many students work until they are exhausted and leave remaining assignments unfinished. A better approach is to decide what is most important to complete immediately and which assignments could, if necessary, be completed later.

4. **Use spare moments.** Think of all the time you spend waiting. You wait for a class to begin, for a ride, for a friend to call, for a pizza to arrive. Instead of wasting this time, you could use it to review a set of lecture notes, work on review questions at the end of a chapter, or review a chemistry lab setup. Always carry with you something you can work on in spare moments.

5. **Learn to combine activities.** Most people think it's impossible to do two things at once, but busy students soon learn that it's possible to combine some daily chores with routine class assignments. Some students, for example, are able to go to a laundry and, while there, outline a history chapter or work on routine assignments. Others review formulas for math or science courses or review vocabulary cards for language courses while walking to classes.

6. **Use lists to keep yourself organized and to save time.** A daily "to do" list is helpful in keeping track of what daily living/household tasks and errands, as well as course assignments, need to be done. As you think of things to be done, jot them down. Then look over the list each morning and try to find the best

way to get everything done. You may find, for instance, that you can stop at the post office on the way to the bookstore, thus saving yourself a trip.

7. **Don't be afraid to admit you're trying to do too much.** If you find your life is becoming too hectic or unmanageable, or if you are facing pressures you can't handle, consider dropping a course. Don't be too concerned that this will put you behind schedule for graduation. More than half of all college students take longer than the traditional time expected to earn their degrees. Besides, you may be able to pick up the course later during a summer session or carry a heavier load during another semester.

FIGHTING THE TENDENCY TO PROCRASTINATE

Have you ever felt that you should work on an assignment, and even wanted to get it out of the way, but could not get started? If so, you may have been a victim of procrastination—putting off tasks that need to be done. Although you know you should review your biology notes this evening, for instance, you procrastinate and do something else instead. Tedious, difficult, or uninteresting tasks are often those that we put off doing. It is often these very tasks, however, that are essential to success in college courses. The following suggestions can help you overcome or control a tendency to procrastinate and put you on track for success.

Give Yourself Five Minutes to Start

If you are having difficulty beginning a task, say to yourself that you will work on it for just five minutes. Often, once you start working, motivation and interest build and you will want to continue working.

Divide the Task into Manageable Parts

Complicated tasks are often difficult to start because they are long and seem unmanageable. Before beginning such tasks, spend a few minutes organizing and planning. Divide each task into parts, and then devise an approach strategy. In other words, list what needs to be done and in what order. In devising an approach strategy for a one-hour biology exam on the topic of cells, one student wrote the following list of subtopics to review:

Cells

atoms and molecules	cell organization
organic molecules	cell functioning
cell theory	cell division

She then decided in what order she would study these topics, which study strategy she would use, and how much time she would devote to each topic.

Clear Your Desk

Move everything from your desk except materials for the task at hand. With nothing else in front of you, you are more likely to start working and less likely to be distracted from your task while working.

Regardless of What You Do, Start!

If you are having difficulty getting started, do something other than sit and stare, regardless of how trivial it may seem. If you are having trouble writing a paper from rough draft notes, for example, start by recopying the notes. Suddenly you'll find yourself rearranging and rephrasing them, and you'll be well on your way toward writing a draft.

Recognize When You Need More Information

Sometimes procrastination is a signal that you lack skills or information. You may be avoiding a task because you're not sure how to do it. You may not really understand why a certain procedure is used to solve a particular type of math problem, for example, so you feel reluctant to do math homework. Similarly, selecting a topic for a term paper may be difficult if you aren't certain of the paper's purpose or expected length. Overcome such stumbling blocks by discussing them with classmates or with your professor.

Think Positively

As you begin a task, send yourself positive messages such as "I'll be able to stick with this" and "It will feel great to have this job done." Avoid negatives such as "This is so boring" and "I can't wait to finish."

Recognize Escape Routes

Some students escape work by claiming they don't have enough time to get everything done. Close analysis of their use of time often reveals that they are wasting valuable time by following one or more escape routes. One such route is needlessly spending time away from your desk: returning library books, going out to pick up take-out food, dropping off laundry, and so on. Another escape route is to overdo routine tasks: meticulously cleaning your room, pressing clothing, or polishing the car. Doing things by hand also consumes time: copying a friend's notes rather than photocopying them or balancing your checkbook by hand rather than using a calculator. Analyze your time carefully to detect and avoid any escape routes such as these.

Avoid "The Great Escape"—Television

For some students, television poses the greatest threat to keeping to their study-time schedule, and certainly it is often the cause of procrastination. If a TV set is on, it is tempting to watch whatever is showing. To overcome this temptation, turn it on and off at specific times for particular programs you want to see. Don't leave it on between programs you intend to watch; if you do, you'll probably continue watching.

EXERCISE 5   DIRECTIONS   Read each situation described, and then answer the questions that follow. Discuss your responses with another student, or write your answers in the spaces provided.

1. In analyzing his amount of committed time, George Andrews filled in a weekly chart, in hours, as follows:

Sleep	56
Breakfast, lunch, dinner (total)	14
Job	35
Time in classes	23
Transportation	10
Personal care	15
Household/family	20
Total	173

George is overcommitted; his total commitments add up to more hours than there are in a week (168). He has to have at least a part-time job in order to pay for school. He is enrolled in science lab technology, so he must spend a lot of class hours in lab. He estimates that he needs 30 hours per week to maintain a high B average this semester. If he schedules this amount of time, he will have virtually no time for leisure and recreation. Look at his chart again. What could he do? What are his choices? Try to find as many alternatives as you can.

_____

_____

2. Susan is a serious student but is having difficulty with her accounting course. She has decided to spend all day Sunday studying accounting. She plans to lock herself in her room and not come out until she has reviewed four chapters. What is wrong with her approach? What study plan would be more effective?

_____

_____

3. Mark realizes that he has three assignments that must be completed in one evening. The assignments are to revise an English composition, to read and highlight ten pages in his anatomy and physiology text, and to recopy a homework assignment for sociology. He decides to get the sociology assignment out of the way first, to do the English composition next (because English is one of his favorite subjects), and then to read the anatomy and physiology text. Evaluate Mark's plan of study.

_____

_____

4. You are taking a course in music appreciation, and your instructor often asks you to listen to a certain part of a concert on FM radio or to watch a particular program on television. You cannot predict when these assignments will be given or at what time you will need to complete them. What could you do to include them in your weekly study schedule?

_____

_____

5. Sam Smith is registered for the following courses, which meet at the times indicated:

Business Management 109   T-Th 12–1:30 P.M.

English 101   M-W-F 11 A.M.–12 Noon

Math 201   T-Th 9–10:30 A.M.

Biology 131   Class M-W-F 2–3 P.M.; Lab W 3–5 P.M.

Psychology 101   M-W-F 9–10 A.M.

The workload for each course is as follows:

Business Management   Two chapters assigned each week; midterm and final exams; one term paper due at the end of the semester

English   One 250-word essay per week

Math   A homework assignment for each class, which takes approximately one hour to complete; a quiz each Thursday

Biology   Preparation for weekly lab; one chapter to read per week; a one-hour exam every three weeks

Psychology   One chapter to read per week; one library reading assignment per week; four major exams throughout the semester

Because Sam has a part-time job, he has the following times available for study:

Between his classes

Evenings: Tuesday, Wednesday

Afternoons: Monday, Thursday, and Friday

Weekends: Saturday morning, all day and evening Sunday

What study schedule would you recommend for Sam? Indicate the times he should study each subject and what tasks he should work on. Use a blank time schedule (Figure 1-5) to plan a schedule for Sam.

LEARNING COLLABORATIVELY

DIRECTIONS Working with another student in your class, exchange and critique the term plans and weekly schedules you wrote in this chapter. Answer the following questions:

1. Where do you see potential problems in the schedule presented?
2. Is enough study time included?
3. Are study times scheduled appropriately? (See suggestions 1–14, pp. 28–29.)
4. Are there "empty hours" that could be used more efficiently?

APPLYING YOUR LEARNING

DIRECTIONS   Working in pairs, analyze this situation and discuss answers to the questions that follow.

Sarah decided she didn't need a time schedule because every day is the same for her. She gets up, makes breakfast, gets her children ready for school, and puts them on the bus. Then she goes to two classes, has lunch, goes to another class, and comes home to study for an hour until her children return. She spends the rest of the afternoon and evening with her husband and children. Recently, Sarah's grades have begun to fall. One of her instructors told her he feels she should spend more time preparing for class.

1. How could making a time schedule help Sarah? What might she learn?
2. Make some suggestions about how Sarah can get more study time.
3. What kinds of changes would she need to make?
4. What important decisions does Sarah need to make?

APPLYING YOUR SKILLS: Sample Textbook Chapter

DIRECTIONS   You will see the above assignment heading in most chapters in this book. This assignment refers you to a sample textbook chapter taken from an interpersonal communication college text titled *Messages: Building Interpersonal Communication Skills*. Each of these assignments will ask you to apply what you learned in the chapter by using the sample textbook chapter. For example, when you learn to identify topic sentences in paragraphs, you will be asked to highlight topic sentences in part of the textbook chapter.

Before you begin a task or assignment it is always useful to decide what you are supposed to learn by completing it. The sample textbook chapter begins on page 513; locate it now and page through it. Do not read it yet! After you have looked at it, write at least three things you hope to discover or improve when reading and studying textbook chapters. List them here.

1. _____

2. _____

3. _____

4. _____

5. _____

QUESTIONS FOR DISCUSSION

1. What are the advantages of working on assignments in several short sessions over a period of time rather than in one longer session all at once?
2. What are some of the ways that you use spare moments and combine activities to help you save time?

3. Why is it more important to overcome procrastination in college than in high school?

4. How can establishing goals and developing plans help you in a job you might hold after finishing college?

SELF-TEST SUMMARY

1. Why should I set goals?

Establishing your goals will eliminate the need to make many day-to-day choices, eliminate conflicts, and keep you focused. Begin by establishing your priorities and following them to achieve your academic goals. Next, compare the time you have allotted to various commitments with the priorities you have assigned to those activities. Finally, build a term plan that you will adjust weekly.

2. What is a term plan?

A term plan is a time schedule that lists all your fixed time commitments, including your classes, transportation time, part-time job hours, sleep, meals, sports, and family commitments. This is your basic time schedule for the semester. From it you can build your weekly schedules easily.

3. What is the value of a weekly time schedule?

A weekly time schedule helps you to plan your study time in advance and avoid last-minute choices of how to use your time best. It is your commitment on paper to how you intend to do what is necessary to accomplish your goals for the week.

4. What can a student on a busy schedule do to save time?

Many students who have heavy family and work responsibilities need to find ways to make the most of their time. They can do this by setting their priorities, organizing their time with lists, using the telephone as a time-saving tool, learning to combine activities, and using their spare moments for study tasks.

5. How can students overcome the urge to procrastinate?

Procrastination can knock even the best students off the success track. To help yourself deal with difficult, tedious, and uninteresting tasks, clear your work area of anything that will distract you, break the task up into manageable parts, get into the task immediately, avoid thinking negatively about it, avoid typical escape routes such as television, and be aware when you need more information and get it.

DIRECTIONS Write the letter of the choice that best completes each statement in the space provided.

CHECKING YOUR RECALL

_____ 1. If you are taking 12 hours of classes, you should expect to study each week for at least
   a. 6 hours.
   b. 12 hours.
   c. 24 hours.
   d. 30 hours.

_____ 2. An example of a well-defined goal is
   a. "I never want to worry about going bankrupt."
   b. "I want to earn a bachelor's degree."
   c. "I want to be a millionaire someday."
   d. "I want to earn a degree in art by the time I am 27."

_____ 3. A term plan is intended to
   a. list all of your unchanging commitments in a semester.
   b. indicate specific study times for each course.
   c. serve as a record of class assignments.
   d. be constantly revised as your weekly schedule changes.

_____ 4. An example of an effective time-saving technique is
   a. waiting as long as possible to complete an assignment.
   b. reviewing class notes while riding on the bus.
   c. eliminating optional assignments from your weekly plan.
   d. studying with a friend.

_____ 5. It is usually best to study for a difficult course
   a. in two or three short blocks of time rather than one long block.
   b. only when you really feel like it.
   c. after a warm-up session.
   d. after you have studied for your easier courses.

APPLYING YOUR KNOWLEDGE

_____ 6. Maurice is a college freshman who just started playing on an intramural water polo team. Maurice was an A/B student in high school and is working a part-time job to help pay for college. Which of the following goals is the most appropriate for Maurice?
   a. I will never get a grade lower than an A in college.
   b. I will make the U.S. Olympic Water Polo Team next year.
   c. I will study for 40 hours each week.
   d. I will graduate from college with at least a 3.0 grade point average within five years.

_____ 7. If you have a biology class on Tuesday mornings, you should plan to study for it on
   a. Monday evenings.
   b. Thursday afternoons.
   c. Friday evenings.
   d. the weekend.

_____ 8. Of the following tasks associated with a math course, the best one to work on early in the evening is
   a. recopying a friend's notes from a class you missed.
   b. learning a difficult method for computing statistics.
   c. copying math formulas from the textbook onto index cards.
   d. checking to make sure you have the assignment written down correctly.

_____ 9. Sarah has an economics examination tomorrow. She has been cramming for four hours straight and is starting to panic. Which of the following suggestions would NOT have helped Sarah to study more effectively?
   a. Studying her easier topics first
   b. Studying in short blocks of time, rather than one long block
   c. Taking a ten-minute break for each hour that she studies
   d. Scheduling her study session at a time when she is alert and feels like studying

QUICK QUIZ   *Continued*   NAME:

_____ 10. Tonight, Justine needs to prepare for a math midterm examination that she'll take tomorrow, make vocabulary flash cards for tomorrow's Russian class, and read three chapters in a novel for her English class in two days. In what order should she most likely attack these assignments?

a. math, Russian, English
b. math, English, Russian
c. Russian, math, English
d. English, Russian, math

MULTIMEDIA *Activities*

Setting Goals and Managing Your Time

1 Go the Web site: http://www.mygoals.com
Opt for the ten-day free trial. Use the software to set specific goals for yourself and to help you create a "Goalplan" for achieving them.

2 Where Does the Time Go?

http://www.ucc.vt.edu/stdysk/TMInteractive.html

Try this online inventory prepared by Virginia Polytechnic Institute and State University to find out how you spend your time each week. Use your results to create a weekly schedule for yourself.

3 Seven-Day Procrastination Plan

http://www.reshall.berkeley.edu/academics/resources/handouts/midterm/7dayprocrastination-study21.doc

Over the next week, use these tips from the Student Learning Center at UC Berkeley to help you accomplish a task or complete a project that you have been putting off.

4 What constitutes success? Close your eyes and imagine yourself at a particular age as a successful person. What do you see? Are you surrounded by friends and family? Do you have a rewarding career? Now, as if you are operating a camera lens, move closer to the image. What details are revealed? Write a list of qualities or conditions that characterize success for you.

5 Write a mission statement for your life. What do you want to accomplish? Is it important to help others? Is having children important? Paste your statement on your mirror so that you will keep seeing your face together with your mission statement.

6 Sketch a picture of yourself overwhelmed by stress. Sketch or write the names of stressors. Choose one and write a goal for completing that activity or solving that problem.

2 Learning Style and Learning Strategies

Why Analyze Your Learning Style?

- ■ You will understand your strengths and weaknesses as a learner and understand how to choose study methods accordingly.
- ■ You will realize why you learn more easily from some instructors than from others.
- ■ You will discover what kinds of learning and thinking are expected in college.

Learning Experiment

Step 1

Study the photograph on the right for one minute.

Step 2

Draw a sketch of one of the people in the photograph.

Step 3

Write two or three sentences describing this person.

Step 4

Compare your drawing and descriptions with those of your classmates by quickly passing them around the room.

The Results

No doubt, some sketches were much better than others. Some were detailed, accurate likenesses; others may have resembled stick figures. Likewise, some students wrote detailed descriptive sentences; others did not. You can conclude that some students have stronger artistic ability than others. Some students have stronger verbal abilities than others. Which students do you expect will do well in an art class? Who will do better on essay exams? Who might consider a career in graphic design? Who should not?

Learning Principle (What This Means to You)

You have strengths and weaknesses as a learner; you should capitalize on your strengths and strive to overcome your weaknesses. In this chapter you will learn to identify strengths and weaknesses and choose study methods accordingly. You will also discover that instructors have unique teaching styles and discover how to adapt to them. Finally, you will learn what kinds of learning and thinking your instructors expect of you.

ANALYZING YOUR LEARNING STYLE

Have you noticed that some types of tasks are easier to learn than others? Have you also discovered that some study methods work better than others? Have you ever found that a study method that works well for a classmate does not work as well for you? These differences can be explained by what is known as *learning style*. Just as you have a unique personality, you also have a unique learning style. People differ in how they learn and in the methods and strategies they use to learn. Your learning style can, in part, explain why some courses are easier than others and why you learn better from one instructor than from another. Learning style can also explain why certain assignments are difficult and other learning tasks are easy.

To begin to understand learning style, think of everyday tasks and activities that you have learned to do easily and well. Think of others that are always troublesome. For example, is reading maps easy or difficult? Is drawing or sketching easy or difficult? Can you assemble items easily? Are tasks that require physical coordination (such as racquetball) difficult? Can you easily remember the lyrics to popular songs? Just as some everyday tasks are easy and others are difficult, so are some academic tasks easy and others more challenging.

The following questionnaire will help you analyze how you learn and enable you to learn more efficiently. Complete the following Learning Style Questionnaire before continuing.

Learning Style Questionnaire

DIRECTIONS   Each item presents two choices. Select the alternative that best describes you. In cases where neither choice suits you, select the one that is closer to your preference. Write the letter of your choice in the blank to the left of each item.

PART ONE

_____ 1. I would prefer to follow a set of
   a. oral directions.
   b. written directions.

_____ 2. I would prefer to
   a. attend a lecture given by a famous psychologist.
   b. read an article written by the psychologist.

_____ 3. When I am introduced to someone, it is easier for me to remember the person's
   a. name.
   b. face.

_____ 4. I find it easier to learn new information using
   a. language (words).
   b. images (pictures).

_____ 5. I prefer classes in which the instructor
   a. lectures and answers questions.
   b. uses films and videos.

_____ 6. To follow current events, I prefer to
   a. listen to the news on the radio.
   b. read the newspaper.

_____ 7. To learn how to operate a fax machine, I would prefer to
   a. listen to a friend's explanation.
   b. watch a demonstration.

PART TWO

_____ 8. I prefer to
   a. work with facts and details.
   b. construct theories and ideas.

_____ 9. I would prefer a job that involved
   a. following specific instructions.
   b. reading, writing, and analyzing.

_____ 10. I prefer to
   a. solve math problems using a formula.
   b. discover why the formula works.

_____ 11. I would prefer to write a term paper explaining
   a. how a process works.
   b. a theory.

_____ 12. I prefer tasks that require me to
   a. follow careful, detailed instructions.
   b. use reasoning and critical analysis.

_____ 13. For a criminal justice course, I would prefer to
   a. discover how and when a law can be applied.
   b. learn how and why it became law.

_____ 14. To learn more about the operation of a high-speed computer printer, I would prefer to
   a. work with several types of printers.
   b. understand the principles on which it operates.

PART THREE

_____ 15. To solve a math problem, I would prefer to
   a. draw or visualize the problem.
   b. study a sample problem and use it as a model.

_____ 16. To remember something best, I
   a. create a mental picture.
   b. write it down.

_____ 17. Assembling a bicycle from a diagram would be
   a. easy.
   b. challenging.

_____ 18. I prefer classes in which I
   a. handle equipment or work with models.
   b. participate in a class discussion.

_____ 19. To understand and remember how a machine works, I would
   a. draw a diagram.
   b. write notes.

_____ 20. I enjoy
   a. drawing or working with my hands.
   b. speaking, writing, and listening.

_____ 21. If I were trying to locate an office on an unfamiliar university campus, I would prefer
   a. a map.
   b. a set of written directions.

PART FOUR

_____ 22. For a grade in biology lab, I would prefer to
   a. work with a lab partner.
   b. work alone.

_____ 23. When faced with a difficult personal problem, I prefer to
   a. discuss it with others.
   b. resolve it myself.

_____ 24. Many instructors could improve their classes by
   a. including more discussion and group activities.
   b. allowing students to work on their own more frequently.

_____ 25. When listening to a lecturer or speaker, I respond more to
   a. the person presenting the ideas.
   b. the ideas themselves.

_____ 26. When on a team project, I prefer to
   a. work with several team members.
   b. divide up tasks and complete those assigned to me.

_____ 27. I prefer to shop and do errands
   a. with friends.
   b. by myself.

_____ 28. A job in a busy office is
   a. more appealing than working alone.
   b. less appealing than working alone.

PART FIVE

_____ 29. To make decisions, I rely on
   a. my experiences and gut feelings.
   b. facts and objective data.

_____ 30. To complete a task, I
   a. can use whatever is available to get the job done.
   b. must have everything I need at hand.

_____ 31. I prefer to express my ideas and feelings through
   a. music, song, or poetry.
   b. direct, concise language.

_____ 32. I prefer instructors who
   a. allow students to be guided by their own interests.
   b. make their expectations clear and explicit.

_____ 33. I tend to
   a. challenge and question what I hear and read.
   b. accept what I hear and read.

_____ 34. I prefer
   a. essay exams.
   b. objective exams.

_____ 35. In completing an assignment, I prefer to
   a. figure out my own approach.
   b. be told exactly what to do.

To score your questionnaire, record the total number of times you selected choice a and the total number of times you selected choice b for each part of the questionnaire. Record your totals in the scoring grid provided.

SCORING GRID		
Part	**Total # of Choice a**	**Total # of Choice b**
Part One	_____ Auditory	_____ Visual
Part Two	_____ Applied	_____ Conceptual
Part Three	_____ Spatial	_____ Verbal
Part Four	_____ Social	_____ Independent
Part Five	_____ Creative	_____ Pragmatic

Now circle your higher score for each part of the questionnaire. The word below the score you circled indicates an aspect of your learning style. Scores in a particular row that are close to one another, such as a 3 and a 4, suggest that you do not exhibit a strong, clear preference for either aspect. Scores that are farther apart, such as a 1 and a 6, suggest a strong preference for the higher-scoring aspect. The next section explains how to interpret your scores and describes these aspects.

Interpreting Your Scores

The questionnaire was divided into five parts; each part identifies one aspect of your learning style. These five aspects are explained below.

Part One: Auditory or Visual Learners

This score indicates the sensory mode you prefer when processing information. Auditory learners tend to learn more effectively through listening, whereas visual learners process information by seeing it in print or other visual modes, including films, pictures, or diagrams. If you have a higher score in auditory than visual, you tend to be an auditory learner. That is, you tend to learn more easily by hearing than by reading. A higher score in visual suggests strengths with visual modes of learning.

Part Two: Applied or Conceptual Learners

This score describes the types of learning tasks and learning situations you prefer and find easiest to handle. If you are an applied learner, you prefer tasks that involve real objects and situations. Practical, real-life learning situations are ideal for you. If you are a conceptual learner, you prefer to work with language and ideas; practical applications are not necessary for understanding.

Part Three: Spatial or Verbal Learners

This score reveals your ability to work with spatial relationships. Spatial learners are able to visualize, or mentally see, how things work or how they are positioned in space. Their strengths may include drawing, assembling things, or repairing. Verbal learners lack skills in positioning things in space. Instead, they tend to rely on verbal or language skills.

Part Four: Social or Independent Learners

This score reveals your preferred level of interaction with other people in the learning process. If you are a social learner, you prefer to work with others—both peers and instructors—closely and directly. You tend to be people-oriented and to enjoy personal interaction. If you are an independent learner, you prefer to work and study alone. You tend to be self-directed or self-motivated and often are goal-oriented.

Part Five: Creative or Pragmatic Learners

This score describes the approach you prefer to take toward learning tasks. Creative learners are imaginative and innovative. They prefer to learn through discovery or experimentation. They are comfortable taking risks and following hunches. Pragmatic learners are practical, logical, and systematic. They seek order and are comfortable following rules.

EXERCISE 1

DIRECTIONS   Write a paragraph describing yourself as a learner. Include aspects of your learning style and give examples from everyday experience that confirm your profile. Explain any results of the Learning Style Questionnaire with which you disagree.

DEVELOPING AN ACTION PLAN FOR LEARNING

Now that you know more about *how* you learn, you are ready to develop an action plan for learning what you read. Suppose you discovered that you are an auditory learner. You still have to read your assignments, which is a visual task. However, to learn the assignment you should translate the material into an auditory form. For example, you could repeat aloud, using your own words, information that you want to remember, or you could tape-record key information and play it back. If you also are a social learner, you could work with a classmate, testing each other out loud.

Figure 2-1, on page 47, lists each aspect of learning style and offers suggestions for how to learn from a reading assignment. To use the figure:

1. Circle the five aspects of your learning style for which you received higher scores. Disregard the others.
2. Read through the suggestions that apply to you.
3. Place a check mark in front of those suggestions you think will work for you. Choose at least one from each category.
4. List the suggestions you chose in the following Action Plan for Learning box.

ACTION PLAN FOR LEARNING

Learning Strategy 1._____

_____

Learning Strategy 2._____

_____

Learning Strategy 3._____

_____

Learning Strategy 4._____

_____

Learning Strategy 5._____

_____

Now that you have listed suggestions to help you learn what you read, the next step is to experiment with these techniques, one at a time. (You may need to refer to the chapters listed in parentheses in Figure 2-1 to learn or review how a certain technique works.) Use one technique for a while, then move on to the next. Continue using the techniques that seem to work; work on revising or modifying those that do not. Do not hesitate to experiment with other techniques listed in the figure; you may find other techniques that work well for you.

Developing Strategies to Overcome Limitations

You should also work on developing the weaker aspects of your learning style. Your learning style is not fixed or unchanging. You can improve areas in which you had low scores. Although you may be weak in auditory learning, for example, many of your professors will lecture and expect you to take notes. If you work on improving your listening and note-taking skills, you can learn to handle lectures effectively. Make a conscious effort to work on improving areas of weakness as well as taking advantage of your strengths.

Several Words of Caution

Ideally, through activities in this section and the use of the questionnaire, you have discovered more about yourself as a learner. However, several words of caution are in order.

1. The questionnaire is a quick and easy way to discover your learning style. Other more formal and more accurate measures of learning style are available. These include *Kolb's Learning Style Inventory* and the *Myers–Briggs Type Indicator.* These tests may be available through your college's counseling, testing, or academic skills centers.
2. There are many more aspects of learning style than those identified through the questionnaire in this chapter. To learn more about other factors affecting learning, see one or both of the tests listed above.

Figure 2-1
Learning Strategies for
Various Learning Styles

Auditory	Visual
1. Tape review notes.	1. Use mapping (see Chapter 15).
2. Discuss/study with friends.	2. Use visualization.
3. Talk aloud when studying.	3. Use CD-ROMs if available.
4. Tape lectures.	4. View videos when available.
	5. Draw diagrams, charts, and maps.

Applied	Conceptual
1. Associate ideas with their application.	1. Use outlining.
2. Take courses with a lab or practicum.	2. Focus on thought patterns (see Chapter 7).
3. Think of practical situations to which learning applies.	3. Organize materials into rules and examples.
4. Use case studies, examples, and applications to cue your learning.	

Spatial	Verbal
1. Draw diagrams; make charts and sketches.	1. Record steps, processes, and procedures in words.
2. Use outlining.	2. Write summaries.
3. Use visualization.	3. Translate diagrams and drawings into language.
4. Use mapping (see Chapter 15).	4. Write your interpretations next to textbook drawings, maps, and graphics.

Social	Independent
1. Interact with the instructor.	1. Use computer-assisted instruction if available.
2. Find a study partner.	2. Enroll in courses using a traditional lecture-exam format.
3. Form a study group.	3. Consider independent study courses.
4. Take courses involving class discussion.	4. Purchase review books and study guides, if available.
5. Work with a tutor.	

Creative	Pragmatic
1. Take courses that involve exploration, experimentation, or discussion.	1. Write lists of steps, processes, and procedures.
2. Use annotation to record impressions and reactions.	2. Write summaries and outlines.
3. Ask questions about chapter content and answer them.	3. Use a structured study environment.
	4. Focus on problem-solving and logical sequence.

3. Learning style is *not* a fixed, unchanging quality. Just as personalities can change and develop, so can learning style change and develop through exposure, instruction, or practice. For example, as you attend more college lectures, your skill as an auditory learner may be strengthened.

4. You probably will not be clearly strong or weak in each aspect. Some students, for example, can learn equally well spatially and verbally. If your scores on one or more parts of the questionnaire were quite close, then you may have strengths in both areas.

5. When most students discover the features of their learning style, they recognize themselves. A frequent comment is "Yep, that's me." However, if for some reason you feel the description of yourself as a learner is incorrect, then do not make changes in your learning strategies on the basis of the outcome. Instead, discuss your style with your instructor or consider taking one of the tests listed in point 1, above.

UNDERSTANDING YOUR INSTRUCTORS' TEACHING STYLES

Just as each student has his or her own learning style, so does each instructor have his or her own teaching style. Some instructors, for example, have a teaching style that promotes social interaction among students. An instructor may organize small group activities, encourage class participation, or require students to work in pairs or teams to complete a specific task. Other instructors offer little or no opportunity for social interaction, as in a lecture class for example.

Some instructors are very applied; they teach by example. Others are more conceptual; they focus on presenting ideas, rules, theories, and so forth. In fact, the same five categories of learning styles identified on pages 44–45 can be applied to teaching styles as well.

To an extent, of course, the subject matter also dictates how the instructor teaches. A biology instructor, for instance, has a large body of factual information to present and may feel he or she has little time to schedule group interaction.

Comparing Learning and Teaching Style

Once you are aware of your learning style and consider the instructor's teaching style, you can begin to understand why you can learn better from one instructor than from another and why you feel more comfortable in certain instructors' classes than in others. When aspects of your learning style match aspects of your instructor's teaching style, you are on the same wavelength, so to speak: the instructor is teaching the way you learn. On the other hand, when your learning style does not correspond to an instructor's teaching style, you may not be as comfortable, and learning will be more of a challenge. You may have to work harder in that class by taking extra steps to reorganize or reformat the material into a form better suited to your learning style. The following section presents each of the five categories of learning–teaching styles and suggests how you might make changes in how you study to accommodate each.

Auditory–Visual

If your instructor announces essential course information (such as paper assignments, class projects, or descriptions of upcoming exams) orally and you are a visual learner, you should be sure to record as much information as possible in your notes. If your instructor relies on lectures to present new material not included in your textbook, taking complete lecture notes is especially important. If your instructor uses numerous visual aids and you tend to be an auditory learner, consider tape-recording summaries of these visual aids.

Applied–Conceptual

If your instructor seldom uses examples, models, or case studies and you are an applied learner, you need to think of your own examples to make the course material real and memorable to you. Leave space in your class notes to add examples. Add them during class if they come to mind; if not, take time as you review your notes to add examples. If your instructor uses numerous demonstrations and examples and you are a conceptual learner, you may need to leave space in your class notes to write in rules or generalizations that state what the examples are intended to prove.

Spatial–Verbal

If you are a spatial learner and your instructor has a verbal teaching style (he or she lectures and writes notes on the board), then you will need to draw diagrams, charts, and pictures to learn the material. On the other hand, if you are a verbal learner and your instructor is spatial (he or she frequently uses diagrams, flowcharts, and so forth), then you may need to translate the diagrams and flowcharts into words in order to learn them easily.

Social–Independent

If your instructor organizes numerous in-class group activities and you tend to be an independent learner, then you will need to spend time alone after class reviewing the class activity, making notes, and perhaps even repeating the activity by yourself to make it more meaningful. If your instructor seldom structures in-class group activities and you tend to be a social learner, try to arrange to study regularly with a classmate or create or join a study group.

Creative–Pragmatic

Suppose your instructor is very systematic and structured in his or her lectures, and, as a creative learner, you prefer to discover ideas through experimentation and free-flowing discussion. In this case, you should consider creating a column in your class notes to record your responses and creative thoughts or reserve the bottom quarter of each page for such annotations. If your instructor is creative and tends to use a loose or free-flowing class format, and you tend to be a pragmatic learner, you may need to rewrite and restructure class notes. If he or she fails to give you specific guidelines for completing activities or assignments, you should talk with your instructor or ask for more information.

EXERCISE 2

DIRECTIONS   Analyze your instructors' teaching styles by completing the following chart for the courses you are taking this semester. List as many teaching characteristics as you can, but do not try to cover every aspect of learning–teaching style.

Course	Instructor's Name	Teaching-Style Characteristics
1.		
2.		
3.		
4.		
5.		
6.		

EXERCISE 3

DIRECTIONS After you have completed the chart in Exercise 2, select one of your instructors whose teaching style does not match your learning style. Write a paragraph describing the differences in your styles. Explain how you will change your study methods to make up for these differences.

MEETING YOUR INSTRUCTORS' EXPECTATIONS

Learning in college is different from learning in high school or on-the-job training. Now that you have a profile of yourself as a learner, it is time to discover what kinds of learning are expected of you. Whether you have just completed high school or are returning to college with work experiences or family responsibilities, you will face new demands and expectations in college. The following sections describe your instructors' expectations.

Take Responsibility for Your Own Learning

In college, learning is mainly up to you. Instructors function as guides. They define and explain what is to be learned, but they expect you to do the learning. Weekly class time is far shorter than in high school. Often there isn't enough time in class for instructors to provide drills, practices, and reviews of factual course content. Instead, college class time is used primarily to introduce content that is to be learned and to discuss ideas. Instructors expect you to learn the material and to be prepared to discuss it in class. *When, where,* and *how* you learn are your choices. Be sure to take into account the five aspects of your learning style as you make these choices.

Focus on Concepts

Each course you take will require that you learn a great many facts, statistics, dates, definitions, formulas, rules, or principles. It is easy to become convinced that learning these is sufficient and to become a robot learner—memorizing facts from texts and lectures and then recalling them on exams and quizzes. Actually, factual information is only a starting point, a base from which to approach the real content of a course. Most college instructors expect you to go beyond facts to analysis—to consider what the collection of facts and details *means.* Many students, however, "can't see the forest for the trees"; they get caught up in specifics and fail to grasp the larger, more important concepts. To avoid this pitfall, be sure to keep the following questions in mind as you read and study:

- Why do I need to know this?
- Why is this important?
- What principle or trend does this illustrate?
- How can I use this information?
- How does this fit in with other course content?

Focus on Ideas, Not "Right Answers"

Through previous schooling, many students have come to expect their answers to be either right or wrong. They assume that learning is limited to memorizing a collection of facts and that their mastery of the course is measured by the number of "right answers" they have learned. Accordingly, they are lost when faced with an essay question such as:

> Defend or criticize the arguments that are offered in favor of capital punishment. Refer to any readings that you have completed.

There is no one right answer to this question. You can either defend the arguments or criticize them. The instructor who asks this question expects you to think and to provide a reasoned, logical, consistent response that draws on information you have acquired through your reading. Here are a few more examples of questions for which there are no single correct answers.

> Do animals think?

> Would you be willing to reduce your standard of living by 15 percent if the United States could thereby eliminate poverty? Defend your response.

> Imagine a society in which everyone has exactly the same income. You are the manager of an industrial plant. What plans, policies, or programs would you implement to motivate your employees to work?

Evaluate New Ideas

Throughout college you will continually meet new ideas; you will agree with some and disagree with others. Don't make the mistake of accepting or rejecting a new idea, however, until you have really explored it and have considered its assumptions and implications. Ask questions such as:

- What evidence is available in support of this idea?
- What opposing evidence is available?
- How is my personal experience related to this idea?
- What additional information do I need in order to make a decision?

Explore Ideas Using a Journal

As you begin college, you will encounter many new ideas and meet many new people, both classmates and instructors, from whom you will discover new approaches and conventions—new ways of looking at and doing things. You will also begin to explore many academic fields that you did not study in high school. It is easy to feel overwhelmed by it all. Sometimes you need to sort out ideas and your reactions to them. Many students find it helpful to keep a journal. A journal is an informal record of your thoughts, ideas, impressions, and reactions. Most students use a spiral-bound notebook, but because a journal is written for you, not your instructor, it may take any form you select and may contain whatever you choose. Some students record impressions and feelings; others record new ideas they want to explore. Writing about your ideas will focus them and clarify your response to them. Journal entries, by the way, are an excellent source of ideas when you have to choose a topic about which to write a paper.

Because learning is a major focus of college, and because you will be reading about new learning strategies throughout this book, consider including in your journal a record of each learning strategy you try and how it works. You will find it helpful to review your journal; often, doing so will suggest which strategies seem to work for each of your courses. A learning journal is discussed in more detail in Chapter 16, pages 373–374.

DEVELOPING ACTIVE LEARNING STRATEGIES

Your instructors also expect you to become an active learner, illustrated by the following situation. A first-year student who had always thought of himself as a B student was getting low C's and D's in his business course. The instructor gave weekly quizzes; each was a practical problem to solve. Every week the student memorized his lecture notes and carefully reread the assigned chapter in his textbook. When he spoke with his instructor about his low grades, the instructor told him that his study methods were not effective and that he needed to become more active and involved with the subject matter. Memorizing and rereading are passive approaches. The instructor suggested that he try instead to think about content, ask questions, anticipate practical uses, solve potential problems, and draw connections between ideas.

Active Versus Passive Learning

How did you learn to ride a bike, play racquetball, or change a tire? In each case you learned by doing, by active participation. College learning requires similar active involvement and participation. Active learning is expected in most college courses and can often make the difference between barely average grades and top grades. Figure 2-2 below lists common college learning situations and contrasts the responses of active and passive learners. The examples in Figure 2-2 show that passive learners do not carry the learning process far enough. They do not go beyond what instructors tell them to do. They fail to think about, organize, and react to course content.

Figure 2-2 Characteristics of Passive and Active Learners	Passive Learners	Active Learners
Class lectures	Write down what the instructor says	Decide what is important to write down
Textbook assignments	Read	Read, think, ask questions, try to connect ideas
Studying	Reread	Consider learning style, make outlines and study sheets, predict exam questions, look for trends and patterns
Writing class assignments	Only follow the professor's instructions	Try to discover the significance of the assignment, look for the principles and concepts it illustrates
Writing term papers	Do only what is expected to get a good grade	Try to expand their knowledge and experience with a topic and connect it to the course objective or content

Active Learning Strategies

When you study, you should be thinking about and reacting to the material in front of you. This is how you make it happen:

1. **Ask questions about what you are reading.** You will find that this helps to focus your attention and improve your concentration.
2. **Consider the purpose behind assignments.** Why might a sociology assignment require you to spend an hour at the monkey house of the local zoo, for example?
3. **Try to see how each assignment fits with the rest of the course.** For instance, why does a section called "Amortization" belong in a business mathematics textbook chapter entitled "Business and Consumer Loans"?
4. **Relate what you are learning to what you already know from the course and from your background knowledge and personal experience.** Connect a law in physics with how your car brakes work, for example.
5. **Think of examples or situations in which you can apply the information.**

Throughout the remainder of this text, you will learn many strategies for becoming an active learner. Active learning also involves active reading. In Chapter 5 you will learn specific strategies for becoming an active reader.

EXERCISE 4

DIRECTIONS   Review each of the following learning situations. Answer each question by suggesting active learning approaches.

1. Having a graded exam returned to you by your history professor. How could you use this as a learning device? _____

   _____

2. Being assigned "Letter from Birmingham Jail" by Martin Luther King, Jr., for your English composition class. What questions would you try to answer as you read? _____

   _____

3. Completing a biology lab. How would you prepare for it? _____

   _____

4. Being assigned by your sociology instructor to read an article in *Newsweek* on crime in major U.S. cities. How would you record important ideas? _____

   _____

THINKING CRITICALLY

In college, your instructors expect you to learn actively, and they also expect you to think critically. A first step in becoming a critical thinker is to become familiar with the types of thinking that college instructors demand. Figure 2-3, on page 54, lists six levels of thinking in order of increasing complexity. Based on a progression of thinking skills developed by Benjamin Bloom and revised by Anderson, they are widely used by educators in many academic disciplines.

Figure 2-3
Levels of Thinking

Level	Examples
REMEMBERING: recalling information, repeating information with no changes	Recalling dates, memorizing definitions for a history exam
UNDERSTANDING: understanding ideas, using rules, and following directions	Explaining a mathematical law, knowing how the human ear functions, explaining a definition in psychology
APPLYING: applying knowledge to a new situation	Using knowledge of formulas to solve a new physics problem
ANALYZING: seeing relationships, breaking information into parts, analyzing how things work	Comparing two poems by the same author
EVALUATING: making judgments, assessing the value or worth of information	Evaluating the effectiveness of an argument opposing the death penalty
CREATING: putting ideas and information together in a unique way, creating something new	Designing a new computer program

The *remembering* level of thinking is basically memorization; this is something you've been doing for years. The *understanding* level is also familiar. If you are able to explain how to convert fractions to decimals, then you are thinking at the comprehension level. At the *applying* level, you apply to a new situation information that you have memorized and understood. When you use your knowledge of punctuation to place commas correctly in a sentence, you are functioning at the application level. The *analyzing* level involves examining what you have learned and studying relationships. When you explain how a microscope works, you are analyzing its operation. *Evaluating* involves making judgments. When you decide what is effective and what is ineffective in a classmate's presentation in a public speaking class, you are evaluating the presentation. The *creating* level requires you to put ideas together to form something new. When you write a paper by drawing on a variety of sources, you are synthesizing them.

Using Levels of Thinking

The last three levels—analyzing, evaluating, and creating—involve critical thinking. Some exam questions require you to remember, understand, and apply. Many objective exams (multiple-choice, true–false) include items that focus on these levels. Essay exams, however, as well as some multiple-choice questions, require thinking at the three higher levels. Participating in class discussions, writing papers, making speeches, and artistic expression (music, painting, and the like) all require analyzing, evaluating, and/or creating. In later chapters, you'll learn more about these levels of thinking when preparing for and taking exams (see Chapters 17 and 18).

Applying Levels of Thinking
READING AND LEVELS OF THINKING

As you read, be sure to think at each level. Here is a list of questions to help you read and think at each level.

Level of Thinking	Questions
REMEMBERING	What information do I need to learn?
UNDERSTANDING	What are the main points and how are they supported?
APPLYING	How can I use this information?
ANALYZING	How is this material organized? How are the ideas related?
	How are the data presented in graphs, tables, and charts related? What trends do they reveal?
EVALUATING	Is this information accurate, reliable, and valuable? Does the author prove his or her points?
CREATING	How does this information fit with other sources (class lectures, other readings, your prior knowledge)?

EXERCISE 5

DIRECTIONS   Identify the level or levels of thinking that each of the following tasks demands.

1. Retelling a favorite family story to your nieces and nephews

   _____

2. Using the principles of time management discussed in Chapter 1 to develop a weekly study plan

   _____

3. Learning the names of the U.S. presidents since World War II

   _____

4. Reorganizing your lecture notes by topic

   _____

5. Writing a letter to the editor of your hometown newspaper praising a recently passed city ordinance that restricts new toxic-waste disposal sites

   _____

6. Writing a term paper that requires library research

   _____

7. Using prereading techniques when reading your speech communication textbook

   _____

8. Listening to speeches by two candidates who are running for mayor and then deciding which one gets your vote

   _____

9. Watching several hours of TV programming to determine the amount of time given to commercials, to public service announcements, to entertainment programs, and to news

_____

10. Writing an article for the campus newspaper explaining why on-campus parking is inadequate

_____

EXERCISE 6

DIRECTIONS   Read "Dimensions of Nonverbal Communication" and answer the questions that follow.

Dimensions of Nonverbal Communication

In recent years, research has reemphasized the important role of physical, or non-verbal, behaviors in effective oral communication. Basically, three generalizations about nonverbal communication should occupy your attention when you are a speaker:

1. *Speakers reveal and reflect their emotional states through their nonverbal behaviors.* Your listeners read your feelings toward yourself, your topic, and your audience from your facial expressions. Consider the contrast between a speaker who walks to the front of the room briskly, head held high, and one who shuffles, head bowed and arms hanging limply. Communications scholar Dale G. Leathers summarized a good deal of research into nonverbal communication processes: "Feelings and emotions are more accurately exchanged by nonverbal than verbal means. . . . The nonverbal portion of communication conveys meanings and intentions that are relatively free from deception, distortion, and confusion."

2. *The speaker's nonverbal cues enrich or elaborate the message that comes through words.* A solemn face can reinforce the dignity of a funeral eulogy. The words "Either do this or do that" can be illustrated with appropriate arm-and-hand gestures. Taking a few steps to one side tells an audience that you are moving from one argument to another. A smile enhances a lighter moment in your speech.

3. *Nonverbal messages form a reciprocal interaction between speaker and listener.* Listeners frown, smile, shift nervously in their seats, and engage in many types of nonverbal behavior. . . . There are four areas of nonverbal commu-nication that concern every speaker: (a) *proxemics,* (b) *movement and stance,* (c) *facial expressions,* and (d) *gestures.*

—Gronbeck et al., *Principles of Speech Communication,* pp. 217–218

1. Remembering: What are the three generalizations?
2. Understanding: Explain how a speaker can reveal his or her emotional state.
3. Applying: Give an example (not used in the excerpt) of how a speaker can reveal his or her emotional state.
4. Analyzing: If nonverbal communication is free of deception, is it possible to tell a lie using body language?
5. Evaluating: How is this information useful and important to me in a public speaking class?
6. Creating: To what extent is this information consistent with what I already know about nonverbal messages?

EXERCISE 7 | **DIRECTIONS**   Read "Body Adornment," in Part Eight, pages 450–453. Then write two questions that require thinking at each of the levels we have discussed (a total of 12 questions).

LEARNING COLLABORATIVELY

DIRECTIONS   Working in groups of two or three, prepare a "Need to Know" list for new students on your campus. Include information you have discovered so far about learning and studying in college. Groups should compare and compile lists and may wish to prepare a handout for next semester's class, post information on the campus Web site, or submit the final list to the college newspaper for publication or to the director of student orientation for use with incoming students.

APPLYING YOUR LEARNING

DIRECTIONS   Form groups of three or four students and analyze the following situation. Discuss answers to the questions that follow.

A history professor has just returned graded midterm exams to her class. One student looks at the grade on the first page, flips through the remaining pages while commenting to a friend that the exam was "too picky," and files it in her notebook. A second student reviews his exam for grading errors and notices one error. Immediately, he raises his hand and asks for an adjustment to his grade. The instructor seems annoyed and tells the student she will not use class time to dispute individual grades. A third student reviews her exam bluebook to identify a pattern of error; on the cover of the bluebook, she notes topics and areas in which she is weak.

1. Compare the three students' responses to the situation.
2. What does each student's response reveal about his or her approach to learning?
3. Analyze the student's response to the instructor's error in grading. What alternatives might have been more appropriate?
4. At what level(s) of thinking was each of the three students functioning?

APPLYING YOUR SKILLS: Sample Textbook Chapter

Read the first section of the Sample Textbook Chapter on page 515, titled "Culture and Cultural Processes."

Answer each of the following questions:

1. Remembering: What is the definition of culture?
2. Understanding: How do people learn cultural roles?
3. Applying: Give an example of an ethnic group.
4. Analyzing: Why would risk takers have greater acculturation potential?
5. Evaluating: Evaluate the seven statements listed on page 515 that are used to measure cultural identity. Are they fair and comprehensive?
6. Creating: Create a list of questions that could be used to evaluate an immigrant's readiness to accept a new culture.

QUESTIONS FOR DISCUSSION

1. What are the most common learning styles in your class? Discuss some subject-specific strategies that those with each style can apply to their studies.
2. How do learning styles relate to choice of major or choice of profession? Discuss majors and jobs that may be most appropriate and inappropriate for the various learning styles.
3. Take a look at the tests you've taken so far in college. Determine which of Benjamin Bloom's types of thinking are present in each exam question. Brainstorm some study strategies to help you prepare for questions in each category.

SELF-TEST SUMMARY

1. Why is it useful to analyze your learning style?

Analyzing your learning style can help you to understand why you may learn better from one instructor than another and why some courses are easier for you than others. Building an awareness of how you learn best and what your limitations are can help you understand how to study more effectively and become a more efficient learner.

2. Why is it important to analyze your instructors' teaching styles?

You may need to make changes in how you learn to suit each instructor's teaching style.

3. What do instructors expect of college students?

In college, students are expected to set their own operating rules, take responsibility for their own learning, and focus on and evaluate ideas and concepts.

4. What does "becoming an active learner" mean?

Active learning is essential to success in college. To become a more effective learner, you should get actively involved with reading assignments, lectures, and class activities by (a) asking questions about class presentations and reading assignments, and (b) looking for the purpose behind learning the information presented.

5. What levels of thinking are expected of college students?

College instructors expect their students to read and think critically. There are six levels of thinking: remembering, understanding, applying, analyzing, evaluating, and creating. Many classroom activities, such as exams, papers, and discussions, require reading and thinking at these levels.

DIRECTIONS Write the letter of the choice that best completes each statement in the space provided.

CHECKING YOUR RECALL

_____ 1. Learning style can be defined as

    a. person's mental ability and capacity for learning.

    b. the speed with which a person can grasp information.

    c. how much information a person remembers.

    d. the methods a person uses best in taking in information.

_____ 2. The primary value of identifying your learning style is that it can help you

    a. become interested in what you are studying.

    b. develop and maintain your concentration.

    c. become more efficient in how you study.

    d. increase your reading rate.

_____ 3. In order to meet your instructors' expectations, you should

    a. focus on "right answers."

    b. accept or reject ideas upon first being exposed to them.

    c. give the instructor responsibility for your learning.

    d. consider what facts and details mean, rather than devoting yourself to memorizing facts only.

_____ 4. After completing a reading assignment, an effective reader should

    a. connect the material to other assigned readings.

    b. decide how difficult the chapter was compared with others.

    c. memorize the vocabulary list.

    d. write down his or her opinion of the material.

_____ 5. An active learner would do all of the following EXCEPT:

    a. Read, think, ask questions, and try to connect ideas.

    b. Predict exam questions and look for trends and patterns.

    c. Do only what is expected to get a good grade.

    d. Try to discover the significance of the assignment and look for the principles and concepts it illustrates.

APPLYING YOUR KNOWLEDGE

_____ 6. After completing the Learning Style Questionnaire, LaVon wanted to find out if she tends to learn better by hearing or by reading. She should look at her score on the

    a. auditory/visual section.

    b. applied/conceptual section.

    c. social/independent section.

    d. creative/pragmatic section.

_____ 7. Jens will graduate from high school in May and go on to college at the state university. He will probably find out that college learning is different from high school learning in that

    a. he will be spending more time each week in class.

    b. he will be expected to take responsibility for his learning.

    c. his instructors will place more emphasis on memorization of facts.

    d. his instructors will spend more time reviewing course content.

_____ 8. Owen learns best using diagrams, charts, and sketches. He frequently uses outlining, visualization, and mapping to help him organize the ideas presented in his classes. Owen can best be described as a

    a. verbal learner.

    b. auditory learner.

    c. spatial learner.

    d. applied learner.

Continued

QUICK QUIZ *Continued*   NAME:

_____ 9. On her physics test, Janiece will be expected to use her knowledge of formulas to solve a new physics problem. Janiece's test will require her to use which level of thinking?

  a. remembering
  b. applying
  c. analyzing
  d. evaluating

_____ 10. Amelia is taking a biology class in which the instructor relies on lectures to present information. Because the course covers so much material, the instructor does not have time to schedule group interaction. If Amelia were a social learner, it would be most helpful for her to

  a. drop the class immediately because it doesn't suit her learning style.
  b. spend time alone after class, reviewing the lecture.
  c. form a study group with students from her class.
  d. tape-record lectures to listen to by herself later.

MULTIMEDIA *Activities*

Learning Style and Learning Strategies

1 Best Teacher Description

http://humanities.byu.edu/elc/teacher/bestteacher

Compiled by a Brigham Young University faculty member, this site lists the characteristics of good teachers as described by students. Choose three of your teachers—past or present—and evaluate them according to the criteria presented here. Then, write a paragraph describing your ideal teacher.

2 Quick Tips: Student–Instructor Differences

http://www.lethbridgecollege.ab.ca/departments/student/learning/quicktip/stu_inst.html

The Learning Centre at Lethbridge Community College in Canada offers these basic guidelines for student–teacher interaction. Examine the chart on rights and responsibilities. Create your own chart about another type of relationship: parent–child, employer–employee, friend–friend, etc.

3 Index of Learning Styles Questionnaire

http://www.engr.ncsu.edu/learningstyles/ilsweb.html

Try another learning style assessment at this site from the North Carolina State University. Compare your results with those from the assessment in this book. How do online tests differ from those on paper? Which do you prefer? Is this a result of your learning style?

4 Write a poem or song about something you learned in a class this week. Could this be a useful study aid for you? Why or why not?

5 Create a visual representation of your learning style analysis by using a bar graph. Shade in each bar in Figure 2-4 to reflect your scores on the Learning Style Questionnaire. What areas would you like to strengthen? How could you accomplish this?

6 Make a list of several classmates or friends, indicating what you think their dominant learning styles are. How could each person help you learn? Which ones would you prefer to study with? Why?

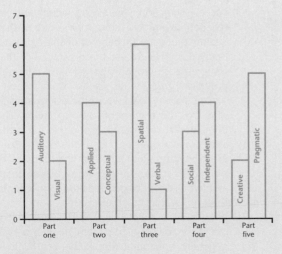

Figure 2-4
Learning Style Questionnaire Scores

3 Improving Learning and Memory

Why Improve Your Learning and Memory Techniques?

■ You will discover how to learn more efficiently.

■ Learning is your primary job while in college; the more you know about it, the more confident and comfortable you will be.

Learning Experiment

Step 1

Suppose you wanted to become a better swimmer. What would you do? List some ideas here:

_____

_____

_____

Step 2

Now read the following paragraph that explains the physics of swimming.

> For every action, there's an equal and opposite reaction. Swimmers move *forward* by pushing *back* against the water (instead of pushing *up* and *out* as many do). The greater the resistance of the water, the greater the forward thrust. And since still water provides greater resistance than water that's already moving backward, the old straight-arm pull isn't the most efficient way to swim. The most effective stroke, instead, is one that's curved so that you're always pushing against a column of "new" or still water. Resistance in the right places is a swimmer's friend. In the wrong places, though, it's an enemy, and it's known as drag. In order to move through water most efficiently, your body must pose as little resistance (drag) as possible. This is called streamlining. To streamline your body, keep it generally horizontal along the central axis (your spine) so that all your energy is used for propelling

your body *directly forward,* and none is wasted by moving it vertically, to the side, or even backward.

—Katz, *Swimming for Total Fitness: A Progressive Aerobic Program,* p. 99

Step 3

Would the paragraph above help you become a better swimmer? Why or why not?

The Results

You probably agreed that the paragraph would be useful. Why? Because it explains how the process works and offers suggestions about how to position your body to move through the water more efficiently.

Learning Principle (What This Means to You)

By reading about the dynamics of swimming, you received an overview of the process. **If you understand how a process works, you will be able to put it to use more easily.** In this chapter you will learn how memory works and learn many practical suggestions for improving your memory. After you have completed this chapter you will be better prepared to learn from both lectures and textbooks.

Have you ever wondered why you can't remember what you have just read? Have you noticed students in your classes who seem to remember everything? Do you wonder how they do it? The answer is not that these other students are brighter than you are or that they have studied twice as long as you have. It is that they have learned *how* to learn and to remember; they have developed techniques for effective learning.

FORGETTING

Forgetting, which is defined as the loss of information stored in memory, is a normal, everyday occurrence. Psychologists have extensively studied the rate at which forgetting takes place. For most people, forgetting occurs very rapidly right after learning and then levels off over time. Figure 3-1 illustrates just how fast forgetting normally occurs and how much information is lost. The figure shows what is known as the *retention curve,* and it shows how much you are able to remember over time.

The retention curve is important to you as a learner. Basically, it suggests that unless you are one of the lucky few who remember almost everything they hear or read, you will forget a large portion of the information you learn unless you do something to prevent it. For instance, the graph shows that your recall of learned information drops to below 50 percent within an hour and to about 25 percent within two days.

Fortunately, certain techniques can prevent or slow down forgetting. These techniques are the focus of the remainder of this book. Throughout the book, you will learn techniques that will enable you to identify what to learn (pick out what is important) and to learn it in the most effective way. Each technique is intended to help you remember more and to slow down your rate of forgetting. For instance, in Chapter 4 you will learn how taking notes during class lectures can help you learn and remember what the lecture is about. In Chapter 16 you will learn a system for reading to learn and remember more.

**Figure 3-1
The Retention Curve**

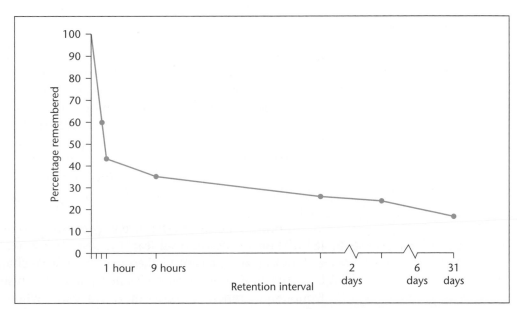

EXERCISE 1 | DIRECTIONS   Apply what you have learned about the rate of forgetting to each of the following study situations. Refer to Figure 3-1.

1. How much information from a textbook chapter can you expect to recall two days after you read it?

   _____

2. How much information from a lecture you attended last week can you expect to remember this week if you did not take any notes on the lecture?

   _____

3. What do you think your level of recall would be if you took notes on a particular lecture but did not review your notes for two weeks?

   _____

4. Why would it be necessary to take notes on a film shown in class if you had to write a reaction paper on it that evening?

   _____

Why Forgetting Occurs

Suppose you have studied a topic but find that on an exam you are unable to remember much about it. There are several possible explanations:

- You never completely learned the information in the first place.
- You did not study the information in the right way.
- You are not asking the right questions or using the right means to remember the information.
- You have forgotten the information.

This chapter will describe how to learn information initially, how to study and review it, and how to use appropriate techniques to recall it.

There are two common reasons why forgetting occurs.

- **Disuse: Use it or lose it!** If you do not use information, you tend to forget it. For example, if you don't use a friend's address, you tend to forget it. If you use it frequently, you will remember it. To make sure you do not forget information you have learned, be sure to use it. Periodic review, discussed later in this chapter on page 72, will help keep information fixed in your memory.
- **Interference.** One type of interference occurs when something new you have learned prevents you from remembering something old you have already learned. If you start studying Spanish, you may find you have difficulty remembering the French you already learned. This type of interference occurs when the new learning is very similar to the old learning. To minimize the effects of interference, try not to study similar subjects back-to-back.

  Another type of interference occurs when something you have already learned prevents you from learning something new. For example, you may call a local store, recently taken over by a large chain store, by its old name because you do not remember its new name. In a history course you may have trouble remembering events in World War I when studying World War II.

To prevent this type of interference, you may have to review the old learning to keep it fresh in your memory. Refer to the section of this chapter titled "How to Review," page 72.

Refer to the section of this chapter titled "How to Review," page 72.

EXERCISE 2

DIRECTIONS   For each of the following situations, use the information above on forgetting to explain why each student described below was experiencing difficulty.

1. Allan was taking both sociology and psychology. Why did he forget what he studied yesterday in sociology after he attended his psychology class today?

   _____

2. Maria carefully read and highlighted each chapter in her business marketing text. She worked hard each week on the assigned chapters, but never looked back at what she had already learned. When a exam was announced, she found she had to relearn much of the information. Why did she forget it?

   _____

3. Kim was taking a history course. She reviewed her lecture notes each afternoon, right after class, and was confident she had learned the information. When an exam was announced, she found she had to relearn a great deal of information. Why did she forget it?

   _____

AN OVERVIEW OF THE LEARNING AND MEMORY PROCESS

Three stages are involved in the memory process: encoding, storage, and retrieval. First, information enters the brain from a variety of sources. This process is known as **encoding.** In a learning situation, you take in information by reading or listening. This information lingers briefly in what is known as **sensory storage** and is then either **stored** or discarded. Momentary or brief storage is called **short-term memory.** Next, information in short-term memory is either forgotten or transferred into more lasting storage called **long-term memory.** Anything that is to be remembered for more than a few seconds must be stored in long-term memory. To place information in long-term memory, one must learn it in some way. Finally, information can be brought back, or remembered, through a process known as **retrieval.** Figure 3-2, on page 66, is a visual model of the learning and memory processes. Refer to it frequently as you read the sections that explain each stage.

How Encoding Works

Every waking moment, your mind is bombarded with a variety of impressions of what is going on around you. Your five senses—hearing, sight, touch, taste, and smell—provide information about your surroundings. Think for a moment of all the signals your brain receives at a given moment. If you are reading, your eyes transmit the visual patterns of the words. But you may also hear a door slamming, a clock ticking, or a dog barking. Your sense of smell may detect perfume or cigarette smoke. Your sense of touch may signal that a pen you are using to

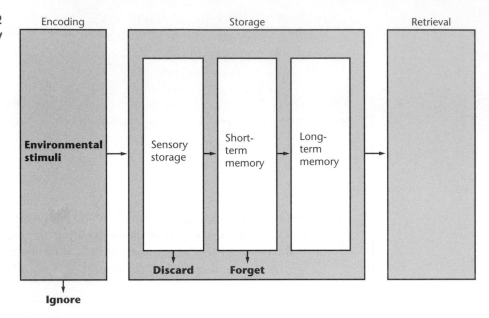

**Figure 3-2
A Model of Memory**

underline will soon run out of ink or that the room is chilly. When you listen to a classroom lecture, you are constantly receiving stimuli—from the professor, from students around you, and from the lecture hall. All these environmental stimuli are transmitted to your brain for very brief sensory storage and interpretation. It is also easy to be distracted by competing stimuli.

How Sensory Storage Works

Information received from your five senses is transmitted through the nervous system to the brain, which accepts and interprets it. The information stays briefly in the nervous system while the brain interprets it; this short period of interpretation is known as **sensory storage**.

How does your mind handle the barrage of information conveyed by your senses? Thanks to what is known as **selective attention**, your brain automatically sorts out the more important signals from the trivial ones. Trivial signals, such as insignificant noises around you, are ignored or discarded. Through the skills of concentration and attention, you can train yourself to ignore other, more distracting signals, such as a dog barking or people talking in the background.

Although your sensory storage accepts all information, data are kept there only briefly, usually less than a few seconds. Then the information either fades or decays or is replaced with new, incoming stimuli. The function of sensory storage, then, is to retain information long enough for you to selectively interpret it and send it to your short-term memory.

How Short-Term Memory Works

Short-term memory holds the information that was sent from your sensory storage system. It is used to store information you wish to retain for only a few seconds. A telephone number, for example, is stored in your short-term memory until you dial it. A lecturer's words are retained until you can record them in your notes. Most researchers agree that short-term memory lasts much less than a minute—perhaps 20 seconds or less. Information can be maintained longer if you practice or rehearse the information (repeating a phone number, for example). When you are introduced to someone, you will not be able to remember the person's name unless you repeat it, thereby learning it, at the time of the introduction. Otherwise, incoming information will force it out of your short-term memory. Similarly, you will not be able to remember what you read in a textbook chapter or heard in a lecture unless you take action to learn and remember it.

EXERCISE 3

DIRECTIONS   Use your knowledge of the memory process to answer the following questions.

1. Observe and analyze the area in which you are sitting. What sensory impressions (sights, sounds, touch sensations) have you been ignoring as a result of selective attention?

   _____

2. Can you remember what you ate for lunch three weeks ago? If not, why not?

   _____

3. Explain why two people are able to carry on a deep conversation at a crowded, noisy party.

   _____

4. Explain why someone who looks up a phone number and then walks into another room to dial it may forget the number.

   _____

5. Suppose you are reading a section of your history text. You come across an unfamiliar word and look up its meaning. Once you have looked up the word, you find that you must reread the section. Why?

   _____

How Long-Term Memory Works

Long-term memory is a relatively permanent store of information. Unlike short-term memory, long-term memory is nearly unlimited in both span (length) and capacity (size). It contains hundreds of thousands of facts, details, impressions, and experiences that you have accumulated throughout your life.

Once information is stored in your long-term memory, you recall it through a process known as **retrieval**. Academic tasks that require you to retrieve knowledge include math or science problems, quizzes and exams, and papers. Retrieval is tied to storage. The manner in which information is stored in your memory affects its availability and how easily you can retrieve it.

ORIGINAL LEARNING

You have to learn something before you can remember it. The manner in which you take in information depends on how well you can remember it. Use the following suggestions for learning information the first time.

Exclude Competing Information

Deliberately exclude everything that does not relate to what you want to remember. For instance, if you are reading, do not sit where there is other competing visual information, such as a television.

Identify Your Purpose

As you read, be sure you know what types and kinds of information you will need to learn and remember. Your purpose will determine how you read and how you study. If you are reading reference material for a research paper, you may need to pay attention to facts and statistics. If you are reading material to prepare for a class discussion, however, you might focus on controversial issues.

Decide What to Learn

It is impossible to learn all the information in your textbook or all the information from several weeks of lectures. Instead, you will need to decide what information to learn and remember and what to pay less attention to. In one class, such as psychology, definitions may be important. In other classes, such as history, they may be less so. For each course, make a list of what you need to learn. Use your syllabus as a guide. Also use textbook chapter review questions to help you.

Use Prereading

You will remember more of what you read if you are familiar with both the content and structure of the material before you begin to read it. Prereading is a technique for becoming familiar with what you read. It is discussed in detail in Chapter 5.

Use Various Sensory Channels

Use as many senses as possible to take in information. When listening to a lecture, for example, pay attention to visual clues the lecturer provides as well as to hearing what he or she says. Taking notes uses a third sense—your sense of touch.

Learn in Your Own Words

It is easy to copy information word-for-word from a textbook or to copy exactly what a lecturer says. If you do so, however, you will never be sure you really understand it and will be able to explain it. Instead, try to record information in your own words. If you are unable to do so, this is a good sign that you do not understand it. (See Chapter 5, "Checking Your Comprehension," for more help.)

Repeat Information Aloud

Many students find that repeating information aloud helps them to learn it. Reading your class notes aloud, for example, may help you keep what you have written in your memory.

Connect New Learning with Old Learning

Isolated, unrelated pieces of information are difficult to learn and retain. If, however, you can link new learning to old, already stored information, it will be easier to store and remember the new information since you have an established memory slot in which to hold it. For example, an economics student could associate the factors influencing the supply and demand curves with practical instances from his family's retail florist business.

Take Advantage of Your Learning Style

In Chapter 2 you completed the Learning Style Questionnaire which identified your strengths as a learner. Be sure to use these strengths as you learn new material. If you are an auditory learner, for example, be sure to repeat information aloud and talk with classmates about course content. If you are a social learner, try to study with classmates.

Use Visualization

Even if you are not a visual learner, visualizing certain types of information is the best way to learn them. Visualizing means creating a mental picture of something in your mind. Your picture or image should be sufficiently detailed to include as much related information as possible. A student taking an anatomy and physiology class could find visualization an effective way to learn the parts of the skeletal system. She could first draw it on paper and then visualize, or mentally draw, the system in her head.

Visualization makes remembering easier because related information is stored in one unified image, and, if you can recall any part of that mental picture, you will be able to retrieve the whole picture.

Organize Information (Chunking)

Learning a large number of individual facts or pieces of information is often a difficult, frustrating task. Organize or reduce information into groups or chunks. Instead of overloading your memory with numerous individual facts, learn organized, meaningful sets of information that you can store as one chunk. Have you ever wondered why social security numbers and phone numbers have dashes? The dashes divide the information into chunks, making them easier to remember.

To organize information, keep the following suggestions in mind:

- **Discover how the material you are studying is connected.** Search for some organizing principle. In studying basic business management skills, for example, you may discover that the skills are divided into technical skills, interpersonal relations skills, and decision-making skills.
- **Look for similarities and differences.** If you are studying types of business, compare and contrast the organization, operation, and efficiency of each type.
- **Look for sequences and for obvious divisions or breaking points within the sequences.** For example, if you are studying the overfishing of oceans as part of an environmental studies class, you could organize the information into past practices, current policies, and unsolved problems.

Use Effective Study Strategies

You can learn more effectively and in less time if you use the right study methods. A major portion of this book is devoted to helping you learn and remember. Table 3-1 provides an easy reference guide to learning strategies.

**Table 3-1
Reference Guide to
Learning Strategies**

Learning Strategy	Chapter Reference
Taking lecture notes, using the recall clue system to study lecture notes	Chapter 4
Prereading, active reading	Chapter 5
Recognizing thought patterns	Chapter 7
Highlighting in textbooks	Chapter 14
Outlining, summarizing, and mapping	Chapter 15
Using the SQ3R system	Chapter 16
Studying for exams	Chapter 17

EXERCISE 4

DIRECTIONS   Use your knowledge of original learning to explain each of the following situations.

1. Two groups of students read a textbook chapter. One group highlighted key ideas on each page; the second group paraphrased and recorded the important ideas from each page. Explain why the second group received higher scores than the first group on a test based on the chapter.

   _____

2. A text that contains photographs is often easier to learn from than one without them. What learning function do the pictures perform?

   _____

3. A business instructor plans to lecture on the process of analyzing job stress. Before class, she draws a diagram of this process on the chalkboard. During the lecture she refers to it frequently. Why did the instructor draw the diagram?

   _____

4. A political science instructor is discussing an essay on world terrorism. He begins the discussion by asking his students to recall recent terrorist acts and what the response to them was. How is the instructor helping his students learn the content of the essay?

   _____

5. A sociology instructor asks her students to read and write a summary of a journal article she has placed on reserve in the library. How is she helping her students learn the material?

   _____

6. A business student studying the characteristics of the levels of management (top, middle, and front-line) did so by thinking of a person he knew who held each position. Of what value was this technique?

   _____

7. A student in a health care degree program was studying conflict resolution. She had to learn ten different resolution strategies. How could she learn them effectively?

_____

8. One group of students read a psychology chapter and took notes on it. Another group read the chapter and took notes as well, but they also discussed the material in a study group. Why did the second group score higher on the exam that was based on that chapter?

_____

9. A business management student was studying the decision-making process. She grouped the steps into three categories: data gathering, analysis, and resolution. What learning technique did she use?

_____

10. A student taking an environmental studies course was studying the topic of water pollution. Before he read the assigned chapter, he recalled several instances of water pollution in his home town. Of what value was this recollection?

_____

EXERCISE 5

DIRECTIONS   Discuss techniques that might help you learn the following sets of information.

1. The process of amending the Constitution for an American government course
2. The factors that influence market price for an economics course
3. Different forms of mental illness for a psychology course
4. Ways to recognize and distinguish the different types of figurative language for a literature course
5. The process of cell division for a biology course
6. Important terms from an introductory sociology course
7. The different types of white collar crimes and their cost to society for a criminology course
8. A comparison of the different kinds of psychoactive drugs for a health course

WHEN TO REVIEW

Some students think that as long as they spend time studying they will get good grades. While it is necessary to spend time studying, it is also very important to plan *when* to study and review so that you get the most out of the time you spend.

Immediate Review

Forgetting occurs most rapidly right after learning. **Immediate review** means reviewing new information as soon as possible after you hear or read it. Think of immediate review as a way of fixing in your mind what you have just learned. Here are some ways to use immediate review:

- **Review your lecture notes as soon as possible after taking them.**
- **Review a textbook chapter as soon as you finish reading it.** Do this by rereading each chapter heading and then rereading the summary.
- **Review all course materials again at the end of each day of classes.**

Periodic Review

Most college semesters are three or four months long. You cannot realistically expect to remember what you learned early in the semester, especially since you are continuing to learn more new information, unless you take active steps to do so. To keep from forgetting what you have learned you will need to review it several times throughout the semester. **Periodic review,** then, means returning to and quickly reviewing previously learned material on a regular basis. Suppose you learned the material in the first three chapters of your criminology text during the first two weeks of the course. Unless you review that material regularly, you are likely to forget it and have to relearn it by the time your final exam is given. Therefore, you should establish a periodic review schedule in which you quickly review these chapters every three weeks or so.

Final Review

Final review means making a last check of material before a test or exam. This should not be lengthy session; instead, it should be a quick once over of everything you have learned. A final review is helpful because it fixes in your mind what you have learned. Be sure to schedule your final review as close as possible to the exam in which you will need to recall it.

HOW TO REVIEW

The worst way to review what you have learned is to simply reread it. Rereading textbook chapters and entire sets of lecture notes is time consuming and produces very poor results. Use the following suggestions to improve how efficiently you review.

Schedule Short Review Sessions

While it is tempting to sit down and say you're not going to move until you can remember a set of information, you will learn more quickly if you schedule several short review sessions rather than one long one. If possible, spread your review over several days, with short sessions scheduled for each day.

Test Yourself

If you study only by rereading chapters or notes, you will never know if you can remember the material. Instead, test yourself. Make up questions and answer them. Study with another student and ask each other questions. Turn the headings in your textbook into questions and answer them. For more about these techniques, see the section on Guide Questions in Chapter 5, page 113. The recall system for notetaking in Chapter 4, page 92, is another way you can test yourself.

Use Numerous Sensory Channels to Store Information

Many students think of reading as the only way to take in information. You can learn better, however, if you use sound and touch, as well. Use listening, writing, drawing or diagramming, and discussion to help you learn more effectively.

Develop Retrieval Clues

A **retrieval clue** is a tag that enables you to pull a piece of information from your memory. Think of your memory as having slots or compartments in which you store information. If you can name or label what is in the slot, you will know where to look to find information that is located in that slot. Think of memory slots as similar to the way kitchen cupboards are often organized, with specific items in specific places. If you need a knife to cut a pizza, you look in the utensils drawer. Similarly, if you have a memory slot labeled "environmental problems," in which you store information related to pollution, its problems, causes, and solutions, you can retrieve information on air pollution by locating the appropriate memory slot. Developing retrieval clues involves selecting a word or phrase that summarizes or categorizes several pieces of information. For example, you might use the phrase "motivation theories" to organize information for a psychology course on instinct, drive, cognitive, arousal, and opponent-process theories and the major proponents of each.

Anticipate Exam Questions

Information in a textbook appears in a different format and with different wording than the wording and format of exam questions. If you study simply by rereading, you have not practiced recognizing the information in different formats and may not realize what information an exam question is asking for. Instead, study for an exam by predicting exam questions and practicing writing answers to them. You will learn more about how to do this in Chapter 17.

Simulate Test Situations

Practice retrieving learned information by simulating test conditions. If you are studying for a math exam, prepare by solving problems. In a horticulture class, if your exam requires you to identify certain plants, then study photos and characteristics of plants. Be sure to model your practice on the event for which you are preparing. It should be the same type of activity and the time limit should be similar.

Overlearn

It is tempting to stop studying as soon as you feel you have learned a given body of information. However, to ensure complete, thorough learning, it is best to plan a few more review sessions. When you learned to drive a car, you did not stop practicing parallel parking after the first time you did it correctly. Similarly, for a botany course, you should not stop reviewing the process of photosynthesis and its place within the carbon cycle at the moment you feel you have mastered it. Instead, use additional review to make the material stick in your mind.

Consider Physical Surroundings

It is easier to recall information when you are in the same setting in which you learned it. Consider reviewing your notes in the lecture hall in which you took them. Also, if possible, study in the room in which you will take a particular exam.

EXERCISE 6

DIRECTIONS Use your knowledge of the memory process to answer the following questions.

1. On many campuses, weekly recitations or discussions are scheduled for small groups to review material presented in large lecture classes. What learning function do these recitation sections perform?

   _____

2. After lecturing on the causes of domestic violence, a sociology instructor showed her class a videotape of an incident of domestic violence. What learning function(s) did the film perform? How would the tape help students remember the lecture?

   _____

3. A student spends more time than anyone else in her class preparing for the midterm exam, yet she cannot remember important definitions and concepts at the time of the exam. Offer several possible explanations of her problem.

   _____

4. A sociology student is studying a chapter on age and the elderly. The exam based on that chapter will contain both multiple-choice items and an essay question. How should she test herself in preparation for the exam?

   _____

5. One student studied for his math exam for three hours the night before the exam. Another student studied for one hour on each of three days before the exam. He studied by creating and answering sample problems. Which student do you think did better on the exam? Why?

   _____

Use Memorization

Memorization is one of the least effective ways of learning, but there is plenty of material that must be learned this way. In chemistry, you have to memorize the periodic table. In history, you will need to memorize dates and historical events. Here are several useful memorization techniques.

- *Mnemonics* **are memory tricks, or aids, that you can devise to help you remember information.** Mnemonics include rhymes, anagrams, words, nonsense words, sentences, and mental pictures that aid in the recall of facts. Do you remember this rhyme? "Thirty days hath September, / April, June, and November. / All the rest have thirty-one / except February, alone, / which has twenty-eight days clear / and twenty-nine in each leap year." The rhyme is an example of a mnemonic device. It is a quick and easy way of remembering the number of days in each month of the year. You may have learned to recall the colors of the rainbow by remembering the name *Roy G. Biv;* each letter in this name stands for one of the colors that make up the spectrum: *R*ed, *O*range, *Y*ellow, *G*reen, *B*lue, *I*ndigo, *V*iolet. Mnemonic devices are useful when you are trying to learn information that has no organization of its own. You will find them useful in reviewing texts and lecture notes as you prepare for exams.

- **Another memory device is called** ***method of loci.*** It involves selecting a familiar object, such as your home or car, and associating items to be remembered with areas in your home or parts of your car. For example, suppose you are trying to remember the four components of language: phonemes, morphemes, syntax, and semantics. Begin by picturing the first location, say the hood of your car. Place phonemes on the hood. Then move to the windshield; place morphemes on the windshield. Place syntax on the steering wheel and semantics on the dashboard. To learn the four components of language, visualize the first location and think of phonemes, associating them together, and so forth. To recall the components, take an imaginary tour of your car. When you think of the hood, you will think of phonemes.

EXERCISE 7

DIRECTIONS   Apply your knowledge of memorization techniques by completing each of the following activities.

1. Make up a rhyme or nonsense word to help you learn something you need to remember for one of your other courses.
2. Try the method of loci technique by trying to remember the last names of your classmates. Then try it out on material for one of your other courses.

EXERCISE 8

DIRECTIONS   Identify your most difficult course. Consider the material you are required to learn and review for the next major test. Spend some time organizing textbook and lecture material that you are sure will be on that test. Make a study plan that uses at least four of the techniques described in this chapter. Show your work to a classmate. Both of you should then offer each other suggestions to make studying more effective.

LEARNING COLLABORATIVELY

DIRECTIONS   Form a pair with another student. If possible, choose a student who is taking or has taken one of the same courses you are taking, or is taking a course in the same field (science, mathematics, business, and so on). Together, prepare a list of strategies for learning the material initially and for reviewing it; give examples from the course or field of study you share. Include strategies that would be helpful to other students taking the course. Make your strategy list available to other class members who may take the course. Select two strategies and begin using them immediately.

APPLYING YOUR LEARNING

Carlos is having difficulty with his human anatomy and physiology course. He feels overwhelmed by the volume of facts and details, as well as the new terminology he must learn. His next assigned chapter is "The Skeletal System." It first discusses functions and types of bones and then describes all the bones in the human skeletal system, including the skull, vertebral column (spine), pelvis (hip), and extremities (arms, legs, feet, and hands). Carlos says that he understands the material as he reads it but cannot remember it later. His instructor gives weekly quizzes as well as hour-long exams.

1. Explain why Carlos understands information as he reads it but cannot recall it later.
2. What can Carlos do to correct his lack of recall?
3. What techniques would help Carlos learn the skeletal system?

APPLYING YOUR SKILLS: Sample Textbook Chapter

DIRECTIONS Select two or more original learning strategies and apply them to the section of the sample textbook chapter titled "Culture and Cultural Processes." Use immediate review when you finish. Review the material periodically. Evaluate the effectiveness of the techniques you have chosen.

QUESTIONS FOR DISCUSSION

1. What strategies do you use to remember the following types of information: people's names; phone numbers; directions; steps in a process; a telephone message? Use the chapter's information to explain why different strategies are needed for these different types of information.
2. Imagine that you are learning about the culture of an African tribe, the artistic style of Monet, or the chemical differences between acids and bases. What could you do to learn that information in each of these situations?
3. Give some examples of mnemonic devices that you have used to help you store information.

SELF-TEST SUMMARY

1. What is forgetting and why does it occur?

Forgetting is the loss of information stored in memory. It occurs through disuse or interference.

2. What are the steps in the learning process?

Encoding is the taking in of information. Information lingers briefly in short-term memory, and is either discarded or transferred to long-term memory. When information is remembered it is called retrieval.

3. What techniques can improve original learning?

Exclude competing stimuli, identify your purpose, decide what to learn, use prereading, use sensory channels, learn in your own words, repeat information aloud, connect new learning with old learning, use your learning style, use visualization, organize information, and use effective study strategies.

4. What are the three types of review?

Three types of review are immediate, periodic, and final.

5. What strategies will help you review effectively?

Use short review sessions, test yourself, use sensory channels, develop retrieval clues, anticipate exam questions, simulate test situations, overlearn, and consider physical surroundings.

DIRECTIONS   Write the letter of the choice that best completes each statement in the space provided.

CHECKING YOUR RECALL

_____ 1. All of the following are types of review except

    a. immediate review.

    b. purposeful review.

    c. periodic review.

    d. final review.

_____ 2. Information remains in your short-term memory for no longer than

    a. a minute.

    b. an hour.

    c. a day.

    d. a week.

_____ 3. Mnemonics involves

    a. making up rhymes or words to help you remember information.

    b. visualizing an event as it happened.

    c. connecting new information with already learned facts.

    d. grouping ideas together based on similar characteristics.

_____ 4. During selective attention, your brain

    a. classifies information into groups or sets.

    b. practices information to learn it.

    c. automatically sorts out important information from trivial signals.

    d. sends information to long-term memory.

_____ 5. If you are unable to explain information in your own words, it is a sign that

    a. you do not understand it.

    b. you did not review it properly.

    c. you did not connect new learning with previous learning.

    d. interference has occurred.

APPLYING YOUR SKILLS

_____ 6. Evan has just attended a chemistry lecture. According to the retention curve, if he does not transfer what he has learned into his long-term memory, he will forget more than half of what he has learned within

    a. an hour.

    b. a day.

    c. three days.

    d. a week.

_____ 7. Caylor is studying in his apartment while his roommates are home. He is concentrating on his studies and ignoring his roommates' chatter and laughter. Caylor is practicing

    a. overlearning.

    b. selective attention.

    c. retrieval.

    d. periodic review.

_____ 8. In her Introduction to Music elective, Katie uses the saying "Every good boy deserves fudge" to help her remember the line notes of the treble clef. This memory trick is an example of

    a. competing stimuli.

    b. a sensory channel.

    c. a visualization.

    d. a mnemonic device.

_____ 9. Zachary has just finished reading a textbook chapter on the causes of World War I. The most effective way for Zachary to store that information he has just learned is for him to

    a. immediately reread the chapter.

    b. move on to a completely different subject.

    c. read the next chapter.

    d. reread the chapter headings and the summary.

_____ 10. If Rosa wanted to develop retrieval clues to help her learn material for her geology class, she would specifically try to

    a. overlearn the material.

    b. store the information in one unified piece.

    c. choose a word or phrase that summarizes several pieces of information.

    d. connect the information with her personal experience.

MULTIMEDIA *Activities*

Improving Learning and Memory

1 Memory Solitaire

http://www.exploratorium.edu/brain_explorer/memory.html

Try this fun memory game and get some good memory-building advice from the Exploratorium in San Francisco. Ask a friend to play too; compare your results. What memory-building techniques work for you?

2 Penny Memory Test

http://www.dcity.org/braingames/pennies/

This site presents a classic test of memory. See how well you do. Create a test like this of your own and test your friends' memories.

3 Online Memory Experiment

http://www.essex.ac.uk/psychology/experiments/memtask.html

How many numbers can you remember in a row? Give this site a try. Practice some memory-building techniques, then try this experiment again.

4 Write down some of your first memories. Why do you think these events stayed with you? Consider encoding, storage, and retrieval.

5 Try to draw a floor plan of some-place you used to go as a child, such as your elementary school or an old friend's house. How much do you remember? Why do you remember certain areas better than others? Do you find that this exercise triggers even more memories?

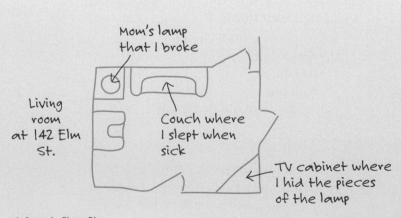

A Sample Floor Plan

4 Taking Notes in Class

Why Take Notes on Lectures?

■ Taking notes keeps your mind on the lecture.

■ Taking notes helps you decide what is important.

■ Taking notes will help you recall the lecture.

■ Your notes will be a valuable study tool.

Learning Experiment

Step 1

Ask a friend to (or your instructor may choose to) read each of the following paragraphs aloud. (Each paragraph may be read aloud twice.) While paragraph 1 is read to you, just listen. While and after paragraph 2 is read to you, write a set of notes that contain its most important ideas.

Paragraph 1

Did you know that use of empty space is a form of communication? How humans use space can communicate as loudly as words and phrases. How close or how far away you stand from another person communicates a message. Research by Edward Hall identifies four types of distance, each of which defines the relationship you establish with others. The first, intimate distance, is not considered appropriate in public (except in crowded places, such as elevators). Family members and spouses may use the intimate distance. Personal distance is the space around you that no one invades unless invited, such as to shake hands. Social distance is the distance at which you operate in daily living—sitting in classrooms, attending a

play, shopping, and so forth. The fourth type, public distance, is used when you are not involved with another person.

Paragraph 2

Communication occurs with words and gestures, but did you know it also occurs through sense of smell? Odor can communicate at least four types of messages. First, odor can signal attraction. Animal species give off scents to attract members of the opposite sex. Humans use fragrances to make themselves more appealing or attractive. Second, smell communicates information about tastes. The smell of popcorn popping stimulates the appetite. If you smell a chicken roasting you can anticipate its taste. A third type of smell communication is through memory. A smell can help you recall an event months or even years ago, especially if the event is an emotional one. Finally, smell can communicate by creating an identity or image for a person or product. For example, a woman may wear only one brand of perfume. Or a brand of shaving cream may have a distinct fragrance, which allows users to recognize it.

(Continued)

Learning Experiment *(Continued)*

Step 2

Wait 24 hours, or until the next class session, then, *without* reading either paragraph or looking at your notes, answer the following questions.

Paragraph 1

Name the four types of distances discussed in the paragraph.

Paragraph 2

Name the four messages that smell can communicate.

Check your answers in the Answer Key at the end of the chapter, page 99.

The Results

You probably got more information correct for paragraph 2 than you did for paragraph 1. Why?

Because you listened to paragraph 2 and then you wrote. In doing this, you used three sensory modes: hearing (listening), touching (writing), and seeing (reading your notes). For paragraph 1, you used only one sensory mode: hearing.

Learning Principle *(What This Means to You)*

You have five senses—five ways of taking in information from the world around you: sight, touch, smell, sound, and taste. **The more senses you use to learn something, the easier it will be to learn.** When you listen to a college lecture, you are using only one sensory mode. If you take notes on the lecture as you listen, you are using your sense of touch as well as your sense of hearing. When you reread the notes after you have written them, you are employing a third sensory mode—sight. In this chapter you will learn how to take notes effectively, how to edit them, and how to develop a system to study them.

SHARPENING YOUR LISTENING SKILLS

The first step in taking good lecture notes is to sharpen your listening skills. The average adult spends 31 percent of each waking hour listening. By comparison, 7 percent is spent on writing, 11 percent on reading, and 21 percent on speaking. Listening, then, is an essential communication skill. During college lectures, listening is especially important: it is your primary means of acquiring information.

Have you ever found yourself not listening to a professor who was lecturing? Her voice was loud and clear, so you certainly could hear her, but you weren't paying attention—you tuned her out. This situation illustrates the distinction between hearing and listening. Hearing is a passive, biological process in which sound waves are received by the ear. Listening, however, is an intellectual activity that involves the processing and interpretation of incoming information. Listening must be intentional, purposeful, and deliberate. You must plan to listen, have a reason for listening, and carefully focus your attention. Use the following suggestions to sharpen your listening skills:

1. **Approach listening as a process similar to reading.**
   When you read, you not only recognize words but also understand, connect, and evaluate ideas. Similarly, listening is not simply a process of hearing words. It is a comprehension process in which you grasp ideas, assess their importance, and connect them to other ideas. All the reading comprehen-

sion skills you will develop in Part Two of this text are useful for listening as well. Focus on identifying main ideas, and on evaluating the importance and connection of details in relation to the main idea. Be alert for transitions—speakers tend to use them more frequently than writers. Also, try to identify patterns of thought to improve both comprehension and recall.

2. **Focus on content, not delivery.**

   It is easy to become so annoyed, upset, charmed, or engaged with the lecturer as an individual that you fail to comprehend the message he or she is conveying. Force yourself to focus on the content of the lecture and disregard the personal style and characteristics of the lecturer.

3. **Focus on ideas as well as facts.**

   If you concentrate on recording and remembering separate, unconnected facts, you are doomed to failure. Remember, your short-term memory is extremely limited in span and capacity, so while you are focusing on facts, it is inevitable that you will ignore some and forget others. Instead, listen for ideas, significant trends and patterns, as well as facts.

4. **Listen carefully to the speaker's opening comments.**

   As your mind refocuses from prior tasks and problems, it is easy to miss the speaker's opening remarks. However, these are among the most important. Here the speaker may establish connections with prior lectures, identify his or her purpose, or describe the lecture's content or organization.

5. **Attempt to understand the lecturer's purpose.**

   If the lecturer's purpose is not stated explicitly, try to reason it out. Is it to present facts, raise and discuss questions, demonstrate a trend or pattern, or present a technique or procedure?

6. **Fill the gap between rate of speech and rate of thinking.**

   Has your mind ever wandered back and forth during a lecture? Although you may be interested in what the speaker is saying, do you seem to have time to think about other things while listening? This is natural, because the rate of speech is much slower than the speed of thought. The average rate of speech is around 125 words per minute, whereas the rate at which you can process ideas is more than 500 words per minute. To listen most effectively, use this gap to think about lecture content. Anticipate what is to follow, think of situations in which the information might be applied, pose questions, or make the information fit your prior knowledge and experience.

7. **Approach listening as a challenging mental task.**

   We all know concentration and attention are necessary for reading, yet many of us treat listening as something that should occur without effort. Perhaps because of the constant barrage of spoken words we are bombarded with through radio, television, and conversation, we assume that listening occurs automatically. Lectures, however, are a concentrated form of oral communication that require you to put higher-level attention and thinking skills into gear.

PREPARING FOR A LECTURE CLASS

Before you attend a lecture class, you should become familiar with the main topic of the lecture and be aware of important subtopics and related subjects.

Understanding the lecture and taking notes will be easier if you have some idea of what the lecture is about. If your instructor assigns a textbook chapter that is related to the lecture, try to read the assignment before attending. If you are unable to read the entire chapter before class, at least preread the chapter to become familiar with the topics it covers. (You will learn about prereading in Chapter 5.) If no reading assignment is given in advance, check your course outline to determine the topic of the lecture. Then preread the sections of your text that are about the topic.

Once you arrive at a lecture class, get organized before it begins. Take your coat off and have your notebook, pen, and textbook chapter (if needed) ready to use. While waiting for class to begin, try to recall the content of the previous lecture: Think of three or four key points that were presented. Check your notes, if necessary. This process will activate your thought processes, focus your attention on course content, and make it easier for you to begin taking notes right away.

HOW TO TAKE LECTURE NOTES

A good set of lecture notes must accomplish three things. First, and most important, your notes must serve as a record or summary of the lecture's main points. Second, they must include enough details and examples so that you can recall the information several weeks later. Third, your notes must in some way show the relative importance of ideas presented and the organization of the lecture.

Record Main Ideas

The main ideas of a lecture are the points the instructor emphasizes and elaborates. They are the major ideas that the details, explanations, examples, and general discussion support. Instructors can give clues to what is important in a lecture. The following are a few ways in which speakers show what is important:

Change in Voice

Some lecturers change the tone or pitch of their voices in order to emphasize major points. A speaker's voice may get louder or softer, or higher or lower, as he or she presents important ideas.

Change in Rate of Speech

Speakers may slow down as they discuss important concepts. Sometimes a speaker goes so slowly that he or she seems to be dictating information. If a speaker giving a definition pauses slightly after each word or phrase, this is a signal that the definition is important and you should write it down.

Listing and Numbering Points

A lecturer may directly state that there are "three important causes" or "four significant effects" or "five possible situations" as he or she begins discussing a particular topic. These expressions are clues to the material's importance.

Frequently, a speaker further identifies or emphasizes the separate, particular facts or ideas that make up the "three causes" or "four effects" with words such as *first, second,* and *finally,* or *one effect, a second effect, another effect,* and *a final effect.*

Writing on the Chalkboard

Some lecturers write key words or outlines of major ideas on the chalkboard as they speak. Not all important ideas are recorded on the chalkboard, but you can be sure that when an instructor does take the time to write a word or phrase on the chalkboard, it is important.

Use of Audiovisuals

Some instructors emphasize important ideas, clarify relationships, or diagram processes or procedures by using audiovisual aids. Commonly used are overhead projectors that project on a screen previously prepared material or information the instructor draws or writes. Also, an instructor may use movies, filmstrips, videotapes, or photographs to emphasize or describe important ideas and concepts.

Direct Announcement

Occasionally, an instructor will announce straightforwardly that a concept or idea is especially important. He or she may begin by saying, "Particularly important to remember as you study is . . ." or "One important fact that you must keep in mind is . . ." The instructor may even hint that such information would make a good exam question. Be sure to mark hints like these in your notes. Emphasize these items with an asterisk or write *Exam?* in the margin.

Nonverbal Clues

Many speakers give as many nonverbal as verbal clues to what is important. Some lecturers walk toward their audience as they make a major point. Others use hand gestures, pound the table, or pace back and forth as they present key ideas. Each speaker is different, but most speakers use some nonverbal means of emphasizing important points.

EXERCISE 1

DIRECTIONS   Select one of your instructors and analyze his or her lecture style. Attend one lecture, and, as you take notes, try to be particularly aware of how he or she lets you know what is important. After the lecture, try to analyze your instructor using the following questions.

1. Did the instructor's voice change? When? How?

_____

2. Did the rate of speaking vary? When?

_____

3. Did the instructor list or number important points?

_____

4. Did the instructor use the chalkboard?

_____

5. Did he or she directly state what was important?

_____

6. What nonverbal clues did the instructor give?

_____

Record Details and Examples

A difficult part of taking notes is deciding how much detail to include with the main ideas. Obviously, you cannot write down everything; lecturers speak at the rate of about 125 words per minute. Even if you could take shorthand, it would be nearly impossible to record everything the lecturer says. As a result, you have to be selective and record only particularly important details. As a rule of thumb, record a brief phrase that summarizes each major supporting detail. Try to write down a phrase for each detail that directly explains or clarifies a major point.

If an instructor gives you several examples of a particular law, situation, or problem, be sure to write down, in summary form, at least one example. Record more than one if you have time. Although at the time of the lecture it may seem that you completely understand what is being discussed, you will find that a few weeks later you really do need the example to boost your recall.

Record the Organization of the Lecture

As you write down the main ideas and important details of a lecture, try to organize or arrange your notes so that you can easily see how the lecture is organized. By recording the organization of the lecture, you will be able to determine the relative importance of ideas, and you will know what to pay the most attention to as you study and review for an exam.

A simple way to show a lecture's organization is to use indentation. Retain a regular margin on your paper. Start your notes on the most important of the topics at the left margin. For less important main ideas, indent your notes slightly. For major details, indent slightly more. Indent even more for examples and other details. The rule of thumb to follow is this: the less important the idea, the more it should be indented. Your notes might be organized like the sample that follows.

> **MAJOR TOPIC**
> Main idea
> > detail
> > detail
> > > example
> Main idea
> > detail
> > detail
> > detail
>
> **MAJOR TOPIC**
> Main idea
> > detail
> > > example

Note that this sample looks like an outline but is missing the Roman numerals (I, II, III), capital letters (A, B, C), and Arabic numerals (1, 2, 3) that are usually contained in an outline. Also note, however, that this system of note taking accomplishes the same major goal as an outline—it separates important information from less important information. This indentation system, like an outline, shows at a glance how important a particular fact or idea is. If the organization of a lecture is obvious, you may wish to use a number or letter system in addition to indenting.

**Figure 4-1
Using Patterns in
Lecture Note Taking**

Pattern	Note-Taking Tips
Comparison–contrast	Record similarities, differences, and basis of comparison; use two columns or make a chart.
Cause–effect	Distinguish causes from effects; use diagrams.
Sequence or order	Record dates; focus on order and sequence; use a time line for historical events; draw diagrams; record in order of importance; outline events or steps in a process.
Classification	Use outline form; list characteristics and distinguishing features.
Definition	Record the general category or class; then list distinguishing characteristics; include several examples.
Enumeration	Record in list or outline form; record the order of presentation.

Lectures are often organized using patterns: definition, time sequence, comparison–contrast, cause–effect, classification, or enumeration. Figure 4-1 lists tips for "customizing" your note taking to each of these patterns. An entire lecture may be organized using one pattern; a history lecture, for example, may use the time sequence pattern throughout. More often, however, several patterns will be evident at various points in a lecture. A psychology professor, for instance, may discuss definitions of motivation and compare and contrast different motivational theories. (Refer to Chapter 7 for a review of organizational patterns and the directional words that signal them.)

The notes in Figure 4-2 and Figure 4-3 (p. 86) show that effective lecture notes should record main ideas, important details, and examples and that they should reflect the lecture's organization. Both sets of notes were taken on the same lecture. One set of notes is thorough and effective; the other is lengthy and does not focus on key ideas. Read and evaluate each set of notes.

Make Note Taking Easier

If you record main ideas, details, and examples using the indentation system to show the lecture's organization, your notes will be adequate. However, there are some tips you can follow to make note taking easier, to make your notes more complete, and to make study and review easier.

Use Ink

Pencil tends to smear and is harder to read.

Use a Standard-Sized Notebook and Paper

Paper smaller than $8\frac{1}{2}$ by 11 inches doesn't allow you to write as much on a page, and it is more difficult to see the overall organization of a lecture if you have to flip through a lot of pages.

Keep a Separate Notebook or Section for Each Course

You need to have your notes for each course together so that you can review them easily.

**Figure 4-2
Notes Showing
Lecture Organization**

A. Social Stratification   Soc. 106
    Defs   9/16
      Soc. Strat.   —hierarchy of ranks that exist in society
      Status   —criteria to find positions in soc.
            2 types
                        1. ascribed status—handed down;
                            inherited
                            ex.: titles, race, wealth, ethnic
                            background
                        2. achieved status—things you control
                            ex.: education, jobs
B. Social Mobility
    Def. —how indiv. moves in hierarchy
          —amt. of movement depends on society
    2 Types
            1. caste—ex.: India—no mobility—you inherit class
               + status
            2. open—large amt. of achieved status—great
               mobility—ex.: USA.

**Figure 4-3
Less Effective,
Unfocused Lecture Notes**

Social Stratification

Social stratification—defined as the ranks that exist in
society—the position that any person has—ascribed
status—it is handed down—
example: titles. A second kind is achieved—it is the kind
you decide for yourself.Social stratification is important
in understanding societies.How a person moves up and down
+ changes his social status is called mobility. Some
societies have a lot of mobility. Others don't have any—
example is India.

There are 2 kinds of movement.
    1. Caste system is when everybody is assigned a class
        and they must stay there without any chance to
        change.
    2. Open—people can move from one to another. This is
        true in the United States.

Date Your Notes

For easy reference later, be sure to date your notes. Your instructor might announce that an exam will cover everything presented after, for example, October 5. If your notes are not dated, you will not know where to begin to study.

Leave Blank Spaces

To make your notes more readable and to make it easier to see the organization of ideas, leave plenty of blank space. If you know you missed a detail or definition, leave additional blank space. You can fill it in later by checking with a friend or referring to your text.

Mark Assignments

Occasionally an instructor will announce an assignment or test date in the middle of a lecture. Of course you will jot it down, but be sure to mark "Assignment" or "Test Date" in the margin so that you can find it easily and transfer it to your assignment notebook.

Mark Ideas that Are Unclear

If an instructor presents a fact or idea that is unclear, put a question mark in the margin. Later, ask your instructor or another student about this idea.

Sit in the Front of the Classroom

Especially in large lecture halls, it is to your advantage to sit near the front. In the front you will be able to see and hear the instructor easily—you can maintain eye contact and observe his or her facial expressions and nonverbal clues. If you sit in the back, you may become bored, and it is easy to be distracted by all the people in front of you. The people seated between you and the instructor create a feeling of distance. You may feel that the instructor is not really talking to you.

Don't Plan to Recopy Your Notes

Some students take each day's notes in a hasty, careless way and then recopy them in the evening. These students feel that recopying helps them review the information. Actually, recopying often becomes a mechanical process that takes a lot of time but very little thought. Time spent recopying can be better spent reviewing the notes in a manner that will be suggested later in this chapter. If, however, you are reorganizing and expanding upon your notes and not just copying them, then rewriting can be useful.

Recognize that Tape-Recording Lectures Is Time-Consuming

In an effort to get complete and accurate notes, some students tape-record very detailed or complicated lectures. After the lecture, they play back the tape and edit their notes, starting and stopping the tape as needed. This is a time-consuming technique, but some students find it a helpful way to build their confidence, improve their note-taking techniques, and assure themselves that their notes are complete. If you decide to tape-record, do so sparingly. Unless your notes are incomplete, listening to a recording requires a great deal of time and often yields little gain. *If you plan to tape-record, be sure to ask your instructor for permission to do so.*

**Figure 4-4
Abbreviations for
Use in Note Taking**

Common Words	Abbreviation	Specialized Words	Abbreviation
and	+	organization	org.
with	w/	management	man.
compare		data bank	D.B.
comparison	comp.	structure	str.
importance	imp't	evaluation	eval.
advantage	adv	management	
introduction	intro	by objective	MBO
continued	con't	management	
		information system	MIS
		organizational	
		development	OD
		communication	
		simulations	comm/sim

Use Abbreviations

To save time, try to use abbreviations instead of writing out long or frequently used words. If you are taking a course in psychology, you do not want to write out *p-s-y-c-h-o-l-o-g-y* each time the word is used. It would be much faster to use the abbreviation *psy.* Try to develop abbreviations that are appropriate for the subject areas you are studying. The abbreviations shown in Figure 4-4 above, devised by a student in business management, will give you an idea of the possibilities. Note that both common and specialized words are abbreviated.

As you develop your own set of abbreviations, be sure to begin gradually. It is easy to overuse abbreviations and end up with notes that are so cryptic as to be almost meaningless.

EXERCISE 2

DIRECTIONS   Select one set of lecture notes from a class you recently attended. Reread your notes and look for words or phrases you could have abbreviated. Write some of these words and their abbreviations in the spaces provided.

Word   **Abbreviation**

_____   _____

_____   _____

_____   _____

_____   _____

_____   _____

_____   _____

_____   _____

Create a Code System

Devise a system by which you record or mark specific types of information in specific ways. For example, number the items in a list, write "ex" next to each

Figure 4-5
Adapting Note Taking to
Your Learning Style

Learning Characteristics	Note-Taking Strategy
Auditory	Take advantage of your advantage! Take thorough and complete notes.
Visual	Work on note-taking skills; practice by tape-recording a lecture; analyze and revise your notes.
Applied	Think of applications (record as annotations). Write questions in the margin about applications.
Conceptual	Discover relationships among ideas. Watch for patterns.
Spatial	Add diagrams and maps, as appropriate, during editing.
Nonspatial	Record lecture's diagrams and drawings—but translate into language during editing.
Social	Review and edit notes with a classmate. Compare notes with others.
Independent	Choose seating in close contact with the instructor; avoid distracting groups of students.
Creative	Annotate your notes, recording impressions, reactions, spinoff ideas, and related ideas.
Pragmatic	Reorganize your notes during editing. Pay attention to the lecturer's organization.

example, or put question marks next to ideas you don't understand. (A system for marking textbooks is given in Figure 14-1, p. 330.)

Make the Most of Your Learning Style

Use your knowledge of your learning style preferences to guide your note taking. By adapting your note-taking strategies to take advantage of your learning style, you will also make study and review easier. Figure 4-5 above offers some suggestions for tailoring your note taking to your learning style.

Overcoming Common Note-Taking Problems

Instructors present lectures differently, use various lecture styles, and organize their subjects in different ways. Therefore, students often have difficulty taking notes in one or more courses. Figure 4-6, page 90, identifies common problems associated with lecture note taking and offers possible solutions.

HOW TO EDIT YOUR NOTES

After you have taken a set of lecture notes, do not assume that they are accurate and complete. Most students find that they missed some information and were unable to record as many details or examples as they would have liked. Even very experienced note takers face these problems. Fortunately, the solution is simple. Don't plan on taking a final and complete set of notes during the lecture. Instead, record just enough during the lecture to help you remember a main idea, detail, or example. Leave plenty of blank space; then, if possible, sit down immediately after the lecture and review your notes. Fill in the missing information. Expand, or flesh out, any details or examples that are not fully explained. This process is called **editing.** It is essentially a process of

Figure 4-6
Common Note-Taking
Problems

Problem	Solution
"My mind wanders and I get bored."	Sit in the front of the room. Be certain to preview assignments. Think about questions you expect to be answered in the lecture.
"The instructor talks too fast."	Develop a shorthand system; use abbreviations. Leave blanks and fill them in later.
"The lecturer rambles."	Preview correlating text assignments to determine organizing principles. Reorganize your notes after the lecture.
"Some ideas don't seem to fit anywhere."	Record them in the margin or in parentheses within your notes, and think about them later during editing.
"Everything seems important." "Nothing seems important."	You have not identified key concepts and may lack necessary background knowledge (see Chapter 5)—you do not understand the topic. Preview related text assignments.
"I can't spell all the new technical terms."	Write them phonetically, the way they sound. Fill in correct spellings during editing.
"The instructor uses terms without defining them."	Write the terms as they are used; leave space to record definitions later, when you can consult the text glossary or a dictionary.
"The instructor reads directly from text."	Mark passages in the text; write the instructor's comments in the margin. Record page references in your notes.

correcting, revising, and adding to your notes to make them complete and more accurate. Editing notes for a one-hour lecture should take no more than five or ten minutes.

If you are unable to edit your notes immediately after a lecture, it is critical that you edit them that evening. The more time that lapses between note taking and editing, the less effective editing becomes. Also, the greater the time lapse, the more facts and examples you will be unable to recall and fill in.

The sample set of lecture notes in Figure 4-7 on page 91 has been edited. The notes taken during the lecture are in black; the additions and changes made during editing are in color. Read the notes, noticing the types of information added during editing.

Editing is also a time for you to think about the notes you've taken—to move beyond the literal knowledge and comprehension levels of thought to the levels that involve critical thinking.

Using a Computer to Organize Your Notes

Consider using a word processor to edit and reorganize your notes. The computer makes it easy to rearrange ideas in a way that makes sense to you or that parallels how they are presented in the textbook chapter. The process of entering your notes into the computer can function as review—a time when you think about, consolidate, or expand on ideas presented in the lecture.

Tips for Keeping a Computerized Notebook

Here are a few tips for keeping computerized lecture notes:

Figure 4-7
Edited Lecture Notes

Anxiety + Defense Mechanisms   10/12

I. Anxiety   generalized
        def gen fear or worry
    Levels
        1. Moderate - productive
                athletes - higher level of phys. functioning
                test-taking - certain am't helps - keeps you alert
        2. Extreme - uncomfortable   ex.: nauseated
                - extremely nervous, hands shaking
                - can be reduced by defense mechanism

II. Defense Mech   scious
        def - uncon devices to protect self and/or keep self
                under control
                ex.: student who is hostile toward teacher
                        explains it to himself by saying that "the
"Types of Def. Mechanism   teacher hates me"
        1. Repression - to drive out of consciousness
                ex.: student - math instructor   student forgets
                        to keep app't with math instructor because
                        he's afraid he will be told he is failing the
                        course.   to anxiety
        2. Regression - reaction by going back to less
            mature behavior
                ex.: college student applying for job but
                        doesn't get it -pouts + says the
                        interviewer cheated + hired son of
                        his best friend.

1. **Create a separate file for each of your courses.**
2. **Transfer your notes onto the computer as soon as possible after each class.** Do so while the lecture is still fresh in your mind.
3. **As you transfer, edit and reorganize your notes.** Use the suggestions given above.
4. **Develop a system.** Designate major topics, key points, definitions, and examples by using different typefaces (bold, capitals, italics) or symbols (asterisks, bullets).
5. **Save your work frequently onto a disk.** You will have a record of your notes in case your hard drive fails.
6. **Print a copy of your notes.** Take them to class because you may want to refer to them during the next lecture.

Integrating Text and Lecture Notes

A continual problem students wrestle with is how to integrate lecture and textbook notes. The computer offers an ideal solution to the integration of textual and lecture notes. The cut-and-paste option enables you to move pieces (sections) of your notes to any desired place in the document. Thus, you can easily integrate text and lecture notes on each major topic.

Applying Levels of Thinking
EDITING NOTES AND LEVELS OF THINKING

As you edit your notes, keep the following questions in mind.

Level of Thinking	Questions
Applying	How can I use this information?
Analyzing	How do these notes fit with other lectures? With the textbook assignment?
Evaluating	How useful is this information? Was it clear and well presented? What additional information do I need? What don't I fully understand?
Creating	What does this all mean? How can I summarize it?

Do not hesitate to add marginal notes, jot down questions, add reactions, draw arrows to show relationships, and bracket sections that seem confusing.

HOW TO STUDY YOUR NOTES

Taking and editing lecture notes is only part of what must be done to learn from your instructor's lectures. You also have to learn and review the material in the notes in order to do well on an exam. To study lecture notes, try to apply the same principles that you use in learning material in your textbooks.

1. **Do not try to learn what is in your notes by reading them over and over.** Rereading is not an efficient review technique because it takes too much time relative to the amount you learn.
2. **As in reading textbook assignments, identify what is important.** You must sort out what you will learn and study from all the rest of the information you have written in your notes.
3. **Have a way of checking yourself—of deciding whether you have learned the necessary information.**

To study lecture notes, you can use a system called the *recall clue system.*

The Cornell Notetaking Recall Clue System

Developed at Cornell University, the recall clue system helps make the review and study of lecture notes easier and more effective. To use the recall clue system, follow these steps:

1. **Leave a two-inch margin at the left side of each page of notes.**
2. **Write nothing in the margin while you are taking notes.**
3. **After you have edited your notes, fill in the left margin with words and phrases that briefly summarize the notes.**

The recall clues should be words that will trigger your memory and help you recall the complete information in your notes. These clues function as memory tags. They help you retrieve from your memory any information that is labeled with these tags. Figure 4-8 on the next page shows a sample of notes in which the recall clue system has been used. When you are taking an exam, the recall clues from your notes will work automatically to help you remember necessary information.

Figure 4-8
Lecture Notes with
Recall Clues Added

Numerical Properties of Atoms   Chem 109
                                                      2/9

I. Prop. related to Temperature + Heat

melting point
   A. Melting Point
      - when particles in a solid move fast
      enough to overcome forces holding them
      together - temp at which this happens =
      melting point.

freezing point
      - Freezing Pt. -temp at which forces
      attracting particles to one another hold
      particles together.

heat of fusion
      - Heat of Fusion -amt. of heat req'd. to
      melt one gram of any substance
      at its melting pt.

boiling point
   B. Boiling Point
      - Point at which molecules of a liquid
      begin to escape as gas.

heat of vap.
      - Heat of vaporization -amt. of heat req'd.
      to change one gram of liquid to a gas
      at its boiling pt.

Condensation pt.
      - Condensation Pt. - point at which gas,
      cooling, changes back to liquid.

spec. heat
   C. Specific Heat
         ex. beach -sand hot, water cold- why?
         Sand + H_2O have different spec. heat
      def. -am't. of heat needed to raise temp.
      of a spec. mass of substance by a
      certain am't.

formula for S.h.
      formula - S.h. = heat in cals.
               mass in grams x temp. diff. in °C
      S.h.   = $\dfrac{cal}{g \times °C}$

A variation on the recall clue system that students have found effective is to write questions rather than summary words and phrases in the margin (see Figure 4-9 on p. 94). The questions trigger your memory and enable you to recall the information that answers your question. The use of questions enables you to test yourself, simulating an exam situation.

Using the Cornell Notetaking Recall Clue System

To study your notes using the recall clue system, cover up the notes with a sheet of paper, exposing only the recall clues in the left margin. Next, read the first recall clue and try to remember the information in the portion of the notes beside it. Then slide the paper down and check that portion to see whether you remembered all the important facts. If you remembered only part of the information, cover up that portion of your notes and again check your recall. Continue checking until you are satisfied that you can remember all the important facts. Then move on to the next recall clue on the page, following the same testing–checking procedure.

To get into the habit of using the recall clue system, mark off with a ruler a two-inch column on the next several blank pages in each of your notebooks.

**Figure 4-9
Lecture Notes with
Recall Questions Added**

Marketing
104

Role of Advertising

What is advertising?	Advertising —Widely used in our economy. —Promotes competition; encourages open system. definition—presentation of a product/service to broad segment of the population.
What are its characteristics?	Characteristics 1. non-personal—uses media rather than person-to- person contact. 2. paid for by seller 3. intended to influence the consumer.
What is the ultimate objective?	Objectives Ultimate objective—to sell product or service

What are the
immediate objectives?
	Immediate objectives
	1. to inform—make consumer
	aware
	   ex. new product available
	2. to persuade—stress value,
	advantages of product
	   ex. results of market
	   research
	3. to reinforce—happens
	after 1 and 2
	—consumers need to be
	reminded about
	prod./service—even if
	they use it.—often done
	through slogans and
	jingles.

Then, when you open your notebook at the beginning of the class, you will be reminded to use the system.

EXERCISE 3 | **DIRECTIONS**   Read the sample set of notes in Figure 4-10. Fill in the recall clues or formulate questions that would help you study and learn the notes.

**Figure 4-10
Sample Lecture Notes**

I. Psychoanalytic theory—created by Sigmund Freud
   A. free association—major diagnostic techniques in psychoanalysis; patient reports whatever comes to mind/holds nothing back.
   B. repression—psych. process of driving ideas out of consciousness.
   C. suppression—conscious of an idea, but won't tell anyone about it.
   D. trauma—particularly disturbing event; most psych. disturbances traceable to a trauma.
   E. interp. of dreams—dreams—fantasies that person believes to be true/have profound influence on personality devlpmt.
   F. Id—power system of personality providing energy.
     1. pleasure principle—all unpleasant events should be avoided.
       a. primary process—normal logic does not operate. ex. bizarre dreams, hallucinations
   G. Ego—strategist of personality/concerned w/what a person CAN do.
     1. reality principle—distinction between real + unreal rather than dist. between pleasure + pain. Satisfies id in a realistic manner.
       a. secondary process—rational, logical, critical.
   H. Superego—"good versus bad," rewards and punishments.
     1. conscience—critical, punitive aspect of superego.

EXERCISE 4

DIRECTIONS For each course you are taking this semester, use the recall clue system for at least one week. Use the recall clues to review your notes several times. At the end of the week, evaluate how well the system works for you.

1. What advantages does it have?

   _____

   _____

   _____

2. Did it help you remember facts and ideas?

   _____

   _____

   _____

3. Are there any disadvantages?

   _____

   _____

   _____

LEARNING COLLABORATIVELY

DIRECTIONS   Working in pairs, bring two sets of lecture notes to class. The first set should be notes taken *before* this chapter on note taking was assigned. The second should be a set of notes taken after this chapter was assigned and should contain editing and recall clues. Assess each other's progress, and suggest areas for further improvement.

APPLYING YOUR LEARNING

Jan is taking an American government course in which class lectures are very important. She has trouble following the lectures and knowing what is important because her instructor does not follow the textbook and often digresses from the topic. The instructor lectures at a fast pace, so Jan feels she is missing important information.

1. What advice would you give Jan for taking lecture notes?
2. How should she study and review her notes?
3. What thought patterns could she expect to find in an American government course?
4. Should Jan tape-record the lectures?
5. Would rewriting or editing her notes be helpful? If so, what changes should she make?

QUESTIONS FOR DISCUSSION

1. What is the difference between hearing and listening? Is it similar to the distinction between reading and understanding?
2. What goals must a good set of lecture notes accomplish?
3. Why is the recall clue system effective in helping you study?
4. Use Figure 4-5 to determine note-taking strategies that are appropriate for your learning style. How can you use these strategies in this class?

SELF-TEST SUMMARY

1. Why should you improve lecture note taking?

Because many college instructors expect you to remember and apply the facts and ideas in their class lectures, it is necessary to take good lecture notes, edit them properly, and develop a system for studying them effectively.

2. What are the characteristics of effective lecture notes?

Effective lecture notes should accomplish three things. First, good notes should summarize the main points of the lecture. Well-taken lecture notes are a valuable aid to study. Second, lecture notes should include enough details and examples so that you can recall and completely understand the information several weeks later. Third, the notes should show the relative importance of ideas and reflect the organization of the lecture.

3. How can you improve your listening skills?

Taking good lecture notes depends on good listening skills. To make your listening more intentional, purposeful, and deliberate, you should apply good reading skills to listening: Focus on content and ideas, not on the speaker's style or on facts alone; pay attention to opening statements; look for the speaker's purpose; and prevent your mind from wandering by focusing your concentration, attention, and thinking skills.

4. Why should you edit your lecture notes?

After taking a set of lecture notes, it is necessary to correct, revise, fill in missing or additional information, and expand your notes. This editing process results in clearer, more accurate notes.

5. How should you study your lecture notes?

The recall clue system is a way of making study and review easier and more effective. During note taking, leave blank a two-inch margin at the left of each page of notes. Later, as you reread your notes, write in the margin words and phrases that briefly summarize the notes. These phrases, or recall clues, trigger your memory and help you recall information in the notes.

DIRECTIONS Write the letter of the choice that best completes each statement in the space provided.

CHECKING YOUR RECALL

_____ 1. A speaker's opening comments typically
   a. identify the organization and purpose of the lecture.
   b. do not contain any important information.
   c. consist only of personal or humorous stories told to get the audience's attention.
   d. will be repeated at the conclusion of the lecture.

_____ 2. The gap between rate of speech and rate of thinking is such that the
   a. speaker has a distinct advantage.
   b. listener has to strain to follow along.
   c. speaker has to allow time for listeners to catch up.
   d. listener has time to think of other things.

_____ 3. One difference between listening and hearing is that listening is
   a. purely biological.
   b. passive.
   c. unintentional.
   d. purposeful.

_____ 4. Instructors often signal what is important during a lecture by doing all of the following except
   a. increasing their rate of speech.
   b. changing the tone or pitch of their voices.
   c. writing on the chalkboard.
   d. listing or numbering points.

_____ 5. Recall clues are intended primarily to
   a. aid your ability to retrieve information.
   b. identify the patterns used in a particular lecture.
   c. reduce the amount of information you must learn.
   d. organize your lecture notes.

APPLYING YOUR SKILLS

_____ 6. Pedro is reviewing the psychology notes he took in class today. The best way for Pedro to review his notes is to
   a. copy his notes over to make them more legible.
   b. expand on details that he didn't have time to write down.
   c. revise his notes while listening to a tape recording of the lecture.
   d. read his notes aloud over and over.

_____ 7. Craig is having trouble taking good notes because his instructor speaks too quickly for him. All of the following strategies might help him _except_
   a. tape-recording the lectures.
   b. using abbreviations.
   c. sitting at the back of the class.
   d. leaving blanks in his notes for filling in missing information later.

_____ 8. Anwali is editing the notes she took during her biology class this morning. This means that Anwali is
   a. grouping the ideas in her notes into paragraphs.
   b. copying the notes over so that they are neater.
   c. memorizing the facts in the notes.
   d. correcting, revising, and adding to her notes to make them more complete and accurate.

_____ 9. Oscar is trying to improve his listening skills during lectures. Oscar should try to
   a. focus on delivery, not content.
   b. memorize unconnected facts.
   c. identify main ideas, relationships, and trends.
   d. come up with mnemonic devices.

_____ 10. Helen has arrived early for an English lecture. The most effective use of her time would be to
   a. review the homework assignment due that day.
   b. begin reading the next textbook chapter assignment.
   c. review her notes from the previous lecture.
   d. chat with friends until the class begins.

MULTIMEDIA *Activities*

Taking Notes in Class

1 Look over the list of abbreviations you can use in your note taking on this Web site from the University of North Dakota, Grand Forks:

http://www.und.nodak.edu/dept/ULC/study/abbrv.html

Are any of these helpful to you? Write an entire paragraph in your own shorthand and then have a friend try to decipher it. How close was your friend?

2 Look over the note-taking systems outlined on this Web site from Caltech, San Luis Obispo:

http://www.sas.calpoly.edu/asc/ssl/notetaking.systems.html

Experiment with them in your classes.

3 Are You a Good Listener?

http://www.effectivemeetings.com/productivity/communication/listener.asp

Although this site is directed toward listening in meetings, it can still apply to the way students conduct themselves during class discussions and group work sessions. Try a variation of the exercise they suggest—choose various points to monitor during your conversations and classes, not just interrupting.

4 Use your note-taking skills in other areas of your life. Try taking notes on your phone calls to help you become a more efficient listener and engaged conversationalist.

5 Ask a friend to take notes on a conversation you are having. Review the notes later. Do the notes accurately reflect what you said? Did your friend leave out information that you thought was important?

> **Answer Key for Learning Experiment**
> Paragraph 1: intimate, personal, social, public
> Paragraph 2: attraction, taste, memory, identity

5 Active Reading Strategies

Why Become an Active Reader?

- Active reading stimulates your thinking.

- Active reading helps you get interested in and stay involved with what you read.

- It makes reading easier by providing you with a mental outline of the material.

- Active reading increases your recall.

Learning Experiment

Step 1

In the space provided, draw the face of a one-dollar bill.

Step 2

Find a one-dollar bill and compare your drawing with it. Notice the features you did not include.

The Result

Although hundreds of one-dollar bills have passed through your hands over the years, you probably did not recall very many features. Why? You did not recall these features because you did not plan to remember them. (No doubt you would have done better if the experiment directed you to study the face of a one-dollar bill for several minutes and then put it away and draw it.)

Learning Principle
(What This Means to You)

We all remember what we intend to remember. If you do not decide what you should remember before reading a textbook chapter, your recall is likely to be poor. On the other hand, if you decide what you need to know before you start, your recall will be much higher. This chapter will demonstrate several techniques that will help you decide what to learn in a textbook chapter. Specifically, you will learn to preread before reading, to discover what you already know about the topic, and to define your purposes for reading. You will also learn to monitor and strengthen your comprehension as you read.

PREREADING AND PREDICTING

Do you check for traffic before crossing a street? Do you check the depth of a pool before diving in? What do you do with an article or chapter before you read it, before you "jump in"? In this section, you will become acquainted with the technique of prereading—a useful way of checking any written material before you read it. Just as most people check traffic before crossing a street or water depth before diving, to be an efficient reader you should check printed materials before reading to become generally familiar with the overall content and organization.

Before reading, you should make predictions about the material. You might make predictions, or educated guesses, about how difficult or interesting the material will be, what topics will be discussed, or how the author will approach the subject. You might also anticipate how the material will be organized—how it progresses from one idea to another.

How to Preread

Your overall purposes in prereading are to identify the most important ideas in the material and note their organization. You look only at specific parts and skip over the rest. The portions to look at in prereading a textbook chapter are described in the following paragraphs. Later you will learn how to adapt this procedure to other types of material.

1. **Read the title and subtitle.**
   The title provides the overall topic of the article or chapter; the subtitle suggests the specific focus, aspect, or approach toward the overall topic.

2. **Read the introduction or first paragraph.**
   The introduction, or first paragraph if there is no introduction, serves as a lead-in to the chapter. It gives you an idea of where the material starts and where it is going.

3. **Read each major heading.**
   The headings function as labels or topic statements for what is contained in the sections that follow them. In other words, a heading announces the major topic of each section.

4. **Read the first sentence under each heading.**
   The first sentence frequently tells you what the passage is about or states the central thought. You should be aware, however, that in some types of material and in certain styles of writing, the first sentence does not function as a central thought. Instead, the opening sentence may function as a transition or lead-in statement, or it may be designed to catch your interest. If the first sentence seems unimportant, read the last sentence; often this sentence states or restates the central thought.

5. **Note any typographical and graphical aids.**
   Italic (slanted) type is used to emphasize important terms and definitions by distinguishing them from the rest of the passage. Note any material that is numbered 1, 2, 3, lettered a, b, c, or presented in list form. Graphs, charts, pictures, and tables are other means of emphasis and usually signal something that is important in the chapter. Be sure to read the captions for pictures and the legends on graphs, charts, and tables. Note words in italic or bold print—usually a definition follows.

6. **Read the last paragraph or summary.**

   The summary or last paragraph gives a condensed view of the chapter and helps you identify key ideas. Often the summary outlines the key points in the chapter.

7. **Read quickly any end-of-article or end-of-chapter material.**

   This might include references, study questions, vocabulary lists, or biographical information about the author. These materials will be useful later as you read and study the article or chapter, and it is important, as part of your prereading, to note whether such materials are included. If there are study questions, it is useful to read them through quickly, because they will indicate what is important in the chapter. If a vocabulary list is included, rapidly skim through it to identify terms you will need to learn as you read.

Demonstration of Prereading

The textbook chapter excerpt seen in Figure 5-1 on the next page has been included to demonstrate what it is like to preread. This excerpt is taken from an introductory text, *Sociology*, by James M. Henslin. To illustrate how prereading is done, these pages have been specially marked. Everything that you should look at or read has been shaded. Preread this excerpt now, reading only the shaded portions of each page.

EXERCISE 1

DIRECTIONS   Answer each of the following questions after you have preread the reading titled "Language" in Figure 5-1 on pages 104–105. Do *not* read the entire selection. Mark T after statements that are true and F after those that are false. Do not look back in the reading to locate the answers. When you finish, check your answers in the answer key at the end of the chapter, page 125, and write your score in the space indicated.

1. Language consists of symbols that communicate   _____
   thoughts and ideas.

2. Language allows us to pass along knowledge and   _____
   experience to the next generation.

3. Language creates confusion about events in the past.   _____

4. Language has little relationship to culture.   _____

5. Language allows people to plan purposeful activities.   _____

Score (number right):   _____

Look back at your score on the quiz in Exercise 1. Probably you got at least half of the questions right, perhaps more. This quiz was a test of the main ideas that were presented in this excerpt. You can see, then, that prereading does familiarize you with the chapter and enables you to identify and remember many of the main ideas it contains. Actually, each part of the chapter that you read while prereading provided you with specific information about the organization and content of the chapter. The following exercise emphasizes how each step in the prereading process gives you useful information about the material to be read.

Figure 5-1
Prereading

PREREADING LANGUAGE

The primary way in which people communicate with one another is through **language**—symbols that can be combined in an infinite number of ways for the purpose of communicating abstract thought. Each word is actually a symbol, a sound to which we have attached a particular meaning. This allows us to use it to communicate with one another. Language itself is universal in the sense that all human groups have language, but there is nothing universal about the meanings given to particular sounds. Thus, like gestures, in different cultures the same sound may mean something entirely different—or may have no meaning at all.

The significance of language for human life is difficult to overstate. As will become apparent from the following discussion, *language allows culture to exist.*

LANGUAGE ALLOWS HUMAN EXPERIENCE TO BE CUMULATIVE   By means of language, we pass ideas, knowledge, and even attitudes on to the next generation, allowing it to build on experiences that it may never undergo. This building process enables humans to modify their behavior in light of what previous generations have learned. Hence, the central sociological significance of language: *Language allows culture to develop by freeing people to move beyond their immediate experiences.*

Without language, human culture would be little more advanced than that of the lower primates. To communicate, we would be limited to the grunts and gestures, which would minimize the temporal dimension of human life. Our communications would be limited to a small time span: events that are now taking place, those that have just taken place, or those that will take place immediately—a sort of "slightly extended present." You can grunt and gesture, for example, that you want a drink of water, but in the absence of language how could you share ideas concerning past or future events? There would be little or no way to communicate to others what event you had in mind, much less the greater complexities that humans communicate—ideas and feelings about events.

LANGUAGE PROVIDES A SOCIAL OR SHARED PAST   Without language, our memories would be extremely limited, for we associate experiences with words and then use words to recall the experience. Such memories as would exist in the absence of language would be highly individualized, for only rarely and incompletely would we communicate them to others, much less discuss them and agree on something. By attaching words to an event, however, and then using those words to recall the event we are able to discuss the event. As we talk about past events, we develop shared understanding about what those events mean. In short, through talk, people develop a shared past.

LANGUAGE PROVIDES A SOCIAL OR SHARED FUTURE   Language also extends our time horizons forward. Because language enables us to agree on times, dates, and places, it allows us to plan activities with one another. Think about it for a moment. Without language, how could you ever plan future events? How could you possibly communicate goals, times, and plans? Whatever planning could exist would be limited to rudimentary communications, perhaps to an agreement to meet at a certain place when the sun is in a certain position. But think of the difficulty, perhaps impossibility, of conveying just a slight change in this simple arrangement, such as "I can't make it tomorrow, but my neighbor can, if that's all right with you."

LANGUAGE ALLOWS SHARED PERSPECTIVES   Our ability to speak, then, provides us a social (or shared) past and future. This is vital for humanity. It is a water-

Figure 5.1
(Continued)

shed that distinguishes us from animals. But speech does much more than this. When we talk with one another, we are exchanging ideas about events; that is, we are sharing perspectives. Our words are the embodiment of our experiences, distilled into a readily exchangeable form, mutually understandable to people who have learned that language. Talking about events allows us to arrive at the shared understandings that form the basis of social life. To not share a language while living alongside one another, however, invites miscommunication and suspicion.

LANGUAGE ALLOWS COMPLEX, SHARED, GOAL-DIRECTED BEHAVIOR
Common understanding enable us to establish a *purpose* for getting together. Let's suppose you want to go on a picnic. You use speech not only to plan the picnic but also to decide on reasons for the picnic—which may be anything from "because it's a nice day and it shouldn't be wasted studying" to "because it's my birthday." Language permits you to blend individual activities into an integrated sequence. In other words, through discussion you decide where you will go; who will drive; who will bring the hamburgers, the potato chips, the soda; where you will meet; and so on. Only because of language can you participate in such a common yet complex event as a picnic—or build roads and and bridges, or attend college classes.

IN SUM   The sociological significance of language is that it takes us beyond the world of apes and allows culture to develop. Language frees us from the present by providing a past and a future. It gives us the capacity to share understandings about the past and develop shared perceptions about the future, as well as to establish underlying purposes for our activities. Consequently, as in the case of planning a picnic, each individual is able to perform a small part of a larger activity, aware that others are carrying out related parts. In this way, language enables a series of separate activities to become united into a larger whole.

EXERCISE 2

DIRECTIONS   Listed below are various parts of an actual textbook chapter or article to which you would refer in prereading. For each item, read the parts and then answer the question that follows.

1. *Sample article*

Title:	"Psychologists Have Proof of ESP"
Source:	*Today's Women* magazine
Question:	Answer with yes or no. Would you expect this article to

   a. be technical?
   b. be highly factual with careful references?
   c. contain accounts of individuals with ESP?
   d. contain opinions?
   e. contain references for further study?

2. *Sample text*

Section heading:	Culture and Technology
Subheadings:	Historical Roots and Trends
	Recent Technological Changes
	Predicted Long-Range Effects
Question:	What clues do you have about how the author arranged ideas in this section of the text?

_____

_____

_____

3. *Sample text*

Title: *Diversity in Families*

Chapter title: "The Social Construction of Intimacy"

Chapter introduction:

Intimacy, like other social relations, is shaped by our surroundings. Therefore, we cannot understand it in isolation from the rest of social life. This chapter is about intimate relationships and the ways in which they are embedded in social circumstances. Intimacy exists in relationships based on friendship, romantic love, and parenthood; it even exists among co-workers (Risman and Schwartz, 1989). Intimacy concerns both women and men, in homosexual as well as heterosexual relationships. Although intimacy need not include either sex or love, our focus is on relationships that encompass both.

In this chapter, we examine intimacy through a sociological lens. We begin by examining the changing historical and societal context giving rise to intimacy as it is defined today. We then look at patterns of courtship and mate selection by connecting them to historical developments. Turning to sexuality, we underscore the macro structural conditions that shape our most private behaviors. Here, we review the facts and trends pertaining to sex in contemporary U.S. society. We also consider some of the social connections between sexual practices and public health and policy issues. Finally, we turn our attention to the ways in which love and sex are patterned differently for various groups.

—Zinn and Eitzen, *Diversity in Families*, p. 205

Questions: a. List the topics the chapter will cover in the order in which you expect they will be covered.

_____

_____

_____

_____

_____

b. Which of the following will the chapter emphasize?
   (1) how intimacy has changed over the past several decades
   (2) that intimacy is affected by other aspects of social life
   (3) the importance of intimacy in long-term relationships
   (4) why courtship and mate selection depend on traditional values

4. *Sample text*

Title: *Our Changing Economy*

Subtitle: *An Introduction to Economics*

Chapter title: "Why Are There Economic Systems?"

Graphic aids: The chapter includes the following graphic aids:
   a. a graph showing the relationship between the production of various types of goods and price

b. a "Beetle Bailey" cartoon that illustrates that choice is associated with cost

c. a picture of objects that have been used as money in various cultures throughout the world

Question: Consider what each graphic tells you about the chapter content.

a. _____

b. _____

c. _____

5. *Sample text*

Title: *The World Today*

Subtitle: *Its Patterns and Cultures*

Chapter title: "Asia"

Section headings: This chapter is divided into four major sections:

a. The Heritage of the Past in the Orient

b. How the People of the Orient Make a Living

c. New Directions for India, Pakistan, and Southeast Asia

d. The People's Republic of China, Democracy, and the Uncommitted Orient

Question: By noting the section titles within this chapter, what do you expect about the organization and content of the chapter?

_____

_____

_____

_____

Prereading Specific Types of Material

Not all reading materials are organized in the same way, and not all reading materials have the same features or parts. Consequently, you must adjust the way you preread to the type of material you are working with. Figure 5-2 on the next page offers suggestions on how to adapt the prereading method to suit what you are reading.

Why Prereading Works

Research studies suggest that prereading increases comprehension and improves recall. Several studies show that prereading is a useful technique for reading textbook chapters. In a classic study done by McClusky, college students were divided into two groups.* One group was taught how to use headings and

*H. Y. McClusky, "An Experiment on the Influence of Preliminary Skimming on Reading," *Journal of Educational Psychology*, 25 (1934): 521–529.

Figure 5-2
How to Adjust
Prereading to the
Material

Type of Material	Special Features to Consider
Textbooks	Title and subtitle
	Preface
	Table of contents
	Appendix
	Glossary
Textbook chapters	Summary
	Vocabulary list
	Review and discussion questions
Articles and essays	Title
	Introductory paragraphs
	Concluding paragraphs (see Chapter 7)
Research reports	Abstract
Articles without headings	First sentences of paragraphs
Tests and exams	Instructions and directions
	Number of items
	Types of questions
	Point distribution
Reference sources	Table of contents
	Index
Newspapers	Headline
	First few sentences
	Section headings
Internet Web sites	Title
	Features listed on home page
	Links (see Chapter 9)
	Sponsor

summaries for prereading; the other group received no instruction. Both groups were given a selection to read and comprehension questions to answer. Results of the study indicated that the group who used headings and summaries read 24 percent faster than, and just as accurately as, the students who did not preread. Prereading is effective for several reasons.

1. **It helps you get interested in and involved with what you will read.** It activates your thinking. Because you know what to expect, reading the material completely is easier.
2. **It provides you with a mental outline of the material you are going to read.** You begin to anticipate the sequence of ideas; you see the relationships among topics; you recognize what approach and direction the author has taken in writing about the subject.
3. **It lets you apply several principles of learning.** You identify what is important, thus establishing an intent to remember.
4. **It functions as a type of rehearsal that enhances recall because it provides repetition of the most important points.**

Prereading is used best with expository, factual material that is fairly well organized. Knowing this, you can see that prereading is not a good strategy to use when reading materials such as novels, poems, narrative articles, essays, or short stories. However, you will find it fairly easy to adapt the prereading technique to other kinds of writing.

EXERCISE 3 | **DIRECTIONS**   Select a chapter from one of your textbooks. To be practical, choose a chapter that you will be assigned to read in the near future. After prereading it, answer the following questions.

1. What is the major topic of the chapter?

   _____

2. How does the author subdivide, or break down, this topic?

   _____

3. What approach does the author take toward the subject? (Does he or she cite research, give examples, describe problems, list causes?)

   _____

4. Construct a brief outline of the chapter.

   _____

Making Predictions

Do you predict what a film will be about and whether seeing it will be worthwhile on the basis of a coming attractions preview? Do you anticipate what a party will be like before attending? This type of prediction or anticipation is typical and occurs automatically. Do you predict what a chapter will discuss before you read it?

Research studies of good and poor readers demonstrate that efficient readers frequently predict and anticipate, both before reading and while they read, both the content and organization of the material. For example, from the title of a textbook chapter, you can predict the subject and, often, how the author will approach it. A business management textbook chapter titled "Schools of Management Thought: Art or Science?" indicates the subject—schools of management—but also suggests that the author will classify the various schools as artistic (creative) or scientific. Similarly, author, source, headings, graphics, photographs, chapter previews, and summaries, all of which you may check during prereading, provide additional information for anticipating content.

Making predictions is a way to expand and broaden your thinking beyond the Remembering and Understanding levels. Predicting forces you to apply your knowledge to new situations (Applying), to examine how ideas fit together (Analyzing), and to put ideas together in unique ways (Creating). For a review of the Levels of Thinking, see Figure 2-3 on page 53.

Efficient readers frequently make predictions about organization as well as content. That is, they anticipate the order or manner in which ideas or information will be presented. For instance, from a chapter section titled "The History of World Population Growth," you can predict that the chapter will be organized chronologically, moving ahead in time as the chapter progresses. A chapter titled "Behavioral *vs.* Situational Approaches to Leadership" suggests that the chapter will compare and contrast the two approaches to leadership.

As efficient readers read, they also confirm, reject, or revise their initial predictions. For example, a student who read the heading "Types of Managers" anticipated that the section would describe different management styles. Then he began reading:

Types of Managers

Now that you have an idea of what the management process is, consider the roles of managers themselves. It is possible to classify managers by the nature of the position they hold. This section will review some of the major categories of managers. The next section will identify how these differences affect a manager's job.

The student immediately revised his prediction, realizing that managers would be classified not by style but by the position they hold. Making predictions and anticipating content and organization are worthwhile because they focus your attention on the material. Further, the process of confirming, rejecting, or revising predictions is an active one—it forces you to concentrate and helps you to understand. Once you know what to expect in a piece of reading, you will find it easier to read.

EXERCISE 4

DIRECTIONS   For the textbook chapter described below, predict which of the following topics might appear in the chapter, and place a check mark next to each.

Textbook title: *Psychology: An Introduction*
Chapter: "Human Development Before Birth"
Headings: The Mechanics of Heredity
Prenatal Development: Influences Before Birth

Topics:

_____   1. Mental abilities of newborns

_____   2. How sex is determined

_____   3. How infants learn speech

_____   4. Intellectual deficits

_____   5. Fetal alcohol syndrome

_____   6. Types of genes

_____   7. Observing the development of emotions

_____   8. Chromosome abnormalities

_____   9. Siblings as behavioral role models

_____   10. Upper body development

EXERCISE 5

DIRECTIONS   Below are listed a textbook title, chapter title, and chapter headings. Place a check mark in front of the statements you predict will appear in the chapter. If possible, also indicate the section in which each statement is most likely to appear. (Indicate by marking 1, 2, 3, 4, or 5 to correspond to the headings in order.)

Textbook title: *America's Problems: Social Issues and Public Policy*
Chapter: "The Family"
Headings: Some Trends in Family Disruption
The Consequences of Family Disruption
Inequality in the Family: Division of Labor in the Home
Work, Family, and Social Supports
The Family as a Crucible of Violence

Statements:

_____   1. Divorce creates social and personal stress for both children and parents.

_____   2. Sex-role stereotypes dictate how much males contribute to housekeeping chores.

_____   3. Street crime takes an enormous toll on citizens and only rarely results in prosecution by the courts.

_____   4. Child and spouse abuse is aggravated by poverty and gender inequality.

_____   5. The continued concentration of minorities in low-paying jobs is a reflection of inequality.

_____   6. Lack of day care for single-parent families creates insurmountable problems.

_____   7. Changing health care policies have reduced public responsibilities for family health care maintenance.

EXERCISE 6 | DIRECTIONS Preread the textbook excerpt titled "Communication Between Women and Men," in Part Eight, pages 466–468. Then make a list of topics you predict it will cover. Next, read the selection. Then review your list of predictions and place a check mark next to those that were correct.

EXERCISE 7 | DIRECTIONS Select a chapter from one of your textbooks. Preread the chapter, and then write a list of predictions about the chapter's content or organization.

DISCOVERING WHAT YOU ALREADY KNOW

Discovering what you already know about a topic will make learning easier because you will be connecting new information to old information already in place. You will find, too, that reading material becomes more interesting once you have connected its topic with your own experience. Comprehension will be easier, too, because you will have already thought about some of the ideas presented in the material.

Suppose you are studying a business textbook and are about to begin reading a chapter on advertising that discusses the objectives of advertising, the construction and design of ads, and the production of ads. Before you begin reading the chapter, you should spend a minute or two recalling what you already know about these topics. Try one or more of the following techniques.

1. **Ask questions and try to answer them.** You might ask questions such as "What are the goals of advertising?" In answering this question, you will realize you already know several objectives: to sell a product, to introduce a new product, to announce sales or discounts, and so on.

2. **Relate the topic to your own experience.** For a topic on the construction and design of ads, think about ads you have heard or read recently. What similarities exist? How do the ads begin? How do they end? This process will

probably lead you to realize that you already know something about how ads are designed.

3. **Free-associate.** On a sheet of scrap paper, jot down everything that comes to mind about advertising. List facts and questions, or describe ads you have recently heard or seen. This process will also activate your recall of information.

At first, you may think you know very little—or even nothing—about a particular topic. However, by using one of the foregoing techniques, you will be surprised to find that there are very few topics about which you know nothing at all. For example, suppose you were about to read a biology chapter on genetics. At first you might think you know nothing about it. Complete Exercise 8 to discover what you do know about genetics.

EXERCISE 8

DIRECTIONS For a chapter on genetics, write a list of questions, experiences, or associations that would help focus your mind on the topic. (Hint: Think of inherited family traits and characteristics; ask questions about eye and hair color.) When you have finished, compare your work with the student sample shown in Figure 5-3.

EXERCISE 9

DIRECTIONS Discover what you already know about the following topics by using at least two of the techniques described in this section for each topic.

Topics
1. Creativity
2. Aggressive behavior
3. Body language

When you have finished, answer the following questions:

1. Did you discover you knew more about the topics than you first thought?
2. Which technique worked best? Why?
3. Might the technique you choose depend on your subject matter?

Figure 5-3
A Student Sample

What eye color is dominant?
Is a tendency to be overweight inherited?
What do genes do?
How many do we have?
What is genetic engineering?
Are aspects of personality inherited?
Can environment influence genetics?
Why do some women have facial hair?
Can genes be defective? If so, what happens?
What do chromosomes do?
Is hair loss hereditary?
Can a person have two eyes each of a different color?

EXERCISE 10 | DIRECTIONS   In Exercise 6 you preread the textbook excerpt titled "Communication Between Women and Men." Discover what you already know about differences in the ways men and women talk and communicate using one of the techniques described in this section.

EXERCISE 11 | DIRECTIONS   Select a chapter from one of your textbooks. Preread it, and use one of the techniques described in this section to discover what you already know about the subject of the chapter.

DEFINING YOUR PURPOSES FOR READING

Have you ever read a complete page or more and then not remembered a thing? Have you wandered aimlessly through paragraph after paragraph, section after section, unable to remember key ideas you have just read, even when you were really trying to concentrate? If these problems sound familiar, you probably began reading without a specific purpose in mind. That is, you were not looking for anything in particular as you read. Guide questions can focus your attention and help you pick out what is important.

Developing Guide Questions

Most textbook chapters use boldface headings to organize chapter content. The simplest way to establish a purpose for reading is to convert each heading into one or more questions that will guide your reading. These are called **guide questions.** As you read, you then look for the answers. For a section with the heading "The Hidden Welfare System," you could ask the questions "What is the hidden welfare system?" and "How does it work?" As you read that section, you would actively search for answers. For a section of a business textbook titled "Taxonomy of Organizational Research Strategies," you could pose such questions as "What is a taxonomy?" and "What research strategies are discussed and how are they used?"

The excerpt that follows is taken from a social problems textbook chapter on problems of education. Before reading it, use the heading to formulate several guide questions and list them here. Then read the passage to find the answers, and fill them in after your questions.

Question 1: _____

_____

Answer: _____

_____

Question 2: _____

_____

Answer: _____

_____

Pink-Collar Occupations

At the beginning of the twentieth century, only about 20 percent of all women were in the labor force; by 1990 that figure exceeded 60 percent, and today there are well over 70 million women in the workforce (U.S. Bureau of the Census, 1990a, 2000). Despite their large representation in the workforce, almost half of all women employed outside the home are in clerical or service work. Sociologist Jessie Bernard (1981) coined the term *pink-collar occupation* to describe clerical work; over 80 percent of all secretaries, typists, stenographers, and other clerical workers are women. The service work category includes occupations such as nursing, child care, household service, and restaurant work. Jobs in clerical and service work come with far less income, power, and prestige than most male-dominated occupations. Both verbal and nonverbal communications are shaped by gender as well as dominant-subordinate positions in the work arena (Johnson, 1994). Patterns in women's employment and incomes are changing, and occupational and other economic opportunities for women are increasing (Huber and Stephens, 2000). For the first time in human history, technology has made it possible for women's economic productivity to equal men's (Huber, 1990). Nevertheless there still exists a distinctive gender-poverty gap, and a higher proportion of women live in poverty in the United States than in most other industrial and postindustrial nations (Casper et al., 1994).

—Thompson and Hickey, *Society in Focus,* p. 320

You probably developed such questions as "What are pink-collar occupations?" or "What occupations are considered to be pink collar?" Then, as you read the section, you found out that pink collar is a term used to describe service work, predominantly done by women. You also discovered that these jobs pay less than male-dominated occupations and have less power and prestige. However, patterns are changing, opportunities are increasing, but a gender-poverty gap still exists. Did the guide questions help you focus your attention and make the paragraph easier to read?

You may find it helpful to jot down your guide questions in the margins of your texts, next to the appropriate headings. These questions are then available for later study. Rereading and answering your questions is an excellent method of review.

Formulating the Right Questions

Guide questions that begin with *What, Why,* and *How* are especially effective. *Who, When,* and *Where* questions are less useful, because they can often be answered through superficial reading or may lead to simple, factual, or one-word answers. *What, Why,* and *How* questions require detailed answers that demand more thought, so they force you to read in greater depth.

For example, "The Fall of the Roman Empire," the title of a section in a history text, could be turned into a question such as "When did the Roman Empire fall?" For this question, the answer is merely a date. This question, then, would not guide your reading effectively. On the other hand, questions such as "How did the Roman Empire fall?" and "What brought about the fall of the Roman Empire?" and "What factors contributed to the fall of the Roman Empire?" would require you to recall important events and identify causes.

Here are a few examples of effective guide questions:

EXERCISE 17

DIRECTIONS   Select a three- to four-page section of a chapter in one of your textbooks. Read the section, and then answer questions 1 and 4 in Exercise 16.

Evaluating Your Comprehension

At times, signals of poor comprehension do not come through clearly or strongly enough. In fact, some students think they have understood what they read until they are questioned in class or take an exam. Only then do they discover that their comprehension was incomplete. Other students find that they understand material on a surface, factual level but that they do not recognize more complicated relationships and implied meanings or do not see implications and applications. Use the following methods to determine whether you really understand what you read.

1. **Set checkpoints.** Race car drivers make pit stops during races for quick mechanical checks and repairs; athletes are subject to frequent physical tests and examinations. These activities provide an opportunity to assess performance and to correct any problems or malfunctions. Similarly, when you are reading, it is necessary to stop and evaluate.

As you preread a textbook assignment, identify reasonable or logical checkpoints: points at which to stop, check, and (if necessary) correct your performance before continuing. Pencil a check mark in the margin to designate these points. These checkpoints should be logical breaking points where one topic ends and another begins or where a topic is broken down into several subtopics. As you reach each of these checkpoints, stop and assess your work using the techniques described below.

2. **Use your guide questions.** Earlier in this chapter, you learned how to form guide questions by using boldface headings. These same questions can be used to monitor your comprehension while reading. When you finish a boldface-headed section, stop and take a moment to recall your guide question and answer it mentally or on paper. Your ability to answer your questions will indicate your level of comprehension.

3. **Ask connection questions.** To be certain that your understanding is complete and that you are not recalling only superficial factual information, ask connection questions. **Connection questions** are those that require you to think about content. They force you to draw together ideas and to discover relationships between the material at hand and other material in the same chapter, in other chapters, or in class lectures. Here are a few examples:

- What does this topic have to do with topics discussed earlier in the chapter?
- How is this reading assignment related to the topics of this week's class lectures?
- What does this chapter have to do with the chapter assigned last week?
- What principle do these problems illustrate?

Connection questions enable you to determine whether your learning is meaningful—whether you are simply taking in information or are using the information and fitting it into the scheme of the course. The best times to ask connection questions are before beginning and after you have finished a chapter or each major section.

4. **Use internal dialogue.** Internal dialogue—mentally talking to yourself—is another excellent means of monitoring your reading and learning. It involves rephrasing to yourself the message the author is communicating or the ideas

you are studying. If you are unable to express ideas in your own words, your understanding is probably incomplete. Here are a few examples of the use of internal dialogue.

- While reading a section in a math textbook, you mentally outline the steps to follow in solving a sample problem.
- You are reading an essay that argues convincingly that the threat of nuclear war is real. As you finish reading each stage of the argument, you rephrase it in your own words.
- As you finish each boldface section in a psychology chapter, you summarize the key points.

EXERCISE 18 | DIRECTIONS   Read "Your Appearance, Good or Bad, Can Affect Size of Your Paycheck" in Part Eight on page 501. Answer the guide questions you wrote in Exercise 14, page 116.

EXERCISE 19 | DIRECTIONS   Choose a section from one of your textbooks. Read it, and then check your understanding by using both guide questions and connection questions. List your questions on a separate sheet of paper.

EXERCISE 20 | DIRECTIONS   Select another section from one of your textbooks, and experiment with the technique of internal dialogue to assess your comprehension. In the space provided here, describe the technique you used and say whether or not it worked.

_____

_____

_____

_____

STRENGTHENING YOUR COMPREHENSION

You have learned how to recognize clues that signal strong or weak understanding of reading material and how to assess your comprehension. This section will offer some suggestions to follow when you realize you need to strengthen your comprehension.

1. **Analyze the time and place in which you are reading.** If you've been reading or studying for several hours, mental fatigue may be the source of the problem. If you are reading in a place with distractions or interruptions, you may not be able to understand what you're reading. (See the Success Workshop on page 11 for suggestions on how to monitor and improve your concentration.)
2. **Rephrase each paragraph in your own words.** You might need to approach complicated material sentence by sentence, expressing each in your own words.
3. **Read aloud sentences or sections that are particularly difficult.** Reading out loud sometimes makes complicated material easier to understand.

4. **Reread difficult or complicated sections.** At times, several readings, in fact, are appropriate and necessary.

5. **Slow down your reading rate.** On occasion, simply reading more slowly and carefully will provide you with the needed boost in comprehension.

6. **Write guide questions next to headings.** Refer to your questions frequently and jot down or underline answers.

7. **Write a brief outline of major points.** This will help you see the overall organization and progression of ideas. (See Chapter 15 for specific outlining techniques.)

8. **Highlight key ideas.** After you've read a section, go back and think about and highlight what is important. Highlighting forces you to sort out what is important, and this sorting process builds comprehension and recall. (Refer to Chapter 14 for suggestions on how to highlight effectively.)

9. **Write notes in the margins.** Explain or rephrase difficult or complicated ideas or sections.

10. **Determine whether you lack background knowledge.** Comprehension is difficult—at times, it is impossible—if you lack essential information that the writer assumes you have. Suppose you are reading a section of a political science text in which the author describes implications of the balance of power in the Third World. If you do not understand the concept of balance of power, your comprehension will break down. When you lack background information, take immediate steps to correct the problem:

    • Consult other sections of your text, using the glossary and index.
    • Obtain a more basic text that reviews fundamental principles and concepts.
    • Consult reference materials (encyclopedias, subject dictionaries, or biographical dictionaries).
    • Ask your instructor to recommend additional sources, guidebooks, or review texts.

EXERCISE 21

DIRECTIONS   The following three paragraphs have been chosen because they are difficult. Assess your comprehension as you read each, paying attention to both positive and negative signals (Figure 5-4, p. 118). After you have read each paragraph, list the signals you received, and indicate what you could do to strengthen your comprehension.

Paragraph 1

The extension of civil rights was not initiated by government act; civil rights were won through a long and bitter struggle of people determined to seize the citizenship that was their birthright. Deprived of political and business opportunities for a century, bright young black men and women turned to the black church to express their hopes, energies, and aspirations. This was particularly true in the segregated South. But during the 1950s the accumulation of change began to wear the edges of racial separation thin. When a young scholar, Martin Luther King, Jr., returned from Boston University to take up the ministry at Dexter Avenue Baptist Church in 1954 in Montgomery, Alabama, he had no hint that a nationwide civil rights movement would soon swirl around him or that his name would be linked with the great march on Washington of 1963 that would help open the floodgates of integration. What made King one of the most famous Americans of his day was the energy of a suppressed American culture, which he articulated into a momentous political and moral awakening. Its successes were his; its failures revealed his limitations and exposed the deepest barriers to equality in American life.

—Wilson et al., *The Pursuit of Liberty,* p. 422

Positive signals: _____

Negative signals: _____

Strengthen comprehension by: _____

Paragraph 2

In intermediary pricing, cost-plus pricing is the dominant mode among intermediaries in the marketing channel, wholesalers and retailers, where it is called *markup pricing.* These marketers deal with large assortments of products and do not have the resources to develop demand schedules for each item. . . . Channel members' prices are not totally unrelated to demand; they do assign different percentage markups to different items based upon sales experience and estimates of consumer price sensitivity. Wholesalers and retailers will quickly lower prices if an item is not selling. Also, the intermediary's price is based upon a markup on manufacturer's selling price, or discount from manufacturer's suggested retail price. The manufacturer may have researched demand and conducted a competitive analysis before setting the price and discount schedules.

—Kinnear, Bernhardt, and Krentler, *Principles of Marketing,* p. 637

Positive signals: _____

Negative signals: _____

Strengthen comprehension by: _____

Paragraph 3

As noted previously, one of the main motivations for zoologists to study development is that it provides insights regarding taxonomic relationships among groups of animals. In the early 19th century the Estonian biologist Karl Ernst von Baer made a number of observations that suggest such a relationship, although he explicitly rejected any evolutionary implications. What is known as von Baer's law states that embryonic development in vertebrates goes from general forms common to all vertebrates to increasingly specialized forms characteristic of classes, orders, and lower taxonomic levels. Thus the early embryos of all vertebrates, whether fish, frog, hog, or human, all look alike. Later it is possible to tell the human embryo from the fish but not from the hog, and still later one can see a difference between these two mammals.

—Harris, *Concepts in Zoology,* p. 130

Positive signals: _____

Negative signals: _____

Strengthen comprehension by: _____

EXERCISE 22

DIRECTIONS   Select three brief sections from your most difficult textbook. Choose three of the suggestions for strengthening your comprehension, and list them here. Try out each suggestion on one textbook section. Evaluate and describe the effectiveness of each.

	Suggestion	**Evaluation**
1.	_____	_____
2.	_____	_____
3.	_____	_____

LEARNING COLLABORATIVELY

DIRECTIONS   Choose another student with whom to work. Each student should select, from one of his or her textbooks, a chapter that he or she has already read. The students should exchange textbooks, and each should preread the selected chapter. The textbook owner should quiz the textbook prereader about what he or she learned from the chapter by prereading. Then the prereader should make predictions about chapter content and organization. Finally, the owner should confirm or deny each prediction.

APPLYING YOUR LEARNING

Malcolm's reading assignment this week for his sociology class consists of a newspaper article, a journal article that does not contain a summary, an essay, and a short story. The class is studying the changing structure of the family during the twentieth century.

1. Describe how Malcolm should preread the newspaper article. What should he be looking for?
2. Describe how Malcolm should preread the journal article.
3. What should Malcolm pay attention to in prereading the essay?
4. The short story was written in 1941 by an American writer. A short story is an unusual assignment in a sociology class. Realizing this, how should Malcolm preread it? What predictions can he make about the story? What should he be looking for as he reads it?
5. Which assignment is most likely to present comprehension problems?
6. How should Malcolm evaluate his comprehension for each?

APPLYING YOUR SKILLS: Sample Textbook Chapter

1. Preread the entire sample textbook chapter, pages 513–532. Predict what topics you expect will be covered in the chapter.
2. Use one of the strategies on pages 111–112 to discover what you already know about the topics covered in the chapter.
3. Write at least five guide questions that would be useful in reading the chapter.
4. Read the section titled "Intercultural Communication," pages 516–518. As you read, be alert for positive and negative comprehension signals.
5. What strategies could you use to strengthen your comprehension? Choose one strategy and reread the section; evaluate the effectiveness of the technique.

QUESTIONS FOR DISCUSSION

1. How well did prereading work for you? If it did not work well, troubleshoot the problem with another student.
2. How do you know when you don't understand what you read? What strategies do you use to improve your understanding?

3. Among the strategies given for improving your comprehension, which seem most helpful? Why? Do you think the strategies should vary from course to course? If so, how?
4. What features do your textbooks offer to help you understand what you read? Which features are most helpful? Why?

SELF-TEST SUMMARY

1. What is prereading?

Prereading is a technique that allows the reader to become familiar with the material to be read before beginning to read it completely. The technique involves checking specific parts of an article or textbook chapter that provide the reader with a mental outline of the content of the material. Prereading makes the actual reading of the material easier and helps the reader understand and remember what she or he reads.

2. How do you preread?

In prereading, the reader should note items such as the title and subtitle, the author and source, the publication or copyright date, the introduction or first paragraph, each major heading and the first sentence under it, typographical aids (italics, maps, pictures, charts, graphs), the summary or last paragraph, and any end-of-chapter or end-of-article materials.

3. Why is it helpful to make predictions about materials you are preparing to read?

Making predictions is a process of connecting what you already know about the subject with the clues you pick up during prereading. Efficient readers not only make predictions but also continually revise and modify them as they read.

4. Why is it valuable to discover what you already know before reading?

Discovering what you already know about a topic before you read will increase your comprehension. Three methods of discovery are questioning, relating to previous experience, and free association.

5. How can I define a purpose for reading?

Before reading, establish a purpose by developing guide questions built from boldface headings and from first sentences of articles or essays without headings. Ask *what, why,* and *how* questions.

6. How can I keep track of comprehension while reading?

Keep track of both positive and negative signals by using these four techniques: establishing checkpoints, using guide questions, asking connection questions, and using internal dialogue.

DIRECTIONS   Write the letter of the choice that best completes each statement in the space provided.

CHECKING YOUR RECALL

_____ 1. The overall topic of a chapter is typically provided in the

   a. title.
   b. first paragraph.
   c. summary.
   d. references.

_____ 2. The first sentence under each boldface heading in a chapter typically

   a. gives the author's qualifications.
   b. tells what the section is about.
   c. explains how the author will approach the topic.
   d. announces the author's purpose for writing.

_____ 3. The primary purpose of free association while reading is to

   a. establish your purpose for reading.
   b. distinguish between important and unimportant information.
   c. discover what you already know about the topic.
   d. outline your beliefs about the topic.

_____ 4. The most useful type of guide questions begin with the word

   a. who.
   b. when.
   c. where.
   d. why.

_____ 5. Making predictions encourages you to do all of the following except

   a. apply your knowledge to new situations.
   b. examine how ideas fit together.
   c. put ideas together in new ways.
   d. memorize facts provided by the text.

APPLYING YOUR SKILLS

_____ 6. Lauren uses prereading of a chapter to help her identify the most important ideas in the material. In prereading, Lauren

   a. memorizes the important facts.
   b. reads the introduction, each major heading, and the summary.
   c. takes notes on the important points in the chapter.
   d. reads the entire selection carefully.

_____ 7. For her British literature course this semester, Rima is required to read a novelette, several poems, three short stories, and selected chapters from a textbook. Of these assignments, the most useful one for Rima to preread would be the

   a. novelette.
   b. poems.
   c. short stories.
   d. textbook chapters.

_____ 8. Cory is trying to assess her comprehension of a chapter she has been reading in an anthropology textbook. One positive signal she should look for is if

   a. everything in the chapter seems important.
   b. she often has to slow down or reread.
   c. the vocabulary is unfamiliar.
   d. she can paraphrase the author's ideas.

_____ 9. Antonio is evaluating his comprehension of a history text. To determine whether he really understands what he has read, Antonio should

   a. read the entire chapter before stopping to assess his level of understanding.
   b. answer guide questions and ask connection questions.
   c. avoid mentally talking to himself in order to keep himself focused on the reading.
   d. skip over information that seems difficult or boring.

_____ 10. Caleb has realized that he needs to strengthen his reading comprehension in his economics class. Caleb should do all of the following except:

   a. copy word for word sections of the text that are difficult to understand.
   b. consult additional sources if he finds he does not have sufficient background knowledge.
   c. rephrase each paragraph in his own words.
   d. read in a quiet place at a time when he has the energy to concentrate.

MULTIMEDIA *Activities*

Active Reading Strategies

1 Write a list predicting four things that will happen to you in school over the next three days. For example, "I'll get my history paper back with an A grade." After three days, check your predictions. Which ones came true? How did you know they would?

Prediction	Outcome
1.	
2.	
3.	
4.	

2 Try reading passages from your textbooks out loud with a study partner. Explain to each other what you heard and ask each other questions to check your comprehension.

3 How to Read an Essay

http://www.studygs.net/reading_essays.htm

This Web site from the University of St. Thomas provides a list of questions to ask yourself when preparing to read an essay, textbook, or article. It includes a link to a useful summary sheet. Print out the summary sheet and use it for your next reading assignment.

4 Practice Reading Comprehension Test

http://www.gsu.edu/~wwwrtp/instrdg.htm

Try this practice test from the University of Georgia Board of Regents. Questions are answered and scored online. You can even take an instructional version which explains the right and wrong answers.

5 Effective Reading Tutorial

http://www.jcu.edu.au/studying/services/studyskills/effreading/index.html

Try this online module from James Cook University in Australia for improving your reading rate and comprehension.

Answer Key for Exercise 1
1. T   2. T   3. F   4. F   5. T

6 Understanding Paragraphs

Why Study Paragraphs?

■ You will learn to identify the important information in paragraphs in your reading assignments.

■ You will see how the ideas in each paragraph fit together.

■ You will improve your own writing with more effective paragraphs.

Learning Experiment

Step 1

Read through list 1 below, spending a maximum of 15 seconds.

List 1	List 2	List 3	List 4
KQZ	BLT	WIN	WAS
NLR	FBI	SIT	THE
XOJ	SOS	LIE	CAR
BTK	CBS	SAW	RUN
YSW	NFL	NOT	OFF

Step 2

Now, cover list 1 with your hand or a piece of scrap paper and write down, in the space provided for list 1, as many items as you can remember.

List 1	List 2	List 3	List 4
___	___	___	___
___	___	___	___
___	___	___	___
___	___	___	___
___	___	___	___

Step 3

Follow steps 1 and 2 for each of the other three lists.

Step 4

Check to see how many items you had correct on each of the four lists.

The Results

Did you recall more items on list 2 than on list 1? Why? Did you remember more items on list 4 than on list 3? As you must now realize, after list 1, each list is more meaningful than the one before it. These lists progress from nonsense syllables to meaningful letter groups to words and, finally, to words that, when strung together, produce further meanings.

Learning Principle (What This Means to You)

You are able to remember information that is meaningful more easily than information that has no meaning. Once you understand how paragraphs are organized, they will become more meaningful and their contents easier to remember. In this chapter you will learn the three essential parts of a paragraph and how they work together to create meaning.

THREE ESSENTIAL ELEMENTS OF A PARAGRAPH

A *paragraph* can be defined as a group of related sentences about a single topic. This chapter focuses on knowledge and comprehension of paragraph structure. It will help you understand and remember what you read. It will also help you write paragraphs more effectively. Once you know how a paragraph is structured, you will be able to apply your knowledge to paragraph writing. A paragraph contains three essential elements:

- The **topic**, the one thing a paragraph is about, is the unifying factor, and every sentence and idea contained in the paragraph is related to the topic.
- The **main idea**, what the author wants to communicate about the topic, is the central or most important thought in the paragraph. Every other sentence and idea in the paragraph is related to the main idea. The sentence that expresses this idea is called the **topic sentence**.
- **Details** are the proof, support, explanation, reasons, or examples that explain the paragraph's main idea.

Each of the following examples contains a group of sentences, but only one is a paragraph. Only that one has the three essential elements. Identify the paragraph.

Cats frequently become aggressive when provoked. Some plants require more light than others as a result of coloration of their foliage. Some buildings, because of poor construction, waste a tremendous amount of energy.

Some plants require more light than others as a result of coloration of their foliage. Some plants will live a long time without watering. Plants are being used as decorator items in stores and office buildings.

Some plants require more light than others as a result of coloration of their foliage. Plants with shades of white, yellow, or pink in their leaves need more light than plants with completely green foliage. For example, a Swedish ivy plant with completely green leaves requires less light per day than a variegated Swedish ivy that contains shades of white, yellow, and green in its leaves.

In the first example, the sentences were unrelated; each sentence was about a different thing, and there was no connection among them.

In the second example, each sentence was about plants—the common topic; however, the sentences together did not prove, explain, or support any particular idea about plants.

In the third example, each sentence was about plants, and all the sentences were about one main idea: that some plants need more light than others because of the coloration of their leaves. Thus, the third example is a paragraph; it has a topic—plants; a main idea—that plants require varying degrees of light due to coloration; and supporting details—the example of the Swedish ivy. The first sentence functions as a topic sentence.

In order to understand a paragraph, a reader must be able to identify the topic, main idea, and details easily. In the following paragraph, each of these parts is identified.

Topic
Sentence | As societies become industrialized, the distribution of workers among various economic activities tends to change in a predictable way. In the early stages, the population is engaged in agriculture and the collection of raw materials for food and shelter. But as technology develops, agricultural workers are drawn into manufacturing and construction.

Topic: distribution of workers

Details

This chapter will focus on identifying these essential elements of the paragraph and help you to read paragraphs more easily. Although the emphasis is on reading paragraphs, you will find this information useful in your own writing as well. Just as a reader must identify these elements, so must a writer structure his or her paragraphs by using these elements.

HOW TO IDENTIFY THE TOPIC

The topic of a paragraph is the subject of the whole paragraph. It is the one thing that the whole paragraph is about. Usually, the topic of a paragraph can be expressed in two or three words. To find the topic of a paragraph, ask yourself this question: What is the one thing the author is discussing throughout the paragraph? Read the following example:

> Magazines are a channel of communication halfway between newspapers and books. Unlike newspapers or books, however, many of the most influential magazines are difficult or impossible to purchase at newsstands. With their color printing and slick paper (in most cases), magazines have become a showplace for exciting graphics. Until the 1940s most consumer (general) magazines offered a diverse menu of both fiction and nonfiction articles and miscellany such as poetry and short humor selections. With television providing a heavy quotient of entertainment for the American home, many magazines discovered a strong demand for nonfiction articles, their almost exclusive content today.
>
> —Agee, Ault, and Emery, *Introduction to Mass Communication*, p. 153

In the example, the author is discussing one topic—magazines—throughout the paragraph. Notice how many times the word *magazines* is repeated in the paragraph. Frequently, the repeated use of a word can serve as a clue to the topic of a paragraph.

EXERCISE 1

DIRECTIONS   Read each of the following paragraphs and then select the topic of the paragraph from the choices given.

1. Part of the exodus of the elderly from the workplace is due simply to their prosperity. Older people have higher disposable incomes than any other age group in the population, and they are using their wealth to consume more leisure. But early retirement is also being prompted by American businesses. Career advancement often slows after age 40; over 60 percent of American corporations offer early retirement plans, while only about 5 percent offer inducements to delay retirement. Even more important is the federal government's tax treatment of the elderly. Individuals age 70 and over, especially those in middle-income brackets, can be subject to a crushing array of taxes. They must pay taxes on up to 85 percent of their Social Security benefits, contribute payroll taxes if they keep working, and bear the loss of $1 in Social Security benefits for every $3 of wage income over about $10,000. Because these taxes can "piggyback" on each other, effective marginal tax rates can become astronomical for the elderly. In fact, for a fairly typical couple trying to supplement their retirement checks, income from work can be subject to a tax rate in excess of 80 percent, so little take-home pay remains after taxes. No wonder so many seniors are saying "no thanks" to seemingly attractive jobs.

   —Miller, *Economics Today*, p. 122

   a. the prosperity of the elderly
   b. why senior citizens are leaving the workplace
   c. unfair taxation of senior citizens
   d. social security benefits for the elderly

2. Children of Native American parents are traditionally socialized through an extensive network of relatives. Along with grandparents, uncles and aunts participate with parents in child care, supervision of children, and assurance of love, and cousins are thus considered as close as siblings. Members of this extended family also teach children their tribal values and beliefs or traditions and rituals. Reflecting a group-oriented culture, the values of cooperation and sharing are emphasized, while competitive behavior is discouraged. Children and adolescents are further encouraged to participate in tribal ceremonies and develop an appreciation for their cultural heritage.

—Thio, *Sociology,* p. 155

a. the structure of Native American families
b. competitive behavior versus cooperation
c. socialization of Native American children
d. the importance of cultural heritage

3. Slavery has taken a number of different forms. War captives and their descendants formed a class of slaves in some societies; in others, slaves were a commodity that could be bought and sold. The rights granted to a slave varied, too. In ancient Greece, a slave could marry a free person, but in the stratified society of the southern United States before the Civil War, slaves were not allowed even to marry each other, because they were not permitted to engage in legal contracts. Still, slaves in the South often lived together as husband and wife throughout their adult lives, forming nuclear families that remained tightly knit until they were separated at the auction block.

—Hicks and Gwynne, *Cultural Anthropology,* p. 270

a. rights of slaves
b. slavery in Greece
c. forms of slavery
d. slavery in the southern United States

4. The simple word "to" has caused a great deal of confusion in many areas of science. For example, consider the phrase, "Birds migrate southward to escape winter." The statement seems harmless enough, but if interpreted literally, it implies that the birds have a goal in mind, or that they are moving under the direction of some conscious force that compels them to escape winter. Philosophers have termed such assumptions *teleology.* (*Teleos* is Greek for *end* or *goal.*) It is commonly used in reference to ideas that go beyond what is actually verifiable and generally implies some inner drive to complete a goal or some directing force operating above the laws of nature.

—Wallace, *Biology: The World of Life,* pp. 31–32

a. forces operating above the laws of nature
b. confusion in language
c. literally interpreted statements
d. teleological assumptions

5. Earth's magnetic field is known to have reversed polarity many times in our planet's history. The *geographic* North and South Poles have of course remained in place, but the *magnetic* north and south poles have changed polarity continually. Marine geophysicists interpreted the magnetic seafloor patterns as indicating that the rock either solidified during a time when Earth's magnetic field was like it is today (a "positive" value) or solidified at another time, when the field was reversed (a "negative" value). In a way, the formation of these magnetic patterns in rocks is similar to a tape recording: the changes in Earth's magnetic field are the signal, which is being recorded on two very slowly moving "tapes" that spread in opposite directions from the ridge.

—Ross, *Introduction to Oceanography,* p. 48

a. polarity of the earth's magnetic field

b. patterns of rocks on the seafloor

c. geographic poles of the earth

d. work carried out by marine geophysicists

6. All surfaces have textures that can be experienced by touching or through visual suggestion. Textures are categorized as either actual or simulated. *Actual* textures are those we can feel by touching, such as polished marble, wood, sand or swirls of thick paint. Simulated (or implied) textures are those created to look like something other than paint on a flat surface. A painter can simulate textures that look like real fur or wood but to the touch would feel like smooth paint. Artists can also invent actual or simulated textures. We can appreciate most textures even when we are not permitted to touch them, because we know, from experience, how they would feel.

—Preble, Preble, and Frank, *Artforms,* p. 71

a. surface textures

b. feeling textures

c. painting textures

d. simulated textures

7. Many people believe that the only way to attain efficiency is through competition. One of the roles of government is to serve as the protector of a competitive economic system. Congress and the various state governments have passed *antitrust legislation.* Such legislation makes illegal certain (but not all) economic activities that might, in legal terms, restrain trade—that is, prevent free competition among actual and potential rival firms in the marketplace. The avowed aim of antitrust legislation is to reduce the power of *monopolies*—firms that have great control over the price of goods they sell. A large number of antitrust laws have been passed that prohibit specific anticompetitive business behavior. Both the Antitrust Division of the Department of Justice and the Federal Trade Commission attempt to enforce these antitrust laws. Various state judicial agencies also expend efforts at maintaining competition.

—Miller, *Economics Today,* p. 98

a. monopolies

b. promoting competition

c. economic efficiency

d. federal legislation

8. Businesses do not operate in a vacuum, but rather exist within a business environment that includes economic, legal, cultural, and competitive factors. Economic factors affect businesses by influencing what and how many goods and services consumers buy. Laws and regulations have an impact on many activities in a business. Cultural and social factors influence the characteristics of the goods and services sold by businesses. Competition affects what products and services a business offers, and the price it charges.

—Nickerson, *Business and Information Systems,* p. 30

a. economic factors in business

b. business activities

c. business environment

d. competition in business

9. Successful social movements almost always spark a reaction from groups that oppose their gains. These reaction groups are sometimes more powerful than the protest movement itself. The Civil Rights movement, for instance, sparked an antifederal government backlash among white southerners during the 1970s and 1980s that contributed to the success of such politicians as George Wallace and the rise of

Republican party fortunes in that region. The Women's movement sparked a powerful backlash among fundamentalist religious groups. The successes of the Environmental movement during the 1970s energized a powerful, well-funded, and well-organized counteroffensive by America's leading corporations and business organizations.

—Greenberg and Page, *The Struggle for Democracy,* p. 291

a. successful social movements
b. the Civil Rights movement
c. the Republican party
d. reaction groups

10. We know that changes in sea level have occurred in the past. In some instances, however, these were not related to changes in the volume of water, as was caused by melting or forming of glaciers. Rather, sea level shifted in response to changes in the shape of the ocean basin itself. Reducing the dimensions of the ocean basin (especially depth) by increasing the rates of subduction or seafloor spreading could cause a rise in sea level worldwide. An increase in the size of the ocean basin could cause a drop in sea level.

—Ross, *Introduction to Oceanography,* p. 62

a. glacier melting and formation
b. the shape of the ocean basin
c. rates of subduction
d. changes in sea level

EXERCISE 2

DIRECTIONS For each of the following paragraphs, read the paragraph and write the topic in the space provided. Be sure to limit the topic to a few words.

1. Energy conservation in the short run and long run will require creative solutions in all areas of business. A few innovative solutions have already surfaced which indicate that business understands the importance of saving energy. The makers of Maxwell House coffee developed a method to save natural gas. The first step in making instant coffee is to brew the coffee just as people do at home, except in 1000-gallon containers. The heat to brew the coffee had come from burning natural gas, and the process left Maxwell House with tons of coffee grounds. The company then had to use trucks (that burned gasoline) to cart the coffee grounds away. Maxwell House realized it could save most of the cost of the natural gas (and the gasoline cost) by burning the grounds to get the heat to brew subsequent batches of coffee. Natural gas is now used only to start the coffee grounds burning.

—Kinnear, Bernhardt, and Krentler, *Principles of Marketing,* pp. 79–81

Topic: _____

2. The characteristic of speed is universally associated with computers. Power is a derivative of speed as well as of other factors such as memory size. What makes a computer fast? Or, more to the point, what makes one computer faster than another? Several factors are involved, including microprocessor speed, bus line size, and the availability of cache. A user who is concerned about speed will want to address all of these. More sophisticated approaches to speed include flash memory, RISC computers, and parallel processing.

—Capron, *Computers,* p. 82

Topic: _____

3. The process of becoming hypnotized begins when the people who will be hypnotized find a comfortable body position and become thoroughly relaxed. Without letting their minds wander to other matters, they focus their attention on a specific object or sound, such as a metronome or the hypnotist's voice. Then, based on both what the hypnotherapist expects to occur and actually sees occurring, she or he tells the clients how they will feel as the hypnotic process continues. For instance, the hypnotist may say, "You are feeling completely relaxed" or "Your eyelids are becoming heavy." When people being hypnotized recognize that their feelings match the hypnotist's comments, they are likely to believe that some change is taking place. That belief seems to increase their openness to other statements made by the hypnotist.

—Uba and Huang, *Psychology*, p. 148

Topic: _____

4. Learning words is an important part of language acquisition. Yet the infinite productivity and flexibility of human language rest on much more than just words: they derive from people's ability to combine words in an incredibly large number of ways, according to rules understood by all users of that language, in order to express novel ideas and fine gradations of meaning. These rules are called syntax, or grammar. Children begin the task of acquiring syntax by expressing single relations such as possession ("Mommy's hat"). They progress to acquire more and more complex grammatical constructions (one child who was nearly 3 said, "I'm sorry I can't do that because it fell over when I pushed it").

—Newcome, *Child Development*, p. 223

Topic: _____

5. Let's now deal with the fact that the human eye contains two distinctly different photoreceptor cells. Both rods and cones exist in our retinas, but they are not there in equal numbers. In one eye, there are approximately 120 million rods, but only 6 million cones; rods outnumber cones approximately 20 to 1. Not only are rods and cones found in unequal numbers, but they are not evenly distributed throughout the retina. Cones are concentrated in the center of the retina, at the fovea. Rods are concentrated in a band or ring surrounding the fovea, out toward the periphery of the retina. These observations have led psychologists to wonder if the rods and cones of our eyes have different functions.

—Gerow, *Essentials of Psychology*, p. 138

Topic: _____

6. Although there were unions in the United States before the American Revolution, they have become major power blocks only in the last 60 years or so. Directly or indirectly, managerial decisions in almost all organizations are now influenced by the effect of unions. Managers in unionized organizations must operate through the union in dealing with their employees instead of acting alone. Decisions affecting employees are made collectively at the bargaining tables and through arbitration, instead of individually by the supervisor when and where the need arises. Wages, hours, and other terms and conditions of employment are largely decided outside of management's sphere of discretion.

—Mosley, Pietri, and Magginson, *Management: Leadership in Action*, p. 317

Topic: _____

7. When a group is too large for an effective discussion or when its members are not well informed on the topic, a panel of individuals may be selected to discuss the topic

for the benefit of others, who then become an audience. Members of a panel may be particularly well informed on the subject or may represent divergent views. For example, your group may be interested in UFOs (unidentified flying objects) and hold a discussion for your classmates. Or your group might tackle the problems of tenants and landlords. Whatever your topic, the audience should learn the basic issues from your discussion.

—Gronbeck et al., *Principles of Speech Communication*, p. 302

Topic: _____

8. It seems obvious that power inequality affects the quality of people's lives. The rich and powerful live better than the poor and powerless. Similarly, power inequality affects the quality of *deviant* activities likely to be engaged in by people. Thus the powerful are more likely to perpetrate profitable crimes, such as corporate crime, while the powerless are more likely to commit unprofitable crimes, such as homicide and assault. In other words, power—or lack of it—largely determines the type of crime people are likely to commit.

—Thio, *Sociology*, p. 181

Topic: _____

9. Automated radio has made large gains, as station managers try to reduce expenses by eliminating some of their on-the-air personnel. These stations broadcast packaged taped programs obtained from syndicates, hour after hour, or material delivered by satellite from a central program source. The closely timed tapes contain music and commercials, along with the necessary voice introductions and bridges. They have spaces into which a staff engineer can slip local recorded commercials. By eliminating disc jockeys in this manner, a station keeps its costs down but loses the personal touch and becomes a broadcasting automaton. For example, one leading syndicator, Satellite Music Network, provides more than 625 stations with their choice of seven different 24-hour music formats that include news and live disc jockeys playing records.

—Agee, Ault, and Emery, *Introduction to Mass Communications*, p. 225

Topic: _____

10. Bone is one of the hardest materials in the body and, although relatively light in weight, it has a remarkable ability to resist tension and other forces acting on it. Nature has given us an extremely strong and exceptionally simple (almost crude), supporting system without giving up mobility. The calcium salts deposited in the matrix give bone its hardness, whereas the organic parts (especially the collagen fibers) provide for bone's flexibility and great tensile strength.

—Marieb, *Essentials of Human Anatomy and Physiology*, p. 119

Topic: _____

HOW TO FIND THE MAIN IDEA

The main idea of a paragraph tells you what the author wants you to know about the topic. The main idea is usually directly stated by the writer in one or more sentences within the paragraph. The sentence that states this main idea is called the **topic sentence**. The topic sentence tells what the rest of the paragraph is about. In some paragraphs, the main idea is not directly stated in any one sentence. Instead, it is left to the reader to infer, or reason out.

To find the main idea of a paragraph, first decide what the topic of the paragraph is. Then ask yourself these questions: What is the main idea—what is the author trying to say about the topic? Which sentence states the main idea? Read the following paragraph:

> The Federal Trade Commission has become increasingly interested in false and misleading packaging. Complaints have been filed against many food packagers because they make boxes unnecessarily large to give a false impression of quantity. Cosmetics manufacturers have been accused of using false bottoms in packaging to make a small amount of their product appear to be much more.

In the preceding paragraph, the topic is false packaging. The main idea is that the Federal Trade Commission is becoming increasingly concerned about false or misleading packaging. The author states the main idea in the first sentence, so it is the topic sentence.

WHERE TO FIND THE TOPIC SENTENCE

Although the topic sentence of a paragraph can be located anywhere in the paragraph, there are several positions where it is most likely to be found. Each type of paragraph has been diagrammed to help you visualize how it is structured.

First Sentence

The most common position of the topic sentence is first in the paragraph. In this type of paragraph, the author states the main idea at the beginning of the paragraph and then elaborates on it.

> The good listener, in order to achieve the purpose of acquiring information, is careful to follow specific steps to achieve accurate understanding. First, whenever possible, the good listener prepares in advance for the speech or lecture he or she is going to attend. He or she studies the topic to be discussed and finds out about the speaker and his or her beliefs. Second, on arriving at the place where the speech is to be given, he or she chooses a seat where seeing, hearing, and remaining alert are easy. Finally, when the speech is over, an effective listener reviews what was said and reacts to and evaluates the ideas expressed.

Usually, in this type of paragraph, the author is employing a deductive thought pattern in which a statement is made at the beginning and then supported throughout the paragraph.

Last Sentence

The second most common position of the topic sentence is last in the paragraph. In this type of paragraph, the author leads or builds up to the main idea and then states it in a sentence at the very end.

> Whenever possible, the good listener prepares in advance for the speech or lecture he or she plans to attend. He or she studies the topic to be discussed and finds out about the speaker and his or her beliefs. On arriving at the place where the speech is to be given, he or she chooses a seat where seeing, hearing, and remaining alert are easy. And when the speech is over, he or she reviews what was said and reacts to and evaluates the ideas expressed. Thus, an effective listener, in order to achieve the purpose of acquiring information, takes specific steps to achieve accurate understanding.

The thought pattern frequently used in this type of paragraph is inductive. That is, the author provides supporting evidence for the main idea first and then states it.

Middle of the Paragraph

Another common position of the topic sentence is in the middle of the paragraph. In this case, the author builds up to the main idea, states it in the middle of the paragraph, and then goes on with further elaboration and detail.

> Whenever possible, the good listener prepares in advance for the speech or lecture he or she plans to attend. He or she studies the topic to be discussed and finds out about the speaker and his or her beliefs. <u>An effective listener, then, takes specific steps to achieve accurate understanding of the lecture.</u> Furthermore, on arriving at the place where the speech is to be given, he or she chooses a seat where it is easy to see, hear, and remain alert. Finally, when the speech is over, the effective listener reviews what was said and reacts to and evaluates the ideas expressed.

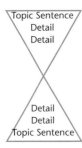

First and Last Sentences

Sometimes an author uses two sentences to state the main idea or states the main idea twice in one paragraph. Usually, in this type of paragraph, the writer states the main idea at the beginning of the paragraph, then explains or supports the idea, and finally restates the main idea at the very end.

> <u>The good listener, in order to achieve the purpose of acquiring information, is careful to follow specific steps to achieve accurate understanding.</u> First, whenever possible, the good listener prepares in advance for the speech or lecture he or she is going to attend. He or she studies the topic to be discussed and finds out about the speaker and his or her beliefs. Second, on arriving at the place where the speech is to be given, he or she chooses a seat where seeing, hearing, and remaining alert are easy. Finally, when the speech is over, he or she reviews what was said and reacts to and evaluates the ideas expressed. <u>Effective listening is an active process in which a listener deliberately takes certain actions to ensure that accurate communication has occurred.</u>

EXERCISE 3

DIRECTIONS Read each of the following paragraphs and underline the topic sentence.

1. First, language consists of a large number of *symbols*. The symbols that make up a language are commonly referred to as *words*. They are the labels that we have assigned to the mental representation of our experiences. When we use the word *chair* as a symbol, we don't use it to label any one specific instance of a chair. We use it to represent our concept of what a chair is. Note that, as symbols, words do not have to stand for real things in the real world. With language, we can communicate about owls and pussycats in teacups; four-dimensional, time-warped hyperspace; and a cartoon beagle that flies his doghouse into battle against the Red Baron. Words are used to stand for our cognitions, our concepts, and we have a great number of them.

   —Gerow, *Essentials of Psychology*, p. 289

2. One important reality with which marketers must contend is that people have *selective perception.* That is, we actually perceive only a very small proportion of all the stimuli with which we are constantly bombarded. For example, most consumers are

exposed to countless advertisements every day on billboards, in magazines and newspapers, and on television or the radio, but they actually are conscious of very few of them. Thus, an important goal for marketers is to make sure that the advertisements for their products are perceived by their target markets.

—Kinnear, Bernhardt, and Krentler, *Principles of Marketing*, p. 191

3. Many people assume that the law is based on the consent of citizens, that it treats citizens equally, and that it serves the best interest of society. If we simply read the U.S. Constitution and statutes, this assumption may indeed be justified. But focusing on the *law on the books,* as William Chambliss (1969) pointed out, may be misleading. The law on the books does indeed say that the authorities ought to be fair and just. But are they? To understand crime, Chambliss argued, we need to look at the *law in action,* at how legal authorities actually discharge their duty. After studying the law in action, Chambliss concluded that legal authorities are actually unfair and unjust, favoring the rich and powerful over the poor and weak.

—Thio, *Sociology,* p. 180

4. The functions of desktop publishing software are similar to those of word processing programs, except that some capabilities are more sophisticated. A user can enter text using the desktop publishing program in the same way that he or she can enter text with a word processing program. In addition, the user can retrieve text from a file created by another program. For example, the user may enter, edit, and save text using a word processing program and then retrieve the saved text using the desktop publishing program.

—Nickerson, *Business and Information Systems,* p. 249

5. Verbal and nonverbal communications exist in a context, and that context to a large extent determines the meaning of any verbal or nonverbal behavior. The same words or behaviors may have totally different meanings when they occur in different contexts. For example, the greeting, "How are you?" means "Hello" to someone you pass regularly on the street but means "Is your health improving?" when said to a friend in the hospital. A wink to an attractive person on a bus means something completely different from a wink that signifies a put-on or a lie. Similarly, the meaning of a given signal depends on the behaviors it accompanies or is close to in time. Pounding a fist on the table during a speech in support of a politician means something quite different from that same gesture in response to news of a friend's death. Divorced from the context, it is impossible to tell what meaning was intended just from examining the signals. Of course, even if you know the context in detail, you still may not be able to decipher the meaning of the verbal or nonverbal message.

—DeVito, *Human Communication,* p. 110

6. The rate of cooling of an object depends on how much hotter the object is than the surroundings. The temperature change per minute of a hot apple pie will be more if the hot pie is put in a cold freezer than if put on the kitchen table. When the pie cools in the freezer, the temperature difference between it and its surroundings is greater. A warm home will leak heat to the cold outside at a greater rate when there is a large difference in the inside and outside temperatures. Keeping the inside of your home at a high temperature on a cold day is more costly than keeping it at a lower temperature. If you keep the temperature difference small, the rate of cooling will be correspondingly low.

—Hewitt, *Conceptual Physics,* p. 279

7. The pawnshop industry has been in decline in most parts of the world. In Great Britain in 1900 there were 3,000 pawnshops; in the 1990s there are fewer than 150.

In the United States, however, the pawnshop business actually grew during the same time period, from under 2,000 to more than 7,000 today. Pawnshops in this country currently make about 40 million loans a year with an aggregate dollar amount over $1 billion. Most of these pawnshops are in the Southeast and Rocky Mountain areas. One of the reasons for the growth of pawnshops is that many states have relaxed their restrictions (called *usury laws*) on the maximum interest rates that can be charged. Pawnshops in these states can now legally charge the high rates needed to stay in business. Further, the percentage of U.S. citizens classified as low-income has risen in recent decades. These individuals cannot get loans from mainstream financial institutions, such as banks and savings and loan associations, and so must turn to alternatives, one of which is the pawnshop.

—Miller, *Economics Today,* p. 213

8. Because faces are so visible and so sensitive, you pay more attention to people's faces than to any other nonverbal feature. The face is an efficient and high-speed means of conveying meaning. Gestures, posture, and larger body movements require some time to change in response to a changing stimulus, whereas facial expressions can change instantly, sometimes even at a rate imperceptible to the human eye. As an instantaneous response mechanism, it is *the* most effective way to provide feedback to an ongoing message. This is the process of using the face as a regulator.

—Weaver, *Understanding Interpersonal Communication,* p. 220

9. Color, a component of light, affects us directly by modifying our thoughts, moods, actions, and even our health. Psychologists, as well as designers of schools, offices, hospitals, and prisons, have acknowledged that colors can affect work habits and mental conditions. People surrounded by expanses of solid orange or red for long periods often experience nervousness and increased blood pressure. In contrast, some blues have a calming effect, causing blood pressure, pulse, and activity rates to drop to below normal levels.

—Preble, Preble, and Frank, *Artforms,* p. 64

10. During photosynthesis in green plants, as the energy of sunlight falls on the green pigment in the leaves, carbon dioxide and the hydrogens of water are used to make food, and water and oxygen are released. The release of oxygen by those first photosynthesizers was a critical step in the direction of life's development. In a sense, the production of oxygen falls into the "good news–bad news" category. It's good news for us, of course, since we need oxygen, but as oxygen began to become a prevalent gas in the atmosphere, it sounded the death knell for many of the early organisms. This is because oxygen is a disruptive gas, as demonstrated by the process of rusting metal. So, in the early days of life on the planet, many life forms were destroyed by the deadly and accumulating gas.

—Wallace, *Biology: The World of Life,* p. 167

RECOGNIZING DETAILS

The **details** in a paragraph are those facts and ideas that prove, explain, support, or give examples of the main idea of the paragraph. Once the topic and main idea have been identified, recognizing the supporting details is a relatively simple matter. The more difficult job is selecting the few key, or most important, details that clearly support the main idea.

All details in a paragraph are related to, and in some way expand, the paragraph's main idea, but not all these details are crucial to the author's central thought. Some details are just meant to describe; others are meant to provide added, but not essential, information; still others are intended merely to repeat or restate the main idea.

On the other hand, the primary supporting details within a paragraph are those statements that carry the primary supporting evidence needed to back up the main idea. To find the primary supporting details in a paragraph, ask yourself the question: What are the main facts the author uses to back up or prove what she or he said about the topic?

In the following paragraph, the topic sentence is underlined twice; the key primary supporting details are underlined once. Notice how the underlined details differ, in the type and importance of the information they provide, from the remaining details in the paragraph.

> <u>The larger-scale and more technologically sophisticated a society, the weaker its ties of marriage,</u> for several reasons. First, in large-scale societies, especially mobile ones like Western society, <u>individuals continually meet new people of the opposite sex.</u> Second, people are likely to <u>live longer</u> in technologically advanced societies, and longevity sometimes <u>leads to marital discontent.</u> Third, <u>many of the functions of marriage</u> in large-scale, technologically sophisticated societies <u>are fulfilled by other institutions.</u> A married person's economic support, for example, does not depend on cooperation with a spouse when both spouses earn paychecks outside their joint household and can continue to do so even if they part.
>
> —Hicks and Gwynne, *Cultural Anthropology,* p. 258

All the underlined details give the primary reasons why marriage ties are weaker in larger-scale, more technologically sophisticated societies. The details in the remainder of the paragraph offer examples or explain these reasons further.

EXERCISE 4

DIRECTIONS   Each of the following statements could function as the topic sentence of a paragraph. After each statement are sentences containing details that may be related to the main idea. Read each sentence and make a check mark beside those with details that can be considered primary support for the main idea statement.

1. *Topic sentence:*

   Licorice is used in tobacco products because it has specific characteristics that cannot be found in any other single ingredient.

   Details:

   _____   a. McAdams and Co. is the largest importer and processor of licorice root.

   _____   b. Licorice blends with tobacco and provides added mildness.

   _____   c. Licorice provides a unique flavor and sweetens many types of tobacco.

   _____   d. The extract of licorice is present in relatively small amounts in most types of pipe tobacco.

   _____   e. Licorice helps tobacco retain the correct amount of moisture during storage.

2. *Topic sentence:*

Many dramatic physical changes occur during adolescence between the ages of 13 and 15.

Details:

_____ a. Voice changes in boys begin to occur at age 13 or 14.

_____ b. Facial proportions may change during adolescence.

_____ c. The forehead tends to become wider, and the mouth widens.

_____ d. Many teenagers do not know how to react to these changes.

_____ e. Primary sex characteristics begin to develop for both boys and girls.

3. *Topic sentence:*

The development of speech in infants follows a definite sequence or pattern of development.

Details:

_____ a. By the time an infant is six months old, he or she can make 12 different speech sounds.

_____ b. Before the age of three months, most infants are unable to produce any recognizable syllables.

_____ c. During the first year, the number of vowel sounds a child can produce is greater than the number of consonant sounds he or she can make.

_____ d. During the second year, the number of consonant sounds a child can produce increases.

_____ e. Parents often reward the first recognizable word a child produces by smiling or speaking to the child.

4. *Topic sentence:*

The two main motives for attending a play are the desire for recreation and the need for relaxation.

Details:

_____ a. By becoming involved with the actors and their problems, members of the audience temporarily suspend their personal cares and concerns.

_____ b. In America today, the success of a play is judged by its ability to attract a large audience.

_____ c. Almost everyone who attends a play expects to be entertained.

_____ d. Plays allow the audience to release tension, which facilitates relaxation.

_____ e. There is a smaller audience that looks to theater for intellectual stimulation.

5. *Topic sentence:*

   In some parts of the world, famine is a constant human condition and exists for a variety of reasons.

   Details:

   _____ a. In parts of Africa, people are dying of hunger by the tens of thousands.

   _____ b. Famine is partly caused by increased population.

   _____ c. Advances in medicine have increased life expectancies, keeping more people active for longer periods of time.

   _____ d. Agricultural technology has not made substantial advances in increasing the food supply.

   _____ e. Because of the growth of cities, populations have become more dense, and agricultural support for these population centers is not available.

6. *Topic sentence:*

   The amount of alcohol an average person consumes has been found to depend on a number of socioeconomic factors such as age, sex, ethnic background, and occupation.

   Details:

   _____ a. Some religions prohibit consumption altogether, and most encourage moderation.

   _____ b. The highest proportion of drinkers is found among people with an educational level of below sixth grade.

   _____ c. People in a lower socioeconomic level drink more than people in a higher socioeconomic level.

   _____ d. In some cultures drinking is common at meals, but these same cultures disapprove of drunkenness.

   _____ e. Farm owners have the highest proportion of non-drinkers, while professionals and businessmen have the highest proportion of drinkers.

7. *Topic sentence:*

   An individual deals with anxiety in a variety of ways and produces a wide range of responses.

   Details:

   _____ a. Anxiety may manifest itself in such physical symptoms as increased heart activity and labored breathing.

   _____ b. Fear, unlike anxiety, is a response to real or threatened danger.

   _____ c. Psychologically, anxiety often produces a feeling of powerlessness, or lack of direct control over the immediate environment.

   _____ d. Temporary blindness, deafness, and loss of the sensation of touch are examples of extreme physical responses to anxiety.

   _____ e. Some people cannot cope with anxiety and are unable to control the neurotic behavior associated with anxiety.

8. *Topic sentence:*

An individual's status or importance within a group affects his or her behavior in that particular group.

Details:

_____ a. High-status individuals frequently arrive late at social functions.

_____ b. Once a person achieves high status, he or she attempts to maintain it.

_____ c. High-status individuals demand more privileges.

_____ d. Low-status individuals are less resistant to change within the group structure than persons of high status.

_____ e. There are always fewer high-status members than low-status members in any particular group.

9. *Topic sentence:*

An oligopoly is a market structure in which only a few companies sell a certain product.

Details:

_____ a. The automobile industry is a good example of an oligopoly, although it gives the appearance of being highly competitive.

_____ b. The breakfast cereal, soap, and cigarette industries, although basic to our economy, operate as oligopolies.

_____ c. Monopolies refer to market structures in which only one industry produces a particular product.

_____ d. Monopolies are able to exert more control and price fixing than oligopolies.

_____ e. In the oil industry, because there are only a few producers, each producer has a fairly large share of the sales.

10. *Topic sentence:*

Advertising can be used to expand consumer choice as well as to limit it.

Details:

_____ a. Food stores that typically advertise their "specials" each Wednesday in the local paper are encouraging consumer choice.

_____ b. Department store advertising often makes the consumer aware of new products and styles, as well as of current prices of products.

_____ c. Misleading or excessive advertising is usually rejected by the consuming public.

_____ d. Exaggerated claims made by some advertisers serve to limit the consumer's actual knowledge and free choice of products.

_____ e. Advertising that provides little or no factual information, but merely attempts to make the brand name well known, actually restricts consumers' free choice.

EXERCISE 5

DIRECTIONS   Read each paragraph and identify the topic and the main idea. Write each in the space provided. Then underline the key supporting details.

1. The extent to which parents will sacrifice for their offspring is familiar to anyone who has watched either a robin tirelessly bringing worms to a nest full of gaping mouths or a human parent writing checks to pay for tuition. Humans are apt to interpret such selflessness as a manifestation of love, but many ethological studies suggest that in birds, at least, the behavior is a motor program. In many species of birds, any gaping mouth will evoke feeding by parents, whether the mouth belongs to their own young or not. European cuckoos and other brood parasites exploit this motor program to their own advantage. A further sign that parental behavior in birds is automatic can be seen when the chicks of gulls stray outside the nest. The parents apparently do not recognize a chick outside the nest, because they stand idly by while they starve to death or are eaten by predators.

    —Harris, *Concepts in Zoology*, p. 420

Topic: _____

Main idea: _____

2. There are a number of reasons why there has been an increase in the demand for nurses, not the least of which is the aging of the U.S. population. Older people use hospitals more and have chronic ailments that require more nursing. Moreover, as hospitals reduce the length of stay of patients, people who are discharged earlier than in previous years need more home care, usually provided by nurses. At the same time as demand has been rising, the supply of nurses has decreased somewhat. The age distribution of women between 18 and 24 has decreased in the past decade. Because this is the group from which nurses traditionally come, there have been fewer potential nurses. In addition, women have more alternatives in the labor market than they did years ago.

    —Miller, *Economics Today*, p. 84

Topic: _____

Main idea: _____

3. Perhaps we can best describe a theory by showing how one can be developed. Suppose someone comes up with an idea—one that explains certain observed phenomena in nature. At first, it is regarded as just that, an idea. But after it has been carefully described and its premises precisely defined, it may then become a *hypothesis*—an idea that can be tested. In a sense, the hypothesis is the first part of an "if . . . then" statement. The "then" predicts the result of the hypothesis, so one can know by testing if the hypothesis is sound. A hypothesis can also stand as a provisional statement for which more data are needed. If rigorous, carefully controlled testing supports the hypothesis, more confidence will be placed in it, until it finally gains the status of a theory. The theory itself, however, may remain unproven and unprovable. A hypothesis, then, is a possible explanation to be tested, whereas a *theory* is a more-or-less verified explanation that accounts for observed phenomena in nature.

    —Wallace, *Biology: The World of Life*, p. 28

Topic: _____

Main idea: _____

4. With young infants, especially those under a year old, it is not possible to assess all components of the emotions we know in adulthood. Lack of language in infancy makes it difficult to know if they are aware of bodily changes such as increased heart

rate or if they have thoughts regarding such things as the possibility of being hurt. Thus, developmental psychologists have concentrated on studying the changes in the brain and body of the infant that follow encounters with situations that would lead to an emotion in an adult, such as stimuli that would elicit pain (e.g., an inoculation), or happiness (e.g., social interaction). They have also coded the facial expressions shown by infants in such situations.

—Newcombe, *Child Development,* p. 152

Topic: _____

Main idea: _____

5. When accomplished writers use the word revision, they don't mean the sort of superficial changes implied in the old elementary school phrase "Copy it over in ink." Revision doesn't even mean writing your paper over again. Instead, it means reading your draft carefully in order to make principled, effective changes in the existing text. It means stepping outside the draft you've created; assessing its strengths and weaknesses as if you were a reader seeing it for the first time; and deciding what parts of the draft need to be expanded, clarified, elaborated, illustrated, reworded, restructured, modified—or just plain cut.

—Anson and Schwegler, *The Longman Handbook for Writers and Readers,* p. 78

Topic: _____

Main idea: _____

6. The final component of a computer is secondary storage, also called auxiliary storage, which stores data not currently being processed by the computer and programs not currently being performed. Its function differs from that of primary storage, which stores the data and instructions that are currently being processed by the computer. For example, if the computer is currently doing payroll processing, then the employee data and the payroll computation program would be stored in the computer's primary storage. Other data and programs that are not currently being used, such as would be needed for sales analysis, would be stored in secondary storage and brought into primary storage when needed. Primary storage is temporary storage, and anything stored in it is lost when the power to the computer is turned off. Secondary storage, however, is permanent storage; anything stored in secondary storage remains there until it is changed even if the power is turned off.

—Nickerson, *Business and Information Systems,* p. 66

Topic: _____

Main idea: _____

7. In any given presidential election, in fact, only a handful of candidates are serious possibilities. So far in American history, these have virtually always been middle-aged or elderly white men, with extensive formal education, fairly high income, and substantial experience as public figures—usually as government officials (especially governors or senators) or military heroes. Movie stars, media commentators, business executives, and others who would be president almost always have to perform lesser government service until they are seriously considered for the presidency. Ronald Reagan, for example, most of whose career was spent acting in motion pictures and on television, served as governor of California before being elected president. Women and racial minorities have been conspicuous by their absence. Civil rights activist and congresswoman Shirley Chisholm made a run for the Democratic party presidential nomination in 1972 but did not get very far.

Representative Pat Schroeder of Colorado tested the waters in 1988 but decided to withdraw. General Colin Powell was among the favorites for the Republican presidential nomination in 1996, according to public opinion polls, but he decided against making a run.

—Greenberg and Page, *The Struggle for Democracy,* p. 190

Topic: _____

Main idea: _____

8. One of the most common targets of populist sentiment has been concentrated economic power and those who exercise it. Andrew Jackson mobilized this sentiment in his fight against the Bank of the United States in the 1830s. The Populist movement of the 1890s directed its political and legislative efforts against the new corporations of the day, especially the banks and the railroads. Corporations were the target of popular hostility during the dark days of the Great Depression and also in the 1970s, when consumer groups made the lives of some corporate executives extremely uncomfortable. Contemporary public opinion polls find strong popular support for free enterprise existing side by side with negative feelings about corporations and corporate leaders.

—Greenberg and Page, *The Struggle for Democracy,* pp. 107–108

Topic: _____

Main idea: _____

9. Complex, organized structures are not easy to maintain. Whether we consider the molecules of your body or the books and papers on your desk, organization tends to disintegrate into chaos unless energy is used to sustain it. (We will explore this tendency more fully in Chapter 6.) To stay alive and function effectively, organisms must keep the conditions within their bodies fairly constant; in other words, they must maintain **homeostasis** (derived from Greek words meaning "to stay the same"). One of the many conditions that organisms regulate is body temperature. Among warm-blooded animals, for example, vital organs such as the brain and heart are kept at a warm, constant temperature despite wide fluctuations in environmental temperature.

—Audesirk, Audesirk, and Byers, *Biology: Life on Earth,* pp. 4–5

Topic: _____

Main idea: _____

10. Mexico City, with a population of 14 to 20 million, leads the world's cities in population. Situated in a high altitude with mountains forming a rim around it, Mexico City is primed for air pollution. Add to this the millions of vehicles without air-pollution control devices, the use of leaded fuel, and the 35,000 industrial sites spewing forth pollutants. A recent ozone reading of 0.35 parts per million was four times the level considered safe in California. Mexico City is attempting to address this severe problem by starting to equip cars with emission controls, eliminating diesel buses, and so forth. However, with the population of the city growing at such a high rate, such attempts may be "too little, too late."

—Glynn, Hohm, and Stewart, *Global Social Problems,* p. 222

Topic: _____

Main idea: _____

TRANSITIONS

Transitions are linking words or phrases used to lead the reader from one idea to another. Figure 6-1 presents a list of commonly used transitions. If you get in the habit of recognizing transitions, you will see that they often guide you through a paragraph, helping you to read it more easily.

In the following paragraph, notice how the underlined transitions lead you from one important detail to the next.

> You need to take a few steps to prepare to become a better note-taker. <u>First,</u> get organized. It's easiest to take useful notes if you have a system. A loose leaf notebook works best because you can add, rearrange, or remove notes for review. If you use spiral or other permanently bound notebooks, use a separate notebook for each subject to avoid confusion and to allow for expansion. <u>Second,</u> set aside a few minutes each day to review the syllabus for your course, to scan the assigned readings, and to review your notes from the previous class period. If you do this just before each lecture, you'll be ready to take notes and practice critical thinking. <u>Finally,</u> prepare your pages by drawing a line down the left margin approximately two inches from the edge of the paper. Leave this margin blank while you take notes so that later you can use it to practice critical thinking.
>
> —Gronbeck et al., *Principles of Speech Communication,* pp. 32–33

Not all paragraphs contain such obvious transitions, and not all transitions serve as such clear markers of major details. Transitions may be used to alert you to what will come next in the paragraph. If you see the phrase *for instance* at the beginning of a sentence, then you know that an example will follow. When you see the phrase *on the other hand,* you can predict that a different, opposing idea

**Figure 6-1
Common Transitions**

Type of Transition	Examples	What They Tell the Reader
Time–sequence	first, later, next, finally	The author is arranging ideas in the order in which they happened.
Example	for example, for instance, to illustrate, such as	An example will follow.
Enumeration	first, second, third, last, another, next	The author is marking or identifying each major point (sometimes these may be used to suggest order of importance).
Continuation	also, in addition, and, further, another	The author is continuing with the same idea and is going to provide additional information.
Contrast	on the other hand, in contrast, however	The author is switching to a different, opposite, or contrasting idea than previously discussed.
Comparison	like, likewise, similarly	The writer will show how the previous idea is similar to what follows.
Cause–effect	because, thus, therefore, since, consequently	The writer will show a connection between two or more things, how one thing caused another, or how something happened as a result of something else.
Summation	thus, in short, to conclude	The writer will state or restate his or her main point.

will follow. Figure 6-1 lists some of the most common transitions used within paragraphs and indicates what they tell you. In the next chapter, you will see that these transitional words also signal the author's organization.

EXERCISE 6   DIRECTIONS   Underline each transition used in the paragraphs in Exercise 5.

UNSTATED MAIN IDEAS

Occasionally, a writer does not directly state the main idea of a given paragraph in a topic sentence. Instead, he or she leaves it up to the reader to infer, or reason out, what the main idea of the paragraph is. This type of paragraph is called **unstated main idea.** This type of paragraph contains only details or specifics that are related to a given topic and substantiate an unstated main idea. To read this type of paragraph, start as you would for paragraphs with stated main ideas. Ask yourself the question for finding the topic: What is the one thing the author is discussing throughout the paragraph? Then try to think of a sentence about the topic that all the details included in the paragraph would support.

Read the paragraph in the following example. First, identify the topic. Then study the details and think of a general statement that all the details in the paragraph would support or prove.

> Suppose a group of plumbers in a community decide to set standard prices for repair services and agree to quote the same price for the same job. Is this ethical? Suppose a group of automobile dealers agree to abide strictly by the used car blue book prices on trade-ins. Is this ethical? Two meat supply houses serving a large university submit identical bids each month for the meat contract. Is this ethical?

This paragraph describes three specific instances in which there was agreement to fix prices. Clearly, the main idea of the author is whether price collusion is ethical, but that main idea is not directly stated in a sentence anywhere within the passage.

EXERCISE 7   DIRECTIONS   In the following paragraphs the main idea is not directly stated. Read each paragraph, identify the topic, and write it in the space provided. Then write a sentence that expresses the main idea of the passage.

1. In 1950, only two cities, London and New York, had populations over 8 million; today there are 20 of these huge cities, 14 of them in developing countries. At present, the total urban population of the developing countries is an estimated 1.3 billion people—more than the total populations of Europe, Japan, and North America combined. At a growth rate of 50 million new urbanites every year, due both to natural increases in resident populations and immigration from rural areas, over half the people in the developing world will live in cities by the year 2020.

   —Hicks and Gwynne, *Cultural Anthropology,* p. 144

Topic: _____

Main idea: _____

2. When a homemaker is killed in an auto accident, that person's family can often sue for the value of the services that were lost. Attorneys (who rely on economists) are often asked to make an attempt to estimate this value to present to the court. They

add up the cost of purchasing babysitting, cooking, housecleaning, and tutoring services. The number turns out to be quite large, often in excess of $30,000 a year. Of course one of the problems in measuring the value of unremunerated housework in such a way is that we could often purchase the services of a full-time live-in house-keeper for less money than if we paid for the services of the various components of housekeeping. And what about quality? Some homemakers serve fabulous gourmet meals; others simply warm up canned and frozen foods. Should they be valued equally? Another problem lies in knowing when to stop counting. A person can hire a valet to help him or her get dressed in the morning. Should we therefore count the time spent in getting dressed as part of unpaid work? Both men and women perform services around the house virtually every day of the year. Should all of those unremu-nerated services be included in a "new" measure of GDP? If they were, measured GDP would be increased dramatically.

—Miller, *Economics Today,* p. 185

Topic: _____

Main idea: _____

3. Most anthropologists make their living by teaching in universities, colleges, and com-munity colleges, and by carrying out university-based research. But a substantial and increasing proportion of anthropologists find employment in nonacademic settings. Museums, for example—especially museums of natural history, archaeology, and art and folklore—have long relied on the expertise of anthropologists. In recent years, anthropologists have been welcome in a greater variety of public and private posi-tions: in government agencies concerned with welfare, drug abuse, mental health, environmental impact, housing, education, foreign aid, and agricultural develop-ment; in the private sector as personnel and ethnic relations consultants and as man-agement consultants for multinational firms; and as staff members of hospitals and foundations.

—Harris, *Cultural Anthropology,* pp. 3–4

Topic: _____

Main idea: _____

4. By 1932 the value of industrial shares had fallen close to 60 percent on the New York and Berlin markets. Unemployment doubled in Germany, and 25 percent of the labor force was out of work in the United States. The middle class, which had invested in the stock market, saw their investments and savings wiped out. In nation after nation, industry declined, prices fell, banks collapsed, and economies stagnated. In the western democracies the depression heightened the feelings of uneasiness that had existed since 1918. In other countries, the tendency to seek authoritarian solutions became even more pronounced. Throughout the world people feared a future marked by lowered standards of living, unemployment, and hunger.

—Wallbank et al., *Civilization Past and Present,* p. 831

Topic: _____

Main idea: _____

5. During the 1960s, police went from walking "beats" to riding in squad cars. While squad cars provided a faster response to emergency calls, they also changed the nature of social interaction between police officers and the public. Much police work had been highly personal, as officers strolled the sidewalks talking to storekeepers and homeowners, but it became much more impersonal, with less contact between officers and citizens. Since the 1960s, technological advances have provided more

elaborate means of communication and surveillance, better-equipped squad cars, and more sophisticated weaponry. Unfortunately criminals have benefited from increased technology as well. This increased technology and other developments have led many city leaders to question contemporary policing practices and some to accentuate the need to reemphasize police–community relations.

— Thompson and Hickey, *Society in Focus*, p. 162

Topic: _____

Main idea: _____

6. Severe punishment may generate such anxiety in children that they do not learn the lesson the punishment was designed to teach. Moreover, as a reaction to punishment that they regard as unfair, children may avoid punitive parents, who therefore will have fewer opportunities to teach and guide the child. In addition, parents who use physical punishment provide aggressive models. A child who is regularly slapped, spanked, shaken, or shouted at may learn to use these forms of aggression in interactions with peers.

— Newcombe, *Child Development*, p. 354

Topic: _____

Main idea: _____

7. In 1920 there was one divorce for every seven marriages in the United States. Fifty years later the rate had climbed to one divorce for every three marriages, and today there is almost one divorce for every two marriages. The divorce rate in the United States is now the highest of any major industrialized nation, while Canada is in a rather distant second place.

— Coleman and Cressey, *Social Problems*, p. 130

Topic: _____

Main idea: _____

8. Chat groups such as you'll find on the commercial Internet Service Providers and the increasingly popular Internet Relay Chat groups enable you to communicate with others in real time (called *synchronous conversation* as opposed to *asynchronous conversation* in which there's a delay between the message-sending and the message-receiving). Real time communication obviously has its advantages; you can ask questions, respond to feedback, and otherwise adjust your message to the specific receivers. One great disadvantage, however, is that you may not find anyone you want to talk with when you log on. Unlike e-mail, you can't leave a message. Chat groups, like listservs and newsgroups, are subject specific and, because there are so many of them (they number in the thousands), you're likely to find some dealing with the topics you're researching. Another advantage of chat rooms and IRC channels is that you can establish one yourself. With other members of your class, you can then discuss the topics you're interested in. The problem with chat groups is that everyone has to be online at the same time.

— DeVito, *The Elements of Public Speaking*, pp. 132–133

Topic: _____

Main idea: _____

9. People's acceptance of a product is largely determined by its package. The very same coffee taken from a yellow can was described as weak, from a dark brown can too

strong, from a red can rich, and from a blue can mild. Even our acceptance of a person may depend on the colors worn. Consider, for example, the comments of one color expert: "If you have to pick the wardrobe for your defense lawyer heading into court and choose anything but blue, you deserve to lose the case. . . ." Black is so powerful it could work against the lawyer with the jury. Brown lacks sufficient authority. Green would probably elicit a negative response.

—DeVito, *Messages,* p. 153

Topic: _____

Main idea: _____

10. Scientific theories arise through *inductive reasoning.* Inductive reasoning is the process of creating a generalization as a result of making many observations that support it, and none that contradict it. Simplistically, the theory that Earth exerts gravitational forces on objects arose from repeated observations of objects falling down toward Earth and from a complete lack of observations of objects "falling up." Likewise, the cell theory arises from the observation that all organisms that have the attributes of life are composed of one or more cells, and that nothing that is not composed of cells shares all these attributes. Once a scientific theory has been formulated, it can be used to support *deductive reasoning.* In science, deductive reasoning is the process of generating hypotheses about how a specific experiment or observation will turn out, based on a well-supported generalization such as a scientific theory. For example, based on the cell theory, if a new organism is found that shares all the attributes of life, scientists can confidently deduce or hypothesize that it will be composed of cells. Of course, the new organism should be carefully scrutinized under the microscope to determine its cellular structure; if compelling new evidence arises, a theory can be modified.

—Audesirk, Audesirk, and Byers, *Biology: Life on Earth,* 2/e, p. 12

Topic: _____

Main idea: _____

EXERCISE 8

DIRECTIONS   Turn to the reading "Your Appearance, Good or Bad, Can Affect Size of Your Paycheck," in Part Eight, page 501. Read each paragraph and identify the topic and main idea. Then place brackets around the topic and underline the sentence that expresses the main idea. If the main idea is unstated, write a brief statement of the main idea in the margin.

EXERCISE 9

DIRECTIONS   Select a three-page section from a textbook that you have been assigned to read. After reading each paragraph, place brackets around the topic and then underline the sentence that states the main idea. If any paragraph has an unstated main idea, write a sentence in the margin that summarizes the main idea. Continue reading and marking until you have completed the three pages.

LEARNING COLLABORATIVELY

DIRECTIONS   Working in pairs, exchange the textbook sections you chose in Exercise 9. Review and critique each other's marking.

APPLYING YOUR LEARNING

Jason is having trouble distinguishing topic sentences from details in his sociology textbook. Imagine that you are Jason's study partner and that he has asked you for help. You have decided that the best way to help him is to explain by using some sample paragraphs.

1. Using "From Bear Teeth to Pearls: Why We Adorn Ourselves" in Part Eight, page 455, select several paragraphs you could use as samples.
2. Outline the advice you will give Jason about distinguishing topic sentences from details.

APPLYING YOUR SKILLS: Sample Textbook Chapter

Highlight the topic sentence of each of the paragraphs under the chapter headings titled "Culture and Cultural Processes" and "Intercultural Processes," on pages 515–518.

QUESTIONS FOR DISCUSSION

1. Do newspaper articles use topic sentences? Why or why not?
2. Are topic sentences used in fiction? Why or why not?
3. Why would a writer choose not to state explicitly the main idea in his or her paragraph?
4. What are some guidelines for knowing when to start a new paragraph?
5. How are the paragraphs typically organized in magazines? Web pages? Newspaper articles?

SELF-TEST SUMMARY

1. What is a paragraph?   A paragraph is a group of related sentences about a single topic. It provides explanation, support, or proof for a main idea (expressed or unexpressed) about a particular topic.

2. What are the essential elements of a paragraph?   A paragraph has three essential elements.
a. Topic: the one thing the entire paragraph is about
b. Main idea: a direct statement or an implied idea about the topic
c. Details: the proof, reasons, or examples that explain or support the paragraph's main idea

3. **Where is the topic sentence most likely to be found?**

A topic sentence expressing the main idea of the paragraph may be located anywhere within the paragraph. It most commonly appears first or last but can also appear in the middle, or both first and last.

4. **How can you identify main ideas that are not stated in a topic sentence?**

Occasionally an author will write a paragraph in which the main idea is not stated in any single sentence. Instead, it is left up to the reader to infer, or reason out, the main idea. To find the main idea when it is unstated, ask yourself the following question: What is the one thing (topic) this paragraph is about, and what is the author saying about this thing (main idea)?

Quick Quiz

NAME:

DIRECTIONS Write the letter of the choice that best completes each statement in the space provided.

CHECKING YOUR RECALL

_____ 1. The topic of a paragraph can be defined as the
   a. subject of the paragraph.
   b. most specific fact in the paragraph.
   c. noun that is the subject of the first sentence.
   d. author's point of view.

_____ 2. The three essential elements of a paragraph are its
   a. proof, reasons, and examples.
   b. topic, main idea, and details.
   c. main idea, topic sentence, and transitions.
   d. topic, transitions, and examples.

_____ 3. The best clue to the topic of a paragraph can be found in the paragraph's
   a. organization.
   b. transitional words.
   c. repeated use of a word.
   d. types of details.

_____ 4. The details of a paragraph are intended to
   a. restate the main idea.
   b. appear before the main idea.
   c. explain or support the topic sentence.
   d. indicate the topic of the next paragraph.

_____ 5. The phrase "to illustrate" indicates the type of transition known as
   a. cause and effect.
   b. example.
   c. comparison.
   d. summation.

APPLYING YOUR SKILLS

_____ 6. Erika is having difficulty identifying topic sentences in the paragraphs she reads. One helpful fact Erika should remember is that the topic sentence of a paragraph is most commonly the
   a. first sentence.
   b. second sentence.
   c. middle of the paragraph.
   d. last sentence.

_____ 7. Courtney is reading a paragraph in which the author has stated the main idea of the paragraph at both the beginning and the end of the paragraph. In this situation, Courtney should expect that
   a. the first statement is more important than the last.
   b. the last statement is more important than the first.
   c. the sentences in between are all examples.
   d. one sentence is a restatement of the other.

_____ 8. You are reading a paragraph in which the author has left the main idea unstated. Which of the following questions can help you find the main idea of the paragraph?
   a. Does the author reveal any bias?
   b. Does the author express an opinion?
   c. Are there any examples in the paragraph?
   d. What does the author want me to know about the topic?

_____ 9. Galen is reading a paragraph with this topic sentence: "One unwelcome result of the increase in sexual activity is a high incidence of teenage pregnancies." Of the following sentences, the detail that does not belong in this paragraph is
   a. an epidemic of teenage pregnancies has captured national attention.
   b. nearly one million teenage girls become pregnant each year.
   c. about 30% of all teenage girls become pregnant once.
   d. teenage boys are traditionally unable to assume financial responsibility.

_____ 10. Diedre is reading a paragraph which arranges ideas in the order in which they happened. Diedre is correct if she identifies this type of pattern as
   a. comparison.
   b. time sequence.
   c. continuation.
   d. enumeration.

153

MULTIMEDIA *Activities*

Understanding Paragraphs

1 Working with a classmate, choose a weekly news magazine. Read the first paragraph in three different articles and discuss what the topic, main idea, and details are. Share the paragraphs and your discussion with the larger group.

2 Visit the Internet Movie Database Web site at http://www.imdb.com

Select a movie to read about. Read the main details, the plot summary, and the combined details parts of the movie description. Which part of the description gives information that is most similar to the main idea of a paragraph? How do you know?

3 Read three article titles from the home page of *National Geographic,* online at http://www.nationalgeographic.com/ngm/

Write down the titles of the articles, the types of transitions you expect for each, and the reasons you expect those types.

Title of Article	Transitions	Reasons
1.		
2.		
3.		

4 What Is a Topic Sentence?

http://www.cerritos.edu/reading/topic1.html

Review how to locate the topic sentence of a paragraph with these tips and exercises from Cerritos College.

7 Following Thought Patterns

Why Learn About Thought Patterns?

■ **Patterns provide a framework for comprehending what you read.**

■ **They enable you to anticipate a writer's flow of thought.**

■ **Patterns help you remember what you read.**

Learning Experiment

Step 1

Study the following five diagrams for a minute. Then cover the diagrams with your hand and draw as many of them as you can recall.

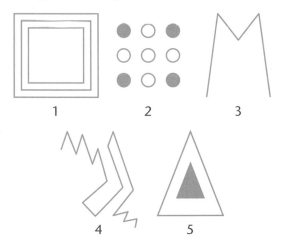

Step 2

Compare your drawings with the original diagrams.

The Results

Did you get the first, second, third, or fifth drawing correct? Why didn't you get the fourth one correct? Diagram 4 had no organization or pattern; the other four diagrams had an organization that you could identify.

Learning Principle
(What This Means to You)

You are able to remember information better if it is organized or if you can detect a pattern. The experiment above demonstrated that you can recall a *diagram* more easily if you can detect a pattern. The same principle applies to ideas. If you can recognize how a writer has organized his or her ideas, you will be able to remember them more easily.

In college you will read a variety of materials; however, most of what you read will be textbooks, which are unique, highly organized information sources. If you become familiar with their organization and structure and learn to follow the writers' thought patterns, you will find that you can read them more easily. This chapter focuses on important features of textbook chapters and essays: (1) their overall structure or progression of ideas, (2) the types of details used to explain each idea, and (3) organizational patterns (how the ideas fit together).

THE ORGANIZATION OF TEXTBOOK CHAPTERS

Reading a chapter can be compared to watching a football game. You watch the overall progression of the game from start to finish, but you also watch individual plays and notice how each is executed. Furthermore, you observe how several plays work together as part of a game strategy or pattern. Similarly, when reading a chapter, you are concerned with the progression of ideas. But you are also concerned with each separate idea and how it is developed and explained. This chapter focuses on important features of textbook chapters and essays.

A textbook is made up of parts, each successively smaller and more limited in scope than the one before it. As a general rule, the whole text is divided into chapters; each chapter may be divided into sections; each section is subdivided by headings into subsections; and each subsection is divided into paragraphs. Each of these parts has a similar structure. Just as each paragraph has a main idea and supporting information, each subsection, section, or chapter has its own key idea and supporting information.

Locate the Controlling Idea and Supporting Information

The controlling idea in a textbook section is the broad, general idea the writer is discussing throughout the section. It is the central, most important thought that is explained, discussed, or supported throughout the section. It is similar to the main idea of a paragraph but is a more general, more comprehensive idea that takes numerous paragraphs to explain.

The controlling idea, then, is developed or explained throughout the section. In this chapter, the section you are reading is called "The Organization of Textbook Chapters." Subheadings are often used to divide a section into smaller units. Each subsection, or group of paragraphs, explains one idea or major concept, the central thought. This subsection is titled "Locate the Controlling Idea and Supporting Information." Each paragraph within a subsection provides one main idea that supports or explains the central thought. As you read each paragraph, you should understand its function and its connection to the other paragraphs in the section. The end of each section is an ideal checkpoint for monitoring your comprehension. Although the number of subheadings and paragraphs will vary, the structure of textbook sections is usually consistent (see Figure 7-1 on p. 157).

On page 158, read the section in Figure 7-2, "Learning," from a chapter in a biology book titled *Biology: The Network of Life*. (Note: Ellipses [. . .] indicate places where text has been omitted from the original.)

Note that paragraph 1 of the section introduces the subject: learning. The paragraph then defines learned behavior and states that only recently has it been studied in animals. the last sentence of the first paragraph states the controlling idea of the section: there are five types of learning. The subheadings divide the remaining text, and each identifies one category of learning. Each group of paragraphs under a subheading explains one type of learning (its central thought). In the first subsection, on imprinting, the third sentence in paragraph 1 states the central thought of the section.

This example shows that the subheadings divided the section into five parts, or subsections. The section began with a general discussion of the subject and was divided into five smaller topics. This progression of ideas from large to small, general to particular, is typical of most textbooks. When you are familiar with and can follow this progression, your textbooks will seem more logical and systematic and will be easier to read.

**Figure 7-1
Organization of a
Textbook Section**

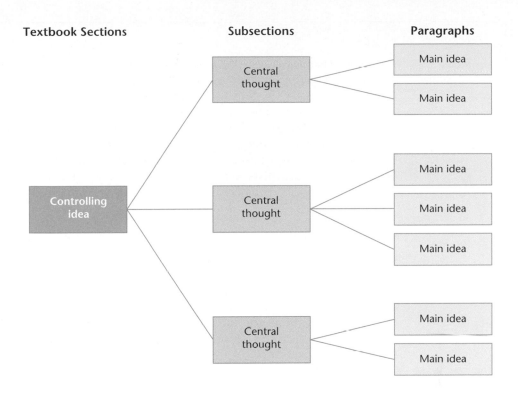

EXERCISE 1

DIRECTIONS   Turn to "Your Appearance, Good or Bad, Can Affect Size of Your Paycheck" in Part Eight on page 501 of this text and complete the following Instructions.

1. Where is the controlling idea of this article expressed? Underline it.
2. The dark-print headings divide the chapter into three parts. Write a sentence expressing the main point of each part.

EXERCISE 2

DIRECTIONS   Read the excerpt "Communication Between Women and Men" in Part Eight on page 466 taken from a sociology textbook chapter. Complete the following instructions.

1. What subject does the article discuss?
2. What is the controlling idea?
3. Underline the central idea of each of the two subsections.
4. Underline the topic sentence of each paragraph.

EXERCISE 3

DIRECTIONS   Choose a three- to four-page section from one of your textbooks that you have already read, and answer the following questions.

1. What is the overall topic or subject discussed in this section?

_____

2. What is the controlling idea?

_____

3. Is the section divided by subheadings? If so, underline the central thought in each subsection.

LEARNING

Introduction of subject

Learned behavior occurs when animals change their responses as a result of experience. Psychologists did a considerable amount of the early work on learning. They have primarily been concerned with human learning, and even when their research has been on animals, it has been with an eye toward using animals to understand human behavior. More recently, biologists have focused directly on animal learning. Although studies on learning have been carried out on a relatively small number of species, a vast amount of information has been generated. Scientists now recognize five major categories of learning: imprinting, habituation, associative learning, latent learning, and insight.

Controlling idea of section

Imprinting

Central thought of subsection

Imprinting is a highly specialized form of learning. In many species, it takes place during the early stages of an animal's life, when attachment to parents, the family, or a social group is critical for survival. Imprinting is a process whereby a young animal forms an association or identification with another animal, object, or class of items. The best-known type of imprinting, called filial imprinting, concerns the behavior of young in following a "mother object." During a critical sensitive period, a young animal is susceptible to imprinting.

Topic sentence

Young animals are not completely indiscriminate in what they follow. For example, a mallard duckling will follow a moving object for the first two months after hatching. It will show a preference, however, for yellow-green objects (the color of its parents) over objects of different colors. Young animals may also be sensitive to sound as well as to sights. Wood ducks respond to a species-specific call in exiting from their nests.

Topic sentence

Imprinting is an important form of learning, because it has both short-term effects on the immediate parent–offspring relationship and long-term effects that become evident in adult animals. For example, lack of imprinting has been shown to result in abnormal adult social behavior in some species. Also, the breeding preferences of many birds are a consequence of early imprinting experiences. As adults, they prefer to mate with birds of their imprinted parents' color or markings. This form of imprinting, which has considerable evolutionary significance as a reproductive isolating mechanism, is called sexual imprinting. The phenomenon can be tested by experiments that allow a bird to be raised by foster parents of a different species. When these young birds mature, they show a sexual preference for mates with the color of their foster parents. Sexual imprinting can have some unusual outcomes, as when hand-reared birds become sexually imprinted on people.

Habituation

Habituation is a simple form of learning . . .

Associative Learning

Habituation is learning that results in the loss of a response that is not relevant or useful to the animal. Associative learning, in contrast, is . . .

Latent Learning . . .

Insight . . .

Figure 7-2
Excerpt from *Biology: The Network of Life*

THE STRUCTURE OF ARTICLES AND ESSAYS

An article or essay usually begins with an **introduction** that presents the thesis statement (or controlling idea). Then one or more paragraphs are devoted to each supporting idea. The main part of the essay, often called the **body**, presents ideas and information that support the thesis statement. A **conclusion** makes a final statement about the subject and draws the article or essay to a close.

You can visualize the organization of an article or essay as follows.

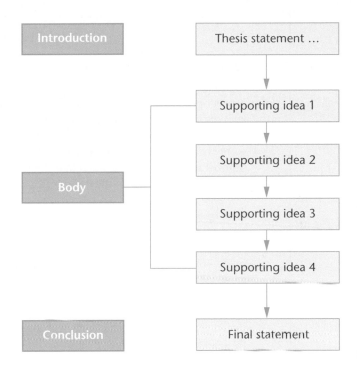

EXERCISE 4

DIRECTIONS   Assume you have been assigned the essay below, "Spare Parts for Human Bodies," by your biology instructor. Read it to answer the following questions.

Introduction:

1. How do the authors try to interest you in the subject?

    _____

2. What is the subject of the essay?

    _____

3. What is the authors' thesis?

    _____

Body:

4. What main supporting ideas do the authors offer to support their thesis?

_____

_____

Conclusion:

5. What is the authors' final statement on tissue engineering?

_____

_____

Spare Parts for Human Bodies

Raul Mercia lost part of his thumb in an industrial accident, but doctors are growing a new one for him. After the accident, doctors harvested some of his bone cells and kept them alive in the laboratory. Later, surgeons grafted a piece of sterile coral, shaped like a thumb bone, onto Mr. Mercia's damaged digit. His cultured bone cells were then seeded onto the coral's surface. In time, the bone cells will increase in number and form a real bone that will replace the biodegradable coral support.

Mr. Mercia was one of the first humans to benefit from a new technology known as tissue engineering, in which new body parts are grown in the laboratory. Researchers have been working for years on techniques to create lab-grown tissues and organs, but the field took a great leap forward in 1995, when scientists produced a mouse with a human ear growing on its back. Actually, it wasn't a real ear, but rather an artificial ear made out of cartilage. To make it, researchers used biodegradable plastic to construct an ear-shaped "scaffold." Then they painted cartilage cells onto the scaffold, and the resulting artificial "ear" was grafted onto the back of a mouse (so that the cartilage cells could be nourished by the mouse's circulatory system). As the cartilage cells reproduced, they spread over the surface of the scaffold and developed into living cartilage tissue in the shape of an ear. Eventually, the biodegradable plastic scaffold disappeared, and the cartilage "ear" could be surgically removed from the mouse. In theory, an ear grown in this manner could be used to replace a damaged or missing human ear.

The success of the rather bizarre ear-on-a-mouse experiment demonstrated our newfound power to manipulate cells, the fundamental units of life. All living things are constructed of cells, including organs and tissues that can be damaged by disease or injury. If scientists can shape cells into a living ear, might they not someday be able to sculpt cells into working livers, kidneys, and lungs? If so, perhaps fewer lives will be lost to failed organs.

By the middle of 2001, Raul Mercia's thumb was developing nicely. His own bone cells were filling the pores in the coral framework, and the new structure retained the shape of a normal thumb bone. Still, Mercia remains one of only a few human recipients of bioengineered tissues. In the lab, however, scientists have managed to grow liver, skin, cartilage, bone, heart valves, tendons, intestines, blood vessels, and breast tissue on pastic scaffolds, and to implant some of these tissues into animals. Researchers continue to refine tissue construction methods and to develop better scaffolding materials. With each passing day, our ability to control the behavior of cells gets a little better. And Raul Mercia will not have to live without a thumb.

It seems that our newfound ability to rearrange the building blocks of life will produce at least some medical benefits. These benefits (and in fact a large proportion of modern medical technology) flow directly from a longstanding scientific endeavor: trying to understand how cells work. Not everyone agrees, however, that we ought to use the fruits of this project to alter the makeup of human bodies.

—Audesirk, Audesirk, and Byers, *Life on Earth,* pp. 51, 64

TYPES OF SUPPORTING INFORMATION

Authors use various types of supporting information to explain the controlling idea of a textbook section. Recognizing these types of supporting information is the key to understanding *how* the author develops and connects his or her ideas.

Examples

Usually a writer gives an example in order to make an idea practical and understandable. An example shows how a principle, concept, problem, or process works or can be applied in a real situation. In the following paragraph, notice how the writer explains the concept of motivation to make a purchase by giving a specific example.

> Motivation is defined as activity toward a goal. It is the basis of all consumer behavior. A basic question marketers must answer is, "What will motivate people to buy my product or service?" When a consumer is motivated, he exists in a state called drive. Drive is generated by tension, which is caused by an unfulfilled need. Consumers strive to reduce the tension by satisfying the need. The need is thus a critical component in the motivation process. When a need is aroused, it becomes a motive or drive stimulating behavior. For example, hunger is a basic need that, when aroused, becomes a motive for satisfying the need, perhaps by stopping at a McDonald's restaurant. Of course, the consumer could satisfy hunger in many other ways. The specific decision to stop at McDonald's is influenced, in turn, by many additional factors.
>
> —Kinnear, Bernhardt, and Krentler, *Principles of Marketing,* p. 143

As you read examples, be sure to look for the connection between the example and the concept it illustrates. Remember that examples are important only for the ideas they illustrate.

Reasons

Certain types of main ideas are most easily explained by giving reasons. Especially in argumentative and persuasive writing, you will find that a writer supports an opinion, belief, or action by discussing why it is appropriate. In the following paragraph, the writer gives reasons *why* oil field development can harm the environment.

> Oil field development has also been shown to have negative environmental impacts. Drilling activities themselves have fairly minimal impact, but much more than drilling is involved in the development of an oil field. Road networks must be constructed, and many sites may be explored in the course of prospecting. These activities can fragment habitats and can be noisy and disruptive enough to affect wildlife. The extensive infrastructure that must be erected to support a full-scale drilling operation typically includes housing for workers, access roads, transport pipelines, and waste piles for removed soil. In addition, ponds may be constructed for collecting sludge, the toxic leftovers that remain after the useful components of oil have been removed
>
> —Brennen and Withgot, *Environment: The Science Behind the Stories,* p. 546

You can see that the writer offers three reasons why oil field development has a negative environmental impact: roads can disrupt habitat and wildlife, an infrastructure must be created, and ponds will be created to collect toxic leftovers.

Description

An author uses description to help you visualize the appearance, organization, or composition of an object, a place, or a process. Descriptions are usually detailed and are intended to help you create a mental picture of what is being described. Read the following description of how movement is depicted in a particular thirteenth-century sculpture.

> To give lifelike feeling, artists often search for ways to create a sense of movement. Sometimes movement itself is the subject or a central quality of the subject. One of the world's most appealing depictions of movement is that of the Dancing Krishna, portraying a moment in India's ancient legend of the god Krishna when Krishna, as a playful child, has just stolen his mother's butter supply and now dances with glee. Bronze provides the necessary strength to hold the dynamic pose as the energy-radiating figure stands on one foot, counterbalancing arms, legs, and torso.
>
> —Preble, Preble, and Frank, *Artforms,* p. 60

You should be able to visualize the pose depicted in this bronze sculpture and even, perhaps, Krishna's facial expression. Each detail contributes to the description a bit of information that, when added to other bits, reveals its appearance.

Facts and Statistics

Another way to support an idea is to include facts or statistics that provide information about the main or controlling idea. Read the following paragraph, and notice how facts and statistics are used to support the idea that the size of the global teenage market is significant.

> Collectively, American teens spent $172 billion in 2001—that's a lot of Slurpees. The spending power of American teens is well known, and lately European companies also are appreciating the vast economic clout of the young. Euroteens also have plenty of cash to spend; a survey of Germans aged 16 to 18 by *Yomag.net,* an online magazine for European teens, found that 60 percent had a job and 92 percent received an allowance, with a significant number receiving both. Another *Yomag.net* survey of teens from other European countries showed that they received a monthly allowance of about ∈ 36.74 (one euro having roughly the same value as a dollar). That figure doesn't compare with the $22.68 *weekly* average that U.S. teens receive, but it's still more than chump change! Indeed, the potential of the global youth market is massive, representing about $100 billion in spending power! This is because of the huge proportion of people in many countries who are very young. For example, consider that while 21 percent of U.S. residents are 14 or younger, these are the corresponding percentages in some other countries.
>
> —Saloman, *Consumer Behavior, Buying, Having, and Being,* p. 503

When reading factual support or explanations, remember these questions: *What? When? Where? How?* and *Why?* They will lead you to the important facts and statistics contained in the passage.

Citation of Research Evidence

In many fields of study, authors support their ideas by citing research that has been done on the topic. Authors report the results of surveys, experiments, and research studies in order to substantiate theories or principles or to lend support to a particular viewpoint. The following excerpt from a psychology textbook reports the results of research conducted to evaluate the ability of chimpanzeees to learn numbers.

> More recent research suggests that chimpanzees may be able to learn numerical as well as linguistic symbols (Beran, 2004; Beran & Rumbaugh, 2001). Researchers trained two chimpanzees to use a joystick to move dots on a computer screen. Then, the chimps were taught to collect specific numbers of dots in association with Arabic numerals. In other words, when *3* was displayed on the screen, the chimp was supposed to use its joystick to move three dots from one location to another. Although the chimps learned the task, they tended to perform poorly with quantities in excess of six or seven. Afterward, the researchers ceased practicing with them because they wanted to find out whether the animals would remember the associations over extended periods of time. When they were restested 6 months later, the chimps were able to perform the task quite well, although they made more errors than when they were first trained. After 3 years, the researchers tested them again and found that they still remembered the symbol–quantity associations.
>
> —Wood, Wood, and Boyd, *Mastering the World of Psychology,* p. 210

When reading research reports, keep the following questions in mind. They will help you see the relationship between the research results and the author's controlling idea.

1. Why was the research done?
2. What did it show?
3. Why did the author include it?

EXERCISE 5

DIRECTIONS   Read the following passages and identify the type of supporting information or detail that is used in each.

1. Three ceramic jars made in different villages in the late nineteenth and early twentieth centuries illustrate similarities and variations within the regional pottery style of the Pueblo peoples of New Mexico. The jars are similar in size and shape, but are different in surface decoration, with each bearing a design that is typical of the pottery produced by the artists of its Pueblo.

   The jar from Acoma Pueblo is decorated in large swaths—the brick-red elements seem to wander over the entire surface, draping over the shoulders of the jar like a garland. This undulating form divides the pot into irregularly shaped large areas.

   On the Zuni jar the design is divided by vertical lines into sections in which other lines define circular triangular areas.

   In San Ildefonso Pueblo, Maria Martinez and her husband developed another distinctive style, seen in our third example. The San Ildefonso jar has contrasting curvilinear and rectilinear shapes. This jar also features the subtle contrast of matte black and shiny black areas.

   —Preble, Preble, and Frank, *Artforms,* pp. 98–99

Type of detail: _____

2. With its long history of immigration, the United States has often been called a **melting pot.** This phrase refers to a mixture of cultures, ideas, and peoples. As the third wave of immigration continues, policymakers have begun to speak of a new **minority majority,** meaning that America will eventually cease to have a White, generally Anglo-Saxon majority. The 2000 census data found an all-time low in the percentage of non-Hispanic White Americans—just over 69 percent of the population. African Americans made up 12 percent of the population, Hispanics 13 percent, Asians 4 percent, and Native Americans slightly less than 1 percent. Between 1980

and 1990, minority populations grew at a much faster rate than the White population. The Census Bureau estimates that by the middle of the twenty-first century, Whites will represent only 52 percent of the population.

Until recently, the largest minority group in the country has been the African-American population. One in eight Americans is a descendent of these reluctant immigrants: Africans who were brought to America by force as slaves. A legacy of racism and discrimination has left a higher proportion of the African-American population economically and politically disadvantaged than the White population. In 2002, the U.S. Census Bureau found that 24 percent of African Americans lived below the poverty line compared to 10 percent of Whites.

Despite this economic disadvantage, African Amercans have recently been exercising a good deal of political power. The number of African-American elected officials has increased by over 500 percent since 1970. African Americans have been elected as mayors of many of the country's biggest cities, including Los Angeles, New York, and Chicago. In 2001, Colin Powell became the first African-American Secretary of State and Condoleezza Rice became the nation's first African-American to serve as the president's National Security Advisor.

—Edwards, Wattenberg, and Lineberry, *Government in America,* pp. 179–180

Type of detail: _____

3. Polls help political candidates detect public preferences. Supporters of polling insist that it is a tool for democracy. With it, they say, policymakers can keep in touch with changing opinions on the issues. No longer do politicians have to wait until the next election to see if the public approves or disapproves of the government's course. If the poll results suddenly turn, government officials can make corresponding mid-course corrections. Indeed, it was George Gallup's fondest hope that polling could contribute to the democratic process by providing a way for public desires to be felt at times other than elections.

Critics of polling, by contrast, think it makes politicians more concerned with the following than leading. Polls might have told the constitutional convention delegates that the Constitution was unpopular, or told Jefferson that people did not want the Louisiana Purchase. Certainly they would have told William Seward not to buy Alaska, known widely at the time as "Seward's Folly." Polls may thus discourage bold leadership.

—Edwards, Wattenberg, and Lineberry, *Government in America,* p. 156

Type of detail: _____

4. In simple, preindustrial societies, most interactions occur in primary groups of kin, friends, and neighbors. By contrast, in present-day industrial societies, secondary-group interactions are very important. A secondary group *consists of two or more people who interact formally and impersonally to accomplish a specific objective.* Sociologists call these activities *instrumental behavior,* because people's interaction with others is not an end in itself, but a means of achieving specific goals. In most secondary relationships, interactions are limited and often brief, rules are important, and people relate to one another in terms of specific roles. For example, professors and students may get to know each other pretty well during a semester, but only in their reciprocal roles. It is rare for either to know where the other lives, the names of her or his spouse and children, or how the other spends her or his leisure time. Secondary groups may be small or large, but all large groups in which regular face-to-face interaction is impossible are secondary groups.

If you examine your daily routine, you will discover that, whereas a few hours each day may be devoted to family and friends, much of the day's activities are embedded in secondary groups. When you visit a restaurant, attend class, shop at the mall, go to church, participate in a club meeting, or have a brief chat with the mail carrier, you are engaging in secondary-group activities. The distinction between primary and secondary groups, however, is not always clear-cut, and in everyday life, groups may include elements of each *ideal type.* For example, when co-workers begin to see each other after work and engage in multifaceted relationships, office relationships may come to include both primary and secondary traits, and primary groups may emerge. When this occurs, co-workers often bend the rules and may sometimes even subvert the group's formal objectives in order to accommodate each other's individual talents, interests, and needs.

—Thompson and Hickey, *Society in Focus,* pp. 135–136

Type of detail: _____

5. In North America, paper, yard debris, food scraps, and plastics are the principal components of municipal solid waste, together counting for over 70% of the waste stream. Even after recycling, paper is the largest component of municipal solid waste in the United Sates, comprising 37% of all waste produced.

   The majority of municipal solid waste comes from packaging and from nondurable goods (products meant to be discarded after a short period of use). In addition, old durable goods and outdated equipment are thrown away as consumers purchase new products. Peoples' drive for more goods, as well as for the newest technologies, has resulted in a great deal of waste generation. In 2000, a total of 232 million tons of municipal solid waste was produced in the United States, almost one ton per person per year. The average American produces over 2.0 kg (4.5 lb) of trash per day.

   Following the United States in per capita solid waste generation are Canada, with 1.7 kg (3.75 lb) per day, and the Nertherlands, with roughly 1.4 kg (3.0 lb) per day. Of developed nations, Germany and Sweden produce the least per capita waste, each country generating just under 0.9 kg (2.0 lb) per day. The relative wastefulness of the U.S. lifestyle, with its excess packaging and reliance on nondurable goods, has caused critics to label the United States "the throwaway society."

—Brennan and Withgott, *Environment: The Science Behind the Stories,* pp. 591–592

Type of detail: _____

6. A consumer's national origin is often a strong indicator of his preferences for specific magazines or TV shows, foods, apparel, and choice of leisure activities. Marketers need to be aware of these differences and sensitivities. Even overseas American restaurants must adapt to local customs. For example, in the Middle East, rules about the mixing of the sexes and the consumption of alcohol are quite strict. Chili's Grill & Bar is known simply as Chili's, and the chain offers a midnight buffet during Ramadan season, when Muslims are required to fast from dawn to dusk. McDonald's in Saudi Arabia offers separate dining areas for single men and women and children. Booths must have screens because women can't be seen eating meat.

—Soloman, Marshall, and Stuart, *Marketing: Real People, Real Choices,* p. 202

Type of detail: _____

7. The first stage of the purchase decision process is problem recognition. It occurs when a person perceives a difference between some ideal state and his or her actual state at a given moment. Consider, for example, a student who is in the market to rent an apartment. For her, the problem-recognition stage may have started when she decided that her dorm was too noisy or perhaps after an argument with her roommate. For a product like shampoo, problem recognition may occur when a consumer sees his favorite brand on sale, or it may be triggered when he notices that the bottle in his shower is almost empty.

Problem recognition may occur gradually. Several weeks may have passed before our student realized how much the noise in the dorm was bothering her. Sometimes, it occurs very quickly. When standing in the check-out line at the grocery store you see your favorite movie star on the cover of *People* and impulsively buy the magazine, you have experienced nearly instantaneous problem recognition. In fact, you have gone through virtually the entire purchase decision process in a matter of moments.

—Kinnear, Bernhardt, and Krentler, *Principles of Marketing*, p. 180

Type of detail: _____

8. According to its proponents, a national primary would bring directness and simplicity to the process for the voters as well as the candidates. The length of the campaign would be shortened and no longer would votes in one state have more political impact than votes in another. The concentration of media coverage on this one event, say its advocates, would increase not only political interest in the nomination decision, but also public understanding of the issues involved.

—Edwards, Wattenberg, and Lineberry, *Government in America*, p. 230

Type of detail: _____

9. When the government sets out to measure the size of the labor force or the number of unemployed, its statisticians obviously cannot interview every single worker or potential worker. Survey data must be used. Although the survey technique is extensive—consisting of almost 60,000 households in almost 2,000 counties and cities in all 50 states and the District of Columbia—it is imperfect. One of the main reasons, argue some economists, is because of the *underground economy.* The underground economy consists of individuals who work for cash payments without paying any taxes. It also consists of individuals who engage in illegal activities such as prostitution, gambling, and drug trafficking.

   Some who are officially unemployed and are receiving unemployment benefits do nonetheless work "off the books." Although they are counted as unemployed by the BLS, they really are employed. The same analysis holds for anyone who works and does not report income earned. The question, of course, is, How big is the underground economy? If it is small, the official unemployment statistics may still be adequate to give a sense of the state of the national economy. Various researchers have come up with different estimates of the size of the underground economy. Professor Peter Guttman believes that it is at least 10 percent of the size of the national economy. Other researchers have come up with estimates ranging from 5 to 15 percent. In dollars and cents that may mean that the underground economy represents between $300 billion and $900 billion a year. How many members of the true labor force work in this economy and their effect on the true unemployment rate is anyone's guess.

—Miller, *Economics Today*, p. 147

Type of detail: _____

10. An enlarger can produce a print of any size—larger, smaller, or the same size as a negative, so it is sometimes more accurately called a projection printer. Most often, however, it is used to enlarge an image. An enlarger operates like a slide projector mounted vertically on a column. Light from an enclosed lamp shines through a negative and is then focused by a lens to expose an image of the negative on printing paper placed at the foot of the enlarger column. Image size is set by changing the distance from the enlarger head (the housing containing lamp, negative, and lens) to the paper; the greater the distance, the larger the image. The image is focused by moving the lens closer to or farther from the negative. The exposure time is con-

trolled by a timer. To regulate the intensity of the light, the lens has a diaphragm aperture with f-stops like those on a camera lens.

—London and Upton, *Photography,* p. 134

Type of detail: _____

RECOGNIZING ORGANIZATIONAL PATTERNS

You have seen that textbook sections are structured around a controlling idea and supporting information and details. The next step in reading these materials effectively is to become familiar with how information is organized.

Recognition of organizational patterns is a useful learning device. It is based on the principle of meaningfulness, which states that things that are meaningful are easier to learn and remember than those that are not. When you fit details into a pattern, you connect them so that each one helps you recall the rest. By identifying how the key details in a paragraph or passage form a pattern, you are making them more meaningful to you and, as a result, making them easier to remember.

Patterns are forms of schemata, or sets of familiar information. Once you recognize that a paragraph or passage follows a particular pattern, its organization becomes familiar and predictable.

Six organizational patterns are commonly used in textbook writing: definition, time sequence, comparison–contrast, cause–effect, classification, and enumeration. A chart that summarizes these patterns is shown in Figure 7-3 on page 180.

To help you visualize each pattern, a diagram will be presented for each. Later, in Chapter 15, you will see that these diagrams, also called maps, are useful means of organizing and retaining information.

These patterns may also appear together in various combinations, producing a mixed pattern. For each of these patterns, particular words and phrases are used to connect details and lead from one idea to another. These words are called **transitional words** because they make a transition, or change, and indicate the direction or pattern of thought. A chart (Figure 7-4) giving examples of types of transitional words appears on page 181.

Definition

The definition pattern defines and explains the meaning of a term or concept. It is one of the most obvious patterns, and you will find it widely used in textbooks. Each academic discipline has its own language or specialized terminology (see Chapter 13). One of the primary tasks of authors of introductory course textbooks is to introduce their readers to this new language that you will find in many textbook sections in which new terms are introduced.

Suppose you were asked to define the word *comedian* for someone unfamiliar with the term. First, you would probably say that a comedian is a person who entertains. Then you might distinguish a comedian from other types of entertainers by saying that a comedian is an entertainer who tells jokes and makes others laugh. Finally, you might mention as examples the names of several well-known comedians who have appeared on television. Although you may have presented it informally, your definition would have followed the standard, classic pattern. The first part of your definition tells what general class or group the term belongs to (entertainers). The second part tells what distinguishes the term from other items in the same class or category. The third part includes further explanation, characteristics, examples, or applications.

This pattern can be visualized as follows:

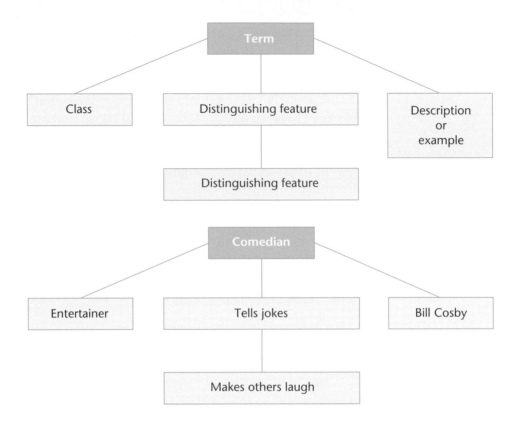

Read the following definition of *society* taken from a sociology textbook.

Society has traditionally been defined as the interacting people who share a common culture—that is, any group of people who speak a common language, share common beliefs and customs, belong to the same institutions and organizations, use the same tools and technology, and consume the same goods. Although the term "society" is sometimes also used to refer to people with a common culture who share the same territory, we prefer not to emphasize this geographical dimension: in modern society it is increasingly possible to share a common culture with people who are geographically dispersed.

—Appelbaum and Chambliss, *Sociology,* p. 55

This definition has three parts: (1) the general class is stated first, (2) the distinguishing characteristics are then described, and (3) further explanation and examples are given. The first sentence states the general class—group of people, interacting people. The same sentence also gives distinguishing characteristics. The remainder of the passage gives further explanation of the term *society*. When reading definitions, be sure to look for each of these parts. Passages that define often use transitional words and phrases such as:

TRANSITIONS FOR THE DEFINITION PATTERN	
refers to	can be defined as
means	consists of
is	

EXERCISE 6

DIRECTIONS   Define each of the following terms by identifying the class it belongs to and describing its distinguishing characteristics.

1. Adolescence
2. Automated teller machine (ATM)
3. Cable television
4. Computer
5. Advertising

Time Sequence and Process

One of the clearest ways to describe events, processes, procedures, and development of theories is to present them in the order in which they occurred. The event that happened first appears first in the passage; whatever occurred last is described last in the passage.

The time sequence pattern can be visualized as follows:

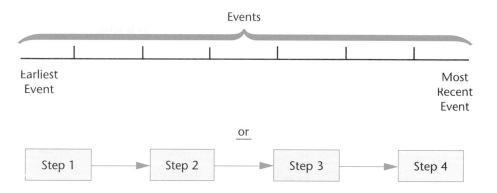

The first drawing is often called a **time line**, the second a **process diagram.** Notice in the following example how the writer proceeds through time, describing the process of communication among members of an organization.

A Business Communication Model

People, not organizations, communicate. An organization's communication system therefore reflects a variety of individuals with different backgrounds, education levels, beliefs, cultures, moods, and needs. When individuals in an organization communicate, what exactly takes place? Let us examine a basic communication model so that we will be better able to understand why communication fails so frequently and what actions managers can take to improve their communication effectiveness. This model illustrates the six most important elements involved in communication between and among organization members:

The *source,* or originator of the message, takes the first step in the communication process. Some event stimulates the need for transmitting ideas, information, or feelings to someone else.

The second step—*encoding*—involves choosing some verbal or nonverbal communication that is capable of transferring meaning, such as spoken or written words, gestures, or actions. One must think not only of what is going to be communicated but also of *how* it will be presented to have the desired effect on the receiver. Thus, the message must be adapted to the level of understanding, interest, *and* needs of the receiver to achieve the desired consequences.

The third step—*transmitting,* or sending the communication from the source to the receiver—reflects the communicator's choice of medium or *distribution channel.* Oral communication may be transmitted through many channels—in person, by telephone, by audio- or videotape. It may take place privately or in a group setting. Written communication may be transmitted by means such as memos, letters, reports, notes, bulletin boards, company manuals, and newsletters. Written communication has the advantage of providing a record for future reference, but the major disadvantage is that it does not allow spontaneous, face-to-face feedback.

The fourth step is *receiving* the message. People receive messages through their five senses—sight, hearing, taste, touch, and smell. Full transmission has not occurred unless a party actually *receives* a message. Many important attempts at communication have failed because the message never got to its intended receiver.

The fifth step of the communication process is *decoding,* which involves providing meaning to the message by the receiver or his or her representative. This meaning is a product of such variables as the receiver's heritage, culture, education, environment, prejudices, and biases, as well as distractions in the surroundings. There is always the possibility that the source's message, when decoded by the receiver, will yield a meaning far different from the one the sender intended. The receiver thus shares a large responsibility for communication effectiveness, for *communication is a two-way street.* Managers and subordinates may occupy both source and receiver roles throughout an interaction.

Step 6 of the process is *feedback*—the responses the receiver gives by further communicating with the sender. Communication is thus a continuous and perpetual process. A person communicates, the receiver responds by further communicating with the original sender or another person, and so forth.

—Mosley, Pietri, and Megginson, *Management,* pp. 333–336

This excerpt could be visualized as follows:

Material presented in terms of a time sequence is relatively easy to read because you know what order the writer will follow. When reading sequential, organized material, pay attention to the order of and connection between events. When studying this material, remember that the order is often as important as the events themselves. To test your memory and to prepare information for study, list ideas in this correct order, or draw a process diagram or time line.

The time sequence pattern uses transitional words to connect the events described or to lead you from one step to another. The most frequently used words are presented in the following box.

TRANSITIONS FOR THE TIME SEQUENCE AND PROCESS PATTERNS		
first	before	following
second	after	last
later	then	during
next	finally	when
as soon as	meanwhile	until

EXERCISE 7

DIRECTIONS   For each of the following topic sentences, make a list of transitional words you expect to be used in the paragraph.

1. Advertising has appeared in magazines since the late 1700s.
2. Large numbers of European immigrants first began to arrive in the United States in the 1920s.
3. The first step in grasping a novel's theme is reading it closely for literal content, including plot and character development.
4. After he left Spain, strong winds blew Columbus and his ships into the middle of the Atlantic.
5. The life cycle of a product consists of the stages a product goes through from when it is created to when it is no longer produced.

Comparison–Contrast

Many fields of study involve the comparison of one set of ideas, theories, concepts, or events with another. These comparisons usually examine similarities and differences. In anthropology, one kinship category might be compared with another; in literature, one poet might be compared with another; in biology, one theory of evolution might be compared with another. You will find that the comparison–contrast pattern appears regularly in the textbooks used in these fields. The comparison–contrast pattern can be visualized in several ways. For material that considers both similarities and differences, the maps below and on the next page are effective.

TOPICS A AND B

Similarities	Differences
_____	_____
_____	_____
_____	_____

For example:

PROFESSOR MILLER AND PROFESSOR WRIGHT

Similarities	Differences
both require class attendance	Miller assigns term paper
both give essay exams	Wright demands class participation
both have sense of humor	age

For material that focuses primarily on differences, you might use the following:

	TOPIC A	TOPIC B
Feature 1	_____	_____
Feature 2	_____	_____
Feature 3	_____	_____
For example:		
Feature	*Professor Smith*	*Professor Jones*
teaching style	lecture	discussion
class atmosphere	formal	casual
type of exam	multiple choice	essay

A comparison–contrast pattern can be organized in one of three ways. A writer comparing two famous artists, X and Y, could use any of the following procedures:

1. Discuss the characteristics of artist X and those of artist Y, and then summarize their similarities and differences.
2. Consider their similarities first, and then discuss their differences.
3. Consider both X and Y together for each of several characteristics. For instance, discuss the use of color by X and Y, then discuss the use of space by X and Y, and then consider the use of proportion by X and Y.

Read the following paragraph, and try to determine which of the preceding patterns is used.

> In their original work both Darwin and that other great innovator who followed him, Gregor Mendel, used deductive reasoning to great effect. Both these giants of biology had been trained in theology. As a result, they were well acquainted with an intellectual tradition based on deduction. And since induction is difficult to apply in a field where so little can be directly observed, perhaps theology provided some of the essential intellectual tools both men needed to develop a viewpoint so different from prevailing theological thinking.
>
> Darwin and Mendel are linked in another fundamental way. Darwin could not explain how successful traits are passed on to successive generations, exposing his theory of natural selection to growing criticism. When Mendel was rediscovered, geneticists were paying a lot of attention to mutations. They still felt that natural selection of variants had a minor part in evolution. The major factor, they believed, was sudden change introduced by mutation. Not until the 1930s did biologists realize, at last, that Darwin's theory of natural selection and Mendel's laws of genetics were fully compatible. Together the two form the basis of population genetics, a major science of today.
>
> —Laetsch, *Plants: Basic Concepts in Botany,* p. 393

DARWIN AND MENDEL

Similarities

both trained in theology	both giants of biology
both developed original viewpoint	held compatible theories

The passage compares the characteristics of the work of Darwin and the work of Mendel. The first paragraph presents their use of deductive reasoning. The second paragraph describes the compatibility of their theories.

In comparison–contrast passages, the way ideas are organized provides clues to what is important. In a passage that is organized by characteristics, the emphasis is placed on the characteristics. A passage that groups similarities and then differences emphasizes the similarities and differences themselves rather than the characteristics.

Transitional words indicate whether the passage focuses on similarities, differences, or both.

TRANSITIONS FOR THE COMPARISON AND CONTRAST PATTERN			
Similarities		**Differences**	
also	too	unlike	nevertheless
similarly	as well as	despite	however
like	both	instead	in spite of
likewise		on the other hand	

EXERCISE 8

DIRECTIONS   For each of the following topic sentences, predict the content of the paragraph. Will it focus on similarities, differences, or both? Also, if you predict that the passage will discuss both similarities and differences, predict the organization of the paragraph that will follow. (Identify the type of organization by its number in the list on page 172 for the comparison–contrast pattern.)

1. Two types of leaders can usually be identified in organizations: informal and formal.

   Content: _____   Organization: _____

2. The human brain is divided into two halves, each of which is responsible for separate functions.

   Content: _____   Organization: _____

3. Humans and primates, such as gorillas and New World monkeys, share many characteristics but are clearly set apart by others.

   Content: _____   Organization: _____

4. Interpersonal communication is far more complex than intrapersonal communication.

   Content: _____   Organization: _____

5. Sociology and psychology both focus on human behavior.

   Content: _____   Organization: _____

Cause–Effect

Understanding any subject requires learning *how* and *why* things happen. In psychology it is not enough to know that people are often aggressive; you also need to know why and how people show aggression. In physics it is not enough to know the laws of motion; you also must understand why they work and how they apply to everyday experiences.

The cause–effect pattern arranges ideas according to why and how they occur. This pattern is based on the relationship between or among events. Some passages discuss one cause and one effect—the omission of a command, for example, causing a computer program to fail.

This relationship can be visualized as follows:

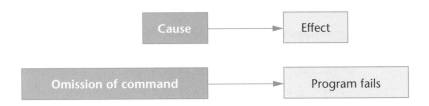

Most passages, however, describe multiple causes or effects. Some may describe the numerous effects of a single cause, such as unemployment producing an increase in crime, family disagreements, and a lowering of self-esteem.

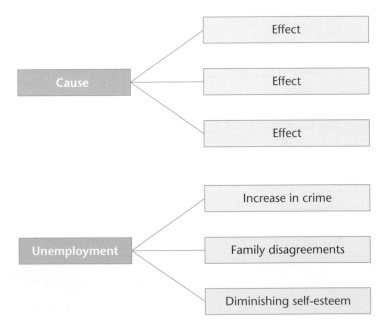

Others may describe the numerous causes of a single effect, such as increased unemployment and poverty along with decreased police protection causing a high crime rate.

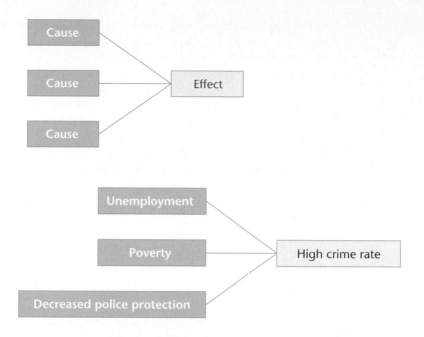

Still others may present multiple causes and effects, such as unemployment and poverty producing an increase in crime and in family disputes.

Read the following passage, which is taken from a business marketing text, and determine which of the following patterns is used:

- single cause–single effect
- single cause–multiple effects
- multiple causes–single effect
- multiple causes–multiple effects

Then draw a diagram in the margin describing this relationship.

Eventually, product class sales begin to decline, sometimes even rapidly. The causes of the decline may be market saturation, new technology, or changes in social values. Since most homes have smoke detectors, sales in that product class have slowed considerably. Compact disc players have significantly slowed sales of cassette tape players. Health conscious consumers have caused a significant decrease in beef consumption in the United States. The decline in volume often results in higher costs. At this stage marketers must eliminate products that are no longer profitable or find ways of cutting operational and marketing costs. Some of these include eliminating marginal dealers and distributors, cutting advertising and sales promotion, and minimizing production costs. These cuts could result in renewed profitability. In effect, the product is "milked"; that is, it is allowed to coast with decreased marketing support as long as it remains profitable.

Of course it is possible that reducing marketing support will hasten the product's demise, and thus decline has been viewed as a self-fulfilling prophecy. Brands that have developed strong consumer loyalty decline slower than products that have not been differentiated from their competitors. It is even possible for individual competitors to do well for quite some time while the product class is in decline. They may be able to garner a larger market share, albeit of a smaller market, as other competitors drop out. Technics and Pioneer continue to produce stereo turntables although distribution is limited.

—Kinnear, Bernhardt, and Krentler, *Principles of Marketing,* p. 290

The passage offers numerous reasons why product sales decline. Numerous causes, then, produce a single effect.

When you read and study ideas organized in a cause–effect pattern, focus on the connection between or among events. To make relationships clearer, determine which of the four cause–effect patterns is used. Transitional words can help you determine the cause–effect relationship.

TRANSITIONS FOR THE CAUSE AND EFFECT PATTERN

Causes	Effects
because	consequently
because of	as a result
since	one result is
one cause is	therefore
one reason is	thus

EXERCISE 9

DIRECTIONS   From the following list of section headings from an American government textbook, predict which sections will be developed using the cause–effect pattern. Place a check mark in front of those you select.

_____ 1. How Public Policies Affect Income

_____ 2. Explaining the Decline of Isolationism in America

_____ 3. Tasks of Political Parties

_____ 4. The Affirmative Action Issue

_____ 5. Political Parties: How Party Loyalty Shifts

_____ 6. Why Bureaucracies Exist

_____ 7. The Organization of National Political Parties

_____ 8. How Lobbyists Shape Policy

_____ 9. Types of Special-Interest Groups

_____ 10. The Nature of the Judicial System

Classification

The classification pattern divides a broad topic into categories. If you were asked to describe types of computers, you might mention mainframes, minicomputers, and microcomputers. By dividing computers into major categories, you are using a pattern known as **classification.**

This pattern is widely used in many academic subjects. For example, a psychology text might explain human needs by classifying them into two categories: primary and secondary. In a chemistry textbook, various compounds may be grouped and discussed according to common characteristics, such as the presence of hydrogen or oxygen. The classification pattern divides a topic into parts, on the basis of common or shared characteristics.

Here are a few examples of topics and the classifications or categories into which each might be divided:

- Movies: comedy, horror, mystery
- Motives: achievement, power, affiliation, competency
- Plant: leaves, stem, roots

You can visualize the classification patterns as follows:

Note how the paragraph that follows classifies the various types of cancers.

> The name of the cancer is derived from the type of tissue in which it develops. Carcinoma (carc = cancer; omo = tumor) refers to a malignant tumor consisting of epithelial cells. A tumor that develops from a gland is called an adenosarcoma (adeno = gland). Sarcoma is a general term for any cancer arising from connective tissue. Osteogenic sarcomas (osteo = bone; genic = origin), the most frequent type of childhood cancer, destroy normal bone tissue and eventually spread to other areas of the body. Myelomas (myelos = marrow) are malignant tumors, occurring in middle-aged and older people, that interfere with the blood-cell-producing function of bone marrow and cause anemia. Chondrosarcomas (chondro = cartilage) are cancerous growths of cartilage.
>
> —Tortora, *Introduction to the Human Body,* p. 56

You can visualize this classification paragraph as follows:

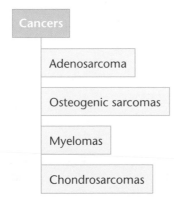

TRANSITIONS FOR THE CLASSIFICATION PATTERN		
several kinds	finally	can be classified as
one type	first	second
another type		

EXERCISE 10

DIRECTIONS   For each of the following topic sentences, supply three pieces of information that might be contained in the paragraph.

1. There are magazines designed for almost every possible interest and every conceivable type of person. _____

   _____

2. Due, in part, to our complicated economic system, there are a number of different types of taxes that are levied. _____

   _____

3. There are several different types of resources a person can turn to when experiencing financial difficulties. _____

   _____

4. There are many types of diet plans; the wise dieter evaluates the benefits of each. _____

   _____

5. Stress comes from a wide variety of situations; however, each situations falls into one of three primary sources. _____

   _____

Enumeration

The primary function of textbooks is to present information. If there is a relationship or connection between or among ideas, this connection is usually emphasized and used to organize information. Many types of information, however, have no inherent order or connection. Lists of facts, characteristics, parts, or categories can appear in any order; thus, writers use a pattern called *enumeration*. In this pattern, the information is often loosely connected with a topic sentence or controlling idea: "There are several issues to be considered . . . " or "There are three problems that may occur when . . ." and so forth. You can visualize the enumeration pattern as follows:

Read the following paragraph, observing how the pattern proceeds from one type of flaw to another.

> The U.S. deposit-insuring agencies have serious design flaws. First, the price of deposit insurance to individual depository institutions was until recently relatively low; the depository institutions are subsidized by the depository insurers. Second, the insurance premium is the same percentage of total deposits for all depository institutions, regardless of the riskiness of the institution's portfolio. Also until recently, all deposit-insuring agencies charged a depository institution about .25 percent of the institution's total (not just insured) deposits. For example, federally insured commercial banks pay a flat fee for the FDIC guarantee of the first $100,000 of each deposit account in the bank. The flaw in this pricing structure is that an individual depository institution's premium is set without regard to its probability of failure, the riskiness of its portfolio, or the estimated cost to the insurer should the institution fail.
>
> —Miller, *Economics Today,* p. 335

One key to reading and studying this pattern is to be aware of how many items are enumerated so you can check your recall of them. It is also helpful to note whether the information is listed in order of importance, frequency, size, or any other characteristic. This will help you organize the information for easier recall.

Transitional words are very useful in locating items in a list. As a writer moves from one item in a list to another, he or she may use transitional words to mark or identify each point.

TRANSITIONS FOR THE ENUMERATION PATTERN	
one	first
another	second
also	finally
too	for example
for instance	in addition

EXERCISE 11

DIRECTIONS   For each of the following topic sentences, supply three pieces of information that might be contained in the paragraph.

1. There are a number of factors wise consumers must consider in deciding which credit card to apply for.
2. Humans have more than just five senses; within the broad category of touch, there are many different kinds of sensation that can be felt.
3. The species of mammals contains many widely different kinds of animals.
4. Scientists find life hard to define, except by describing its characteristics.
5. Because the purpose of a résumé is to sell the qualities of the person writing it, it should include several important kinds of information.

Mixed Patterns

In many texts, sections and passages combine one or more patterns. In defining a concept or idea, a writer might explain a term by comparing it with something similar or familiar. In describing an event or process, a writer might include reasons for or causes of an event or might explain why the steps in a process must be followed in the prescribed order.

Read the following paragraph and determine which two patterns are used.

> The error of ascribing to animals the thoughts, emotions, and motivations of humans is now rejected by most behavioral scientists as anthropomorphic (from the Greek words meaning "man" and "form"). The banishing of anthropomorphism was due largely to the behaviorist school of psychology, which argued that one could only observe animal behavior, not try to infer the mental states underlying it. Later behaviorists, like B. F. Skinner, went even further, arguing that mental states, such as free will, did not occur even in humans. The behaviorist approach to animal behavior has produced more experimentally testable theories than the anthropomorphic approach, but most of these theories have been based on studies of the albino laboratory rat under extremely artificial conditions. Behaviorists have therefore been accused of replacing the anthropomorphic view of animals with a "ratomorphic" view of humans. For zoologists, the behavior of rats under laboratory conditions is not only a poor model for the behavior of humans, it is also a poor model for the natural behavior of rats.
>
> —Harris, *Concepts in Zoology,* p. 402

Two approaches to the study of animal behavior—*anthropomorphic* and *behaviorist*—are defined, but for purposes of explanation, the terms are also compared. Therefore, the paragraph combines a definition pattern with a comparison–contrast pattern.

When reading mixed patterns, do not be overly concerned with identifying or labeling each pattern. Instead, look for the predominant pattern that carries the overall organization.

Figures 7-3 and 7-4 present a review of the organizational patterns and of transitional words commonly used with each pattern. Although this chapter has focused on the use of these patterns in textbook writing, you will find such patterns in other academic situations as well. For example, your professor may organize her or his lecture by using one or more of these patterns and may use transitional words to enable you to follow the line of thought. On exams, especially essay exams, you will find questions that require you to organize information in terms of one or more of the organizational patterns. (Refer to Chapter 17 for more information on essay exam questions.)

Figure 7-3
Summary of
Organizational Patterns

Pattern	Characteristics
Definition	Explains the meaning of a term or phrase; consists of class, distinguishing characteristics, and explanation
Time sequence/Process	Describes events, processes, procedures
Comparison–contrast	Discusses similarities and/or differences among ideas, theories, concepts, objects, or persons
Cause–effect	Describes how one or more things cause or are related to another
Classification	Explains by dividing a topic into parts or categories
Enumeration	Organizes lists of information: characteristics, features, parts, or categories

Figure 7-4
Summary of
Transitional Words

Thought Pattern		Transitional Words
Definition		refers to, means, can be defined as, consists of
Time sequence/Process		first, second, later, before, next, as soon as, after, then, finally, meanwhile, following, last, during, when, until
Comparison–contrast	*Similarities:*	also, similarly, like, likewise, too, as well as, both
	Differences:	unlike, on the other hand, instead, despite, nevertheless, however, in spite of
Cause–effect	*Causes:*	because, because of, since, one cause is, one reason is
	Effects:	consequently, as a result, one result is, therefore, thus
Classification		several kinds, one type, first, second, finally
Enumeration		one, another, also, too, for instance, first, second, finally, for example, in addition

Organizational patterns and transitional words are also useful in organizing your own ideas and presenting them effectively in written form. As you write papers and complete written assignments, these patterns will provide a basis for relating and connecting your ideas and presenting them in a clear and understandable form. The transitional words are useful as transitions, leading your reader from one idea to another.

EXERCISE 12

DIRECTIONS   Assume that each of the following sentences or groups of sentences is the beginning of a textbook section. On the basis of the information contained in each, predict what organizational pattern is used throughout the passage. Look for transitional words to help you identify the pattern.

1. In large businesses, clerical jobs are usually very specialized in order for the work to be accomplished in the most efficient manner. As a result, clerical work is very often routine and highly repetitive. _____

2. There are clear limitations to population growth and the use of natural resources. First, the food supply could be exhausted as a result of water, mineral, and soil depletion. _____

3. Unlike the statues of humans, the statues of animals found at Stone Age sites are quite lifelike. _____

4. When a patient enters a mental hospital, he is carefully tested and observed for 24 hours. Then a preliminary decision is made concerning medication and treatment. _____

5. One shortcoming of the clinical approach in treating mental illness is that definitions of normal behavior are subjective. Another shortcoming of the approach is that it assumes that when a patient has recovered, he will be able to return to his previous environment. _____

6. Most of the world's news is transmitted by Western news agencies. Third World nations regard this dominance as oppressive and feel that action must be taken to develop their communication networks. _____

EXERCISE 13

DIRECTIONS Read each of the following passages, and identify the main organizational pattern used in each.

1. TAMPERING WITH GENES, OR GENETIC ENGINEERING? Genetic engineering, as the name implies, involves manipulating genes to achieve some particular goal. Some people object to the entire idea of tailoring molecules with such profound implications for life. Where could it lead? Would we have the wisdom not to unleash something terrible on the earth?

   Perhaps the greatest threat of recombinant techniques, some would say, lies in [their] very promise. The possibilities of such genetic manipulation seem limitless. For example, we can mix the genes of anything—say, an ostrich and a German shepherd. This may bring to mind only images of tall dogs, but what would happen if we inserted cancer-causing genes into the familiar *E. coli* that is so well adapted to living in our intestines? What if the gene that makes botulism toxin, one of the deadliest poisons known, were inserted into the DNA of friendly *E. coli* and then released into some human population? One might ask, "But who would do such a terrible thing?" Perhaps the same folks who brought us napalm and nerve gas.

   Another, less cynical concern is that well-intended scientists could mishandle some deadly variant and allow it to escape from the laboratory. Some variants have been weakened to prevent such an occurrence; but we should remember that even though smallpox was "eradicated" from the earth, there were two minor epidemics in Europe caused by cultured experimental viruses that had escaped from a lab. One person died of a disease that technically didn't exist.

   —Ferl, Wallace, and Sanders, *Biology: The Realm of Life*, pp. 252–253

Organizational pattern: _____

2. In 1965 Congress sought to rectify the special health care problems of elderly Americans by adopting Medicare. Medicare is part of the Social Security system and covers 40 million people. Part A of Medicare provides hospitalization insurance and short-term nursing care; Part B, which is voluntary, permits older Americans to purchase inexpensive coverage for doctor fees and other nonhospital medical expenses. Because the number of elderly Americans grows rapidly—and because the cost of medical care is growing just as fast (Medicare cost about $250 billion in 2002)—the funding of health care for the elderly is one of the country's most pressing public policy issues.

   —Edwards, Wattenberg, and Lineberry, *Government in America*, p. 593

Organizational pattern: _____

3. PERMANENT SETTLERS Numerous factors account for the growing number of immigrants, worldwide. First, as noted, the planet has been experiencing tremendous population growth, mostly in the less developed regions which do not have sufficient numbers of jobs for the working-age population. One option for unemployed or underemployed citizens in the LDCs (Less Developed Countries) is to migrate to an MDC (More Developed Country) in the hope of finding work. For example, World Bank labor force figures suggest that 10 percent of Mexico's domestic labor force resides in the United States. A second reason for increased migration from LDCs to MDCs is the loss of jobs in LDCs caused by modern electronic machines that displace

human beings. Increased mechanization characterizes the labor forces of LDCs just as it does the MDCs. A third reason for the increase in worldwide migration is environmental degradation. Environmental problems such as deforestation, desertification, and polluted water supplies often result in people moving to other countries to escape these problems.

—Glynn, Hohm, and Stewart, *Global Social Problems,* p. 154

Organizational pattern: _____

4. THE MARXIAN ANALYSIS   Karl Marx was born in Trier, Germany, to middle-class Jewish parents who had converted to Protestantism. He attended the University of Berlin as a doctoral candidate in philosophy, instead of studying law as his father desired. At the university he joined a circle that followed some aspects of Hegel's thought. After finishing his degree, he could not find a university position and so returned to the Rhineland where he began writing for a local newspaper. The injustices he saw around him and his reading of the French socialists Henri de Saint-Simon and Pierre Joseph Proudhon led him to concentrate on the economic factors in history. He went to Paris to continue his studies, met Engels, and was expelled by the authorities in 1845. From there he went first to Belgium and finally to England where, after 1848, he spent most of the rest of his life.

An uncompromising hostility to capitalism drove Marx's work. He stated in the *Manifesto* that communists "openly declare that their ends can be attained only by the forcible overthrow of all existing social conditions." Virtually every day he made his way to the British Museum where he waged intellectual war on capitalism by doing research for his major works, especially *Das Kapital.*

—Wallbank et al., *Civilization Past and Present,* vol. 2, p. 671

Organizational pattern: _____

5. PROTEINS   Proteins are much more complex in structure than carbohydrates or lipids and are involved in numerous physiological activities. Proteins are largely responsible for the structure of body cells. Some proteins in the form of enzymes function as catalysts to speed up certain chemical reactions. Enzymes are very important in regulating chemical reactions in cells to help maintain homeostasis. Other proteins assume an important role in muscular contraction. Antibodies are proteins that defend the body against invading microbes. Some types of hormones are proteins.

Chemically, proteins always contain carbon, hydrogen, oxygen, and nitrogen, and sometimes sulfur. *Amino acids* are the building blocks of proteins. There are at least 20 different amino acids. In protein formation, amino acids combine to form more complex molecules; the bonds formed between amino acids are called *peptide bonds.*

—Tortora, *Introduction to the Human Body,* p. 30

Organizational pattern: _____

6. COUNCILS AND COMMITTEES   Councils and committees are advisory groups found in many different kinds of societies. We have briefly mentioned councils among the Shavante, Tetum, and Qashgai. They meet in public and are usually made up of informally appointed elders. *Committees* differ from councils in that they meet privately. Moreover, whereas councils are typical of simpler political organizations, committees are more characteristic of states. But the two kinds of groups can and often do coexist within the same political organization. When this occurs, councils are superior to committees, whose tasks and powers are delegated to them by councils.

Councils tend to be consensus-seeking bodies, while committees are more likely to achieve agreement by voting (although either kind of body may reach decisions in either way). Consensus seeking is typical of small social groups whose members have frequent personal interaction. Once a council or committee increases to more than about 50 members, decision by consensus is no longer possible. Voting is typical of larger groups whose members do not see much of one another in daily life and who owe their main allegiance not to other group members but to people (perhaps many millions) outside the council or committee. Members may in fact represent these outside people, as is the case with the U.S. Congress.

—Hicks and Gwynne, *Cultural Anthropology,* p. 304

Organizational pattern: _____

7. BELIEFS Beliefs consist of a system of propositions and assertions about the nature of reality. They provide people and societies with a fundamental orientation to the world and answer questions about human origins, proper relations among people, and the destiny of humans and the universe. Simple societies answer these questions with myth and folklore; complex societies answer them with religion and science. Beliefs also include simple observations about the physical and social worlds, or "truths" about nature and people.

Beliefs are social constructions. Although they are typically accepted as truths by the members of a society, beliefs are based not only on objective reality but on social agreement. Moreover yesterday's beliefs and the common sense of the present are the falsehoods and "myths" of tomorrow. For example, the word "lunatic" is derived from the popular nineteenth-century belief that a full moon causes madness, a belief that has folk origins in Europe and even deeper associations in simple cultures. Today, such thinking is derisively labeled "superstition."

—Thompson and Hickey, *Society in Focus,* p. 65

Organizational pattern: _____

8. INTERPERSONAL VERSUS MASS COMMUNICATION Personal or interpersonal channels of communication can occur in social settings when friends or acquaintances share information. Such word-of-mouth communication is a very powerful source of information for consumers. Word-of-mouth communication is usually not under the control of the marketer. Commercial sources of interpersonal communication usually come in the form of personal selling efforts.

Nonpersonal channels of communication, as defined earlier, do not involve direct communication between sender and receiver. Instead, information is shared through mass communication. Advertising, sales promotion, and publicity use nonpersonal techniques. Both interpersonal and mass communication are important in marketing.

A mass communication, such as an advertisement in a magazine, can more accurately deliver the same message to a larger audience than can an interpersonal communication such as a salesperson's presentation to a customer. The latter changes with each attempt to communicate. The cost of reaching an individual through the mass media is substantially lower as well. However, mass communication is one-way, it is less likely to gain the potential audience's selective attention, and it suffers from slow and, many times, inaccurate feedback.

Interpersonal communication has the benefits of being fast, and allowing two-way feedback. A buyer can respond instantly to a salesperson's presentation, and the salesperson can ask for clarification of the response. The greater flexibility in feedback allows the communicator to counter objections from the buyer and thus attain a greater change in attitude and behavior than is possible with mass communication. Interpersonal communication is much more efficient than mass communication. Unfortunately, when used for a large audience, interpersonal communication is slow and very expensive. Hence marketers must compare the efficiency of using a particular type of communication with the cost involved. This comparison is referred to as the *communication-promotion paradox.*

—Kinnear, Bernhardt, and Krentler, *Principles of Marketing,* pp. 475–476

Organizational pattern: _____

9. OBSERVATIONAL LEARNING   Much social learning occurs in situations where learning would not be predicted by traditional conditioning theory, because a learner has made no active response and has received no tangible reinforcer. The individual, after simply watching another person exhibiting behavior that was reinforced or punished, later behaves in much the same way, or refrains from doing so. This is known as observational learning. Cognition often enters into observational learning in the form of expectations. In essence, after observing a model, you may think, "If I do exactly what she does, I will get the same reinforcer to avoid the same punisher." A younger child may be better behaved than his older sister because he has learned from the sister's mistakes.

   This capacity to learn from watching as well as from doing is extremely useful. It enables you to acquire large, integrated patterns of behavior without going through the tedious trial-and-error process of gradually eliminating wrong responses and acquiring the right ones. You can profit immediately from the mistakes and successes of others. Researchers have demonstrated that observational learning is not special to humans. Even octopuses are capable of changing their behavior after merely observing the performances of another member of the species.

—Zimbardo and Gerrig, *Psychology and Life,* p. 337

Organizational pattern: _____

10. THE NERVOUS SYSTEM   The peripheral nervous system is divided into two parts: the somatic (bodily) nervous system and the autonomic (self-governing) nervous system. The somatic nervous system, sometimes called the skeletal nervous system, controls the skeletal muscles of the body and permits voluntary action. When you turn off a light or write your name, your somatic system is active. The autonomic nervous system regulates blood vessels, glands, and internal (visceral) organs like the bladder, stomach, and heart. When you happen upon the secret object of your desire and your heart starts to pound, your hands get sweaty, and your cheeks feel hot, you can blame your autonomic nervous system.

—Wade and Tavris, *Psychology,* p. 77

Organizational pattern: _____

EXERCISE 14   DIRECTIONS   Read "The Talk of the Sandbox" in Part Eight on page 470. Identify the organizational pattern that is used throughout the reading.

LEARNING COLLABORATIVELY

DIRECTIONS   Locate and mark, in one of your textbooks or in Part Eight of this text, several paragraphs that are clear examples of thought patterns discussed in Chapter 7. Write the topic sentence of each paragraph on a separate index card. Once your instructor has formed small groups, choose a group "reader" who will collect all the cards and read each sentence aloud. Groups should discuss each and predict the pattern of the paragraph from which the sentence was taken. The "finder" of the topic sentence should then confirm or reject the prediction and quote sections of the paragraph if necessary.

APPLYING YOUR LEARNING

Suzanne is writing a research paper on "male and female language" for her sociology class. She has collected a great deal of information through research and interviews, but she is having difficulty organizing it. Some of the subtopics on which she has collected information are listed below.

Subject of Paper:

Male and Female Language

Subtopics:

- Research studies on use of language in adolescent, sex-separate peer groups
- Men's language patterns
- Women's language patterns
- Stages of language development in infants and children
- Physical differences in areas of men's and women's brains that control language functioning
- Types of games children play and how they involve language

1. What possible *overall* organizational pattern could her paper follow?
2. What organizational pattern(s) might she follow in developing the section of her paper that deals with each of the topics above?
3. What types of details do you anticipate that Suzanne will include to develop each subtopic?

APPLYING YOUR SKILLS: Sample Textbook Chapter

1. Draw a diagram similar to that on page 157 showing the structure of the sample textbook chapter.
2. For each heading in the entire chapter, predict the thought pattern the section will follow.
3. Choose three headings and read the sections they introduce. Confirm or revise your prediction of the pattern each followed. Highlight transitional words and phrases that suggest the pattern followed.

QUESTIONS FOR DISCUSSION

1. Which type of organizational pattern do you think is used most frequently by college students? Why? Which pattern is used most frequently within each subject area?
2. Think about the various essay examinations you've taken in recent months. Which types of supporting information did you use to explain the controlling idea of your answer? How can you improve your ability to organize an essay question on an examination?
3. Compare the organization of several textbooks. How are the texts organized similarly? How are they different? Which style seems best suited for the topic the text presents?

4. How do newspapers, magazines, television shows, radio programs, and documentary films organize information presented? Which type of organization is most typical in each medium?

5. What type of supporting evidence is typically found in each of the media listed in question 4? How do you know when supporting evidence is sufficient?

SELF-TEST SUMMARY

1. Why is it important to become familiar with the organization of your textbooks?

Textbooks are unique, highly organized sources of information. Becoming familiar with their organization and structure and learning to follow the writer's thought patterns are important textbook reading skills. A textbook is divided into parts: chapters, sections, subsections, and paragraphs. Although each is successively smaller in size and more limited in scope, each follows a similar organization and is built around a single idea with details that support and explain it.

2. What types of supporting information are used in textbooks?

Textbook writers explain ideas by providing various types of supporting information: examples, description, facts and statistics, and citation of research evidence.

3. What are the six common organizational patterns?

The organizational patterns are definition, time sequence/process, comparison–contrast, cause–effect, classification, and enumeration.

4. How can you tell which organizational pattern is being used in a section or paragraph?

By paying close attention to the specific words and phrases a writer uses to connect ideas and lead from one idea to another, you can usually identify the pattern being used. These *transitional words* that show the direction or pattern of thought are different for each of the common organizational patterns.

4. Why is it helpful to recognize the pattern or organization of a paragraph or passage you are reading?

When you recognize that what you are reading follows a specific pattern, you will be better able to follow the ideas being presented and to predict what will be presented next. You will find that you have connected the important details so that recalling one idea will help you recall the others, and as a result, it will be easier to learn and remember them.

DIRECTIONS   Write the letter of the choice that best completes each statement in the space provided.

CHECKING YOUR RECALL

_____ 1. The controlling idea in a textbook section is similar to the main idea of a paragraph *except* that the
   a. paragraph's main idea is more general.
   b. paragraph's main idea is more comprehensive.
   c. textbook section's controlling idea relies on fewer supporting details.
   d. textbook section's controlling idea takes several paragraphs to explain.

_____ 2. The supporting ideas and information are usually presented in an essay's
   a. thesis statement.
   b. introduction.
   c. body.
   d. summary.

_____ 3. The type of supporting information that is used primarily to create a mental picture consists of
   a. research evidence.
   b. comparisons.
   c. reasons.
   d. description.

_____ 4. The primary purpose of an example is to
   a. support ideas with facts and statistics.
   b. highlight differences between two ideas.
   c. illustrate how an idea can be applied to a real situation.
   d. help the reader visualize a process.

_____ 5. Transitional words and phrases such as "on the other hand" and "however" suggest the organizational pattern called
   a. comparison–contrast.
   b. cause-and-effect.
   c. enumeration.
   d. time sequence.

APPLYING YOUR SKILLS

_____ 6. For Louise's biology paper, she wants to explain the various stages that a pol-
liwog goes through before becoming a frog. The best way for her to present this information would be to use a
   a. time sequence pattern.
   b. cause-and-effect pattern.
   c. classification pattern.
   d. definition pattern.

_____ 7. Dean is writing a research paper using the cause–effect organizational pattern. Of the following topics, the one most likely to be written by Dean is
   a. measurement of personality traits.
   b. sources of stress.
   c. limitations of objective tests.
   d. classification of mental disorders.

_____ 8. Mykaela is attempting to identify organizational patterns in articles she is reading for her economics class. To help her identify the comparison and contrast pattern, Mykaela should look for
   a. the meaning of a term or phrase.
   b. events, processes, and procedures.
   c. differences among similar situations.
   d. "if . . . then" relationships.

_____ 9. Miguel wrote a paper in which he stated that several factors, including unemployment, poverty, and decreased police protection, were responsible for the current high crime rate in his city. The cause–effect pattern that Miguel used in his paper was
   a. single cause–single effect.
   b. multiple causes–single effect.
   c. single cause–multiple effects.
   d. multiple causes–multiple effects.

_____ 10. Kelli is writing an article for the college newspaper listing the wide variety of activities available on campus. Kelli is using enumeration as the organizational pattern for this information because the list
   a. has no inherent order or connection.
   b. is based on the relationship between events.
   c. has its own specialized terminology.
   d. focuses primarily on why and how things happen.

MULTIMEDIA *Activities*

Following Thought Patterns

1 Visit the "Today in History" page at the Library of Congress Web site,

http://memory.loc.gov/ammem/today/today.html

Read one of the articles. What is the subject of the article? What is the controlling idea?

2 Rhetorical Patterns for Organizing Documents

http://www.ecf.utoronto.ca/~writing/handbook-rhetoric.html

The University of Toronto presents this site that reviews the ways that information is organized.

3 Logic Patterns

http://bsc.edu/~emoore/lspage3.html

Try these online logic pattern activities from the Teacher's Lab, the Annenberg/CPB Math and Science Project.

4 You will find controlling ideas and supporting evidence in all kinds of reading material, not only in textbooks. Look at this football card, for example. What types of supporting evidence for the player's excellence—examples, reasons, descriptions, facts and statistics, research evidence—do you find?

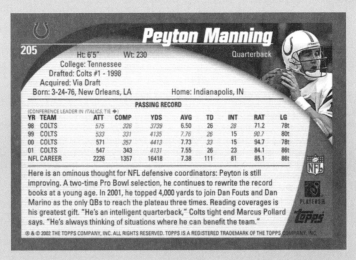

5 Think about another course you are taking or have taken. For each of the organizational patterns listed in Figure 7-3, give one specific example of information that was organized using that pattern.

8 Reading Graphics and Technical Writing

Why Read Graphics?

■ Graphics—pictures of information—help you study complex ideas quickly and efficiently.

■ Graphics condense and organize information that may be complicated and difficult to remember.

■ Graphics display trends and patterns in a clear form so you can better see differences or changes.

Learning Experiment

Step 1

Read the following paragraph and answer the question that follows.

Of all living things, 75.7 percent are animals; 15.4 percent are plants; 4.6 percent are protists; 4.1 percent are fungi; 2 percent are bacteria. Within the animal kingdom, the largest group is insects comprising 72.7 percent of all animal species. Vertebrates represent 3.9 percent, while Arachnids represent 5.7 percent of animal species. Mollusks represent 5.3 percent, Crustaceans represent 3.0 percent, roundworms represent 1.9 percent, and miscellaneous species represent 7.5 percent. Among the vertebrates, fishes comprise 48 percent, reptiles comprise 14 percent, birds comprise 19 percent, mammals comprise 9 percent, and amphibians comprise 10 percent.

Question: What single species comprises the smallest percentage of vertebrates?

Step 2

Study the circle graphs in Figure 8-1 and answer the question that follows.

Question: What single species comprises the smallest percentage of vertebrates?

The Results

For which question was it easier to locate the answer? Which took less time to answer? Why? The second question was easier because the graphs presented a visual representation. You could easily see which portion of the circle labelled vertebrate was the smallest.

Learning Principle
(What This Means to You)

Visualization enables you to grasp ideas, see relationships, and recall information easily. At times, textbook authors will present information visually; other times you may have to create your own visual images. In this chapter you will learn to use visual aids as a learning tool.

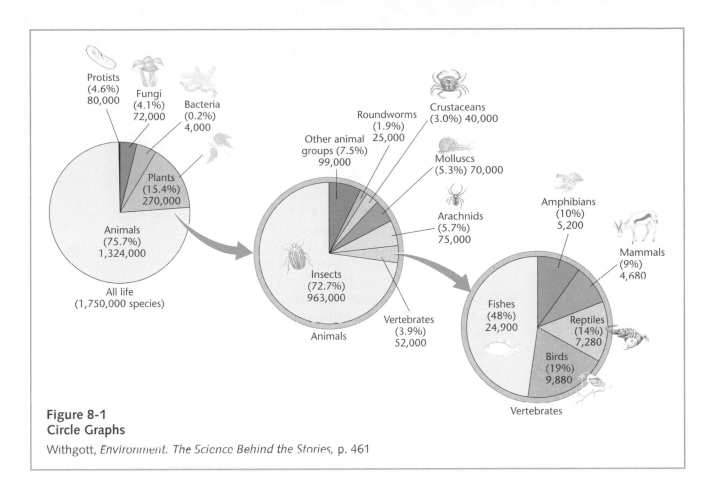

Figure 8-1
Circle Graphs

Withgott, *Environment. The Science Behind the Stories*, p. 461

READING GRAPHICS

Highly detailed specific information is often an integral part of course content. For instance, a sociology course may involve crime-rate statistics, a chemistry course is concerned with the characteristics of atomic particles, and an art history course focuses on historical periods.

These kinds of highly specialized information are presented in two unique ways: (1) graphics and (2) technical writing. The term *graphics* refers to all forms of visual representation of information, including maps, charts, tables, and diagrams. Textbooks in many academic disciplines use graphics to organize and present information. *Technical writing* is the compact, precise, and detailed presentation of factual information intended for practical use or application. Applications may include, for example, solving a problem in chemistry, writing a computer program, or operating a fax machine. College courses in the sciences, applied technologies, business, and specialized careers all demand technical reading skills. The purpose of this chapter is to present strategies for reading graphics and for approaching technical writing.

Some students are tempted to skip over graphs, tables, and diagrams. Stopping to study graphics requires time and seems to interrupt the flow of reading. Others think, incorrectly, that because the accompanying text explains the graphic, the graphic is unimportant. Actually, graphics are usually *more* important than the paragraphs that surround them. They are included to call your attention to, emphasize, and further explain the subject at hand.

Reading graphics enables you to analyze and synthesize information. It is never enough (and it is often unnecessary) to know each individual piece of information presented in a graph or chart. Instead, you must draw together the information to determine what it *means*.

Here is a general strategy for reading graphics. More specific suggestions for each type of graphic will follow.

1. **Read the title or caption.** The title will identify the subject and may suggest what relationship is being described.
2. **Determine how the graphic is organized.** Read the column headings or labels on the horizontal and vertical axes.
3. **Identify the variables.** Decide what is being compared with what or what relationship is being described.
4. **Anticipate the purpose.** On the basis of what you have seen, predict what the graphic is intended to show. Is its purpose to show change over time, describe a process, compare costs, or present statistics?
5. **Determine scale, values, or units of measurement.**
6. **Study the data to identify trends or patterns.** Note changes, unusual statistics, and any unexplained variations.
7. **Draw connections with the chapter content.** Take a moment to discover why the graphic was included and what concepts or key points it illustrates or explains.
8. **Make a brief summary note.** In the margin, jot a brief note about the trend or pattern the graphic emphasizes. Writing will crystallize the idea in your mind, and your note will be useful when you review.

TYPES OF GRAPHICS

There are many types of graphics; each accomplishes specific purposes for the writer, and each describes a particular relationship.

Applying Levels of Thinking
GRAPHICS AND LEVELS OF THINKING

Reading graphics involves several levels of thinking. Your first task is to comprehend the information presented in the graphic. Then you move to analysis, synthesis, and evaluation by focusing on what the graph means or how it can be interpreted. Here is a list of questions to guide your thinking about graphics.

Level of Thinking	Question
Remembering and Understanding	What factual information does the graphic present?
Applying	How can this information be applied to ideas presented in the chapter or to my own experience?
Analyzing	What changes or variations occur in the data?
Evaluating	Of what use or value are these trends or patterns?
Creating	What trends or patterns are evident?

Figure 8-2
A Sample Table

HUMAN POPULATION TRENDS, 1900–2100					
	POPULATION (MILLIONS)				
	1900	1950	2000	2025	2100
Developing regions (total)	1,070	1,681	4,837	6,799	8,748
Africa	133	224	872	1,617	2,591
Asia[a]	867	1,292	3,419	4,403	4,919
Latin America	70	165	546	779	1,238
Developed regions (total)	560	835	1,284	1,407	1,437
Europe, USSR, Japan, Oceania[b]	478	669	987	1,062	1,055
Canada, United States	82	166	297	345	382
World total	1,630	2,516	6,121	8,206	10,185

[a]Excludes Japan.
[b]Includes Australia and New Zealand.
Mix, Farber, and King, *Biology: The Network of Life,* p. 165.

Tables

A table is an organized display of factual information, usually numbers or statistics. Its purpose is to present large amounts of information in a condensed and systematically arranged form. It's easy to make comparisons between or among data. Take a few minutes to study the table in Figure 8-2. Then use the tips listed below.

1. **Determine how the data are classified or divided.** The table shown in Figure 8-2 classifies population growth by year and subdivides it by region (developing or developed).
2. **Make comparisons and look for trends or patterns.** This step involves looking at the rows and columns, noting how each compares with the others. Look for similarities, differences, and sudden changes or variations. Underline or highlight unusual or outstanding data. Try to note increases or decreases that seem unusually high or low. Also note trends in the data. For example, in Figure 8-2, you might note that Asia has the highest population by far at every point or that population growth is projected to slow down in the twenty-first century in developed regions.
3. **Draw conclusions.** Decide what the data mean and what they suggest about the subject at hand. Examine the paragraphs that correspond to the table for clues, or sometimes direct statements, about the purpose of the graph. You can conclude from Figure 8-2 that the world population in general has grown tremendously since 1900 and that a vast majority of the growth has occurred in developing countries.

EXERCISE 1

DIRECTIONS   Study the table in Figure 8-3 (p.194) and answer the questions that follow.

1. Which income level had the smallest percentage of people that attended political meetings or rallies?
2. What income level tried most to influence the votes of others?

Figure 8-3
A Sample Table

POLITICAL PARTICIPATION BY FAMILY INCOME

The following table shows, by their income status, the percentage of the adult population who said they participated in various forms of political activity.

	Gave $ to a party or candidate	Attended political meetings/rallies	Tried to influence votes of others
Family Income			
very low	3	5	21
low	3	3	22
middle	5	4	26
high	12	7	35
very high	25	15	43

Source: National Election Study
Edwards, Wattenberg, and Lineberry, *Government in America,* p. 113.

3. What percentage of the middle-income population gave money to a party or candidate?
4. What percentage of the high-income population attended political meetings or rallies?
5. Which income level was consistently the most involved in politics?

Graphs

There are two primary types of graphs: bar graphs and linear graphs. Each plots a set of points on a set of axes.

Bar Graphs

A bar graph makes comparisons between quantities or amounts. It is particularly useful in showing changes that occur with passing time. Bar graphs usually are designed to emphasize differences. The graph shown in Figure 8-4 (p. 195) displays the percentage of the world's population living in urban areas. It makes it easy to see at a glance how the percentage of city dwellers will increase until the year 2025.

Multiple Bar Graphs

A multiple bar graph displays at least two or three comparisons simultaneously. Figure 8-5 (p. 195) compares male and female preferences for private brands of food products by age group.

Stacked Bar Graphs

In a stacked bar graph, instead of bars being arranged side by side, they are placed one on top of another. This variation is often used to emphasize whole/part relationships—that is, to show what part of an entire group or class a particular item accounts for. Stacked bar graphs also make numerous comparisons possible. The graph in Figure 8-6 (p. 196) enables you to compare responses to a question about care of elderly parents by religion and race and shows a national response as well.

**Figure 8-4
A Sample Bar Graph**

Kaufman and Franz,
*Biosphere 2000:
Protecting the Global
Environment,* p. 143

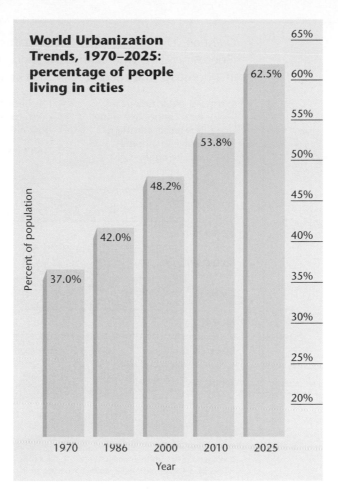

**Figure 8-5
A Sample Multiple Bar
Graph**

Pride and Ferrell,
*Marketing: Concepts and
Strategies,* p. 329

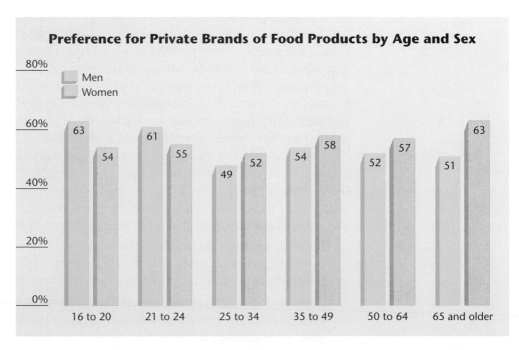

**Figure 8-6
A Sample Stacked
Bar Graph**

Skolnick, *The Intimate
Environment:
Exploring Marriage
and Family*, p. 443

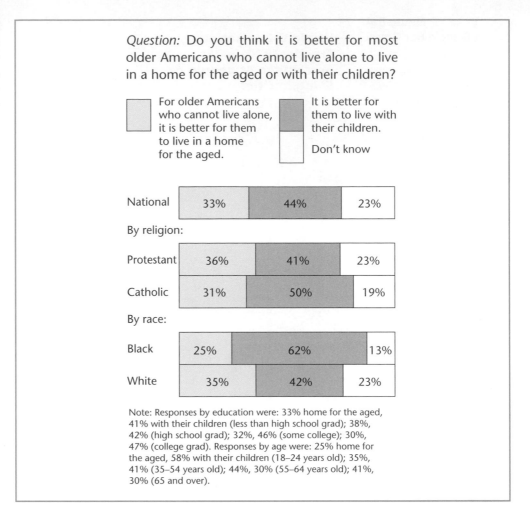

Question: Do you think it is better for most older Americans who cannot live alone to live in a home for the aged or with their children?

☐ For older Americans who cannot live alone, it is better for them to live in a home for the aged.

☐ It is better for them to live with their children.

☐ Don't know

National	33%	44%	23%

By religion:

Protestant	36%	41%	23%
Catholic	31%	50%	19%

By race:

Black	25%	62%	13%
White	35%	42%	23%

Note: Responses by education were: 33% home for the aged, 41% with their children (less than high school grad); 38%, 42% (high school grad); 32%, 46% (some college); 30%, 47% (college grad). Responses by age were: 25% home for the aged, 58% with their children (18–24 years old); 35%, 41% (35–54 years old); 44%, 30% (55–64 years old); 41%, 30% (65 and over).

Linear Graphs

In a linear graph, or line graph, points are plotted along a vertical and a horizontal axis and then connected to form a line. A linear graph allows more data points than a bar graph. Consequently, it is used to present more detailed and/or larger quantities of information. A linear graph may represent the relationship between two variables; if so, it consists of a single line. More often, however, linear graphs are used to compare relationships among several variables, and multiple lines are included. The graph shown in Figure 8-7 shows the changes in population percentages for various minority groups from 1995 to 2050.

Linear graphs are generally used to display continuous data—data that are connected in time or events that occur in sequence. The data in Figure 8-7 move from 1995 to 2050.

Single linear graphs can display one of three general relationships: positive, negative, or independent. Each of these is shown in Figure 8-8.

Positive relationship. When the variables increase or decrease at the same time, the relationship is positive and is shown by a line that climbs up from left to right. In graph A, as years in school increase, so does income.

Inverse (or negative) relationship. When one variable increases as the other decreases, the relationship is inverse, or negative. In graph B, as the years of education increase, the number of children decreases.

**Figure 8-7
A Sample Linear Graph**

United States
Census Bureau

Edwards, Wattenberg, and
Lineberry, *Government in
America*, p. 180

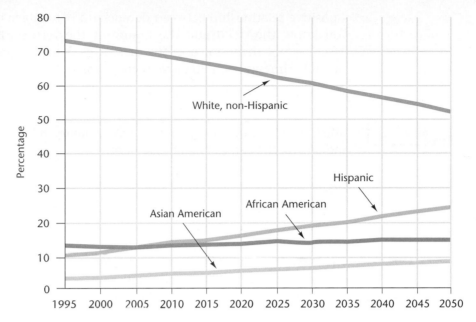

**Figure 8-8
Linear Graph
Relationships**

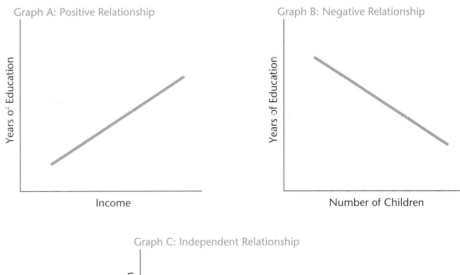

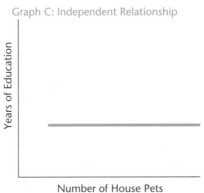

Independent relationship. When the variables have no effect on each other, the relationship is independent. In graph C, years in school have no effect on number of house pets.

The linear graph in Figure 8-7 shows an overall positive relationship between year and all three non-white groups. Between 1900 and 2025, we can see a steady increase in percentage of the population each group comprises, indicating a positive relationship between decade and percentage of the population. Once you know the trend and the nature of the relationship that a linear graph describes, jot them down in the margin next to the graph. These notes will be valuable timesavers as you review the chapter.

EXERCISE 2

DIRECTIONS   Study the graphs shown in Figures 8-9 through 8-11 (pp. 199–200) and answer the corresponding questions.

Figure 8-9: A Multiple Bar Graph (p. 199)

1. What is the purpose of the graph in Figure 8-9?
2. From which social group do Republicans receive the greatest support?
3. From which social group do Democrats receive the greatest support?
4. In which social groups is there the largest split between Democrats and Republicans? In which social groups is there the smallest split?
5. With which part is a female Hispanic over 65 years of age likely to affiliate herself?

Figure 8-10: Stacked Bar Graphs (pp. 199–200)

1. What is the purpose of the two graphs?
2. What age group is projected to increase the most by 2050?
3. In 2000, in which age groups were there more men than women alive?
4. Which age groups will show the least amount of change from 2000 to 2050?

Figure 8-11: A Linear Graph (p. 200)

1. What variables does Figure 8-11 compare?
2. At what stages are women more satisfied than men?
3. Is there a positive, a negative, or an independent relationship between marital satisfaction and child rearing?
4. At what stage(s) is men's satisfaction increasing while women's satisfaction is decreasing?
5. What overall trend does this graph display?

Charts

Four types of charts are commonly used in college textbooks: pie charts, organizational charts, flowcharts, and pictograms. Each is intended to display a relationship, either quantitative or cause–effect.

Pie Charts

Pie charts, sometimes called circle graphs, are used to show whole/part relationships or to show how given parts of a unit have been divided or classified. They let the reader compare the parts with each other as well as compare each part with the whole. Figure 8-12 (p. 201), taken from a health textbook, shows the percentages of deaths from different cardiovascular diseases. It provides a clear visual as well as a statistical comparison of these eight different categories.

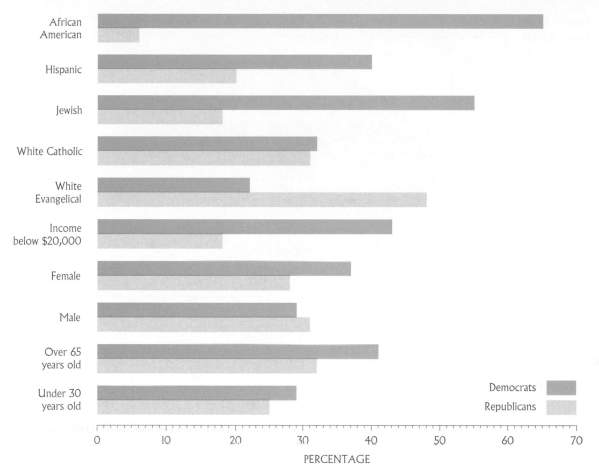

Figure 8-9
A Multiple Bar Graph
Source: Pew Research Center *[http://people-press.org/commentary/display.php3?AnalysisID=95]*
Edwards, Wattenberg, and Lineberry, *Government in America*, p. 180

Figure 8-10
A Stacked Bar Graph

U.S. Census Bureau,
International Data Base.

Wright, *Environmental
Science: Toward a
Sustainable Future*, p. 139

(Continued)

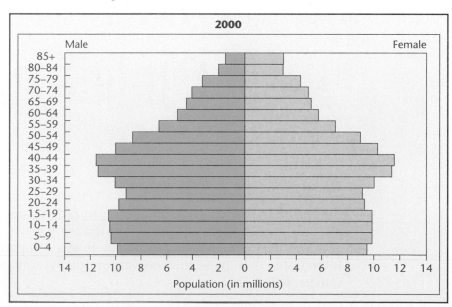

Population Profiles of the United States

**Figure 8-10
A Stacked Bar Graph**
(Continued)

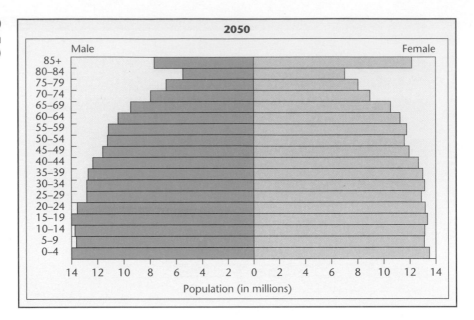

**Figure 8-11
A Linear Graph**

Rollins, *Journal of
Marriage and the
Family*, p. 26

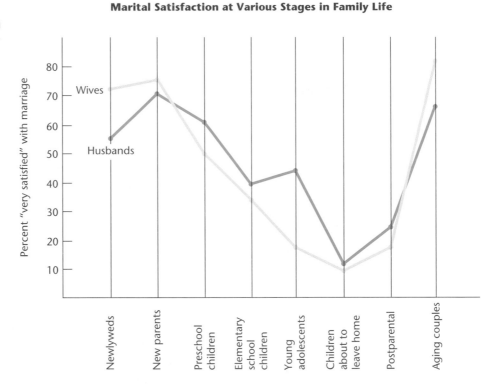

Organizational Charts

An organizational chart divides an organization, such as a corporation, a hospital, or a university, into its administrative parts, staff positions, or lines of authority. Figure 8-13 shows the structure of a company organized by function. It indicates that there are four major subdivisions and depicts divisions of responsibility for each.

**Figure 8-12
A Sample Pie Chart**

Donatelle, *Health: The Basics*, p. 288

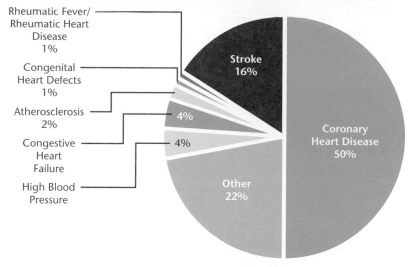

PERCENTAGE BREAKDOWN OF DEATHS FROM CARDIOVASCULAR DISEASES

**Figure 8-13
A Sample
Organizational Chart**

Hitt et al., *Management*, p. 241

Flowcharts

A flowchart is a specialized type of chart that shows how a process or procedure works. Lines or arrows are used to indicate the path (route or routes) through the procedure. Various shapes (boxes, circles, rectangles) enclose what is done at each stage or step. You could draw, for example, a flowchart to describe how to apply for and obtain a student loan or how to locate a malfunction in your car's electrical system. The flowchart shown in Figure 8-14 (p. 202), taken from a business information systems textbook, describes how a payroll system functions. The chart reveals a four-step process and describes the parts of each step.

To read flowcharts effectively, use the following suggestions:

1. **Determine what process the flowchart shows.**
2. **Next, follow the chart, using the arrows and reading each step.** Start at the top or far left of the chart.
3. **When you've finished, describe the process in your own words.** Try to draw the chart from memory without referring to the text. Compare your drawing with the chart, and take note of anything you forgot or misplaced.

**Figure 8-14
A Sample Flowchart**

Nickerson, *Business
and Information
Systems*, p. 309

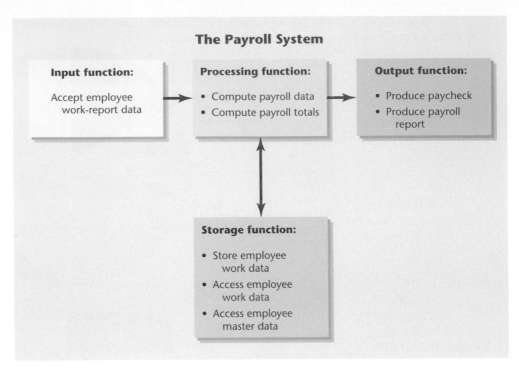

**Figure 8-15
A Sample Pictogram**

Donatelle, *Health: The Basics*, p. 386

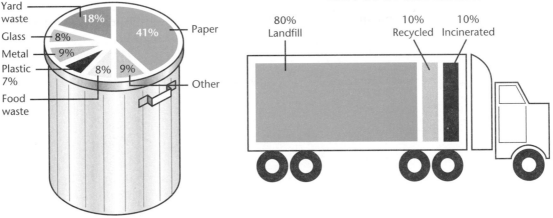

Pictograms

A combination of a chart and a graph, a pictogram uses symbols or drawings (such as books, cars, or buildings), instead of bars or lines, to represent specified amounts. This type of chart tends to be visually appealing, makes statistics seem realistic, and may carry an emotional impact. For example, a chart that uses stick-figure drawings of pregnant women to indicate the number of abortions performed each year per state may have a greater impact than statistics presented in numerical form. A sample pictogram is shown in Figure 8-15 above. This pictogram uses a garbage can to represent the types of trash and a truck to represent what happens to the trash.

EXERCISE 3   DIRECTIONS   Study the charts shown in Figures 8-16 below and 8-17 on page 204, and answer the corresponding questions.

Figure 8-16: Pie Charts

1. What is the purpose of the charts?
2. From which source does the largest percentage of the federal budget come?
3. What percentage of the federal budget is used for national defense?
4. Are the pie charts more or less effective than a bar graph containing the same data? Why?

Figure 8-17: A Flowchart

1. What process does this flowchart describe?
2. What is the purpose of the boxes that mention Richard?
3. Invent another situation and another person that could be used to replace the boxes describing Richard's behavior.
4. What other outcomes are possible for Richard?

Diagrams

Diagrams often are included in technical and scientific as well as business and social science texts to explain processes. Diagrams are intended to help you see relationships between parts and understand what follows what. Figure 8-18 (p. 205), taken from a biology textbook, depicts a plant stem and shows how a plant's history is revealed by stem growth.

Reading diagrams differs from reading other types of graphics in that diagrams often correspond to fairly large segments of text, and you have to switch back and forth frequently between the text and the diagram to determine what part of the process each paragraph refers to.

Because diagrams of processes and their corresponding text are often difficult, complicated, or highly technical, plan on reading these sections more than once. Use the first reading to grasp the overall process. In later readings, focus on

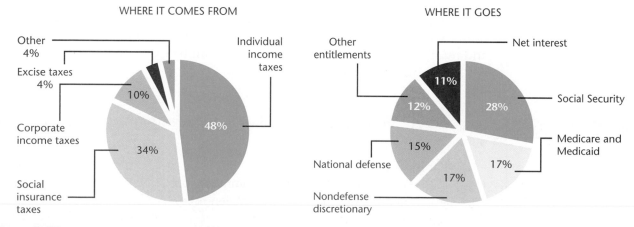

THE FEDERAL GOVERNMENT DOLLAR

WHERE IT COMES FROM

- Other 4%
- Excise taxes 4%
- Corporate income taxes 10%
- Social insurance taxes 34%
- Individual income taxes 48%

WHERE IT GOES

- Other entitlements 12%
- Net interest 11%
- National defense 15%
- Nondefense discretionary 17%
- Medicare and Medicaid 17%
- Social Security 28%

Figure 8-16
Pie Charts

Edwards, Wattenberg, and Lineberry, *Government in America*, p. 474

Figure 8-17
A Sample Flowchart

Solomon, *Consumer Behavior*, p. 293

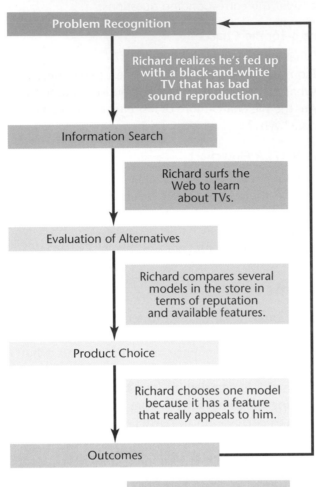

STAGES IN CONSUMER DECISION MAKING

Problem Recognition

Richard realizes he's fed up with a black-and-white TV that has bad sound reproduction.

Information Search

Richard surfs the Web to learn about TVs.

Evaluation of Alternatives

Richard compares several models in the store in terms of reputation and available features.

Product Choice

Richard chooses one model because it has a feature that really appeals to him.

Outcomes

Richard brings home the TV and enjoys his purchase.

the details of the process, examining each step and understanding the progression to the next.

One of the best ways to study a diagram is to redraw it without referring to the original, including as much detail as possible. Or test your understanding and recall of the process explained in a diagram by explaining it, step by step in writing, using your own words.

EXERCISE 4

DIRECTIONS   Study the diagram shown in Figure 8-19 (p. 206) and answer the questions that follow.

1. What is the purpose of the diagram?
2. What amendment process is most commonly used?
3. Name two processes that have never been used.

Maps

Maps describe relationships and provide information about location and direction. They are commonly found in geography and history texts, and they also

**Figure 8-18
A Sample Diagram**

Wallace, *Biology: The World of Life*, p. 321

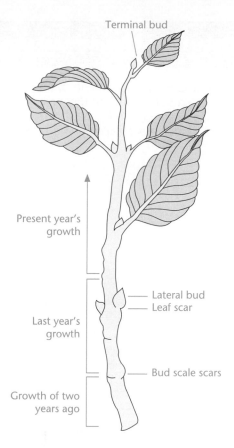

The growth area of a stem. One can read a bit of the plant's history by noting the distance between bud scale scars, the distance being greater for good years when the stem has been able to grow rapidly.

appear in ecology, biology, and anthropology texts. Although most of us think of maps as describing distances and locations, maps also are used to describe placement of geographical and ecological features such as areas of pollution, areas of population density, and political data (voting districts).

When reading maps, use the following steps:

1. **Read the caption.** This identifies the subject of the map.
2. **Use the legend or key to identify the symbols or codes used.**
3. **Note distance scales.**
4. **Study the map, looking for trends or key points.** Often the text that accompanies the map states the key points that the map illustrates.
5. **Try to create a mental picture of the map.**
6. **As a learning and study aid, write, in your own words, a statement of what the map shows.**

Now look at the map shown in Figure 8-20 (p. 207). Its key depicts boxes with various numbers of days in a school year; the more days per year, the larger the box. Using this code, you can quickly locate those countries with the most and fewest school days by looking for the largest and smallest boxes. For example, Japanese students attend school the most days (243), whereas Belgian students attend the fewest (168). You can also observe that in general, nations in

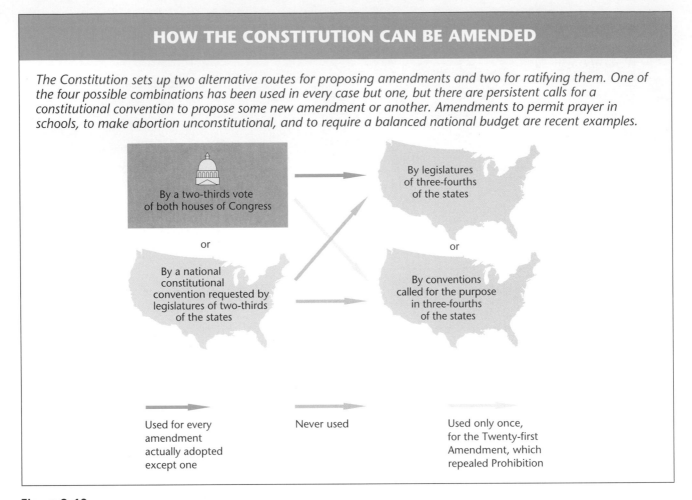

HOW THE CONSTITUTION CAN BE AMENDED

The Constitution sets up two alternative routes for proposing amendments and two for ratifying them. One of the four possible combinations has been used in every case but one, but there are persistent calls for a constitutional convention to propose some new amendment or another. Amendments to permit prayer in schools, to make abortion unconstitutional, and to require a balanced national budget are recent examples.

Figure 8-19
A Diagram

Edwards, Wattenberg, and Lineberry, *Government in America*, p. 47

the Far East have the most school days, whereas students in North and South America attend far fewer days.

Cartoons

Cartoons are included in textbooks to make a point quickly or simply to lighten the text by adding a touch of humor about the topic at hand. Cartoons usually appear without a title or legend and there is often no reference within the text to the cartoon.

Cartoons can make abstract ideas and concepts concrete and real. Pay close attention to cartoons, especially if you are a visually-oriented learner. They may help you recall ideas easily by serving as a recall clue that triggers your memory of related material.

The cartoon shown in Figure 8-21 appears in a sociology textbook chapter titled "Socialization and Gender." It appears on a page that dicusses gender roles learned during childhood.

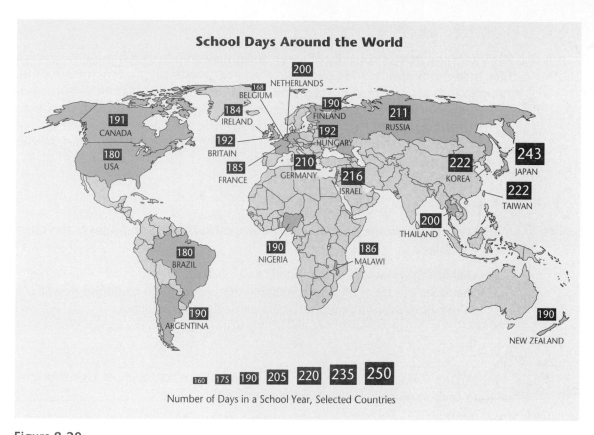

Figure 8-20
A Sample Map

Applebaum and Chambliss, *Sociology*, p. 427

Figure 8-21
A Sample Cartoon

Photographs

Although sometimes considered an art form instead of a graphic, photographs, like other graphics, can be used in place of words to present information. Photographs also are used to spark your interest and, often, to draw out an emotional response or feeling. The caption on a photograph often provides a clue to its intended meaning. As you study a photograph, ask "What is my first overall impression?" and "What details did I notice first?" These questions will lead you to discover the purpose of the photograph.

EXERCISE 5

DIRECTIONS   Study the photographs shown in Figure 8-22 and answer the questions that follow.

1. What are the photographs intended to emphasize?
2. What does this set of photographs show that a paragraph could not describe?
3. List details in the photograph that are particularly compelling.

EXERCISE 6

DIRECTIONS   Indicate what type(s) of graphic(s) would be most useful in presenting each of the following sets of information:

1. Damage done to ancient carved figures by sulfur dioxide in the air
2. A comparison of the types of products the United States imports with those it exports
3. Changes in worker productivity each year from 1970 through 2000 in Japan, France, Germany, and the United States
4. The probabilities of being murdered, broken down by various racial and ethnic groups in the United States
5. Foreign revenue, total revenue, foreign operating profit, foreign assets, and total assets for the ten largest American multinational corporations
6. Living arrangements (one parent, two parents, neither parent) for white, black, and Spanish-origin children under 18 years of age in 1960, 1970, 1980, 1990, and 2000
7. The basic components of a robot's manipulator arm
8. A description of how the AIDS virus affects the immune system
9. Sites of the earliest Neanderthal discoveries in Western Europe
10. Number of receipts of, and profits for, three types of businesses: sole proprietorships, partnerships, and corporations

READING TECHNICAL WRITING

Technical writing is commonly thought of as something science or engineering students read. Actually, technical writing is by no means restricted to traditional technical or scientific fields. Technical writing is what most of us are called on to read in our daily lives as well as in many academic courses. Here are a few examples of situations, both everyday and academic, that require reading technical writing.

**Figure 8-22
Photographs**

Everyday Situations

1. Reading directions to set up your programmable telephone
2. Assembling a bicycle from printed instructions
3. Consulting a repair manual to troubleshoot problems in your car's engine

Academic Situations

1. Reading end-of-the-year financial reports to assess a corporation's financial health for a business class project

2. Consulting the *Journal of Abnormal Psychology* to complete a psychology term paper on characteristics of the manic-depressive personality
3. Referring to a technical manual to find out how to save a file in a new word processing program

Technical writing, then, is an important part of everyday activities and of many academic disciplines. Technical reading skills are essential in both the everyday and the academic world. This portion of the chapter will discuss and describe technical writing and offer suggestions for reading it effectively.

How Technical Writing Is Different

You already know that technical writing is different, but do you know how it differs from other types of writing? Take a moment now and think about what you already know about technical writing.

Now expand your knowledge by comparing several sample pieces of writing, one of which is a technical one. All of the following excerpts concern the same topic: birds. After you have read all three, complete Exercise 7.

Sample 1

"You would know the heron if you saw it," the stranger continued eagerly. "A queer, tall white bird with soft feathers and long thin legs. And it would have a nest perhaps in the top of a high tree, made of sticks, something like a hawk's nest."

Sylvia's heart gave a wild beat; she knew that strange white bird, and had once stolen softly near where it stood in some bright green swamp grass, away over at the other side of the woods. There was an open place where the sunshine always seemed strangely yellow and hot, where tall, nodding rushes grew, and her grandmother had warned her that she might sink in the soft black mud underneath and never be heard of more. Not far beyond were the salt marshes just this side of the sea itself, which Sylvia wondered and dreamed much about, but never had seen, whose great voice could sometimes be heard above the noise of the woods on stormy nights.

—Jewett, Sarah, "A White Heron"

Sample 2

At once a voice arose among
   The bleak twigs overhead
In a full-hearted evensong
   Of joy unlimited;
An aged thrush, frail, gaunt, and small
   In blast-beruffled plume,
Had chosen thus to fling his soul
   Upon the growing gloom.

—Hardy, Thomas, "The Darkling Thrush"

Sample 3

THRUSH. In the large thrush family of birds are some of the finest singers—the robin, the bluebird, and the nightingale, as well as those commonly known as thrushes. Although most of them are feathered in browns and buffs, some thrushes—such as the robin and the bluebird—have bright colors.

Whatever the color of the parent birds, all young thrushes have spotted breasts until their first autumn molt. Some species nest and live in trees, others on the ground; some feed on insects, others on fruits. In England the mavis, or song thrush, the missel thrush, and the nightingale are the best-known species. In the United States the wood thrush, the hermit thrush, and the veery are among the best known of the family. These are slender brown birds.

The wood thrush often nests in wooded city lots. The hermit prefers secluded northern forests. The veery's home is in low, wet woodlands with dense underbrush. They lay three or four greenish-blue eggs. The willow thrush is a western subspecies of the veery. (See also *Birds; Bluebird; Nightingale; Robin.*)

The scientific name of the thrush family is Turdidae; of the wood thrush, *Hylocichla mustelina;* of the hermit thrush, *H. guttata;* of the veery and willow thrush, *H. fuscescens.*

—*Compton's Interactive Encyclopedia,* p. 495

Sample 1, an excerpt from an essay titled "A White Heron," presents an everyday description of the heron—a sense of oddness and awkwardness is revealed through the description.

Sample 2 is an excerpt from a poem titled "The Darkling Thrush," by Thomas Hardy. Here the bird and its song are presented in contrast to a gloomy depressing scene.

Sample 3, an excerpt from an encyclopedia entry on thrushes, presents factual information about the bird's appearance and habitat.

DIRECTIONS By comparing and contrasting the three samples just given, list additional features of technical writing that you have discovered. Then compare your list with the information that appears in Figure 8-23 (p. 212).

Tips for Reading Technical Material

Use the following suggestions about reading rates, rereading, prereading, reading text, and visualization when reading technical material.

Adjust Your Reading Rate

Because technical writing is factual and contains numerous illustrations, diagrams, and sample problems, you should read more slowly. Plan on spending twice as long reading a technical textbook as you spend reading nontechnical texts.

Plan on Rereading

Do not expect to understand everything the first time you read the assignment. It is helpful to read an assignment once rather quickly to get an overview of it. Then reread it to learn the details.

Preread Carefully

Because technical material often deals with unfamiliar subject matter about which you have little or no background knowledge, prereading is a particularly important skill.

Alternate Between Reading Text and Studying Graphics

Drawings and illustrations are referred to frequently in surrounding text. Consequently, it is often necessary to alternate between text and graphics. Page

**Figure 8-23
Characteristics of
Technical Writing**

Characteristic	Description
Purpose	To supply the reader with needed information to perform a task, understand a situation, solve a problem, make a decision.
Fact density	Facts are abundant and usually are presented as compactly as possible.
Exact word choice	Meaning must be clear and without possibility of confusion or misinterpretation.
Technical/specialized vocabulary	Because meaning must be exact, technical or specialized vocabulary is often introduced. These words have specific meanings within the field or discipline and often serve as shortcuts to the lengthy descriptions or details that would be necessary if nonspecialized language were used.
Abbreviations and notation systems	An extensive system of abbreviation and notations (signs and symbols) is used. These are also shortcuts to writing out complete words or meanings and are often used in diagrams, formulas, and drawings.
Graphics	Most technical writing contains numerous drawings, charts, tables, diagrams, or graphs. They are included to clarify, help you visualize, and emphasize key information.
Examples and sample problems	Technical textbooks often contain numerous examples and sample problems. These are included to illustrate how information is used and instructions are applied.
Specific formats	Technical writing often follows specific formats. A lab report has a specific organization. A psychologist's case report has specific categories. Research reports in the sciences typically include a statement of problem, a description of experimental design, and so forth.

arrangement is often confusing, and a diagram and the paragraph that explains it may not be on the same page. Other times, a diagram may appear before it is referred to in the text. Use the following strategy:

1. **Notice the types of illustrations and drawings as you preread the material.**
2. **As soon as a graphic is mentioned in the text, locate and study it. Titles, captions, and labels are important.**
3. **If a graphic appears before its text reference, notice its title, and keep reading until it is introduced.**
4. **Plan to stop reading frequently to refer to graphics.** For instance, when reading about the function of specific parts of a piece of equipment, each time a specific part is mentioned, refer to the diagram and locate the part. Then read the description of its function.

Use Visualization

Visualization is a process of creating mental pictures or images. As you read, try to visualize the process or procedure being described. Make your image as specific and detailed as possible. Visualization will make reading these descriptions easier, as well as improve your ability to recall details. Here are a couple of examples of how students use visualizations.

- A nursing student reading about methods of arranging intravenous tubing for administering two solutions simultaneously visualized the arrangement of clamps, tubing, and bottles
- A communications student studying types of nonverbal communication visualized himself using each form

Now read the following description of paramecia and try to visualize as you read.

> If you should find yourself with a microscope and unable to resist examining the water of a scummy pond, you would likely find great numbers of tiny protozoans. Some of these would be covered with tiny, hairlike cilia. Protists that bear cilia at some stage in the life cycle comprise the phylum ciliophora. The most familiar of these are the Paramecia. Paramecia (singular, Paramecium) are recognizable by their slipper shape, which is maintained by their outer thickened membrane, the pellicle. The pellicle, while holding its form, is flexible enough to enable the paramecium to bend around objects as it furiously swims through the water propelled by the wave-like actions of the cilia covering its body. Behind its rounded anterior (or front) end lies a deep oral groove into which food is swept by other cilia. The food is then forced through a mouthlike pore (cytostome) at the end of the groove and into a bulbous opening, which will break away and move into the cytoplasm as a food vacuole.
>
> —Wallace, *Biology: The World of Life*, pp. 237–38

Tips for Studying Technical Material

Use the following suggestions to learn technical material:

Study Daily

Because technical material may be unfamiliar, frequent contact with the material is necessary if you are to remember it.

Reserve Large Blocks of Time

Large blocks of time are often necessary to complete projects, lab write-ups, or problem sets. Also, technical material requires a particular mind-set, which, once you've established it, is worth continuing.

Learn Technical Vocabulary

Understanding the technical vocabulary in your discipline is essential. For technical and applied fields, it is especially important to learn to pronounce technical terms and use them in your speech and writing. To establish yourself as a professional in the field and to communicate effectively with other professionals, it is vital to speak and use the language. Use the suggestions in Chapter 13 for learning specialized terminology.

Study by Drawing Diagrams and Pictures

Although your textbook may include numerous drawings and illustrations, there is not sufficient space to have drawings for every process. An effective learning strategy is to draw diagrams and pictures whenever possible. These should be fast sketches; be concerned with describing parts or processes, and do not worry about artwork or scale drawings. For example, a student studying air conditioning and refrigeration repair drew a quick sketch of a unit he was to repair in his lab before he began to disassemble it, and he referred to sketches he had drawn in his notebook as he diagnosed the problem.

Focus on Concepts and Principles

Because technical subjects are so detailed, many students get lost in details and lose sight of the concepts and principles to which the details relate. Keep a sheet on which you record information you need to refer to frequently in the front of your notebook for easy reference. Include constants, conversion formulas, metric equivalents, and commonly used abbreviations.

Integrate Lab, Lecture, and Classroom Activities

Many technical courses have a required lab. Because the lab is scheduled separately from the lecture and has its own unique format, you may fail to see the lab as an integral part of the course. The lab is intended to help you understand and apply principles and techniques used in your course and gives you an opportunity to ask questions. Use the following tips for handling lab work:

- Be prepared before going to lab. Read the manual or assignment once to understand its overall purpose and a second time to understand the specific procedures. Make notes or highlight key information.
- Ask questions before you make a mistake. Because procedures can be time-consuming to repeat, ask questions first.
- Be sure you understand the purpose of each step before you perform it.
- Analyze your results and do the follow-up report as soon as possible. The best time to study your results is while the experiment and procedures are still fresh in you mind. If you finish the lab work early, stay and discuss results and interpretations with other students or your lab instructor.
- Follow the required format closely when writing your report.

Use the Glossary and Index

Because of the large number of technical terms, formulas, and notations you will encounter, it is often necessary to refer to definitions and explanations. Place a paper clip at the beginning of the glossary and a second at the index so you can find them easily.

Highlight Selectively

Everything looks (and often is) important in texts, and it is easy to fall into the habit of overhighlighting. Avoid this pitfall by reading a whole paragraph or section before highlighting. Then go back and mark only key terms and concepts. Do not try to highlight all useful facts. Refer to Chapter 14 for suggestions on how to highlight effectively.

Use Outlining

Many students find outlining to be an effective study and review technique. Some texts include chapter outlines, but even though your text may have one, make your own. It is the process of making the outline that is important. Outlining forces you to decide what pieces of information are important and

Figure 8-24
A Sample
Summary Sheet

Month(s)	Activity
1–2	raise head—45 degrees
3	roll—front to back
4	sit with support
6	sit alone
7–12	crawl and creep
7	pull to stand
9	sidestepping
11	stand alone
12	walk

how they are related and then to express the ideas in your own words. Refer to Chapter 15 for specific suggestions on taking outline notes.

Learn Processes and Procedures

Procedures, directions, installations, repairs, instructions, and diagnostic checking procedures all follow the process pattern. To read materials written in this pattern, you must not only learn the steps but also learn them in the correct order. To study process material, use the following tips:

1. **Prepare study sheets that summarize each process.** For example, a psychology student learning the steps in motor development of infants wrote the summary shown in Figure 8-24.
2. **Test your recall by writing out the steps from memory.** Recheck periodically by mentally reviewing each step.
3. **For difficult or long procedures, write each step on a separate index card.** Shuffle the pack and practice putting the cards in the correct order.
4. **Be certain you understand the logic behind the process.** Figure out why each step is done in a specific order.

EXERCISE 8 DIRECTIONS Turn to the article titled "Communication Between Women and Men" in Part Eight on page 466. Write a brief outline for the section titled "Speaking Different Genderlects."

LEARNING COLLABORATIVELY

DIRECTIONS Bring a copy of your local newspaper, a magazine, or *USA Today* to class. After your instructor forms groups, each group should select and tear out four or five graphics. For each graphic, your group should identify the type of graphic, analyze its purpose, and identify the trend or pattern it reveals. In your group, discuss what other types of graphics could be used to accomplish the author's purpose. Working together, your group should choose one graphic to submit to the instructor with a brief summary of your analysis.

APPLYING YOUR LEARNING

Elaine is a liberal arts major who is taking a biology class to fulfill her science requirement. Her reading assignment for this week includes a chapter on plant reproduction and development. It includes numerous complicated diagrams of reproductive life cycles of conifers (a type of evergreen tree) and flowering plants. Elaine is unsure how to approach reading and understanding the material. She is also frustrated because some of the diagrams appear before the part of the chapter that explains them. The chapter also describes, but does not illustrate, the reproductive stages of ferns, mosses, and algae.

1. Give some suggestions to help Elaine read and study the chapter.
2. How should she read and study the diagrams in the chapter?
3. How can Elaine learn and understand the life cycles not illustrated in the chapter?
4. What general suggestions would you offer to help Elaine succeed in a science course that contains a great deal of technical material?

APPLY YOUR SKILLS: Sample Textbook Chapter

1. Evaluate Figure 9-1 on page 516. What is its purpose?
2. The text includes five photographs. What is the purpose of each? Answer the "Skills Viewpoint" text that accompanies each photo.
3. Why were the cartoons on pages 518 and 525 included? What chapter content do they illustrate?
4. Study Table 9-1 on page 524 and read the corresponding text. What is its purpose? Answer the question posed in the text within the table.

QUESTIONS FOR DISCUSSION

1. What are the characteristics of good graphic material? When creating graphics, which of these characteristics are most important to consider? Bring some examples of good and bad graphics to class to review and critique.
2. Identify the types of technical writing a person might frequently encounter in various types of careers. What are some ways that you can become more familiar with these types of information before beginning your chosen career?
3. Do you prefer to read essays and texts with or without graphics? Which learning styles are best suited for graphics use?
4. Examine a paper that you recently wrote. Where could you have added graphics to make your points more clearly?

SELF-TEST SUMMARY

1. What steps can be taken to read graphic material more effectively?

Graphics condense information and enable the reader to see patterns, identify trends, observe variations, and interpret information. To get the most from all types of graphics, you should begin by reading the title or caption and determining how the graphic is organized, what its purpose is, what variables are being presented, and what scale, values, or units of measurements are being used. You should then study the data to identify trends and patterns and to draw connections with the content of the chapter. Finally, making marginal notes will aid your further reading and review.

2. What are the common types of graphics and what is the function of each?

Tables condense and systematically arrange data. Bar graphs, multiple bar graphs, and stacked bar graphs make comparisons between quantities or amounts. Line graphs display data that have continuous values. Charts, including pie charts, organizational charts, flowcharts, and pictograms, display relationships, either quantitative or cause–effect. Diagrams explain processes. Maps provide information about location or direction. Cartoons add humor or may make a point quickly. Photographs spark interest and may draw out an emotional response.

3. How is technical writing different from other types of writing?

Technical writing is unique and distinct from other types of writing. It is action oriented, supplying information that the reader needs to perform a task, solve a problem, or make a decision. Technical writing presents many facts in a small space, so it is precise in word choice; uses a technical, specialized vocabulary; includes special abbreviations and notations; and contains graphics, examples, and sample problems for clarity. Finally, different types of technical writing follow their own specific formats that are different from most other types of writing.

4. How should technical material be read?

When reading technical material, you should plan to read at about half the speed you use with nontechnical writing. You should preread carefully and read the material at least twice. It is important to study any graphics carefully as you are reading the text, and it is helpful to visualize and create a mental picture of what is being described.

5. How can technical material be studied more effectively?

To study technical material more effectively, it is important to study daily in large blocks of time in order to stay focused. You should make an extra effort to learn technical vocabulary by referring frequently to your text's glossary and index. Focusing on concepts and principles, on integrating information from labs, lectures, and classroom activities, and on drawing diagrams and pictures will keep you from getting lost in details. When reading and reviewing, highlight selectively or outline, and prepare study sheets on the important information, procedures, or processes.

DIRECTIONS Write the letter of the choice that best completes each statement in the space provided.

CHECKING YOUR RECALL

_____ 1. All of the following strategies are effective for reading graphics *except*

a. predicting what the graphic is intended to show.

b. identifying the variables.

c. ignoring titles or captions.

d. drawing connections with chapter content.

_____ 2. The primary purpose of tables is to

a. elicit an emotional response.

b. display events that occur in a specific sequence.

c. illustrate parts of a process.

d. present factual information, such as numbers or statistics, in a condensed form.

_____ 3. All of the following statements about graphs are true *except*

a. bar graphs usually are designed to emphasize similarities.

b. multiple bar graphs display two or three comparisons simultaneously.

c. stacked bar graphs show bars placed one on top of another.

d. linear graphs present more detailed information than bar graphs.

_____ 4. When a cartoon appears in a textbook, it typically is intended to do all of the following *except*

a. help make abstract concepts more realistic.

b. make a point quickly.

c. add humor to the topic.

d. correspond to a specific reference in the text.

_____ 5. When you are reading technical writing, you should plan on

a. understanding everything the first time you read the assignment.

b. highlighting all facts and details.

c. reading more slowly.

d. skipping the graphics when you read the text.

APPLYING YOUR SKILLS

_____ 6. Gabriel is writing a paper about the American judicial system. The best way for him to show the levels of the federal court system, from the Supreme Court on down, would be in

a. a pictogram.

b. a process diagram.

c. a pie chart.

d. an organizational chart.

_____ 7. Coran has a chemistry lab in conjunction with his chemistry course. He should always remember to

a. keep his lab work and classroom activities as separate as possible.

b. be as creative as possible when he writes his lab report.

c. understand the purpose of each step in an experiment before he performs it.

d. wait until the next lab meets to complete his follow-up report.

_____ 8. In writing a report for her public policy class, Cayla is appropriately using a flow chart. Cayla's report probably deals with the

a. organization of a county school system.

b. process by which an immigrant becomes a U.S. citizen.

c. percentage of a typical college student's budget that goes to various expenses.

d. difference in salaries between workers in rural and urban areas.

_____ 9. As Philip prereads his economics assignment, he notices that there are many diagrams in this lesson. Philip can assume the diagrams are designed to

a. situate events in time.

b. clarify causes and effects.

c. illustrate parts of a process.

d. make statistics seem more realistic.

_____ 10. Nina is interviewing for an internship as a technical writer. One thing Nina should know about technical writing is that it

a. is factually dense.

b. uses only nonspecialized language.

c. never uses abbreviations.

d. typically does not include examples or sample problems.

MULTIMEDIA *Activities*

Reading Graphics and Technical Writing

1 Make a poster featuring your favorite band or musical artist. Include photos and biographical information. Make your own graphics to show tour dates, record sales, or awards won. How does creating a display like this enhance your understanding of the artist? How does it help others understand your admiration for the artist?

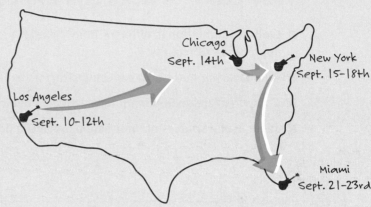

2 Draw some cartoons with your friends about college life. Don't worry about your drawing ability—just have fun and try to convey a humorous comment on being a student.

3 American Photographs: The First Century

http://americanart.si.edu/collections/exhibits/helios/amerphotos.html

Enjoy this online exhibit from the Smithsonian American Art Museum. How do you think people responded to these photographs when they were first shown? What relevance do they have for us today? Pick one photograph that stands out. Write a list of words describing the feelings evoked by the photo.

"Just think, in a few seconds we'll have to start paying off our student loans."

4 'Twas The Night Before Christmas

http://www.night.net/christmas/twas-the-night.html
http://www.night.net/christmas/technicalxmas.html

Compare these two versions of this classic holiday poem. The one written in technical language is meant to be humorous, of course, but note how it illustrates the characteristics of technical writing. Try writing a technical version of how you spent your day. Give it to some friends and see if they can figure out what you did.

9 Reading and Evaluating Electronic Sources

Why Learn to Read and Evaluate Electronic Sources?

- Online information is different from the information on a printed page and needs to be approached differently.

- An increasing number of college instructors expect their students to use electronic sources.

- Computers are an important means of communication and source of information in the workplace.

- Some useful sources of information are available only online.

Learning Experiment

Step 1

Study the following formula for converting temperature from Celsius (C) to Fahrenheit (F). Then, without looking back, write it in the space provided on the next page.

$$F = 1.8C + 32$$

Formula: _____

Step 2

Study the following cartoon. What does it say about parent-child relationships?

Step 3

Briefly describe how you studied each of the preceding tasks. Did you complete them in the same way?

"They got extinct because they didn't listen to their mommies."

The Results

You probably studied the formula differently than the cartoon. You may have repeated the formula or rewrote it until you remembered it. However, with the cartoon you had to look for a meaning implied by its caption and the drawing.

Learning Principle
(What This Means to You)

You study different types of material differently, depending on the nature of the material and on what you are expected to do once you have studied it. In this chapter you will learn to read and study electronic sources differently than you do print sources.

Increasingly, college students are finding the Internet to be a valuable and useful resource. The Internet is a worldwide network of computers through which you can access a wide variety of information and services. Through the Internet, you can access the World Wide Web, a system of Internet servers that allow exchange of information through specially formatted documents. It connects a vast array of resources (documents, graphics, and audio and visual files) and allows users to move from one to another easily and rapidly.

Although in most courses your textbook is still your primary source of information, more and more instructors are expecting their students to use the Internet to supplement their textbooks or obtain additional, more current information by visiting Web sites. (Textbooks, no matter how up-to-date they may be, often do not contain information from the year prior to their publication.) Other instructors expect their students to consult Internet sources in researching a topic for a paper. Many students, too, are finding valuable information on personal or special interests on the Internet.

For example, Maria Valquez, a student majoring in liberal arts, over the course of a week conducted the following activities using electronic sources:

- Ordered a music CD from Amazon.com, an online book and music store
- Visited an online writing center (http://owl.english.purdue.edu), for help with an English paper
- Searched for Web sites on the topic of tattooing for a sociology research paper
- Exchanged e-mail with friends
- Checked the weather in her hometown, in anticipation of a weekend trip
- Visited a Latino student Web site for ideas for organizing a Latino student group on her campus

Electronic sources are becoming increasingly important in many students' academic and personal lives. Therefore, it is important to know how Web sites are structured, how to locate useful sources, how to evaluate the sources you locate, how these sources differ from print sources, and how to navigate through them in an efficient way. It is also important to know how to use information you find on the Internet in papers you write without being guilty of cyberplagiarism.

Although this chapter focuses on using electronic sources, you should realize that the Internet is not always the best source of information. Sometimes it is easier and quicker to find a piece of information in a book or other traditional sources.

HOW TO LOCATE ELECTRONIC SOURCES ON THE WEB

Begin by gaining access to the Internet. In addition to a computer you will need a modem and a browser, such as Microsoft's Internet Explorer or Apple's Safari. You will also need an Internet service provider (ISP) to connect your computer to the Internet. Your college's computer center, your telephone or cable company, or a commercial service provider such as America Online can connect you. You will need a name you use online, called a **username**, and a password. If you need help getting started, check with the staff in your college's computer lab.

Identifying Keywords

To search for information on a topic, you need to come up with a group of specific words that describe your topic; these are known as **keywords.** It is often necessary to narrow your topic in order to identify specific keywords. For example, if you searched the topic "homeschooling," you would find thousands of sources. However, if you narrowed your topic to "homeschooling of primary grade children in California," you would identify far fewer sources.

Searching Web Resources

There are three basic groups of search tools you can use to locate information: subject directories, search engines, and metasearch engines.

Subject directories classify Web resources by categories and subcategories. Some offer reviews or evaluations of sites. Use a subject directory when you want to browse the Web using general topics or when you are conducting a broad search. For example, a subject directory is helpful if you are looking for sites about parenting issues or want to find a list of organizations for animal welfare. INFOMINE (http://infomine.ucr.edu) and Yahoo! (http://www.yahoo.com) are two useful directories.

A search engine is a computer program that helps you locate information on a topic. You instruct a search engine to search for certain keywords, and it provides connections to documents that contain the keywords. Depending on your topic, some search engines are more useful than others. In addition, each search engine may require a different way of entering the keywords. For example, some may require you to place quotation marks around a phrase ("capital punishment"); other times you may need to use plus signs or ANDs and ORs between keywords ("homeschooling" + "primary grades" + "California"; "homeschooling" AND "primary grades" AND "California" OR "Oregon"), which is called Boolean searching. The quotation marks around "primary grades" will create a search for those words as a phrase, rather than as single terms. Many search engines allow you to search for phrases in this way. Still other search engines are menu-based, allowing you to fill in blanks to indicate whether you want to use phrase searching or Boolean searching. Be sure to use the "help" feature when you use a new search engine to discover the best way to enter keywords.

If you are searching for a very specific or obscure topic or if you are having trouble finding information, you can use a metasearch engine. These tools search a number of search engines at the same time and combine all the results in a single listing. Table 9-1 describes several popular search and metasearch engines.

EXERCISE 1   **DIRECTIONS**   Use one of the search tools listed in Table 9-1 to locate three sources on one of the following topics. Then use a different search engine or subject directory to search for the same topic again. Compare your results. Which search tool was easier to use? Which yielded more sources?

1. Prescription drugs for depression
2. Church attendance in America
3. Your favorite movie
4. Oil drilling in Alaska

Table 9-1
Useful Search and
Metasearch Engines

Name	URL	Description
Google	www.google.com	An extensive and very popular tool. Has basic and advanced (menu-based) searching. Many extra features such as translation, domain/file-type searches, and filtering. Online help provided.
Yahoo!	www.yahoo.com	Biggest subject directory on the Web. Pages are organized in a searchable directory. A few advanced features available. Internet portal and site recommendations.
INFOMINE	http://infomine.ucr.edu/	Academic and research sites compiled, organized, and annotated by college and university librarians. Basic and advanced searching (tips provided). Users can submit sites for inclusion.
Exalead	http://www.exalead.com/	Features special navigation and design. Offers related terms and categories. Includes a thumbnail of the Web sites in the results list and opens the site in a viewing frame.
Kartoo	http://www.kartoo.com/	A metasearch engine that features a unique results list. The results are arranged visually in a concept map format.
Ixquick	www.ixquick.com	A metasearch engine covering at least nine other search tools. Features music, picture, and news searches. Search results are rated.

EVALUATING INTERNET SOURCES

Although the Internet contains a great deal of valuable information and resources, it also contains rumor, gossip, hoaxes, and misinformation. In other words, not all Internet sources are trustworthy. You must evaluate a source before accepting it. Here are some guidelines to follow when evaluating Internet sources.

Discover the Purpose of a Web Site

There are millions of Web sites and they vary widely in purpose. Table 9-2 on the next page summarizes five primary types of Web sites.

EXERCISE 2

DIRECTIONS   Using the information in Table 9-2, determine the purpose of five of the following Web sites. Some sites may have more than one purpose. Be sure to investigate the whole site carefully and explain your choices.

1. Typing Injury FAQ Home Page: http://www.tifaq.com/
2. Tibetan Children's Educational and Welfare Fund: http://www.tcewf.org/index.html
3. Realty Times: http://realtytimes.com/

4. Psalmist School of Music: http://www.psalmist.biz/
5. College Finder: http://www.college-finder.info/
6. Israel—A Country Study: http://lcweb2.loc.gov/frd/cs/iltoc.html
7. Senator Chuck Schumer: http://schumer.senate.gov/
8. Center for Science in the Public Interest: http://www.cspinet.org/
9. Meridian: http://www.ncsu.edu/meridian/
10. Professor Hunt's Dog Page: http://www.cofc.edu/~huntc/dogpage.html

Evaluate the Content of a Web Site

When evaluating the content of a Web site, evaluate its appropriateness, its source, its level of technical detail, its presentation, its completeness, and its links.

Evaluate Appropriateness　To be worthwhile a Web site should contain the information you need. That is, it should answer one or more of your search questions. If the site touches only upon answers to your questions but does not address them in detail, check the links on the site to see if they lead you to more detailed information. If they do not, search for a more useful site.

Evaluate the Source　Another important step in evaluating a Web site is to determine its source. Ask yourself "Who is the sponsor?" and "Why was this site put up on the Web?" The sponsor of a Web site is the person or organization who paid for its creation and placement on the Web. The sponsor will often suggest the purpose of a Web site. For example, a Web site sponsored by Nike is designed to promote its products, while a site sponsored by a university library is designed to help students learn to use its resources more effectively.

Type	Purpose and Description	Domain	Sample Sites
Informational	To present facts, information, and research data. May contain reports, statistical data, results of research studies, and reference materials.	.edu or .gov	http://www.haskins.yale.edu/ http://www.census.gov/
News	To provide current information on local, national, and international news. Often supplements print newspapers, periodicals, and television news programs.	.com or .org	http://news.yahoo.com/ http://www.theheart.org/index.cfm
Advocacy	To promote a particular cause or point of view. Usually concerned with a controversial issue; often sponsored by nonprofit groups.	.com or .org	http://www.goveg.com/ http://www.bradycampaign.org/
Personal	To provide information about an individual and his/her interests and accomplishments. May list publications or include the individual's résumé.	Varies . . . may contain .com, .org, .biz, .edu, .info May contain a tilde (~)	http://www.jessamyn.com/ http://www.srmi.biz/resumeJohn.html http://www.maryrussell.info/ http://www.plu.edu/~chasega/
Commercial	To promote goods or services. May provide news and information related to products.	.com, .biz, .info	http://www.nmgroup.biz/ http://www.alhemer.com/ http://www.vintageradio.info/

Table 9-2
Types of Web Sites

If you are uncertain of who sponsors a Web site, check its URL, its copyright, and the links it offers. The ending of the URL often suggests the type of sponsorship, as you can see in Table 9-2. The copyright indicates the owner of the site. Links may also reveal the sponsor. Some links may lead to commercial advertising; others may lead to sites sponsored by nonprofit groups, for example.

Another way to check the ownership of a Web site is to try to locate the site's home page. You can do this by using only the first part of its URL—up to the first slash (/) mark. For example, suppose you found this information on Medicare on the Internet and you wanted to track its source. Its URL is http://www.phaa.net.au/friends_of_medicare/factsheet1.html. This page deals with Medicare, but it begins by talking about Australia. If you go back in the URL to http://www.phaa.net.au you will discover that the sponsoring organization is the Public Health Association of Australia.

Evaluate the Level of Technical Detail   A Web site's level of technical detail should be suited to your purpose. Some sites may provide information that is too sketchy for your search purposes; others assume a level of background knowledge or technical sophistication that you lack. For example, if you are writing a short, introductory-level paper on global warming, information on the University of New Hampshire's NASA Earth Observing System site (http://www.eos-ids.sr.unh.edu/) may be too technical and contain more information than you need, unless you have some previous knowledge in that field.

Evaluate the Presentation   Information on a Web site should be presented clearly; it should be well written. If you find a site that is not clear and well written, you should be suspicious of it. If the author did not take time to present ideas clearly and correctly, he or she may not have taken time to collect accurate information, either.

Evaluate Completeness   Determine whether the site provides complete information on its topic. Does it address all aspects of the topic that you feel it should? For example, if a Web site on Important Twentieth Century American Poets does not mention Robert Frost, then the site is incomplete. If you discover that a site is incomplete, search for sites that provide a more thorough treatment of the topic.

Evaluate the Links   Many reputable sites supply links to other related sites. Make sure that the links are current. Also check to see if the sites to which you were sent are reliable sources of information. If the links do not work or the sources appear unreliable, you should question the reliability of the site itself. Also determine whether the links provided are comprehensive or only present a representative sample. Either is acceptable, but the site should make clear the nature of the links it is providing.

EXERCISE 3 | DIRECTIONS   Evaluate the content of two of the following sites. Explain why you would either trust or distrust the site for reliable content.

1. http://www.circleofpoets.com
2. http://www.earlham.edu/~peters/knotlink.htm
3. http://www.age-of-the-sage.org/psychology/

Evaluate the Accuracy of a Web Site

When using information on a Web site for an academic paper, it is important to be sure that you have found accurate information. One way to determine the accuracy of a Web site is to compare it with print sources (periodicals and books) on the same topic. If you find a wide discrepancy between the Web site and the printed sources, do not trust the Web site. Another way to determine a site's accuracy is to compare it with other Web sites that address the same topic. If discrepancies exist, further research is needed to determine which site is more accurate.

The site itself will also provide clues about the accuracy of its information. Ask yourself the following questions:

- **Are the author's name and credentials provided?** A well-known writer with established credentials is likely to author only reliable, accurate information. If no author is given, you should question whether the information is accurate.
- **Is contact information for the author included on the site?** Sites often provide an e-mail address where the author may be contacted.
- **Is the information complete or in summary form?** If it is a summary, use the site to find the original source. Original information has less chance of error and is usually preferred in academic papers.
- **If opinions are offered, are they presented clearly as opinions?** Authors who disguise their opinions as facts are not trustworthy. (See "Distinguish Between Fact or Opinion" in Chapter 10, p. 248.)
- **Does the writer make unsubstantiated assumptions or base his or her ideas on misconceptions?** If so, the information presented may not be accurate.
- **Does the site provide a list of works cited?** As with any form of research, sources used to put information up on a Web site must be documented. If sources are not credited, you should question the accuracy of the Web site.

It may be helpful to determine whether the information is available in print form. If it is, try to obtain the print version. Errors may occur when the article or essay is put up on the Web. Web sites move, change, and delete information, so it may be difficult for a reader of an academic paper to locate the Web site that you used in writing it. Also, page numbers are easier to cite in print sources than in electronic ones.

EXERCISE 4

DIRECTIONS   Evaluate the accuracy of two of the following Web sites:

1. http://www.amguard.net/
2. http://www.krysstal.com/democracy.html
3. http://www.idausa.org/facts/pg.html

Evaluate the Timeliness of a Web Site

Although the Web is well known for providing up-to-the-minute information, not all Web sites are current. Evaluate a site's timeliness by checking the following dates:

- The date on which the Web site was mounted (put up on the Web)
- The date when the document you are using was added
- The date when the site was last revised
- The date when the links were last checked

This information is usually provided at the end of the site's home page or at the end of the document you are using.

EXERCISE 5

DIRECTIONS   Evaluate the timeliness of two of the following Web sites, using the directions given for each site.

1. http://www.hwg.org/resources/?cid=30
   See when these links were last checked. Find out the consequences by checking the links yourself.
2. http://www.chebucto.ns.ca/Urbancap/
   Evaluate whether this site contains up-to-date information and links on the Community Access Program in Nova Scotia.
3. http://www.journalists.org/2003conference/
   Explain what information on this site might be useful even though the event is over. How would you find out current information for this conference?

WHY ELECTRONIC TEXT REQUIRES NEW READING STRATEGIES

Reading electronic text (also called hypertext) is very different from reading traditional printed text such as textbooks or magazines or newspaper articles. The term electronic text, as used in this chapter, refers to information presented on a Web site. It does not refer to articles and essays that can be downloaded from Searchbank or from an e-journal, for example. Because Web sites are unique, they require a different mind-set and different reading strategies. If electronic text is new or unfamiliar to you, you need to change the way you read and the way you think when approaching Web sites. If you attempt to read Web sites the same way you read traditional text, you may lose focus or perspective, miss important information, or become generally disoriented. Text used on Web sites, often called hypertext, is different in the following ways from traditional print text.

- **Reading Web sites may involve paying attention to sound, graphics, and movement, as well as words.** Your senses, then, may pull you in several different directions simultaneously. Banner advertisements, flashing graphics, and colorful drawings or photos may catch your attention. Some Web sites are available in two formats—graphical and text-only. This is most common for academic sites. If you are distracted by the graphics, check to see if a text-only version of the site is available.
- **Text on Web sites comes in brief, independent screenfuls, sometimes called nodes.** These screenfuls tend to be brief, condensed pieces of information. Unlike traditional text, they are not set within a context, and background information is often not supplied. They do not depend on other pages for meaning either. In traditional print text, paragraphs and pages are dependent—in order to comprehend one, you often must have read and understood a previous one. Electronic pages are often intended to stand alone.
- **Text on Web sites may not follow the traditional main idea–supporting details organization of traditional paragraphs.** Instead, the screen may appear as a group of topic sentences without detail.

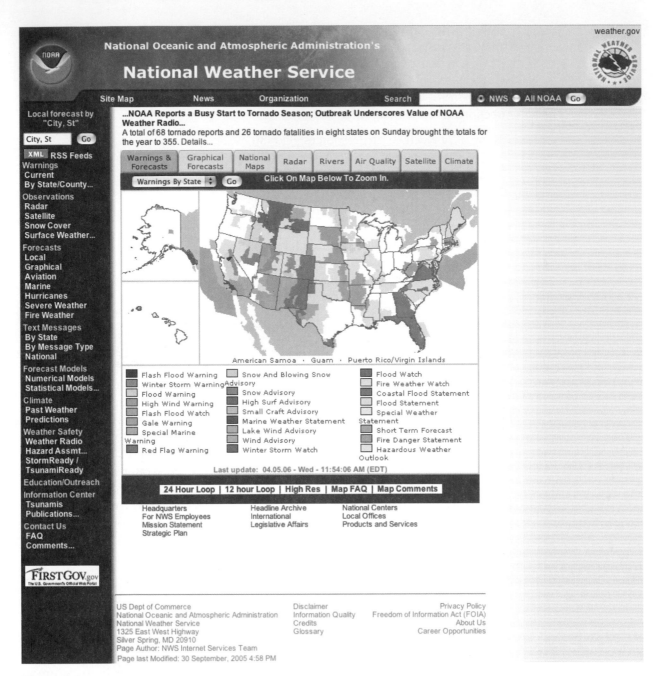

Figure 9-1
A Sample Home Page

- **Web sites are multidirectional; traditional text progresses in a single direction.** When reading traditional text, a reader usually follows a single direction, working through the text from beginning to end as written by the author. Web site text is multidirectional; each electronic reader creates his or her own unique text by following or ignoring different paths. Two readers of the same Web site may read entirely different material, or the same material in a different order. For example, one user of the National Weather Service site (http://www.nws.noaa.gov/) shown in Figure 9-1 might start off by checking the map of weather warnings; another might follow the link to tsunami information; a third might choose to use the search option to locate information on a particular topic.

- **Web site text requires readers to make decisions.** Because screens have menus and links, Web site readers must always make choices. They can focus on one aspect of the topic and ignore all others, for example, by following a path of links. Readers of print text, however, have far fewer choices to make.

- **Web sites allow readers the flexibility to choose the order in which to receive the information.** Partly due to learning style, people prefer to acquire information in different sequences. Some may prefer to begin with details and then, from the details, come to understand underlying rules or principles. Others may prefer to begin in the opposite way. Electronic sources allow readers to approach the text in any manner compatible with their learning style. A pragmatic learner may prefer to move through a site systematically, either clicking or ignoring links as they appear on the screen from top to bottom, for example.

- **Web sites use new symbol systems.** Electronic texts introduce new and sometimes unfamiliar symbols. A flashing or blinking light may suggest a new feature on the site, and an underlined word or a word in a different color may suggest a link. Sound effects, too, may have meanings. For example, on a children's Web site a child can have a book read aloud. An auditory signal may indicate when to turn the page. Icons and drawings may be used in place of words. A drawing of a book, for example, may indicate that print sources are available.

EXERCISE 6

DIRECTIONS   Visit one of the Web sites suggested for one of the World Wide Web activities in Part Eight of this book (p. 464, p. 481, p. 494, p. 512) or locate a different Web site on one of the topics. Write a list of characteristics that distinguish it from the print articles in Part Eight on the same topic.

DEVELOPING NEW WAYS OF THINKING AND READING

Reading electronic sources demands a different type of thinking than reading print sources. A print source is linear—it progresses in a straight line from idea to idea. Electronic sources, due to the presence of links, tend to be multidirectional; you can follow numerous paths.

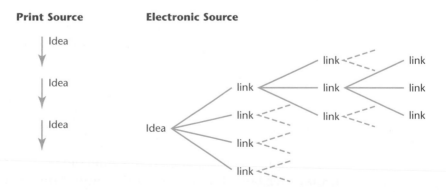

Reading electronic text also requires new strategies. To read electronic text easily and effectively you must first understand how it is different (see the preceding section) and realize that you must change and adapt how you read. Here are some specific suggestions.

Focus on Your Purpose

Focus clearly on your purposes for visiting the site. What information do you need? Because you must create your own path through the site, unless you fix in mind what you are looking for, you may wander aimlessly, wasting valuable time, or even become lost, following numerous links that lead you farther and farther away from the site at which you began.

Get Used to the Site's Design and Layout

Each Web site has unique features and arranges information differently.

1. **When you reach a new site, spend a few minutes discovering how it is organized.** Scroll through it quickly to determine how it is organized and what information is available. Ask yourself the following questions:
   - What information is available?
   - How is it arranged on the screen?
   - Can you search the site using a search option or box?
   - Is there a site map?

   Especially on large and complex sites, you have a number of different choices for locating the information you need. Be sure to spend time exploring your choices before choosing a particular path for your search. The Literature, Arts, and Medicine Database on New York University's Web site (http://endeavor.med.nyu.edu/lit-med/lit-med-db/) shown in Figure 9-2 is a good example. Suppose you are searching for information on how people with mental illnesses have been depicted over time in paintings, books, and movies. Using this database, you can locate information in a variety of ways. One choice is to browse the annotations for each category. This method is not very efficient since the database contains over one thousand annotations. However, browsing is a good way to acquaint yourself with the kinds of information presented for each entry. Another choice is to do a full-text keyword search. This method is likely to result in a large list of records, some of which will not be relevant to your search. A third way is to click on the list of keywords and then find the subject that best matches your topic. In this case, "mental illness" is listed. Choosing this keyword from the list will then bring a list of works pertaining directly to your topic.

2. **Expect the first screen to grab your attention and make a main point.** Web site authors know that many people who read a Web page do not scroll down to see the next screenful.

3. **Get used to the Web site's design before you attempt to obtain information from the site.** Your eye may have a tendency to focus on color or movement, rather than on print. Because some Web sites are highly visual, they require visual as well as verbal thinking. The author intends for you to respond to photos, graphics, and animation.

4. **Consider both the focus and the limitations of your learning style.** Are you a spatial learner? If so, you may have a tendency to focus too heavily on

61st Edition-April 2006

What's New in This Edition

Literature, Arts, & Medicine Database

April, 2006

Art
Annotations
Artists
Meet the Artist
Viewing Room*
Annotated Art Books
Art in Literature

Literature
Annotations
Authors
Meet the Authors*
Listening Room*
Reading Room*

Performing Arts
Film/Video
 Annotations
 Screening Room*
Theater*

Editors' Choices
Choices
Editor's Biosketch
Indexes
Book Order Form

Search Options
Text Search (ALL)
Keyword
Annotator

*Asterisks indicate
multimedia*

Comments/Inquiries

©New York University
1993-2006

10 Year Anniversary Book, *Editors' Choices from The Literature, Arts, and Medicine Database,* (see order form) and its corresponding on-line version (see left panel): editor-annotators discuss the literature, art, and films they consider most valuable for medical humanities teaching and related scholarship (published October 2003)

NEW MATERIAL

10 New Art Annotations

6 New Artists

3 New Film Annotations

23 New Literature Annotations

17 New Authors

CHANGES:

The word "serum" in Pamela's Moore's annotation of the novel, Arrowsmith has been changed to "material."

ADDITIONS:

We have added an editorial note to the commentaries in the annotations of author James Frey's A Million Little Pieces and My Friend Leonard.

Links have been made to newly annotated art work by Vincent van Gogh, "Self-Portrait" and "Self-Portrait with Bandaged Ear"; Gustav Klimt's "Hope, II"; Hollis Sigler's "to Kiss the Spirits" and "Hoping to Bring Her Life Together"; Alice Bailly's "Self-Portrait;; Paul Gauguin's "Where Do We Come From"; Albrecht Dürer's "The Temptation of the Idler"; Anish Kapoor's sculpture, "Cloud Gate"; Marc Quinn's sculpture, "Alison Lapper Pregnant " (see also the Viewing Room).

See Meet the Artist for biographical information on newly added artists Vincent Van Gogh, Hollis Sigler, Alice Bailly, and Anish Kapoor.

Newly annotated poetry by Marilyn Hacker, "Migraine Sonnets," is linked to her audio reading of the poems.

New links have been made to texts and audio of the following poetry: Dannie Abse's "In the Theatre"; Galway Kinnell's "After Making Love We Hear Footsteps"; J. D. McClatchy's "My Mammogram"; Les Murray's "The Last Hellos" (see also the Reading Room and the Listening Room).

TOTAL DATABASE CONTENTS

104 Art Annotations
 64 Artists
186 Film Annotations
2187 Literature Annotations
1297 Authors
 135 Keywords

NEXT EDITION

The next edition of the Literature, Arts, and Medicine Database will be available in July, 2006

TOP

Figure 9-2
A Sample Web Page

Site Map of Literature, Arts, and Medicine Database, http://endeavor.med.nyu.edu/lit-med/lit-med-db/. © New York University 1993–2006. Database is produced at New York University School of Medicine. Reprinted by permission.

231

the graphic elements of the screen. If, on the other hand, you tend to focus on words, you may ignore important visual elements or signals. If you focus *only* on the words and ignore color and graphics on a particular screen, you probably will miss information or may not move through the site in the most efficient way.

Pay Attention to How Information Is Organized

Because you can navigate through a Web site in many different ways, it is important to have the right expectations about Web site organization and to make several decisions before you begin. Some Web sites are much better organized than others. Some have clear headings and labels that make it easy to discover how to proceed; others do not and will require more thought before you begin. For example, if you are reading an article with as many as 10 or 15 underlined words (links), there is no prescribed order to follow and these links are not categorized in any way. Below are some suggestions on how to stay organized when using a Web site.

1. **Use the site map, if provided, to discover what information is available and how it is organized.** A sample site map for the Web site of ARTSEDGE, a national arts and education network sponsored by the John F. Kennedy Center for the Arts, is shown in Figure 9-3 (p. 233). Notice that the links are categorized into "Teach" (teaching resources), "Connect" (connections), "Explore" (media activities), and so forth, making the map useful for site users.
2. **Consider the order in which you want to take in information.** Choose an order in which to explore links; avoid randomly clicking on them. Doing so is somewhat like randomly choosing pages to read out of a reference book. Do you need definitions first? Do you want historical background first? Your decision will be influenced partly by your learning style.
3. **Consider writing brief notes to yourself as you explore a complicated Web site.** Alternatively, you could print the home page and jot notes on it. You can also save Web pages on a disk or on your computer, as a text file.
4. **Expect shorter, less detailed sentences and paragraphs.** Much online communication tends to be briefer and more concise than in traditional sources. As a result, you may have to mentally fill in transitions and make inferences about the relationships among ideas. For example, you may have to infer similarities and differences or recognize cause and effect connections.

EXERCISE 7 DIRECTIONS Visit two Web sites on the same topic. Write a few sentences comparing and contrasting their organization and design.

Use Links to Find the Information You Need

Links are unique to electronic text. Here's how to use them.

1. **Plan on exploring links to find complete and detailed information.** Links, both remote links (those that take you to another site) and related links within a site, are intended to provide more detailed information on topics introduced on the home page.

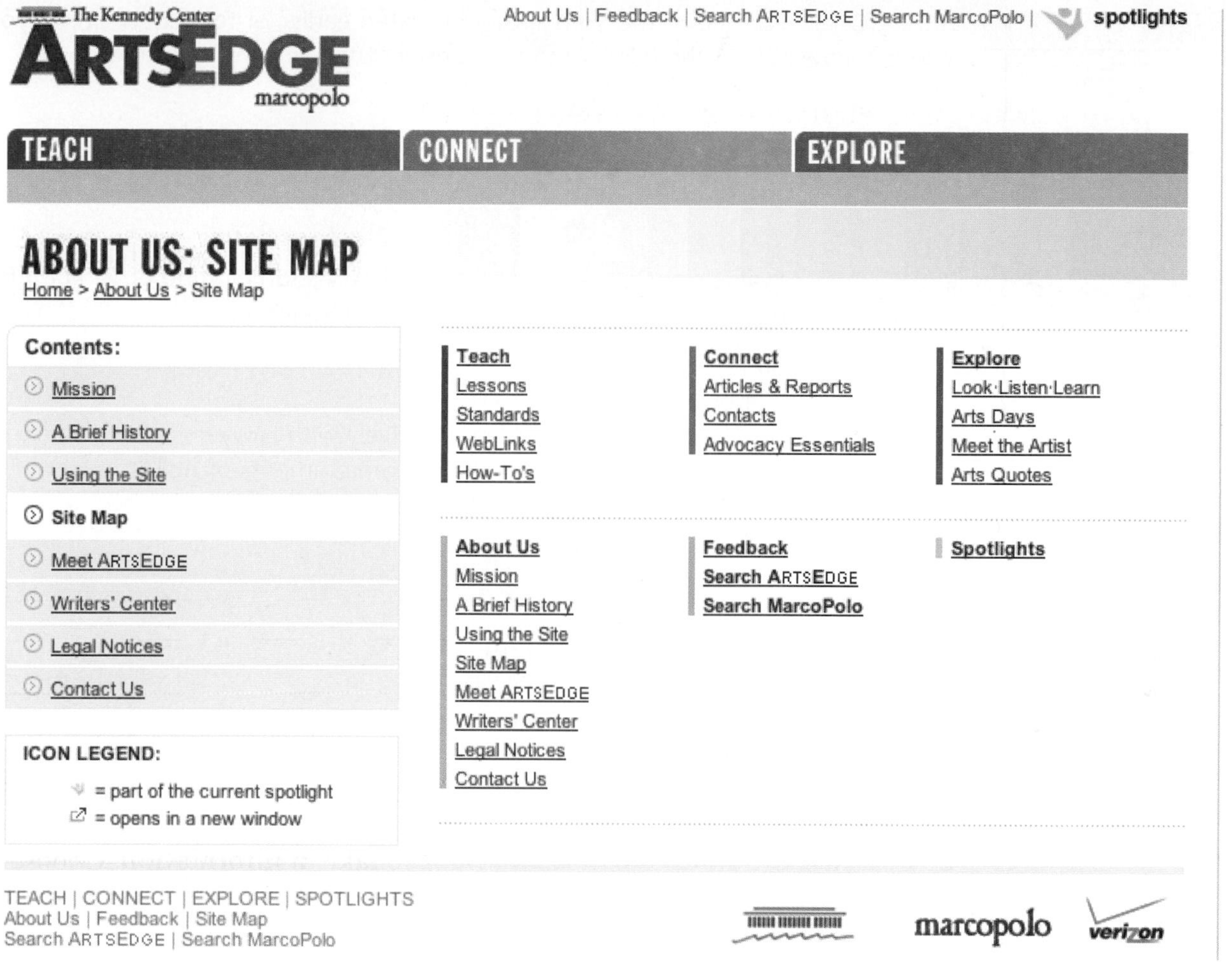

Figure 9-3
A Sample Site Map

2. **As you follow links, be sure to bookmark your original site and other useful sites you come across so you can find them again.** Bookmarking is a feature of your Internet browser that allows you to record Web site addresses and access them later by simply clicking on the site name. Different browsers use different terms for this function. Netscape and Safari use the term *Bookmarks;* Microsoft's Internet Explorer calls it *Favorites.*

3. **If you use a site or a link that provides many pages of continuous text, print the material and read it offline.**

4. **If you find you are lacking background on a topic, use links to help fill in the gap or search for a different, less technical Web site on the same topic.**

5. **Learn to use your browser's history feature if you get lost.** Most Internet browsers have a history feature that allows you to backtrack or retrace the links you followed in a search. In Netscape, for example, click "Back" to move back one link at a time; "History" keeps track of all searches over a given period and allows you to go directly to a chosen site, rather than backtracking step-by-step.

EXERCISE 8

DIRECTIONS   For one of the Web sites you visited earlier or for a new site of your choice, follow at least three links and then answer the following questions:

1. What type of information did each contain?
2. Was each source reliable? How do you know?
3. Which was the easiest to read and follow? Why?

EXERCISE 9

DIRECTIONS   Evaluate each of the sites listed below. Assign a rating of 1–5 (1 = low reliability; 5 = high reliability). Be prepared to discuss your ratings.

1. A Virtual Visit to Expo '74
   http://expo74.brandx.net/
2. Ten Commandments of How to Work Effectively with Lawyers
   http://web.mit.edu/e-club/hadzima/ten-commandments-of-how-to-work-with-lawyers.html
3. School TV
   http://www.schooltv.com/
4. U.S. Economy at a Glance
   http://www.bls.gov/eag/eag.us.htm
5. How to Communicate with Journalists
   http://www.fair.org/index.php?page=122

Change Your Reading Strategies for Reading Electronic Text

Reading electronic text is relatively new to the current generation of college students. (This will no doubt change with the upcoming generations who, as children, will learn to read both print and electronic text.) Most current college students and teachers first learned to read using print text. We have read print text for many more years than electronic text; consequently, our brains have developed numerous strategies or "work orders" for reading traditional texts. Our work orders, however, are less fully developed for electronic texts. Electronic texts have a wider variety of formats and more variables to cope with than traditional texts. A textbook page is usually made up of headings, paragraphs, and an occasional photo or graphic. Web sites may have vibrant color, banner advertisements, and music as well as words.

Reading is not only different, but it also tends to be slower on the computer screen than for print sources. In a book your eyes can see the layout of two full pages. From the two pages you can see headings, division of ideas, and subtopics. By glancing at a print page, you can make an initial assessment of what it contains. You can tell, for example, if a page is heavily statistical (your eye will see numbers, dates, symbols) or is anecdotal (your eye will see capitalized proper names, quotation marks, and numerous indented paragraphs for dialogue, for example). Because you have a sense of what the page contains and how it is organized, you can read somewhat faster. Because a screen holds fewer words, you get far less information before you begin to read.

EXERCISE 10

DIRECTIONS   In groups of two or three students, consider one aspect of learning style. For each, discuss the tendencies, limitations, and implications this particular learning style may have for reading electronic text. How would a pragmatic learner approach a Web site? How might this differ from how a creative learner might approach it?

EXERCISE 11 | **DIRECTIONS** Locate two Web sites that you think are interesting and appealing. Then answer the following questions:

1. How does each use color?
2. How does each use graphics?
3. Is sound or motion used? If so, how?

AVOIDING CYBERPLAGIARISM WHEN READING AND CONDUCTING RESEARCH ON THE WEB

As you write papers for college classes, you will probably use electronic sources to locate the information you need. As you read and take notes, and later, as you write the paper, you need to know the rules for indicating that you have taken information or ideas from the work of other people. You identify your sources in order to help readers find a source if they want to look into the ideas of that author further, as well as to give credit to the person who originally wrote the material or thought of the idea. **Plagiarism** means borrowing someone else's ideas or exact wording without giving that person credit. If you take information on Frank Lloyd Wright's architecture from a reference source, but do not indicate where you found it, you have plagiarized. If you take the six-word phrase "Martinez, the vengeful, despicable drug czar" from an online news article on the war on drugs without putting quotation marks around it and noting the source, you have plagiarized. Plagiarism is intellectually dishonest because you are taking someone else's ideas or wording and passing them off as your own. There are academic penalties for plagiarism. You may receive a failing grade on your paper or you may fail the entire course. At some institutions you can even be academically dismissed.

Cyberplagiarism is a special type of plagiarism; it involves borrowing information from the Internet without giving credit to the source posting the information. It is also called **cut and paste plagiarism**, referring to the ease with which a person can copy something from an Internet document and paste it into his or her own paper. Numerous Web sites offer student papers for sale on the Internet. The term **cyberplagiarism** also refers to using these papers and submitting them as one's own.

What Constitutes Plagiarism

Plagiarism can be intentional (planned) or unintentional (done by accident or oversight). Either way it carries the same academic penalty. If you buy a paper from an Internet site or deliberately copy and paste a section of an article from a Web site into your paper, your plagiarism is intentional. If you take notes from a source and copy exact wording, forget to enclose the wording in quotation marks, and later use that exact wording in your paper, your plagiarism is unintentional, but it is still dishonest. Here are some guidelines that will help you understand exactly what is considered plagiarism.

- Plagiarism is the use of another person's words without giving credit to that person.
- Plagiarism uses another person's theory, opinion, or idea without listing where the information was taken from.

- Plagiarism results when another person's exact words are not placed inside quotation marks. Both the quotation marks and a citation (reference) to the original source are needed.
- Paraphrasing (rewording) another person's words without giving credit to them is plagiarism.
- Using facts, data, graphs, charts, and so on without stating where they were taken from is plagiarism.
- Using commonly known facts or information is not plagiarism and you need not give a source for your information. For example, the fact that Neil Armstrong set foot on the moon in 1969 is widely known and so does not require documentation.

Avoiding Cyberplagiarism

Use the following suggestions to avoid unintentional plagiarism.

- If you copy exact words from any source, put them in quotation marks in your notes, along with the publication information: the author, title, publisher, date of publication, and page number of the source, or, for Web sites, the author, name of the site or page, date of publication, and URL. Be sure to consult a style manual for details on how to indicate in your paper which material is borrowed and how to set up a list of the works you used in your paper.
- List sources for all the information you include in your notes regardless of whether it takes the form of direct quotations, paraphrases, or summaries of someone else's ideas.
- Never copy and paste directly from a Web site into your paper without enclosing the words in quotation marks and listing the source.
- List the source for any information, facts, ideas, opinions, theories, or data you use from a Web site.
- When paraphrasing someone else's words, change as many words as possible and try not to follow the exact same organization. Credit where the information came from.
- Write paraphrases without looking at the original text so you will rephrase it in your own words.

EXERCISE 12   DIRECTIONS   Read the following passage from *Sociology for the Twenty-First Century* by Tim Curry, Robert Jiobu, and Kent Schwirian. Place a check mark next to each statement that is an example of plagiarism.

Mexican Americans. Currently, *Mexican Americans* are the second-largest racial or ethnic minority in the United States, but by early in the next century they will be the largest group. Their numbers will swell as a result of continual immigration from Mexico and the relatively high Mexican birth rate. Mexican Americans are one of the oldest racial-ethnic groups in the United States. Under the terms of the treaty ending the Mexican-American War in 1848, Mexicans living in territories acquired by the United States could remain there and were to be treated as American citizens. Those that did stay became known as "Californios," "Tejanos," or "Hispanos."[1]

_____   a. Mexican Americans are the second-largest minority in the United States. Their number grows as more people immigrate from Mexico.

_____ b. After the Mexican-American War, those Mexicans living in territories owned by the U.S. became American citizens and were called "Californios," "Tejanos," and "Hispanos" (Curry, Jiobu, and Schwirian, 207).

_____ c. "Mexican Americans are one of the oldest racial-ethnic groups in the United States."

_____ d. The Mexican-American War ended in 1848.

LEARNING COLLABORATIVELY

DIRECTIONS   Working with another student, select a topic of mutual interest. Discuss it, narrow it down, and write two or three specific research questions. Working independently, use the Internet to locate answers to your research questions. When you have finished, compare your answers and the sources from which you obtained them.

APPLYING YOUR LEARNING

Robert has been assigned to write a paper on a contemporary issue. He chooses the topic of gun control. He uses a search engine, finds the Web site of the National Rifle Association, and bases his paper on the information he finds there.

1. Discuss what is wrong with Robert's research strategy.
2. Offer suggestions for what he could do to improve his paper.

APPLYING YOUR SKILLS: Sample Textbook Chapter

Choose one of the search engines listed on page 223. Locate and evaluate several sources that address the topic of ethnocentrism. Evaluate the content, accuracy, and timeliness of each site.

QUESTIONS FOR DISCUSSION

1. What are some Web sites you and your classmates frequently use for academic research? What characteristics make these sites particularly helpful?
2. What are some of the techniques you use to avoid plagiarism? Is it harder or easier to avoid cyberplagiarism? Why?
3. What are some of the risks when using the Internet for research? How can you minimize these risks?

SELF-TEST SUMMARY

1. How can you locate sources on the World Wide Web?	To locate sources, identify keywords and use a search engine or metasearch engine.
2. How can you evaluate a Web site?	Evaluate a Web site by discovering its purpose and considering its content, accuracy, and timeliness.
3. In what ways are Web sites different from print text?	Web sites involve graphics, sound, color, and animation. Language tends to be brief; screens are independent. Due to the use of links, Web sites are multidirectional. They require decision making and permit flexibility.
4. How should you read an electronic text?	Identify the purpose of the source or site. Familiarize yourself with the site's design and layout. Pay attention to how information is organized and use links to find the information you need.
5. What is cyberplagiarism?	Cyberplagiarism refers to the borrowing of information from the Internet without giving credit to the source posting the information.

Quick Quiz

DIRECTIONS Write the letter of the choice that best completes each statement in the space provided.

CHECKING YOUR RECALL

_____ 1. When you are reading electronic text, it is most important to
   a. follow as many links as possible.
   b. concentrate on the words and ignore the graphics.
   c. scroll down to the next page.
   d. focus on your purpose for visiting the site.

2. Commercial Web sites
   a. contain only advertising.
   b. offer links to competitors' products.
   c. may include news and product information.
   d. never provide links to informational sites.

_____ 3. Which of the following is *not* a clue to the timeliness of a Web site?
   a. the date the Web site was put on the Web.
   b. the date the Web site was last revised.
   c. the date the author's biography was last revised.
   d. the date when the links were last checked.

_____ 4. The sponsorship of a Web site may provide clues about its
   a. purpose.
   b. timeliness.
   c. structure.
   d. user-friendliness.

_____ 5. A metasearch engine
   a. searches only sources beyond a specified date.
   b. combines electronic and print sources into one directory.
   c. eliminates the necessity to use keywords to initiate a search.
   d. searches a number of search engines and combines the results into a single listing.

APPLYING YOUR SKILLS

_____ 6. Angel needs to write a paper on a current civil rights issue. She is doing some preliminary research on the Internet by previewing a variety of sites. After she finalizes her choice of topic, she will want to visit some of the sites again. The best way for Angel to record Web site addresses so she can access them again later is to
   a. download the addresses onto a diskette.
   b. print out the addresses on paper.
   c. bookmark the addresses in her Internet browser.
   d. send her an e-mail with the addresses she wants to revisit.

_____ 7. Kevin is interested in examining the death penalty issue and wants to compare both pro and con viewpoints. Kevin should check a number of different
   a. commercial Web sites.
   b. personal Web sites
   c. advocacy Web sites.
   d. news Web sites.

_____ 8. Which of the following questions will help you evaluate the accuracy of a Web site?
   a. Does the author state his or her purpose?
   b. Are the author's name and credentials provided?
   c. Who designed the Web site?
   d. Does the URL end in .com?

_____ 9. Zara wants to locate information about a recent terrorist attack in a foreign country. Which of the following types of Web sites should she choose?
   a. advocacy
   b. news
   c. personal
   d. informational

_____ 10. Sam is writing a research paper using various Web pages as resources. To avoid cyberplagiarism, Sam can do all of the following *except*
   a. read information provided by Web sites and not list them as sources.
   b. write a paper on a topic already found on the Internet.
   c. cut and paste information from the Internet into his own paper without crediting the source.
   d. write a paper that consists mostly of quotations and paraphrased information.

MULTIMEDIA *Activities*

Reading and Evaluating Electronic Sources

1 Work with a friend to design a Web site addressing a social issue that is important to you. Write a mission statement, and decide how you would like the site to look, what sorts of information to include, and what types of links you would list. Sketch your ideas out on paper, and consider actually putting it up on the Web sometime.

2 Keep a log of your computer use. For three days, record when, where, and why you spent time on a computer. Ask friends, classmates, and family members to do the same. Compare your results, and then compile them in a chart.

3 Worst of the Web/Best of the Web

http://www.worstoftheweb.com/
http://www.webbyawards.com/webby5/current.Php

Explore some links from these sites and try to determine why they were given their respective "awards." Do you have sites that you return to over and over? What about them appeals to you? What types of sites do you avoid? Why?

4 How to Choose a Search Engine or Directory

http://library.albany.edu/internet/choose.html

The University at Albany Libraries presents this clear, thorough chart suggesting the best search tools for specific needs. Experiment with sites that are new to you and make notes describing your experiences. Which special searches would be most useful for academic applications?

5 Web Site Evaluation Worksheet

http://www.pace.edu/library/instruct/webevalworksheet.htm

Print out this worksheet from the Pace University Library and use it to evaluate the Web sites that you visit on a regular basis.

10 Evaluating the Author's Message

Why Learn to Evaluate What the Author Says?

■ You will understand your reading assignments more fully if you become a critical thinker. Textbook reading requires critical thinking.

■ You will become more successful at taking tests if you read and think critically. Taking tests requires critical thinking.

■ You will write more effective papers if you apply critical thinking skills.

Learning Experiment

Step 1

Read the following paragraph on school voucher systems and highlight important ideas.

> In the late 1960s, a new idea began to receive considerable publicity. It was vintage USA: If there were more competition among schools, perhaps schools would be better. After all, people were entitled to more freedom in choosing where their children would be educated. This idea inspired proposals for voucher plans. Public schools have a virtual monopoly on public funds for education, and children attend schools depending, for the most part, on where they live. A voucher plan can change this situation. In a sense, parents, not schools, receive public money. They receive it in the form of a *voucher*, which they use to pay for their children's attendance at the schools of their choice. The schools receive money from the government in return for the vouchers. The greater the number of parents who choose a particular school, the more money it receives. The idea is to force the public schools to compete with each other, and with private and parochial schools, for "customers." Presumably, good schools would attract plenty of students, and poor schools would be forced either to improve or close.
>
> —Thio, *Sociology*, pp. 376–377

Step 2

Read the following paragraph on homeschooling and then answer the questions that follow, either alone, as part of a classroom discussion group, or with a friend or classmate.

> There has been phenomenal growth in the number of children who receive their formal education at home. In the late 1970s there were only about 12,500 such children, but today the number has soared to more than 500,000 and is still increasing rapidly. Before 1994, most of the home-schooling parents were fundamentalist Christians who believed that religion was either abused or ignored in the public school. But today two thirds of the families reject public education for secular reasons: poor teaching, crowded classrooms, or lack of safety. Many of the older children, though, enroll in public schools part time, for a math class or a chemistry lab, or for after-school activities such as football or volleyball. Most home-schooling parents have some college education, with median incomes between $35,000 and $50,000. Over 90 percent are white.
>
> —Thio, *Sociology*, p. 377

(Continued)

Learning Experiment   *(Continued)*

1. What are the advantages and disadvantages of homeschooling for the child?
2. What credentials should parents be required to demonstrate in order to teach their own children?
3. Do you think a home-schooled child would learn as much or more than a traditionally schooled child? Why?

Step 3

On which topic—voucher systems or homeschooling—do you feel you would be better prepared to write a paper, make a speech, or lead a discussion group?

The Results

You most likely feel better prepared to work with the topic of home-schooling. Why? Probably because the discussion questions that you answered after reading provoked your thinking and opened up your mind to new ideas. By discussing the topic of homeschooling, you used the principle of elaboration.

Learning Principle *(What This Means to You)*

Elaborating, or thinking about and reacting to what you read, helps you to remember more of what you read and prepares you to write about and discuss the ideas. This chapter will show you how to improve your critical reading skills by reacting to and analyzing what you read. You will learn to make inferences, ask critical questions, and analyze arguments effectively. You will learn to handle exam questions, class discussions, and written assignments that demand critical reading and thinking more effectively.

MAKE INFERENCES AS YOU READ

The photograph shown on page 243 was taken from a sociology textbook. What do you think is happening? Where is it happening? How do the participants feel toward one another?

To answer these questions, you used what you saw in the photo to make reasonable guesses. The process you went through is called making an inference. An **inference** is a reasoned guess about what you don't know based on what you do know. We all make inferences throughout our daily lives. If a friend is late, you may predict that she was delayed in traffic, especially if you know she often is so delayed. If you see a seated man frequently checking his watch, you can infer that he is waiting for someone who is late.

As you read, you also need to make inferences frequently. Authors do not always directly state exactly what they mean. Instead, they may only hint at or suggest an idea. You have to reason out or infer the meaning an author intends (but did not say) on the basis of what he or she did say. For instance, suppose a writer describes a character as follows:

> As Agatha studied Agnes, she noticed that her eyes appeared misty, her lips trembled slightly, and a twisted handkerchief lay in her lap.

From the information the author provides, you may infer that Agnes is upset and on the verge of tears. Yet the writer does not say any of this. Instead, the author implies her meaning through the description she provides.

How to Make Inferences

There are no specific steps to follow in making inferences. Each inference depends on the situation and the facts provided as well as on your knowledge and experience with the situation. Following are a few general guidelines for making inferences.

1. **Be sure you understand the literal meaning first.** You need knowledge and comprehension of the stated ideas and facts before you can move to higher levels of thinking, of which making inferences is a part. For each paragraph, then, you should identify the topic, main idea, supporting details, and organizational pattern.

2. **Ask yourself questions.** Ask yourself questions such as:
   - What is the author trying to suggest through the stated information?
   - What do all the facts and ideas point toward or seem to add up to?
   - For what purpose did the author include these facts and details?

   To answer these questions, you must add together the individual pieces of information to arrive at an inference. Making an inference is somewhat like putting together a complicated picture puzzle in which you try to make each piece fit with all the rest of the pieces to form something recognizable.

3. **Use clues provided by the writer.** A writer often provides numerous hints that point you toward accurate inferences. For instance, a writer's choice of words often suggests his or her attitude toward a subject. Try to notice descriptive words, emotionally charged words, and words with strong positive or negative connotations. Here is an example of how the choice of words can lead you to an inference:

   Grandmother had been an <u>unusually attractive</u> young woman, and she carried herself with the <u>graceful confidence</u> of a <u>natural charmer</u> to her last day.

The underlined phrases *unusually attractive, graceful confidence,* and *natural charmer* suggest that the writer feels positive about her grandmother. However, in the following example, notice how the underlined words and phrases create a negative image of the person.

The <u>withdrawn</u> child <u>eyed</u> her teacher with a <u>hostile disdain</u>. When directly spoken to, the child responded in a <u>cold</u> but carefully respectful way.

In this sentence, the underlined words suggest that the child is unfriendly and that she dislikes the teacher.

4. **Consider the author's purpose.** An awareness of the author's purpose is often helpful in making inferences. If an author's purpose is to convince you to purchase a particular product, as in an advertisement, you already have a clear idea of the types of inferences the writer hopes you will make as you begin reading. For instance, here is a magazine ad for a stereo system:

If you're in the market for true surround sound, a prematched system is a good way to get it. The components in our system are built for each other by our audio engineers. You can be assured of high performance and sound quality.

It is clear that the writer's purpose is to encourage you to buy a prematched stereo system.

5. **Verify your inference.** Once you have made an inference, be sure to check that it is accurate. Look back at the stated facts to be sure you have sufficient evidence to support the inference. Also, be sure you have not overlooked other equally plausible or more plausible inferences that could be drawn from the same set of facts.

EXERCISE 1

DIRECTIONS   Read the following passages and then answer the questions. The answers are not directly stated in the passage; you will have to make inferences in order to answer the questions.

Passage A

The Lion's Share

The lion, the jackal, the wolf, and the hyena had a meeting and agreed that they would hunt together in one party and share equally among them whatever game they caught.

They went out and killed an antelope. The four animals then discussed which one of them would divide the meat. The lion said, "Whoever divides the meat must know how to count."

Immediately the wolf volunteered, saying, "Indeed, I know how to count."

He began to divide the meat. He cut off four pieces of equal size and placed one before each of the hunters.

The lion was angered. He said, "Is this the way to count?" And he struck the wolf across the eyes, so that his eyes swelled up and he could not see.

The jackal said, "The wolf does not know how to count. I will divide the meat."

He cut three portions that were small and a fourth portion that was very large. The three small portions he placed before the hyena, the wolf, and himself. The large portion he put in front of the lion, who took his meat and went away.

"Why was it necessary to give the lion such a large piece?" the hyena said. "Our agreement was to divide and share equally. Where did you ever learn how to divide?"

"I learned from the wolf," the jackal answered.

"Wolf? How can anyone learn from the wolf? He is stupid," the hyena said.

"The jackal was right," the wolf said. "He knows how to count. Before, when my eyes were open, I did not see it. Now, though my eyes are wounded, I see it clearly."

—Courlander, *The King's Drum and Other African Stories,* pp. 110–111

1. What did the jackal learn from the wolf?
2. Although "The Lion's Share" is a folktale, it does make a point. Summarize the message this story offers.

Passage B

What's Best for the Child

In many states, there are no regulations governing the number of infants a staff   1
member may care for. In those where there are, many states allow five or six. In Wisconsin, where I live, the maximum is four infants per worker. [According to the National Association for the Education of Young Children, 29 states require this four-to-one ratio, while only three—Kansas, Maryland, and Massachusetts—require a three-to-one ratio. Most of the remaining states have five-to-one or six-to-one ratios.]   2

Consider the amount of physical care and attention a baby needs—say 20 minutes for feeding every three hours or so, and 10 minutes for diapering every two hours or so, and time for the care giver to wash her hands thoroughly and sanitize the area after changing each baby. In an eight-and-a-half-hour day, then, a care giver working under the typical four-to-one ratio will have 16 diapers to change and 12 feedings to give. Four diaper changes and three feedings apiece is not an inordinate amount of care over a long day from the babies' point of view.

But think about the care giver's day: Four hours to feed the babies, two hours and   3
40 minutes to change them. If you allow an extra two and a half minutes at each changing to put them down, clean up the area, and thoroughly wash your hands, you can get by with 40 minutes for sanitizing. (And if you think about thoroughly washing your hands 16 times a day, you may begin to understand why epidemics of diarrhea and related diseases regularly sweep through infant-care centers.)

That makes seven hours and 20 minutes of the day spent just on physical care—if   4
you're lucky and the infants stay conveniently on schedule.

Since feeding and diaper changing are necessarily one-on-one activities, each infant   5
is bound to be largely unattended during the five-plus hours that the other three babies are being attended to. So, if there's to be any stimulation at all for the child, the care giver had better chat and play up a storm while she's feeding and changing.

Obviously, such a schedule is not realistic. In group infant care based on even this   6
four-to-one ratio, babies will not be changed every two hours and they will probably not be held while they're fed.

They also will not get the kind of attention and talk that is the foundation of lan-   7
guage development. If a child is deprived of language stimulation for eight to ten hours a day, how much compensation—how much "quality time"—can concerned parents provide in the baby's few other waking hours at home?

—Conniff, *The Progressive*

1. What is the author's attitude about infant care in a typical day care program?
2. What is the author implying when in the third paragraph she says ". . . if you think about thoroughly washing your hands 16 times a day, you may begin to understand why epidemics of diarrhea and related diseases regularly sweep through infant-care centers"?
3. In paragraph 7, what is the author's purpose in using the word *compensation* in referring to the parents' time with their babies at home?
4. Do you think the author would favor laws that mandate infant–worker ratios? Why?

Passage C

Stiff Laws Nab Deadbeats

The sight of deadbeat dad king Jeffrey Nichols nabbed, cuffed and jailed in New York for ducking $580,000 in child support ought to shake up other scofflaws.

A few years ago, Nichols almost surely would have escaped his responsibilities. His wealth enabled him to run to Toronto, Boca Raton, Fla., and Charlotte, Vt., and he got away with it for five years. He defied three states' court orders to pay up.

He was finally caught because in the past few years local, state and federal governments have finally gotten serious about child support.

A law Congress passed in 1992 required the FBI to chase child-support cheats when they cross state lines. Nichols became a target, culminating in his arrest.

As the scale of such enforcement has grown, it has prompted occasional criticism—particularly about use of Internal Revenue Service records to track down deadbeats. But there's no doubt it's needed.

There are 7 million deadbeat parents, 90% of them dads. If all paid what they are supposed to, their children would have $34 billion more—money that sometimes has to come from the taxpayers instead.

—McMiller, *USA Today*

1. In paragraph 1, the author states that the sight of Nichols jailed "ought to shake up other scofflaws." What is the author implying?
2. Why do you think Nichols became a target of the FBI?
3. Why would the use of Internal Revenue Service records to track down deadbeats receive criticism?
4. Why do you think 90 percent of deadbeat parents are dads?
5. In what way(s) is money taken from the taxpayers when deadbeat parents do not meet their payments?

EVALUATE THE SOURCE

Textbook information can usually be accepted as reliable and well researched. Not all other sources, however, are as worthy of your trust. Not all authors and publishers apply equally high standards of research and verification of information. Not all sources are equal in their levels of detail and technical accuracy, which depend in part on their intended audience. Consequently, checking the source can help you evaluate the accuracy and completeness of the information it contains. Suppose you were doing a research paper on the economic advantages of waste recycling. You found that each of the following sources contained information on recycling. Which do you predict would contain the type of information that would be most useful in writing a term paper?

- An article in *Reader's Digest* titled "Stiffer Laws for Waste Recycling"
- A newspaper editorial titled "Why I Recycle"
- A brochure published by the Waste Management Corporation explaining the benefits of recycling to its potential customers
- An article in *BusinessWeek* titled "Factors Influencing an Economic Boom: Recycling and Waste Management"

The *Reader's Digest* article is limited to discussing laws that regulate recycling and will not focus on its advantages. The newspaper editorial is likely to contain personal opinion rather than factual information. The brochure may be biased (see p. 252), because it was written to convince potential customers that they need the company's services. The best source will be the article in *BusinessWeek*. It is concerned with economic effects of recycling and is likely to contain fairly detailed factual information.

Knowledge and awareness of your sources, then, can help you locate information and evaluate material you are given to read. Suppose you are asked to read an article from *Time* magazine on the relationship between diet and heart disease. You would not expect it to have the same level of detail or analysis as an article in the *Journal of the American Medical Association.*

If you are unfamiliar with a source, you can still evaluate it in several ways. One way is to look for footnotes, endnotes, or a list of references. These features suggest that the author consulted other sources and/or authorities to write his or her article. Another approach is to verify the information by checking additional sources. A third is to check with college librarians; they are familiar with a variety of sources and may be able to tell you whether a particular source is considered reliable.

EXERCISE 2

DIRECTIONS   Predict how useful and appropriate each of the following sources will be for the situation described. Rate each as "Very Appropriate," "Possibly Useful," or "Not Appropriate."

1. *Source:* A *Time* magazine article on American eating habits
   Situation: You are collecting information for a research paper on food cravings for your health and nutrition class.
2. *Source:* A book titled *Junk and Collectibles: The History of Flea Markets*
   Situation: You are preparing a speech on flea markets for your public speaking class.
3. *Source:* The *Human Ecologist,* a periodical dealing with environmental health issues
   Situation: You are writing a letter to the editors of your local newspaper opposing the construction of a chemical waste treatment plant in your neighborhood; you need evidence about possible dangers.
4. *Source:* A classified ad for a Toyota
   Situation: You are shopping for a used car.
5. *Source:* A newsletter published by the Sierra Club, a group devoted to environmental protection
   Situation: You are writing a paper evaluating whether the lumber industry acts responsibly toward the environment.

EXAMINE THE AUTHOR'S QUALIFICATIONS

To evaluate printed material, the competency of the author also must be considered. If the author lacks expertise in or experience with the subject, the material he or she produces may not meet an acceptable level of scholarship and accuracy.

Depending on the type of material you are using, you have several means of checking the qualifications of an author. In textbooks, the author's credentials may be described in one of two places. The author's college or university affiliation, and possibly his or her title, may appear on the title page beneath the author's name. Second, in the preface of the book, the author may indicate or summarize his or her qualifications for writing the text. In nonfiction books and general market paperbacks, a synopsis of the author's credentials and experiences may be included on the book jacket or the back cover. However, in other types of material, little effort is made to identify the author or his or her qualifications. In newspapers, magazines, and reference books, the reader is given little or no information about the writer. You are forced to rely on the judgment of the editors or publishers to assess an author's authority.

If you are familiar with an author's work, then you can anticipate the type of material you will be reading and predict the writer's approach and attitude toward the subject. If, for example, you found an article on world banking written by former President Carter, you could predict it will have a political point of view. If you were about to read an article on John Lennon written by Ringo Starr, one of the other Beatles, you could predict the article might possibly include details of their working relationship from Ringo's point of view.

DISTINGUISH BETWEEN FACT OR OPINION

When working with any source, try to determine whether the material is factual or an expression of opinion. Facts are statements that can be verified—that is, proved to be true or false. Opinions are statements that express feelings, attitudes, or beliefs and are neither true nor false. Here are a few examples of each:

Facts

1. More than one million teenagers become pregnant every year.
2. The costs of medical care increase every year.

Opinions

1. Government regulation of our private lives should be halted immediately.
2. By the year 2025, most Americans will not be able to afford routine health care.

Facts that are taken from a reputable source or verified can be accepted and regarded as reliable information. Opinions, on the other hand, are not reliable sources of information and should be questioned and carefully evaluated. Look for evidence that supports the opinion and indicates that it is reasonable. For example, opinion 2 above is written to sound like a fact, but look closely. What basis does the author have for making that statement?

Some authors are careful to signal the reader when they are presenting an opinion. Watch for words and phrases such as:

apparently	this suggests	in my view	one explanation is
presumably	possibly	it is likely that	according to
in my opinion	it is believed	seemingly	

Other authors do just the opposite; they try to make opinions sound like facts, as in opinion 2 above.

In the following excerpt from a social problems textbook, notice how the author carefully distinguishes factual statements from opinion by using qualifying words and phrases (underlined).

Economic Change, Ideology, and Private Life

It seems clear that there has been a major change in attitudes and feelings about family relationships since the eighteenth century. It is less clear how and why the change came about. One question debated by researchers is: In what social class did the new family pattern originate—in the aristocracy, as Trumbach (1978) believes, or in the upper gentry, as Stone (1977) argued, or in the working class, as Shorter (1975) contended? Or was the rise of the new domesticity a cultural phenomenon that affected people in all social categories at roughly the same time? Carole Shammas (1980) <u>has found evidence</u> of such a widespread cultural change by looking at the kinds of things people had in their homes at various times in the past, as recorded in probate inventories. She found that in the middle of the eighteenth century all social classes experienced a change in living habits; even working-class households now contained expensive tools of domesticity, such as crockery, teapots, eating utensils, and so on. Thus, <u>according to Shammas,</u> the home was becoming an important center for social interaction, and family meals had come to occupy an important place in people's lives.

—Skolnick, *The Intimate Environment: Exploring Marriage and the Family,* p. 95

Other authors, however, mix fact and opinion without making clear distinctions. This is particularly true in the case of informed opinion, which is the opinion of an expert or authority. Ralph Nader represents expert opinion on consumer rights, for example. Textbook authors, too, often offer informed opinion, as in the following statement from an American government text:

The United States is a place where the pursuit of private, particular, and narrow interests is honored. In our culture, following the teachings of Adam Smith, the pursuit of self-interest is not only permitted but actually celebrated as the basis of the good and prosperous society.

—Greenberg and Page, *The Struggle for American Democracy,* p. 186

The author of this statement has reviewed the available evidence and is providing his expert opinion on what the evidence indicates about American political culture. The reader, then, is free to disagree and offer evidence to support an opposing view.

EXERCISE 3

DIRECTIONS   Read each of the following statements and identify whether it sounds like fact, opinion, or informed opinion.

_____ 1. United Parcel Service (UPS) is the nation's largest deliverer of packages.

_____ 2. United Parcel Service will become even more successful because it uses sophisticated management techniques.

_____ 3. UPS employees are closely supervised; new drivers are accompanied on their rounds, and time logs are kept.

_____ 4. The best way to keep up with world news is to read the newspaper.

_____ 5. A community, as defined by sociologists, is a collection of people who share some purpose, activity, or characteristic.

_____ 6. The mayor of our city is an extraordinarily honest person.

_____ 7. To a dieter, food is a four-letter word.

_____ 8. According to a leading business analyst, most television advertising is targeted toward high-spending consumer groups.

_____ 9. Americans spend $13.7 billion per year on alternative medicine and home remedies.

_____ 10. A survey of Minnesota residents demonstrated that lotteries are played most frequently by those who can least afford to play.

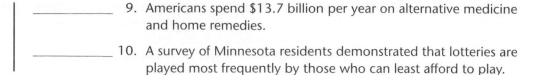

EXERCISE 4   DIRECTIONS   Read or reread "The Talk of the Sandbox: How Johnny and Suzy's Playground Chatter Prepares Them for Life at the Office" in Part Eight on page 470. Deborah Tannen is a nationally known expert on the communication styles of men and women. Underline five statements of informed opinion contained in the excerpt.

EXERCISE 5   DIRECTIONS   Using one of your own textbooks from another course, identify three statements of fact and three statements of informed opinion.

IDENTIFY THE AUTHOR'S PURPOSE

Author's purpose refers to the reason(s) a writer has for writing. Here are a few examples: Textbook authors write to inform and present information. Advertising copy writers write to sell products or services. Comic strip writers write to amuse, entertain, or provide social commentary. Essay writers write to inform, describe, or persuade.

Recognizing an author's purpose can help you decide what critical questions to ask. It can also provide a means of evaluating the material. Ask yourself: How effectively did the author accomplish what he or she set out to accomplish?

For many types of material, the author's purpose is obvious. You know, for example, that the directions on a toy carton are written to tell you how to assemble it and that an advertisement is written to sell a product or service. Other times, the author's purpose is less obvious. To find the author's purpose, use the following suggestions:

1. **Consider the source and its intended purpose.** A writer may want to reach a general-interest audience (anyone who is interested in the subject) or appeal to specific segments of the population. Most newspapers and periodicals such as *Time* and *Newsweek* appeal to a general-interest audience. The *Journal of American Medicine, Skiing Today,* and the *World of Antiques* appeal to specific audiences with specialized interests. Also, a writer may intend his or her writing for an audience with particular political, moral, or religious attitudes. Articles in the *Atlantic Monthly* often appeal to those with a conservative political viewpoint, whereas the *Catholic Digest* appeals to a particular religious group. The source can suggest certain biases, priorities, or political views. If the source does not clearly identify the intended audience, then the level of language, the choice of words, and the complexity of the ideas, examples, or arguments used will often suggest the audience the writer has in mind. Once you have identified a potential audience, you can begin to consider what it is the writer wants to communicate to that audience.
2. **Consider the point of view.** Point of view is the perspective from which an article or essay is written. A review of a rock concert, for example, may be described from the point of view of someone in the music industry or from that of someone who is a classical music fan. A controversial issue may be discussed from a more objective point of view, examining both sides of the

issue, or from a more subjective point of view, in which the author favors one side of the issue. Point of view might be described as the way an author looks at or approaches his or her subject. Accordingly, point of view can often suggest the author's purpose in writing.

3. **Decide whether the writer tries to prove anything about the subject.** Try to determine whether the article is written to persuade you to accept a certain point of view or to perform a certain action. For instance, a writer may write to convince you that inflation will cause a national disaster, or that inflicting the death penalty is morally wrong, or that the best jobs are available in health-related fields.

EXERCISE 6

DIRECTIONS   For each of the following passages, identify the author's purpose.

Passage 1

Legal Issues and the Internet

Can existing laws solve problems on the Internet that involve libel, privacy, censorship, and copyright? Is it possible, or desirable, to regulate the content of millions of communication acts that take place daily on this international highway? If so, to whom should the laws primarily apply—to the operators of the online services or to their users? And how can the rights of the creators of those materials be protected?

These are some of the questions still largely unanswered in the complex, almost anarchic, cyberspace world of the 1990s.

—Agee et al., *Introduction to Mass Communication*, p. 466

Purpose: _____

_____

Passage 2

Hunger in Rural America

Rural America is where the highest percentages of hungry people are to be found, says George Sanders, director of the Alabama Coalition Against Hunger. The irony is not lost on him: People in rural communities—where the United States raises most of the food it uses to feed not only its own citizens but much of the world as well—go hungry themselves. That's because the infrastructure of rural communities is designed to get food out, not to distribute it within, says Sanders.

Many rural people, though they are eligible, do not get food stamps or other government food support. One reason is that social service agencies don't have offices in small communities, so visiting the right government office to maintain the paperwork can mean a 100-mile odyssey.

Also, people in rural towns are sometimes unwilling to apply for food stamps because it's hard to protect their privacy. Those who do may travel to other communities to avoid using food stamps at the grocery where they've shopped all their lives.

And while urban food pantries can expect monthly shipments of food surpluses from the federal government, rural pantries get shipments only quarterly, making planning difficult. That is, it would be difficult, Sanders says, if rural communities *had* pantries. Most don't. Sparsely populated counties are hard pressed to maintain a volunteer staff at a food pantry, says Sanders.

He and other advocates say that hunger cannot be eliminated unless policymakers reappraise the nation's current food-assistance system, which simply doesn't work anymore.

—Clarke, *Salt*

Purpose: _____

_____

Passage 3

Momentum and Energy

Nearly two decades before Newton's *Principia* was published, the Royal Society of London called for experimental studies of the behavior of colliding objects. Responses were received from several of Newton's contemporaries, including Sir Christopher Wren and Christian Huygens (1629–1695). Their observations led to the discovery of laws governing the exchange of momentum and energy between two colliding objects. These ideas were known to Newton and influenced his work. Their most important result was the law of conservation of linear momentum. According to this law, the total momentum after a collision is the same as the total momentum before the collision. This law made a key contribution to the growing understanding of mechanics.

Momentum as stated in Newton's second law is often called linear momentum to distinguish it from the angular momentum associated with rotational motion, which we will discuss in Chapter 9. The independent laws concerning the conservation of energy and of linear momentum are among the most basic laws in contemporary physics. Although we will derive these laws from Newton's laws of motion, in some respects they are even more fundamental and far-reaching than Newton's laws. For example, even in situations where Newton's laws do not apply, such as speeds approaching the speed of light or dimensions on atomic scales, these conservation laws are still valid. The use of conservation laws is one of the most fundamental ways of describing nature.

For simplicity, we focus on one conservation law at a time. Here we want to emphasize the conservation of momentum. However, in some cases we will first apply conservation of momentum and then use conservation of mechanical energy. In the next chapter we will examine collisions in which the laws of conservation of momentum and of conservation of kinetic energy are applied simultaneously.

—Jones and Childers, *Contemporary College Physics,* p. 188

Purpose: _____

_____

BE ALERT FOR BIAS

Bias refers to an author's partiality, inclination toward a particular viewpoint, or prejudice. A writer is biased, for example, if she or he takes one side of a controversial issue and does not recognize opposing viewpoints. Perhaps the best example of bias occurs in advertising. A magazine advertisement for a new snack cracker, for instance, describes only positive selling features: taste, low cholesterol, convenience, and crunch. The ad does not recognize the cracker's negative features: that it's high in calories, high in fat, and so on. In some material, the writer is direct and forthright in expressing his or her bias; at other times, the bias is less obvious and is left for the reader to discover through careful analysis.

Read the following description of rock and rap music:

People used to tap their feet and smile when they listened to American popular music. Now many of us sit open-mouthed and stare: at "speed metal" rockers with roadkill hair who, despite a certain virtuosity on guitar, treat music as a form of warfare; at "grunge" bands in thrift-shop flannels who throw tantrums and smash their instruments; at "gangsta" rappers in baggy gear who posture as rapists, drug dealers, prostitutes, murderers, and terrorists. Tune in to MTV, and you will occasionally come across something wonderful. But more likely the sonic abuse and verbal–visual ugliness will appall and repel you.

"Turn that racket down," we yell, realizing that we sound just like our parents. So we chalk the problem up to age, telling ourselves that people prefer the music of their youth, and that's all there is to it. But this explanation conjures up a most unlikely prospect: today's teenagers 60 years from now attending Saturday-night dances in their retirement communities, their eyes misting over to the sounds of Megadeth, Sonic Youth, and Niggaz With Attitude. Such a future seems unlikely for the obvious but underappreciated reason that much of today's popular music evokes only the more intense, unsettling emotions of youth: anxiety, lust, anger, aggression. In the narrow gauge of its effects, such music could not be more different from the best of American popular music, which balances those emotions with tenderness, grace, and wit. Indeed, the great vigor of our music has always been its ability to blend opposites.

—Bayles, *Wilson Quarterly*

In this passage, the author's bias against rock and rap music is clear. The author's choice of words—*sonic abuse*, *verbal–visual ugliness*, and *roadkill hair*—reveals a negative attitude. Note, too, that the author's selection of detail is biased; no positive aspects of rock or rap are mentioned.

To identify bias, apply the following steps:

1. **Pay attention to emotional language.** Does the author use numerous positive or negative terms to describe the subject?
2. **Notice descriptive language.** What impression is created? How does the author make you feel?
3. **Look for opposing viewpoints.** Does the author present or ignore disadvantages, limitations, and alternative solutions?

EXERCISE 7

DIRECTIONS   Read each of the following statements, and place a check mark in front of any that reveal bias.

___ 1. Hydrogen is by far the best choice for an alternative fuel.

___ 2. Intelligent design should not be taught in schools along with evolution.

___ 3. In 1913, Arthur Whynne created the first crossword puzzle.

___ 4. The Swim to Stay Fit Program gives students an excellent way to get in shape.

___ 5. A third of all students today buy their back-to-school items online.

EXERCISE 8

DIRECTIONS   Describe the author's bias in each of the following statements.

1. Those clamoring to shut down the farmers, however, should look hard at the prospect of a prairie full of subdivisions and suburban pollution: car exhaust, lawn and garden fertilizers, woodstoves, sewage. Certainly, the smoke from field burning is an annoyance, particularly to the hard-hit Sandpoint area, and to some it's a health hazard. But the benefits the sturdy farmers produce 50 weeks of the year shouldn't be dismissed casually.

—Oliveria, "Burning Will Go; That's Not All Good," *Spokesman Review* (July 24, 2002)

2. Cruises are one of the best buys in vacationing today. Prices have not increased in over a decade yet the amenities on board have improved year after year. And the service is second to none. Passengers are pampered by employees at every turn; by the pool, in the many dining rooms, in the casino, and in their cabins, with a steward on call 24 hours a day.

—Adapted from Cook, Yale, Marqua, *Tourism: The Business of Travel*, p. 245

3. While world leaders once again pledged to help Africa, the many poor people in another part of the developing world, Latin America, attract little notice. There is a reason for that oversight: all but a wretched pair (Haiti and Nicaragua) of Latin American countries are officially classed as "middle-income" and all (except Cuba) are democracies. Latin America is less of a stain on the world's conscience.

—"Not Always With Us," *The Economist* (September 2005)

4. NASCAR can't make vague rules. This bunch of young race-car drivers is high-strung and emotional. They're hot-headed, and they react to everything quickly. They don't have the wisdom and patience of an older driver. They are young men who are wired to the max. They're coiled up like a snake all the time, and they're ready to strike at anybody or anything.

—Waltrip, "Calling Dr. Phil: NASCAR Needs Black-and-White Penalties,"
FOXSports.com (September 2005)

EXERCISE 9

DIRECTIONS Read the following passage. Underline words and phrases that reveal the author's bias.

Jerry's Got to Be Kidding
Why Disabled People Aren't Laughing

People with disabilities are outraged by the backward practices of telethons, the worst of which is the Jerry Lewis Muscular Dystrophy Association (MDA) Telethon. Some of us demonstrated against last fall's Labor Day telethon. As a writer–activist and a severely disabled person who must use a power wheelchair to get around, I helped lead a vigil outside the telethon in Los Angeles, as did others in Chicago, Denver, and other cities.

Do I watch the telethon? Yes, on tape, in manageable doses to avoid a stroke. Jerry Lewis' comedy career began with crude imitations of disabled people. He continues with smarmy, self-glorifying performances of songs like "The Wind Beneath My Wings" while mugging, beaglelike, at the camera or one of his disabled "kids." He encapsulates everything that disabled people wish to escape.

I have polio, not muscular dystrophy. Nevertheless, the stigma created by the telethon smears *all* physically disabled people. And those without muscular dystrophy do not even receive any of the MDA's stingy services.

—Bolte, *In These Times*

ANALYZE THE AUTHOR'S TONE

In speech, a speaker's tone of voice often reveals his or her attitude toward the subject and contributes to the overall message. Tone is also evident in a piece of writing, and it too contributes to meaning. Recognizing an author's tone is often important because tone can reveal feelings, attitudes, or viewpoints not directly stated by the author. An author's tone is achieved primarily through word choice and stylistic features such as sentence pattern and length.

Tone, then, often reveals feelings. Many human emotions can be communicated through tone—disapproval, hate, admiration, disgust, gratitude, and forcefulness are examples. Now read the following passage, paying particular attention to the feeling it creates.

What You Don't Know About Indians
Native American Issues Are Not History

Most Americans, even those deeply concerned about issues of justice, tend to speak of Indian issues as tragedies of the distant past. So ingrained is this position that when the occasional non-Indian does come forward on behalf of *today's* Indian cause—Marlon Brando, William Kunstler, Robert Redford, Jane Fonda, David Brower—they are all dismissed as "romantics." People are a bit embarrassed for them, as if they'd stepped over some boundary of propriety.

The Indian issue is *not* part of the distant past. Many of the worst anti-Indian campaigns were undertaken scarcely 80 to 100 years ago. Your great-grandparents were already alive at the time. The Model-T Ford was on the road.

And the assaults continue today. While the Custer period of direct military action against Indians may be over in the United States, more subtle though equally devastating "legalistic" manipulations continue to separate Indians from their land and their sovereignty.

—Mander, *Utne Reader*

Here the author's tone is concerned and serious. He is concerned about Native American issues and current legal manipulations.

An author's bias is often revealed in his or her tone. To identify an author's tone, ask yourself: How does the author feel about his or her subject and how are these feelings revealed?

EXERCISE 10

DIRECTIONS   Describe the tone of each of the following passages.

1. The caller's voice does not hold together well. I can tell he is quite old and not well. He is calling from Maryland.

   "I want four boxes of the Nut Goodies," he rasps at me after giving me his credit card information in a faltering hurry.

   "There are 24 bars in each box," I say in case he doesn't know the magnitude of his order. Nut Goodies are made here in St. Paul and consist of a patty of maple cream covered with milk chocolate and peanuts. Sort of a Norwegian praline.

   "OK, then make it five boxes but hurry this up before my nurse gets back."

   He wants the order billed to a home address but sent to a nursing home.

   "I've got Parkinson's," he says. "I'm 84."

   "OK, sir. I think I've got it all. They're on the way." I put a rush on it.

   "Right. Bye," he says, and in the pause when he is concentrating God knows how much energy on getting the receiver back in its cradle, I hear a long, dry chuckle.

   One hundred and twenty Nut Goodies.

   Way to go, buddy.

   —Swardson, *City Pages*

   Tone: _____

   _____

2. **Gleanings**

   So these three economists are on one of those Washington week-in-review shows. You know, the kind where reliable gray men with bad haircuts wear sincere gray suits and everybody talks to each other with pained grimaces like they're reunited school chums harboring a deadly secret ("She's *all* of our problem now, Finchley"). At prediction time, the grayest of the men says the economy is about to shoot toward unprecedented growth, the slate-colored one warns of triple-dip recession-sugar cone extra and the steely guy says "no change." Three different pointy heads, one economy, three totally different predictions. These are the experts? What the hell kind of job is that?

   —Durst, *"We Don't Know Squat"*

   Tone: _____

   _____

3. **What You Need**

You need a large wooden frame and enough space to accommodate it. Put comfortable chairs around it, allowing for eight women of varying ages, weight, coloring, and cultural orientation. It is preferable that this large wood frame be located in a room in a house in Atwater or Los Banos or a small town outside Bakersfield called Grasse. It should be a place that gets a thick, moist blanket of tule fog in the winter and be hot as blazes in the summer. Fix plenty of lemonade. Cookies are a nice complement.

When you choose your colors, make them sympathetic to one another. Consider the color wheel of grammar school—primary colors, phenomena of light and dark; avoid antagonism of hues—it detracts from the pleasure of the work. Think of music as you orchestrate the shades and patterns; pretend that you are a conductor in a lush symphony hall; imagine the audience saying *Ooh* and *Ahh* as they applaud your work.

—Otto, *How to Make an American Quilt*

Tone: _____

_____

EVALUATE THE DATA AND EVIDENCE

Once you have understood a writer's argument by identifying what is asserted and how, the next step is to evaluate the soundness, correctness, and worth of the reasons and evidence that support the assertion. As a critical reader, your task is to assess whether the evidence is sufficient to support the claim. Let's look at a few types of evidence that are often used.

Facts

Be sure the facts are taken from a reliable source and are verifiable.

Personal Experience

Writers often substantiate their ideas through experience and observation. Although a writer's personal account of a situation may provide an interesting perspective on an issue, personal experience should not be accepted as proof. The observer may be biased or may have exaggerated or incorrectly perceived a situation.

Examples

Examples can illustrate or explain a principle, concept, or idea. To explain what aggressive behavior is, your psychology instructor may offer several examples: fighting, punching, and kicking. Examples should not be used by themselves to prove the concept or idea they illustrate, as is done in the following passage:

The American judicial system treats those who are called for jury duty unfairly. It is clear from my sister's experience that the system has little regard for the needs of those called as jurors. My sister was required to report for jury duty the week she was on vacation. She spent the entire week in a crowded, stuffy room waiting to be called to sit on a jury and never was called.

The sister's experience does sound unfair, but it, by itself, does not prove anything about the entire judicial system.

Statistics

Many people are impressed by statistics—the reporting of figures, percentages, averages, and so forth—and assume that they are irrefutable proof. Actually, statistics can be misused, misinterpreted, or used selectively to give other than the most objective, accurate picture of a situation. Suppose you read that magazine X has increased its readership by 50 percent while magazine Y had only a 10 percent increase. From this statistic, some readers might assume that magazine X has a wider readership than magazine Y. However, obtaining complete information may well reveal that this is not true. The missing, but crucial, statistic is the total readership of each magazine prior to the increase. If magazine X had a readership of 20,000 and increased it by 50 percent, its readership would total 30,000. However, if magazine Y's readership was already 50,000, a 10 percent increase (bringing the new total to 55,000) would still give it the larger readership, despite the fact that it made the smaller increase. Always approach statistical evidence with a critical, questioning attitude.

Statistics are often presented in graphical form. Writers use graphs to make points dramatically. At times they may exaggerate certain data by manipulating how the graph is drawn or by their choice of what scale to use.

Comparisons and Analogies

Comparisons and analogies (extended comparisons) serve as illustrations and are often used in argument. Their reliability depends on how closely the comparison corresponds, or how similar it is, to the situation to which it is being compared. For example, Martin Luther King, Jr., in his famous letter from the Birmingham jail, compared nonviolent protesters to a robbed man. To evaluate this comparison, you would need to consider how the two are similar and how they are different. In general, no two things are exactly the same.

Appeal to Authority

A writer may quote a well-known person or expert on the issue. Unless the well-known person is knowledgeable or experienced with the issue, his or her opinion is not relevant. Whenever an expert is cited, be certain that the expert offers support for her or his opinion.

Cause–Effect Relationships

A writer may argue that when two events occurred in close sequence, one caused the other. In other words, a writer may assume a cause–effect relationship when none exists. For example, suppose unemployment decreased the year a new town mayor was elected. The mayor may claim she brought about the decrease in unemployment. However, the decrease may have been caused by factors the mayor was not involved with, such as a large corporation opening a branch within the town and creating new jobs.

Relevancy and Sufficiency of Evidence

Once you have identified the evidence used to support an argument, the next step is to decide whether the writer has provided enough of the right kind of evidence to lead you to accept his or her claim. This is always a matter of judgment; there are no easy rules to follow. You must determine (1) whether the evidence provided directly supports the statement and (2) whether sufficient evidence has been provided.

Suppose an article in your campus newspaper urges the elimination of mathematics as a required course at your college. As evidence, the student offers the following:

> Mathematics does not prepare us for the job market. In today's world, calculators and computer programs have eliminated the need for the study of mathematics.

This evidence neither directly supports the statement nor provides sufficient evidence. First, calculators and computer programs do not substitute for an understanding of mathematical principles. Second, the writer does nothing to substantiate his idea that mathematics is irrelevant to the job market. The writer should provide facts, statistics, expert opinion, or other forms of documentation.

EXERCISE 11

DIRECTIONS   For each of the following statements, discuss the type or types of evidence that you would need in order to support and evaluate the statement.

1. Individuals must accept primary responsibility for the health and safety of their children.
2. Apologizing is often seen as a sign of weakness, especially among men.
3. There has been a steady increase in illegal immigration over the past 50 years.
4. More college women than college men agree that euthanasia should be legal.
5. Car advertisements sell fantasy experiences, not a means of transportation.

ANALYZE ARGUMENTS

An argument has three essential parts:

- issue
- claim
- support

First, an argument must address an **issue**—a problem or controversy about which people disagree. Abortion, gun control, animal rights, capital punishment, and drug legalization are all examples of issues. Second, an argument must take a position on an issue. This position is called a **claim.** An argument may claim that capital punishment should be outlawed or that medical use of marijuana should be legalized. Finally, an argument offers **support** for the claim. Support consists of reasons and evidence that the claim is reasonable and should be accepted. An argument may also include a fourth part—a **refutation.** A refutation considers opposing viewpoints and attempts to disprove or discredit them.

Here is an example: baseball players' use of steroids is an issue. A claim could be made that baseball players' use of steroids is unhealthy and unfair and that owners and players need to take the issue seriously. Support for the claim could include reasons why steroid use is unhealthy and unfair. An opposing viewpoint to the author's argument may be that steroid use creates enhanced performance, which makes the game more fun and competitive for fans. This argument could be refuted by providing evidence that fans dislike extraordinary feats of performance and would prefer to see the game played without the use of performance-enhancing drugs.

For most issues, more than one claim is possible. For example, on the issue of gun control, here are three possible claims:

- All handguns should be legal.
- No handguns should be legal.
- Some handguns should be legal for certain individuals.

Consider the issue of abortion. Here are three possible claims:

- No abortions should be allowed.
- All abortions should be legal.
- Some abortions should be allowed under special circumstances.

An argument, then, takes one position on an issue and provides reasons and evidence that its claim is sound or believable.

EXERCISE 12

DIRECTIONS   For each of the following issues, identify at least two claims and write a sentence expressing each.

1. Immigration laws restricting entry into the United States

   _____

   _____

2. Drug testing in the workplace

   _____

   _____

3. Smoking in public places

   _____

   _____

EXERCISE 13

DIRECTIONS   For each of the following essay titles, predict the issue and claim that the essay addresses.

1. "Organic Farming: Quality and Environmental Care"
2. "Park Neighbors Applaud Curfew"
3. "Limited Access Limits Votes of Disabled"
4. "Global Warming Linked to Hurricanes"
5. "Solar Energy: An Energy Alternative Whose Time Has Come"

Types of Support

Three common types of support are reasons, evidence, and emotional appeals. A **reason** is a general statement that supports a claim. It explains why the writer's viewpoint is reasonable and should be accepted. In an argument opposing steroid use by baseball players, two primary reasons are

- it is unhealthy, and
- it is unfair.

Evidence consists of facts, statistics, experiences, comparisons, and examples that demonstrate why the claim is valid. To support the claim that steroids are unhealthy, a writer could offer medical facts that demonstrate that steroids are dangerous to one's health. Alternatively, the writer could provide an example of a player who used steroids and describe his health problems.

Emotional appeals are ideas that are targeted toward needs or values that readers are likely to care about. Needs include physiological needs (food, drink, shelter) and psychological needs (sense of belonging, sense of accomplishment, sense of self-worth, sense of competency). In an argument against steroid use, the writer could appeal to a reader's sense of fairness—players should not be allowed to succeed by using drugs rather than natural talent. The writer could also appeal to the reader's sense of nostalgia by mentioning baseball traditions that are being corrupted. An argument favoring gun control, for example, may appeal to a reader's need for safety, while an argument favoring restrictions on sharing personal or financial information may appeal to a reader's need for privacy and financial security.

EXERCISE 14

DIRECTIONS   Identify the type(s) of evidence used to support each of the following brief arguments.

1. Many students have part-time jobs that require them to work late afternoons and evenings during the week. These students are unable to use the library during the week. Therefore, library hours should be extended to weekends.
2. Because parents have the right to determine their children's sexual attitudes, sex education should take place in the home, not at school.
3. No one should be forced to inhale unpleasant or harmful substances. That's why the ban on cigarette smoking in public places was put into effect in our state. Why shouldn't there be a law to prevent people from wearing strong colognes or perfumes, especially in restaurants, since the sense of smell is important to taste?

Reading an Argument

When reading arguments, use the following steps:

READING ARGUMENTS

1. **Identify the issue.** What controversial question or problem does the argument address?
2. **Identify the claim/position, idea, or action the writer is trying to convince you to accept.** Often, a concise statement of this key point appears early in the argument or in the introduction of a formal essay. The author often restates this key point.
3. **Read the entire article or essay completely, more than once if necessary.** Underline key evidence that supports the author's claim.
4. **Evaluate the types of evidence the author provides.** Does he or she offer statistics, facts, or examples? Is the evidence relevant and sufficient?
5. **Watch for conclusions.** Words and phrases such as *since, thus, therefore, accordingly, it can be concluded, it is clear that, it follows that,* and *hence* are signals that a conclusion is about to be given.
6. **Reread the argument and examine its content and structure.** What is stated? What is implied or suggested?
7. **Write a brief outline of the argument, listing its key points.**

Now read the following brief argument, applying the steps listed above.

Misstep on Video Violence
USA Today

In the booming world of video games, there are more than a few dark corners: Murder and mayhem. Blood and gore. Explicit sex and abuse of women. In one of the best-selling series, Grand Theft Auto, car stealing is accompanied by drug use, shootouts that kill police and bystanders, and simulated sex with comely prostitutes who are beaten with baseball bats afterward.

Small wonder some parents are concerned over what game-crazed teens may be up to. And small wonder, too, that legislators in several states are playing to these concerns by trying to outlaw the sale of violent and sexually explicit games to minors. A bill banning the sale of such games to anyone younger than 18 is awaiting the governor's signature in Illinois. A similar proposal is moving in the Michigan Legislature. The issue has been raised this year in at least nine other states and the District of Columbia. But to what useful end?

This is the latest chapter in a very old story. When teenage entertainment offends adult sensibilities—think Elvis Presley's pulsating hips or the arrival on newsstands of Hugh Hefner's Playboy—the first response is to see the new phenomenon as a threat to social order. The second is to attempt to ban it. Parents—former teenagers all—seem to forget history's lesson: The bans never work. And they're probably not constitutional, anyway. Courts have ruled that today's sophisticated video games are protected as creative expression. If communities want to limit access, they must show overriding evidence that the games pose a public threat. That evidence does not exist.

Lawmakers and activist groups assert that the thrill of engaging in virtual criminal activity will spur teens to try the real thing. But the violent crime rate has gone down nearly 30% since the first bloody shoot-'em-up games debuted in the early 1990s. Youth crime rates have dropped even more. And a Federal Trade Commission survey found parents already involved in 83% of video-game purchases and rentals for minors.

Judges have repeatedly rejected as flawed the studies that advocates say show a link between fantasy violence and anti-social behavior. To the extent there is a threat, it is mainly to the individual, vulnerable teenager, and it can be addressed only by parents.

Unknown to many parents, they're getting some help. The game industry's rating system classifies games in six categories from "early childhood" to "adults only" and requires detailed content descriptions. Also, newer models of popular games include parental controls that can block their use for age-inappropriate games. Manufacturers have announced an expanded ratings-education program, and major retailers are tightening their restrictions on sales to minors.

There will always be a market for the dark, tasteless, even the outrageous, and parents ought to keep kids away from it. But even with the best intentions of legislators, the problem is beyond their reach. New laws are likely to give parents only the false impression that someone else is solving that problem for them.

—USA Today, June 6, 2005

The issue discussed in the argument is legislation banning video violence. The author takes the position that legislation is not effective in controlling video violence.

The author offers the following reasons:

- The bans never work. He cites the examples of Elvis Presley and *Playboy* magazine.
- The bans may not be constitutional.
- The games do not pose a public threat. He or she offers statistics that violent crime is dropping since video games came on the market.

- Many parents already monitor video game use.
- The game industry already classifies the games, gives details of their content, and plans a ratings education program.
- Retailers are tightening restrictions on sales to minors.

EXERCISE 15

DIRECTIONS   Read the argument below, paying particular attention to the type(s) of evidence used. Then answer the questions that follow.

Death Penalty Debate Finally Produces Useful Result
USA Today

For the past half century, the nation has been locked—deadlocked might be a better word—in a bitter debate over the death penalty. But what if there is a middle ground? With little fanfare, a compromise has been gaining favor for more than a decade, drawing support as DNA evidence has exonerated inmates on death row. Last week, it reached a milestone. Texas, site of one in three executions, gave juries the option to sentence defendants in capital cases to life without parole rather than death.

All but one death-penalty state, New Mexico, now offers that choice, a marked change from the era when life sentences were a meaningless illusion. But why stop at making life without parole just an optional alternative to execution? It is a fitting replacement, assuring severe punishment for the worst of crimes but with a safety valve to protect those falsely accused or wrongly sentenced.

Evidence of the need pours in weekly now. Five times in the past seven months, the Supreme Court has had to rein in state courts that mishandled death penalty cases. On Monday, the court ordered a new sentencing trial in a Pennsylvania case involving shoddy work by the lawyer for an accused murderer. Last week, the court sent back cases from Texas and California that reeked of racial discrimination in jury selection. Earlier, the court ruled against Texas (again) and Missouri (twice) in cases of excluding relevant evidence, making defendants appear in shackles and executing juveniles.

Just last week at the state level:

- An Oklahoma appeals court ordered a new trial for a man sentenced to death in a 1982 murder on the basis of testimony from a police chemist who has since been fired for poor and unreliable lab work.
- An Illinois man jailed for eight months and facing the death penalty in his daughter's death was released when a long-overdue DNA test finally came back—negative.
- A former North Carolina judge urged the state Legislature to impose a two-year moratorium on executions.

Against this backdrop, the rate of executions has dropped 40% from its onetime high.

Since the death penalty was reinstated in 1976, the Supreme Court has tried to make clear that it is to be applied carefully and evenhandedly. Nevertheless, cases of incompetent lawyering, suppression of evidence, local prejudice and other affronts to justice keep appearing. The result is evident in the numbers who narrowly escaped execution: While 972 people have been put to death since the 1970s, at least 119 have been taken off death row because of evidence they were wrongly convicted or sentenced.

According to a Gallup Poll in May, 74% of the public supports the death penalty, but backing for capital punishment drops to 56% when respondents are given the alternative of life without parole. Even in Texas, a Scripps-Howard poll last October found that while 75% supported the death penalty, 78% favored the option of life without parole.

Already, life without the death penalty is the norm in a growing number of states. In addition to the 12 that don't allow it, five others have had no executions in more than 30 years; six have used it only once in that time. Abolishing the death penalty and using life without parole instead can't fix all the injustices exposed in courts across the nation. But at least no one would be executed as a result.

—*USA Today,* June 22, 2005

1. What is the issue? _____

2. What is the claim?_____

3. What types of evidence are used? _____

4. Is the evidence convincing? _____

5. Is there sufficient evidence? Why or why not?_____

6. What action is called for?_____

LEARNING COLLABORATIVELY

DIRECTIONS   Bring to class a brief (two- to three-paragraph) newspaper article, editorial, film review, and so on. Working in groups of three or four students, each student should read his or her piece aloud or distribute copies. The group should discuss and evaluate (1) the source of the material, (2) the author's qualifications, (3) whether more facts or opinions are represented, (4) the author's purpose, (5) any bias, and (6) the tone of the passage. Your group should choose one article and submit your findings to the class or instructor.

APPLYING YOUR LEARNING

Ian is taking a business course in which he is studying forms of business ownership: sole proprietorships, partnerships, corporations, cooperatives, syndicates, and joint ventures. He read and highlighted his textbook and attended all class lectures. To prepare for an essay exam, Ian made a study sheet summarizing the characteristics of each form of ownership. When Ian read the following exam question, he knew he was in trouble.

Exam Question

Suppose you are the sole proprietor of a successful car wash. The owner of a competing car wash suggests that you form a partnership. Another competitor suggests that you enter into a joint venture to explore expansion opportunities. And a major car wash chain offers you a management position and stock in the corporation if you sell out. Write an essay explaining what factors you would consider in making a decision.

1. What levels of thinking did Ian use in preparing for the exam?
2. Why was Ian in trouble? That is, what types of thinking does the question demand?
3. How should Ian have prepared for the exam?

APPLYING YOUR SKILLS: Sample Textbook Chapter

1. Describe the tone of the sample textbook chapter.
2. The author is a professor at Hunter College of the City University of New York. What further information would you need to evaluate his qualifications to write the book from which this chapter was taken?
3. Do an Internet search using Google or another search engine and locate information about Professor DeVito. Use this information to evaluate his qualifications.

QUESTIONS FOR DISCUSSION

1. Think about editorials that you've read in your school or local paper. What makes a great editorial? What makes a poor editorial? What techniques can an author use to present his or her argument and supporting evidence in an editorial?
2. Why is making inferences helpful in college studies? What subjects most frequently require you to make inferences?
3. Why is critical thinking particularly important when using Web sites?
4. What types of evidence are typically used in articles related to the topics you are studying? What types of questions should you ask when dealing with these various types of evidence?

SELF-TEST SUMMARY

1. What is an inference?	An inference is a reasoned guess about what you do not know based on information that you do have.
2. Why is it important to check the source of material?	Not all sources are reliable or trustworthy.
3. Why should you check the author's qualifications?	Not all authors are qualified to write about their subjects. From an unqualified author you may get incomplete or incorrect information.
4. What is the difference between facts and opinions?	Facts are statements that can be verified as correct. Opinions express feelings, attitudes, and beliefs and are neither true nor false.
5. How can you identify an author's purpose?	You can identify an author's purpose by considering the source, the point of view, and persuasive statements of the author's writing.
6. What is author bias?	Author bias refers to an author's partiality or inclination to express only one viewpoint.
7. What is tone?	Tone is an expression of the author's attitude toward his or her subject.
8. What are seven types of evidence?	Evidence includes facts, personal experience, examples, statistics, comparisons and analogies, appeal to authority, and cause–effect relationships.
9. What are the three parts of an argument?	An argument addresses an issue, takes a position or makes a claim, and presents reason and evidence to support the position.

Quick Quiz

NAME:

DIRECTIONS Write the letter of the choice that best completes each statement in the space provided.

CHECKING YOUR RECALL

_____ 1. A fact is a statement that
   a. can be verified.
   b. is true.
   c. has no proof.
   d. expresses an opinion.

_____ 2. Statistics must be evaluated primarily because they may
   a. include too many facts.
   b. have appeared in another source first.
   c. have been manipulated.
   d. be based on another person's research.

_____ 3. All of the following questions indicate a higher level of thinking *except:*
   a. What are the author's qualifications?
   b. Is the material fact or opinion?
   c. What is the literal meaning of the material?
   d. What is the author's purpose?

_____ 4. One characteristic of biased writing is that it
   a. analyzes examples in great detail.
   b. favors a particular viewpoint.
   c. presents evidence objectively.
   d. consists primarily of untrue statements.

_____ 5. The author's position in an argument can best be described as the
   a. author's paraphrase of the issue.
   b. author's collection of relevant evidence.
   c. idea the author wants you to agree with.
   d. concept the author is refuting.

APPLYING YOUR SKILLS

_____ 6. Antonio arrived several minutes late for his sociology class and discovered the room empty and dark. He decided that the class must have been canceled and went to the library instead. In this situation, Antonio reached his decision by making
   a. an informed opinion.
   b. an inference.
   c. a generalization.
   d. a connotation.

_____ 7. In her research on homeschooling, Raquel has encountered the following statements. The one that is an example of an opinion is
   a. over half a million children are homeschooled annually.
   b. home-schooled children completely miss out on all those normal social advantages that a child in public school gets every day.
   c. most parents who homeschool their children have had at least one year of college.
   d. most homeschooling parents are middle-class, with median incomes between $35,000 and $50,000.

_____ 8. Robert has a literature assignment in which he has to identify Jane Austen's tone in *Persuasion*. In this assignment, he will be looking specifically for Austen's
   a. feelings about her subject.
   b. purpose for writing.
   c. style of writing.
   d. use of historical information.

_____ 9. Analise wants to identify bias in the articles she has found while researching the need for increased security in courtrooms. Analise can assume an article is biased when the author
   a. presents both sides of a controversial issue.
   b. includes numerous facts and statistics as evidence.
   c. attempts to appeal to a general-interest audience.
   d. uses primarily positive or negative terms to describe the subject.

_____ 10. Trevor has been asked to evaluate the argument presented by the author of an article on the use of the atomic bomb in World War II. As a critical reader, Trevor should evaluate an argument primarily by deciding whether the
   a. author's ideas agree with his own.
   b. evidence is relevant and sufficient.
   c. author's personal experience is interesting and believable.
   d. supporting details are presented dramatically.

265

MULTIMEDIA *Activities*

Evaluating the Author's Message

1 The next time you are making weekend plans with your family or friends, have each person create an argument to try to convince the rest of the group to choose his or her proposed activity. Share these with a classmate by e-mail, by phone, or in person, and analyze the types of evidence used. Who presented the strongest case?

2 Sharpen your critical thinking skills by playing games. There are many board and card games that you may have played that call for strategy, logic, and inference. Host a game night where each person brings a challenging game and a snack.

3 Brain Teasers and Puzzles

http://www.brainbashers.com/

Try some of the challenges in this huge database of puzzles, and be sure to view the optical illusions too. Try making up some of your own to stump your classmates.

4 Look for evidence of critical thinking skills on TV or in the movies. Write down examples of characters making inferences, evaluating evidence, and creating arguments.

5 Identifying the Argument of an Essay

http://commhum.mccneb.edu/argument/summary.htm

Try this online tutorial in critical reasoning from Metropolitan Community College in Nebraska. Complete the exercises and make notes about the new concepts you learn.

6 Critical Thinking Forum

http://www.criticalthinking.org/forum/index.php?board=11.0

Monitor this forum for college and university students about critical thinking from the Foundation for Critical Thinking. Make a list of topics addressed in the forum and note your thoughts on these topics. Consider posting some of your ideas.

11 Evaluating the Author's Technique

Why Evaluate the Author's Technique?

■ You will learn to evaluate and interpret an author's message.

■ You will become more successful in reading and evaluating a wide range of authors and sources.

■ You will be able to select accurate, reliable information to include in papers and speeches.

Learning Experiment

Step 1

Read each of the statements shown in Step 2.

Step 2

Place a check mark in front of each statement that you think is true, for which you do not need further information, and which you could safely use in a research paper, provided that it came from a reliable source.

_____ 1. The governor of our state is a loose cannon.

_____ 2. They say that the economy is booming and will show further improvement over next year.

_____ 3. The tendency to prefer products and people from one's own culture over those from other cultures is known as ethnocentrism.

_____ 4. Politicians are a greedy, lazy bunch.

_____ 5. People in glass houses shouldn't throw stones.

_____ 6. Senator Whiner's foreign policies were criticized and then defeated.

The Results

Did you check only statement 3? If so, this shows that you are a questioning, critical thinker. All of the other statements are questionable. You need further explanation, evidence, or more information before you can accept them as reliable.

Learning Principle
(What This Means to You)

Reading with a critical eye and a questioning attitude are important skills. This chapter will show you how to recognize the various techniques writers can use to mislead, misguide, or even deceive a reader. You will learn how to spot emotional language, interpret figurative language, examine generalizations and assumptions, and study manipulative language.

PAY ATTENTION TO CONNOTATIVE LANGUAGE

If you were wearing a jacket that looked like leather but was made out of man-made fibers, would you prefer it be called *fake* or *synthetic?* Would you rather be part of a *crowd* or a *mob?* Would you rather be called *thin* or *skinny?*

Each of the pairs of words above has basically the same meaning. A *crowd* and a *mob* are both groups of people. Both *fake* and *synthetic* refer to something manmade. If the words have similar meanings, why did you choose *crowd* rather than *mob* and *synthetic* rather than *fake?* While the pairs of words have similar primary meanings, they carry different shades of meaning; each creates a different image or association in your mind. This section explores these shades of meaning, called connotative meanings.

All words have one or more standard meanings. These meanings are called **denotative meanings.** Think of them as those meanings listed in the dictionary. They tell us what the word names. Many words also have connotative meanings. **Connotative meanings** include the feelings and associations that may accompany a word. For example, the denotative meaning of *sister* is a female sibling. However, the word carries many connotations. For some, *sister* suggests a playmate with whom they shared their childhood. For others the term may suggest an older sibling who watched over them. Let us take another example, the word *breakfast.* Its denotative meaning is "a morning meal," but its connotative meaning to many may suggest grabbing food on the run. To others it may suggest a leisurely start to the day.

Connotations can vary from individual to individual. The denotative meaning for the word *flag* is a piece of cloth used as a national emblem. To many, the American flag is a symbol of patriotism and love of one's country. To some people, though, it may mean an interesting decoration to place on their clothing. The word *dog* to dog lovers suggests a loyal and loving companion. To those who are allergic to dogs, however, the word *dog* connotes discomfort and avoidance—itchy eyes, a runny nose, and so forth.

Writers and speakers use connotative meanings to stir your emotions or to bring to mind positive or negative associations. Suppose a writer is describing how someone drinks. The writer could choose words such as *gulp, sip, slurp,* or *guzzle.* Each creates a different image of the person. Connotative meanings, then, are powerful tools of language. When you read, be alert for meanings suggested by the author's word choice. When writing or speaking, be sure to choose words with appropriate connotations.

EXERCISE 1

DIRECTIONS   For each of the following pairs of words, underline the word with the more positive connotation.

1. suspicious	curious
2. simple	plain
3. shove	nudge
4. immature	youthful
5. mistake	blunder
6. welcome	allow
7. junk	salvage
8. enthusiastic	fanatic
9. timid	shy
10. easygoing	lazy

EXERCISE 2

DIRECTIONS For each word listed, write a word that has similar denotative meaning but a negative connotation. Then write a word that has a positive or neutral connotation.

WORD	NEGATIVE CONNOTATION	POSITIVE or NEUTRAL CONNOTATION
Example: slow	sluggish	gradual
1. large	_____	_____
2. persuade	_____	_____
3. characteristic	_____	_____
4. uncommon	_____	_____
5. work	_____	_____
6. protect	_____	_____
7. toss	_____	_____
8. lecture	_____	_____
9. obtain	_____	_____
10. smart	_____	_____

EXERCISE 3

DIRECTIONS Discuss the differences in the connotative meaning of each of the following sets of words. Consult a dictionary, if necessary.

1. refuge: retreat—shelter—hideout
2. original: unusual—strange—creative
3. sensitive: responsive—thin-skinned—emotional
4. enemy: adversary—opponent—rival
5. tolerant: permissive—liberal—soft
6. routine: regular—predictable—boring
7. trick: prank—feat—hoax
8. complaint: protest—criticism—gripe
9. fascinate: charm—hypnotize—seduce
10. careful: cautious—particular—fussy

EXAMINE FIGURATIVE LANGUAGE

Figurative language makes a comparison between two unlike things that share one common characteristic. If you say that your apartment looked as if it had been struck by a tornado, you are comparing two unlike things—your apartment and the effects of a tornado. Figurative language makes sense creatively or imaginatively, but not literally. You mean that the apartment is messy and disheveled. Figurative language is a powerful tool that allows writers to create images or paint pictures in the reader's mind. We all know the devastation caused by a tornado and have a visual picture of it. Figurative language also allows writers to suggest an idea without directly stating it. If you say the mayor bellowed like a bear, you are suggesting that the mayor was animal-like, loud, and forceful, but you have not said so directly. By planting the image of bear-like behavior, you have communicated your message to your reader.

There are three primary types of figurative language—similes, metaphors, and personification. A **simile** uses the words *like* or *as* to make the comparison:

The computer hums like a beehive.

After 5:00 P.M. our downtown is as quiet as a ghost town.

A **metaphor** states or implies the relationship between the two unlike items. Metaphors often use the word *is*.

The computer lab is a beehive.

After 5:00 P.M. our downtown is a ghost town.

Personification compares humans and nonhumans according to one characteristic, attributing human characteristics to ideas or objects. If you say "the wind screamed its angry message," you are giving the wind the humanlike characteristics of screaming, being angry, and communicating a message. Here are some other examples:

The sun mocked us with its relentless glare.

After two days of writer's block, her pen started dancing across the page.

Because figurative language is a powerful tool, be sure to analyze the author's motive for using it. Often, a writer uses figurative language as a way of describing rather than telling. A writer could say "The woman blushed" (telling) or "The woman's cheeks filled with the glow of a fire" (describing). Other times, however, figurative language is a means of suggesting ideas or creating impressions without directly stating them. When evaluating figurative language, ask the following questions:

- Why did the writer make the comparison?
- What is the basis or shared characteristic of the comparison?
- Is the comparison accurate?
- What images does the comparison suggest? How do these images make you feel?
- Is the comparison positive or negative?
- Are several different interpretations possible?

EXERCISE 4

DIRECTIONS   Explain the comparison in each of the following examples of figurative language.

1. The rain moved like a curtain across the lake.
2. At the busy playground, the child was glued to her mother's side.
3. Every time the locker room door opened, a pungent bouquet of dirty socks, wet towels, and sweaty boys smacked us in the face.
4. The roast beef was as tough as an old boot.
5. After hours of delays, the weary passengers were herded like sheep through the airport and onto a hotel shuttle bus.

EXERCISE 5

DIRECTIONS   Discuss how the writer of each of the following passages uses figurative language to create a specific impression.

1. Aliens have invaded Hollywood. Helped by new computer graphics technology that has simplified the creation of weird-looking extraterrestrials, the silver screen is now crawling with cosmic critters eager to chow down on us, abduct us, or just tick us off as they total our planet. Why are aliens suddenly infesting the local multiplex? Partly it's because after the collapse of the Soviet Union, Hollywood had to hunt around for a new source of bad guys. But our own space program has also convinced many among the popcorn-eating public that visiting other worlds will be a walk in the park for any advanced species.

—Bennett, Shostak, and Jakosky, *Life in the Universe*, p. 2

2. A frequent objection is that poetry ought not to be studied at all. In this view, a poem is either a series of gorgeous noises to be funneled through one ear and out the other without being allowed to trouble the mind, or an experience so holy that to analyze it in a classroom is as cruel and mechanical as dissecting a hummingbird.

—Kennedy and Gioia, *Literature: An Introduction to Fiction, Poetry, and Drama*, p. 454

3. Thick as a truck at its base, the Brazil-nut tree rises 10 stories to an opulent crown, lord of the Amazon jungle. It takes the tree a century to grow to maturity; it takes a man with a chain saw an hour to cut it down. "It's a beautiful thing," nods Acelino Cardoso da Silva, a 57-year-old farmer. "But I have six hungry people at home. If the lumberman turns up, I'll sell."

—Margolis, "A Plot of Their Own," *Newsweek* (January 21, 2002)

EXERCISE 6

DIRECTIONS   Convert each of the following statements to an expression of figurative language.

Example: The daffodils bloomed. The daffodils covered the hillside like a bright yellow blanket.

1. People cried at the movie.
2. I was embarrassed.
3. We ate too much.
4. The fireworks were beautiful.
5. It snowed a lot last night.

WATCH FOR MISSING INFORMATION

Writers mislead by omission. Writers may omit essential details, ignore contradictory evidence, or selectively include only details that favor their position. They may also make incomplete comparisons, use the passive voice, or use unspecified nouns and pronouns.

Suppose, in describing homeschooling, an author states, "Many children find homeschooling rewarding." But what is the author not telling us? If the author does not tell us that some children find homeschooling lonely and feel isolated from their peers, the author is not presenting a fair description of homeschooling. The writer has deliberately omitted essential details that a reader needs to understand homeschooling.

Suppose the same writer describes a research study that concludes that homeschooled children excel academically. The writer, to be fair, should also report that other studies have demonstrated that homeschooled children do not differ in academic achievement from traditionally educated students. In this case, the writer has ignored contradictory evidence, reporting only evidence that he or she wants the reader to know.

In describing a homeschool environment, suppose the writer reports that "the home environment is ideal" and goes on to describe features such as comfortable home surroundings, flexible scheduling, and supportive parental mentoring. To be fair, the writer should also point out what the home environment lacks. A home environment may lack a library of instructional software, collaborative learning activities with classmates, or the services of learning support specialists. The writer, then, selectively reported details, telling us what was positive and omitting negative details.

Suppose the writer concludes his or her article on homeschooling by saying, "Homeschooling is the better route to follow to produce a well-educated child." What the writer has not told us is what route homeschooling is better than. Is it better than a private school? Is it better than a public school? Is it better than hiring a private tutor? The writer has made an incomplete comparison.

One way writers avoid revealing information is to use a particular sentence structure that does not identify who performed a specified action. In the sentence *The cup broke,* you do not know who broke the cup. In the sentence *The bill was paid,* you do not know who paid the bill. This sentence pattern is called the passive voice. Here are a few more examples of the passive voice. In each, notice what information is missing.

The tax reform bill was defeated.

The accounting procedures were found to be questionable.

The oil spill was contained.

Another way writers avoid revealing information is to use nouns and pronouns that do not refer to a specific person or thing. The sentence *They said it would rain by noon* does not reveal who predicted rain. The sentence *It always happens to me* does not indicate what always happens to the writer. Here are a few more examples:

They say the enemy is preparing to attack.

Anyone can get rich with this plan; many people have already.

Politicians don't care about people.

To be sure you are getting full and complete information, ask the following questions:

- What important information is omitted? (What have you not told me?)
- What contradictory evidence is not reported?
- Has the author selectively reported details to further his or her cause?
- Does the author explain incomplete comparisons?
- What else do I need to know?

To answer these questions, it may be necessary to do additional reading or research, either on the Internet or in your college library. Try to locate another article on the same topic and notice what additional information is included.

EXERCISE 7

DIRECTIONS   For each of the following statements, indicate what information is missing.

1. They were denied health insurance.
2. Ticket prices have doubled this year.
3. Anyone can get a fake I.D.
4. Our schools are safer.
5. Real estate prices are inflated in parts of the country.

BE ALERT FOR GENERALIZATIONS

Suppose you are reading an article that states that "Artists are temperamental people." Do you think that every artist who ever painted a portrait or composed a song is temperamental? Can you think of exceptions? This statement is an example of a generalization. A **generalization** is a statement about an entire group (musicians) based on known information about part of the group (musicians the writer has met or observed). A generalization requires a leap from what is known to a conclusion about what is unknown. Generalizations may be expressed using words such as *all, always, none,* or *never.* Some statements may imply but not directly state that the writer is referring to the entire group or class. The statement "Musicians are temperamental people" suggests but does not directly state that all musicians are temperamental. Here are a few more generalizations:

> Rich people are snobs.
>
> Chinese food is never filling.
>
> Pets are always troublesome.

The key to evaluating generalizations is to evaluate the type, quality, and amount of evidence given to support them. Here are a few more generalizations. What type of evidence would you need to convince you that each is or is not true?

> College students are undecided about future career goals.
>
> Fast food lacks nutritional value.
>
> Foreign cars outperform similar American models.

For the generalization about college students, you might need to see research studies about college students' career goals, for example. And then, even if studies did conclude that many college students are undecided, it would not be fair to conclude that every single student is undecided. If no evidence is given, then the generalization is not trustworthy and should be questioned.

You can also evaluate a generalization by seeing whether the author provides specifics about the generalization. For the statement "Pets are always troublesome," ask what kind of pets the author is referring to—a pet potbellied pig, an iguana, or a cat? Then ask what is meant by troublesome—does it mean the animal is time consuming, requires special care, or behaves poorly?

Another way to evaluate a generalization is to try to think of exceptions. For the generalization *Medical doctors are aloof and inaccessible,* can you think of a doctor you have met or heard about who was caring and available to his or her patients? If so, the generalization is not accurate in all cases.

EXERCISE 8

DIRECTIONS   Read each of the following statements and place a check mark before each generalization.

____ 1. Motorcyclists are thrill-seekers.

____ 2. Houses are not built like they used to be.

____ 3. In the United States, hurricane season lasts from June 1 to November 30.

____ 4. Cars equipped with diesel engines are about 25 percent more efficient than regular cars.

____ 5. People who visit online chat rooms are looking for trouble.

EXERCISE 9

DIRECTIONS   Read each of the following paragraphs and underline each generalization.

1. Students who attend coeducational middle and high schools are at a disadvantage. Teenage boys and girls always learn better in single-sex classrooms, without the constant distraction of the opposite sex.

2. Travelers are fed up with their treatment by the airlines. Flight delays occur even in good weather, and the constant overbookings leave passengers scrambling to find another flight. On top of the inconvenience, tickets cost a fortune.
3. Motorists never give pedestrians the right of way. Once they get behind the wheel of a car, people believe that they own the road; yielding to someone on foot would never occur to someone driving a car.

EXERCISE 10

DIRECTIONS   For each of the following generalizations, indicate what questions you would ask and what types of information you would need to evaluate the generalization.

1. No one writes letters anymore.
2. The weather is always perfect in San Diego.
3. All of the instructors at the college are dedicated to helping students.
4. People who work at home have a better quality of life.
5. Cosmetic surgery is only for the very wealthy and the very vain.

EXAMINE THE AUTHOR'S ASSUMPTIONS

Suppose a friend asked you, "Have you stopped cheating on your girlfriend?" This person, perhaps not a friend after all, is making an assumption. He or she is assuming that you already have been cheating. An **assumption** is an idea or principle the author accepts as true and makes no effort to prove or substantiate. Usually, it is a beginning or premise on which he or she bases the remainder of the statement. Assumptions often use words such as *since, if,* or *when.* Here are a few more examples:

- You're not going to make that mistake again, are you? (The assumption is that you have already made the mistake at least once.)
- When you're mature, you'll realize you made a mistake. (The assumption is that you are not mature now.)
- You are as arrogant as your sister. (The assumption is that your sister is arrogant.)
- My dog is angry. (The assumption is that dogs have and can express emotions.)

Each of the above statements makes no attempt to prove or support the hidden assumption; it is assumed to be true.

Authors often make assumptions and make no effort to prove or support them. For example, an author may assume that television encourages violent behavior in children and proceed to argue for restrictions on TV viewing. Or a writer may assume that protests against a government are wrong and suggest legal restrictions on how and when protests may be held. If a writer's assumption is wrong or unsubstantiated, then the statements that follow from the assumption should be questioned. If television does not encourage violent behavior, for example, then the suggestion to restrict viewing should not be accepted unless other reasons are offered.

EXERCISE 11

DIRECTIONS   Read each of the following statements and then place a check mark before those choices that are assumptions made by the writer of the statement.

___ 1. Since fossil-fuel resources are dwindling, it is imperative that we begin converting to nuclear energy now.
   a. It can be accurately predicted when fossil fuels will run out.
   b. People who oppose nuclear power are not realistic.
   c. Nuclear power is the only alternative to fossil fuels.

___ 2. Many cultural treasures, such as paintings and other artifacts, were wrenched from their country of origin during times of war; these national treasures should be returned and displayed in their rightful homes.
   a. These artifacts were taken forcibly and illegally.
   b. Some artifacts were taken in an effort to safeguard them from damage.
   c. There is an appropriate and safe place for such artifacts to be displayed in their country of origin.

___ 3. Hip-hop music and "gangsta rap" encourage violence and criminal behavior; therefore, these types of music should be subject to government censorship.
   a. It is the government's responsibility to censor music.
   b. Criminal behavior is a result of hip-hop music and gangsta rap.
   c. Other forms of entertainment feature violence and criminal behavior.

EXERCISE 12

DIRECTIONS   For each statement listed below, identify at least one assumption.

1. Musicians should let their songs be downloaded for free. The profits they make on sales of their CDs more than make up for any losses they may have from fans' file sharing.
2. Adding essay items to standardized tests will make the tests impossible to grade objectively.
3. Sports teams should be banned from using Native American names or references; teams such as the Braves and the Redskins are showing extreme disrespect to Native Americans.
4. Shopping online is the most efficient way to purchase clothing and other household items.
5. Sodas and other carbonated beverages have no place in our schools; school vending machines should contain bottled water, juice, or sports drinks only.

WATCH FOR MANIPULATIVE LANGUAGE

Authors can shape their readers' thinking and response to their message by the language they choose to express that message. Writers use a variety of language manipulation techniques to achieve a particular effect, to communicate their message in a particular way, and to appeal to specific groups of people. These techniques include clichés, jargon, allusions, euphemisms, doublespeak, and hyperbole.

Clichés

A **cliché** is a tired, overused expression. Here are a few examples:

Curiosity killed the cat.

Bigger is better.

Absence makes the heart grow fonder.

He is as blind as a bat.

These everyday expressions have been overused; they are so frequently used that they no longer carry a specific meaning. They have become pat expressions, used by authors without much thought or creativity. Because the expressions are so common, many readers tend to accept them at face value rather than to evaluate their meaning and appropriateness. When you recognize a cliché, ask yourself the following questions:

- Why did the writer use the cliché?
- Why did the writer not use a fresh, original expression instead?

Numerous clichés used throughout a piece of writing may suggest that the author has not thought in depth about the topic or has not made the effort to express his or her ideas in an interesting and unique way.

- **Is the author trying to gloss over or skip over details by using a cliché?** Clichés often oversimplify a situation that is complex. In trying to decide which courses to register for, a student may say, "Don't put off till tomorrow what you can do today." Actually the student *could* register today, but it may be better to wait until he or she has had time to think, do research, and talk to others about course selection.
- **Is the author trying to avoid directly stating an unpopular or unpleasant idea?** Suppose you are reading an article on controlling world terrorism. After describing recent acts of terrorism, the writer concludes the article with the cliché, "What will be, will be." What does this cliché really say? The expression is a common one and is generally accepted. However, in this context, the cliché suggests (but does not directly state) that nothing can be done about terrorism, an unpopular viewpoint that would receive criticism if directly expressed.
- **Is the cliché fitting and appropriate?** Suppose in writing an article on college financial aid, the writer admonishes students not to spend their financial aid loan before they receive it, by saying, "Don't count your chickens before they are hatched." The writer's audience would be better served if the writer, instead, had offered more detail, explaining that loan checks are often delayed, and that spending money before it is received may cause serious financial problems.
- **What does the use of clichés reveal about the author?** Use of clichés may signal that an author is not fully aware of his or her audience or interested in accommodating them. A writer who packs an article full of clichés is not aware that his or her readers prefer fresh, descriptive information, rather than standard clichés.

EXERCISE 13

DIRECTIONS For each of the following clichés, explain its meaning and then think of a situation in which it would be untrue or inappropriate.

1. There's no time like the present.
2. No pain, no gain.
3. Don't judge a book by its cover.
4. Every cloud has a silver lining.
5. If you can't take the heat, get out of the kitchen.

EXERCISE 14

DIRECTIONS Replace each of the following clichés with more specific information that fits the context of the sentence.

1. Joe had worked at the firm for a year but he was still low man on the totem pole.
2. The councilman promised to turn over a new leaf after he was convicted of bribery and extortion.
3. We wanted to sell our house quickly, so when our agent brought a prospective buyer we put all our cards on the table.
4. The caterers were two hours late and the band was awful, but the straw that broke the camel's back was seeing the guest of honor's name misspelled on the cake.
5. The new teacher may seem strict but she has a heart of gold.

Allusions

Allusions are references to well-known religious, literary, artistic, or historical works or sources. A writer may refer to a biblical verse, a character in a famous poem or novel, a line in a well-known song, or a historical figure such as Napoleon or George Washington. An allusion makes a connection or points to similarities between the author's subject and the reference. Writers usually assume that educated readers will recognize and understand their allusions. Here are a few examples of allusions:

- A writer describes a person as having the patience of Job. In the Bible, Job is a righteous man whose faith was tested by God.
- An article on parental relationships with children refers to the Oedipus complex. Oedipus was a figure in Greek mythology who unknowingly killed his father and married his mother. He blinded himself when he discovered what he had done. The Oedipus complex is controversial but refers to a child's tendency to seek sexual fulfillment from a parent of the opposite sex.

If you encounter an allusion you do not understand, check it on the Internet using a search engine such as Google (www.google.com) by typing in the key words of the allusion. The following reference sources may also be helpful:

Merriam-Webster's Dictionary of Allusions

Dictionary of Historical Allusions and Eponyms

The Facts on File Encyclopedia of Word and Phrase Origins

Allusions can make writing interesting and connected to the past. Some authors, however, may include numerous literary or scholarly allusions to give their writing the appearance of scholarship. Do not be overly impressed by a writer's use of allusions, particularly obscure ones. A writer may use allusions to divert readers' attention from the lack of substantive detail or support. When evaluating a writer's use of allusions, ask the following questions:

- What does the allusion mean?
- Why did the author include the allusion?
- What does the allusion contribute to the overall meaning of the work?

EXERCISE 15   DIRECTIONS   For each of the following statements, explain the meaning of the allusion.

1. The investigation into city politics has opened a Pandora's box.
2. The cruise ship appeared Brobdingnagian next to the fishing boat.

3. Thanks to a good samaritan, our flat tire was changed and we were on our way again in less than an hour.
4. The latest cell phones have a Big Brother aspect to them, allowing parents to constantly monitor their children's locations and activities.
5. When it comes to investing, my brother-in-law certainly has the Midas touch.

Euphemisms

What do these sentences have in common?

> He suffered combat fatigue.
>
> The company is downsizing.
>
> Capital punishment is controversial.

Each uses an expression called a euphemism. A **euphemism** is a word or phrase that is used in place of a word that is unpleasant, embarrassing, or otherwise objectionable. The expression *combat fatigue* is a pleasant way to refer to the psychological problems of veterans caused by their experiences in war, *downsizing* replaces the word *firing*, and *capital punishment* is a substitute for *death penalty*.

The word *euphemism* comes from the Greek roots *eu-*, meaning "sounding good," and *-pheme*, meaning "speech." Euphemisms have a long history going back to ancient languages and cultures. Ancient people thought of names as an extension of things themselves. To know and say the name of a person or object gave power over the person or thing. Thus, calling something by its name was avoided, even forbidden. God, Satan, deceased relatives, and hunted animals would often be referred to indirectly. For example, in one culture God was called The Kindly One; the bear was called The Grandfather. Today, many euphemisms are widely used in both spoken and written language. Here are a few more examples:

> The foreign spy was put out of circulation. (the spy was killed)
>
> He was hit by friendly fire. (accidentally shot during combat by a member of his own military)
>
> My brother works as a sanitation engineer. (janitor or garbage collector)

Euphemisms tend to minimize or downplay something's importance or seriousness. They are often used in politics and advertising. They can be used to camouflage actions or events that may be unacceptable to readers or listeners if bluntly explained. For example, the phrase *casualties of war* may be used instead of the phrase *dead soldiers* to lessen the impact of the attack. To say that a politician's statement was *at variance with the truth* has less impact and is less forceful than to say that the politician lied.

A writer may use a euphemism to alter your perception of a situation by lessening its harshness, ugliness, severity, or seriousness. When a writer uses a euphemism, substitute the everyday meaning of the euphemism and notice whether the writer's message changes.

EXERCISE 16

DIRECTIONS For each of the underlined euphemisms, write a substitution that does not minimize or avoid the basic meaning of the term.

Example: We took our old refrigerator to the <u>sanitary landfill</u>.
<u>We took our old refrigerator to the dump.</u>

1. Her grandmother passed away after a long illness.
2. Several ferryboat passengers experienced severe motion discomfort and became violently ill.
3. The department store offers a wide selection of plus sizes.
4. They finally made the difficult decision to have their dog put to sleep.
5. Because of our financial status, we bought a pre-owned vehicle.

LEARNING COLLABORATIVELY

Each student should bring a copy of a current popular magazine to class. Choose a feature article and examine it for each of the topics covered in this chapter. Analyze why each was included and its possible effect on unsuspecting readers.

APPLYING YOUR SKILLS: Sample Textbook Chapter

1. What assumptions does the textbook chapter author make about your knowledge and experience with the chapter topic?
2. Identify five generalizations that the author makes.
3. Reread the chapter's introduction, page 514.
   - Identify words that have strong connotative meanings.
   - What is the tone of this excerpt?
   - What information did the author omit?
   - What generalizations are made?
   - What euphemisms are used?

QUESTIONS FOR DISCUSSION

1. Discuss the types of publications in which you might expect a writer to purposefully omit information.
2. Create a figurative expression to describe one characteristic of a close friend.
3. Brainstorm a list of clichés that you are tired of hearing and would like to avoid using in your speech and writing.
4. Create a list of connotative meanings that may exist for one of the following words: *birthday, patriotism, paycheck,* or *dinner.*

SELF-TEST SUMMARY

1. What is connotative language?

Connotative language refers to the feelings and associations that may accompany a word.

2. What is figurative language? What are three types of figurative language?

Figurative language is a comparison that makes sense imaginatively but not literally. Similes make comparisons using the words *like* or *as.* Metaphors make the comparison more directly, often using the word *is.* Personification compares humans and nonhumans according to one characteristic.

3. **What information might an author purposefully omit?**

An author may omit essential information or contradictory evidence that doesn't support his or her argument.

4. **What is a generalization?**

A generalization is a statement about an entire group based on known information about only part of the group.

5. **What is an assumption?**

An assumption is an idea or principle that the author accepts as true and makes no effort to prove or substantiate.

6. **What is a cliché?**

A cliché is a tired, overused expression.

7. **What is an allusion?**

An allusion is a reference to well-known religious, literary, artistic, or historical works or sources.

8. **What is a euphemism?**

A euphemism is a word or phrase that in used in place of a word that is unpleasant, embarrassing, or objectionable.

Quick Quiz

NAME:

DIRECTIONS Write the letter of the choice that best completes each statement in the space provided.

CHECKING YOUR RECALL

_____ 1. The standard, dictionary meaning of a word is known as its
   a. connotative meaning.
   b. denotative meaning.
   c. figurative meaning.
   d. inferred meaning.

_____ 2. A generalization can be defined as a
   a. principle or idea that an author accepts as true and makes no effort to prove.
   b. comparison between two unlike things that share one common characteristic.
   c. statement expressing feeling, attitudes, or beliefs that are neither true nor false.
   d. statement about a whole group based on information about part of the group.

_____ 3. An author who uses the passive voice may be trying to avoid
   a. identifying who performed a particular action.
   b. explaining incomplete comparisons.
   c. including contradictory evidence.
   d. revealing details that favor one position.

_____ 4. An assumption can be defined as an idea or principle that the author
   a. attempts to disprove.
   b. approaches logically.
   c. disagrees with.
   d. accepts as true without attempting to prove.

_____ 5. Figurative language compares
   a. several images.
   b. two unlike things.
   c. many similar things.
   d. several descriptive images.

APPLYING YOUR LEARNING

_____ 6. The statement "The cousins fought like cats and dogs" is a example of
   a. an allusion.
   b. a cliché.
   c. doublespeak.
   d. jargon.

_____ 7. The statement "She's got the Midas touch when it comes to making money" is an example of
   a. a euphemism.
   b. doublespeak.
   c. jargon.
   d. an allusion.

_____ 8. The statement "The veterinarian said that our cat would have to be put to sleep" is an example of
   a. a euphemism.
   b. a cliché.
   c. doublespeak.
   d. a generalization.

_____ 9. A word that describes a person who is intelligent but which also has a negative connotation is
   a. smart.
   b. bright.
   c. egghead.
   d. wise.

_____ 10. Of the following statements, the one that expresses a generalization is
   a. "I learned more than I ever expected to in this course."
   b. "That course was my favorite."
   c. "Dr. Fassell is a biology professor."
   d. "All of the instructors at the college are dedicated to helping students."

MULTIMEDIA *Activities*

Evaluating the Author's Technique

1 Euphemism Chart

Look over this collection of euphemisms from a journalism class at New York University.

http://www.nyu.edu/classes/copyXediting/euphemisms.html

What can you add to this list that would be relevant to journalists? Try looking in a magazine or newspaper for ideas. Why is it important for reporters to know current language usage?

2 Sports Jargon

All sports have their own specific terminology. Read this article by a student at Swarthmore College in which several sports terms are defined.

http://phoenix.swarthmore.edu/2005-03-24/sports/14854

Read the sports section in your school or town newspaper. Highlight all the words you consider to be jargon. Could these articles be written without jargon?

3 Similes and Metaphors

Print out this list of similes and metaphors from the North East Wales Institute of Higher Education.

http://www.newi.ac.uk/englishresources/workunits/ks3/langmedia/all/simandmet1.pdf

Write down what you think each expression means. Compare your thoughts with your classmates.

> To begin with, he (Mendel) needed <u>true-breeding plants,</u> plants that showed little variation from generation to generation.[2]
>
> The <u>mean</u>—the mathematical average of a set of numbers—will determine whether grades will be based on a curve.

Finally, an author may simply insert a synonym directly within the sentence.

> Another central issue, that of the right of a state to withdraw or <u>secede</u> from the Union, was simply avoided.[3]

EXERCISE 1

DIRECTIONS   In each sentence, locate the part of the sentence that gives a definition or synonym of the underlined word. Underline this portion of the sentence.

1. A <u>democracy</u> is a form of government in which the people effectively participate.[4]
2. The amount of heat that it takes to melt one gram of any substance at its melting point is called the <u>heat of fusion.</u>[5]
3. <u>Linoleic acid</u> is an essential fatty acid necessary for growth and skin integrity in infants.[6]
4. When a gas is cooled, it <u>condenses</u> (changes to a liquid) at its condensation point.[7]
5. But neither a monkey nor an ape has thumbs long enough or flexible enough to be completely <u>opposable,</u> able to reach comfortably to the tips of all the other fingers, as is required for our delicate yet strong precision grip.[8]

Example/Illustration Context Clues

Authors frequently explain their ideas and concepts by giving specific, concrete examples or illustrations. Many times, when an example is given that illustrates or explains a new term, you can figure out the meaning of the term from the example. Suppose, for instance, that you frequently confuse the terms *fiction* and *nonfiction* and you are given the following assignment by your instructor: *Select any nonfiction book and write a critical review; you can choose from a wide range of books, such as autobiographies, sports books, how-to manuals, commentaries on historical periods, and current consumer-awareness paperbacks.* From the examples given, you can easily see that *nonfiction* refers to books that are factual, or true.

Writers sometimes give you an advance warning or signal that they are going to present an example or illustration. Phrases that signal an example or illustration to follow include *for example, for instance, to illustrate, such as, included are,* and so on. Read the following examples:

> Some everyday, common <u>solutions</u> include gasoline, antifreeze, soda water, seawater, vodka, and ammonia.
>
> Specifically, management of a New York bank developed a strategic plan to increase its customers by making them see banks as offering a large variety of services rather than just a few <u>specialized services</u> (cashing checks, putting money into savings accounts, and making loans).[9]

EXERCISE 2

DIRECTIONS   Read each sentence and write a definition or synonym for each underlined word. Use the illustration/example context clue to help you determine word meanings.

1. Maria enjoys all <u>equestrian</u> sports, including jumping, riding, and racing horses.

   _____

2. Murder, rape, and armed robbery are <u>reprehensible</u> crimes.

   _____

3. Psychological disturbances are sometimes traceable to a particular <u>trauma</u> in childhood. For example, the death of a parent may produce long-range psychological effects.

   _____

4. To <u>substantiate</u> his theory, Watson offered experimental evidence, case study reports, testimony of patients, and a log of observational notes.

   _____

5. Many <u>phobias</u> can seriously influence human behavior; the two most common are claustrophobia (fear of confined spaces) and acrophobia (fear of heights).

   _____

6. <u>Homogeneous</u> groups, such as classes made up entirely of boys, social organizations of people with high IQs, country clubs, and wealthy families, have particular roles and functions.

   _____

Contrast Context Clues

It is sometimes possible to figure out the meaning of an unknown word from a word or phrase in the context that has an opposite meaning. To use a simple example, in the sentence "Sam was thin, but George was obese," a contrast of opposites is set up between George and Sam. The word *but* signals that an opposite or contrasting idea is to follow. By knowing the meaning of *thin* and knowing that George is the opposite of thin, you figure out that *obese* means "not thin," or *fat*.

Most often when an opposite or contrasting meaning is given, a signal word or phrase in the sentence indicates a change in the direction of the thought. Most commonly used are these signal words or phrases: *on the other hand, however, although, whereas, but, nevertheless, on the contrary.* Note the following example:

> The Federalists, from their <u>pessimistic</u> viewpoint, believed the Constitution could protect them by its procedures, whereas the more positive Anti-Federalists thought of the Constitution as the natural rights due to all people.

In the preceding example, if you did not know the meaning of the word *pessimistic,* you could figure it out because a word appears later in the sentence that gives you a clue. The sentence is about the beliefs of two groups, the Federalists and the Anti-Federalists. The prefix *anti-* tells you that they hold opposite or differing views, and *whereas* also signals a contrast. If the Federalists are described as pessimistic and their views are opposite those of the Anti-Federalists, who are described as more positive, you realize that *pessimistic* means the opposite of positive, or negative.

Here is another example:

> Most members of Western society marry only one person at a time, but in other cultures <u>polygamy</u> is common and acceptable.

In this sentence, by the contrast established between Western society and other cultures, you can infer that *polygamy* refers to the practice of marriage to more than one person at a time.

EXERCISE 3

DIRECTIONS   Read each sentence and write a definition or synonym for each underlined word. Use the contrast context clue to help you determine the meaning of the word.

1. The philosopher was <u>vehement</u> in his objections to the new grading system; the more practical historian, on the other hand, expressed his views calmly and quietly.

_____

2. The mayor was <u>dogmatic</u> about government policy, but the assistant mayor was more lenient and flexible in his interpretations.

_____

3. Instead of evaluating each possible solution when it was first proposed, the committee decided it would <u>defer</u> judgment until all possible solutions had been proposed.

_____

4. The two philosophical theories were <u>incompatible:</u> One acknowledged the existence of free will; the other denied it.

_____

5. Cultures vary in the types of behavior that are considered socially acceptable. In one culture, a man may be <u>ostracized</u> for having more than one wife, whereas in other cultures, a man with many wives is an admired and respected part of the group.

_____

Context Clues in the Logic of a Passage

One of the most common ways in which context provides clues about the meaning of an unknown word is through logic or general reasoning about the content of a sentence or about the relationship of ideas within a sentence. Suppose that before you read the following sentence you did not know the meaning of the word *empirical*.

> Some of the questions now before us are <u>empirical</u> issues that require evidence directly bearing on the question.[10]

From the way *empirical* is used in the sentence, you know that an empirical issue is one that requires direct evidence, and from that information you can infer, or reason, that *empirical* has something to do with proof or supporting facts.

Now suppose that you did not know the meaning of the term *cul-de-sac* before reading the following sentence:

> A group of animals hunting together can sometimes maneuver the hunted animal into a <u>cul-de-sac:</u> out onto a peak of high land, into a swamp or river, or into a gully from which it cannot escape.[11]

From the mention of the places into which a hunted animal can be maneuvered—a gully, a peak, or a swamp—you realize that the hunters have cornered the animal and that *cul-de-sac* means a blind alley or a situation from which there is no escape.

EXERCISE 4

DIRECTIONS   Read each of the following sentences and write a synonym or definition for each underlined word or term. Look for context clues in the logic of the passage to help you figure out the meaning of each word.

1. Religious or ethical convictions make the idea of capital punishment, in which a life is willingly, even legally, extinguished, a <u>repugnant</u> one.

   _____

2. The former Berlin Wall, originally built with enough force and strength to separate East and West Germany, was <u>impervious</u> to attack.

   _____

3. When the judge pronounced the sentence, the convicted criminal shouted <u>execrations</u> at the jury.

   _____

4. The police officer was <u>exonerated</u> by a police review panel of any possible misconduct or involvement in a case of police bribery.

   _____

5. The editor would not allow the paper to go to press until certain passages were <u>expunged</u> from an article naming individuals involved in a political scandal.

   _____

EXERCISE 5

DIRECTIONS   Each of the following sentences contains an underlined word or phrase whose meaning can be determined from the context. Underline the part of the sentence that contains the clue to the meaning of the underlined words. Then, in the blank below, identify what type of context clue you used.

1. <u>Separation of powers</u> is the principle that the powers of government should be separated and put in the care of different parts of the government.[12]

   _____

2. Samples of moon rock have been analyzed by <u>uranium dating</u> and found to be about 4.6 billion years old, or about the same age as the earth.[13]

   _____

3. Like horses, human beings have a variety of <u>gaits;</u> they amble, stride, jog, and sprint.[14]

_____

4. In the past, <u>malapportionment</u> (large differences in the populations of congressional districts) was common in many areas of the country.[15]

_____

5. Tremendous <u>variability</u> characterizes the treatment of the mentally retarded during the medieval era, ranging from treatment as innocents to being tolerated as fools to persecution as witches.[16]

_____

EXERCISE 6

DIRECTIONS   Read each of the following paragraphs. For each underlined word, use context to determine its meaning. Write a synonym or brief definition in the space provided.

1. In the laboratory, too, nonhuman primates have accomplished some surprising things. In one study, chimpanzees compared two pairs of food wells containing chocolate chips. One pair might contain, say, five chips and three chips, the other four chips and three chips. Allowed to choose which pair they wanted, the chimps almost always chose the one with the higher combined total, showing some sort of <u>summing ability</u>. Other chimps have learned to use <u>numerals</u> to label quantities of items and simple sums. Two rhesus monkeys, named Rosencrantz and Macduff, learned to <u>order</u> groups of one to four symbols according to the number of symbols in each group (e.g., one square, two trees, three ovals, four flowers). Later, when presented with pairs of symbol groups containing five to nine symbols, they were able to point to the group with more symbols, without any further training. This is not exactly algebra, but it does suggest that monkeys have a <u>rudimentary</u> sense of number.

—Wade & Tavris, *Psychology,* p. 337

a. summing ability _____

b. numerals _____

c. order _____

d. rudimentary _____

2. **Territoriality**

Many animals that live in groups share a home range. In winter, for example, many birds flock together in a home range. After the spring migration to their new habitats, however, most male birds undergo a Jekyll-to-Hyde <u>transformation</u> and establish a territory that they vigorously defend against other males of their species. As noted before, sticklebacks, as well as numerous other animals, also establish territories. The essential difference between a home range and a territory is that the territory is, by definition, defended against <u>encroachment</u> by others of the same species. Male birds <u>advertise</u> possession of their territories by songs and visual displays. An <u>intruding</u> male's song or plumage is the releaser for territorial aggression by the resident. Resident males will often attack a tape recorder playing another male's song or a <u>tuft</u> of feathers the same color as the male's breeding plumage. The only way for a male bird to lurk about within the territory of another is to keep quiet and out of sight.

Such "lurkers" are less likely to breed, however, because the songs and display are also required to attract females.

In some species a territory may be occupied by two or more males and their mates. Wolves are the classic illustration of a species that defends a group territory. The average wolf pack is an extended family of from five to eight individuals with a territory of a few hundred square kilometers. An <u>alpha male</u> and an <u>alpha female</u> lead the pack. They define the pack's territory by releasing a pheromone during a characteristic raised-leg urination about every 450 meters as they patrol its perimeter. To wolves from neighboring territories these <u>olfactory</u> boundary markers are, in one sense at least, nothing to sniff at. Packs of wolves have been seen abandoning a deer chase rather than cross into another pack's territory.

—Harris, *Concepts in Zoology*, p. 417

a. transformation _____

b. encroachment _____

c. advertise _____

d. intruding _____

e. tuft _____

f. alpha male _____

g. alpha female _____

h. olfactory _____

3. Many animals communicate by chemical signals, which have the unique advantage of <u>persisting</u> for some time after the messenger has left the area. They also have the advantage that they will be detected only by those with receptors that respond to the chemical, so they are less likely to attract predators. Some chemical messages have a hormone-like ability to <u>induce</u> specific behavioral responses in recipients in the same species. Such chemical messages are called <u>pheromones.</u> The best-known pheromones are insect sex attractants, many of which have been isolated and chemically analyzed. The first such pheromone to be studied was bombykol, which is produced in minute amounts by glands near the anus of the female silk moth *Bombyx mori*. The glands from half a million females had to be processed to yield 12 mg of pheromone. (One lab worker was reportedly overheard complaining, "The end is always in sight, but the work is never done.") A single molecule of bombykol is enough to <u>evoke</u> an action potential from the antenna of a male silk moth, and several hundred molecules are enough to make the male fly upwind, toward the female.

—Harris, *Concepts in Zoology*, pp. 408–409

a. persisting _____

b. induce _____

c. pheromones _____

d. evoke _____

4. Certain personal <u>characteristics</u> may explain who among the extremely poor are more likely to become homeless. These characteristics have been found to include chronic mental problems, alcoholism, drug addiction, serious criminal behavior, and physical health problems. Most of the extremely poor do not become homeless

because they live with their relatives or friends. But those who suffer from any of the personal <u>disabilities</u> just mentioned are more likely to wear out their welcome as <u>dependents</u> of their parents or as <u>recipients</u> of aid and money from their friends. After all, their relatives and friends are themselves likely to be extremely poor and already living in crowded housing. We should be careful, though, not to <u>exaggerate</u> the <u>impact</u> of personal disabilities on homelessness. To some degree, personal disabilities may be the <u>consequences</u> rather than the cause of homelessness.

—Thio, *Sociology,* p. 235

a. characteristics _____

b. disabilities _____

c. dependents _____

d. recipients _____

e. exaggerate _____

f. impact _____

g. consequences _____

ANALYZING WORD PARTS

Mark and Elaine were taking a course in biology. While walking to class one day, Mark complained to Elaine, "I'll never be able to learn all this vocabulary!" They agreed that they needed some system, because learning each new word separately would be nearly impossible. Have you felt the same way in some of your courses?

The purpose of this section is to present a system of vocabulary learning. This system works for specific courses in which a great deal of new terminology is presented, as well as for building your overall, general vocabulary. The approach is based on analyzing word parts. Many words in the English language are made up of word parts called *prefixes, roots,* and *suffixes.* Think of these as beginnings, middles, and endings of words. These word parts have specific meanings, and when added together, they can help you figure out the meaning of the word as a whole. Let's begin with a few words from biology.

poikilotherm   homeotherm   endotherm   ectotherm

You could learn the definition of each term separately, but learning would be easier and more meaningful if you could see the relationship among the terms.

Each of the four words has as its root *-therm,* which means "heat." The meaning of the prefix, or beginning, of each word is given below.

poikilo-	=	changeable
homeo-	=	same or constant
endo-	=	within
ecto-	=	outside

Knowing these meanings can help you determine the meaning of each word.

poikilotherm	=	organism with variable body temperature (i.e., cold-blooded)
homeotherm	=	organism with stable body temperature (i.e., warm-blooded)
endotherm	=	organism that regulates its temperature internally
ectotherm	=	organism that regulates its temperature by taking in heat from the environment or giving off heat to the environment

When you first start using this method, you may not feel that you're making progress; in this case, you had to learn four prefixes and one root to figure out four words. However, what may not yet be obvious is that these prefixes will help unlock the meanings of numerous other words, not only in the field of biology but also in related fields and in general vocabulary usage. Here are a few examples of words that include each of the word parts we have analyzed:

therm-	**poikilo-**	**homeo- (homo-)**	**ecto-**	**endo-**
thermal	poikilocyte	homeostasis	ectoparasite	endocytosis
thermodynamics	poikilocytosis	homogeneous	ectoderm	endoderm

The remainder of this section will focus on commonly used prefixes, roots, and suffixes that are used in a variety of academic disciplines. In various combinations, these will unlock the meanings of thousands of words. For example, more than 10,000 words begin with the prefix *non-*.

Once you have mastered the prefixes, roots, and suffixes given in this chapter, you should begin to identify word parts that are commonly used in each of your courses. For example, Figure 12-1 shows a partial list made by one student for a psychology course. Keep these lists in your course notebooks or use index cards, as described later in this chapter.

Figure 12-1
A Sample List of Prefixes

Psychology
neuro– nerves, nervous system   path– feeling, suffering
phob– fear   homo– same
auto– self   hetero– different

Before learning specific prefixes, roots, and suffixes, it is useful to be aware of the following points:

1. **In most cases, a word is built on at least one root.**
2. **Words can have more than one prefix, root, or suffix.**
   - Words can be made up of two or more roots (*geo / logy*).
   - Some words have two prefixes (*in / sub / ordination*).
   - Some words have two suffixes (beauti / *ful / ly*).
3. **Words do not always have both a prefix and a suffix.**
   - Some words have neither a prefix nor a suffix (read).
   - Others have a suffix but no prefix (read / *ing*).
   - Others have a prefix but no suffix (*pre* / read).

4. **Roots may change in spelling as they are combined with suffixes.** Some common variations are noted on page 295.

5. **Sometimes you may identify a group of letters as a prefix or root but find that it does not carry the meaning of the prefix or root.** For example, in the word *internal*, the letters *inter* should not be confused with the prefix *inter-*, meaning "between." Similarly, the letters *mis* in the word *missile* are part of the root and are not the prefix *mis-*, which means "wrong" or "bad."

Prefixes

Prefixes, appearing at the beginning of many English words, alter or modify the meaning of the root to which they are connected. In Figure 12-2 (p. 294), common prefixes are grouped according to meaning.

EXERCISE 7

DIRECTIONS   Use the prefixes listed in Figure 12-2 to help determine the meaning of each of the underlined words in the following sentences. Write a brief definition or synonym for each. If you are unfamiliar with the root, you may need to check a dictionary.

1. The instances of <u>abnormal</u> behavior reported in the mass media are likely to be extreme.

   _____

2. The two theories of language development are not fundamentally <u>incompatible,</u> as originally thought.

   _____

3. When threatened, the ego resorts to <u>irrational</u> protective measures, which are called defense mechanisms.

   _____

4. Freud viewed the <u>interplay</u> among the id, ego, and superego as of critical importance in determining behavioral patterns.

   _____

5. The long-term effects of continuous drug use are <u>irreversible.</u>

   _____

EXERCISE 8

DIRECTIONS   Write a synonym or brief definition for each of the following underlined words. Check a dictionary if the root is unfamiliar.

1. a <u>substandard</u> performance _____

2. to <u>transcend</u> everyday differences _____

3. <u>telecommunications</u> equipment _____

4. a <u>hypercritical</u> person _____

5. a <u>retroactive</u> policy _____

6. <u>superconductive</u> metal _____

Figure 12-2
Common Prefixes

Prefix	Meaning	Sample Word
Prefixes indicating direction, location, or placement		
circum-	around	circumference
com-, col-, con-	with, together	compile
de-	away, from	depart
ex-/extra-	from, out of, former	ex-wife
hyper-	over, excessive	hyperactive
inter-	between	interpersonal
intro-/intra-	within, into, in	introduction
mid-	middle	midterm
post-	after	posttest
pre-	before	premarital
re-	back, again	review
retro-	backward	retrospect
sub-	under, below	submarine
super-	above, extra	supercharge
tele-	far	telescope
trans-	across, over	transcontinental
Prefixes referring to amount or number		
bi-	two	bimonthly
equi-	equal	equidistant
micro-	small	microscope
mono-	one	monocle
multi-	many	multipurpose
poly-	many	polygon
semi-	half	semicircle
tri-	three	triangle
uni-	one	unicycle
Prefixes meaning "not" (negative)		
a-, an-, ab-	not	asymmetrical
anti-	against	antiwar
contra-	against, opposite	contradict
dis-	apart, away, not	disagree
mis-	wrong, bad	misunderstand
non-	not	nonfiction
pseudo-	false	pseudoscientific
un-	not	unpopular

7. <u>extracurricular</u> activities _____

8. <u>postoperative</u> nursing care _____

9. a blood <u>transfusion</u> _____

10. <u>antisocial</u> behavior _____

11. to <u>misappropriate</u> funds _____

12. a <u>microscopic</u> organism _____

13. a <u>monotonous</u> speech _____

14. a <u>pseudointellectual</u> essay _____

15. a <u>polysyllabic</u> word _____

Roots

Roots carry the basic or core meaning of a word. Hundreds of root words are used to build words in the English language. Thirty of the most common and most useful are listed in Figure 12-3. Knowing the meanings of these roots will assist you in unlocking the meanings of many words. For example, if you know that the root *dic-* or *dict-* means "tell" or "say," then you have a clue to the meanings of such words as *predict* (to tell what will happen in the future), *contradiction* (a statement that is contrary or opposite), and *diction* (wording or manner of speaking).

Figure 12-3
Common Roots

Root	Meaning	Sample Word
aster, astro	star	astronaut
aud, audit	hear	audible
bio	life	biology
cap	take, seize	captive
chron(o)	time	chronology
corp	body	corpse
cred	believe	incredible
dict, dic	tell, say	predict
duc, duct	lead	introduce
fact, fac	make, do	factory
geo	earth	geophysics
graph	write	telegraph
log, logo, logy	study, thought	psychology
mit, miss	send	dismiss
mort, mor	die, death	immortal
path	feeling, disease	sympathy
phone	sound, voice	telephone
photo	light	photosensitive
port	carry	transport
scop	seeing	microscope
scribe, script	write	inscription
sen, sent	feel	insensitive
spec, spic, spect	look, see	retrospect
tend, tent, tens	stretch, strain	tension
terr, terre	land, earth	territory
theo	god	theology
ven, vent	come	convention
vert, vers	turn	invert
vis, vid	see	invisible
voc	call	vocation

EXERCISE 9   DIRECTIONS   Write a synonym or brief definition for each of the underlined words. Consult Figures 12-2 and 12-3 as necessary.

1. a <u>monotheistic</u> religion _____

2. a <u>subterranean</u> tunnel _____

3. a <u>chronicle</u> of events _____

4. a <u>conversion</u> chart _____

5. <u>exportation</u> policies _____

6. leading an <u>introspective</u> life _____

7. to <u>speculate</u> on the results _____

8. <u>sensuous</u> music _____

9. a <u>versatile</u> performance _____

10. an <u>incredible</u> explanation _____

11. infant <u>mortality</u> rates _____

12. the <u>tensile</u> strength of a cable _____

13. a <u>vociferous</u> crowd _____

14. a logical <u>deduction</u> _____

15. a <u>corporate</u> earnings report _____

Suffixes

Suffixes are word endings that often change the part of speech of a word. For example, adding the suffix *-y* to a word changes it from a noun to an adjective and shifts the meaning—for example, *cloud, cloudy*. Often several different words can be formed from a single root word with the addition of different suffixes. Here is an example:

Root: *Class*
        classify
        classification
        classic

Common suffixes are grouped according to meaning in Figure 12-4.

**Figure 12-4
Common Suffixes**

Suffix	Sample Word
Suffixes that refer to a state, condition, or quality	
-able	touchable
-ance	assistance
-ation	confrontation
-ence	reference
-ic	aerobic
-ible	tangible
-ion	discussion
-ity	superiority
-ive	permissive
-ment	amazement
-ness	kindness
-ous	jealous
-ty	loyalty
-y	creamy
Suffixes that mean "one who"	
-ee	employee
-eer	engineer
-er	teacher
-ist	activist
-or	editor
Suffixes that mean "pertaining to" or "referring to"	
-al	autumnal
-ship	friendship
-hood	brotherhood
-ward	homeward

EXERCISE 10

DIRECTIONS   Write a synonym or brief definition of each of the underlined words. Consult a dictionary if necessary.

1. acts of <u>terrorism</u> _____

2. a <u>graphic</u> description _____

3. a <u>materialistic</u> philosophy _____

4. <u>immunity</u> to disease _____

5. <u>impassable</u> road conditions _____

6. a speech <u>impediment</u> _____

7. <u>intangible</u> property _____

8. <u>instinctive</u> behavior _____

9. <u>interrogation</u> techniques _____

10. the communist <u>sector</u> _____

11. obvious <u>frustration</u> _____

12. <u>global</u> conflicts _____

13. in <u>deference</u> to _____

14. <u>piteous</u> physical ailments _____

15. Supreme Court <u>nominee</u> _____

EXERCISE 11   DIRECTIONS   The following terms were taken from "The Decorated Body" in Part Eight, pages 460–464. Locate the terms in the reading and write a brief definition of each. Use both context clues and word parts and a dictionary, if necessary.

1. unbearable (para. 1) _____

2. transformed (para. 2) _____

3. millennia (para. 3) _____

4. aesthetically (para. 4) _____

5. unornamented (para. 5) _____

6. communal (para. 5) _____

7. pretexts (para. 8) _____

8. inscription (para. 9) _____

9. brutish (para. 10) _____

10. homogeneous (para. 12) _____

EXERCISE 12   DIRECTIONS   From a chapter in one of your textbooks, make a list of words with multiple word parts. Using Figures 12-2, 12-3, and 12-4, define as many as you can. Check the accuracy of your definitions using your book's glossary or a dictionary.

LEARNING COLLABORATIVELY

DIRECTIONS   The instructor will choose a reading selection from Part Eight and divide the class into groups. In your groups, locate and underline at least five difficult words in the selection that can be defined by analyzing word parts and/or using context clues. Work together with group members to determine the meaning of each word, checking a dictionary to verify and expand meanings.

APPLYING YOUR LEARNING

Imagine that Jon is taking one of your courses with you. He is having difficulty figuring out and remembering new terms presented in the text and in lectures.

1. Photocopy several pages from your notes and from your text where new terms are introduced.
2. Explain to Jon what context clues the professor and the author are using.
3. Share with Jon your system for building up a content-specific vocabulary.

APPLYING YOUR SKILLS: Sample Textbook Chapter

1. Identify ten words from the chapter that are essential for you to learn. Enter them in a vocabulary log.
2. Select one word from the chapter and draw a word map of it.

QUESTIONS FOR DISCUSSION

1. Discuss in which academic courses learning word parts would be most useful. In which courses would it be less useful?
2. Which type(s) of context clues is used most frequently in college textbooks?
3. In which of your textbooks do you find the definition context clue most commonly used?
4. In classroom lectures, how do instructors explain the meaning of unfamiliar terms?

SELF-TEST SUMMARY

1. What is a context clue?	The context—the words around an unknown word—frequently contains clues that help you figure out the meaning of the unknown word.
2. What are the four basic types of context clues? Define each.	There are four basic types of context clues. a. *Definition:* A brief definition or synonym of an unknown word may be included in the sentence in which the word is used. b. *Example/illustration:* Writers may explain their words and ideas by giving specific, concrete examples. c. *Contrast:* The meaning of an unknown word can sometimes be determined from a word or phrase in the context that has the opposite meaning. d. *Logic of the passage:* The meaning of an unknown word can sometimes be determined through reasoning or by applying logic to the content of the sentence or paragraph.
3. How can learning word parts improve your vocabulary?	Learning word parts enables you to figure out the meaning of an unknown word by analyzing the meanings of its parts—prefixes, roots, and suffixes.

QUICK QUIZ

DIRECTIONS Write the letter of the choice that best completes each statement in the space provided.

CHECKING YOUR RECALL

_____ 1. If you encounter an unfamiliar word when you are reading, the *first* strategy you should try is to

    a. look it up in a dictionary.
    b. pronounce it out loud.
    c. analyze its parts.
    d. figure out its meaning from the words around it.

_____ 2. Teresa read this sentence in her biology class syllabus: "We will study fission— the act of splitting into parts—during our unit on cells." The type of context clue in this situation is

    a. a definition.
    b. an example.
    c. an illustration.
    d. a contrast.

_____ 3. The word or phrase that signals an example context clue is

    a. on the other hand.
    b. however.
    c. for instance.
    d. nevertheless.

_____ 4. All of the following statements about word parts are true *except*

    a. words always have at least one prefix, one root, and one suffix.
    b. roots may change in spelling as they are combined with suffixes.
    c. some words have more than one root.
    d. words can have more than one prefix or suffix.

APPLY YOUR SKILLS

DIRECTIONS Each of the following sentences contains a word whose meaning can be determined from the context. Select the choice that most clearly states the meaning of the underlined word as it is used in the sentence.

_____ 5. The tour guide assured us that the trail was safe for travel, but it looked <u>precarious</u> to the rest of the group.

    a. unknown
    b. unsafe
    c. narrow
    d. messy

_____ 6. The comedian <u>satirized</u> the tourists in the front row, making fun of the way they were dressed.

    a. complimented
    b. ridiculed
    c. ignored
    d. spoke to

_____ 7. The actor often portrayed <u>taciturn</u> characters, but in the television interview he was quite chatty.

    a. talkative
    b. relaxed
    c. quiet
    d. unpleasant

DIRECTIONS Each of the following underlined words contains a root and a prefix and/or suffix. Using your knowledge of roots, prefixes, and suffixes, choose the best definition for each word.

_____ 8. Martin is <u>hypersensitive</u> about his mother's health.

    a. considerate
    b. complimentary
    c. overly concerned
    d. indifferent

_____ 9. The scientist used a <u>chronograph</u> as part of her experiment.

    a. sound system
    b. light-sensitive film
    c. scale
    d. time-measuring instrument

_____ 10. To treat the inflammation, the patient must receive shots <u>intramuscularly</u>.

    a. within the muscle
    b. next to the muscle
    c. between muscles
    d. away from the muscle

MULTIMEDIA *Activities*

Using Context and Word Parts

1 All around us, words from other languages are mixed in with English. Take notice of foreign words and phrases you encounter in your daily life. Write them down, define them, and state their language of origin. For example, you may hear a consumer reporter use the Latin phrase, *caveat emptor!* (Let the buyer beware!)

2 The meaning of a word can change over time. Watch some old movies and listen carefully to the dialogue. Use context clues to figure out the meanings of unfamiliar phrases and slang. Consult a slang dictionary or ask an older person to explain what you don't understand.

3 Commonly Misused Words

http://www.cmu.edu/styleguide/trickywords.html#misused

Be on the lookout for these easy-to-confuse words listed here by Carnegie Mellon University. Which words would you add to this list? Which words surprised you? Write a paragraph on the importance of proper usage. Why does it matter as long as people know what you mean?

4 Word Game of the Day

http://www.m-w.com/game/

Have fun building your vocabulary with these puzzles from Merriam-Webster. Challenge your friends.

5 Context Quiz

Try this online quiz that tests your ability to figure out which verb to use in context:

http://www.quia.com/quiz/105496.html

After you are done, look up any words you did not know in a dictionary.

13 Expanding Your Vocabulary

Why Expand Your Vocabulary?

■ Your vocabulary is a reflection of you, and a strong vocabulary creates a positive image.

■ Broadening your vocabulary will improve the clarity of your thinking.

■ Your reading and writing skills will improve as your vocabulary improves.

■ A strong vocabulary will contribute to both academic and career success.

Learning Experiment

Step 1

Study the following list of words and meanings (list A) for one to two minutes.

List A

contrive—to plan with cleverness; to devise
comprise—to consist of
revulsion—feeling of violent disgust
retaliate—to return in kind, to get even with
repertoire—a collection of skills or aptitudes; a collection of artistic or musical works to be performed

Step 2

Study list B for one to two minutes. Then, for each word, write a sentence using the word.

List B

ambivalent—uncertain or undecided about a course of action
infallible—incapable of making a mistake
mundane—commonplace, ordinary
relentless—unyielding, unwilling to give in
déjà vu—the impression of having seen or experienced something before

Step 3

Wait two days and then take the following quiz. Cover the two lists above before you begin the quiz.

Match each word in column A with its meaning in column B. Write the letter from column B in the blank provided.

	Column A	Column B
_____	1. revulsion	a. to return in kind
_____	2. comprise	b. undecided
_____	3. repertoire	c. feeling of violent disgust
_____	4. contrive	d. feeling of experiencing something again
_____	5. retaliate	e. collection of skills or aptitudes

_____ 6. ambivalent   f. to consist of

_____ 7. relentless   g. ordinary

_____ 8. infallible   h. incapable of
error

_____ 9. déjà vu   i. to create a
clever plan

_____ 10. mundane   j. unwilling to
give in

Step 4

Check your answers using the key at the end of the chapter, page 318.

The Results

Questions 1–5 were based on list A; Questions 6–10 were based on list B. You probably got more questions right for list B than for list A. Why? For list B, you used each word in a sentence. By using each word in a sentence you were practicing it. Practice is a part of a technique known as rehearsal, which means going back over material you are attempting to learn.

Learning Principle
(What This Means to You)

Rehearsal improves both your ability to learn and your ability to recall information. To expand your vocabulary, be sure to practice using words you identify as important to learn, whether they are part of your general vocabulary or the specialized terminology of your courses. This chapter will help you to identify the words you need to add to your vocabulary and to use the resources that can expand your vocabulary.

GENERAL APPROACHES TO VOCABULARY EXPANSION

Expanding your vocabulary requires motivation, a positive attitude, and skills, and the first of these is the most important. To improve your vocabulary, you must be willing to work at it, spending both time and effort to notice and learn new words and meanings. Unless you intend to remember new words you hear or read, you will probably forget them. Your attitude toward reading will also influence the extent to which your vocabulary develops. If you enjoy reading and you read a broad range of subjects, you will frequently encounter new words. On the other hand, if you read only when required to do so, your exposure to words will be limited. Finally, your skills in using reference sources, in handling specialized terminology, and in organizing a system for learning new words will influence your vocabulary development.

This chapter will focus on the skills you need to build your vocabulary. Before you continue, however, read the following suggestions for expanding your vocabulary.

Read Widely

One of the best ways to improve your vocabulary is by reading widely and diversely, sampling many different subjects and styles of writing. Through reading, you encounter new words and new uses for familiar words. You also see words used in contexts that you have not previously considered.

College is one of the best places to begin reading widely. As you take elective and required courses, you are exposed to new ideas as well as to the words that express them clearly and succinctly. While you are a student, use the range of required and elective reading to expand your vocabulary.

Use Words You Already Know

Most people think they have just one level of vocabulary and that this can be characterized as large or small, strong or weak. Actually, everyone has at least four levels of vocabulary, and each varies in strength.

1. Words you use in everyday speech or writing
   Examples: *sharp, teeth, parent, visit, steak, illness*
2. Words you know but seldom or never use in your own speech or writing
   Examples: *lethal, legitimate, lawful, landscape, laid-back*
3. Words you've heard or seen before but cannot fully define
   Examples: *logistics, lament, lackadaisical, latent, latitude*
4. Words you've never heard or seen before
   Examples: *lanugo, lagniappe, laconic, lactone, lacustrine*

In the spaces provided below, list five words that fall under each of these four categories. It will be easy to think of words for category 1. Words for categories 2 through 4 may be taken from the following list.

activate	delicate	impartial
alien	delve	impertinent
attentive	demean	liberate
congruent	focus	logic
connive	fraught	manual
continuous	garbanzo	meditate
contort	gastronome	osmosis
credible	havoc	resistance
deletion	heroic	voluntary

Category 1	*Category 2*	*Category 3*	*Category 4*
_____	_____	_____	_____
_____	_____	_____	_____
_____	_____	_____	_____
_____	_____	_____	_____
_____	_____	_____	_____

To build your vocabulary, try to shift as many words as possible from a less familiar to a more familiar category. This task is not easy. You start by noticing words. Then you question, check, and remember their meanings. Finally, and most important, you use these new words often in your speech and writing.

Look for Five-Dollar Words to Replace One-Dollar Words

Some words in your vocabulary are general and vague. Although they convey meaning, they are not precise, exact, or expressive. Try to replace these one-dollar words with five-dollar words that convey your meaning more directly. The word *good* is an example of a much-overused word that has a general, unclear meaning in the following sentence:

The movie was so good, it was worth the high admission price.

Try substituting the following words in the preceding sentence: *exciting, moving, thrilling, scary, inspiring*. Each of these gives more information than the word *good*. These are the types of words you should strive to use in your speech and writing.

Build Your Word Awareness

Get in the habit of noticing new or unusual words when reading and listening. Learn to pay attention to words and notice those that seem useful. One of the first steps in expanding your vocabulary is to develop a word awareness. At the college level, many new words that you learn do not represent new concepts or ideas. Instead, they are more accurate or more descriptive replacements for simpler words and expressions that you already know and use. Once you begin to notice words, you will find that many of them automatically become part of your vocabulary.

Your instructors are a good resource for new words. Both in formal classroom lectures and in more casual discussions and conversations, many instructors use words that students understand but seldom use. You will hear new words and technical terms that are particular to a specific discipline.

Other good sources are textbooks, collateral reading assignments, and reference materials. If you are like most students, you understand many more words than you use in your own speech and writing. As you read, you will encounter many words you are vaguely familiar with but cannot define. When you begin to notice these words, you will find that many of them become part of your vocabulary.

Consider Working with a Vocabulary Improvement Program

If you feel motivated to make improvements in a concentrated program of study, consider setting aside a block of time each week to work with a vocabulary improvement program. A variety of paperbacks on the market are designed to help you improve your vocabulary. The average bookstore should have several to choose from. Computer programs, some in game formats, have also been designed to strengthen general vocabulary. Check with your college's learning lab or library to see what is available.

USING REFERENCE SOURCES

Once you have developed a sense of word awareness and have begun to identify useful words to add to your vocabulary, the next step is to become familiar with the references you can use to expand your vocabulary.

Dictionaries: Which One to Use

Students often ask, "Which dictionary should I use?" There are several types of dictionaries, each with its own purpose and use. A pocket or paperback dictionary is an inexpensive, shortened version of a standard dictionary. It is small enough to carry with you to your classes and is relatively inexpensive.

A collegiate dictionary is a larger, more inclusive dictionary. Although a pocket dictionary is convenient, it is also limited. A pocket edition lists about 55,000 words, whereas a collegiate dictionary lists up to 150,000 words. The collegiate edition also provides much more information about each word.

Several standard dictionaries are available in both desk and paperback editions. These include *Webster's New World Dictionary of the American Language, Merriam-Webster's Collegiate Dictionary,* and the *American Heritage Dictionary of the English Language.*

Another type is the unabridged dictionary, which can be found in the reference section of any library. The unabridged edition provides the most information on each word in the English language.

Whether you purchase a collegiate or a pocket dictionary will depend on your needs as well as on what you can afford. It would be ideal to have both. A pocket dictionary is sufficient for checking spelling and for looking up common meanings of unfamiliar words. To expand your vocabulary by learning additional meanings of words or to do any serious word study, you need a desk dictionary.

Many dictionaries of different types are available on the Internet. Two of the most widely used English print dictionaries, those by Merriam-Webster and American Heritage, have Internet versions. Both of these sites (http://www.m-w.com/ and http://www.yourdictionary.com/index.shtml) feature an audio component with which the user can hear how a word is pronounced. Specialized dictionaries in all fields also have places in cyberspace. From medical terminology to foreign languages, Web searchers can find vocabulary help for almost all their needs.

Use of the Dictionary

Most students are familiar with the common uses of a dictionary: (1) to look up the meaning of words one doesn't know and (2) to check the spelling of words. A dictionary can be useful in many other ways because it contains much more than just word meanings. For most entries you will find a pronunciation key, word origin, part(s) of speech, variant spellings, and synonyms. At the beginning or end of many desk dictionaries, you will find information on language history and manuscript form, lists of symbols, and tables of weights and measures.

A dictionary is the basic tool for expanding your vocabulary. Get in the habit of consulting your dictionary whenever you see or hear a somewhat familiar word that you don't use and can't define precisely. Locate the word, read each meaning, and find the one that fits the way the word was used when you read or heard it. Use the vocabulary card system suggested later in this chapter to record and learn these words.

EXERCISE 1

DIRECTIONS   Use a desk dictionary to answer the following questions.

1. What does the abbreviation *obs.* mean?

   _____

2. What does the symbol *c.* stand for?

   _____

3. How many meanings are listed for the word *fall?*

   _____

4. How is the word *phylloxera* pronounced? (Record its phonetic spelling.)

   _____

5. What is the plural spelling of *addendum?*

_____

6. Can the word *protest* be used other than as a verb? If so, how?

_____

7. The word *prime* can mean first or original. List some of its other meanings.

_____

8. What does the French expression *savoir faire* mean?

_____

9. List three synonyms for the word *fault.*

_____

10. List several words that are formed using the word *dream.*

_____

Thesauruses

A thesaurus, or dictionary of synonyms, is a valuable reference for locating a precise, accurate, or descriptive word to fit a particular situation. Suppose you are searching for a more precise term for the expression *looked over,* as used in the following sentence:

> My instructor looked over my essay exam.

The thesaurus lists the synonyms given in Figure 13-1. Right away you can identify a number of words that are more specific than the phrase *looked over.* The next step, then, is to choose from the list the word that most closely

VERBS **12. see, behold, observe, view, witness, perceive, discern, spy,** espy, descry, **sight,** have in sight, make out, spot [coll.], twig [coll.], discover, notice, distinguish, recognize, ken [dial.], **catch sight of,** get a load of [slang, U.S.], take in, look on *or* upon, cast the eyes on or upon, **set** *or* **lay eyes on, clap eyes on** [coll.]; pipe, lamp, nail, peg [all slang]; **glimpse,** get *or* catch a glimpse of; see at a glance, see with half an eye; see with one's own eyes.

13. look, peer, direct the eyes, turn *or* bend the eyes, lift up the eyes; **peek, peep,** pry, take a peep *or* peek; play at peekaboo *or* bopeep; get an eyeful [coll., U.S.].

14. look at, take a look at, take a gander at [slang, U.S.], have a looksee [slang, U.S.], look on *or* upon, gaze at *or* upon; **watch, observe,** pipe [slang], **view, regard;** keep in sight *or* view, hold in view; look after, follow; spy upon.

15. scrutinize, survey, eye, ogle, contemplate, look over, give the eye [slang], give the once-over *or* double-O [slang, U.S.]; examine, **inspect 484.31;** size up [coll.], take one's measure [slang].

16. gaze, gloat, fix~, fasten *or* rivet the eyes upon, keep the eyes upon; eye, ogle; **stare,** look [coll.], goggle, **gape, gawk** [coll.], gaup *or* gawp [dial.], gaze open-mouthed; crane, crane the neck; rubber, **rubberneck,** gander [all slang, U.S.]; look straight in the eye, look full in the face, hold one's eye *or* gaze, stare down; strain the eyes.

17. glare, glower, look daggers.

18. glance, glimpse, glint, cast a glance, glance at *or* upon, take a glance at, take a slant *or* squint at [slang].

19. look askance *or* **askant,** give a side-long look, cut one's eye [slang], glime [dial.]; squint, look asquint; cock the eye; **look down one's nose** [coll.].

20. leer, leer the eye, look leeringly, give a leering look.

21. look away, avert the eyes; look another way, break one's eyes away, stop looking, turn away from, turn the back upon; drop one's eyes *or* gaze, cast one's eyes down; avoid one's gaze, cut eyes [coll.].

Figure 13-1
A Sample Thesaurus Entry

suggests the meaning you want to convey. The easiest way to do this is to test out, or substitute, various choices in your sentence to see which one is most appropriate; check the dictionary if you are not sure of a word's exact meaning.

Many students misuse the thesaurus by choosing words that do not fit the context. *Be sure to use words only when you are familiar with all their shades of meaning.* Remember, a misused word is often a more serious error than a wordy or imprecise expression.

The most widely used thesaurus was originally compiled by the English scholar Peter Roget and is known today as *Roget's Thesaurus;* it is readily available in an inexpensive paperback edition.

EXERCISE 2

DIRECTIONS   Replace the underlined word or phrase in each sentence with a more descriptive word or phrase. Use a thesaurus to locate your replacement.

1. When Sara learned that her sister had committed a crime, she was <u>sad.</u>
2. Compared with earlier chapters, the last two chapters in my chemistry text are <u>hard.</u>
3. The instructor spent the entire class <u>talking about</u> the causes of inflation and deflation.
4. The main character in the film was a <u>thin,</u> talkative British soldier.
5. We went to see a <u>great</u> film that won the Academy Award for best picture.

Subject Area Dictionaries

Many academic disciplines have specialized dictionaries that list important terminology used in that field. They give specialized meanings and suggest how and when to use a word. For the field of music there is the *New Grove Dictionary of Music and Musicians,* which lists and defines the specialized vocabulary of music. Other subject area dictionaries include *Taber's Cyclopedic Medical Dictionary, A Dictionary of Anthropology,* and *A Dictionary of Economics.*

Be sure to find out whether there is a subject area dictionary for your courses and area of specialization. Most of these dictionaries are available only in hardbound copies, and they are likely to be expensive. Many students, however, find them to be worth the initial investment. You will find that most libraries have copies of specialized dictionaries in their reference section.

EXERCISE 3

DIRECTIONS   List below each course you are taking this term. Using your campus library or the Internet, find out whether a subject area dictionary is available for each discipline. If so, list their titles below.

Course   **Subject Area Dictionary**

_____   _____

_____   _____

_____   _____

_____   _____

LEARNING SPECIALIZED TERMINOLOGY

Each subject area can be said to have a language of its own—its own set of specialized words that makes it possible to describe and accurately discuss topics, principles and concepts, problems, and events related to the subject area.

One of the first tasks that both college instructors and textbook authors face is the necessity of introducing and teaching the specialized language of an academic field. This task is especially important in introductory, first-semester courses in which a student studies or encounters the subject area for the first time. In an introduction to psychology course, for instance, you often start by learning the meaning of *psychology* itself—what the study is devoted to, what it encompasses, how it approaches situations, events, and problems. From that point you move on to learn related terms: *behavior, observations, hypothesis, experiment, variables, subjects,* and so forth.

Often the first few class lectures in a course are introductory. They are devoted to acquainting students with the nature and scope of the subject area and to introducing the specialized language.

The first few chapters in a textbook are introductory, too. They are written to familiarize students with the subject of study and acquaint them with its specialized language. In one economics textbook, 34 new terms were introduced in the first two chapters (40 pages). In the first two chapters (28 pages) of a chemistry book, 56 specialized words were introduced. A sample of the words introduced in each of these texts is given below. From these lists you can see that some of the terms are common, everyday words that take on a specialized meaning; others are technical terms used only in that subject area.

New Terms: Economics Text	New Terms: Chemistry Text
capital	matter
ownership	element
opportunity cost	halogen
distribution	isotope
productive contribution	allotropic form
durable goods	nonmetal
economic system	group (family)
barter	burning
commodity money	toxicity

Recognition of specialized terminology is only the first step in learning the language of a course. More important is the development of a systematic way of identifying, marking, recording, and learning the specialized terms. Because new terminology is introduced in both class lectures and course textbooks, it is necessary to develop a procedure for handling the specialized terms in each.

EXERCISE 4

DIRECTIONS   Turn to the reading "Stem-cell Therapy: Promise and Reality," in Part Eight, page 490. Identify as many new terms as you can, and record them in the space provided below.

Total number of specialized words: _____

Examples of specialized vocabulary: _____

_____

_____

_____

_____

EXERCISE 5 | DIRECTIONS   Select any two textbooks you are currently using. In each, turn to the first chapter and check to see how many specialized terms are introduced. List the total number of such terms. Then list several examples.

Textbook 1: _____   Textbook 2: _____
                    (title)   *(title)*

Total number of specialized words: _____   Total number of specialized words: _____

Examples of Specialized Words   **Examples of Specialized Words**

1. _____   1. _____

2. _____   2. _____

3. _____   3. _____

4. _____   4. _____

5. _____   5. _____

6. _____   6. _____

7. _____   7. _____

Specialized Terminology in Class Lectures

As a part of your note-taking system, develop a consistent way of separating new terms and definitions from other facts and ideas. You might circle or draw a box around each new term; or, as you edit your notes (make revisions, changes, or additions to your notes after taking them), underline each new term in red; or mark "def." in the margin each time a definition is included. The mark or symbol you use is a matter of preference; the important thing is to find some way to identify definitions for further study. In addition, as part of your editing process, check each definition to be sure that it is complete and readable. Also, if you were not able to record any explanation or examples of new terms, add them as you edit. If the definitions you recorded are unclear, check with a friend or with your instructor. The last step in handling new terminology presented in class lectures is to organize the terms into a system for efficient study. One such system will be suggested later in this chapter.

Specialized Terminology in Textbooks

Textbook authors use various means to emphasize new terminology as they introduce it. In some texts, new vocabulary is printed in italics, boldface type, or colored print. Other texts indicate new terms in the margin of each page. The most common means of emphasis, however, is a new-terms list or vocabulary list at the beginning or end of each chapter.

While you are reading and highlighting important facts and ideas, you should also mark new terminology. Be sure to mark definitions and to separate them from other chapter content. (The mark or symbol you use is your choice.)

Occasionally in textbooks, you may meet a new term that is not defined or for which the definition is unclear. In this case, check the glossary at the back of the book for the meaning of the word. Make a note of the meaning in the margin of the page.

The glossary, a comprehensive list of terms introduced throughout the text, is an aid that can help you learn new terminology. At the end of the course, when you have covered all or most of the chapters, the glossary can be used to review terminology. Use the glossary to test yourself; read an entry, cover up the meaning, and try to remember it; then check to see whether you were correct. As you progress through a course, however, the glossary is not an adequate study aid. A more organized, systematic approach to learning unfamiliar new terms is needed.

USE WORD MAPPING TO EXPAND YOUR VOCABULARY

Word mapping is a visual method of expanding your vocabulary. It involves examining a word in detail by considering its meanings, synonyms (words similar in meaning), antonyms (words opposite in meaning), part(s) of speech, word parts, and usages. A word map is a form of word study. By the time you have completed the map, you will find that you have learned the word and are ready to use it in your speech and writing.

Here is a sample map for the word *intercept*.

Word Map

Original sentence using the word Antivirus programs intercept unwanted and dangerous e-mail attachments.

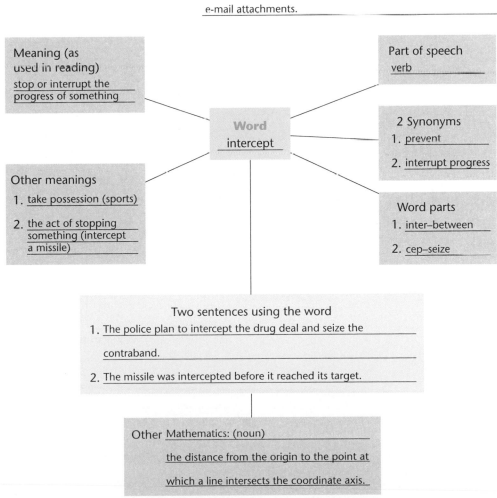

Meaning (as used in reading)
stop or interrupt the progress of something

Other meanings
1. take possession (sports)
2. the act of stopping something (intercept a missile)

Word
intercept

Part of speech
verb

2 Synonyms
1. prevent
2. interrupt progress

Word parts
1. inter–between
2. cep–seize

Two sentences using the word
1. The police plan to intercept the drug deal and seize the contraband.
2. The missile was intercepted before it reached its target.

Other Mathematics: (noun)
the distance from the origin to the point at which a line intersects the coordinate axis.

Use the following steps in completing a word map:

1. **Write the sentence containing the word at the top of the map.**
2. **Look the word up in your dictionary.** Figure out which meaning fits the context of the sentence and write it in the box labeled "Meaning (as used in reading)."
3. **In the "Part of speech" box, write in the word's part(s) of speech as used in context.**
4. **Study the dictionary entry to discover other meanings of the word.** Write them on the map in the box labeled "Other meanings."
5. **Find or think of two synonyms (words similar in meaning), and write them in the "Synonyms" box.** You might need a thesaurus for this.
6. **Analyze the word's parts and identify any prefixes, roots, or suffixes.** Write each word part and its meaning in the space provided.
7. **At the bottom of the map write two sentences using the word.**
8. **In the box labeled "Other," include any other interesting information about the word.** You might include antonyms, restrictive meanings, or word history.

EXERCISE 6 | DIRECTIONS Using a dictionary, complete a word map for one of the new words you are learning in one of your other courses.

Word Map

Original sentence using the word _____

_____

Meaning (as used in reading)
_____
_____
_____

Word

Part of speech
_____

2 Synonyms
1. _____
2. _____

Other meanings
1. _____
2. _____
3. _____

Word parts
1. _____

Two sentences using the word

1. _____
_____
_____
2. _____
_____

Other	_____
	_____

SYSTEMS OF LEARNING VOCABULARY

Here are two effective ways to organize and learn specialized or technical vocabulary for each of your courses.

The Vocabulary Card System

Once you have identified and marked new terminology, both in your lecture notes and in your textbook, the next step is to organize the words for study and review. One of the most efficient and practical ways to accomplish this is the vocabulary card system. Use a 3-by-5-inch index card for each new term. Record the word on the front and its meaning on the back. If the word is particularly difficult, you might also include a guide to its pronunciation. Underneath the correct spelling of the word, indicate in syllables how the word sounds. For the word *eutrophication* (a term used in chemistry to mean "overnourishment"), you could indicate its pronunciation as "you-tro-fi-kay'-shun." On the back of the card, along with the meaning, you might want to include an example to help you remember the term more easily. A sample vocabulary card, front and back, is shown in Figure 13-2.

Use these cards for study, for review, and for testing yourself. Go through your pack of cards once, looking at the front and trying to recall the meaning on the back. Then reverse the procedure; look at the meanings and see whether you can recall the terms. As you go through the pack in this way, sort the cards into two piles: words you know and words you don't know. The next time you review the cards, use only cards in the "don't know" pile for review. This sorting procedure will help you avoid wasting time reviewing words you have already learned. Continue to review the cards until you are satisfied that you have learned each new term. To prevent forgetting, review the entire pack of cards periodically.

The Computerized Vocabulary File

Using a word processing program, create a computer file for each of your courses. Daily or weekly, review both textbook chapters and lecture notes and

**Figure 13-2
A Sample Vocabulary
Card**

Front of Card

conglomerate

con - glom' - er - it

Back of Card

def.: an organization comprising two or more companies that produce unrelated products.
ex.: Nichols company owns a shoe factory, vineyards in France, soft drink factories, and Sara Jane pastry company.

enter specialized and technical terms that you need to learn. Use a two-column or table format, entering the word in one column, its meaning in the other. You might subdivide or code your file by textbook chapter so that you can review easily when exams or quizzes on particular chapters are announced.

Your files can be used in several different ways. If you alphabetize the words, you have created a glossary that will serve as a handy reference. Keep a print copy handy as you read new chapters and review lecture notes. When studying the words in your file, try scrambling the words to avoid learning them in a fixed order.

EXERCISE 7   **DIRECTIONS**   Select two or three sets of notes on a particular topic from any course you are taking. Prepare a set of vocabulary cards for the new terms introduced. Review and study the cards.

EXERCISE 8   **DIRECTIONS**   Select one chapter from any of the textbooks you are currently using. Prepare a vocabulary card for each new term introduced in the chapter. Review and study the cards.

LEARNING COLLABORATIVELY

DIRECTIONS   After listing 20 unfamiliar words and their meanings on the chalkboard, the instructor will divide the class into two groups. Group 1 should record each word on an index card, writing the word on the front and its meaning on the back. Group 2 should copy the words in a list on a piece of notebook paper, writing the meaning to the right of each word. Both groups will be given five minutes to study the words (which have been erased from the chalkboard). Members of Group 1 should study by testing themselves using their index cards. Members of Group 2 should study by rereading their lists. During the next class, both groups should take a test on the words. Tally and compare scores of each group, and discuss what this experiment demonstrates about vocabulary learning.

APPLYING YOUR LEARNING

Erika is taking a human anatomy course and is having difficulty understanding and learning all the new vocabulary items. Her instructor uses many specialized words in lectures. Often Erika is unable to spell the words correctly, and sometimes she cannot write down the entire definition.

1. Is there a dictionary you would recommend that Erika use?
2. How can Erika separate out these new terms in her lecture notes?
3. How can Erika use the glossary in her textbook to help her study for exams?
4. How can she use the vocabulary card system to study?

APPLYING YOUR SKILLS: Sample Textbook Chapter

1. Use context to define each of the following words used in the chapter:

   a. acculturation (p. 515) _____

   b. cultural filters (p. 516)_____

   c. explicitly (p. 519) _____

   d. modest (p. 520) _____

   e. discrepancies (p. 524) _____

2. Use word parts as well as context to define each of the following words:

   a. unidirectional (p. 515)_____

   b. interracial (p. 517) _____

   c. insensitive (p. 519)_____

   d. overattribution (p. 524)_____

   e. credibility (p. 525) _____

3. Complete the Vocabulary Quiz on page 531.

QUESTIONS FOR DISCUSSION

1. What are some ways that you learn new vocabulary? Explain the methods that are particularly effective for you in various classes and subject areas.
2. What are the advantages of using a large vocabulary when you write?
3. What are an author's responsibilities related to vocabulary when writing for various audiences?
4. One challenge of accepting a new job is learning the specialized vocabulary used by the people who work in a chosen field, company, or department. What are some ways that a new employee can most effectively deal with new vocabulary?

SELF-TEST SUMMARY

1. **What can you do to expand your overall vocabulary?**

Expanding your vocabulary is a relatively simple process and does not require large investments of time or money. It will be most helpful to develop a sense of word awareness—to pay attention to and notice words. Wide reading can expose you to new words and new uses of familiar words. In your speech and writing, you should try to use more exact and expressive words to convey your meaning more clearly and directly. Finally, you might try a vocabulary building program, either book- or computer-based. You can obtain help and information at your college learning laboratory.

2. Which reference sources are helpful in vocabulary building?

References that are useful in expanding your vocabulary include a dictionary, a thesaurus, and subject area dictionaries. Owning both a pocket and a desk dictionary is helpful for quick reference and serious word study. A good thesaurus is an indispensable reference for selecting the best word for a particular situation. Subject area dictionaries are very helpful in locating meanings and uses of specialized terms for the different academic disciplines.

3. How can you identify which specialized terms to learn?

Specialized terminology—those words used within an academic discipline—are especially important to learn. While taking notes and reading textbooks, pay special attention to these words. When taking lecture notes, it is helpful to distinguish new terms and definitions by circling them, highlighting them in a coded color, or labeling them in the margins of your notes. Your textbooks will often make special terms stand out by using italics, bold print, or color. You should also mark any other terms that are new to you. Further, you can consult each chapter's vocabulary list for terms to learn and can use your text's glossary as a study aid.

4. What is a word map?

A word map is a visual method of expanding your vocabulary by examining part(s) of speech and summarizing word parts and word usages.

5. How can you use the vocabulary card system to help you learn new vocabulary?

Once general and specialized vocabulary have been identified, the vocabulary card system provides an easy and efficient way to learn each. It involves using 3-by-5-inch cards for study, review, and self-testing. Each card should contain a word and its pronunciation on one side and its meaning and an example on the other. Study these cards by looking at one side and then at the other and then reversing the process. Sort them into piles: "words learned" and "words to be learned." Concentrate on the words you haven't learned until you master them all. Keep them fresh in your memory by reviewing them often and testing yourself frequently.

NAME:

DIRECTIONS   Write the letter of the choice that best completes each statement in the space provided.

CHECKING YOUR RECALL

_____ 1. A thesaurus lists a word's
   a. synonyms.
   b. translations.
   c. abbreviations.
   d. history.

_____ 2. In a textbook, the glossary is typically located
   a. in the margin of each page.
   b. at the beginning of each chapter.
   c. at the end of each chapter.
   d. at the end of the book.

_____ 3. Specialized vocabulary includes words and phrases that
   a. have a different meaning in another language.
   b. are used in a particular subject area.
   c. must be defined each time they are used.
   d. are used casually in speech.

_____ 4. All of the following characterize a strong vocabulary *except*
   a. substituting long words for short words.
   b. speaking with precise, descriptive language.
   c. using unusual meanings for common words.
   d. applying technical terms in specific disciplines.

_____ 5. In most dictionaries, you can find all of the following information about a word *except* its
   a. pronunciation.
   b. origin.
   c. part of speech
   d. opposite meaning.

APPLYING YOUR SKILLS

_____ 6. Preston wants to expand his vocabulary and has asked his friends for advice. All of the following suggestions are efficient ways for Preston to expand his vocabulary *except*
   a. reading a wide range of subjects and styles.
   b. developing an awareness of new or unusual words.
   c. replacing the general words in his vocabulary with more descriptive words.
   d. avoiding the use of specialized terminology.

_____ 7. Olivia needs detailed information about a variety of words for a project in her English class. The source that will provide her with the most information on each word in the English language is
   a. a pocket dictionary.
   b. a collegiate dictionary.
   c. a subject area dictionary.
   d. an unabridged dictionary.

_____ 8. Davis needs to determine the meaning of some technical engineering terms. The best sources for the meanings of the technical terms include all of the following *except*
   a. his instructor's presentations.
   b. a subject area dictionary.
   c. his textbook.
   d. a thesaurus.

_____ 9. Detra plans to use the vocabulary card system to help her learn material for a botany course. When she creates her cards, she should be sure to
   a. record as many definitions on each card as possible.
   b. keep the cards in alphabetical order at all times.
   c. include a pronunciation guide for difficult words.
   d. review the whole set of cards every time.

_____ 10. Ron has noticed that his economics instructor often introduces specialized vocabulary in class lectures. When this happens, Ron should
   a. find the term in his text and highlight it.
   b. record it on a separate list.
   c. disregard it if he doesn't know what it means.
   d. record and mark it in his notes.

MULTIMEDIA *Activities*

Expanding Your Vocabulary

1 Carry a small notebook with you to record new words that you come across in your daily life. Look up the definitions and try to use them when appropriate.

2 Vocabulary Quizzes

http://grammar.ccc.commnet.edu/grammar/vocabulary.htm

Pick a few of these vocabulary quizzes from Capital Community College to complete online (scroll to the bottom of the page for quizzes). Use a dictionary if necessary. Evaluate your performance. Choose some words from the quizzes to learn using techniques from this chapter.

3 Draw pictures of new creatures, machines, plants (anything!) and make up names for them. Then write an explanation of each name.

4 Banished Words

http://www.lssu.edu/banished/current/default.html

Look over this list of words voted the most misused, overused, or useless words of the year. Do you agree with these choices? What words might you add?

5 A Word a Day

http://www.wordsmith.org/awad/index.html

Sign up to receive a word a day in your e-mail or read a newsletter about words on this interesting site for language fans. Use the new words in your writing and speech.

> **Answer Key for Learning Experiment**
> 1. c 2. f 3. e 4. i 5. a 6. b 7. j 8. h 9. d 10. g

14 Textbook Highlighting and Marking

Why Learn to Highlight and Mark Your Textbooks?

- Highlighting and marking force you to sort ideas, deciding which are important and which are not.

- Highlighting and marking keep you physically active while you read and help focus your attention on the material.

- Highlighting and marking help you remember what you read.

- Highlighting and marking force you to weigh and evaluate what you read.

- Highlighting and marking help you see the organization of facts and ideas and connections between them.

Learning Experiment

Step 1

Study the following diagram of the human brain. Estimate how long it would take you to learn all the parts of the brain shown in the diagram.

Step 2

Now, using the same diagram, estimate how long it would take you to learn only the four principal parts of the brain.

Principal Parts of the Human Brain

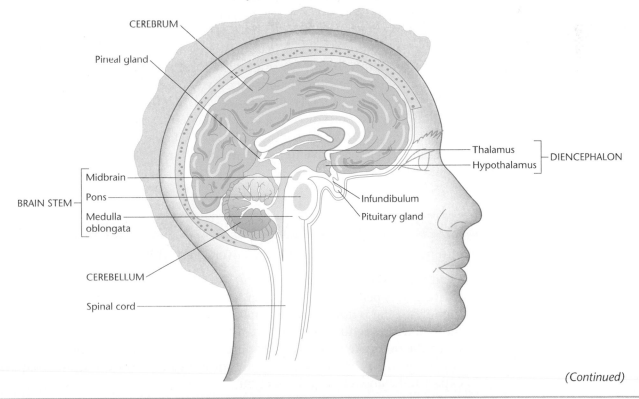

(Continued)

THE PROBLEM OF TEXTBOOK REVIEW

As you have already discovered, most college courses involve lengthy and time-consuming reading assignments. Just completing the reading assignments is a big job. Have you begun to wonder how you will ever go back over all those textbook chapters when it's time for an exam?

Let's suppose that it takes you at least four hours to carefully read a 40-page chapter for one of your courses. Assume that your text has ten chapters of approximately 40 pages each. It would take a total of 40 hours, then, to read completely through the text once. Suppose that your instructor is giving a final exam that will cover the entire text. If the only thing you did to prepare for the final was to reread the whole text, then it would take close to another 40 hours to study for the exam; and one additional reading is no guarantee that you will pass the exam.

Now consider this: If you had highlighted and marked important ideas and facts as you were first reading the chapters, when you were ready to review, you would have to read and study only what you marked. If you had marked or highlighted 15 to 20 percent of the chapter material, you would have cut your rereading time by 80 to 85 percent, or 32 hours! Of course, to prepare effectively for the exam, you would have to review in other ways besides rereading, but you would have time left to do this.

HOW TO HIGHLIGHT TEXTBOOKS

To learn how to highlight textbooks effectively, start with the following guidelines:

1. **Read first; then highlight.** As you are reading to develop skill in highlighting, it is better to read a paragraph or section first and then go back and highlight what is important to remember and review. Later, when you've had more practice highlighting, you may be able to highlight while you read.
2. **Read the boldface headings.** Headings are labels, or overall topics, for what is contained in that section. Use the headings to form questions that you expect to be answered in the section.

3. **After you have read the section, go back and highlight the parts that answer your questions.** These will be parts of sentences that express the main ideas, or most important thoughts, in the section. In reading and highlighting the following section, you could form questions like those suggested and then highlight as shown.

Questions to Ask

What are primary groups?

What are secondary groups?

Primary and Secondary Groups

It is not at all surprising that some students used their families as a reference group. After all, families are the best examples of the groups Charles Cooley (1909) called *primary* chiefly because they "are fundamental in forming the social nature and ideals of the individual." In a primary group the individuals interact informally, relate to each other as whole persons, and enjoy their relationship for its own sake. This is one of the two main types of social groups. In the other type, a secondary group, the individuals interact formally, relate to each other as players of particular roles, and expect to profit from each other.

—Thio, *Sociology,* p. 100

4. **As you identify and highlight main ideas, look for important facts that explain or support the main idea, and highlight them too.**
5. **When highlighting main ideas and details, do not highlight complete sentences.** Highlight only enough so that you can see what is important and so that your highlighting makes sense when you reread. Note how only key words and phrases are highlighted in the following passage.

Gossip

There can be no doubt that everyone spends a great deal of time gossiping. In fact, gossip seems universal among all cultures (Laing 1993), and among some it's a commonly accepted ritual (Hall 1993). Gossip refers to third party talk about another person; the word **gossip** "now embraces both the talker and the talk, the tattler and the tattle, the newsmonger and the newsmongering" (Bremner 1980, p. 178). Gossip is an inevitable part of daily interactions; to advise anyone not to gossip would be absurd. Not gossiping would eliminate one of the most frequent and enjoyable forms of communication.

In some instances, however, gossip is unethical (Bok 1983). First, it's unethical to reveal information that you've promised to keep secret. Although this principle may seem too obvious to even mention, it seems violated in many cases. For example, in a study of 133 school executives, board presidents, and superintendents, the majority received communications that violated an employee's right to confidentiality (Wilson and Bishard 1994). When it is impossible to keep something secret (Bok offers the example of the teenager who confides a suicide plan), the information should be revealed only to those who must know it, not to the world at large. Second, gossip is unethical when it invades the privacy that everyone has a right to, for example, when it concerns matters that are properly considered private and when the gossip can hurt the individuals involved. Third, gossip is unethical when it's known to be false and is nevertheless passed on to others.

—DeVito, *The Interpersonal Communication Book,* p. 191

ASPECTS OF EFFECTIVE HIGHLIGHTING

For your highlighting to be effective and useful to you as you study and review, it must follow four specific guidelines.

1. **The right amount of information must be highlighted.**
2. **The highlighting must be regular and consistent.**
3. **It must be accurate.**
4. **It must clearly reflect the content of the passage.**

Suggestions for implementing these guidelines and examples of each are given in the following paragraphs.

Highlight the Right Amount

Students frequently make the mistake of highlighting either too much or too little. If you highlight too much, the passages you have marked will take you too long to reread when you are studying later. If you highlight too little, you won't be able to get any meaning from your highlighting as you review it.

Too Much Highlighting

Iran, which had served as an area of competition between the British and the Russians since the nineteenth century, became a bone of contention between the United States and the Soviet Union after World War II. As the result of an agreement between the British and the Russians in 1941, Shah Mohammad Reza Pahlavi (1919–1980) gained the Iranian throne. After the war he asked foreign troops to withdraw from his country, but following the slow return of the Soviet army to its borders, aggressive activities of the Iranian Communist party (Tudeh), and an assassination attempt on the Shah's life, Iran firmly tied itself to the West.

—Wallbank et al., *Civilization Past and Present,* pp. 1012–1013

Too Little Highlighting

Iran, which had served as an area of competition between the British and the Russians since the nineteenth century, became a bone of contention between the United States and the Soviet Union after World War II. As the result of an agreement between the British and the Russians in 1941, Shah Mohammad Reza Pahlavi (1919–1980) gained the Iranian throne. After the war he asked foreign troops to withdraw from his country, but following the slow return of the Soviet army to its borders, aggressive activities of the Iranian Communist party (Tudeh), and an assassination attempt on the Shah's life, Iran firmly tied itself to the West.

Effective Highlighting

Iran, which had served as an area of competition between the British and the Russians since the nineteenth century, became a bone of contention between the United States and the Soviet Union after World War II. As the result of an agreement between the British and the Russians in 1941, Shah Mohammad Reza Pahlavi (1919–1980) gained the Iranian throne. After the war he asked foreign troops to withdraw from his country, but following the slow return of the Soviet army to its borders, aggressive activities of the Iranian Communist party (Tudeh), and an assassination attempt on the Shah's life, Iran firmly tied itself to the West.

Almost all of the first passage is highlighted. To highlight nearly all of the passage is as ineffective as not highlighting at all, because it does not distinguish important from unimportant information. In the second passage, only the main point of the paragraph is highlighted, but very sketchily—not enough detail is included. The highlighting in the third passage is effective; it identifies the main idea of the paragraph and includes enough details to make the main idea clear and understandable.

As a rule of thumb, try to highlight no more than one-quarter to one-third of each page. This figure will vary, of course, depending on the type of material you are reading. Here is another example of effective highlighting. Note that approximately one-third of each paragraph is highlighted.

Living with Pain

Temporary pain is an unpleasant but necessary part of life, a warning of disease or injury. Chronic pain, which is ongoing or recurring, is another matter, a serious problem in itself. Back injuries, arthritis, migraine headaches, serious illnesses such as cancer—all can cause unrelieved misery to pain sufferers and their families. Chronic pain can also impair the immune system, and such impairment can put patients at risk of further complications from their illnesses.

At one time, the only way to combat pain was with drugs or surgery, which were not always effective. Today, we know that the experience of pain is affected by attitudes, and that treatment must take into account psychology as well as biology. Even social roles can influence a person's response to pain. For example, although women tend to report greater pain than men do, a real-world study of people who were in pain for more than six months found that men suffered more severe psychological distress than women, possibly because the male role made it hard for them to admit their pain.

—Wade and Tavris, *Invitation to Psychology,* p. 182

Develop a Regular and Consistent System of Highlighting

As you develop your textbook highlighting skills, you should focus on this second guideline: Develop a system for deciding what type of information you will highlight and how you will mark it. First, decide what type of information you want to mark. Before marking anything, decide whether you will mark only main ideas or mark main ideas and details. You should also decide whether you will highlight or mark definitions of new terminology and, if so, how you will distinguish them from other information marked in the paragraph. Second, it is important to use consistently whatever system and type of highlighting you decide on so that you will know what your highlighting means when you review it. If you sometimes mark details and main ideas and other times highlight only main ideas, at review time you will find that you are unsure of what passages are marked in what way, and you will be forced to reread a great deal of material.

You may decide to develop a system for separating main ideas from details, major points from supporting information. When you review highlighting done this way, you will immediately know what is the most important point of the paragraph or section, and you will not get bogged down in the details—unless you need to. One such system uses one color of marker for main points and a different color for details. Another approach is to use asterisks and brackets to call attention to the main points.

Each of the following paragraphs has been highlighted using one of the suggested systems. You will notice that the paragraphs vary in the type of information marked in each.

Version 1: Use of Color

Barriers to Listening

There are several reasons why people are poor listeners. One reason is that the complex human mind can comprehend many more words per minute than speakers can produce. Listeners can process more than 400 spoken words per minute, yet the average speaker only produces between 125 and 175 words per minute. This time lag between slower speaking rates and faster rates of thinking is known as the **speech–thought differential.** Stated in a different way, the listener needs only 15 seconds of every minute to comprehend the spoken message. The resulting time lag creates special problems. In this excess time, listeners' thoughts may begin to stray. Can you recall a time when you began listening to a speaker, but soon found yourself thinking about lunch, or an upcoming test, or a date? This tendency for our thoughts to stray poses many problems for the speaker trying to convey an understandable message, especially if the subject matter is complex.

—Gronbeck et al., *Principles of Speech Communication,* p. 25

Version 2: Use of Brackets and Asterisks

Barriers to Listening

* There are several reasons why people are poor listeners. One reason is that the complex human mind can comprehend many more words per minute than speakers can produce. Listeners can process more than 400 spoken words per minute, yet the average speaker only produces between 125 and 175 words per minute. This time lag between slower speaking rates and faster rates of thinking is known as the * **speech–thought differential.** Stated in a different way, the listener needs only 15 seconds of every minute to comprehend the spoken message. The resulting time lag creates special problems. In this excess time, listeners' thoughts may begin to stray. Can you recall a time when you began listening to a speaker, but soon found yourself thinking about lunch, or an upcoming test, or a date? This tendency for our thoughts to stray poses many problems for the speaker trying to convey an understandable message, especially if the subject matter is complex.

EXERCISE 1

DIRECTIONS   Read the following passage. Then evaluate the effectiveness of the highlighting, making suggestions for improvement.

Scarcity of Human Fossils

Unfortunately humans are a maddeningly poor source of fossils. In 1956, the paleontologist G. H. R. von Koenigswald calculated that if all the then-known fragments of human beings older than the Neanderthal people were gathered together they could be comfortably displayed on a medium-sized table. Although many more fossils of early hominids have been found since then, discoveries are still rare.

Why are human fossils so scarce? Why can one go to good fossil sites almost anywhere in the world and find millions of shell remains or thousands of bones of extinct reptiles and mammals, while peoples earlier than Neanderthal are known from only a handful of sites at which investigators, working through tons of deposits, pile up other finds by the bushel basket before recovering a single human tooth?

There are many reasons. First, the commonness of marine fossils is a direct reflection of the abundance of these creatures when they were alive. It also reflects the tremendous span of time during which they abounded. Many of them swarmed through the waters of the earth for hundreds of millions of years. Whey they died, they sank and were covered by sediments. Their way of life—their life in the water—preserved them, as did their extremely durable shells, the only parts of them that now remain. Humans, by contrast, have never been as numerous as oysters and clams. They existed in small numbers, reproduced slowly and in small numbers, and lived a relatively long time. They were more intelligent than, for example, dinosaurs and were perhaps less apt to get mired in bogs, marshes, or quicksands. Most important, their way of life was different. They were not sea creatures or exclusively riverside browsers but lively, wide-ranging food-gatherers and hunters. They often lived and died in the open, where their bones were gnawed by scavengers, were trampled on, and were bleached and decomposed by the sun and rain. In hot climates, particularly in tropical forests and woodlands, the soil is likely to be markedly acid. Bones dissolve in such soils, and early humans who lived and died in such an environment had a very poor chance of leaving remains that would last until today. Finally, human ancestors have been on earth only a few million years. There simply has not been as much time for them to leave their bones as there has been for some of the more ancient species of animals.

—Campbell and Loy, *Humankind Emerging,* pp. 22–23

EXERCISE 2

DIRECTIONS   Read each passage and then highlight the main ideas and important details in each. You may want to try various systems of highlighting as you work through this exercise.

1. **The Relationship Between Publicity and Public Relations**

   Publicity and public relations are closely related. While the public-relations role in organizations involves many communications approaches including institutional advertising and personal selling by senior corporate executives, publicity is often the cornerstone of a company's public-relations efforts. A firm's successful public-relations efforts, for example, might be largely the result of publicity it has managed to attract. When Chevron Oil sponsors research aimed at improving the environment, news reports that carry the story (publicity) are instrumental in furthering the image of the company (public relations).

   Publicity is generally a short-term strategy whereas a firm's public relations are ongoing. It is also important to note that a firm controls its public-relations efforts. The company designs its public-relations program to provide positive information about itself and its products. Because publicity is not generated internally, the organization cannot control it.

   Both publicity and public relations are important components of an organization's integrated marketing communications. When carefully planned, with an understanding of the target audience's interests, publicity and public relations can effectively promote a company with little expense.

   —Kinnear, Bernhardt, and Krentler, *Principles of Marketing,* p. 537

2. **Beliefs**

   Beliefs consist of a system of propositions and assertions about the nature of reality. They provide people and societies with a fundamental orientation to the world and answer questions about human origins, proper relations among people, and the destiny of humans and the universe. Simple societies answer these questions with myth and folklore; complex societies answer them with religion and science. Beliefs also include simple observations about the physical and social worlds, or "truths" about nature and people.

   Beliefs are social constructions. Although they are typically accepted as truths by the members of a society, beliefs are based not only on objective reality but on social agreement. Moreover yesterday's beliefs and the common sense of the present are the falsehoods and "myths" of tomorrow. For example, the word "lunatic" is derived from the popular nineteenth-century belief that a full moon causes madness, a belief that has folk origins in Europe and even deeper associations in simple cultures. Today, such thinking is derisively labeled "superstition."

The belief systems of simple societies are generally well integrated and stable and contain few contradictions. In contrast, complex societies—in particular, industrial societies—include multiple and competing belief systems that usually contain many contradictions. For example, Fundamentalist Christianity and science each contain a logically consistent body of beliefs and underlying premises, but the two present very different views of reality. Because of competing ideologies, or beliefs that support, rationalize, or legitimize various social arrangements, people in industrial societies are often more critical of their beliefs than are people in simple societies. Their beliefs are also apt to change at a much faster rate.

—Thompson and Hickey, *Society in Focus,* p. 65

3. **Policies to Reduce Unemployment**

The Employment Act of 1946 gave the U.S. government responsibility for establishing policies to achieve the maximum practical level of employment in the nation. Before deciding on a policy for full employment, it is necessary to identify the causes of unemployment. Then policymakers can design programs to remedy each type. Economists classify unemployment into three categories, depending on the cause: frictional, cyclical, and structural.

Frictional Unemployment. Some portion of total unemployment includes workers who are unemployed because of "frictions" in the movement of workers from job to job or among workers entering the labor force for the first time.

Frictional unemployment is common in a growing economy and reflects the healthy expansion or decline of different sectors of the economy. Markets and production techniques are constantly changing to reflect changes in consumer demand. Workers must move out of declining industries and into expanding industries. If there were no frictional unemployment, expanding industries would have to bid up the wages of employed workers, aggravating tendencies toward inflation.

In recent years, frictional unemployment has come to constitute a larger portion of total employment. This is primarily because of the growing numbers of married women and teenagers in the job market, with typically higher rates of entry and reentry into the labor force than adult male workers.

Frictional unemployment is, by definition, temporary. Its effects may be relieved by better job information and aids to worker mobility. For example, workers can be provided job counseling, or they can be paid grants to finance a move to a new location where jobs are more plentiful.

Cyclical Unemployment. A more serious problem than frictional unemployment is cyclical unemployment—unemployment associated with cycles of economic activity. The Great Depression provides the most obvious example of cyclical unemployment. During the Great Depression, the unemployment rate reached as high as 25 percent of the labor force.

Typically, economic activity grows in spurts. Periods of growth and prosperity are followed by slower growth or decline. Once homes are equipped with all the latest consumer gadgets, demand for consumer goods diminishes. Retailers cut back on inventories and cancel orders to wholesalers. The whole economic system seems to pause before the next round of innovations creates new gadgets, and the cycle begins again.

Cyclic swings in employment are most severe in industries producing durable goods. Purchase of a VCR, microwave oven, or personal computer can be postponed if consumers are worried about their jobs. Cyclical swings are less severe in industries producing nondurable goods and services. Purchases of food, clothing, and health services, for instance, cannot generally be postponed.

In past business cycles, blue-collar production workers were more likely to suffer unemployment than white-collar professional or supervisory workers. Professional and supervisory workers have specialized functions and, often, employment contracts that formerly made dismissal difficult. These workers suffered severely in the recession of 1990–91, however.

Expansionary fiscal and monetary policy make prolonged cyclical unemployment less a threat to our economic system today than in former years.

Structural Unemployment. The kind of unemployment that is most damaging to our prosperity and social health is the growing problem of structural unemployment. *Structural unemployment* is caused by an imbalance between the structure of the labor force, on the one hand, and the requirements of modern industry, on the other. Unless available labor skills correspond to the needs of business firms, there will be unemployment. In fact, there may be severe unemployment at the same time there are job vacancies. Structural unemployment is worsened by the entry of untrained workers (such as teenagers) into the labor force.

The greatest needs in business today are for skilled workers and for workers in the growing service sector. For example, there are extreme shortages of workers in machine trades, some types of engineering, nursing, and transportation.

Policies to remedy structural unemployment include federal and state programs to train workers in new skills, better job information and counseling, and private on-the-job training.

—McCarty, *Dollars and Sense: An Introduction to Economics,* pp. 272–273

Highlight Accurately

A third guideline for marking textbooks is to be sure that the information you highlight accurately conveys the content of the paragraph or passage. In a rush, students often overlook the second half of the main idea expressed in a paragraph, miss a crucial qualifying statement, or mistake an example or (worse yet) a contrasting idea for the main idea. Read the following paragraph and evaluate the accuracy of the highlighting.

> It has long been established that the American legal court system is an open and fair system. Those suspected to be guilty of a criminal offense are given a jury trial in which a group of impartially selected citizens are asked to determine, based upon evidence presented, the guilt or innocence of the person on trial. In actuality, however, this system of jury trial is fair to everyone except the jurors involved. Citizens are expected and, in many instances, required to sit on a jury. They have little or no choice as to the time, place, or any other circumstances surrounding their participation. Additionally, they are expected to leave their job and accept jury duty pay for each day spent in court in place of their regular on-the-job salary. The jury must remain on duty until the case is decided.

In the preceding paragraph, the highlighting indicates that the main idea of the paragraph is that the legal system that operates in American courts is open and fair. The paragraph starts out by saying that the legal system has long been established as fair, but then it goes on to say (in the third sentence) that the system is actually unfair to one particular group—the jury. In this case, the student who did the highlighting missed the real main statement of the paragraph by mistaking the introductory contrasting statement for the main idea.

Make Your Highlighting Understandable for Review

As you highlight, keep the fourth guideline in mind: Be certain that your highlighting clearly reflects the content of the passage so that you will be able to reread and review it easily. Try to highlight enough information in each passage so that the passage reads smoothly when you review it.

Read these two examples of highlighting of the same passage. Which highlighting is easier to reread?

Version 1

Capital may be thought of as manufactured resources. Capital includes the tools and equipment that strengthen, extend, or replace human hands in the production of goods and services. Hammers, sewing machines, turbines, bookkeeping machines, and component parts of finished goods—all are capital goods. Even the specialized skills of trained workers can be thought of as a kind of human capital. Capital resources permit "roundabout" production: producing goods indirectly with a kind of tool rather than directly by physical labor.

To construct a capital resource requires that we postpone production of consumer goods and services today so that we can produce a tool that will enable us to produce more goods and services in the future. To postpone production of wanted goods and services is sometimes a painful decision, particularly when people are poor and in desperate need of goods and services today.

—McCarty, *Dollars and Sense,* pp. 213–214

Version 2

Capital may be thought of as manufactured resources. Capital includes the tools and equipment that strengthen, extend, or replace human hands in the production of goods and services. Hammers, sewing machines, turbines, bookkeeping machines, and component parts of finished goods—all are capital goods. Even the specialized skills of trained workers can be thought of as a kind of human capital. Capital resources permit "roundabout" production: producing goods indirectly with a kind of tool rather than directly by physical labor.

To construct a capital resource requires that we postpone production of consumer goods and services today so that we can produce a tool that will enable us to produce more goods and services in the future. To postpone production of wanted goods and services is sometimes a painful decision, particularly when people are poor and in desperate need of goods and services today.

A good way to check to see if your highlighting is understandable for review is to reread only your highlighting. If parts are unclear right away, you can be sure it will be more confusing when you reread it a week or a month later. Be sure to fix ineffectual highlighting in one paragraph before you continue to the next paragraph.

TESTING YOUR HIGHLIGHTING

As you are learning highlighting techniques, it is important to check to be certain that your highlighting is effective and will be useful for review purposes. To test the effectiveness of your highlighting, take any passage that you highlighted in Exercise 2 and reread only the highlighting. Then ask yourself the following questions:

1. **Have I highlighted the right amount or do I have too much or too little information highlighted?**
2. **Have I used a regular and consistent system for highlighting?**
3. **Does my highlighting accurately reflect the meaning of the passage?**
4. **As I reread my highlighting, is it easy to follow the train of thought or does the passage seem like a list of unconnected words?**

EXERCISE 3 | **DIRECTIONS** Read the first five paragraphs of "Move Over, Big Brother" in Part Eight on p. 506. Highlight the main ideas and important details. When you have finished, test your highlighting by asking the four preceding questions. Make any changes that will make your highlighting more consistent, accurate, or understandable.

EXERCISE 4 | **DIRECTIONS** Choose a three- to four-page passage from one of your textbooks. Read the selection and highlight the main ideas, the important details, and any key terms that are introduced. When you have finished, test your highlighting by asking the four questions listed on page 328, and make any changes that will improve your highlighting.

MARKING A TEXTBOOK

As you were highlighting paragraphs and passages in the earlier part of this chapter, you may have realized that highlighting alone is not sufficient, in many cases, to separate main ideas from details and both of these from new terminology. You may have seen that highlighting does not easily show the relative importance of ideas or indicate the relationship between facts and ideas. Therefore, it is often necessary to mark, as well as highlight, selections that you are reading. Suggestions for marking are shown in Figure 14-1 on the next page.

Two versions of the same paragraph, excerpted from *Messages* by DeVito, follow. The first version contains only highlighting, whereas both highlighting and marking are used in the second. Which version more easily conveys the meaning of the passage?

Version 1

Cultural Time

Two types of cultural time are especially important in nonverbal communication. In American culture, *formal time* is divided into seconds, minutes, hours, days, weeks, months, and years. Other cultures may use phases of the moon or the seasons to delineate time periods. In some colleges courses are divided into 50- or 75-minute periods that meet two or three times a week for 14-week periods called semesters. Eight semesters of 15 or so 50-minute periods per week equal a college education. Other colleges use quarters or trimesters. As these examples illustrate, formal time units are arbitrary. The culture establishes them for convenience.

Informal time refers to the use of general time terms—for example, "forever," "immediately," "soon," "right away," "as soon as possible." This area of time creates the most communication problems because the terms have different meanings for different people.

Attitudes toward time vary from one culture to another. In one study, for example, the accuracy of clocks was measured in six cultures—Japanese, Indonesian, Italian, English, Taiwanese, and North American (U.S.). The Japanese had the most accurate and Indonesians had the least accurate clocks. A measure of the speed at which people in these six cultures walked found that the Japanese walked the fastest, the Indonesians the slowest.

—DeVito, *Messages*, pp. 161–162

Figure 14-1
Textbook Marking

Type of Marking		Example
Circling unknown words	def	. . . redressing the apparent (asymmetry) of their relationship . . .
Marking definitions	def	To say that the balance of power favors one party over another is to introduce a disequilibrium.
Marking examples	ex	. . . concessions may include negative sanctions, trade agreements . . .
Numbering lists of ideas, causes, reasons, or events		. . . components of power include self-image, population, natural resources, and geography
Placing asterisks next to important passages	*	Power comes from three primary sources . . .
Putting question marks next to confusing passages	?→	. . . war prevention occurs through institutionalization of mediation . . .
Making notes to yourself	check def in soc text	. . . power is the ability of an actor on the international stage to . . .
Marking possible test items	T	There are several key features in the relationship . . .
Drawing arrows to show relationships		. . . natural resources . . . control of industrial manufacturing capacity
Writing comments, noting disagreements and similarities	Can terrorism be prevented through similar balance?	. . . war prevention through balance of power is . . .
Marking summary statements	sum	. . . the greater the degree of conflict, the more intricate will be . . .

Version 2

Cultural Time

def Two types of cultural time are especially important in nonverbal communication. In American culture, [formal time] is divided into seconds, minutes, hours, days, weeks, months, and years. Other cultures may use phases of the moon or the seasons to delineate time periods. In some colleges courses are divided into 50- or 75-minute
examples periods that meet two or three times a week for 14-week periods called semesters. Eight semesters of 15 or so 50-minute periods per week equal a college education. Other colleges use quarters or trimesters. As these examples illustrate, formal time units are arbitrary. The culture establishes them for convenience.
def [Informal time] refers to the use of general time terms—for example, "forever," "immediately," "soon," "right away," "as soon as possible." This area of time creates

the most communication problems because the terms have different meanings for different people.

cultural differences

Attitudes toward time vary from one culture to another. In one study, for example, the accuracy of clocks was measured in six cultures—Japanese, Indonesian, Italian, English, Taiwanese, and North American (U.S.). The Japanese had the most accurate and Indonesians had the least accurate clocks. A measure of the speed at which

research study

people in these six cultures walked found that the Japanese walked the fastest, the Indonesians the slowest.

As you can see, in version 2 the two types of cultural time are easy to identify. Boxing the two types makes them immediately noticeable and distinguishes them from the remainder of the passage.

Critical Comments

When you highlight, you are operating at the knowledge and comprehension levels of thinking (see Chapter 2, p. 54). Marking is an opportunity to record your thinking at other levels.

Applying Levels of thinking
MARKING AND LEVELS OF THINKING

Here are some examples of the kinds of marginal notes you might make.

Level of Thinking	Marginal Notes
Applying	Jot notes about how to use the information.
Analyzing	Draw arrows to link related material.
Evaluating	Comment on the worth, value, relevance, and timeliness of ideas.
Creating	Record ideas about how topics fit together; make notes connecting material to lectures; condense ideas into your own words.

Writing Summary Notes

Writing summary words or phrases in the margin is one of the most valuable types of textbook marking. It involves pulling ideas together and summarizing them in your own words. This process forces you to think and evaluate as you read and makes remembering easier. Writing summary phrases is also a good test of your understanding. If you cannot state the main idea of a section in your own words, you probably do not understand it clearly. This realization can serve as an early warning signal that you may not be able to handle a test question on that section.

The following sample passage has been included to illustrate effective marking of summary phrases. First, read through the passage. Then look at the marginal summary clues.

Cross-Cultural Conclusions

At this juncture, after analyzing organized crime in various societies, we may reach several conclusions about the subject.

hierarchical

First, organized crime is basically the same across societies in being a *hierarchical* organization that engages in crime activities. Organized crime differs from one society to another only in intraorganizational unity and criminal activities. Members' loyalty to the crime organization seems stronger in Japan and Hong Kong than in the United States and Italy today. The Hong Kong Triads engage in drug trafficking much more extensively than their counterparts in other countries. The Triads, along with their peers in Japan, Italy, and Russia, seem to have penetrated legitimate business and politics more deeply than the crime organizations in the United States.

not uniquely American

Second, there is no validity to the suggestion of Bell's well-known theory that organized crime is a uniquely American way for ambitious poor people in the United States to realize the American dream. There is nothing unique about American organized crime as a ladder of success for the ambitious poor. Organized crime serves the same function in other countries.

stronger outside U.S.

Third, organized crime is more pervasive, influential, or powerful in Italy, Japan, and Hong Kong than in the United States. The reason may be partly cultural in that organized crime in foreign countries is more socially acceptable and integrated into the legitimate world of business and politics. The reason may also be partly economic: the less mature the capitalism of a country is, the less controllable and hence more prevalent its organized crime is. This point shows most clearly in the contrast between the United States and Russia.

difficult to get rid of

Fourth, it is extremely difficult, if not impossible, to get rid of organized crime, as shown by the failure of anti-syndicate measures in various countries. This is particularly true in Japan and Hong Kong because of the underworld's deeper penetration into the conventional upperworld. By comparison, however, the American authorities are more successful in prosecuting mobsters, especially in recent years. Does this mean that we can ever hope to eradicate organized crime in the United States? Let us take a closer look at this issue.

—Thio, *Deviant Behavior*, pp. 311–312

Summary notes are most effectively used in passages that contain long and complicated ideas. In these cases, it is simpler to write a summary phrase in the margin than to highlight a long or complicated statement of the main idea and supporting details.

To write a summary clue, try to think of a word or phrase that accurately states, in brief form, a particular idea presented in the passage. Summary words should trigger your memory of the content of the passage.

EXERCISE 5

DIRECTIONS Read the following textbook selection. Then mark as well as highlight important information contained in the passage.

Basis of Social Organization

Although monkeys and apes differ from each other in important ways, they share many characteristics. Of these, certainly the most interesting is that they are all social species (except perhaps the orangutan) and their societies are highly organized. We first need to ask ourselves several questions. What are the advantages of social life? Why are so many mammal and bird species social and why have the Hominoidea developed this characteristic to such lengths? Four kinds of advantage are usually proposed by zoologists:

1. Several pairs of eyes are better than one in the detection of predators and in their avoidance. Defense by a group is also far more effective. Three or four male baboons constitute an impressive display and can frighten any predator, even a lion. A lone baboon is a dead baboon.

2. Competing for large food patches is more successful when done by groups rather than by individuals. We shall see that some monkeys' social groups subdivide when food is sparse and widely scattered.

3. Reproductive advantages accrue from social groups because regular access to the opposite sex is ensured.

4. Social groups permit extensive socialization with peers and elders and the opportunity to learn from them. Among animals such as the higher primates, this is a factor of the greatest importance.

These factors are probably the most important in bringing about the selection of social life in animals such as primates. Although considerable variation may occur within a species, especially under different environmental conditions, only a few Old World primate species (including the gibbons and siamang, a large gibbon) normally live in groups consisting only of an adult male, a female, and their young. The orang is unique in being more-or-less solitary. The remaining Old World monkeys and apes all live in social groups that number as high as 500 individuals but most commonly number between 10 and 50.

But how are these societies organized? Far from being a structureless collection of rushing, squalling animals, primate societies are remarkably complex and stable. Order is maintained in primate societies through a complex interrelationship of several factors. One factor is the animals' prolonged period of dependence: infant apes and monkeys, like human infants, are far from self-sufficient, and maintain a close relationship with their mothers longer than most other animals.

—Campbell and Loy, *Humankind Emerging*, pp. 127 128

EXERCISE 6   DIRECTIONS   Turn to the reading on page 506 in Part Eight that you highlighted to complete Exercise 3. Review the section and add marking and summary words that would make the section easier to study and review.

EXERCISE 7   DIRECTIONS   Choose a three- or four-page excerpt from one of your textbooks. Highlight and mark main ideas, important details, and key terms. Include summary words, if possible.

LEARNING COLLABORATIVELY

DIRECTIONS   Your instructor will choose a reading from Part Eight and divide the class into two groups for an out-of-class assignment. One group should highlight the reading but make no other markings. The second group should both highlight and mark the reading. During the next class session, students may quiz each other to determine which group is better prepared for (1) an essay exam, (2) a multiple-choice exam, and (3) class discussion.

APPLYING YOUR LEARNING

Jin Lon always highlights her psychology textbook but often wonders whether her highlighting is effective. She usually highlights complete sentences because she is afraid she will miss something important. Sometimes she uses just one marker, and other times she uses two different colored markers. She usually highlights about half of each paragraph. As she reads, she notices things that she thinks could be on an exam, makes a mental note, and continues reading. She doesn't make any notes in the margins because she is unsure what to write.

1. How could Jin Lon determine whether her highlighting is effective?
2. Evaluate Jin Lon's highlighting technique.
3. Should she continue to use two highlighting systems?
4. How could she make better note of possible exam questions?
5. What advice could you give her on marking her textbooks?

APPLYING YOUR SKILLS: Sample Textbook Chapter

1. Read and highlight the sections of the chapter titled "Cultural Differences" and "Improving Intercultural Communication." Test the effectiveness of your highlighting using the suggestions on page 328.
2. Choose one section of the chapter and add markings. How did the markings make the section easier to reread and study?

QUESTIONS FOR DISCUSSION

1. Highlighting becomes more challenging as the density of the material increases. Discuss the systems you use to highlight and mark texts in various subject areas.
2. Why is highlighting frequently a new skill learned in college? Why do many college students tend to highlight too much? Why is a regular and consistent highlighting system important?
3. Evaluate your own ability to highlight effectively. What are your strengths? What are your weaknesses?

SELF-TEST SUMMARY

1. Why should you highlight and mark chapters when you read them?

Reading textbook chapters is a long and time-consuming process. As you read, you encounter a great deal of information that you know you will need to study and review for your next exam or quiz. To be able to locate this information quickly when you study, it is necessary to highlight and mark important information as you read. Without a system of highlighting and marking, you need to reread an entire chapter in order to review it effectively.

2. What guidelines should you follow for effective highlighting?

Highlight the right amount. Develop a regular and consistent system of highlighting. Highlight accurately. And make your highlighting understandable for later review. It is also wise to have a system for marking as well as highlighting.

3. Why should you supplement your textbook highlighting with marking?

Marking involves the use of marginal notes, summary words, and symbols that can make a passage easier to review. Marking can help you to organize the information you have highlighted by showing the relative importance of, or the relationships between, facts and ideas.

4. Why do highlighting
   and marking work as a way
   to prepare for study?

Highlighting and marking are an effective way to prepare yourself for study because they take advantage of a number of learning principles. This method forces you to focus your concentration by keeping you physically active, makes you think about and evaluate the information, helps you grasp the organization of the material, and provides you with a way to check your understanding.

DIRECTIONS Write the letter of the choice that best completes each statement in the space provided.

CHECKING YOUR RECALL

_____ 1. In general, you should highlight no more than about
  a. one-tenth of each page.
  b. one-third of each page.
  c. one-half of each page.
  d. three-fourths of each page.

_____ 2. The primary purpose of highlighting is to
  a. increase your reading rate.
  b. make review and study more efficient.
  c. learn to highlight the right amount.
  d. increase your review time.

_____ 3. When you are reading a textbook assignment, you should try to highlight all of the following *except*
  a. main ideas.
  b. important definitions.
  c. complete sentences.
  d. possible exam questions.

_____ 4. You should highlight for all of the following reasons *except* to
  a. help you remember what you read.
  b. keep you physically active while you read.
  c. make you decide which ideas are important.
  d. guarantee that you'll understand the material the first time you read it.

_____ 5. One difference between highlighting and marking is that, typically,
  a. highlighting shows the relative importance of ideas.
  b. highlighting indicates the relationship between facts and ideas.
  c. marking requires you to operate at higher levels of thinking.
  d. marking can be done without reading the text.

APPLYING YOUR SKILLS

_____ 6. Jameson has read and highlighted a text assignment. To study for his upcoming examination, he should

  a. review his highlighting.
  b. reread the chapter.
  c. go back and revise his highlighting.
  d. never need to look at it again.

_____ 7. Oliver is trying to decide what he should highlight in his psychology text. In making his decision, he should pay particular attention to
  a. paragraph length.
  b. page layout.
  c. graphics.
  d. boldfaced headings.

_____ 8. Caitlyn wants to test the effectiveness of her highlighting. She should ask herself all of the following questions *except:*
  a. Have I highlighted the right amount of information?
  b. Does my highlighting accurately reflect the meaning of the passage?
  c. Have I varied my system for highlighting to make it more interesting?
  d. Is my highlighting understandable for review?

_____ 9. Barbara has finished highlighting and marking a chapter in her physics text and is now writing summary notes. If Barbara is working effectively, she is most likely
  a. pulling ideas together and summarizing them in her own words.
  b. taking notes based only on the summary of a chapter.
  c. highlighting a long or complicated section first.
  d. recording her impression of the material's value.

_____ 10. Your friend Danae is struggling with learning to mark information in her textbooks. The most you can suggest is that she should
  a. mark only the information that has not been highlighted.
  b. include comments on the author's style.
  c. make sure someone else can understand your notes.
  d. think about the information and evaluate it as you read.

MULTIMEDIA *Activities*

Textbook Highlighting and Marking

1 Get creative with your highlighters. Buy a set of different-colored highlighters and use them not only for your textbooks, but also for your planner, calendar, letters to friends or family, cards, notes, maps, shopping lists, and doodling. Add some color to your everyday documents while getting comfortable with your new tools.

2 Practice your highlighting skills with a friend. Each of you should buy the same newspaper or magazine. Pick some articles to highlight and then compare your techniques. Be prepared to justify your choices and to offer constructive criticism.

3 Textbook Marking

http://www.byu.edu/ccc/learning/txt-mkg.php

Learn some strategies and look at actual markings at this Brigham Young University site. Use them during your next textbook reading assignment. Write a paragraph about the advantages of highlighting and marking. Imagine you are trying to sway someone who thinks it is wrong to write in books.

4 Icons, Font, Style, and Color Codes Used in the Course Material

http://faculty.frostburg.edu/cosc/htracy/cosc120/Codes.htm

Look over the conventions a Frostburg State University instructor uses in material for online learning. How effective do you think these graphics would be? Create a special code for your planner, calendar, or journal. Try using symbols, stamps, or stickers.

5 Highlighting

Review this information from Clemson University about textbook highlighting:

http://www.clemson.edu/collegeskills/sec3pg10.htm

How does the format of the explanation help to reinforce the content of the explanation? Try the quiz on note taking; evaluate your strengths and weaknesses.

15 Methods of Organizing Information

Why Organize Information from Your Textbooks?

■ You will learn the material as you organize it.

■ You will develop useful study aids.

■ You will increase the amount of material you can remember.

Learning Experiment

Step 1

Read the following description of the steps involved in a conversation.

> Conversation takes place in at least five steps: opening, feedforward, business, feedback, and closing. It is convenient to divide any act—and conversation is no exception—into chunks or stages and view each stage as requiring a choice of what to say and how to say it. In this model the conversation process is divided into five stages, each of which requires that you make a choice as to what you'll do. The first step is to open the conversation, usually with some kind of greeting: "Hi. How are you?" "Hello, this is Joe." It is a message that establishes a connection between two people and opens the channels for more meaningful interaction. At the second step, you usually provide some kind of feedforward, which gives the other person a general idea of the conversation's focus: "I've got to tell you about Jack," "Did you hear what happened in class yesterday?" or "We need to talk about our vacation plans." At the third step, you talk "business," the substance or focus of the conversation. The term "business" is used to emphasize that most conversations are goal directed; you converse to fulfill one or several of the general purposes of interpersonal communication: to learn, relate, influence, play or help. The fourth step is the reverse of the second. Here you reflect back on the conversation to signal that as far as you're concerned the business is completed: "So you want to send Jack a get-well card," "Wasn't that the craziest class you ever heard of?" or "I'll call for reservations, and you'll shop for what we need."

> —DeVito, *The Interpersonal Communication Book,* p. 266

Step 2

Now, draw a diagram or write an outline that explains the process of conversation.

The Results

Did drawing the diagram or writing an outline help you learn or understand the steps in conversation? Why? In order to diagram or outline, you had to grasp the process and make it fit within a framework. Through these activities you were consolidating, or putting together, the information. You organized it and made connections among the ideas presented.

Learning Principle (What This Means to You)

Consolidation is a process in which information settles, gels, or takes shape. The key to learning large amounts of information is to organize and consolidate it. Basically, this involves looking for patterns, differences, similarities, or shared characteristics and then grouping, rearranging, and reducing the information into manageable pieces. In this chapter you will learn three methods of consolidating information from either textbooks or lectures: outlining, summarizing, and mapping.

ORGANIZING BY OUTLINING

Outlining is an effective way of organizing the relationships among ideas. It involves both analysis and synthesis of ideas. From past experiences, many students think of an outline as an exact, detailed, organized listing of all information in a passage; they consider outlining as routine copying of information from page to page and, therefore, avoid doing it.

Actually, an outline should *not* be a recopying of ideas. Think of it, instead, as a means of pulling together important information and recording it to show how ideas interconnect. It is a form of note taking that provides a visual picture of the structure of ideas within a textbook chapter.

Outlining has many advantages, one being that you learn while you do it. Outlining forces you to think about the material you read and to sort out the important ideas from those that are less important. Because it requires you to express ideas in your own words and to group them, outlining reveals whether you have understood what you read. Finally, thinking about, sorting, and expressing ideas in your own words is a form of repetition, or rehearsal, that helps you to remember the material.

How to Develop an Outline

To be effective, an outline must show (1) the relative importance of ideas and (2) the relationship between ideas. The easiest way to achieve this is to use the following format.

I. Major topic
   A. First major idea
      1. First important detail
      2. Second important detail
   B. Second major idea
      1. First important detail
         a. Minor detail or example
      2. Second important detail
II. Second major topic
   A. First major idea

Note that the more important ideas are closer to the left margin, whereas less important details are indented toward the middle of the page. A quick glance at an outline indicates what is most important and how ideas support or explain one another.

Here are a few suggestions for developing an effective outline.

1. **Don't get caught up in the numbering and lettering system.** Instead, concentrate on showing the relative importance of ideas. How you number or letter an idea is not as important as showing what other ideas it supports or explains. Don't be concerned if some items don't fit exactly into outline format.

2. **Be brief; use words and phrases, never complete sentences.** Abbreviate words and phrases where possible.

3. **Use your own words rather than lifting most of the material from the text.** You can use the author's key words and specialized terminology.
4. **Be sure that all information underneath a heading supports or explains it.**
5. **All headings that are aligned vertically should be of equal importance.**

Now study the sample outline in Figure 15-1, which is based on the first five paragraphs of "Communication Between Women and Men" in Part Eight on page 466.

How Much Information to Include

Before you begin to outline, decide how much information to include. An outline can be very brief and cover only major topics, or, at the other extreme, it can be very detailed, providing an extensive review of information.

How much detail you include in an outline should be determined by your purpose in making it. For example, if you are outlining a collateral reading assignment for which your instructor asked that you be familiar with the author's viewpoint and general approach to a problem, then little detail is needed. On the other hand, if you are outlining a section of an anatomy and physiology text for an upcoming objective exam, a much more detailed outline

Figure 15-1
A Sample Outline

I. Communication between Women and Men
   A. Differences
      1. Men—use language of status and independence
      2. Women—use language of connection & intimacy
   B. Genderlects
      1. def—different linguistic styles between men and women
      2. failure to understand genderlects creates problems
         a) ex—Linda & Josh
            1. Linda—wanted to be involved
            2. Josh—wanted to be independent
      3. purposes of communication
         a. men—to give information
         b. women—to express feelings
         c. men & women—cross purposes = miscommunication
      4. Public communication
         a. men—topics: business, food, sports
         b. women— topics: people, business, health
         c. mixed groups—topics: follow style of men only groups

Figure 15-2
A Sample Computer
Outline

I. ARGUMENTATION

 A. **Definition**—process of putting forth a claim or proposition supported by reasons

   1. others examine the argument and offer counterarguments
   2. rule governed—unlike other forms of public speaking
   3. is a form of "mutual truth-testing"

 B. **Four Social Conversions That Arguments Follow**

   1. *Bilaterality*—requires 2 people or 2 messages
     a. message open for examination by the other person
     b. arguer understands that others may offer opposing messages
       (1) ex. seller of new car
       (2) candidates for political office
   2. *Self-risk*—opening ideas to others involves risk
     a. ideas may fail

is needed. To determine the right amount of detail, ask yourself: What do I need to know? What type of test situation, if any, am I preparing for?

Outlining Using a Computer

Word processing programs are particularly helpful for writing outlines. The tab key makes indenting easy and systematic, and you can devise a system by which you use different typefaces to designate the relative importance of ideas. For example, you might use capital letters and boldface for major topics, lowercase boldface for the most important supporting ideas, and regular type for details and examples. An example is shown in Figure 15-2. Alternatively, you might use symbols to distinguish various types of information—an asterisk for important ideas, brackets for key definitions, and so forth.

Word processing programs enable you to move text readily. Consequently, you can rearrange information easily, grouping ideas on a specific topic together. You will find this capability particularly useful when preparing study sheets for essay exams and when writing papers.

When to Use Outlining

Outlining is useful in a variety of situations.

1. **When you are using reference books or reading books you do not own, outlining is an effective way of taking notes.**
2. **When you are reading material that seems difficult or confusing, outlining forces you to sort ideas, see connections, and express them in your own words.**

3. **When you are asked to write an evaluation or critical interpretation of an article or essay, it is helpful to outline briefly the factual content.** The outline will reflect the development and progression of thought and will help you analyze the writer's ideas.

4. **In courses where order or process is important, an outline is particularly useful.** In a data processing course, for example, in which various sets of programming commands must be performed in a specified sequence, making an outline is a good way to organize the information.

5. **In the natural sciences, in which classifications are important, outlines help you record and sort information.** In botany, for example, one important focus is the classification and description of various plant groups. Making an outline will enable you to list subgroups within each category and to keep track of similar characteristics.

EXERCISE 1

DIRECTIONS Read each of the following passages and complete the outline that follows it.

1. **Fibromyalgia**

   Although there are many diseases today that seem to defy our best medical tests and treatments, one that is particularly frustrating is **fibromyalgia,** a chronic, painful, rheumatoid-like disorder that affects as many as 5 to 6 percent of the general population. Persons with fibromyalgia experience an array of symptoms including headaches, dizziness, numbness and tingling, itching, fluid retention, chronic joint pain, abdominal or pelvic pain, and even occasional diarrhea. Suspected causes have ranged from sleep disturbances, stress, emotional distress, and viruses, to autoimmune disorders; however, none have been proven in clinical trials. Because of fibromyalgia's multiple symptoms, it is usually diagnosed only after myriad tests have ruled out other disorders. The American College of Rheumatology identifies the major diagnostic criteria as:

   - History of widespread pain of at least 3 months' duration in the axial skeleton as well as in all four quadrants of the body.
   - Pain in at least 11 of 18 paired tender points on digital palpitation of about 4 kilograms of pressure.

   —Adapted from Donnatelle, *Health: The Basics,* p. 346

   I. Fibromyalgia—chronic rheumatoid-like disorder

   A. Affects _____ % of population

   B. Symptoms

       1. headaches, _____, numbness, tingling, itching, _____, joint pain, abdominal or _____ pain, diarrhea

   C. Suspected _____

       1. Sleep disturbances, _____, _____, viruses, autoimmune disorders

   D. Major diagnostic criteria

       1. _____

       2. _____

2. **Gathering Data in Foreign Countries**

Conducting market research around the world is big business for U.S. firms. Among the top 50 U.S. research firms, over 40 percent of revenues come from projects outside the United States. However, market conditions and consumer preferences vary widely in different parts of the world, and there are big differences in the sophistication of market research operations and the amount of data available to global marketers.

For these reasons, choosing an appropriate data collection method is difficult. In some countries many people may not have phones, or low literacy rates may interfere with mail surveys. Local customs can be a problem as well. Offering money for interviews is rude in Latin American countries. Saudi Arabia bans gatherings of four or more people except for family or religious events, and it's illegal to stop strangers on the street or knock on the door of someone's house! Cultural differences also affect responses to survey items. Both Danish and British consumers, for example, agree that it is important to eat breakfast, but the Danish sample may be thinking of fruit and yogurt whereas the British sample is thinking of toast and tea. Sometimes these problems can be overcome by involving local researchers in decisions about the research design, but even so care must be taken to ensure that they fully understand the study's objectives and can relate what they find to the culture of the sponsoring company.

Another problem with conducting marketing research in global markets is language. It is not uncommon for researchers to mistranslate questionnaires, or for entire subcultures within a country to be excluded from research. For example, there are still large areas in Mexico where native Indian tribes speak languages other than Spanish, so researchers may bypass these groups in surveys. To overcome these difficulties, researchers use a process called *back-translation*, which requires two steps. First, a questionnaire is translated into the second language by a native speaker of that language. Second, this new version is translated back into the original language to ensure that the correct meanings survive the process. Even with precautions such as these, however, researchers must interpret data obtained from other cultures with care.

—Solomon, *Marketing,* p. 135

I. Market research in foreign countries

    A. Big business for U.S. firms

        1. _____ of U.S. research firms' revenue comes from foreign projects

        2. _____ and consumer preferences vary widely

        3. differences in sophistication and _____

    B. Choice of data collection methods _____

        1. no _____

        2. _____

        3. _____ customs

        4. cultural differences affect _____

        5. problems may be overcome by using _____

    C. Language problems

        1. _____

        2. _____

3. overcome problems using back-translation

a. _____

b. _____

3. **The Family: Basic Concepts**

The **family** is *a social institution, found in all societies, that unites people in coopera-tive groups to oversee the bearing and raising of children.* Family ties are also called **kinship,** *a social bond, based on blood, marriage, or adoption.* All societies have families, but exactly who people count among their kin has varied through his-tory and varies today from one culture to another. In the United States, most people regard a **family unit** as *a social group of two or more people, related by blood, marriage, or adoption, who usually live together.* Here, as elsewhere, families form around **marriage,** *a legally sanctioned relationship, involving economic coop-eration as well as normative sexual activity and childbearing, that people expect to be enduring.*

Today, however, some people object to defining only married couples and chil-dren as "families" because it implies a single standard of moral conduct. Also, because business and government programs generally use this conventional defini-tion, unmarried but committed partners—whether heterosexual or homosexual—are excluded from health care and other benefits. More and more, however, organiza-tions are coming to recognize *families of affinity,* that is people with or without legal or blood ties who feel they belong together and want to define themselves as a family.

The U.S. Bureau of the Census, too, uses the conventional definition of family. Thus, sociologists who use Census Bureau data describing "families" must accept this definition. But the national trend is toward a more inclusive definition of family.

—Macionis, *Society: The Basics,* p. 308

I. The Family

A. Definitions

1. _____: social institution found in all societies that unites people in cooperative groups to oversee _____

2. kinship: family ties, a social bond, based on _____

3. _____: social group of _____ related by blood, marriage, or adoption, usually living together

4. marriage: _____

B. Objections to Definitions

1. only married couples with children—single _____

2. unmarried partners _____

3. _____: used to describe people with or without legal or blood ties who _____

a. recognized by _____

b. not used by _____

c. _____

EXERCISE 2

DIRECTIONS   Turn to the article titled "Civil Liberties and the Constitution" in Part Eight on page 496. Write a brief outline of the section titled "The Right to Privacy."

EXERCISE 3

DIRECTIONS   Write a brief outline of Chapter 14 of this text, "Textbook Highlighting and Marking." Assume you are preparing for an essay exam on the chapter.

EXERCISE 4

DIRECTIONS   Write a brief outline of this chapter. Assume you are preparing for a multiple-choice exam on the chapter.

EXERCISE 5

DIRECTIONS   Choose a section from one of your textbooks and write a brief outline that reflects the organization and content of that section.

SUMMARIZING

A **summary** is a brief statement or list of ideas that identifies the major concepts in a textbook section. Its main purpose is to record the most important ideas in an abbreviated and condensed form. It is a synthesis of ideas. A summary is briefer and less detailed than an outline. It goes one step beyond an outline by pulling together the writer's thoughts and making general statements about them. In writing a summary or making summary notes, you may indicate how the writer makes his or her point or note the types of supporting information the writer provides.

Writing a summary forces you to go beyond separate facts and ideas and consider what they mean as a whole. Summarizing encourages you to consider such questions as "What is the writer's main point?" and "How does the writer prove or explain his or her ideas?" It is also a valuable study technique that will clarify the material.

How to Summarize

Although most students think of a summary as a correctly written paragraph, a summary written for your own study and review purposes may be in either paragraph or note format. If you choose a note format, however, be sure that you record ideas and not just facts. The section that follows lists tips for writing summaries. Before reading them, read the selection titled "What Numbers Can Be Crunched Offshore?" and the sample summary shown in Figure 15-3 (p. 346).

What Numbers Can Be Crunched Offshore?

Planning on an accounting career for job security? If so, you might want to take a second look at what's happening with *business process outsourcing (BPO)*. Worldwide finance and accounting outsourcing will top $38 billion in 2004, up from $12 billion just five years earlier. BPO is the use of third parties to perform services (not manufacturing) that a company would otherwise do internally. Universities and hospitals, for example, outsource cafeteria operations to food service firms, retailers outsource human resources (HR) activities to HR firms, and manufacturing companies outsource shipping and delivery activities to UPS, FedEx, and other delivery specialists that do the job better, at lower cost.

Figure 15-3
A Sample Summary

Business process outsourcing (BPO) is the use of third parties to do some of the work that a company's own employees would ordinarily do. BPO has increased dramatically between 1999 and 2004. Companies use BPO because they believe that their companies should concentrate on their primary activities and not be bothered with side issues, such as accounting. Offshoring, also called offshore outsourcing, is the use of third parties in foreign countries. The largest increase in the use of offshoring has been in behind-the-scenes office services where little customer contact or individualization is required. Examples are reading x-rays and basic accounting services. Some companies are beginning to offshore more complicated accounting services. When this is done, one of the offshore company's employees maybe relocated within the hiring company.

The outsourcer's basic philosophy is that businesses do best when they focus on their core activities, rather than getting side tracked into noncore activities that, for many firms, includes accounting. "Finance and accounting take up a lot of time and energy, " says Accenture partner John Gillespie. "There are generally a lot of people involved, lots of staff development, staff planning, accounting controls, processing issues, and a lot of routine stuff that frankly you don't need your high flyers in finance to be worried about. Outsourcing allows client companies to focus on their core business."

Offshore outsourcing *(off-shoring)*—using third parties in other countries—is expected to surpass $24 billion for U.S. business processes in 2007. The biggest area of growth is in back-office professional services that have low customer contact and require little customization—radiology analysis (for example, x-rays, CT scans, MRIs), computer software and information technology development, engineering (for example, product design, testing, and analysis), and basic accounting services. Standardized processes are easily exported for service abroad thanks to the Internet's global reach. Accounting's basic number-crunching activities—payroll, accounts receivable, accounting, inventory valuation—are easily outsourced because the same accounting rules apply to all customers.

Beyond the basics, however, companies are beginning to outsource more intricate accounting activities, too, including stock and margin accounting, financial accounting, management accounting, real estate accounting, tax compliance, and even internal auditing. For these more customized processes, one of the outside company's employees may be co-located to the outsourcer's facility because good interaction with the client and thorough understanding of its business practices are needed. Data for these more customized accounting activities are transmitted for off-shore processing, then results are transmitted back to the outsourcer.

—Griffin, *Business*, p. 471

Define Your Purpose

Before writing a summary, take a moment to consider your purpose for writing it. In summarizing part of a philosophy textbook chapter, your purpose may be to familiarize yourself with arguments famous philosophers made, or your purpose might be to develop a time line of how philosophy has developed. Your purpose will help you determine how much and what kind of information you want to include in your summary. If you are trying to summarize philosophical arguments, details and examples will be important, but if you are trying to create a basic time line of the development of philosophy, you will be less interested in details and examples. Gear your summary toward what you are trying to learn from the selection. In the sample summary in Figure 15-3, the student's purpose is to understand outsourcing and offshoring.

Identify the Main Point

When you begin to write a summary, first identify the author's main idea. Once you find it, write a statement that expresses it. This statement will help you to focus your summary. Just as with an outline, a summary starts with a main idea and moves on to include details and further information. In the summary in Figure 15-3, the main point is that outsourcing, and, in particular, offshoring, is increasing in use.

Include Key Supporting Information

After you have located the main point, look for the most important information used by the author to support his or her main idea. Include only key reasons, facts, or events. The information about why outsourcing is used and the types of jobs that are outsourced is included in the summary in Figure 15-3.

Identify Key Definitions

Make a point to include definitions of key terms, new principles, theories, or procedures that are explained in the text. As you write the summary, underline or highlight essential words or phrases as you define them so that you will be able to locate them easily when reviewing. In Figure 15-3, the definitions of *BPO* and *offshoring* are included.

Evaluate the Importance of Details

You will probably want to include some details in your summary; however, the amount of detail needed will vary depending on the type and amount of recall you need. For example, in a passage in an American history textbook about the kinds of protests the colonists organized against British taxes, the examples of the protests themselves are important details and have historical significance. But if you are summarizing a mathematics textbook passage that explains different types of theorems, you would not want to include the examples showing the theorems at work, since the examples are included only to help you understand the theorems themselves.

It can also be useful to include details such as examples in a summary when you have difficulty understanding or remembering a concept.

Consider the Author's Attitude and Approach

It may be appropriate to include the author's attitude and approach toward the subject, depending on the type of material you are summarizing. Additionally, you may want to include the author's purpose for writing the passage. If, for example, you are summarizing an argument or persuasive essay on welfare reform, it would be important to note the author's attitude, approach, and purpose.

General Summary Writing Tips

Keep your summary objective and factual. Think of it as a brief report that reflects the writer's ideas and does not include your own evaluation of them. You are not writing an analysis of the passage, you're simply trying to boil down the basic facts and information presented in the passage.

Use a word processor to write summaries, since this will make it easy for you to move pieces of them around and group related summaries together. Because your understanding of a topic grows and expands as you learn more about it and as the course progresses, you may be able to take several summaries, and eventually combine them into one. Don't feel as if you've wasted your time with the earlier summaries, though. Writing summaries is a process that allows you to think about the topic, and by putting concepts and facts in your own words, you increase your understanding.

When to Use Summaries

Summaries are particularly useful in learning situations in which factual, detailed recall is not needed.

Preparing for Essay Exams

Summarizing ideas to be learned for possible exam topics is an excellent way to study for an essay exam. Because essay exam questions often require you to summarize information you have learned on a particular topic, writing summaries is a good way to practice taking the exam.

Reading Literature

When reading literature, you are most often required to interpret and react to the ideas presented. To do so, you must be sure you are familiar with the basic plot (in fiction) or literal presentation of ideas (in nonfiction). Writing a plot summary (describing who did what, when, and where) for fiction and a content summary for nonfiction will help you be certain you have mastered the literal content.

Collateral Reading Assignments

In many undergraduate courses, instructors give additional reading assignments in sources other than your textbook. These assignments may be given to supplement information in the text, to present a different or opposing viewpoint, to illustrate a concept, or to show practical applications. Usually, in-depth recall of particular facts and information is not expected. Your instructor probably wants you to understand the main points and their relation to topics covered in the text or in class; therefore, a brief summary is a useful study aid for collateral readings.

Laboratory Experiments/Demonstrations

A summary is a useful means of recording the results of a laboratory experiment or class demonstration in a natural science course. Although laboratory reports usually require a format that includes careful reporting of procedures and listing of observations, a summary is often included. Reviewing summaries is an efficient way of recalling the purposes, procedures, and outcomes of lab and classroom experiments conducted throughout the semester.

EXERCISE 6

DIRECTIONS   After reading each selection, circle the letter of the choice that best summarizes it.

1. **The Right to Counsel and the Miranda Warnings**

   It was not until the Warren Court made its landmark rulings in *Escobedo v. Illinois* (1964) and *Miranda v. Arizona* (1966) that the full implications of the Fifth and Sixth Amendments for police interrogations were spelled out for state courts. The *Escobedo* case involved a claim that the defendant, Danny Escobedo, had been forced to make incriminating statements during interrogation. These statements led to his conviction on charges of murdering his brother-in-law. The Supreme Court noted that despite repeated requests to see his lawyer, Escobedo did not have an attorney present during questioning, and therefore his confession was made without the advice of counsel, in violation of the Sixth Amendment. The Court ruled that suspects have the right to the advice of counsel during police questioning to ensure that any confession they make is voluntary.

   The Court went further in the *Miranda* case. This 1966 case was decided along with three others, all of which dealt with the admissibility of statements obtained from suspects during police interrogations after they had been arrested. Ernesto Miranda's name happened to be at the top of the list, and he became famous because of it.

   In deciding *Miranda* and the other cases, the Court ruled not only that arrested suspects have the right to counsel, but also that the police must clearly inform them of that right before any questioning begins. Ernesto Miranda had been convicted of rape and kidnapping largely on the basis of a confession he made following nearly two hours of intense police interrogation. The Court took into account the ability of experienced police interrogators to induce confessions from intimidated suspects; with his attorney present, Miranda might not have succumbed to the menacing interrogation. The right to have counsel present during questioning undergirds the Fifth Amendment right against self-incrimination.

   In its decision, the Court ruled that police must inform arrested suspects of certain rights *before* any interrogation begins. The **Miranda warnings** resulted.

   —Barlow, *Criminal Justice in America*, p. 327

   a. *Escobedo v. Illinois* was decided in 1964 by the Warren Court. Danny Escobedo had been convicted of murdering his brother-in-law. The Court overturned his conviction. *Miranda v. Arizona* was decided in 1966. Ernesto Miranda had been convicted of rape and kidnapping and confessed after a two-hour police interrogation. The conviction was overturned by the Court.
   b. Fifth and Sixth Amendments rights in state courts were spelled out in two cases. First, *Escobedo v. Illinois* decided that suspects have the right to counsel during police questioning to make sure any confession is voluntary. This is based on the Sixth Amendment. Second, *Miranda v. Arizona* decided that police must clearly inform suspects of the right to counsel before questioning them and that this is part of the Fifth Amendment right against self-incrimination. Miranda warnings were the result of this.
   c. Escobedo was forced to make incriminating statements during interrogation and wasn't permitted to see his lawyer. Miranda confessed to police and probably would not have if he had had an attorney present.
   d. The Sixth Amendment resulted from the *Escobedo* case about the right to counsel. The Fifth Amendment was adopted after the *Miranda* case spelled out the right to be informed of the right to counsel before being questioned by police during an interrogation.

2. **Assimilation**

Assimilation is *the process by which minorities gradually adopt patterns of the dominant culture.* Assimilation involves changing styles of dress, values, religion, language, and friends.

Many people think of the United States as a "melting pot," in which different nationalities blend together. But, in truth, rather than everyone "melting" into some new cultural pattern, most minorities have adopted the dominant culture established by the earliest settlers. Why? Assimilation is both the avenue to upward social mobility and a way to escape the prejudice and discrimination directed against more visible foreigners (Newman, 1973).

The amount of assimilation varies by category. For example, Germans and Irish have "melted" more than Italians, and the Japanese more than the Chinese or Koreans. Multiculturalists, however, oppose assimilation because it suggests minorities are "the problem" and defines them (rather than majority people) as the ones who need to do all the changing.

—Macionis, *Society: The Basics,* p. 253

a. The United States is a melting pot where many different cultures are assimilated. Minorities who assimilate melt into the new cultural pattern by adopting the dominant culture.

b. Assimilation is a process in which minorities adopt the pattern of the dominant culture. This varies by category. In the United States, Germans and Irish have assimilated more than Japanese, Chinese, or Koreans.

c. Multiculturalists study assimilation, the way minorities change to become part of the dominant culture established by the earliest settlers. Assimilation makes the minorities the problem.

d. Assimilation is a process through which minorities gradually adopt patterns of the dominant culture—for example, styles of dress, values, religion, language, and friends. It occurs because it is a way for minorities to gain upward social mobility and to escape discrimination. Multiculturalists oppose it since it forces minorities to do all the changing.

3. **Lunar Cycles**

Many ancient civilizations paid particular attention to the lunar cycle [cycles of the moon], often using it as the basis for lunar calendars. The months on lunar calendars generally have either 29 or 30 days, chosen to make the average agree with the approximately 29-$\frac{1}{2}$-day lunar cycle. A 12-month lunar calendar has only 354 or 355 days, or about 11 days less than a calendar based on the tropical year. Such a calendar is still used in the Muslim religion, which is why the month-long fast of Ramadan (the ninth month) begins about 11 days earlier with each subsequent year.

Other lunar calendars take advantage of the fact that 19 years is almost precisely 235 lunar months. Because this fact was discovered in 432 B.C. by the Babylonian astronomer Meton, the 19-year period is called the **Metonic cycle.** A lunar calendar can be synchronized to the Metonic cycle by adding a thirteenth month to 7 of every 19 years (making exactly 235 months in each 19-year period), thereby ensuring that "new year" comes on approximately the same date every nineteenth year. The Jewish calendar follows the Metonic cycle, adding a thirteenth month in the third, sixth, eighth, eleventh, fourteenth, seventeenth and nineteenth years of each cycle. This also explains why the date of Easter changes each year: The New Testament ties the date of Easter to the Jewish festival of Passover, which has its date set by the Jewish lunar calendar. In a slight modification of the original scheme, most Christians now celebrate Easter on *the first Sunday after the first full moon after March 21*; if the full moon falls on Sunday, Easter is the following Sunday.

—Bennett et al., *The Cosmic Perspective,* p. 57

a. The lunar cycle was the basis for lunar calendars in ancient civilizations. The average lunar cycle is $29\frac{1}{2}$ days. The average lunar calendar had 354 or 355 days. This type of calendar is used by Muslims. Since 19 years is 235 lunar months, the Metonic cycle adds a thirteenth month to 7 of every 19 years. The Jewish calendar follows this cycle, and the date of the Christian celebration of Easter is determined by this calendar.

b. Easter was originally calculated by determining the date of Passover. Now it is determined based on the moon. It is the first Sunday after the first full moon after March 21. If the full moon is a Sunday, Easter is the next Sunday.

c. The Metonic cycle was discovered by Meton in 432 B.C. Lunar calendars are synchronized to the Metonic cycle by adding a thirteenth month to 7 out of every 19 years. The new year then starts on the same date every nineteenth year.

d. The Muslim religion uses a lunar calendar. Each month has 29 or 30 days and the year has 11 fewer days than a tropical year calendar. Ramadan, the ninth month, begins about 11 days earlier every year because of this calendar. The date of Easter is determined by the Jewish calendar.

4. **Designing Your Fitness Program**

Once you commit yourself to becoming physically active, you must decide what type of fitness program is best suited to your needs. Good fitness programs are designed to improve or maintain cardiorespiratory fitness, flexibility, muscular strength and endurance, and body composition. A comprehensive program could include a warm-up period of easy walking followed by stretching activities to improve flexibility, then selected strength development exercises, followed by performance of an aerobic activity for 20 minutes or more, and concluding with a cool-down period of gentle flexibility exercises.

The greatest proportion of your exercise time should be spent developing cardiovascular fitness, but you should not exclude the other components. Choose an aerobic activity you think you will like. Many people find **cross training**—alternate-day participation in two or more aerobic activities (i.e., jogging and swimming)—less monotonous and more enjoyable than long-term participation in only one aerobic activity. Cross training is also beneficial because it strengthens a variety of muscles, thus helping you avoid overuse injuries to muscles and joints.

—Donatelle, *Health: The Basics*, p. 282

a. A good fitness program includes a warm-up period of easy walking, stretching, strength development exercises, a 20-minute aerobic activity, and a cool-down period of flexibility exercises.

b. Good fitness programs improve or maintain cardiorespiratory fitness, flexibility, muscular strength and endurance, and body composition. A program's focus should be on cardiovascular fitness but should include other components. Cross training, alternate-day participation in two or more aerobic activities, strengthens a variety of muscles.

c. It is important to choose a fitness program that is best suited to your needs. You should choose an aerobic activity you like. Cross training reduces boredom and is more enjoyable than just one aerobic activity. It helps avoid overuse injuries to muscles and joints as well.

d. Cardiovascular fitness is the most important component of a fitness program. A cool-down period is recommended. Jogging and swimming are two aerobic activities that can be done together in cross training. A comprehensive fitness program will include the different components of body composition.

EXERCISE 7

DIRECTIONS   Read each of the following selections and then complete the summaries that follow them by filling in the blanks.

1. **Tsunami or Seismic Sea Wave**

An occasional wave that momentarily but powerfully influences coastlines is the tsunami. **Tsunami** is Japanese for "harbor wave," named for its devastating effect where its energy is focused in harbors. Tsunami often are reported incorrectly as "tidal waves," but they have no relation to the tides. They are formed by sudden, sharp motions in the sea floor, caused by earthquakes, submarine landslides, or eruptions of undersea volcanoes. Thus, they properly are called *seismic sea waves*.

—Christopherson, *Geosystems*, p. 470

Summary: A _____ (also called a tsunami) is a wave that powerfully influences coastlines and is formed by _____ caused by

_____. It has devastating effects on

_____.

2. **Types of Evidence Presented in Court**

The outcome of a trial usually hinges on the presentation of evidence. Attorneys for the prosecution and defense have two major types of evidence they can offer in support of their case: **demonstrative evidence** and **testimonial evidence.** Demonstrative evidence consists of physical objects—for example, the bloody glove presented in the O.J. Simpson trial, a weapon, fingerprints, blood samples, DNA, stolen property, tire or shoe prints, business records, computer files, and written or videotaped confessions. Testimonial evidence consists of oral evidence given under oath either in the courtroom or in *depositions* taken before attorneys for both sides and recorded by a court reporter.

—Barlow, *Criminal Justice in America*, p. 439

Summary: Two types of _____ can be presented in court.

_____ is physical objects. Testimonial evidence is

_____ or _____.

3. **Store Image**

When people think of a store, they often have no trouble portraying it in the same terms they might use in describing a person. They might use words like *exciting, depressed, old-fashioned, tacky,* or *elegant.* **Store image** is how the target market perceives the store—its market position relative to the competition. For example, Bloomingdale's department store is seen by many as chic and fashionable, especially compared to a more traditional competitor such as Macy's. These images don't just happen. Just as brand managers do for products, store managers work hard to create a "personality."

—Solomon, *Marketing*, p. 418

Summary: _____ is how the target market perceives a

_____ and its market position relative to

_____. Store managers must work hard to create

_____.

4. **Hay Fever**

Perhaps the best example of a chronic respiratory disease is **hay fever.** Usually considered to be a seasonally related disease (most prevalent when ragweed and flowers are blooming), hay fever is common throughout the world. Hay fever attacks, which are characterized by sneezing and itchy, watery eyes and nose, cause a great deal of misery for countless people. Hay fever appears to run in families, and research indicates that lifestyle is not as great a factor in developing hay fever as it is in other chronic diseases. Instead, an overzealous immune system and an exposure to environmental allergens including pet dander, dust, pollen from various plants, and other substances appear to be the critical factors that determine vulnerability. For those people who are unable to get away from the cause of their hay fever response, medical assistance in the form of injections or antihistamines may provide the only possibility of relief.

—Donatelle, *Health: The Basics,* p. 338

Summary: Hay fever is a chronic _____ that is seasonably

related and common _____. It is characterized by _____.

It runs in families and is not affected by _____. Overzealous

immune systems and _____ determine vulnerability. It can be

treated with _____.

5. **Aging and Culture**

Culture shapes how we understand growing old. In low-income countries, old age gives people great influence and respect because they control most land and have wisdom gained over a lifetime (Sheehan, 1976; Hareven, 1982). A preindustrial society, then, is usually a **gerontocracy,** *a form of social organization in which the elderly have the most wealth, power and privileges.*

But industrialization lessens the social standing of the elderly. Older people typically live apart from their grown children, and rapid social change renders much of what seniors know obsolete, at least from the point of view of the young. A problem of industrial societies, then, is **ageism,** *prejudice and discrimination against the elderly.*

—Macionis, *Society: The Basics,* p. 77

Summary: _____ affects how we regard aging.

_____ societies are usually gerontocracies, where the elderly

have the most _____. In _____ societies, the

elderly live apart from their families and have obsolete knowledge.

_____, which means prejudice and _____

against older people, becomes a problem.

EXERCISE 8   DIRECTIONS   Read the following selection and then complete the summary by filling in the blanks.

Catalogs

A **catalog** is a collection of products offered for sale in book form, usually consisting of product descriptions accompanied by photos of the items. Catalogs came on the scene within a few decades of the invention of moveable type in the fifteenth century, but they've come a long way since then. The early catalogs pioneered by Montgomery Ward and other innovators such as Sears were designed for people in remote areas who lacked access to stores.

Today the catalog customer is likely to be an affluent career woman with access to more than enough stores but who does not have the time or desire to go to them. According to the Direct Marketing Association, over two-thirds of the U.S. adult population orders from a catalog at least once in a year. Catalog mania extends well beyond clothing and cosmetics purchases. Dell and Gateway 2000, direct-selling computer companies, each have annual sales of over $1 billion. Recent catalog entries by computer giants IBM and Compaq are signs that ordering even a complex and expensive purchase such as a computer by mail is becoming common for many shoppers.

Although established retailers such as Bloomingdale's or JCPenney publish catalogs, others are start-ups by ambitious entrepreneurs who cannot afford to open a store. For example, a housewife named Lillian Hochberg began by selling handbags through the mail. Today the Lillian Vernon catalog mails out more than 137 million copies each year. As we saw with Neiman-Marcus, many stores use catalogs to complement their in-store efforts. In fact, more than half of the top 50 department stores use this selling technique. This allows the store to reach people who live in areas too small to support a store. Although catalogs can be an efficient way to reach shoppers, they can also be an expensive way to do business. Catalog retailers must expect to mail out 10 to 20 books for every order they receive, and paper and printing costs are rising steadily.

—Solomon, *Marketing,* p. 427

Summary: A catalog is _____.

Typical catalog customers are _____. Two-thirds of the U.S.

population _____. Catalog sales of _____ are

becoming common. Fifty percent of all department stores use catalogs to

_____. Catalogs allow stores to reach people who

_____. Catalogs can be an _____ way

to do business since _____.

EXERCISE 9 | **DIRECTIONS** Write a brief summary of the textbook excerpt subtitled "Observational Learning" on page 185 of this text.

EXERCISE 10 | **DIRECTIONS** Write a summary of "Body Adornment," which begins on page 450 in Part Eight.

EXERCISE 11 | **DIRECTIONS** Refer to the section from one of your textbooks that you used to complete Exercise 5 on page 345. Write a summary of the information presented in this section.

MAPPING: A VISUAL MEANS OF ORGANIZING IDEAS

Mapping is a visual method of organizing information. It involves drawing diagrams to show how ideas or concepts in an article or chapter are related. Mapping provides a picture, or visual representation, of how ideas are developed and connected. Maps group and consolidate information and make it easier to learn. How much you use mapping will depend on your learning style. Some students, especially those with a visual learning style, prefer mapping to outlining. Other students find mapping to be freer and less tightly structured than outlining. The degree to which you use mapping will also depend on the types of courses you are taking. Some types of information are more easily learned by using mapping than are others.

Maps can take numerous forms. You can draw them in any way that shows the relationships among ideas. They can be hand drawn or drawn using a word processor's capability to box and block type. Figure 15-4 shows the types of information to include in a map, depending on the desired level of detail. Figure 15-5 on the next page shows two sample maps. Each was drawn to show the organization of the section "Checking Your Comprehension" in Chapter 5 of this book. Refer to pages 117–120; then study each map.

How to Draw Maps

Think of a map as a picture or diagram that shows how ideas are connected. Use the following steps in drawing a map:

1. Identify the overall topic or subject, and write it in the center or at the top of the page.
2. Identify the major supporting information that is related to the topic. Write each fact or idea on a line connected to the central topic.
3. As you discover a detail that further explains an idea already mapped, draw a new line branching from the idea it explains.

**Figure 15-4
A Model Map**

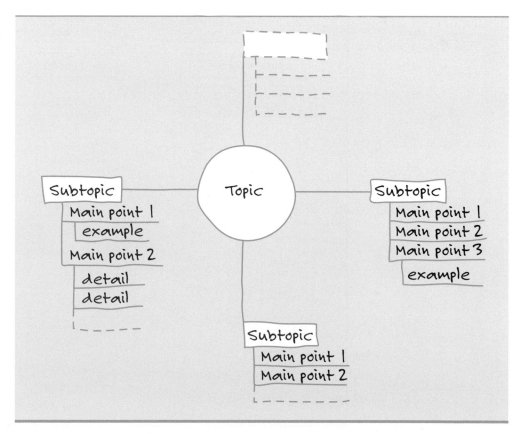

**Figure 15-5
Sample Maps**

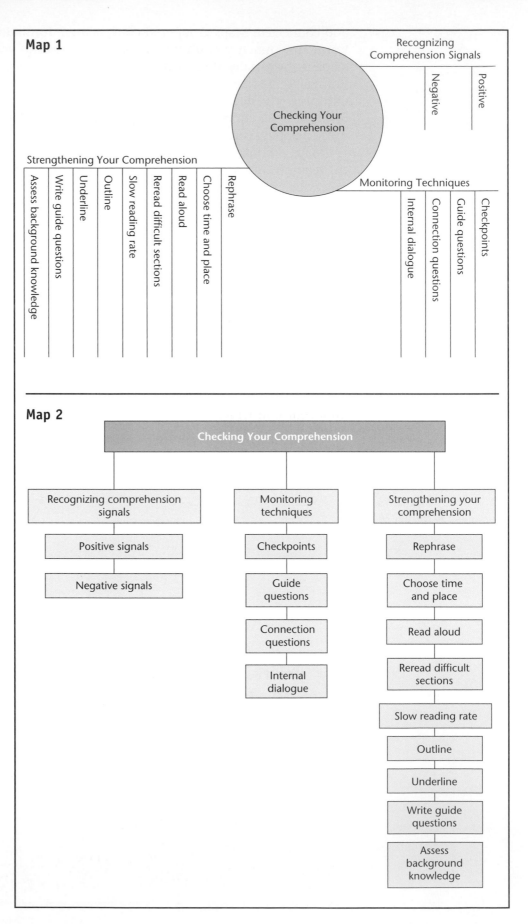

How you arrange your map will depend on the subject matter and how it is organized. Like an outline, it can be either quite detailed or very brief, depending on your purpose.

EXERCISE 12   DIRECTIONS   Draw a map showing the organization of any section of Chapter 1 in this text.

EXERCISE 13   DIRECTIONS   Turn to the reading "Stem-cell Therapy: Promise and Reality" on page 490 in Part Eight. Draw a map showing how the article is organized.

EXERCISE 14   DIRECTIONS   Select a section from one of your textbooks. Draw a concept map that reflects its organization.

Specialized Types of Maps

Maps may take numerous forms. This section presents five types of maps useful for organizing specific types of information: time lines, process diagrams, part/function diagrams, organizational charts, and comparison–contrast charts.

Time Lines

In a course in which chronology of events is the central focus, a time line is a useful way to organize information. To visualize a sequence of events, draw a single horizontal line and mark it off in yearly intervals, just as a ruler is marked off in inches, and then write events next to the appropriate year. The time line in Figure 15-6, for example, was developed for an American history course in which the Vietnam War was being studied. It shows the sequence of events and helps you to visualize the order in which things happened.

Figure 15-6
A Time Line

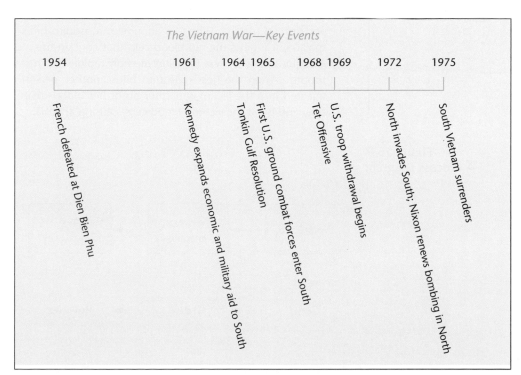

The Vietnam War—Key Events

| 1954 | 1961 | 1964 | 1965 | 1968 | 1969 | 1972 | 1975 |

French defeated at Dien Bien Phu

Kennedy expands economic and military aid to South

Tonkin Gulf Resolution

First U.S. ground combat forces enter South

Tet Offensive

U.S. troop withdrawal begins

North invades South; Nixon renews bombing in North

South Vietnam surrenders

DIRECTIONS   The following passage reviews the ancient history of maps. Read the selection, and then draw a time line that helps you visualize these historical events. (Remember that B.C. refers to time before the birth of Christ, and such numbers increase as time moves back in history.)

In Babylonia, in approximately 2300 B.C., the oldest known map was drawn on a clay tablet. The map showed a man's property located in a valley surrounded by tall mountains. Later, around 1300 B.C., the Egyptians drew maps that detailed the location of Ethiopian gold mines and that showed a route from the Nile Valley to the mines. The ancient Greeks were early mapmakers as well, although no maps remain for us to examine. It is estimated that in 300 B.C. they drew maps showing the earth to be round. The Romans drew the first road maps, a few of which have been preserved for study today. Claudius Ptolemy, an Egyptian scholar who lived around 150 A.D., drew one of the most famous ancient maps. He drew maps of the world as it was known at that time, including 26 regional maps of Europe, Africa, and Asia.

Process Diagrams

In the natural sciences, as well as in other courses such as economics and data processing, processes are an important part of course content. A diagram that visually presents the steps, variables, or parts of a process will aid learning. A biology student, for example, might use Figure 15-7, which describes the food chain and shows how energy is transferred through food consumption. Note that this student included an example, as well as the steps in the process, to make the diagram clearer.

DIRECTIONS   The following paragraph describes the process through which malaria is spread by mosquitoes. Read the paragraph, and then draw a process diagram that shows how this process occurs.

Malaria, a serious tropical disease, is caused by parasites, or one-celled animals, called protozoa. These parasites live in the red blood cells of humans as well as in female anopheles mosquitoes. These mosquitoes serve as hosts to the parasites and carry and spread malaria. When an anopheles mosquito bites a person who already has malaria, it ingests the red blood cells that contain the malaria parasites. In the host mosquito's body, these parasites multiply rapidly and move to its salivary glands and mouth. When the host mosquito bites another person, the malaria parasites are injected into the victim and enter his or her bloodstream. The parasites again multiply and burst the victim's blood cells, causing anemia.

Figure 15-7
A Process Diagram

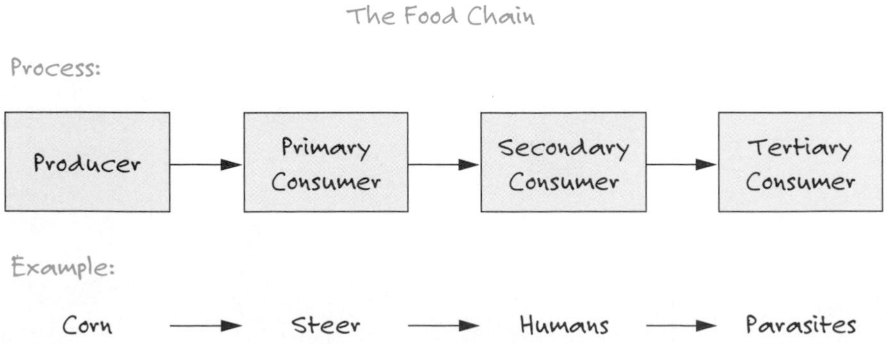

The Food Chain

Process:

| Producer | → | Primary Consumer | → | Secondary Consumer | → | Tertiary Consumer |

Example:

Corn → Steer → Humans → Parasites

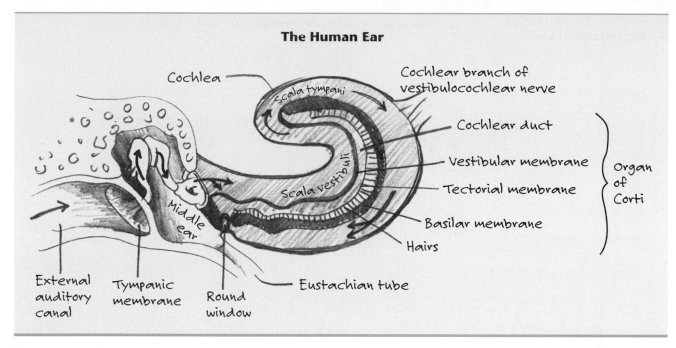

The Human Ear

Figure 15-8
A Part/Function Diagram

Part/Function Diagrams

In courses that deal with the use and description of physical objects, labeled drawings are an important learning tool. In a human anatomy and physiology course, for example, the easiest way to study the parts and functions of the inner, middle, and outer ear is to use a drawing of the ear. You can study the material and make a sketch of the ear, then test your recall of ear parts and their function. Refer to Figure 15-8 above for a sample part/function diagram.

EXERCISE 17   DIRECTIONS   The following paragraph describes the Earth's structure. Read the paragraph, and then draw a diagram that will help you visualize how the Earth's interior is structured.

> At the center is a hot, highly compressed *inner core,* presumably solid and composed mainly of iron and nickel. Surrounding the inner core is an *outer core,* a molten shell primarily of liquid iron and nickel with lighter liquid material on the top. The outer envelope beyond the core is the *mantle,* of which the upper portion is mostly solid rock in the form of olivine, an iron–magnesium silicate, and the lower portion chiefly iron and magnesium oxides. A thin coat of metal silicates and oxides (granite), called the *crust,* forms the outermost skin.
>
> —Berman and Evans, *Exploring the Cosmos,* p. 145

Organizational Charts

When you are reviewing material that is composed of relationships and structures, organizational charts are useful study aids. Suppose that in a business management course, you are studying the organization of a small temporary clerical employment agency. If you drew and studied the organizational chart shown in Figure 15-9 on page 360, the structure would become apparent and easy to remember.

**Figure 15-9
An Organizational Chart**

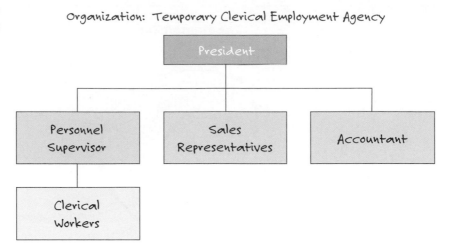

Organization: Temporary Clerical Employment Agency

EXERCISE 18

DIRECTIONS The following paragraph describes one business organizational structure that is studied in management courses. Read the paragraph, and then draw a diagram that will help you visualize this type of organization.

It is common for some large businesses to be organized by *place,* with a department for each major geographic area in which the business is active. Businesses that market products for which customer preference differs from one part of the country to another often use this management structure. Departmentalization allows each region to focus on its own special needs and problems. Often the president of such a company appoints several regional vice presidents, one for each part of the country. Then each regional office is divided into sales districts, each supervised by a district director.

Comparison–Contrast Charts

A final type of visual aid that is useful for organizing factual information is the comparison–contrast chart. Based on the categorization principle of learning, this method of visual organization divides and groups information according to similarities or common characteristics. Suppose that in a marketing and advertising course, you are studying three types of market survey techniques: mail, telephone, and personal interview surveys. You are concerned with factors such as cost, level of response, time, and accuracy. In your text, this information is discussed in paragraph form. To learn and review this information in an efficient manner, you could draw a chart such as the one shown in Figure 15-10 on the next page.

EXERCISE 19

DIRECTIONS The following passage describes the major physical differences between humans and apes. Read the selection, and then arrange the information into a chart that would make the information easy to learn.

Numerous physical characteristics distinguish humans from apes. While apes' bodies are covered with hair, the human body has relatively little hair. While apes often use both their hands and feet to walk, humans walk erect. Apes' arms are longer than their legs, while just the reverse is true for humans. Apes have large teeth, necessary for devouring coarse, uncooked food, and long canine teeth for self-defense and fighting. By comparison, human teeth are small and short. The ape's brain is not as well developed as that of the human being. Humans are capable of speech, thinking, and higher-level reasoning skills. These skills enable humans to establish culture, thereby placing the quality and level of human life far above that of apes.

**Figure 15-10
A Comparison–Contrast
Chart**

Market Survey Techniques			
Type	Cost	Response	Accuracy
Mail	usually the cheapest	higher than phone or personal interview	problems with misunderstanding directions
Phone	depends on phone service	same as personal interview	problems with unlisted phones and homes w/out phones
Personal interview	most expensive	same as phone	problems with honesty when asking personal or embarrassing questions

Humans are also set apart from apes by features of the head and face. The human facial profile is vertical, while the ape's profile is *prognathous,* with jaw jutting outward. Humans have a chin; apes have a strong lower jaw, but no chin. Human nostrils are smaller and less flaring than those of the ape. Apes also have thinner, more flexible lips than human beings.

Man's upright walk also distinguishes him from apes. The human spine has a double curve to support his weight, while an ape's spine has a single curve. The human foot is arched both vertically and horizontally but, unlike the ape's, is unable to grasp objects. The human torso is shorter than that of apes. It is important to note that many of these physical traits, while quite distinct, differ in degree rather than in kind.

EXERCISE 20

DIRECTIONS   Draw a comparison–contrast chart showing the differences in communication between men and women. Use the reading "Communication Between Women and Men" in Part Eight, page 466, as your source.

LEARNING COLLABORATIVELY

DIRECTIONS   Your instructor will choose a reading from Part Eight and divide the class into three groups. Members of one group should outline the material, another group should draw maps, and the third should write summaries. When the groups have completed their tasks, the class members should review each other's work. Several students should read their summaries aloud, draw their maps, and write their outlines on the chalkboard. Discuss which of the three methods seemed most effective for the material and how well prepared each group feels for (1) an essay exam, (2) a multiple-choice exam, and (3) a class discussion.

APPLYING YOUR LEARNING

Ken's courses this semester include History of the British Empire, Business Management, Biology, and Introduction to Anthropology. The history course requirements include several collateral reading assignments from books placed on reserve in the library and an essay final exam. The anthropology text contains several chapters and lectures explaining how humans evolved and the relationships of other species to humans; a short-answer and essay final exam will be given. The biology course involves textbook reading, lectures, labs, and multiple-choice exams. The business management course focuses, in part, on the organization and structure of corporations; two multiple-choice and true/false exams will be given.

1. In which course(s) do you think Ken will need to use outlining? Why?
2. In which course(s) do you think Ken will need to use summarizing? Why?
3. Recommend a mapping strategy Ken might use for each course. Explain why each recommended approach is appropriate.

APPLYING YOUR SKILLS: Sample Textbook Chapter

1. Write an outline of the section titled "Recognize Culture Shock," pages 528–530.
2. Write a summary of the section titled "Avoid Overattribution," page 524.
3. Draw a comparison and contrast chart of the section titled "Individualist and Collectivist Cultures," page 518.

QUESTIONS FOR DISCUSSION

1. Why is it important to determine what type of test situation, if any, you are preparing for before you begin to outline?
2. In what types of learning situations are summaries most helpful to you? How and when have you used summaries in the past? What makes a particularly effective summary?
3. Share some maps that you have created for various classes. What makes the maps particularly effective?
4. List some learning situations in which time lines, process diagrams, part/function diagrams, organizational charts, and comparison–contrast charts can be most helpful to you and your classmates.

SELF-TEST SUMMARY

1. What is an outline and what are its advantages?	Outlining is a way to organize information to indicate the relative importance of ideas and the relationships among them. When done correctly, it helps you to sort ideas, test your understanding, and recall the material.
2. What is a summary and what are its advantages?	Summarizing is the process of recording a passage's most important ideas in a condensed, abbreviated form. A summary not only helps you to organize the facts and ideas presented in the text but also enables you to go beyond the facts and react to them critically.
3. What is mapping and what are its advantages?	Mapping creates a visual representation of the information and shows relationships. Five types of concept maps are time lines, process diagrams, part/function diagrams, organizational charts, and comparison–contrast charts. Mapping is versatile in that it enables you to adjust to both the type of information you are recording and its unique organization. Grouping and consolidating information in different ways makes it easier to learn and remember.

Quick Quiz

NAME:

DIRECTIONS   Write the letter of the choice that best completes each statement in the space provided.

CHECKING YOUR RECALL

_____ 1. Outlining can best be described as
   a. listing information to be learned.
   b. recopying detailed ideas and examples.
   c. recording facts in alphabetical order.
   d. organizing ideas to show relationships.

_____ 2. Outlining requires you to do all of the following *except*
   a. think about the material you read.
   b. decide the relative importance of ideas.
   c. put ideas into your own words.
   d. include your opinion of the information.

_____ 3. The main purpose of a summary is to
   a. reflect the organization of ideas.
   b. present a brief review of information.
   c. raise questions about the material.
   d. provide a detailed record of content.

_____ 4. A summary should always include
   a. the author's main point.
   b. examples.
   c. a list of graphics.
   d. your own opinion.

_____ 5. The most useful type of map for organizing information according to similarities of common characteristics is
   a. an organizational chart.
   b. a process diagram.
   c. a comparison–contrast chart.
   d. a time line.

APPLYING YOUR SKILLS

_____ 6. Four students created outlines from a chapter in their economics text. Which student probably created the most effective outline?
   a. Ron included only the information that fit into the outline format he chose.
   b. Emily focused on outlining the author's attitudes.

   c. Michel ensured that his outline expressed at least four levels of ideas.
   d. Li-Min showed the relative importance of ideas.

_____ 7. Dominique needs to complete the following tasks. The task for which writing a summary would be most helpful would be
   a. preparing for an essay exam in sociology.
   b. keeping track of the steps to follow in solving calculus problems.
   c. learning a list of terms and definitions for a biology course.
   d. learning the characteristics of different types of mental illness for a psychology class.

_____ 8. In Yolanda's music class, she drew a diagram showing the various parts of an electric guitar and what each part does. The type of concept map she created in this situation is called
   a. an organizational chart.
   b. a time line.
   c. a process diagram.
   d. a part/function diagram.

_____ 9. Mimi is taking a sociology course in which the focus is social problems. Her instructor has distributed a list of articles, of which she is expected to read ten. The most effective way for her to record the information from her reading would be to prepare
   a. a detailed outline of each article.
   b. index cards for each article.
   c. a summary of each article.
   d. a time line to organize the articles.

_____ 10. In a course on child development, James is studying the development and changes in the human brain prior to birth. The most effective method of study in this situation would be for him to
   a. write a brief summary.
   b. draw a process diagram.
   c. create an organizational chart.
   d. draw a part/function diagram.

MULTIMEDIA *Activities*

Methods of Organizing Information

1 Organize information about your life. Create an outline of your day or of your future plans; make a time line about yourself; construct a family tree.

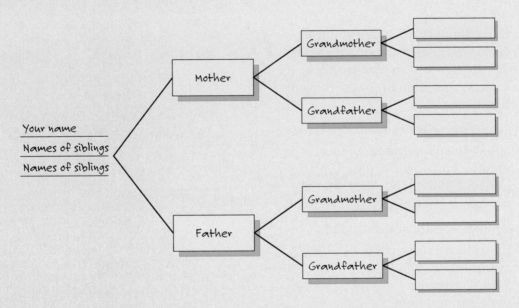

2 Think about careers that interest you and make a comparison–contrast chart listing the pros and cons of each profession. You could include characteristics such as education required, salary, challenges, prestige, flexibility, and independence.

Career	Pros	Cons

3 Explore this interactive outline of the student handbook for engineering students at Boston University.

http://www.bu.edu/eng/handbook/

How effective is the outline format for this subject matter? How does hypertext enhance the online outline experience? Imagine you are creating a Web site about your life. Design the interactive outline around which you could build the site.

4 PBS Time Lines:

http://www.pbs.org/deepspace/timeline/index.html
http://www.pbs.org/kera/usmexicanwar/timeline/index.html
http://www.pbs.org/wgbh/amex/telephone/timeline/
http://www.pbs.org/wnet/pharaohs/timeline1.html
http://www.pbs.org/wgbh/amex/eleanor/timeline/index.html

Many of the programs on PBS have accompanying Web sites with time lines. Visit the Internet pages listed above and evaluate their design and content. How well do they clarify the sequence of events and their importance? Write down your thoughts about the concept of time. Explain how you organize the passage of time in your own mind.

5 Kinds of Concept Maps

http://classes.aces.uiuc.edu/ACES100/Mind/c-m2.html

View these examples of the different types of concept maps. Using ideas, relationships, situations, and experiences from your own life, create a simple concept map of each type.

16 Study and Review Strategies

Why Learn Review Strategies?

■ You forget material rapidly unless you review what you have learned.

■ If you review what you have learned regularly, you won't have to cram before exams.

Learning Experiment

Step 1

Make a list of five to ten tasks (sports, hobbies, household duties, etc.) you can perform well. For each, indicate how you know you are proficient at the task.

Step 2

Make a list of two to five things you might want to learn to do at some point in your lifetime (write a novel, ride horseback, race cars, etc.). For each, indicate how you will measure your success.

The Results

For each task, either those at which you are proficient or those you would like to learn, you were able to suggest some measure or yardstick by which you can evaluate your proficiency or success.

Learning Principle (What This Means to You)

To know whether you have accomplished something, you need some measurement standard. To know whether you have learned something, you also need to test or measure your learning. **For academic learning, self-testing, often through writing, is an effective way to measure what you have learned.** In this chapter you will discover several learning strategies that involve review and self-testing. Even though you have read a textbook chapter and highlighted or outlined it, you cannot be certain that you have learned the material or will be able to apply it on exams. Study and review must follow reading and organizing.

LEARNING THROUGH WRITING

Writing is a form of recoding or processing information by rearranging, rephrasing, or regrouping it so that it becomes more meaningful and easier to recall. Outlining, summarizing, and mapping, each described in the preceding chapter, are forms of writing and recoding and contribute to learning. This section will discuss three other ways to use writing to learn: paraphrasing, self-testing, and keeping a learning journal.

Paraphrasing

A paraphrase is a restatement of a passage's ideas in your own words. The author's meaning is retained, but your wording, *not* the author's, is used. We use paraphrasing frequently in everyday speech. For example, when you relay a message from one person to another, you convey the meaning but do not use the person's exact wording. A paraphrase can be used to make a passage's meaning clearer and often more concise. A paraphrase, then, moves you from a knowledge level in which you can recall information to a comprehension level in which you understand the ideas presented. Paraphrasing is also an effective learning and review strategy in several situations.

First, paraphrasing is useful for portions of a text for which exact, detailed comprehension is required. For example, you might paraphrase the steps in solving a math problem, the process by which a blood transfusion is administered, or the levels of jurisdiction of the Supreme Court. Figure 16-1 shows a paraphrase written by a biology student studying the functioning of the human heart.

Paraphrasing is also a useful way to be certain you understand difficult or complicated material. If you can express the author's ideas in your own words,

**Figure 16-1
A Sample Paraphrase**

Passage	Paraphrase
What does the separation of the two halves of the heart have to do with efficiency? The two halves are essentially two hearts, one serving the lungs, the other serving the body. When CO_2-laden blood enters the right atrium from the large veins (the *superior vena cava* from above and the *inferior vena cava* from below), it is pumped from the atrium to the right ventricle. Contraction of the right ventricle sends the blood through the *pulmonary arteries* to the lungs. Here the blood picks up oxygen and releases carbon dioxide before returning to the left atrium via the *pulmonary veins*. The left atrium pumps the blood into the left ventricle, which then contracts to send the blood into the large aorta, which immediately branches before looping downward, carrying the blood on the first leg of its long journey through the body, bearing its gift of oxygen. —Wallace, *Biology: The World of Life*, p. 434	Blood-filled CO_2 enters the right atrium of the heart from the superior vena cava and the inferior vena cava. It is pumped to the right ventricle, where a contraction moves it through the pulmonary arteries into the lungs, where it exchanges CO_2 for O_2 and then returns through the pulmonary veins to the left atrium. From the left atrium it is pumped to the left ventricle, then to the large aorta, and from there it carries O_2 to the rest of the body.

Figure 16-2
A Comparison of
Paraphrases

Passage: Neurons

Individual neurons do not form a continuous chain, with each neuron directly touching another, end to end. If they did, the number of connections would be inadequate for the vast amount of information the nervous system must handle. Instead, individual neurons are separated by a minuscule space called the synaptic cleft, where the axon terminal nearly touches a dendrite or the cell body of another. The entire site—the axon terminal, the cleft, and the membrane of the receiving dendrite or cell body—is called a synapse. Because a neuron's axon may have hundreds or even thousands of terminals, a single neuron may have synaptic connections with a great many others. As a result, the number of communication links in the nervous system runs into the trillions or perhaps even the quadrillions.

Although we seem to be born with nearly all the neurons we will ever have, many synapses have not yet formed at birth. Research with animals shows that axons and dendrites continue to grow as a result of both physical maturation and experience with the world, and tiny projections on dendrites called spines increase both in size and in number. Throughout life, new learning results in the establishment of new synaptic connections in the brain, with stimulating environments producing the greatest changes (Greenough & Anderson, 1991; Greenough & Black, 1992). Conversely, some unused synaptic connections are lost as cells or their branches die and are not replaced (Camel, Withers, & Greenough, 1986). The brain's circuits are not fixed and immutable; they are continually developing and being pruned in response to information and to challenges and changes in the environment.

—Wade and Tavris, *Psychology*, pp. 124–125

Paraphrase 1: Demonstrates Lack of Understanding

Neurons don't connect with each other because it would be too much information for the nervous system. They have trillions or even quadrillions of links and hundreds or thousands of terminals. They also have clefts, membranes, and synapses—the receiving dendrite or cell body. We seem to be born with all of them that we will ever have. Spines or dendrites become more and bigger, and some of their branches aren't replaced. The brain's circuits cannot be fixed, but are pruned.

Paraphrase 2: Demonstrates Understanding

Neurons are separated from each other by tiny spaces or clefts between the axon of one and the dendrite of another. These three parts make up a synapse. Because of synapses, neurons can make more connections with each other than if they had to touch. This allows for trillions of links in the nervous system. The number of synapses we have is constantly changing. Unused connections vanish, and learning causes our axons and dendrites to grow and make new synaptic connections.

you can be certain you understand it, and if you find yourself at a loss for words—except for those of the author—you will know your understanding is incomplete. Figure 16-2 shows two students' paraphrases of an excerpt from a difficult passage. Paraphrase 1 shows that the student had difficulty—the student wrote in generalities and was unable to connect ideas. In contrast, paraphrase 2 carries the meaning of the passage and demonstrates the student's high level of understanding.

Paraphrasing is a useful strategy for working with material that is stylistically complex, poorly written, or overly formal, awkward, or biased. Many technical manuals, for example, are poorly written and require the reader to struggle to obtain meaning. An essay written in the 1700s may use language patterns different from those you are accustomed to. In such situations, it is helpful to cut through the language barrier and express the content as simply as possible in your own words. Figure 16-3 below shows how a student simplified a complicated discussion about the disappearance of oral poetry from Germany.

Use the following suggestions to paraphrase effectively:

1. **Read slowly and carefully.**
2. **Read the material through entirely before writing anything.**
3. **As you read, pay attention to exact meanings and relationships among ideas.**
4. **Read each sentence and express the key idea in your own words.** Reread the original sentence; next, look away and write your own sentence. Then reread the original and add anything you missed.
5. **Don't try to paraphrase word by word.** Instead, work with ideas.
6. **For words or phrases that you are unsure of or are not comfortable using, check a dictionary to locate a more familiar meaning.**
7. **You may combine several original sentences into a more concise paraphrase.**
8. **Follow the author's arrangement (order) of ideas unless you have a specific reason for changing them.**
9. **When finished, reread your paraphrase and compare it with the original for completeness and accuracy.**

Figure 16-3
Paraphrasing to
Simplify

Passage

The heroic oral poetry of the ancient Germanic peoples, which survived in Iceland and was there committed to writing, disappeared gradually from among the continental Germans in the course of the Middle Ages, and for a long time no adequate substitute took its place. Heathen gods and heathen manners were honored in those poems, and the Church could not approve of either, much less foster their preservation in writing. Thus the numerous German dialects came to be represented during their "old" period, roughly from 500 A.D. to 1000 A.D., almost exclusively by utilitarian and devotional works, and no secular literature worthy of the name was created.

—Parzival

Paraphrase

Germanic heroic oral poetry, although written down in Iceland, disappeared from Germany in the Middle Ages because it celebrated heathen religion that would not be tolerated by the Church. German dialects were thus not written until they became old (500 A.D. to 1000 A.D.) and then only in religious and practical contexts.

EXERCISE 1

DIRECTIONS Write a paraphrase for each of the following excerpts.

1. The tides are important for several reasons. Tidal mixing of nearshore waters removes pollutants and recirculates nutrients. Tidal currents also move floating animals and plants to and from their usual breeding areas in estuaries to deeper waters. People who fish frequently follow tidal cycles to improve their catch, because strong tidal currents concentrate bait and smaller fish, thus attracting larger fish. When sailing ships were more common, departures or arrivals in a harbor had to be closely linked to the tidal cycle.

—Ross, *Introduction to Oceanography*, p. 239

2. The *stomach* is a muscular sac that churns the food as it secretes mucus, hydrochloric acid, and enzymes that begin the digestion of proteins. The food is meanwhile sealed in the stomach by two sphincters, or rings of muscles, one at either end of the stomach. After the mixing is completed, the lower sphincter opens and the stomach

begins to contract repeatedly, squeezing the food into the small intestine. A fatty meal, by the way, slows this process and makes us feel "full" longer. This is also why we're hungry again so soon after a low-fat Chinese dinner.

The *small intestine* is a long convoluted tube in which digestion is completed and through which most nutrient products enter the bloodstream. Its inner surface is covered with tiny, fingerlike projections called *villi*, which increase the surface area of the intestinal lining. Furthermore, the surface area of each villus is increased by about 3000 tiny projections called *microvilli*. Within each villus is a minute lymph vessel surrounded by a network of blood capillaries. While the digested products of certain fats move directly into the lymph vessel, the products of protein and starch digestion move into the blood capillaries.

—Wallace, *Biology: The World of Life,* p. 443

3. *Section 7.* (1). All bills for raising revenue shall originate in the House of Representatives; but the Senate may propose or concur with amendments as on other bills.

(2). Every bill which shall have passed the House of Representatives and the Senate, shall, before it become a law, be presented to the President of the United States; if he approve he shall sign it, but if not he shall return it, with his objections to that House in which it shall have originated, who shall enter the objections at large on their journal, and proceed to reconsider it. If after such reconsideration two thirds of that House shall agree to pass the bill, it shall be sent, together with the objections, to the other House, by which it shall likewise be reconsidered, and if approved by two thirds of that House, it shall become a law. But in all such cases the votes of both Houses shall be determined by yeas and nays, and the names of the persons voting for and against the bill shall be entered on the journal of each House respectively. If any bill shall not be returned by the President within ten days (Sundays excepted) after it shall have been presented to him, the same shall be a law, in like manner as if he had signed it, unless the Congress by their adjournment prevent its return, in which case it shall not be a law.

—U.S. Constitution

EXERCISE 2 DIRECTIONS   Write a paraphrase of the second paragraph of "Move Over, Big Brother" in Part Eight, on page 506.

EXERCISE 3 DIRECTIONS   Write a paraphrase of a two- to three-paragraph excerpt from one of your textbooks. Choose a passage that is difficult or stylistically complex.

Self-Testing

Have you ever taken an exam for which you studied hard and felt prepared, only to find out you earned just an average grade? Although you spent time reviewing, you did not review in the right ways; you probably focused on recalling factual information. Many college professors demand much more of their students than factual recall of textbook and lecture content. They expect their students to react, evaluate, and apply ideas. They require their students to be able to compare and synthesize sources and integrate ideas.

Consequently, a study approach that includes only factual recall is inadequate. Strategies such as rereading, underlining, writing an outline, and drawing maps are useful and important because they enable you to learn literal content. However, you must use additional and different strategies to focus on higher levels of thinking: applying, analyzing, evaluating, and creating.

Writing can facilitate and clarify your thinking. Writing is a way of seeing your ideas. Once you've seen some, others will follow. Writing will help you generate ideas, discover relationships, and grasp applications.

Self-testing is a study strategy that uses writing to discover and relate ideas. It involves writing possible exam questions and drafting answers to them. This activity combines the use of factual recall with interpretation and evaluation. Self-testing is an active strategy that gets you involved with the material and forces you to think about, organize, and express (in your own words) ideas. Self-testing is also a sensible and effective way to prepare for an exam. How would you prepare for a typing or keyboarding exam? By keyboarding. How would you prepare to run a marathon? By running. Similarly, you should prepare for an exam by testing yourself.

Constructing potential test questions is fun and challenging and can be done with a classmate or in groups. It is usually best to write answers yourself, however, to get maximum benefit from the technique. After writing, compare and discuss your answers with classmates. If you prefer to work alone, be sure to verify your answers by referring to your text and/or lecture notes.

What kinds of questions you ask depends on the type of material you are learning as well as on the type or level of analysis your instructor expects. Sample questions for various types of material that you may be required to study are listed in Figure 16-4 on the next page.

To construct and answer possible test questions, use the following hints:

1. Do not waste time writing multiple-choice or true/false questions. They are time-consuming to write, and you know the answer before you start.
2. Matching tests are useful, but they are limited to information that requires only factual recall.
3. Open-ended questions that require sentence answers are best because they tend to require more levels of thought.
4. Consult Figure 16-4 for ideas on how to word your questions.
5. You are interested in long-term retention of information, so it is best to write the questions one day and answer them a day or two later.
6. As you answer your questions, respond in complete sentences. Writing complete sentences usually involves more careful and deliberate thought and therefore leads to more effective learning.
7. Take time to review and critique your answers. This process will also contribute to learning.
8. Rewrite any answers that you found to be poor or incomplete. This repetition will facilitate learning.
9. Save your answers, and review them once again the evening before the exam.

Many students who use self-testing as a review strategy are pleasantly surprised when they take their first exam: they discover that some (or many!) of their questions actually appear on the exam. This discovery boosts their confidence during the exam and saves them time as well. As you will see later in this chapter, self-testing is an important part of the SQ3R system—a systematic approach to learning and study.

**Figure 16-4
Questions to Provoke
Thought**

Type of Material	Questions
Reports of research studies and experiments	What was the purpose of the study? What are the important facts and conclusions? What are its implications? How can these results be used?
Case studies	What is the case intended to illustrate? What problems or limitations does it demonstrate? To what other situations might this case apply?
Models	How was the model derived? What are its applications? What are its limitations? Do other models of the same process exist?
Current events	What is the significance of the event? What impact will this have in the future? Is there historical precedent?
Supplementary readings	Why did your instructor assign the reading? How is it related to course content? What key points or concepts does the reading contain? Does the reading present a particular viewpoint?
Sample problems	What processes or concepts does the problem illustrate? What is its unique feature? How is it similar to and different from other problems?
Historical data (historical reviews)	Why were the data presented? What trends or patterns are evident? How is this information related to key concepts in the chapter or article?
Arguments	Is the argument convincing? How is the conclusion supported? What persuasive devices does the author use? Do logical flaws exist? Is the author's appeal emotional?
Poetry	What kinds of feelings does the poem evoke? What message or statement is the poet making? How does the poet use language to create feelings?
Essays	What is the author's purpose? What thought patterns are evident? How does the author support his or her key point (thesis)?
Short stories	What does the title mean? Beyond the plot, what does the story really mean? (What is the theme?) What kinds of comments does it make about life? How do the plot, setting, and tone contribute to the overall meaning?

EXERCISE 4   DIRECTIONS   Write a list of questions that might be asked on an exam covering one of the chapters that you have already read in this book. Answer them and then verify the correctness of your answers by consulting the chapter.

EXERCISE 5   DIRECTIONS   Write a list of questions for an upcoming exam in one of your courses. Answer each one. Save your questions, and after you have taken the exam, mark those that appeared on the exam. (Do not expect the actual questions to use the same wording or format as those you constructed.)

Applying Levels of Thinking
SELF-TESTING AND LEVELS OF THINKING

When you use the strategy of self-testing, be sure to ask questions at all six levels of thinking.

Level of Thinking	Types of Questions to Ask
Knowing	What is . . . ? When did . . . ? Who was . . . ?
Understanding	Explain how . . . Define . . . Describe the process by which . . .
Applying	Give an example of how . . . Think of a situation in which . . . How can you use . . . ?
Analyzing	Why does . . . ? What trends are evident?
Evaluating	What is the value, importance, or significance of _____? How effectively does . . . ?
Creating	How is _____ related to _____? What are the similarities or differences between _____ and _____?

Keeping a Learning Journal

As you have seen throughout this book, there is a wide range of study and review alternatives. Do not expect to know right away what strategies will work for you or what modifications to make. Instead, you will need to experiment with different variations until you are satisfied with the results. Some students find it effective to keep a learning journal—an informal written record of the techniques they have tried, how well these techniques worked, and what problems they encountered. Writing the journal helps you to sort and evaluate techniques. The journal also serves as a record and is useful to reread as you revise or consider new approaches. Keep a separate journal—perhaps a spiral or steno notebook or section—for each of your most challenging courses. A sample learning journal entry is shown in Figure 16-5 on the next page. It was written as the student applied several of the techniques in this chapter to her biology textbook.

Your journal may include a wide range of observations, comments, and reactions. Consider including the following:

- General reactions to course content
- Unique features of assignments
- What you like and what you don't like about the course
- Problems encountered with a particular assignment
- Techniques that worked (and *why*)
- Techniques that didn't work (and *why*)
- New ideas for approaching the material
- Changes you made in using various techniques
- Analysis and reactions to exams after you take them and again when they are returned

Figure 16-5
Sample Learning Journal

Paraphrasing It is difficult not to use the same words.
I was unable to find a paraphrase for scientific words.
I learned the material very well, though, because I spent
so much time thinking about it.

Self-testing This was very helpful and helped me to focus
on important parts of the chapter. I'm going to keep the
questions I wrote and use them while studying for the
final exam.

SQ3R This was really effective, and I improved on it by
highlighting the answer I found to the question I asked.
This helped to focus my reading. Asking and answering
the question out loud also helped since I'm an auditory
learner. I also drew maps and diagrams and I reread
them out loud.

Be sure to date your entries and indicate the particular chapters or assignments to which they apply. Some students also find it helpful to record the amount of time spent on each assignment.

Once you've made several entries for a particular course, reread your entries and look for patterns. Try to discover what you are doing right, what needs changing, and what changes you'll make. Then write an entry summarizing your findings.

EXERCISE 6

DIRECTIONS   For each course you are taking this semester, create a learning journal. Experiment with self-testing as a means of reviewing a particular chapter in each course. Then write a journal entry describing how you used self-testing, how you modified the technique to suit the course, and how effective you felt it to be.

A CLASSIC SYSTEM: SQ3R

In 1941, a psychologist named Francis P. Robinson developed a study-reading system called SQ3R that integrates study and review with reading. The SQ3R system, which is based on principles of learning theory, was carefully researched and tested and has been used ever since by millions of students. Continuing experimentation has confirmed its effectiveness. Since that time, SQ3R has been taught to thousands of college students and has become widely recognized as the classic study-reading system.

As a step toward developing your own personalized system, look at SQ3R as a model. Once you see how and why SQ3R works, you can modify or adapt it to suit your own academic needs.

Steps in the SQ3R System

The SQ3R system involves five basic steps that integrate reading and study techniques. As you read the following steps, some of them will seem similar to the skills you have already learned.

S—Survey

Try to become familiar with the organization and general content of the material you are to read.

1. **Read the title.**
2. **Read the lead-in or introduction.** (If it is extremely long, read just the first paragraph.)
3. **Read each boldface heading and the first sentence that follows it.**
4. **Read titles of maps, charts, or graphs; read the last paragraph or summary.**
5. **Read the end-of-chapter questions.**
6. **After you have surveyed the material, you should know generally what it is about and how it is organized.**

The Survey step is the technique of prereading that you learned in Chapter 5.

Q—Question

Try to form questions that you can answer as you read. The easiest way to do this is to turn each boldface heading into a question. (The section of Chapter 5 titled "Defining Your Purposes for Reading" discusses this step in depth.)

R—Read

Read the material section by section. As you read each section, look for the answer to the question you formed from the heading of that section.

R—Recite

After you finish each section, stop. Check to see whether you can answer your question for the section. If you can't, look back to find the answer. Then check your recall again. Be sure to complete this step after you read each section.

R—Review

When you have finished the whole reading assignment, go back to each heading; recall your question and try to answer it. If you can't recall the answer, be sure to look back and find the answer. Then test yourself again.

The SQ3R method ties together much of what you have already learned about active reading. The first two steps activate your background knowledge and establish questions to guide your reading. The last two steps provide a means of monitoring your comprehension and recall.

Why SQ3R Works

Results of research studies overwhelmingly suggest that students who are taught to use a study-reading system understand and remember what they read much better than students who have not been taught to use such a system.

In a classic study designed to test the effectiveness of the SQ3R system,* the reading rates and comprehension levels of a group of college students were measured before and after they learned and used the SQ3R system. After students learned the SQ3R method, the average reading rate increased by 22 percent; the comprehension level increased by 10 percent.

If you consider for a moment how people learn, it becomes clear why study-reading systems are effective. One major way to learn is through repetition. Consider the way you learned the multiplication tables. Through repeated practice and drills, you learned $2 \times 2 = 4$, $5 \times 6 = 30$, $8 \times 9 = 72$, and so forth. The key was repetition. Study-reading systems provide some of the repetition necessary to ensure learning. Compared with the usual once-through approach to reading textbook assignments, which offer one chance to learn, SQ3R provides numerous repetitions and increases the amount learned.

SQ3R has many psychological advantages over ordinary reading. First, surveying (prereading) gives you a mental organization or structure—you know what to expect. Second, you always feel that you are looking for something specific rather than wandering aimlessly through a printed page. Third, when you find the information you're looking for, it is rewarding; you feel you have accomplished something. And if you can remember the information in the immediate- and long-term recall checks, it is even more rewarding.

EXERCISE 7

DIRECTIONS   Read the article titled "Stem-cell Therapy: Promise and Reality?" beginning on page 490, using the SQ3R method. The following SQ3R worksheet will help you get started. Fill in the required information as you go through each step.

SQ3R Worksheet

S—Survey: Read the title of the article, the introduction, and each boldface heading, and look at any pictures that appear.

1. What is the article about?

   _____

2. What major topics are included?

   _____

Q—Question 1: Turn the first heading into a question.

   _____

   _____

R—Read: Read the material that follows the first heading, looking for the answer to your question.

R—Recite: Reread the heading and recall the question you asked. Briefly answer this question in your own words without looking at the section. Check to see whether you are correct.

   _____

   _____

*F. P. Robinson, *Effective Study* (New York: Harper & Row, 1941), p. 30.

Q—Question 2: Turn the second heading into a question.

_____

_____

R—Read: Read the material that follows the second heading, looking for the answer to your question.

R—Recite: Briefly answer the question.

_____

_____

Q—Question 3: Turn the third heading into a question.

_____

_____

R—Read: Read the material that follows the third heading, looking for the answer to your question.

R—Recite: Briefly answer the question.

_____

_____

Q—Question 4: Turn the fourth heading into a question.

_____

_____

R—Read: Read the material that follows the fourth heading, looking for the answer to your question.

R—Recite: Briefly answer the question.

_____

_____

Now complete the review step.

R—Review: Look over the entire article by rereading the headings. Try to answer the question you made from each heading.

Answer to Question 1:

_____

_____

Answer to Question 2:

_____

_____

Answer to Question 3:

_____

_____

Answer to Question 4:

_____

_____

Check to see that your answers are correct.

UPDATING AND REVISING THE SQ3R SYSTEM

Now that you are familiar with the basic SQ3R system, it is time to modify it to suit your specific needs. As mentioned previously, the SQ3R method was developed in the 1940s, more than 60 years ago. Over these many years, considerable research has been done and much has been discovered about the learning process. Consequently, it is now possible to expand on the original SQ3R method by adding more recent techniques and strategies. Figure 16-6 lists the steps in the SQ3R method and indicates how you can expand each step to make it work better for you. Most of the techniques listed have been described in previous chapters, as indicated in the table.

As shown in Figure 16-6, the Survey step is really a get-ready-to-read step, along with the Question step. The Read step becomes much more than simply the see-words step. It involves interacting with the text, thinking, anticipating, and reacting. The Recite step can involve much more than answering the questions posed in the Question step. As you identify important information, grasp relationships, and understand key concepts, you might change your highlighting, add to your marking, write notes or questions, self-test, summarize, outline, or draw maps. The final step, Review, can be expanded to include paraphrasing, self-testing, and the review of highlighting, annotation, outlines, and maps.

One popular modification of the SQ3R system is the addition of a fourth R— "Rite"—creating an SQ4R system. SQ4R recognizes the importance of writing, note taking, outlining, and summarizing in the learning process.

Add an "Evaluate" Step

Because critical thinking is an important part of learning, many students add an Evaluate step to the SQ3R system. The Review step assures you that you have

Figure 16-6
Expanding SQ3R

SQ3R Steps	Additional Strategies
Survey	Preread (Chapter 5) Activate your background and experience (Chapter 5) Predict (Chapter 5)
Question	Ask guide questions (Chapter 5)
Read	Check your understanding (Chapter 5) Highlight and mark (Chapter 14) Anticipate thought patterns (Chapter 7)
Recite	Outline (Chapter 15) Summarize (Chapter 15) Map (Chapter 15)
Review	Paraphrase (Chapter 16) Self-test (Chapter 16) Review highlighting, outlines, and maps (Chapters 14, 15)

mastered the material at the knowledge and comprehension levels of thinking. An Evaluate step encourages you to sit back and *think* about what you have read. To get started, ask yourself questions such as:

- Why is this information important?
- How can I use it?
- How does it fit with the class lectures?
- How is this chapter related to previously assigned ones?
- Does the author provide enough evidence to support his or her ideas?
- Is the author biased?
- What are the author's tone and purpose?

Consider Your Learning Style

In Chapter 2, you completed a learning style questionnaire to discover characteristics of your learning style. These characteristics are important to consider in deciding how to modify SQ3R to work best for you. For instance, if you are a visual learner, you might sketch a map showing the organization of the chapter as part of the Survey step. Then, as part of the Recite step, include additional mapping. An auditory learner, during the Survey step, might predict and tape-record what he or she expects the chapter to cover and replay the tape before and after reading. In addition, the questions could be taped during the Question step and then played back and answered as part of the Recite step.

EXERCISE 8

DIRECTIONS   Review the results of the Learning Style Questionnaire on page 11. Then write a list of the changes you might make to the SQ3R method for one of your courses.

ADAPTING YOUR SYSTEM FOR DIFFERENT ACADEMIC DISCIPLINES

Various academic disciplines require different kinds of learning. In an English composition and literature class, for example, you learn skills of critical interpretation, whereas in a chemistry course you learn facts, principles, and processes. A history course focuses on events, their causes, their significance, and their long-term trends.

Because different courses require different types of learning, they also require different types of reading and study; therefore, you should develop a specialized study-reading approach for each subject. The following subjects are some of the academic disciplines most commonly studied by beginning college students, for which changes in a study-reading system are most important. For each, possible modifications in a study-reading system are suggested.

Mathematics

Sample problems are an important part of most math courses; therefore, you would add a Study the Problems step, in which you would try to see how the problems illustrate the theory or process explained in the chapter. This step might also include working through or reviewing additional practice problems.

Literature

When reading novels, essays, short stories, or poetry in a composition and literature class, you are usually asked to interpret, react to, and write about what you read. For reading literature, then, you might drop the Recite step, use the Review step for the literal content (who did what, when, and where?), and add two new steps: Interpret and React. In the Interpret step, you would analyze the characters, their actions, and the writer's style and point of view to determine the writer's theme or message. In the React step, you might ask questions such as "What meaning does this have for me? How effectively did the writer communicate his or her message? Do I agree with this writer's view of life?" You should make notes about your reactions, which can be a source of ideas if a paper is assigned.

Sciences

Prereading is particularly important when you are reading and studying biology, chemistry, physics, or another science, because most of the material is new. You might quickly read each end-of-chapter problem to discover what principles and formulas are emphasized in that chapter. The sciences emphasize facts, principles, formulas, and processes; therefore, build in a Write or Record step in which you highlight, outline, or write study sheets.

Social Sciences

Introductory courses in the social sciences (psychology, sociology, anthropology, economics, political science, and the like) often focus on a particular discipline's basic problems or topics. These courses introduce specialized vocabulary and the basic principles and theories on which the discipline operates.

For social science courses, then, build a Vocabulary Review step into your study-reading system. A Write or Highlight step is also needed to provide an efficient method for review and study.

Other Academic Disciplines

This brief chapter does not permit discussion of modifications for every academic discipline. Probably you are taking one or more courses that we have not mentioned. To adapt your study-reading system to these courses, ask yourself the following questions:

1. What type of learning is required? What is the main focus of the course? (Often the preface or the first chapter of your text will answer these questions. The instructor's course outline or objectives may be helpful.)
2. What must I do to learn this type of material?

Learn to "read" the instructor of each course. Find out what each expects, what topics and types of information each feels are important, and how your grades are determined. Talk with other students in the course or with students who have already taken the course to get ideas for useful ways of studying.

EXERCISE 9

DIRECTIONS Three textbook excerpts appear in Part Eight (pp. 450, 466, and 496). Each represents a different academic discipline. How would you modify the SQ3R system to study-read each textbook excerpt?

1. Sociology

_____

_____

_____

_____

2. Communication

_____

_____

_____

_____

3. Political Science

_____

_____

_____

_____

EXERCISE 10

DIRECTIONS List each of the courses you are taking. Then briefly indicate what changes in your study-reading system you intend to make for each course.

_____

_____

_____

_____

_____

_____

LEARNING COLLABORATIVELY

DIRECTIONS Your instructor will divide the class into three groups and select one of the readings in Part Eight. As an out-of-class assignment, the members of one group should _only_ read the assignment (they should not use SQ3R or preread or review). A second group should preread (see Chapter 5) but should not review. A third group should use the SQ3R system. During the next class meeting, your instructor will quiz you and will report which group earned the highest scores. The class should evaluate their scores and draw conclusions about the relative effectiveness of the study methods used.

APPLYING YOUR LEARNING

Sharon is a visual, conceptual, and pragmatic learner. She is taking an astronomy course and is finding the textbook complicated. She is having difficulty understanding and completing reading assignments. Exams in astronomy are a combination of multiple-choice and essay. She is also taking Introduction to Women's Studies. Many of the readings are newspaper articles about current events and essays about the history of women's roles. The exam will be an essay exam.

1. What reading techniques and learning strategies using writing would you recommend to Sharon to help her with her astronomy text?
2. How can Sharon prepare for her essay exam? What specific suggestions can you make on the basis of the types of readings assigned for the course?
3. How might Sharon adapt SQ3R for her astronomy course?
4. How might Sharon adapt SQ3R for Introduction to Women's Studies?

APPLYING YOUR SKILLS: Sample Textbook Chapter

1. Write a paraphrase of the first paragraph under the heading "Individualist and Collectivist Cultures," on page 518.
2. Write ten questions you could use to self-test yourself on the content of this sample textbook chapter.
3. Use the SQ3R method on this chapter. Use a worksheet similar to the one shown on pages 376–378. Evaluate the effectiveness of the method. What worked? What would you change, add, or do differently?

QUESTIONS FOR DISCUSSION

1. In what everyday situations have you used paraphrasing?
2. What makes paraphrasing and self-testing particularly effective?
3. What questions can you ask your professors to improve the effectiveness of self-testing in specific classes?
4. Discuss your use of SQ3R. What worked? What do you need to change?
5. What types of study-reading systems are effective for each learning style represented in your class? Why are these systems effective for each group?

SELF-TEST SUMMARY

1. **Why is paraphrasing a useful study strategy?**

Paraphrasing, the restatement of a passage's ideas in your own words, is a particularly useful strategy for recording the meaning and checking your comprehension of detailed, complex, precise, or poorly or unusually written passages. When you use your own words rather than the author's, the meaning of the passage is expressed in a clearer and more concise way than the original, making it easier to study and review.

2. **What are the advantages of self-testing?**

Self-testing emphasizes interpretation and application of the information being learned. Writing possible exam questions and drafting answers to them causes you to think about and organize ideas and to express them in your own words. It also gives you a way to practice for an upcoming exam.

3. **How can a learning journal help you find the study techniques that work for you?**

By keeping a written record of your reactions, comments, and assessments of learning strategies for individual courses, you can discover which strategies work best for you and how to modify them to be even more useful. Rereading your journal entries periodically and summarizing your impressions can help you see what is working, as well as what needs changing and how to change it.

4. **What is the SQ3R study-reading system?**

The SQ3R method is a classic five-step method of study and review. The steps are Survey, Question, Read, Recite, and Review.

5. **Why is it effective?**

The SQ3R study method has several advantages over ordinary reading. By building a mental framework on which to fit information, searching actively for important facts, going through the repetitions involved in the three Rs, and feeling rewarded when you find the answers to your questions, you can improve your comprehension and recall of study material.

6. **How can you adapt your study-reading system for different academic disciplines?**

The SQ3R method should be adapted to suit the unique characteristics of various academic disciplines. The system can also be expanded to include additional and/or newer techniques and strategies. Considering the focus of the course, the type of learning required, and what you must do to learn the material will guide you in adapting and expanding your study-reading system.

QUICK QUIZ

DIRECTIONS   Write the letter of the choice that best completes each statement in the space provided.

CHECKING YOUR RECALL

_____ 1. Self-testing is a study strategy that involves

    a. writing and answering possible exam questions.

    b. taking a graded exam at home or in another location outside the class.

    c. rewriting the end-of-chapter questions in a textbook.

    d. using old exams and quizzes to study for an exam.

_____ 2. Of the following self-test questions, the one that requires the highest level of thinking is:

    a. Who were the major literary figures during the Great Depression?

    b. When did Allen Ginsberg write "Howl"?

    c. How does Walt Whitman connect poetic devices and emotion in "To a Locomotive in Winter"?

    d. Where was Langston Hughes born?

_____ 3. The "S" step of SQ3R is similar to

    a. summarizing.

    b. prereading.

    c. outlining.

    d. categorizing.

_____ 4. The Recite step of SQ3R primarily involves

    a. becoming familiar with the organization and general content of the material you are about to read.

    b. forming questions that you can answer as you read.

    c. checking to see if you can answer the questions you formed for each section.

    d. going back over the material once you have read it.

_____ 5. When you are developing your own study-reading system, it is most important to consider

    a. your learning style.

    b. what you dislike most about studying.

    c. how much time each of your assignments requires.

    d. how many of the SQ3R steps you can eliminate.

APPLYING YOUR SKILLS

_____ 6. As part of a music theory assignment, Joshua has been asked to paraphrase an article describing the evolution of the blues. To paraphrase effectively, Joshua should do all of the following *except*

    a. read slowly and carefully.

    b. follow the author's arrangement of ideas.

    c. read the material before writing anything.

    d. paraphrase word by word.

_____ 7. Nora has decided to use paraphrasing to help her learn a chapter in her linguistics textbook. Her primary focus in paraphrasing should be on

    a. evaluating the material for relevance.

    b. recording her reactions to the author's point of view.

    c. thinking of practical applications for the material.

    d. restating the author's meaning in her own words.

_____ 8. Garrett's academic advisor recommends that Garrett begin using a learning journal. Garrett's advisor most likely wants Garrett to

    a. keep track of each week's assignments.

    b. transcribe tape-recorded lectures.

    c. record and evaluate learning strategies.

    d. outline difficult textbook chapters.

_____ 9. Emma is using the SQ3R system to study a chapter in her physics textbook. She should do the Review step of SQ3R

a. while she is reading the chapter.
b. while she is forming questions.
c. after she has completed a section.
d. after she has completed the assignment.

_____ 10. Luis is creating a study-reading system for a modern fiction course. In this situation, he should probably add a

a. Study Problems step.
b. Vocabulary Review step.
c. Paraphrase step.
d. React and Interpret step.

MULTIMEDIA *Activities*

Study and Review Strategies

1 Kyoto National Museum

http://www.kyohaku.go.jp/eng/tenji/index.html

Write down some questions that you would expect to be answered about the artwork at this Japanese museum. Include questions from each of the six levels of thinking. Then, view one of the past exhibits featured on the Web site and find the answers to your questions. Review the information and write a short essay or teach a friend about what you learned.

Level of Thinking	Questions
Knowing	
Understanding	
Applying	
Analyzing	
Evaluating	
Creating	

2 Textbook Reading

http://www.dartmouth.edu/~acskills/success/reading.html

Dartmouth College offers several online handouts designed to help students read textbooks effectively and efficiently. Two featured documents are "Six Reading Myths" and "Harvard Report on Reading." Read them over and discuss with your classmates how these documents apply to your current experiences. Offer each other suggestions for improving your reading skills.

3 SQ3R Worksheet

Try using this worksheet from Northern Virginia Community College for your next textbook reading assignment:

http://www.nv.cc.va.us/home/diwilson1/SQ3RAssignmentSheet.htm

Evaluate whether this system worked well for you. Adapt it to your particular needs.

4 Try writing out what you would like to say to your employer, doctor, or instructors before you talk to them. How does this technique prepare you for a conversation?

5 Watch an informational program on TV or see a documentary. Paraphrase on paper the ideas and facts presented. Explain what you learned to a friend or family member. Did you understand and remember more than you usually do when viewing these types of materials?

17 Preparing for Exams

Why Learn to Prepare for Exams?

■ Preparing well for exams helps you tie together the facts and concepts you have learned.

■ Better preparation for exams will help you achieve better grades.

■ If you prepare well for your exams, you will minimize stress.

Learning Experiment

Imagine you are taking a statistics class and must learn to calculate the median of a set of numbers.

Step 1

Read the following paragraph defining the term *median.*

> Because it can be affected by extremely high or low numbers, the mean is often a poor indicator of central tendency for a list of numbers. In cases like this, another measure of central tendency, called the **median,** can be used. The *median* divides a group of numbers in half; half the numbers lie above the median, and half lie below the median.
>
> Find the median by listing the numbers *in order* from *smallest* to *largest.* If the list contains an *odd* number of items, the median is the *middle number.*
>
> If a list contains an *even* number of items, there is no single middle number. In this case, the median is defined as the mean (average) of the *middle two* numbers.

Step 2

Applying the definition above, circle the median in each of the following groups of numbers.

17, 24, 6, 9, 10, 2, 44
7, 13, 9, 4

Which step was more useful in helping you learn the formula?

The Results

Most students find step 2 more useful. Why? In step 1 all you do is read. In step 2 you apply the explanation to two sets of numbers. Step 2 forces you to use and apply the information contained in step 1. By practicing computing the median, you come to understand it.

Learning Principle
(What This Means to You)

One of the best ways to prepare for a test is to simulate the test conditions. To prepare for an exam, then, practice answering the types of questions you think will be on the test. Do not just read or reread as step 1 required you to do. This chapter will offer many ideas on preparing for exams and will show you ways to study by simulating test conditions for both objective and essay tests. You will also learn how to organize your review, identify what to study, analyze and synthesize information, and learn and remember what is important.

ORGANIZING YOUR STUDY AND REVIEW

Studying is the most important thing you can do to increase your chance of passing an exam. When exam papers are returned, you may hear comments like "I spent at least ten hours studying. I went over everything, and I still failed the exam!" Students frequently complain that they spend large amounts of time studying and do not get the grades they think they deserve. Usually the problem is that although they did study, they did not study the best way. The first thing to do, well in advance of the exam, is to get organized. The timing of your review sessions is crucial to achieving good test results. Organize your review sessions, using the suggestions discussed in the following sections.

Organize Your Time

1. **Schedule several review sessions at least a week in advance of an exam.** Set aside specific times for daily review, and incorporate them into your weekly schedule. If you are having difficulty with a particular subject, set up extra study times.
2. **Spend time organizing your review.** Make a list of all chapters, notes, and handouts that need to be reviewed. Divide the material, planning what you will review during each session.
3. **Reserve time the night before the exam for a final, complete review.** Do not study new material during this session. Instead, review the most difficult material, checking your recall of important facts or information for possible essay questions.

Find Out About the Exam

When studying for an exam or test, find out whether it will be objective, essay, or a combination of both. If your instructor does not specify the type of exam when he or she announces the date, ask during or after class. Most instructors are willing to tell students what type of exam will be given—sometimes they simply forget to mention it when announcing the exam. If an instructor chooses not to tell you, do not be concerned; at least you have shown that you are interested and are thinking ahead.

Be sure you know what material the exam will cover. Usually your instructor will either announce the exam topics or give the time span that the exam will cover. Also, find out what your instructor expects of you and how he or she will evaluate your exam. Some instructors expect you to recall text and lecture material; others expect you to agree with their views on a particular subject; still others encourage you to recall, discuss, analyze, or disagree with the ideas and information they have presented. You can usually tell what to expect by the way quizzes have been graded or classes have been conducted.

Attend the Class Before the Exam

Be sure to attend the class prior to the exam. Cutting class to spend the time studying, though tempting, is a mistake. During this class, the instructor may give a brief review of the material to be covered or offer last-minute review suggestions. Have you ever heard an instructor say "Be sure to look over . . . " prior to an exam? Also, listen carefully to how the instructor answers students' questions; these answers will provide clues about what the exam will emphasize.

Consider Studying with Others

Depending on your learning style, it may be helpful to study with another person or with a small group of students from your class. Be sure to weigh the following advantages and disadvantages of group study. Then decide whether group study suits your learning style.

Group study can be advantageous for the following reasons:

1. **Group study forces you to become actively involved with the course content.** Talking about, reacting to, and discussing the material aids learning. If you have trouble concentrating or staying focused when studying alone, group study may be useful.
2. **One of the best ways to learn something is to explain it to someone else.** By using your own words and thinking of the best way to explain an idea, you are analyzing it and testing your own understanding. The repetition involved in explaining something you already understand also strengthens your learning.

Group study can, however, have disadvantages.

1. **Unless everyone is serious, group study sessions can turn into social events in which very little studying occurs.**
2. **Studying with the wrong people can produce negative attitudes that will work against you.** For example, the "None of us understands this and we can't all fail" attitude is common.
3. **By studying with someone who has not read the material carefully or attended classes regularly, you will waste time reviewing basic definitions and facts that you already know, instead of focusing on more difficult topics.**

EXERCISE 1 | **DIRECTIONS**   Plan a review schedule for an upcoming exam. Include material you will study and when you will study it.

IDENTIFYING WHAT TO STUDY

In preparing for an exam, review every source of information—textbook chapters and lecture notes—as well as sources sometimes overlooked, such as old exams and quizzes, the instructor's handouts, course outlines, and outside assignments. Talking with other students about the exam can also be helpful.

Textbook Chapters

You must review all chapters that were assigned during the period covered by the exam or that are related to the topics covered in the exam. Review of textbook chapters should be fairly easy if you have kept up with weekly assignments, used your own variation of a study-reading system, and marked and underlined each assignment.

Lecture Notes

In addition to textbook chapters, review all relevant notes. This, too, is easy if you have used the note-taking and editing system presented in Chapter 4.

Previous Exams and Quizzes

Be sure to keep all old tests and quizzes, which are valuable sources of review for longer, more comprehensive exams. Most instructors do not repeat the same test questions, but old quizzes list important facts, terms, and ideas. The comprehensive exam will probably test your recall of the same information through different types of questions.

Look for Patterns of Error

Pay particular attention to items that you got wrong; try to see a pattern of error.

1. **Are you missing certain types of questions?** If so, spend extra time on these questions.
2. **Are there certain topics on which you lost most of your points?** If so, review these topics.
3. **Are you missing questions at a particular level of thinking?** Use a grid like the one shown in Figure 17-1 to analyze what type of questions you are getting wrong. If you discover, for example, that you are getting knowledge and comprehension questions wrong, include more factual review in your study plans. On the other hand, if you are missing numerous synthesis questions, you need to focus more on drawing connections between and among your study topics.

Identify the Levels of Thinking Your Instructor Emphasizes

The grid shown in Figure 17-2 on page 391 can also be used to identify the level of thinking your instructor requires on exams. For example, some instructors may emphasize application; others may focus on analysis and synthesis of information. You can see that the exam analyzed in Figure 17-2 emphasized comprehension and application questions. To discover your instructor's emphasis, go through a previous exam, question by question, identifying and marking each question's type in the grid. Once you have discovered your instructor's emphasis, adjust your study methods accordingly. Include more factual review if knowledge and comprehension are emphasized. Be sure to consider practical situations and uses if application questions are frequently asked.

Figure 17-1
Sample Grid for Analysis of Errors

Level of Question	Exam 1 Wrong Answers	Exam 2 Wrong Answers			
Remembering	0	1			
Understanding	2	0			
Applying	7	5			
Analyzing	1	2			
Evaluating	1	0			
Creating	0	0			

Figure 17-2
Sample Grid for
Determining Your
Instructor's Emphasis

Level of Thinking	Exam 1 Question Numbers	Exam 2 Question Numbers
Remembering	5, 8, 25	
Understanding	1, 3, 18, 19, 21, 22, 24	
Applying	2, 5, 6, 7, 10, 11, 12, 14, 16, 20	
Analyzing	4	
Evaluating	13, 17	
Creating	9, 15, 23	

Instructors' Handouts

Instructors frequently distribute duplicated sheets of information, such as summary outlines, lists of terms, sample problems, maps and charts, or explanations of difficult concepts. Any material that an instructor prepares for distribution is bound to be important. As you review these sheets throughout the course, date them and label the lecture topic to which they correspond. Keep them together in a folder or in the front of your notebook so that you can refer to them easily.

Outside Assignments

Out-of-class assignments might include problems to solve, library research, written reactions or evaluations, or lectures or movies to attend. If an instructor gives an assignment outside of class, the topic is important. Because of the limited number of assignments that can be given in a course, instructors choose only those that are most valuable. You should therefore keep your notes on assignments together for easy review.

Talk with Other Students

Talking with classmates can help you identify the right material to learn. By talking with others, you may discover a topic that you have overlooked or recognize a new focus or direction.

EXERCISE 2

DIRECTIONS   Construct a grid like the one shown in Figure 17-2. Use it to analyze the level(s) of thinking your instructor emphasized on one of your previous exams.

ANALYZING AND SYNTHESIZING INFORMATION

Once you have identified what material to learn, the next step is to draw together, analyze, and synthesize the information. Synthesis is an important critical-thinking skill because it forces you to see connections among ideas. In your close study of chapters and lecture notes, it is easy to get lost in details and lose sight of major themes or processes. When concentrating on details, you can miss significant points and fail to see relationships. Exams often measure your awareness of concepts and trends as well as your recall of facts, dates, and definitions. The following suggestions will help you learn to synthesize information.

Get a Perspective on the Course

To avoid focusing too narrowly on details and to obtain perspective on the course material, step back and view the course from a distance. Imagine that all your notes, textbook chapters, outlines, and study sheets are arranged on a table and that you are looking down on them from a peephole in the ceiling. Then ask yourself: What does all that mean? When put together, what does it all show? Why is it important?

Look for Relationships

Study and review consist of more than just learning facts. Try to see how facts are related. In learning the periodic table of chemical elements, for example, you should do more than just learn names and symbols. You should understand how elements are grouped, what properties the elements in a group share, and how the groups are arranged.

Look for Patterns and the Progression of Thought

Try to see why the material was covered in the order in which it was presented. How is one class lecture related to the next? To what larger topic or theme are several lectures connected? For class lectures, check the course outline or syllabus that was distributed at the beginning of the course. Because it lists major topics and suggests the order in which they will be covered, your syllabus will be useful in discovering patterns.

Similarly, for textbook chapters, try to focus on the progression of ideas. Study the table of contents to see the connection between chapters you have read. Often chapters are grouped into sections based on similar content.

Watch for the progression or development of thought. Ask yourself: What is the information presented in this chapter leading up to? What does it have to do with the chapter that follows? Suppose that in psychology you had covered a chapter on personality traits and next were assigned a chapter on abnormal and deviant behavior. You would want to know what the two chapters have to do with each other. In this case, the first chapter on personality establishes the standards or norms by which abnormal and deviant behavior are determined.

Interpret and Evaluate

Do not let facts and details camouflage important questions. Remember to ask yourself: What does this mean? How is this information useful? How can this be applied to various situations? Once you have identified the literal content, stop, react, and evaluate its use, value, and application.

Prepare Study Sheets

The study sheet system is a way of organizing and summarizing complex information by preparing a mini-outline. It is most useful for reviewing material that is interrelated, or connected, and needs to be learned as a whole rather than as separate facts. Types of information that should be reviewed on study sheets include:

1. Theories and principles
2. Complex events with multiple causes and effects
3. Controversial issues—pros and cons
4. Summaries of philosophical issues
5. Trends in ideas or data
6. Groups of related facts

Look at the sample study sheet in Figure 17-3, which was made by a student preparing for a psychology exam that would cover a chapter on stress. You will note that the study sheet organizes information on two approaches to coping with stress and presents that information in a form that permits easy comparison.

To prepare a study sheet, first select the information to be learned. Then outline the information, using as few words as possible. Group together important points, facts, and ideas related to each topic.

EXERCISE 3

DIRECTIONS   Prepare a study sheet for the selection "Increased Hurricane Activity Tied to Global Warming," which begins on page 482 in Part Eight. Use the following three headings in your study sheet: Hurricane Activity; Cause: Warm Water; and Global Warming and Climate Change Research.

EXERCISE 4

DIRECTIONS   Prepare a study sheet for a topic you are studying in one of your courses. Include all the information you need to learn in order to prepare for an exam.

**Figure 17-3
A Sample Study Sheet**

	Problem-Focused Approach	Emotion-Focused Approach
Purpose	solving the problem causing stress	changing or managing the emotions the problems caused
Example	learning about a disability and how to live with it	expressing grief and anger to get it out of your system
How it is accomplished	1. define the problem 2. learn about the problem and how to fix it 3. take steps to fix the problem	1. reappraisal 2. comparisons 3. avoidance 4. humor

LEARNING AND MEMORIZING

The methods and procedures you use to learn and to remember information depend on the type of exam for which you are preparing. You would study and learn information differently for a multiple-choice test than for an essay exam.

Exams can be divided into two basic types: objective and essay. Objective tests include short-answer tests in which you choose one or more answers from several that are given, or supply a word or phrase to complete a statement. Multiple-choice, true/false, matching, and fill-in-the-blank questions appear on objective tests. In each of these, the questions are constructed so that the answers you choose are either right or wrong; scoring is completely objective, or free from judgment.

Essay tests require you to answer questions in your own words. You have to recall information, organize it, and present it in an acceptable written form. This is different from recognizing the correct answer among several choices or recalling a word or phrase. Because essay exams differ from objective tests, you must use different methods in preparing and reviewing for them.

Review for Objective Tests

Objective tests usually require you to recognize the right answer. On a multiple-choice test, for example, you have to pick the correct answer from the choices given. On matching tests, you have to recognize which two items go together. One goal in reviewing for objective tests, then, is to become so familiar with the course material that you can recognize and select the right answers.

Use Highlighting and Marking

Your highlighting of reading assignments can be used in several ways for review. First, reread your highlighting in each chapter. Second, read the chapter's boldface headings and form a question for each, as you did in the Question step in the SQ3R system. Try to answer your question; then check your highlighting to see whether you were correct. Finally, review special marks you may have included. If, for example, you marked new or important definitions with a particular symbol, then you should go through the chapter once and note these terms, checking your recall of their meanings.

Use the Recall Clues in Your Lecture Notes

Go back through each set of lecture notes and check your recall by using the marginal recall clue system. Test yourself by asking questions and trying to remember answers. Mark in red ink things you have trouble remembering. Then use ink of a different color the second time you go through your notes, marking information you still can't recall.

Use Study Aids

Use all study sheets, outlines, summaries, and organizational charts and diagrams that you have prepared to review and learn course content. To learn the information on a study sheet or outline, first read through it several times. Then take the first topic, write it on a sheet of paper, and see whether you can fill in the information under the topic on your study sheet or outline. If you can't recall all the information, test yourself until you have learned it. Continue in this way with each topic.

Use the Index Card System

The index card system is an effective way of reviewing for objective tests. Using 3-by-5-inch index cards (or just small sheets of paper), write part of the information on the front, the remainder on the back. To review the dates of important events, write the date on the front, the event on the back; to review vocabulary, put each term on the front of a card and its definition on the back. See the sample index cards shown in Figure 17-4, which were made by a student preparing for an objective exam in biology.

To study these cards, look at the front of each and try to remember what is written on the back. Then turn the card over to see whether you are correct. As you go through your pack of cards, sort them into two stacks—those you know and those you don't remember. Then go back through the stack of those you don't know, study each, and retest yourself, again sorting the cards into two stacks. Continue this procedure until you are satisfied that you have learned all the information. Go through your cards in this manner two or three times a day for three or four days before the exam. On the day of your exam, do a final, once-through review so that the information is fresh in your mind.

The index card system has several advantages. First, it is time-efficient; by sorting the cards, you spend time learning what you do not know and do not waste time reviewing what you have already learned. Second, by having each item of information on a separate card rather than in a list on a single sheet of paper, you avoid the danger of learning the items in a certain order. If you study

**Figure 17-4
Sample Study Cards**

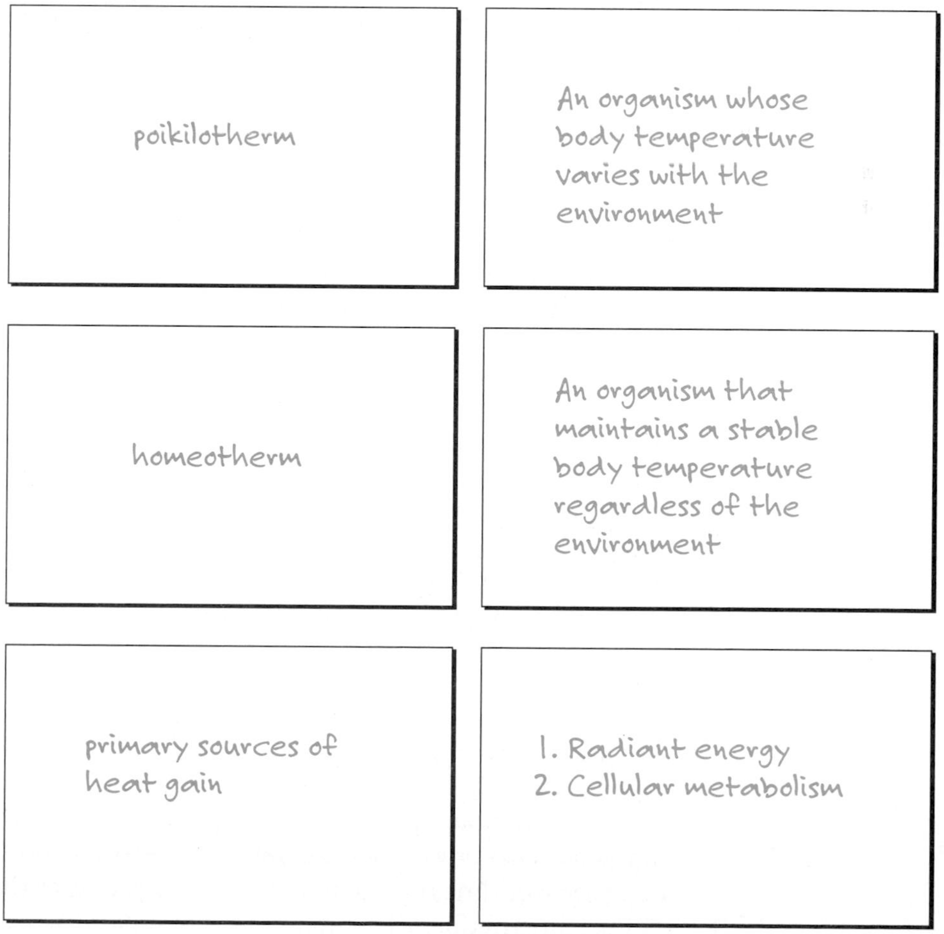

poikilotherm	An organism whose body temperature varies with the environment
homeotherm	An organism that maintains a stable body temperature regardless of the environment
primary sources of heat gain	1. Radiant energy 2. Cellular metabolism

a list of items, you run the risk of being able to remember them only in the order in which they are written on the list. When a single item appears out of order on an exam, you may not remember it. By sorting and occasionally shuffling your index cards, you avoid learning information in a fixed order. A third advantage of the index card system is that these cards are easy to carry in a pocket or purse. It is therefore easier for you to space your review of the material. If you carry them with you, you can study in spare moments—even when you don't have textbooks or notebooks with you. Moments usually wasted waiting in supermarket lines, doctors' offices, gas stations, or traffic jams can be used for study.

The index card system is more appropriate for learning brief facts than for reviewing concepts, ideas, and principles or for understanding sequences of events, theories, and cause–effect relationships. For this reason, it works best when you are studying for objective tests that include short-answer questions such as fill-in-the-blanks.

Test Yourself

Check to be sure you have learned all the necessary facts and ideas. By testing yourself before the instructor tests you, you are preparing in a realistic way for the exam. If you were entering a marathon race, you would prepare for the race by running—not by playing golf. The same is true of test taking; you should prepare for a test by testing yourself—not by simply rereading chapters or pages of notes. You can test yourself in any of the following ways:

- Use recall clues for your lecture notes (see Chapter 4, p. 92).
- Draw and label maps (see Chapter 15, p. 354).
- Write partially completed outlines. Fill in the blanks from memory.
- Use vocabulary cards (see Chapter 13, p. 313).
- Work with a classmate, testing each other by making up sample questions and answering them.

EXERCISE 5 | **DIRECTIONS** Prepare a set of index cards (at least 20) for a chapter or section of a chapter you are studying in one of your courses. Then learn the information on the cards, using the sorting technique described in this section.

Review for Essay Exams

Essay exams demand extensive recall. Starting with a blank sheet of paper, you are required to retrieve from your memory all the information that answers the question. Then you must organize that information and express your ideas about it in acceptable written form.

To review for an essay exam, first identify topics that may be included in the exam. Then predict actual questions and write outline or rough-draft answers.

Select Probable Topics

In choosing topics to study, you attempt to predict what questions will be included on the exam. There are several sources from which you can choose topics. First, you can use boldface textbook headings to identify important topics or subtopics. End-of-chapter discussion questions and recall clues written in the margins of your lecture notes may also suggest topics. Remember to check the course outline distributed by your instructor at the beginning of the course. This outline frequently contains a list of major topics covered in the course.

Study the Topics Selected

Once you have made your choices, identify which aspects of the topics might be tested. Perhaps the best source of information is your instructor, who probably has been consciously or unconsciously giving clues all semester about what the most important topics are. Train yourself to watch and listen for these clues. Specifically, look for your instructor's approach, focus, and emphasis with respect to the subject matter. Does your history instructor emphasize causes and dates of events? Or is he or she more concerned with the historical importance and lasting effects of events? Is your ecology instructor concerned with specific changes that a pollutant produces or its more general environmental effects?

Write Possible Questions

Next, write actual questions that you think your instructor might ask. Study the sample essay questions in Figure 18-1 on page 414 to get an idea of how they are written. Be sure to predict questions at all levels of thinking.

Applying Levels of Thinking

PREPARING FOR ESSAY EXAMS AND LEVELS OF THINKING

Level of Thinking	What to Ask
Knowing and Understanding	These levels require recall of facts; remembering dates, names, definitions, and formulas falls into these categories. The five "W" questions—Who? What? Where? When? and Why?—are useful to ask.
Applying	This level of thinking requires you to use or apply information. The following two questions best test this level: In what practical situations would this information be useful? What does this have to do with what I already know about the subject?
Analyzing	Analysis involves seeing relationships. Ask questions that test your ability to take ideas apart, find cause–effect relationships, and discover how things work.
Evaluating	This level involves making judgments and assessing value or worth. Ask questions that challenge sources, accuracy, long-term value, importance, and so forth.
Creating	This level involves pulling ideas together. Ask questions that force you to look at similarities and differences.

Write Outline or Rough-Draft Answers

Once you have identified possible exam questions, the next step is to practice answering them. Do not take the time to write out full, complete sentences. Instead, collect and organize the information you would include in your answer, and record it in brief note or outline form, listing the information you would include.

If you are using a computer to organize lecture notes and notes taken from textbook chapters, it is easy to prepare a study sheet. You can copy sections from both sources to create a study sheet on each topic.

**Figure 17-5
A Sample Key-Word
Outline**

> Problem vs. Emotion
>   Purpose
>   Example
>   how accomplished

Use Key-Word Outlines

As a convenient way to remember what your draft answer includes, make a key-word outline of your answer. For each item in your draft, identify a key word that will trigger your memory of that idea. Then list and learn these key words. Together, these words form a mini-outline of topics and ideas to include in an essay on this topic. A key-word outline is shown in Figure 17-5.

Predicting and answering possible examination questions is effective for several reasons. Predicting forces you to analyze the material, not just review it. Drafting answers forces you to express ideas in written form. Through writing, you will recognize relationships, organize your thoughts, and discover the best way to present them.

EXERCISE 6

DIRECTIONS   Assume you are preparing for an essay exam in one of your courses. Predict several questions that might be asked for one textbook chapter and write them in the space provided. Try to write questions that require different levels of thinking.

_____

_____

_____

_____

_____

EXERCISE 7

DIRECTIONS   Choose one of the essay exam questions that you wrote in Exercise 6. Prepare a study sheet that summarizes the information on the topic. Then reduce that information on your study sheet to a key-word outline.

LEARNING COLLABORATIVELY

DIRECTIONS   Each student should write five essay questions based on the three readings included in Thematic Group D, "Civil Liberties," in Part Eight, pages 496–512. Working in groups of three or four students, compare and evaluate your questions, revise several strong ones, and categorize each question using the levels of thinking described in Chapter 2 on page 54. Finally, choose one question to submit to the class. After each group has presented its question, the class will identify the level(s) of thinking that each question demands and discuss which is the hardest and which is the easiest.

APPLYING YOUR LEARNING

Art is taking a psychology course in which grades are based on four multiple-choice exams. Each exam contains 50 items worth two points and is machine-scored. When exams are returned, students receive their answer sheets but do not receive the questions themselves. On the first exam, Art earned 68 points, which is a high D grade. For the second exam, he spent more time studying but only earned 72, a C−. When Art visited his instructor in her office and asked for advice on how to improve his grade, the instructor handed Art copies of the first two exams and said, "Spend a half hour or so with each of these; I'm sure you'll discover what's going wrong."

1. What things should Art look for in the exams?
2. What kinds of notes should he make, if any, about the exams?
3. How should Art use each of the following in preparing for his next multiple-choice exam?
   - index cards
   - lecture notes
   - summaries of textbook chapters

APPLYING YOUR SKILLS: Sample Textbook Chapter

1. Describe how you would prepare for an objective test on this chapter.
2. Describe how you would prepare for an essay exam on this chapter.

QUESTIONS FOR DISCUSSION

1. Under what conditions have study groups been effective in helping you study?
2. What are some ground rules your group could establish to help ensure your valuable time is spent well?
3. Review several previous exams, quizzes, or tests from one of your other courses. Discuss whether this review was beneficial.

SELF-TEST SUMMARY

1. How can you get organized to study and review for exams?

Organizing for study and review requires planning and scheduling your time so that you can review all the material carefully and thoroughly. You should begin at least a week before the exam to plan what material you will study each day and at what specific times you will study, and you should plan time for a complete review the evening before the exam. Attending the last class before the exam can provide you with useful hints, and group study can be helpful for certain individuals and circumstances.

2. How can you identify what to study?

In order to identify what to study, it is important to review all of your sources of information. To determine what material is to be learned, you should review all textbook chapters assigned; your lecture notes; exams and quizzes you have taken; classroom handouts; and notes on outside assignments. From these sources and discussion with other students, you will arrive at the topics most likely to be covered on the exam.

3. How can you organize these facts and ideas and synthesize them into a meaningful body of information to be studied?

To synthesize the information presented in a course, it is helpful to "step back" and look at the larger picture of the meaning of the course. Look at relationships between ideas, note patterns in the course syllabus and your textbook's table of contents, and see past the details to the important questions regarding the use, value, and application of this information. Preparing study sheets or mini-outlines can help in this process.

4. How can you best learn and memorize the information for objective and essay exams?

Learning and memorizing, the final steps in preparing for exams, require learning the material in a manner that is most appropriate for the type of exam you will take. For objective exams, you should review all highlighting and marking, the recall clues in your lecture notes, and any study aids you have prepared throughout the course. By using the index card system and testing yourself, you can be sure you have learned all the important facts and ideas. For essay exams, you should begin by predicting probable exam questions. Next, you should study the topics selected by preparing a study sheet from which you can review and write a clear, concise essay. Finally, prepare a key-word outline or mini-outline that will guide you when writing answers to the questions you predicted earlier.

DIRECTIONS Write the letter of the choice that best completes each statement in the space provided.

CHECKING YOUR RECALL

_____ 1. As you prepare for an exam, you should do all of the following *except*
    a. spend time organizing your review.
    b. skip the class prior to the exam so you can study.
    c. find out what type of exam it will be.
    d. set aside specific times for daily review.

_____ 2. The best reason to review previous exams and quizzes before an exam is to
    a. try to identify important facts, terms, and ideas.
    b. look for questions that will be repeated on the exam.
    c. eliminate some areas of study.
    d. replace extensive textbook review.

_____ 3. A common mistake students make when studying for an exam is to
    a. begin reviewing too far ahead of the exam.
    b. study with other students.
    c. look for relationships among ideas.
    d. fail to interpret facts and details.

_____ 4. A study sheet is most similar to
    a. a mini-outline.
    b. an organizational chart.
    c. a self-test.
    d. a learning journal.

_____ 5. Of the following review situations, index cards would be most useful for
    a. comparing Thoreau and Whitman for a literature class.
    b. studying the theory of relativity in physics.
    c. learning definitions for an anatomy and physiology class.
    d. studying the events leading up to America's involvement in Vietnam for a history class.

APPLYING YOUR SKILLS

_____ 6. By looking at old exams, Evan has determined that his marketing instructor tends to emphasize essay questions at the application level of thinking. Therefore, Evan should predict essay questions that ask students to
    a. recall facts, dates, names, and definitions.
    b. use information in practical situations.
    c. find cause-and-effect relationships.
    d. assess the long-term value of the information.

_____ 7. Alicia is studying her American government textbook before an exam. If she wanted to find out the textbook's progression of ideas, she would probably consult the text's
    a. appendix.
    b. preface.
    c. table of contents.
    d. first chapter.

_____ 8. Sheri has analyzed her patterns of error on history exams and discovered that she frequently gets knowledge and comprehension questions wrong. One way that she should adjust her study methods is to focus more on
    a. connections between topics.
    b. factual review.
    c. practical situations and uses.
    d. out-of-class assignments.

_____ 9. Keith is preparing for an essay exam in his world history class. The first step Keith should take is to
    a. identify topics that may be included on the exam.
    b. predict actual questions.
    c. write sample essay answers.
    d. create a key-word outline.

_____ 10. Spencer is preparing for an essay test. He should use a key-word outline to
    a. trigger his memory of ideas he wants to include in an essay.
    b. serve as a guide for study and review.
    c. organize his study.
    d. test his understanding of a topic.

MULTIMEDIA *Activities*

Preparing for Exams

1 Evaluate your past test preparation techniques. Write down the ways you have studied in the past. How successful were these techniques for you? Did you study differently for different subjects? In what ways? How can you adapt old study habits to your new learning strategies? Discuss these issues with your classmates.

2 List information that you have memorized—phone numbers, song lyrics, commercial jingles, friends' birthdays, and so forth. Evaluate the content of your list. What motivated you to memorize this information? What motivates you to memorize and learn information for your classes? How can you reward yourself for your hard work?

3 Ten Traps of Studying

http://caps.unc.edu/content/view/73/01

Avoid these studying traps with help from the University of North Carolina at Chapel Hill. Print out the list and highlight the traps that apply to you. Make a list of the strategies you can use to improve your study habits. Post the list where you can see it often.

4 Test Preparation

http://www.studygs.net/tst.prp1.htm

Read these tips, techniques, and suggestions for preparing for exams from the University of St. Thomas. Write down your feelings about taking tests. What happens to you emotionally and physically? What is your philosophy on test taking? Are tests necessary? Why or why not?

5 Reasons to Review Tests

http://www.mtsu.edu/~studskl/rtrned.html

Middle Tennessee State University offers a dozen practical reasons to look over your returned tests. When else might it be useful to examine your mistakes? Create a chart that describes some mistakes you have made in school, at home, and on the job. What did you do? Why was it wrong? How did you fix it? What did you learn?

18 Taking Exams

Why Learn How to Take Exams?

■ You will be required to take plenty of exams in your college career.

■ Exams may be an important part of admission to graduate school, the job application process, and licensing and certification for various careers.

■ Knowing how to approach an exam can earn you extra grade points.

Learning Experiment

Step 1

Here is a multiple-choice test item from a psychology exam:

> Modern psychological researchers maintain that the mind as well as behavior can be scientifically examined primarily by
>
> a. observing behavior and making inferences about mental functioning.
> b. observing mental activity and making inferences about behavior.
> c. making inferences about behavior.
> d. direct observation of behavior.

If you know the correct answer, circle it now.

Step 2

If you did not know the correct answer, use your reasoning skills to determine the best answer and circle it.

Hints:

1. Which choices do *not* refer to both the mind and behavior? (Answer: choices c and d)
2. Which choice contains an activity that cannot be easily done? (Answer: b—mental activity cannot be observed without specialized medical equipment.)

The Results

Using the hints above, you probably were able to eliminate choices b, c, and d.

Learning Principle (What This Means to You)

Although you probably did not know the correct answer, you were able to figure it out. **When taking exams, trust your reasoning skills to help you figure out correct answers.** In this chapter you will learn how to sharpen your reasoning skills for all types of exams. The manner in which you approach an exam, how you read and answer objective questions, and how carefully you read, organize, and write your answers to an essay exam can influence your grade. This chapter discusses each of these aspects of becoming test-wise and also considers a problem that interferes with many students' ability to do well on exams: test anxiety.

403

GENERAL SUGGESTIONS FOR TAKING EXAMS

The following suggestions will help you approach classroom exams in an organized, systematic way.

Bring Necessary Materials

When going to any exam, be sure to take along any materials you might be asked or allowed to use. Be sure you have an extra pen, and take a pencil in case you must make a drawing or diagram. Take paper—you may need it for computing figures or writing essay answers. Take along anything you have been allowed to use throughout the semester, such as a pocket calculator, conversion chart, or dictionary. If you are not sure whether you may use them, ask the instructor.

Get There on Time

It is important to arrive at the exam room on time, or a few minutes early, to get a seat and get organized before the instructor arrives. If you are late, you may miss instructions and feel rushed as you begin the exam.

If you arrive too early (15 minutes ahead), you risk anxiety induced by panic-stricken students questioning each other, trading last-minute memory tricks, and worrying about how difficult the exam will be.

Sit in the Front of the Room

If you have a choice, the most practical place to sit in an exam room is at the front. There you often receive the test first and get a head start. There, also, you are sure to hear directions and corrections and can easily read any changes written on the chalkboard. Finally, it is easier to concentrate at the front of the room. At the back, you are exposed to distractions, such as a student dropping papers or cheating, or the person in front who is already two pages ahead of you.

Preread the Exam

Before you start to answer any of the questions, take a minute or two to quickly page through the exam, noting the directions, the length, the types of questions, and the general topics covered. Prereading provides an overview of the whole exam. Prereading also helps eliminate the panic you may feel if you go right to the first few questions and find that you are unsure of the answers.

Plan Your Time

After prereading the exam, you will know the numbers and types of questions included. You should then estimate how much time you will spend on each part of the exam. The number of points each section is worth (the point distribution) should be your guide. If, for example, one part of an exam has 20 multiple-choice questions worth one point each and another part has two essays worth 40 points each, you should spend much more time answering the essay questions than working through the multiple-choice items. If the point distribution is not indicated on the test booklet, you may want to ask the instructor what it is.

As you plan your time, be sure to allow three to four minutes at the end of the exam to review what you have done, answering questions you skipped and making any necessary corrections or changes.

To keep track of time, wear a watch. Many classrooms do not have wall clocks, or you may be sitting in a position where the clock is difficult to see.

If you were taking an exam with the following distribution of questions and points, how would you divide your time? Assume the total exam time is 50 minutes.

Type of Question	Number of Questions	Total Points
Multiple-choice	25 questions	25 points
True/false	20 questions	20 points
Essay	2 questions	55 points

You should probably divide your time like this:

Prereading	1–2 minutes
Multiple-choice	15 minutes
True/false	10 minutes
Essay	20 minutes
Review	3–4 minutes

Because the essays are worth twice as many points as either of the other two parts of the exam, it is necessary to spend twice as much time on the essay portion.

Read the Questions Carefully

Most instructors word their questions so that what is expected is clear. A common mistake students make is to read more into the question than is asked for. To avoid this error, read the question several times, paying attention to how it is worded. If you are uncertain what is asked for, try to relate the question to the course content. Don't anticipate hidden meanings or trick questions.

EXERCISE 1

DIRECTIONS For each of the exams described below, estimate how you would divide your time.

1. Time limit: 75 minutes

Type of Question	Number of Questions	Total Points
Multiple-choice	20 questions	40 points
Matching	10 questions	10 points
Essay	2 questions	50 points

How would you divide your time?

Prereading	_____	minutes
Multiple-choice	_____	minutes
Matching	_____	minutes
Essay	_____	minutes
Review	_____	minutes

2. Time limit: 50 minutes

Type of Question	Number of Questions	Total Points
True/false	15 questions	30 points
Fill-in-the-blank	15 questions	30 points
Short answer	10 questions	40 points

How would you divide your time?

Prereading   _____ minutes

True/false   _____ minutes

Fill-in-the-blank   _____ minutes

Short answer   _____ minutes

Review   _____ minutes

HINTS FOR TAKING OBJECTIVE EXAMS

When taking objective exams—usually multiple choice, true/false, or matching—remember the following hints, which may net you a few more points.

Read the Directions

Before answering any questions, read the directions. Often an instructor may want the correct answer marked in a particular way (underlined rather than circled). The directions may contain crucial information that you must know in order to answer the questions correctly. If you were to ignore directions such as the following and assume the test questions were of the usual type, you could lose a considerable number of points.

True/False Directions

Read each statement. If the statement is true, mark a T in the blank to the left of the item. If the statement is false, add and/or subtract words in such a way as to make the statement true.

Multiple-Choice Directions

Circle all the choices that correctly complete the statement.

Without reading the true/false directions, you would not know that you should correct incorrect statements. Without reading the multiple-choice directions, you would not know that you are to choose more than one answer.

Leave Nothing Blank

Before turning in your exam, be sure you have answered every question. If you have no idea about the correct answer to a question, guess—you might be right. On a true/false test, your chances of being correct are 50 percent; on a four-choice multiple-choice question, your odds are 25 percent.

Students frequently turn in tests with some items unanswered because they leave difficult questions blank, planning to return to them later. Then, in the rush to finish everything, they forget to go back to them. The best way to avoid this problem is to enter what look like the best answers and mark the question numbers with an X or a check mark; then, if you have time at the end of the exam, you can give them more thought. If you run out of time, at least you will have attempted to answer them.

Look for Clues

If you encounter a difficult question, choose what seems to be the best answer, mark the question so that you can return to it, and keep the item in mind as you go through the rest of the exam. Sometimes you will see some piece of information later in the exam that reminds you of a fact or idea. At other times you may notice information that, if true, contradicts an answer you have already chosen.

Don't Change Answers Without Good Reason

When reviewing your exam answers, don't make a change unless you have a specific reason for doing so. If a later test item made you remember information for a previous item, by all means make a change. If, however, you are just having second thoughts about an answer, leave it alone. Your first guess is usually the best one.

Hints for Taking True/False Tests

When taking true/false tests, watch for words that qualify or change the meaning of a statement; often, just one word makes it true or false. Consider the following oversimplified example.

All dogs are white.

Some dogs are white.

The first statement is obviously false, whereas the second is true. In each statement, only one word determined whether the statement was true or false. Of course, the words and statements are much more complicated on college true/false exams, but you will find that one word often determines whether a statement is true or false. Read the following examples:

All paragraphs must have a stated main idea.

Spelling, punctuation, and handwriting *always* affect the grade given to an essay answer.

When taking notes on a lecture, try to write down *everything* the speaker says.

In each of these examples, the italicized words modify—or limit—the truth of the statement. When reading a true/false statement, look carefully for any limiting words, such as *all, some, none, never, always, usually, frequently,* and *most of the time.* Overlooking these words may cost you several points on an exam.

Read Two-Part Statements Carefully

Occasionally, you may find a statement with two or more parts. In answering these items, remember that both or all parts of the statement must be true in order for it to be correctly marked true. If part of the statement is true and another part is false, then mark the statement false. Here is an example.

The World Health Organization (WHO) has been successful in its campaign to eliminate smallpox and malaria.

Although it is true that WHO has been successful in eliminating smallpox, malaria is still a world health problem and has not been eliminated. Because only part of this statement is true, it should be marked false.

Look for Negative and Double-Negative Statements

Test items that use negative words or word parts can be confusing. Words such as *no, none, never, not,* and *cannot* and beginnings of words such as *in-, dis-, un-, it-,* and *ir-* are easy to miss and always alter the meaning of the statement. For items that contain negative statements, make it a habit to underline or circle them as you read.

Statements that contain two negatives, such as the following, are even more confusing.

> It is not unreasonable to expect Vietnam veterans to continue to be angry about their exposure to Agent Orange.

In reading these statements, remember that two negatives balance or cancel out each other. "Not unreasonable," then, can be interpreted to mean "reasonable."

Make Your Best Guess

When all else fails and you are unable to reason out the answer to an item, use these three last-resort rules of thumb:

1. **Absolute statements tend to be false.** Because there are very few things that are always true and for which there are no exceptions, your best guess is to mark statements that contain words such as *always, all, never,* or *none* as false.
2. **Mark any item that contains unfamiliar terminology or facts as false.** If you've studied the material thoroughly, trust that you would recognize as true anything that was a part of the course content.
3. **When all else fails, it is better to guess true than false.** It is more difficult for instructors to write false statements than true statements. As a result, many exams have more true items than false.

EXERCISE 2

DIRECTIONS   The following true/false test is based on content presented in the reading "Your Appearance, Good or Bad, Can Affect the Size of Your Paycheck" in Part Eight on page 501. Read each item. Then find and underline the single word that, if changed or deleted, could change the truth or falsity of the statement. In the space provided at the left, indicate whether the statement is true or false by marking T for true and F for false.

_____ 1. All of the tropical rainforests in Cote d'Ivoire have dwindled away.

_____ 2. The *Proceedings of the National Academy of Sciences* identified six types of human activities that enhance the Earth's resources.

_____ 3. An ecological footprint is the amount of space needed to supply all of the demands of one person.

_____ 4. Human activities have reduced the productivity of the Earth's forests and grasslands by 50 percent.

_____   5. Overgrazing and deforestation decrease the productivity of land in developing countries.

_____   6. One-quarter of the world's agricultural land is suffering moderate to severe erosion.

_____   7. Water supplies beneath the ground are called aquifers.

_____   8. Neither China nor India is rapidly depleting aquifers to supply its needs.

_____   9. The total world fish harvest has gradually declined since its peak in the late 1960s.

_____   10. The standard of living in developed countries is much higher than that of the rest of the world.

Hints for Taking Matching Tests

Matching tests require you to select items in one list that can be paired with items in a second list. Use the following tips to complete matching tests:

1. **Before answering any items, glance through both lists to get an overview of the subjects and topics the test covers.** Next, try to discover a pattern. Are you asked to match dates with events, terms with meanings, people with accomplishments?
2. **Answer the items you are sure of first, lightly crossing off items as you use them.**
3. **Don't choose the first answer you see that seems correct; items later in the list may be better choices.**
4. **If the first column consists of short words or phrases and the second is made up of lengthy definitions or descriptions, save time by "reverse matching"; that is, look for the word or phrase in column 1 that fits each item in column 2.**

Hints for Taking Short-Answer Tests

Short-answer tests require you to write a brief answer, usually in list or sentence form. Here is an example:

> List three events that increased U.S. involvement in the Vietnam War.

In answering short-answer questions, be sure to:

1. **Use point distribution as a clue to how many pieces of information to include.** For a nine-point item asking you to describe the characteristics of a totalitarian government, give at least three ideas.
2. **Plan what you will say before starting to write.**
3. **Use the amount of space provided, especially if it varies for different items, as a clue to how much you should write.**

Hints for Taking Fill-in-the-Blank Tests

Items that ask you to fill in a missing word or phrase within a sentence require recall of information rather than recognition of the correct answer. It is important, therefore, to look for clues that will trigger your recall.

1. **Look for key words in the sentence, and use them to decide what subject matter and topic the item covers.**
2. **Decide what type of information is required.** Is it a date, name, place, or new term?
3. **Use the grammatical structure of the sentence to determine the type of word called for.** Is it a noun, verb, or qualifier?

Hints for Taking Multiple-Choice Tests

Multiple-choice exams are among the most frequently used types of exams and are often the most difficult. The following suggestions should improve your success in taking multiple-choice tests.

Read all choices first, considering each.

Do not stop with the second or third choice, even if you are sure that you have found the correct answer. Remember, on most multiple-choice tests, your job is to pick the *best* answer, and the last choice may be better than the preceding answers.

Some multiple-choice tests include combinations of previously listed choices.

See the following test item:

> Among the causes of slow reading is (are)
> a. lack of comprehension.
> b. reading word by word rather than in phrases.
> c. poorly developed vocabulary.
> d. making too few fixations per line.
> e. a and b
> f. a, b, and c
> g. a, b, c, and d

The addition of choices that are combinations of previous choices tends to be confusing. Treat each choice, when combined with the stem, as a true or false statement. As you consider each choice, mark it true or false. If you find more than one true statement, select the choice that contains the letters of all the true statements you identified.

Use logic and common sense.

Even if you are unfamiliar with the subject matter, it is sometimes possible to reason out the correct answer. The following item is taken from a history exam on Japanese–American relations after World War II:

> Prejudice and discrimination are
> a. harmful to our society because they waste our economic, political, and social resources.
> b. helpful because they ensure against attack from within.
> c. harmful because they create negative images of the United States in foreign countries.
> d. helpful because they keep the majority pure and united against minorities.

Through logic and common sense, it is possible to eliminate choices b and d. Prejudice and discrimination are seldom, if ever, regarded as positive, desirable, or helpful, because they are inconsistent with democratic ideals. Having narrowed your answer to two choices, a or c, you can see that choice a offers a stronger, more substantial reason why prejudice and discrimination are harmful. What other countries think of the United States is not as serious as the waste of economic, political, and social resources.

Study any items that are very similar.

When two choices seem very close and you cannot choose between them, stop and examine each. First, try to express each in your own words. Then analyze how they differ. Often this process will lead you to recognize the correct answer.

Look for qualifying words.

As in true/false tests, the presence of qualifying words is important. Because many statements, ideas, principles, and rules have exceptions, you should be careful in selecting items that contain such words as *best, always, all, no, entirely,* and *completely,* all of which suggest that something is always true, without exception. Also be careful of statements that contain such words as *none, never,* and *worst,* which suggest things that without exception are never true. Items containing words that provide for some level of exception or qualification are more likely to be correct; a few examples are *often, usually, less, seldom, few, more,* and *most.*

In the following example, note the use of italicized qualifying words:

In most societies
a. values are *highly* consistent.
b. people *often* believe and act on values that are contradictory.
c. *all* legitimate organizations support the values of the majority.
d. values of equality *never* exist alongside prejudice and discrimination.

In this question, items c and d contain the words *all* and *never,* suggesting that those statements are true without exception. Thus, if you did not know the answer to this question based on content, you could eliminate items c and d on the basis of the level of qualifiers.

Some multiple-choice questions require application of knowledge or information.

You may be asked to analyze a hypothetical situation or to use what you have learned to solve a problem. Here is an example taken from a psychology test:

Carrie is uncomfortable in her new home in New Orleans. When she gets dressed up and leaves her home and goes to the supermarket to buy the week's groceries, she gets nervous and upset and thinks that something is going to happen to her. She feels the same way when walking her four-year-old son Jason in the park or playground.
   Carrie is suffering from
   a. shyness.
   b. a phobia.
   c. a personality disorder.
   d. hypertension.

In answering questions of this type, start by crossing out unnecessary information that can distract you. In the preceding example, distracting information includes the woman's name, her son's name, where she lives, why she goes to the store, and so forth.

Answer the items using your own words.

If a question concerns steps in a process or the order in which events occur, or any other information that is likely to confuse you, ignore the choices and use the margin or scrap paper to jot down the information as you can recall it. Then select the choice that matches what you wrote.

Avoid selecting answers that are unfamiliar or that you do not understand.

A choice that looks complicated or uses difficult words is not necessarily correct. If you have studied carefully, a choice that is unfamiliar to you is probably incorrect.

Pick the choice that seems most complete.

As a last resort, when you do not know the answer and are unable to eliminate any of the choices as wrong, guess by picking the one that seems complete and contains the most information. This is a good choice because instructors are always careful to make the best answer completely correct and recognizable. Such a choice often becomes long or detailed.

Make educated guesses.

In most instances, you can eliminate one or more of the choices as obviously wrong. Even if you can eliminate only one choice, you have increased your odds of being correct on a four-choice item from 1 in 4 to 1 in 3. If you can eliminate two choices, you have improved your odds to 1 in 2, or 50 percent. Don't hesitate to play the odds and make a guess—you may gain points.

HINTS FOR TAKING STANDARDIZED TESTS

At various times in college, you may be required to take a standardized test, which is a commercially prepared, timed test used nationally or statewide to measure skills and abilities. Your score compares your performance with that of large numbers of other students throughout the state or the country. The SAT and ACT are examples of standardized tests; many graduate schools require a standardized test as part of their admission process. Following are a few suggestions for taking this type of test:

1. **Most standardized tests are timed, so the pace you work at is a critical factor.** You need to work at a fairly rapid rate, but not so fast as to make careless errors.
2. **Don't plan on finishing the test.** Many of the tests are designed so that no one finishes.
3. **Don't expect to get everything right.** Unlike classroom tests or exams, you are not expected to get all of the answers correct.
4. **Find out if there is a penalty for guessing.** If there is none, then use the last 20 or 30 seconds to randomly fill in an answer for each item that you have not had time to answer. The odds are that you will get one item correct for every four items that you guess.
5. **Get organized before the timing begins.** Line up your answer sheet and test booklet so you can move between them rapidly without losing your place.

HINTS FOR TAKING ESSAY EXAMS

Essay questions are usually graded on two factors: what you say and how you say it. It is not enough, then, simply to include the correct information. The information must be presented in a logical, organized way that demonstrates your understanding of the subject you are writing about. There can be as much as one whole letter grade difference between a well-written and a poorly written essay, although both contain the same basic information. This section offers suggestions for getting as many points as possible on essay exams.

Read the Question

For essay exams, reading the question carefully is the key to writing a correct, complete, and organized answer.

Read the directions first.

The directions may tell you how many essays to answer and how to structure your answer, or they may specify a minimum or maximum length for your answer.

Study the question for clues.

The question usually includes three valuable pieces of information. First, the question tells you the *topic* you are to write about. Second, it contains a *limiting word* that restricts and directs your answer. Finally, the question contains a *key word* or phrase that tells you how to organize and present answers. Read the essay question in this example.

> *(key word) (limiting word)   (topic)   (limiting word)   (topic)*
> Compare the causes of the Vietnam War with the causes of the Korean War.

In this example you have two topics—the Vietnam War and the Korean War. The question also contains a limiting word that restricts your discussion of these topics and tells you what to include in your answer. In this sample question, the limiting word is *causes*. It tells you to limit your answer to a discussion of events that started, or caused, each war. Do not include information about events of the war or its effects. The key word in the sample question is *compare*. It means you should consider the similarities, and possibly the differences, between the causes of the two wars. When directed to compare, you already have some clues as to how your answer should be written. One possibility is to discuss the causes of one war and then the causes of the other and finally to make an overall statement about their similarities. Another choice is to discuss one type of cause for each of the wars, and then go on to discuss another type of cause for each. For instance, you could discuss the economic causes of each and then the political causes of each.

There are several common key words and phrases used in essay questions. They are listed in Figure 18-1 on page 414. Some questions require only knowledge and comprehension, but most require the higher-level thinking skills of applying, analyzing, evaluating, and creating.

**Figure 18-1
Key Words Used in
Essay Questions**

Key Words	Example	Information to Include
Understanding		
Discuss	Discuss Laetrile as a treatment for cancer.	Consider important characteristics and main points.
Enumerate	Enumerate the reasons for U.S. withdrawal from Vietnam.	List or discuss one by one.
Define	Define thermal pollution and include several examples.	Give an accurate meaning of the term with enough detail to show that you really understand it.
Applying		
Illustrate	State Boyle's law and illustrate its use.	Explain, using examples that demonstrate or clarify a point or idea.
Analyzing		
Compare	Compare the causes of air pollution with those of water pollution.	Show how items are similar as well as different; include details or examples.
Contrast	Contrast the health-care systems in the United States with those in England.	Show how the items are different; include details or examples.
Explain	Explain why black Americans are primarily city dwellers.	Give facts, details, or reasons that make the idea or concept clear and understandable.
Describe	Describe the experimentation that tests whether plants are sensitive to music.	Tell how something looks or happened, including how, who, where, and why.
Justify	Justify former President Carter's attempt to rescue the hostages in Iran.	Give reasons that support an action, event, or policy.
Evaluating		
Evaluate	Evaluate the strategies our society has used to treat mental illness.	React to the topic in a logical way. Discuss the merits, strengths, weaknesses, advantages, or limitations of the topic.
Criticize	Criticize the current environmental controls to combat air pollution.	Make judgments about quality or worth; include both positive and negative aspects.
Prove	Prove that ice is a better cooling agent than water.	Demonstrate or establish that a concept or theory is correct, logical, or valid.
Creating		
Trace	Trace the history of legalized prostitution in Nevada.	Describe the development or progress of a particular trend, event, or process in chronological order.
Summarize	Summarize the arguments for and those against offering sex education courses in public schools.	Cover the major points in brief form; use a sentence-and-paragraph form.

Watch for Questions with Several Parts

A common mistake that students often make is to fail to answer all parts of an essay question, perhaps because they get involved with answering the first part and forget about the remaining parts. Questions with several parts come in two forms. The most obvious form is as follows:

> For the U.S. invasion of Grenada, discuss the
> a. causes.
> b. immediate effects.
> c. long-range political implications.

A less obvious form that does not stand out as a several-part question is the following:

> Discuss *how* the Equal Rights Amendment was developed and *why* it has aroused controversy.

When you find a question of this type, underline or circle the limiting words to serve as a reminder.

Make Notes as You Read

As you read a question the first time, you may begin to formulate an answer. When this occurs, jot down a few key words that will bring these thoughts back when you are ready to organize your answer.

EXERCISE 3

DIRECTIONS   Read each of the following essay questions. For each question, underline the topic, circle the limiting word, and place a box around the key word.

1. Discuss the long-term effects of the trend toward a smaller, more self-contained family structure.
2. Trace the development of monopolies in the late nineteenth and early twentieth centuries in America.
3. Explain one effect of the Industrial Revolution on each of three of the following:
   a. transportation
   b. capitalism
   c. socialism
   d. population growth
   e. scientific research
4. Discuss the reason why, although tropical plants have very large leaves and most desert plants have very small leaves, cactus grows equally well in both habitats.
5. Describe the events leading up to the War of 1812.
6. Compare and contrast the purpose and procedures in textbook marking and lecture note taking.
7. Briefly describe a complete approach to reading and studying a textbook chapter that will enable you to handle a test on that material successfully.
8. List four factors that influence memory or recall ability and explain how each can be used to make study more efficient.
9. Summarize the techniques a speaker or lecturer may use to emphasize the important concepts and ideas in a lecture.
10. Explain the value and purpose of the prereading technique and list the steps involved in prereading a textbook chapter.

EXERCISE 4   **DIRECTIONS**   Write ten possible essay questions for a course you are taking. *Be sure to write at least one question at each level of thinking.*

Organize Your Answer

As mentioned earlier, a well-written, organized essay often gets a higher grade than a carelessly constructed one. Read each of these examples and notice how they differ. Each essay was written in response to this instruction on a psychology final exam: Describe the stages involved in the memory process.

Example 1

Memory is important to everybody's life. Memory has special ways to help you get a better recollection of things and ideas. Psychologists believe that memory has three stages: encoding, storage, and retrieval.

In the encoding stage, you are putting facts and ideas into a code, usually words, and filing them away in your memory. Encoding involves preparing information for storage in memory.

The second stage of memory is storage. It is the stage that most people call memory. It involves keeping information so that it is accessible for use later in time. How well information is stored can be affected by old information already stored and newer information that is added later.

The third step in memory is retrieval, which means the ability to get back information that is in storage. There are two types of retrieval—recognition and recall. In recognition, you have to be able to identify the correct information from several choices. In recall, you have to pull information directly from your memory without using the recognition type of retrieval.

Example 2

Memory is very complicated in how it works. It involves remembering things that are stored in your mind and being able to pull them out when you want to remember them. When you pull information out of your memory it is called retrieval. How well you can remember something is affected by how you keep the information in your mind and how you put it in. When keeping, or storing, information you have to realize that this information will be affected by old information already in your memory. Putting information in your memory is called encoding, and it means that you store facts and ideas in word form in your memory. Information stored in your memory can also be influenced by information that you add to your memory later.

There are two ways you can retrieve information. You can either recognize it or recall it. When you recognize information you are able to spot the correct information among other information. When you recall information you have to pull information out of your head. Recall is what you have to do when you write an essay exam.

While these two essays contain practically the same information, the first will probably receive a higher grade. In this essay, it is easy to see that the writer knows that the memory process has three stages and knows how to explain each. The writer opens the essay by stating that there are three stages and then devotes one paragraph to each of the three stages.

In the second essay, it is not easy to identify the stages of memory. The paragraphs are not organized according to stages in the memory process. The writer does not write about one stage at a time in a logical order. Retrieval is mentioned first; then storage and retrieval are discussed further. At the end, the writer returns to the topic of retrieval and gives further information.

Here are a few suggestions to help you organize your answer.

1. **Think before you start to write.** Decide what information is called for and what you will include.
2. **Make a brief word or phrase outline of the ideas you want to include in your answer.**
3. **Study your word outline and rearrange its order.** You may want to put major topics and important ideas first and less important points toward the end, or you may decide to organize your answer chronologically, discussing events early in time near the beginning and mentioning more recent events near the end. The topic you are discussing will largely determine the order of presentation.
4. **If the point value of the essay is given, use that information as a clue to how many separate points or ideas may be expected.** For an essay worth 25 points, for example, discussion of five major ideas may be expected.

Use Correct Paragraph Form

Be sure to write your answers in complete, correct sentences and to include only one major point in each paragraph. Each paragraph should have a main idea, usually expressed in one sentence. The remainder of the paragraph should explain, prove, or support the main idea you state. Also, use correct spelling and punctuation.

Begin Your Answer with a Thesis Statement

Your first sentence should state what the entire essay is about and suggest how you intend to approach it. If a question asks you to discuss the practical applications of Newton's three laws of motion, you might begin by writing, "Newton's laws of motion have many practical applications." Then you should proceed to name the three laws and their practical applications, devoting one paragraph to each law. If you have time, your final paragraph may summarize or review the major points you covered in the essay.

Make Your Main Points Easy to Find

Because many essay exam readers have a large number of papers to read in a short period of time, they tend to skim (look for key ideas) rather than read everything; therefore, state each main point at the beginning of a new paragraph. For lengthy answers or multipart questions, you might use headings or the same numbering used in the question. Use space (skip a line) to divide your answers into different parts.

Include Sufficient Explanation

Instructors often criticize essay answers because they fail to explain or to support ideas fully. If you include only one major idea per paragraph, you avoid this danger and force yourself to explain major points. Also, if you answer an essay question with the intent of convincing your instructor that you have learned the material, then you are likely to include enough explanation. Another rule of thumb is useful: Too much information is better than too little.

Avoid Opinions and Judgments

Unless the question specifically asks you to do so, do not include your personal reaction to the topic. When you are asked to state your reactions and opinions, include reasons to support them.

Make Your Answer Readable

An instructor cannot help having personal reactions to your answer. Try to make those reactions positive by handing in a paper that is as easy to read as possible. It is annoying to an instructor to try to read poor handwriting and carelessly written answers.

1. **Use ink—it is easier to read than pencil and is less likely to smear.**
2. **Use clean, unwrinkled $8\frac{1}{2}$-by-11-inch paper.** Reading a handful of small sheets is difficult and confusing.
3. **Number your pages and put your name on each sheet.**
4. **Do not scratch out sentences you want to omit.** Draw a single line through each and write *omit* in the margin.
5. **If the paper is thin or the ink runs, write on only one side.**
6. **Leave plenty of space between questions.** Leave a one- to two-inch margin at each side. The instructor will need space to write comments.

Proofread Your Answer

After you have written an essay, read it twice. Before reading your essay the first time, read the question again. Then check to see that you have included all necessary facts and information and that you have adequately explained each fact. Add anything you feel improves your answer. Then read the essay a second time, checking and correcting all the mechanical aspects of your writing. Check for hard-to-read words and errors in spelling and punctuation. Again, make all necessary corrections.

If You Run Out of Time

Despite careful planning of exam time, you may run out of time before you finish writing one of the essays. If this happens, try to jot down the major ideas that you would discuss fully if you had time. Often, your instructor will give you partial credit for this type of response, especially if you mention that you ran out of time.

If You Don't Know the Answer

Despite careful preparation, you may forget an answer. If this should happen, do not leave a blank page; write something. Attempt to answer the question—you may hit upon some partially correct information. The main reason for writing something is to give the instructor a chance to give you a few points for trying. If you leave a blank page, your instructor has no choice but to give you zero points. Usually when you lose full credit on one essay, you automatically eliminate your chance to get a high passing grade.

EXERCISE 5

DIRECTIONS Organize and write a response to one of the following essay questions.

1. Six organizational patterns are commonly used in textbook writing: comparison–contrast, definition, time sequence, cause–effect, classification, and enumeration. Discuss the usefulness of these patterns in predicting and answering essay exam questions.
2. Describe three strategies that have improved your reading skills. Explain why each is effective.
3. Describe your approach to time management. Include specific techniques and organizational strategies that you have found effective.

CONTROLLING TEST ANXIETY

Do you get nervous and anxious just before an exam begins? If so, your response is normal; most students feel some level of anxiety before an exam. In fact, research indicates that some anxiety is beneficial and improves your performance by sharpening your attention and keeping you alert.

Research also shows that very high levels of anxiety can interfere with test performance. Some students become extremely nervous and emotional and lose their concentration. Their minds seem to go blank, and they are unable to recall material they have learned. They also report physical symptoms: their hearts pound, it is difficult to swallow, or they break out in a cold sweat.

Test anxiety is a complicated psychological response to a threatening situation, and it may be related to other problems and past experiences. The following suggestions are intended to help you ease test anxiety. If these suggestions do not help, the next step is to discuss the problem with a counselor.

Be Sure Test Anxiety Is Not an Excuse

Many students say they have test anxiety when actually they have not studied and reviewed carefully or thoroughly. The first question, then, that you must answer honestly is this: Are you in fact *unprepared* for the exam, and do you therefore have every reason to be anxious?

Get Used to Test Situations

Psychologists who have studied anxiety use processes called "systematic desensitization" and "simulation" to reduce test anxiety. Basically, these are ways of becoming less sensitive to or disturbed by tests by putting yourself in testlike conditions. These techniques are complicated processes often used by trained therapists, but here are a few ways you can use these processes to reduce test anxiety:

1. **Become familiar with the building and room in which the test is given.** Visit the room when it is empty and take a seat. Visualize yourself taking a test there.
2. **Develop practice or review tests.** Treat them as real tests, and work on them in situations as similar as possible to real test conditions.
3. **Practice working with time limits.** Set an alarm clock and work only until it rings.
4. **Take as many tests as possible, even though you dislike them.** Always take advantage of practice tests and make-up exams. Buy a review book for

the course you are taking or a workbook that accompanies your text. Treat each section as an exam, and have someone else correct your work.

Control Negative Thinking

Major factors that contribute to test anxiety are self-doubt and negative thinking. Just before and during an exam, test-anxious students often think, "I won't do well." "I'm going to fail." "What will my friends think of me when I get a failing grade?" This type of thinking predisposes you to failure; you are telling yourself that you expect to fail. By thinking in this way, you undermine your own chances for success.

One solution to this problem is to send yourself positive rather than negative messages, such as, "I have studied hard and I deserve to pass." "I know that I know the material." "I know I can do it!" And remember, being well prepared is one of the best ways to reduce test anxiety.

Compose Yourself Before the Test Begins

Don't take an exam on an empty stomach; you will feel queasy. Have something light or bland to eat. Some students find that a brisk walk outside before going to an exam helps to reduce tension.

Before you begin the test, take 30 seconds or so to calm yourself, to slow down, and to focus your attention. Take several deep breaths, close your eyes, and visualize yourself calmly working through the test. Remind yourself that you have prepared carefully and have every reason to do well.

Answer Easy Questions First

To give yourself an initial boost of confidence, begin with a section of the test that seems easy. This will help you to work calmly, and you will prove to yourself that you can handle the test.

LEARNING COLLABORATIVELY

DIRECTIONS   Each member of the class should write an answer to the following essay question, which is based on the reading "The Talk of the Sandbox: How Johnny and Suzy's Playground Chatter Prepares Them for Life at the Office" in Part Eight, page 470.

> Explain how the roles boys and girls assume when they play is similar to the roles they will assume in the workplace.

You may not refer to the reading as you write your answer. Working in pairs, compare your answers, noting the strengths and weaknesses of the essays. Then rewrite and combine your answers to produce a stronger or more nearly complete response.

APPLYING YOUR LEARNING

Maria is taking an American history course. The instructor announced that the next exam will cover only three chapters on the Constitution—its origins, history, and current applications and interpretations. Further, students are allowed to bring their textbook and both lecture and study notes to class and use them during the exam. As most students breathed a sigh of relief, the instructor cautioned, "It's not as easy as you think!" Still, many students in the class are not preparing for this exam at all. Maria knows she should prepare, but she is uncertain about what to do.

1. What type of questions (multiple-choice, true/false, short answer, or essay) do you think Maria's exam will contain?
2. Why would the instructor allow students to bring materials to the exam? What types of learning is she emphasizing? What is she not emphasizing?
3. How should Maria prepare for this exam?

APPLYING YOUR SKILLS: Sample Textbook Chapter

1. Write an answer to one of the following essay questions:
   a. Name and define the four stages of culture shock.
   b. What is the difference between high-context cultures and low-context cultures? Give examples.
   c. Explain the difference between individualist and collectivist orientations.
2. Answer each of the following multiple-choice questions.

Multiple Choice *(from DeVito, Accompanying Web Site for* Messages.*)*

_____ 1. The process through which one develops a cultural identity is

    a. cultural assimilation.
    b. enculturation.
    c. collectivism.
    d. intercultural communication.

_____ 2. A culture in which competition is promoted is

    a. high-context.
    b. individualist.
    c. collectivist.
    d. low-context.

_____ 3. In a _____ culture, women are supposed to be modest, oriented to maintaining the quality of life, and tender.

    a. feminine
    b. masculine
    c. collectivist
    d. individualist

_____ 4. "She's a bad driver because she's a woman" is an example of

    a. disparagement.
    b. overattribution.
    c. ethnocentrism.
    d. accommodation.

_____ 5. Which of the following terms would be inappropriate to use when referring to someone with a disability?

    a. seizure

    b. person with cerebral palsy

    c. wheelchair user

    d. disabled person

_____ 6. If you have a disability you should NOT

    a. ask someone to push your chair for you.

    b. ignore it when people appear to be uncomfortable with your disability.

    c. talk about your disability.

    d. be understanding with people who are uncomfortable with you disability.

_____ 7. Unique cultural _____ influence the messages you receive and how you receive them.

    a. filters

    b. rules

    c. mores

    d. barriers

_____ 8. Communication between Italian Americans and German American is

    a. international communication.

    b. interracial communication.

    c. intercultural communication.

    d. interethnic communication.

_____ 9. Communication between African Americans and Asian Americans is

    a. international communication.

    b. interracial communication.

    c. interethnic communication.

    d. intercultural communication.

_____ 10. When the author says that culture differs by orientation, he is referring to

    a. high-context vs. low-context.

    b. masculine vs. feminine.

    c. individualist vs. collectivist.

    d. ethnocentrism vs. openness

QUESTIONS FOR DISCUSSION

1. What techniques do you use to overcome test anxiety? What techniques are particularly effective for various types of examinations?

2. What types of exams are the least stressful for people with each learning style? What can people do to become more relaxed when taking various types of examinations?

3. Why do professors use various types of objective and essay tests in order to evaluate student learning? From the professor's perspective, what are the advantages and disadvantages of using each type of examination?

4. Why do you think a person's first guess on a multiple-choice test item is usually the best one?

SELF-TEST SUMMARY

1. How can you improve the way you take most exams?

You can improve your exam grades by approaching tests in a systematic, organized manner. This involves taking the necessary materials, arriving on time, deliberately choosing a seat in a nondistracting section of the room, prereading the exam, planning the time you will devote to various sections of the exam, and reading the questions carefully.

2. What can you do to improve the way you take most objective exams?

When taking any type of objective exam, read the directions carefully, leave nothing blank, and look for clues that will help you recall the information. When taking true/false tests, you should also read two-part statements carefully and be aware of negative words or word parts. When you have no idea of the answer, make your best guess by marking extreme statements and those that contain unfamiliar terms as false and all others as true.

For multiple-choice tests, you should make educated guesses by reading the choices carefully, narrowing them down by using reasoning power, paying attention to qualifying words, and considering the choices in light of what you know about the topic. When all else fails, eliminate unfamiliar or confusing items and choose an answer that seems complete.

When taking short-answer tests, use the point distributions and the amount of space provided to determine how much to write, and plan what to write beforehand.

For fill-in-the-blank tests, decide what kind of information is being asked for by the key words in, and grammatical structure of, the sentence.

3. What can you do to improve the way you take essay exams?

When taking an essay exam, it is important to read the question carefully, reading the directions, noting all parts, and looking for clues in the question to determine exactly what type of response your instructor wants. Essay answers should be carefully organized and written in an easy-to-read form. This can be achieved by including a topic sentence in each paragraph, using numbering and headings, including enough information to prove your point, and stating opinions and judgments only when the question asks for them. Take pains to make your answer readable, and carefully proofread for accuracy, grammar, and mechanics. If you run out of time or your memory fails, you may be able to earn some credit by jotting down an outline or writing something relevant to the subject of the essay on the page.

4. How can you control test anxiety?

Too much test anxiety can seriously affect your performance on exams. You can relieve it by being prepared for the exam; becoming familiar with the testing location, conditions, and time limits; controlling negative thoughts; taking time to compose yourself near the time of the exam; and beginning with the easy questions for an initial boost of confidence.

DIRECTIONS Write the letter of the choice that best completes each statement in the space provided.

CHECKING YOUR RECALL

_____ 1. The best way to approach an exam is to
   a. plan to arrive at least 30 minutes before the exam begins.
   b. sit near the back of the class.
   c. bring only a pencil with you.
   d. preread the exam before you answer any questions.

_____ 2. Neil's history exam has a total of 100 points, divided as follows: ten multiple-choice questions worth 20 points, five short-answer questions worth 20 points, five true/false questions worth 10 points, and one essay question worth 50 points. Based on this information, Neil should plan to spend most of his time on the
   a. true/false questions.
   b. short-answer questions.
   c. multiple-choice questions.
   d. essay question.

_____ 3. One thing to remember when taking an objective exam is that
   a. the directions for all objective tests are the same.
   b. you should leave difficult questions blank.
   c. absolute statements tend to be true.
   d. your first guess is usually the best one.

_____ 4. An example of a limiting word in a true/false statement is
   a. always.
   b. however.
   c. when.
   d. because.

_____ 5. On a multiple-choice test, the qualifying word most likely to indicate a correct statement is
   a. always.
   b. usually.
   c. best.
   d. worst.

APPLYING YOUR SKILLS

_____ 6. All of the following suggestions can help improve your performance on multiple-choice exams _except_
   a. choosing the answer that seems most complete.
   b. using logic and common sense.
   c. answering the item first in your own words.
   d. choosing the answer that is unfamiliar to you.

_____ 7. Graham is taking a standardized test for admission to college. One thing he should know about this type of test is that
   a. it is most important that he finish the test.
   b. he is expected to get most of the answers correct.
   c. he should guess on all the items he doesn't know, regardless of how the test is scored.
   d. he should work at a fairly quick rate because the test is probably timed.

_____ 8. In order to reduce test anxiety, you should try to do all of the following _except_
   a. become familiar with the testing location.
   b. avoid taking practice tests and make-up exams.
   c. control negative thinking.
   d. practice working within time limits.

_____ 9. Of the following essay exam questions, the one that asks you to give reasons that support an idea is:
   a. Define symbiosis and give several examples.
   b. Evaluate the strategies our society uses to deal with homelessness.
   c. Justify President George W. Bush's use of the military against Iraq.
   d. State Boyle's law and illustrate its use.

_____ 10. When you are writing an essay exam answer, you should typically try to do all of the following _except_
   a. begin with a thesis statement.
   b. use correct paragraph form.
   c. provide sufficient explanation.
   d. include your personal reaction to the topic.

MULTIMEDIA *Activities*

Taking Exams

1 Create a mutiple-choice test about yourself for others to take. Include about ten questions such as "What is my favorite snack?" or "What instrument have I always wanted to play?" and give four choices. Distribute the test to friends and family. How well do you think they know you?

2 Watch a movie with some friends. After the movie, have each person write a test question that requires a paragraph answer. Take the test and compare your answers. How do the test questions reveal each person's perspective of the film?

3 Practice Test Made by Students

http://www.mtsu.edu/~studskl/practest.html

Students from Middle Tennessee State University created this practice test that reviews how to take true/false and multiple-choice exams. Test yourself!

4 Special Suggestions for Problem Tests

http://caps.unc.edu/content/view/71/0/1/3/

The University of North Carolina at Chapel Hill offers some useful tips for taking exams that involve solving math or science problems. List some other specialized tests (for example, a driver's license test) and specific preparation techniques. Try to think of tests that are given outside of the academic realm.

5 Test Taking Skills

http://www.cla.purdue.edu/asc/resources/tt_skills.pdf

This site from Purdue University gives suggestions to help students "show what they know." Imagine that you will be giving a presentation based on this Web site. Create a poster, graphic organizer, or speech that teaches these suggestions.

19 Improving Your Reading Rate and Flexibility

Why Learn to Improve Your Reading Rate?

- Reading takes time; if you can learn to read faster, you will save time.

- Not everything on a page is equally important. If you can learn to read selectively, you will save time.

Learning Experiment

Step 1

The following paragraph discusses one method by which new products are developed. Read the paragraph only until you get to the words "STOP HERE."

> Me-toos are products that are new to a firm but not new to the marketplace. Companies create "me-toos" because they believe there is room in the market for another competitor, and the projected returns outweigh the risks. For example, STOP HERE when McDonald's decided to enter the fast-food breakfast business, its product was new to the company even though a fast-food breakfast was not new to the market. Procter & Gamble has entered the "me-too" game with both disposable training pants and ultra-thin diapers—two offerings that enable the firm to play catch-up with diaper developments by Kimberly-Clark.

Step 2

Based on what you read, predict what the remainder of the paragraph will contain and write it below.

_____

_____

_____

_____

Step 3

Now, go back and check: Did you predict accurately?

The Results

You have probably discovered that you can predict the content of paragraphs from their topic sentences. The experiment above demonstrates that some parts of a paragraph are more important than others.

Learning Principle (What This Means to You)

Successful students read and learn selectively. You should not read every paragraph in the same way. Instead, you should vary your technique and approach depending on the nature of the assignment and what you are expected to learn from it. This chapter will show you how to adjust your reading rate and reading technique to suit the material you are reading and your purpose for reading it. You will also learn how to skim and scan, alternatives to reading a text in its entirety.

427

BUILDING YOUR READING RATE

Reading rate, the speed at which you read, is measured in words per minute (wpm). What should be your reading rate? Is it better to be a fast reader or a slow reader? Does a good reader read every word? You should be able to read at 100, 200, 300, and 400 wpm; you should be both a fast *and* a slow reader; good readers are often "word skippers." These answers may seem strange or even contradictory, but they are nevertheless true. You should strive to improve your reading rate in order to become a more efficient reader, but you should also be able to change your rate and method of reading to fit different situations and different types of reading material.

To read faster, you must improve your capacity to process information rapidly. Instead of thinking about your eyes and how they move, concentrate on getting information quickly from the printed page. Reading at a faster rate involves understanding ideas and how they interrelate.

By working through this book, you have learned skills and techniques that have improved your comprehension. Many techniques that improve comprehension also improve rate. Reading faster is often a combination of pushing yourself to higher reading speeds on different types of materials and learning and applying several new techniques. The following suggestions will help you to read faster.

Avoid Roadblocks to Reading Efficiency

Certain poor reading habits often carry over from when you first learned to read. These are (1) moving your head as you read, (2) moving your lips as you read, and (3) using your finger or pen to keep your place on the line. Each of these habits can slow you down and contribute to poor comprehension.

Moving Your Head

Moving your head rather than just your eyes across the line of print prevents you from reading at even a normal rate and also creates strain and muscle fatigue. Ask someone to check to see whether you move your head while reading; this person should check when you are not consciously thinking about the problem. One of the easiest ways to break this habit is to sit with your elbow up on your desk with your hand cupping your chin. If you start to move your head, you will feel your hand and forearm move, and this will remind you to correct the habit.

Moving Your Lips

Moving your lips limits your reading rate. The average adult rate of speech (pronouncing words out loud) is 125 words per minute, whereas the average adult rate for silent reading is 250 to 300 words per minute. Thus, moving your lips can really slow your silent reading down—by as much as half. However, there is one situation in which lip movement may be appropriate. When you are reading something that is extremely difficult or complicated, you may find that moving your lips or even whispering aloud as you read helps you to understand the material.

To eliminate this habit, sit in a position in which part of your hand or your fingers touch your lips. If you move your lips while reading, you will feel the movement on your hand or fingers.

Keeping Your Place on the Line

Another bad habit is keeping your place on a line of print by moving your finger or a pen or pencil across the line as you read. This practice causes very slow, word-by-word reading. The solution is simple—tightly grasp the book with both hands. This will prevent you from following across the line with your finger or another object. Be careful you don't cheat and slide your thumb down the margin as a guide to where you are on the page. If you have tried unsuccessfully to control this habit, an eye exam is advisable. Inability to keep one's place on the line is one symptom of a need for corrective lenses.

Preread to Familiarize Yourself with the Material

In Chapter 5, you learned that prereading is a means of improving your comprehension by becoming familiar with the organization and content of material before you begin to read it. In addition to improving your comprehension, prereading increases your reading speed. Because prereading enables you to anticipate the flow of ideas, you will find yourself able to read the material more rapidly.

Try to Eliminate Regressions

As your eyes move across a line, they normally proceed from left to right. Occasionally, instead of moving to the next word, your eyes move backward, or regress, to a word in the same line or in a line already read. Regressions (backward movements) scramble word order, thus creating confusion that slows your pace. Although even very good readers make regressions, your rate and comprehension will improve if you can reduce the number of regressions. The following suggestions will help you eliminate or reduce regressions:

1. **Be conscious of the tendency to regress, and force yourself to continue reading.** Do not allow yourself to regress until you have finished a sentence. Then, if the meaning is still unclear, reread the entire sentence.
2. **If you frequently regress to a word or phrase on a previous line, you might try sliding a 5-by-8-inch index card down the page as you read.** Use the card to cover the lines you have finished reading. This technique will help you break the habit of regression because when you look back, the line will be covered.

Read in Meaning Clusters

Most college students read word by word, looking at each word and then moving to the next one. A more efficient way to read is to combine words that naturally go together. Try not to think of a sentence as a string of single words. Instead, think of it as several word clusters, or phrases. Look at the following sentence:

> The math instructor told her class about the quiz.

"The" does not convey any meaning by itself. While "math" does have meaning, it is intended to describe the next word, "instructor." Rather than reading the first three words separately, try to think of them together as a meaningful phrase—"the math instructor." The remainder of the sentence could then be read as two additional phrases: "told her class" and "about the quiz."

The following brief paragraph has been divided into meaningful word groups separated by slashes. Read the paragraph; as you read, try to see and think of each cluster as a unit of thought rather than as two or three separate words.

> In order / to protect themselves / against loss / drivers purchase / liability insurance. / There are / two types of / liability insurance. / Bodily injury liability / provides payment / if you / are injured / in an accident. / Property damage liability / covers you / when your car / damages the property / of others.

Note that words that make sense together are grouped together. Words are grouped with the words they explain or modify.

To see whether you can group words into meaningful clusters, divide the following paragraph with slashes. The first two lines have been done for you.

> The United States / has changed / in the past one hundred years / from an agricultural economy / to an industrial economy / and has become / the world's first / service economy. What does the term *service* mean? There is no widely accepted definition in marketing. In fact, there is no clear distinction between those firms that are part of a marketing channel for products and those firms that market services. Restaurants are often classified as food distributors because they compete with supermarkets, but restaurants also provide services to customers.
>
> —Kinnear, Bernhardt, and Krentler, *Principles of Marketing*, p. 654

Once you begin reading in word clusters, you will find that meaning falls into place more easily, thus enabling you to read somewhat faster.

Learn to Pace Yourself

An established method of improving your reading rate is *pacing*, which requires maintaining a preestablished rate. Pacing means pushing yourself to read faster than your normal speed while maintaining your level of comprehension. There are numerous ways to pace yourself in order to increase your speed; the following are among the most common methods:

1. **Use an index card.** Slide a 3-by-5-inch card down the page as you read, moving it so that it covers up lines as you read them. This technique will force you along and keep you moving rapidly. Move the card down the page at a fixed pace, and try to keep up while reading. How fast you move the card will depend on the size of the print and the length of the line, so it will vary for each new piece of material you read. At first you will need to experiment to find an appropriate pace. Try to move at a pace that is slightly uncomfortable and that you are not sure you can maintain.
2. **Use your hand or index finger, or a pen or pencil.** Use your hand or index finger, or a pen or pencil, in the same manner as the index card. As with using an index card, using your hand does not completely obstruct your view of the page and allows you to pick up clues from the layout of the page (to see that a paragraph is ending, that a graphic example is to follow, and so on).
3. **Use a timer or clock.** Start by measuring what portion of a page you can read in a minute. Then set a goal for yourself: Determine how many pages you will attempt to read in a given period of time. Set your goal slightly above what you could read at your current rate. For example, suppose that in a particular book you can read half a page in a minute. You might set as your goal to read five pages in nine minutes (forcing yourself to read a little more

than a half-page per minute). The next day, try to read five pages in eight or eight and a half minutes. Use an alarm clock or timer to let you know when you have used up your time.

EXERCISE 1

DIRECTIONS   Select a magazine or newspaper article that you are interested in or a section of a paperback you are reading. Using one of the pacing techniques described in this section, try to increase your current reading speed by approximately 50 wpm. Record your results in the space provided.

Article title: _____

Estimated number of words: _____

Finishing time: _____

Starting time: _____

Reading time: _____

Words per minute: _____

Estimated level of comprehension: _____

Use Rereading to Build Speed

Although rereading is not an effective way to learn, it is an effective method of building your reading speed. Rereading at a slightly faster pace prepares you for reading new material faster. Rereading gets you moving at a faster rate and serves as a practice or trial run for reading new material faster.

To reread for speed increase, use the following steps:

1. **Select an article or passage, and time yourself reading it as you normally would for careful or leisure reading.**
2. **Compute your speed in words per minute after you finish reading.**
3. **Take a break (five minutes or so).** Then reread the same selection, timing yourself again. Push yourself to read faster than you read the first time.
4. **Compute your speed again.** You should be able to reread the selection at a faster rate than you read it initially.
5. **Read a new selection, pushing yourself to read almost as fast as you** *re*read the first selection.

EXERCISE 2

DIRECTIONS   Choose two magazine or newspaper articles that you are interested in reading. Follow the preceding steps for rereading to build speed. Record your results below.

Article 1

Title: _____

Estimated number of words: _____

First reading

Time: _____

Words per minute: _____

Second reading

Time: _____

Words per minute: _____

Article 2

Title: _____

Estimated number of words: _____

First (only) reading

Time: _____

Words per minute: _____

DEVELOPING YOUR READING FLEXIBILITY

The way writers write, the words they use, how they put words together, and how clearly they can express ideas all contribute to how easy it is to read a passage and to how fast it can be read. The type of material you are reading also has a major influence on how fast you can read with good comprehension. Finally, your purpose for reading is an important factor related to both rate and comprehension. If you are reading a magazine article for enjoyment, your purpose is different from when you are reading a textbook chapter to prepare for an exam. If you are paging through the newspaper, your purpose differs from your purpose when you are reading a poem for your English literature class.

As you can see from Figure 19-1, no one should have just one reading rate. Instead, your reading rate should vary according to *what* you are reading and *why* you are reading it. Adjusting your rate in response to the material and to your purpose for reading is called *reading flexibility.*

Learning to adjust your rate according to style, content, and purpose will require a conscious effort at first. If you are now in the habit of reading everything at the same pace, as most college students are, then you will need to force yourself to make an assessment of the particular reading material before

Method of Reading	Range of Speed	Purpose of Reading	Types of Material
Analytical reading	Under 100 wpm	Detailed comprehension: analysis, evaluation, critique	Poetry, argumentative writing
Study reading	150–250 wpm	High comprehension and high recall	Textbooks, library research
Casual reading	250–400 wpm	Moderate comprehension of main ideas, entertainment, enjoyment, general	Novels, newspapers, magazines
Accelerated reading	Above 600 wpm	Overview of material; rapid location of a specific fact	Reference material, magazines, novels, nonfiction

Figure 19-1
Types of Reading

deciding how fast you can read it. When you use the technique of prereading, you are only a small step away from adjusting your rate. By prereading, you familiarize yourself with the overall content and organization of the material. You may also include, as part of your prereading, a step in which you pay particular attention to the overall difficulty of the material. While prereading, you will sample enough of the actual writing to be able to assess the level of complexity of both the language and the content.

Deciding how much to speed up or slow down for a particular article is a matter of judgment. Through experience, you will become able to judge how much you can afford to alter your speed. It is not important to know precisely how much to increase your speed. Rather, the important thing is to develop *flexibility.* Here is a step-by-step procedure you can follow that will help you build the habit of varying your reading rate:

1. **Choose a time and place for reading that will help rather than hinder your concentration.** Choose a time when you are alert and your state of mind is conducive to study.
2. **Preread the material.** As you preread, assess the difficulty of both the writing style and the content. Are there a lot of difficult words? Are the sentences long and complicated? How factual is the material? How much background information do you have on the subject?
3. **Define your overall purpose for reading.** Your purpose will determine the level of comprehension and the degree of retention that you require. Are you reading for enjoyment, looking up facts, or reading a text chapter to prepare for an exam?
4. **Decide what rate would be appropriate for reading this particular material.**
5. **After you've finished the first page of the reading material, stop and evaluate.** Can you understand and remember what you are reading? Can you summarize the ideas in your own words?

You Don't Have to Read Everything

Before you begin to read flexibly, you must accept the notion that there is nothing sacred about the printed word. Many students erroneously believe that anything that appears in print must be true, valuable, and worth reading. Actually, the importance and value of printed information are affected by whether you need to learn it or whether you can use it in a practical way. Depending on the kind of material and on your purpose for reading it, many times you may need to read only some parts and skip over others. You might read selectively in the following situations:

1. **A high level of comprehension is not needed.** If you are not trying to remember a major portion of the facts and details, then you might concentrate on reading only main ideas. This method of reading only main ideas is called *skimming.* Specific techniques for skimming are presented later in the chapter.
2. **You are searching for specific information.** If you are looking up the date of a historical event in your history text, you skip over everything in the chapter except the exact passage that contains the information. This technique of skipping everything except the specific information for which you are looking is called *scanning.* Practice in scanning techniques is included later in the chapter.

3. **You are familiar with what you are reading.** In a college chemistry course, for example, you might find that the first few chapters of your text are very basic if you have already studied high school chemistry. You can therefore afford to skip basic definitions and explanations and examples of principles that you already know. Do not, however, decide to skip an entire chapter or even large sections within it; there just may be some new information included. You may find that more exact and detailed definitions are given or that a new approach is taken toward a particular topic.

4. **The material does not match your purpose in reading.** Suppose that, in giving an assignment in your physics text, your instructor told you to concentrate only on theories, laws, and principles presented in the chapter. As you begin reading the chapter, you find that the first topic discussed is Newton's law of motion, but the chapter also contains a biographical sketch of Newton giving detailed information about his life. Because your purpose in reading the chapter is to focus on theories, laws, and principles, it is appropriate to skip over much of the biographical information.

5. **The writer's style allows you to skip information (portions).** Some writers include many examples of a particular concept or principle. If, after reading two or three examples, you are sure that you understand the idea being explained, just quickly glance at the remaining examples. Unless they present a new aspect or different point of view, skip over them. Other writers provide detailed background information before getting into a discussion of the intended topic. If a chapter starts out by summarizing information that was covered in a chapter you just read last week, it is not necessary to read this information again carefully unless you feel you need to review.

EXERCISE 3

DIRECTIONS   Each of the following items suggests a reading situation and describes the material to be read. After reading each item, decide whether the reader should (a) read the material completely, (b) read parts and skip other parts, or (c) skip most of the material.

_____ 1. Your history instructor has assigned each student to read a historical novel for the purpose of getting a realistic picture of what life was like and how people lived during a certain period. As you are reading, you come to a detailed two-page description of the types of gowns Southern women wore to a particular party. How should you read these two pages?

_____ 2. You are doing research for a sociology term paper on the world population explosion. You are looking for information and statistics on recent population trends. You have located several books from the 1940s on the topic of population growth in the United States. How should you read these books?

_____ 3. Your nursing instructor has just returned a test on a chapter describing the nursing process. She indicates that the class's overall performance on this test was poor and suggests that the chapter be reviewed. You received a grade of 79 on the test. How should you reread this chapter?

_____ 4. Your biology professor has assigned a number of brief outside readings along with the chapters in your regular textbook. He has put them on reserve in the college library for the use of all his classes. This is the only place where they can be used. He did not say whether you would be tested on these readings. How should you read them?

_____ 5. You have just attended English class, where your instructor discussed Milton's *Paradise Lost*. During his discussion, he made numerous references to Dante's *Inferno*. You have never read this second work but think it's important to know something about it. How should you read it?

Skimming Techniques

As you know, the term **skimming** refers to the process of reading only main ideas within a passage and simply glancing at the remainder of the material. Skimming is used to get an overall picture of the material, to become generally familiar with the topics and ideas presented, or to get the gist of a particular work. Usually skimming is an end in itself; that is, skimming is all you intend to do with the article. You do not intend to read it more intensively later. You are willing to settle for an overview of the article, giving up a major portion of the details.

At this point, you may be thinking that skimming seems similar to the technique of prereading. If so, you are correct. Prereading is actually a form of skimming. To be more precise, there are three forms of skimming: *preread skimming, skim-reading,* and *review skimming.* Preread skimming assumes that you plan to read the entire article or chapter and that you are prereading as a means of getting ready to read. Skim-reading refers to situations in which skimming is the only coverage you plan to give the material. Review skimming assumes that you have already read the material and are going back over it as a means of study and review.

We discussed prereading in Chapter 5. Skimming to review after reading is part of the reading-study systems, such as SQ3R, discussed in Chapter 16. This chapter will focus on skim-reading techniques.

Demonstration of Skimming

The sample article in Figure 19-2 (p. 436) has been included to demonstrate what skimming is like. The parts of the passage that should be read while skimming are shaded.

How to Skim-Read

Your purpose in skimming is to get an overall impression of the content of a reading selection. The technique of skimming involves selecting and reading those parts of the selection that contain the most important ideas and merely glancing at the rest of the material. Below is a step-by-step procedure to follow in skimming for main ideas.

1. **Read the title.** If the piece is an article, check the author, publication date, and source.
2. **Read the introduction.** If it is very long, read only the first paragraph completely. Read the first sentence of each paragraph. Usually the first sentence is a statement of the main idea of that paragraph.

**Figure 19-2
An Example of Skimming**

FROM A VEGETARIAN: LOOKING AT HUNTING FROM BOTH SIDES NOW

Deer hunting season opened Nov. 18, and as the gunfire resumes in our woodlands 1 and fields so will the perennial sniping between hunters and animal rights supporters. I always feel caught in the cross-fire on this matter, because I have been a vegetarian and animal rights advocate for over 25 years, but I also have friends I respect who are hunters. I've learned the issue is not as black-and-white as I once believed.

Growing up with many beloved pets and no hunters in my life, I assumed these 2 people were bloodthirsty animal haters. When, in my 20s, I read the great humanitarian Albert Schweitzer's writings on reverence for life, I became a vegetarian and even more contemptuous of hunters.

But I had to revise my opinion after seeing the classic 1981 African film, "The 3 Gods Must Be Crazy." The hero, a good-hearted bushman, slays a small gazelle, then tenderly strokes her, apologizing for taking her life. He explains his family is hungry and thanks her for providing food. I was stunned: a hunter practicing reverence for life! Later, I learned that Native American tradition has the same compassionate awareness about life lost so another life may be sustained.

My position softened further several years ago when Alex Pacheco, a leading 4 animals-rights activist, spoke here. Detailing inhumane practices at meat-packing plants and factory farms, he said the most important thing anyone could do to lessen animal suffering was to stop eating meat. I decided to work toward being vegan (eating no animal products) and reluctantly admitted that hunters were not the animal kingdom's worst enemies. However, I still disliked them.

What really changed my perspective was getting to know some hunters per- 5 sonally, through my job at a Red Cross blood-donation center. Some of my co-workers and a number of our donors are civic-minded people who donate blood (which most people don't) but also shed animal blood with their guns and arrows. Confronting this paradox brought me some realizations.

First, hunters are like any group that differs from me: lacking personal experi- 6 ence of them made it easier to demonize them. They aren't monsters. I don't know if any of them apologizes to or thanks his kill as the hungry bushman did but I do know they aren't cruel, sadistic or bloodthirsty—quite the opposite, as I later discovered.

Second, these people aren't just amusing themselves by ending a life; they are 7 acquiring food. This death that sustains another life has a meaning that, for example, fox hunting does not. To the animal, this distinction may mean little. But it is significant when considering a person's intentions.

Also, I was informed that hunters don't "like to kill." They enjoy the outdoors, 8 the camaraderie and the various skills involved. (One of these skills, the "clean kill," is prized precisely because it minimizes suffering.) Like vegetable gardeners, they enjoy providing food [for] themselves and their families with their own hands. Like those who fish, they enjoy a process of food acquisition that involves an animal's death, but not because it does. Again, this may seem a small point (especially to the prey), but I feel it is meaningful from the standpoint of the hunter's humanity.

In addition, I've come to see a certain integrity in hunters as meat-eaters who 9 "do their own dirty work." Packaged cold-cuts and fast-food burgers mask the fact of lives bled out on the killing floor. Hunters never forget this, for they accept personal responsibility for it.

Furthermore, were I an animal that had to die to feed a human, I'd rather it 10 happen one-on-one, at the hands of that person in the woods that were my home, than amidst the impersonal mass-production machinery of a meat factory. Either way is death, but one way has more dignity, less fear and less suffering.

There are bad hunters who trespass, shoot domestic animals, hunt intoxicated 11 or disregard that cardinal rule of hunting's unwritten code of ethics: wounded prey must not be allowed to suffer. Las Thanksgiving morning in Chestnut Ridge Park, I found a fresh trail fo deer tracks in the snow, heavily splashed with blood. It was horrible.

One of my hunter co-workers was also upset when I told him about it, and had 12 this story. He himself was able to hunt only one day last season and sighted a small, wounded doe. As a student on a tight budget with a family, he hunts for food and would have preferred to ignore the doe's plight and meet his license limit with a large buck. Instead, he devoted a long, difficult day to trailing her until he was close enough to end her suffering. This was a act of mercy and even self-sacrifice, not the action of a heartless person insensitive to animals. It was reverence for life. He claims many hunters would do and have done the same.

And I realized that compassion has many faces, some of the truest the most 13 unexpected.

—The Buffalo News

3. **Read any headings and subheadings.** When taken together, the headings form an outline of the main topics that are covered in the material.
4. **Notice any pictures, charts, or graphs; these are usually included to emphasize important ideas, concepts, or trends.**
5. **If you do not get enough information from the headings or if you are working with material that does not have headings, read the first sentence of each paragraph.**
6. **Glance at the remainder of the paragraph.**
   - Notice any italicized or boldfaced words or phrases. These are key terms used throughout the selection.
   - Look for any lists of ideas within the text of the material. The author may use numerals, such as 1, 2, and 3, to organize the list or may include signal words such as *first, second, one major cause, another cause,* and the like.
   - Look for unusual or striking features of the paragraph. You may notice a series of dates, many capitalized words, or several large-figure numbers.
7. **Read the summary or last paragraph.**

EXERCISE 4

DIRECTIONS   Skim each of the following selections. Then summarize each article in the space provided.

Selection 1: "Are There Perfect Answers About Greenness?"

_____

_____

_____

Selection 2: "Aromatherapy: The Nose Knows?"

_____

_____

_____

Selection 3: "Sleep: The Great Restorer"

_____

_____

_____

1. **Are There Perfect Answers About Greenness?**

   A growing list of U.S. firms have decided—for public relations, staff morale, and other reasons—to be socially responsible about the environment. This is called going "green." For example, Lever Brothers, a manufacturer of household products, has led the pack in recycling plastic bottles. DuPont has campaigned for chemical companies to take voluntary environmental initiatives. Monsanto, a chemical giant, took the lead in reducing air pollution long before passage of the Clean Air Act of 1990. Downy Fabric Softener can now be purchased in a "refill" pack.

   Also, small firms in many businesses—bakers, painters, dry cleaners, and printing companies—have taken steps to comply with the law. Kinko's, a copying and business service firm, recycles paper and toner. Hannaford Brothers supermarkets, located in New England, offer shoppers canvas bags rather than plastic or paper bags. There is a lot of interest in and action toward being a responsible business and in achieving a "green," livable environment. However, there is also some debate about what is best.

   In November 1990 McDonald's Corporation said it would phase out its use of polystyrene foam containers in favor of paper. McDonald's decision was based on evidence suggesting that the chemicals used in producing polystyrene were harmful to the environment. Now studies and researchers have suggested that the foam containers may be better for the environment than paper ones because the loss of trees used to produce paper is environmentally destructive. To settle similar debates, researchers have used a life-cycle analysis procedure to tote up every environmental risk associated with making, using, and disposing of products. In an unpublished study it sponsored, McDonald's claims that paper has lower environmental costs in most, if not all, respects. Therefore McDonald's will stick with paper.

   The environmentally correct decision regarding greenness is equally unclear in the diaper industry. In a study sponsored by Procter & Gamble, the manufacturer of Luvs and Pampers disposable diapers, it was found that cloth diapers consume more than three times as much energy, cradle to grave, as disposables do. But a study sponsored by the National Association of Diaper Services found the opposite.

   The diaper duel illustrates the toughest issue in life-cycle analysis; how to compare different kinds of environmental harm. Cloth diapers use about 60 percent more water and [create a] greater volume of water pollution than disposables do. But disposables generate more than seven times as much trash, hence filling landfills, and they take more energy to produce. Biodegradable disposables, the hoped-for compromise, only biodegrade in the sunlight, not when buried in a landfill.

   Can all products be separated into good and bad categories? The public would like simple answers: foam or paper? disposables or cloth? It doesn't appear, however, that life-cycle analysis or any present analytical methodology is going to provide simple answers. Costs, green benefits, research to support and oppose, common sense, and leadership are all factors that society, the government, and individuals will have to weigh in making decisions about ecological issues.

   —Kinnear, Bernhardt, and Krentler, _Principles of Marketing,_ p. 61

2. **Aromatherapy: The Nose Knows?**

   Humans rely much less on their sense of smell than do other mammals, for whom smells may be the chief way of perceiving the environment, more so than hearing or vision. But we do distinguish (and react in various ways to) a wide range of smells.

The aroma of apples cooking with cinnamon calls up homey visions; a sour smell warns us that the milk has spoiled, an acrid one that something is burning. All sensations are important to cooks, lovers, physicians, and a host of others. Yet most people today live in a scent-impoverished world, thanks largely to indoor plumbing, soap, hot running water, and washable fabrics.

Back to Nature?

It's not surprising that the idea of "aromatherapy"—using inhaled or applied scents to influence behavior and mood or even to treat disease—has recently surfaced or, more correctly, resurfaced. The contemporary version of it, according to J. R. King, a psychologist at the University of Warwick, England, is part of the "back to nature" movement and the backlash against scientific medicine. Modern aromatherapy originated in France, rose to prominence throughout Europe (especially the United Kingdom), and is now growing in popularity in the U.S. and Canada. It's based on people's prior psychological associations with specific smells.

Aromatherapy involves the use of "essential oils"—that is, essences of different plant fragrances. Those believed to have stimulating or relaxing effects include nutmeg, lily-of-the-valley, neroli oil (from orange blossoms), valerian oil, and many, many others. These natural oils are not quite as natural as their vendors claim. To produce an oil such as lavender or gardenia, the plant must be highly processed—pounded, steamed, and heated. These oils can then be diffused in the air—you can paint your light bulbs with them, for example, or sprinkle your linens. They can also be applied to the skin as ointment or during massage.

Some aromatherapy claims are truly extravagant: that essential oils can fight bacteria as effectively as antibiotics, can boost immunity, alleviate arthritis pain, and (applied topically) cure herpes simplex and shingles. Most promoters of aromatherapy don't go this far. A recent catalogue offering essential oils ($12 for a tiny 10-milliliter bottle), plastic aromatherapy diffusers ($34), and a "decoder card" for essential oils ($10) makes no medical claims but alludes simply to "healthier states of mind," "tranquillity," and "coaxing the mind and body into harmonious balance."

The Adaptive Nose

It wouldn't be hard to demonstrate that lavender oil won't cure herpes, but not much scientific work has been done on the psychological effects of aromatherapy, which tend to be backed up by personal testimonial. There's no argument, of course, that the sense of smell has emotional connections, or that it can influence mood. Smells can also affect mental and physical performance. Some malls and stores waft scents toward shoppers, hoping to soften customer resistance—a kind of Muzak for the nostrils. Like Muzak itself, it might strike some people as an infringement of personal privacy.

One problem in studying the effect of aromatherapy is that a person's belief is very important—if you think bergamot oil smells wonderful, you'll probably feel soothed by it—and it's hard to disguise this scent so as to have a "blinded" experiment. Another problem in designing a study is that we tend to get used to odors rapidly. The odor that overwhelms us one moment may hardly be apparent to us five minutes later. Also, reactions to scents are highly personal. What smells sweet and clean to one nose may be sharp and unpleasant to another. Essential oils are not universally pleasant or benign. Some are toxic if swallowed, or can cause skin irritation or induce headache and nausea in some people. In *Aromatherapy: An A–Z*, Patricia Davis lists 35 essential oils (including tansy, wintergreen, wormwood, savory, sassafras, and bitter almond) that should never be used in therapy. Fennel, hyssop, sage, and wormwood, she says, can trigger attacks in epileptics.

Pro-Aroma vs. No Aroma

And there's always the question of allergies. Cosmetics with fragrances cause skin eruptions in some people. Indeed, the trend in cosmetics these days is "fragrance-free," since such products are less likely to cause problems. Actually, as aromatherapy has grown in popularity, another movement is menacing it. People who believe they have "multiple chemical sensitivities" have campaigned to ban perfumes from public areas. Some California cities already have ordinances restricting the use of fragrances. Who indeed does not gag at certain aromas, maybe even gardenia oil? This dispute may well be beyond a rational solution.

Dollars and Scents

The chief benefit of aromatherapy so far has been not so much for the public as for marketers—perfuming mall air, adding supposedly alluring scents to thousands of products from furniture waxes to new cars, and the marketing of essential oils and various gadgets to diffuse them. This is usually harmless, unless you're allergic. But smells don't cure diseases, nor is aromatherapy an adjunct to medicine or an essential component of a healthy life.

—*Berkeley Wellness Letter*

3. **Sleep: the Great Restorer**

Sleep serves at least two biological purposes in the body: *conservation* of energy so that we are rested and ready to perform during high-performance daylight hours, and *restoration* so that neurotransmitters that have been depleted during waking hours can be replenished. This process clears the brain of daily minutiae as a means of preparing for a new day. Getting enough sleep to feel ready to meet daily challenges is a key factor in maintaining optimal physical and psychosocial health.

All of us can identify with that tired, listless feeling caused by sleep deprivation during periods of high stress. Either we can't find enough hours in the day for sleep, or once we get into bed, we can't fall asleep or stay asleep. **Insomnia**—difficulty in falling asleep quickly, frequent arousals during sleep, or early morning awakening—is a common complaint among 20 to 40 percent of Americans. Insomnia is more common among women than among men, and its prevalence is correlated with age and low socioeconomic status.

Some people have difficulty getting a good night's rest due to other sleep disorders. **Sleep apnea,** a condition in which a person may experience hundreds of episodes of breathing stoppage during a normal night's sleep, is increasingly common. Typically caused by upper respiratory tract problems in which weak muscle tone allows part of the airway to collapse, sleep apnea results in poor air exchange. This in turn causes a rise in blood pressure and low oxygen supply in the blood. Sleep apnea may do more than just disrupt sleeping cycles; in some cases, it can actually pose a serious health risk.

How much sleep each of us needs to feel refreshed depends on many factors. There is a genetically based need for sleep, different for each species. Sleep duration is also controlled by *circadian rhythms*, which are linked to the hormone *melatonin*. People may also control sleep patterns by staying up late, drinking coffee, getting lots of physical exercise, eating a heavy meal, or using alarm clocks. The most important period of sleep, known as the time of *rapid eye movement, or REM, sleep*, is essential to feeling rested and refreshed by sleep. This is the period of deepest sleep, during which we dream. If we miss this period of sleep, then we are left feeling groggy and sleep deprived.

Though many people turn to over-the-counter sleeping pills, barbiturates, or tranquilizers to get some sleep, the following methods for conquering sleeplessness are less harmful.

- *If your sleeplessness arises from worry or grief, try to correct what's bothering you.* If you can't correct it yourself, confide in a friend, join a support group, or find a qualified counselor to help you.
- *Don't drink alcohol or smoke before bedtime.* Alcohol can disrupt sleep patterns and make insomnia worse. Nicotine also makes you wakeful.

- *Avoid eating a heavy meal in the evening, particularly at bedtime.* Don't drink large amounts of fluid before retiring, either.
- *Eliminate or reduce consumption of caffeinated beverages except in the morning or early afternoon.*
- *Try a mid-afternoon nap, when circadian rhythms make you especially sleepy.* But avoid taking multiple catnaps—a practice that will keep you awake at night when you should be sleeping.
- *Spend an hour or more relaxing before retiring.* Read, listen to music, watch TV, or take a warm bath.
- *If you're unable to fall asleep, get up and do something rather than lie there.* Don't bring work to bed. If you wake up in the middle of the night and can't fall asleep again, try reading for a short time. Counting sheep or reconstructing a happy event or narrative in your mind may lull you to sleep.
- *Avoid reproaching yourself.* Don't make your sleeplessness a cause for additional worry. Insomnia is not a crime. Not everyone needs eight hours of sleep. You can feel well—and be quite healthy—on less. Don't worry that you have to make up lost sleep. One good night's sleep will reinvigorate you.

—Donatelle, *Access to Health,* pp. 40–41

Scanning Techniques

Scanning is a method of selective reading that is used when you are searching for a particular fact or the answer to a question. Scanning can best be described as a looking rather than a reading process. As you look for the information you need, you ignore everything else. When you finish scanning a page, the only thing you should know is whether it contained the information you were looking for. You should *not* be able to recall topics, main ideas, or details presented on the page. You already use the technique of scanning daily: you regularly scan telephone books, television listings, and indexes. The purpose of this section is to help you develop a rapid, efficient approach for scanning.

Use the following step-by-step procedure to become more skilled in rapidly locating specific information:

1. **State in your mind the specific information you are looking for.** Phrase it in question form if possible.
2. **Try to anticipate how the answer will appear and what clues you might use to help you locate the answer.** If you are scanning to find the distance between two cities, you might expect either digits or numbers written out as words. Also, a unit of measurement, probably miles or kilometers, will appear after the number.
3. **Determine the organization of material.** It is your most important clue to where to begin looking for information. Especially when you are looking up information contained in charts and tables, the organization of the information is crucial to rapid scanning.
4. **Use headings and any other aids that will help you identify which sections might contain the information you are looking for.**
5. **Selectively read and skip through likely sections of the passage, keeping in mind the specific question you formed and your expectations of how the answer might appear.** Move your eyes down the page in a systematic way. There are various eye movement patterns, such as the "arrow pattern" (straight down the middle of the page) and the "Z pattern" (zig-zagging down the page). It is best to use a pattern that seems comfortable and easy for you.

6. When you reach the fact you are looking for, the word or phrase will stand out, and you will notice it immediately.

7. When you have found the needed information, carefully read the sentences in which it appears in order to confirm that you have located the correct information.

EXERCISE 5

DIRECTIONS   Scan each passage to locate and underline the answer to the question stated at the beginning of each.

1. *Question:* Why was an Irish militia supposedly formed?

Passage

Revolution in America also brought drastic changes to Ireland. Before 1775, that unhappy island, under English rule, had endured centuries of religious persecution, economic exploitation, and political domination. During the war, however, Henry Gratton (1746–1820) and Henry Flood (1732–91), two leaders of the Irish Protestant gentry, exploited English weakness to obtain concessions. An Irish militia was formed, supposedly to protect the coasts against American or French attacks. With thousands of armed Irishmen behind them, the two leaders resorted successfully to American methods. In February 1782, a convention in Dublin, representing 80,000 militiamen, demanded legislative independence, which the English Parliament subsequently granted. An Irish legislature could now make its own laws, subject to veto only by the English king. Ireland thus acquired a status denied the American colonies in 1774.

—Wallbank et al., *Civilization Past and Present,* Vol. 2, p. 533

2. *Question:* How does the cost of in-home retailing compare with suburban rates?

Passage

In-home retailing involves the presenting of goods to customers in a face-to-face meeting at the customer's home or by contacting the customer by telephone. This solicitation can be done without advance selection of consumers or follow-ups based upon prior contact at stores, or by phone or mail. The well-known Tupperware party fits in this category. Here a person has a social gathering where everyone knows a sales presentation will be made. Besides Tupperware, the largest companies operating in this type of retailing are Avon (cosmetics), Electrolux (vacuum cleaners), Amway (household products), World Book (encyclopedia and books), Shaklee (food supplements), Home Interiors and Gifts (decorative items), L. H. Stuart (jewelry and crafts), Stanley Home Products (household products), and Kirby (vacuum cleaners). Despite the great cost savings of having no store and no inventory, labor costs make this form of retailing expensive. Expenses are estimated to average about 50 percent of sales, compared to about 26 percent for all retailing.

—Kinnear, Bernhardt, and Krentler, *Principles of Marketing,* p. 388

3. *Question:* Who are secondary relatives?

Passage

Generally, relations with kin outside the parent-child unit play a significant role in American family life. But the strength of those ties and the functions they serve are extremely diverse. They vary according to the kind of relationship—parent, grandparent, cousin, uncle—as well as with social class, ethnic group, occupation, and region of the country. Indeed, in rural areas of the United States today, many families are still focused on extended kin—not just grandparents, but "secondary relatives" like aunts, uncles, cousins, and others. Table 5.1 illustrates the contrasts between this extended kin version of family values, and the kind of familism centered around nuclear or primary family relationships—husbands and wives, parents and children.

—Skolnick, *The Intimate Environment: Exploring Marriage and the Family,* p. 107

4. *Question:* What is a spiff?

Passage

Manufacturers often sponsor *contests* with prizes like free merchandise, trips, and plaques to dealers who reach certain specified sales levels. Additionally, they may get free *merchandise allowances* or even *money bonuses* for reaching sales performance goals. Once in a while, there is a sweepstakes, where "lucky" dealers can win substantial prizes. For example, Fisher-Price Toys had great success with a sweepstakes that gave cooperating dealers a chance to win a trip to Puerto Rico. These types of programs may also be directed at in-store sales personnel for their individual sales performances. A direct payment by a manufacturer to a channel member salesperson is called a *spiff.* This is very common at the consumer level for consumer durables and cosmetics, and at the wholesale level for beer and records. Another version of a spiff is when retailers pay their salespeople to push certain items. Clearly, this practice makes it possible for consumers to be deceived by a salesperson attempting to earn *push money.* As a result, these types of payments are controversial.

—Kinnear, Bernhardt, and Krentler, *Principles of Marketing,* p. 495

5. *Question:* What were the objectives of the New Deal?

Passage

In the 1932 elections, Franklin D. Roosevelt, only the third Democrat to be elected to the presidency since 1860, overwhelmed Hoover by assembling a coalition of labor, intellectuals, minorities, and farmers. The country had reached a crisis point by the time he was to be inaugurated in 1933, and quick action had to be taken in the face of bank closings. Under his leadership, the New Deal, a sweeping, pragmatic, often hit-or-miss program, was developed to cope with the emergency. The New Deal's three objectives were relief, recovery, and reform. Millions of dollars flowed from the federal treasury to feed the hungry, create jobs for the unemployed through public works, and provide for the sick and elderly through such reforms as the Social Security Act. In addition, Roosevelt's administration substantially reformed the banking and stock systems, greatly increased the rights of labor unions, invested in massive public power and conservation projects, and supported families who either needed homes or were in danger of losing the homes they inhabited.

—Wallbank et al., *Civilization Past and Present,* Vol. 2, p. 781

LEARNING COLLABORATIVELY

DIRECTIONS   Your instructor will assign one of the readings in Part Eight or distribute an article of his or her choice. Choose a partner to work with. One student should read the article completely; the other should skim it. Then quiz each other and draw conclusions about the relative efficiency of skimming compared with that of reading. Also, list situations in which skimming would and would not be an appropriate strategy.

APPLYING YOUR LEARNING

Carla has been assigned a term paper for her business marketing class. In the paper, Carla is supposed to select a popular product, such as Pepsi or Reebok sneakers, survey its marketing history, analyze and critique its current marketing strategies, and make recommendations for widening the product's market. Carla began with encyclopedias and then checked the online card catalog, searched the shelves for related books, checked the *Reader's Guide to Periodical Literature,* and consulted the *Business Index* to locate journal articles.

1. Identify the reading strategies Carla might use for each source.

   - Encyclopedia: _____

   - Card catalog: _____

   - Shelved books: _____

   - *Reader's Guide to Periodical Literature:* _____

   - *Business Index:* _____

2. Evaluate Carla's approach to research for this assignment.

APPLYING YOUR SKILLS: Sample Textbook Chapter

Scan the page listed to find the answer to each of the questions listed below.

   a. page 519: Of what type of culture are Thai, Apache, and Mexican examples?
   b. page 520: In Japan, are boys or girls noiser?
   c. page 524: What are the two forms overattribution may take?
   d. page 527: What two cultures are used as an example of the difference in meaning of the word *woman?*
   e. page 528: Explain what communication accommodation theory is.

QUESTIONS FOR DISCUSSION

1. Why is it important to become proficient with skimming and scanning techniques? How might you use these techniques in various professions and hobbies?
2. Why do college students tend to skip the prereading stage? Why is this stage so important in understanding various types of material?
3. Where and when do you read most effectively? Under what conditions are you best able to concentrate on technical material?

SELF-TEST SUMMARY

1. What techniques can you use to improve your overall reading rate?

You can improve your reading rate by eliminating roadblocks, prereading, eliminating regression, reading in meaningful clusters, pacing, and rereading for speed.

2. What factors influence reading flexibility?

The type of material being read, the way the writer's ideas are expressed, and your purpose for reading all influence the rate and method of reading you use.

3. Is it always necessary to read every word on a page?

Many types of material do not require a thorough, beginning-to-end, careful reading. There are also many situations in which reading everything is not necessary; reading some parts is more appropriate.

4. When should I read selectively?

It is effective to read selectively in situations in which you need only main ideas, you are looking for specific facts or the answer to a question, you are highly familiar with the content of the material, or the material contains information that is not related to your purpose. Finally, with certain types of material and styles of writing, you can skip information.

5. What is skimming?

Skimming is a process of reading only main ideas and simply glancing at the remainder of the material. There are three basic types of skimming: preread skimming, skim-reading, and review skimming. The type of skimming used depends on the reader's purpose.

6. What is scanning?

Scanning is a method of selective reading that is used when one is searching for a particular fact or the answer to a question.

DIRECTIONS   Write the letter of the choice that best completes each statement in the space provided.

CHECKING YOUR RECALL

_____ 1. All of the following statements about reading are true *except*

   a. the speed at which you read is measured in words per minute (wpm).

   b. you should be able to read at several speeds.

   c. good readers often skip words.

   d. you should read every paragraph the same way.

_____ 2. Your reading rate can be improved by all of the following techniques *except*

   a. prereading.

   b. rereading.

   c. pacing.

   d. regressing.

_____ 3. Of the following sentences, the one that is divided into meaningful clusters is

   a. The professor / of psychology / waited patiently / to submit / his grades / to the registrar.

   b. The professor / of psychology / waited / patiently / to / submit / his / grades / to / the registrar.

   c. The / professor of / psychology waited / patiently to / submit his / grades to / the registrar.

   d. The professor of / psychology waited / patiently to submit / his / grades to / the registrar.

_____ 4. Reading flexibility refers to your ability to

   a. comprehend and recall what you read.

   b. adjust your rate to suit the material you are reading.

   c. predict points the author will make.

   d. adjust your comprehension to suit your rate.

_____ 5. Reading selectively is most appropriate for material that

   a. does not require a high level of comprehension.

   b. is unfamiliar.

   c. provides little or no background information.

   d. does not include any examples.

APPLYING YOUR SKILLS

_____ 6. Your reading rate would typically be fastest for material such as

   a. poetry.

   b. argumentative writing.

   c. textbooks.

   d. novels.

_____ 7. The primary objective of skimming is to

   a. locate a particular fact within a passage.

   b. get an overall picture of the material.

   c. find examples that support the material.

   d. make sure you understand the idea explained in a passage.

_____ 8. Jamil is writing a history paper and needs to find the date on which the United States entered World War I. The most appropriate reading technique for her to use in this situation is

   a. preread skimming.

   b. skim-reading.

   c. review skimming.

   d. scanning.

_____ 9. Woody has just finished review skimming a chapter in his physical therapy text. This information indicates that he

   a. plans to read the entire chapter later.

   b. is prereading as a way of getting ready to read.

   c. does not plan to give the chapter any more coverage.

   d. has already read the chapter and is going back over it.

_____10. Francine adjusts her reading rate based on the purpose of her reading assignments. In general, her reading rate should be slowest when her purpose for reading is to

   a. analyze or evaluate the material.

   b. be entertained.

   c. obtain an overview of the material.

   d. locate a specific fact.

MULTIMEDIA *Activities*

Improving Your Reading Rate and Flexibility

1 Attend an exhibit at a museum. Set a time limit for yourself for seeing and reading everything in the exhibit. Afterward, write a comprehensive review.

2 Watch a silent movie with titles or a foreign film with subtitles. How have your new reading skills improved your ability to enjoy these types of motion pictures?

3 Effective Reading Tutorial

http://www.jcu.edu.au/studying/services/studyskills/effreading/index.html

Try this online module for improving your reading skills from James Cook University in Australia.

4 Skimming and Scanning Scientific Material

http://www.ucc.vt.edu/stdysk/skimming.html

This online handout from Virginia Tech offers suggestions for reading more effectively in the sciences. Try skimming and scanning a newspaper or magazine with a friend. Test each other on what you read. What types of information did you tend to remember?

5 Personal Reading Improvement

Print out this plan from California Polytechnic State University for increasing your speed and comprehension.

http://sas.calpoly.edu/asc/ssl/personalrdgimprov.doc

Try following these suggestions until you have improved. Evaluate the worthiness of this type of plan.

THEME **A** BODY ADORNMENT

Sociology/Cultural Anthropology

A–1   Textbook Excerpt: Body Adornment

David Hicks and Margaret A. Gwynne

1 We use the term *body adornment* to refer to the voluntary and reversible (as opposed to permanent) changes people make to the outward appearance of their bodies. These changes include wearing clothing and jewelry, using cosmetics (which in many societies are applied to the body as well as to the face), and styling and coloring the hair.

Clothing

2 Human beings almost completely lack the external physical protection from the natural environment that other animals possess, such as tough hides, hard shells, layers of feathers, or thick coats of fur. Even people living in tropical climates, where no insulation against cold weather is needed, must protect their bodies from the sun, rain, stinging insects, thorny vegetation, or rough surfaces. No doubt for this reason, the vast majority of people wear clothes. The native people of Australia, called the Aborigines, were an exception; most were reportedly naked when first contacted by Westerners. But (as far as we know) for practical reasons, few societies in the past, and none today, completely lack a tradition of clothing the body.

3   Garments protect their wearers, but have another, equally important, function as well: to convey messages, both about individual clothes wearers and about the culture or subculture of which they are a part (Barnes and Eicher 1992; Kaiser 1990). One of these is the message of sexual identity. Few societies depend totally on anatomical differences to distinguish males from females. In most, different styles of clothing confirm the differences between the two sexes. Contemporary Western society is unusual in that certain items of casual wear, such as jeans, T-shirts, and jogging shoes are considered appropriate for both males and females. In India, women wear saris, men wear dhotis—never the reverse.

4   Wearing clothes seems not to depend on any innate human sense of modesty, for there is no universal agreement about which parts of the body should be kept hidden from view. In many (but by no means all) societies, the sexual organs, especially those of adults, are kept covered, but in other societies they are intentionally exposed. Sometimes clothing both covers and accentuates simultaneously; Western women's bras and Pacific men's penis sheaths both conceal and emphasize parts of the body. Depending on the society, other parts of the body—the hair, the lower part of the face, the ankles, the female midsection (to name just a few)—are either well hidden or intentionally exposed to public view.

---

anatomical
related to the structure of the body

dhotis
loin cloths worn by Hindu men in India

innate
inborn, possessed at birth

In some cultures, women traditionally wear garments that hide both their faces and bodies. Faces may be shielded by light fabric through which women can see enough to get about, heavier fabric in which eye holes have been cut, or full masks of leather or even metal. In the Hadramaut region of South Yemen (see map on page 452), a woman wears her culture's traditional garb.

5   Another message clothes convey is self-identity. If you were shown close-up photographs of the faces—and only the faces—of two young males, you might be able to determine their approximate ages, ethnic origins, states of health, and moods, but you would have trouble determining which was the face of a punk rocker and which a preppy. Whole-body photographs of the same two males, however—one in a metal-studded leather jacket, combat boots, and spiked hairdo; the other in an oxford-cloth shirt, madras slacks, deck shoes, and short, slicked-down hair—would give you a great deal of information about the different interests and values of these two individuals, provided the cultural context was one with which you were familiar.

6   The interests and values expressed by the appearances of these two individuals are not merely personal. Clothing reflects cultural as well as personal beliefs and ideals, and it is the cultural rather than the personal aspects of clothing that most interest anthropologists. What can we learn about the worldview of a given society from the way its members dress? In what values do the society's members collectively believe? What can clothes tell us about who is socially, politically, or economically **dominant** in the society and who is not? About the relationships between the sexes in the society and the attitudes of members of one sex toward members of the other? About the people's sense of national or ethnic identity, their conservative or liberal inclinations, even their religious beliefs?

7   Head coverings are a good example of the range of ideas that can be transmitted by a single item of clothing. The custom of covering the head, and sometimes the face as well, with a piece of cloth is widespread among females in Middle Eastern societies. Women wear headcloths ranging in size from small kerchiefs to large, enveloping semicircles of cloth that cover the entire body, including the head and sometimes much of the face. These veils are the external expression of deeply rooted Middle Eastern customs and collective ideas (Fernea and Fernea 1987), some of which find their origins in the Muslim religion.

dominant
having the most influence or control

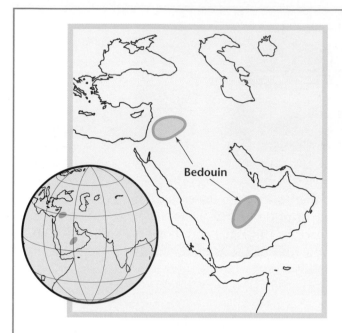

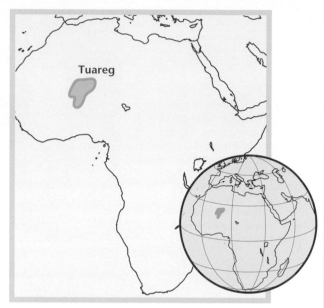

grievous
causing grief or pain

obstructed
got in the way of, hindered

8   The Middle Eastern custom of veiling originated in the time of the prophet Muhammad (A.D. 570–632), founder of Islam, as an outward symbol of religious identity. Muhammad's wives, so the story goes, were once mistaken for slaves—a grievous insult. To avoid future confusion, female followers of Muhammad began to wear veils (Fernea and Fernea 1987:106). But if its first cultural message was one of religious identity, veiling soon began to send a message about social status as well. Because it obstructed both movement and vision, the veil made performing certain tasks very difficult. A poor woman obliged to labor in the fields could not wear one. Thus, wearing this garment soon began to suggest a privileged life-style and high social status. This notion remains widely held today.

9   Veiling delivers other cultural messages too. Many Middle Easterners believe that females have strong sexual appetites and that their sexual behavior reflects directly on the honor of their families. For some, a family's honor rests in part on controlling women's sexuality (Lindholm and Lindholm 1985:234). To protect women from sexual temptation, and males from the uncontrollable lust of dangerous women who might ruin their good names, the physical seclusion of women, a custom known as purdah, has been practiced since the time of Muhammad. Houses may be surrounded by high walls, and women may spend their entire lives virtually imprisoned behind them. Wrapping a woman in a garment that conceals her body from public view is another reflection of the same idea. Today, a Middle Eastern woman wearing a veil on a public street is signaling "hands off!" A man who approaches a veiled woman invites serious trouble, for he is shaming both the woman and her family. This does not mean that a woman wearing a veil is necessarily repressed, inhibited, or even ultraconservative. A modern Muslim woman's veil may conceal a T-shirt, jeans, and sneakers.

10   Another cultural notion associated with veiling is modesty. Among the Bedouin, Arabic-speaking nomads of the Middle East (see map), modesty is an essential component of personal honor and respectability (Abu-Lughod 1986, 1987). The honorable person keeps his or her distance from members of the opposite sex (except for close relatives); casts the eyes shyly downward; moves with formality; and refrains from eating, smoking, talking, or laughing in certain social situations. Young, unmarried women show that they are modest and respectable by wearing kerchiefs on their heads. Married women wear black head-cloths that can be drawn protectively across the face when they are in the presence of certain men, such as in-laws. To display one's modesty in this way is a matter of pride for the Bedouin, who consider this behavior "a sign of respect for the social and moral system" (1987:29).

11   These examples show that in the Middle East, the cultural meanings attached to wearing a veil (or not wearing one) are many. Depending on where and in what style it is being worn, the veil can symbolize a woman's faith, the idea of protection (both from danger and from temptation), the notion of women as temptresses who must not be allowed to distract men, status and wealth, and personal modesty. And although we have been discussing the veil as an article of female apparel, among the Tuareg, camel pastoralists of North Africa (see map), men wear veils because lips are considered obscene.

12   Westerners, too, convey messages with their clothing. In church, a woman's hat or kerchief is a mark of her religious faith; at a party, her expensive beaded dress suggests her wealth and thus her social status. Her white bridal gown symbolizes her purity, and her bridal veil her modesty. When she wears a bikini she does so not to express faith, wealth, social status, purity, or modesty but rather to show off her attractive body. Her message is one of good health, self-discipline, self-esteem, and interest in attracting the attention of the opposite sex.

Source: Cultural Anthropology, pp. 373–376.

REVIEWING THE READING

DIRECTIONS   Write the letter of the choice that best completes each statement in the space provided.

Checking Your Comprehension

_____   1. The main purpose of this selection is to

a. explain how clothing protects our bodies.
b. describe how clothing is used by people to convey messages.
c. demonstrate why women should not wear veils.
d. discuss Middle Eastern culture.

_____   2. The central thought of this selection is that

a. climate has the greatest impact on how people dress.
b. clothing types are determined mainly by religion.

        c. a society's beliefs and customs directly impact the clothes people wear.

        d. unlike in other countries, clothing in America does not convey messages.

_____ 3. The main point of paragraph 10 is that among Bedouin people, veiling

        a. prevents eating or smoking.
        b. suppresses women.
        c. keeps sand out of people's eyes.
        d. represents the culture's belief in modesty.

_____ 4. According to the author, clothing may be used to show all of the following *except*

        a. creativity.
        b. modesty.
        c. social status.
        d. marital status.

_____ 5. Paragraph 11 uses the enumeration pattern to present

        a. the types of head covering worn in the Middle East.
        b. the cultural meanings of veiling.
        c. men's attitudes toward veiling.
        d. the types of cultures where veils are traditionally worn by women.

Checking Your Vocabulary

_____ 6. A change that is *reversible* (paragraph 1)

        a. is easy to hide.
        b. has different meanings.
        c. shows cultural meaning.
        d. is not permanent.

_____ 7. Something *external* (paragraph 2) is

        a. ugly.
        b. brave.
        c. outside.
        d. hidden.

_____ 8. To *accentuate* (paragraph 4) something is to

        a. say it out loud.
        b. hold it close.
        c. correct it.
        d. emphasize it.

_____ 9. If a belief is *cultural* (paragraph 9), it

    a. is not real.

    b. has to do with religion.

    c. is hidden.

    d. has to do with a society or culture.

_____ 10. *Purdah* (paragraph 9) is a custom that

    a. physically secludes women.

    b. involves elaborately decorating cloth.

    c. protects women from religious injustice.

    d. occurs in Africa.

A–2   From Bear Teeth to Pearls: Why We Adorn Ourselves

Catherine Clifford

1 Suppose you were given a choice: You could have makeup and accessories or you could have clothes, but not both. If you took the clothes, you might be smart, but you'd make a lousy cavewoman. Because while we regard food, clothing and shelter as basic necessities, earlier Homo sapiens apparently sported baubles, bangles and proto-cosmetics long before they bothered with body coverings.

2 What's the big deal about a bunch of junk jewelry and body paint that made it more important than keeping warm? It's that the seemingly frivolous art of decorating yourself—be it with bear teeth or bugle beads—has roots that go deep into human identity. And there's a paradox at the heart of why we daub and decorate our bodies: Self-ornamentation is a visual résumé of our societal roles, written in our culture's language, yet it can also be one of the most potent mediums to express individuality.

3 The point of puttin' on the Ritz for primitives was simple: In a nonliterate society, what you wore or how you were painted, scarred or tattooed told volumes about who you were. "Adornment was really a mode of communication, and the message always had to do with group life," explains Ruth P. Rubinstein, professor of sociology at the Fashion Institute of Technology (FIT) in New York City. "In some societies, for example, adornment was used the way we use wedding rings: to identify marital status and establish membership in a particular segment of society." It might say where you were from (to this day, some Moroccan women wear tattoos on their face and hands that identify their village) or what your role was.

4 "Adornment was always something both men and women used," adds Valerie Steele, author of *Paris Fashion: A Cultural History* (Oxford University Press, 1988) and an adjunct professor at FIT. "If anything, men favored ornamentation more because it symbolized their position as chief or priest or warrior." This at-a-glance inventory might also convey sexual information—although it must have been hard to guess wrong about gender if no one wore clothes.

Homo sapiens
species of modern human beings

frivolous
silly, not worthy of serious attention

puttin' on the Ritz
idiom meaning to make a show of wealth or extravagence

A Modern Example of Body Adornment

Cultural Creations

5   One crucial component is, of course, getting everyone to agree about who wears what. "There are no universal symbols—they are necessarily culturally created—but some things, by their form, are chosen to express certain attributes, like a shape that naturally suggests a phallic symbol," says Steele. "Or the color red—every culture does something different with it, but since it's the color of blood, it's frequently connected with life force, sexuality, passion or anger." Similarly, gold (the element, that is) seems to be worn for unusually consistent reasons. "Jewelry arose out of a desire to integrate supernatural powers," says Rubinstein. "It was thought that through gold you could adopt the power of the sun, and through stones, the powers of the underlying universe."

6   But when you get right down to it, the rules that this says that about you had to originate somewhere. "Whoever was in authority might create rules based on their associations," says Rubinstein. For instance, the New Testament gave jewelry a second meaning by proscribing it as seductive centuries ago. But an individual might also adopt certain ornaments that he felt would make him more powerful, and others copied him.

7   The mix of motivations—to stress similarity yet also stand out—is largely responsible for fashion pressures on women. "The importance—and speed—of fashion changes in Western culture over the

proscribing
forbidding

past few centuries seem related to a new value being placed on individual expression," says Claudia Brush Kidwell, curator of costumes for the Smithsonian's American History Museum and coeditor of *Men and Women: Dressing the Part* (Smithsonian Institution Press, 1989). "When individual accomplishment and setting oneself apart become critical, trying new things with clothes and adornment is a logical extension." At the same time, as the growth of capitalism caused men to view their role and therefore their appearance as strictly business, that left women, by default, with the job of enhancing everyone's social scenery. "As men's fashions became more restricted, women not only continued the tradition of playing with materials and trimmings and creating their 'look,' but also it became more important," explains Kidwell. "The duty to be beautiful is a 19th-century concept that is still promoted and commercialized." So two of the strongest directives women get are: Be an individual. And/but be beautiful. Using accoutrements from snazzy shoes to sequined hair bows is one way to satisfy both.

Personal Talismans

8   What makes one woman choose shoes while another goes with bows? The experts' answer: Who knows? "We can look at society and what certain choices mean in a cultural context," says Rubinstein. "For instance, bows imply a restriction of sexuality, something that can be opened but is held back. Polka dots came from the Roman tradition of a circle representing continuity. But we can't explain why you wear something, because that's too personal. Our sense of what is pretty or appealing dates back to early childhood, to what we saw our mothers, grandmothers or fathers wearing. We may favor very different styles than they did, but the real markers of personality—a preference for a specific color blue or a particular kind of jewelry—come from very individual associations."

talismans
objects believed to possess magical powers

9   Some trappings are so rich with resonance that they become modern-day equivalents of primitive talismans. A given item could be family-linked or it could be something you wore when you were at a weight you liked or on the night you met your boyfriend. Whatever, its magic is so private that it's an amulet no one else would recognize and that you might not be entirely aware of yourself. But much as we still don ceremonial robes like bridesmaids' dresses or gray funeral suits, many of us continue to practice a semi-serious mysticism with our sartorial frills.

sartorial
related to clothing

10   Even the most direct statements in self-decoration can be obscure, since the culturewide sources of possible associations are endless. Bits and pieces of various ethnic heritages may show up on our ears or around our necks. Borrowing from other cultures could be a way of displaying qualities that are supposedly characteristic—Latin flamboyance, Eastern mystery—or simply showing worldliness.

flamboyance
elaborate, richly colored

11   Gold indicates wealth, whether you're an inner-city teenager or a society matron, but obviously within very different contexts. Status-y trappings may be an attempt to imitate the upper classes or a flat-out

Trump-like brag about being rich enough to buy extravagant trinkets. (Incidentally, why is it that, when it comes to displays of wealth, more is more up to a point, beyond which it is too much? Because, according to Steele, in the 17th century middle-class people started acquiring more money than many aristocrats, who then scrambled to find new ways of showing superiority that money couldn't buy—in fact, negated. "It takes a certain sensibility to really believe that less is more," says Steele.) As each force in fashion—safari, status, ethnic, athletic, animal print, high-tech—ripples out from its source, it retains less and less of its original message and starts slapping against other waves.

12   On top of all that, points out Steele, there's irony: the current tendency to play any theme not straight but with a wink—wearing an armful of fake "status" watches—so that your kind of people (those who get the joke) recognize you as a kindred spirit. That we still use ornamental objects to signal our identities is unarguable, but not only is the message often less exact, it also tends to vary. "The woman who wears elegant gold earrings one day may wear big pink plastic hoops the next," says Steele. "She hasn't changed, nor has her culture, but there are so many choices now, all of which are acceptable, that there's more freedom to emphasize different aspects of yourself."

13   And that's where you get, finally, to the real fun. Medium and message aside, fooling around with your exterior decoration is being frivolous in the best sense. "Indulging in extra makeup or crazy jewelry says 'Look at me!' in a way—a healthy way—that we might not be comfortable saying straight out," says New York City psychologist Arlene Kagle. "Taking pleasure in resembling a hot rocker one night out of the year doesn't mean you secretly want to put Madonna out of business. It's just that there's a little slice of you that, with the right decoration, you can let out to play. It's similar to one reason people have affairs—they want to experience something new."

14   There's also a pleasure even more primitive than playing with identity: exploring the senses. "Little children are sensual beings," says Kidwell. "They like the feel of soft stuff, they like to drape things around their necks, they like feathers, they like to dab themselves with paint. It doesn't matter whether they're male or female. What matters is the fun of stimulating the senses, the fun of creation."

15   It's worth remembering. The reasons for painting and primping and decorating ourselves like Christmas trees are serious and significant . . . to a point. But there's a wild-card element that makes it all unpredictable and, sometimes, pure pleasure—a visual and emotional perk that's one part science, one part art.

Source: Health, August 1989.

REVIEWING THE READING

DIRECTIONS   Write the letter of the choice that best completes each statement in the space provided.

Checking Your Comprehension

_____ 1. The author wrote this selection in order to

    a. show the many ways art influences our lives.
    b. describe how people choose clothing.
    c. explain why jewelry is an important industry.
    d. explain why people decorate their bodies.

_____ 2. The central point of this selection is that

    a. jewelry does not need to be expensive to look good.
    b. animal prints are popular in fashion.
    c. jewelry and fashion accessories are used to share information.
    d. living outdoors is unhealthy.

_____ 3. Paragraph 8's main idea is that scientists can explain what body decorations mean, but not

    a. how much they are worth.
    b. where they can be found.
    c. why each person chooses certain items.
    d. how many items each person will select.

_____ 4. One of the reasons people experiment with fashion items is to

    a. try something new.
    b. stay busy.
    c. disguise themselves.
    d. spend money.

_____ 5. Fashion pressures on women are explained in Paragraph 7 using

    a. enumeration.
    b. time sequence.
    c. comparison–contrast.
    d. cause and effect.

Checking Your Vocabulary

_____ 6. _Supernatural_ (paragraph 5) powers are

    a. beyond what is normal.
    b. childlike.
    c. developed through adornment.
    d. forbidden in most societies.

_____ 7. _Directives_ (paragraph 7) are

    a. comparisons.
    b. lists.
    c. offers.
    d. orders.

_____ 8. A *talisman* (paragraph 9) is a(n)

    a. item with personal meaning.
    b. man who performs magic.
    c. ticket to attend a cultural event.
    d. message from the dead.

_____ 9. *Resembling* (paragraph 13) another person means you

    a. owe him or her money.
    b. look like him or her.
    c. hang around with him or her.
    d. bother him or her.

_____ 10. An *unpredictable* (paragraph 15) event is

    a. unusual.
    b. not adorned.
    c. not expected.
    d. unwanted.

A–3   The Decorated Body

France Borel

1 Human nakedness, according to social custom, is unacceptable, unbearable, and dangerous. From the moment of birth, society takes charge, managing, dressing, forming, and deforming the child—sometimes even with a certain degree of violence. Aside from the most elementary caretaking concerns—the very diversity of which shows how subjective the motivation is—an **unfathomably** deep and universal tendency pushes families, clans, and tribes to rapidly modify a person's physical appearance.

2   One's genuine physical makeup, one's given anatomy, is always felt to be unacceptable. Flesh, in its raw state, seems both intolerable and threatening. In its naked state, body and skin have no possible existence. The organism is acceptable only when it is transformed, covered with signs. The body only speaks if it is dressed in artifice.

3   For millennia, in the four quarters of the globe, mothers have molded the shape of their newborn babies' skulls to give them silhouettes conforming to **prevalent** criteria of beauty. In the nineteenth century, western children were tightly **swaddled** to keep their limbs straight. In the so-called primitive world, children were scarred or tattooed at a very early age in rituals which were repeated at all the most important steps of their lives. At a very young age, children were fitted with belts, necklaces, or bracelets; their lips, ears, or noses were pierced or stretched.

4   Some cultures have designed sophisticated appliances to alter physical structure and appearance. American Indian cradleboards crushed the skull to flatten it; the Mangbetus of Africa wrapped a knotted rope made of bark around the child's head to elongate it into a sugarloaf shape, which was considered to be **aesthetically** pleasing.

unfathomably
difficult or impossible to understand

prevalent
widely or commonly occurring

swaddled
wrapped tightly in cloth

aesthetically
conforming to commonly held ideas of beauty

An Example of Body Adornment

scarification
the making of superficial incisions in the skin by cutting or scratching

The feet of very young Chinese girls were bound and spliced, intentionally and irreversibly deforming them, because this was seen to guarantee the girls' eventual amorous and matrimonial success.[1]

5   Claude Lévi-Strauss said about the Caduveo of Brazil: "In order to be a man, one had to be painted; whoever remained in a natural state was no different from the beasts."[2] In Polynesia, unless a girl was tattooed, she would not find a husband. An unornamented hand could not cook, nor dip into the communal food bowl. Pink lips were despicable and ugly. Anyone who refused the test of the tattoo was seen to be marginal and suspect.

6   Among the Tivs of Nigeria, women called attention to their legs by means of elaborate scarification and the use of pearl leg bands; the best decorated calves were known for miles around. Tribal incisions behind the ears of Chad men rendered the skin "as smooth and stretched as that of a drum." The women would laugh at any man lacking these incisions, and they would never accept him as a husband. Men would subject themselves willingly to this custom, hoping for scars deep enough to leave marks on their skulls after death.

7   At the beginning of the eighteenth century, Father Laurent de Lucques noted that any young girl of the Congo who was not able to bear the pain of scarification and who cried so loudly that the operation had to be stopped was considered "good for nothing."[3] That is why, before marriage, men would check to see if the pattern traced on the belly of their intended bride was beautiful and well-detailed.

8   The fact that such motivations and pretexts depend on aesthetic, erotic, hygienic, or even medical considerations has no influence on the result, which is always in the direction of transforming the appearance of the body. Such a transformation is wished for, whether or not it is effective.

9   The body is a supple, malleable, and transformable prime material, a kind of modeling clay, easily molded by social will and wish. Human skin is an ideal subject for inscription, a surface for all sorts of marks which make it possible to differentiate the human from the animal. The physical body offers itself willingly for tattooing or scarring so that, visibly and recognizably, it becomes a social entity.

10   The absolutely naked body is considered as brutish, reduced to the level of nature where no distinction is made between man and beast. The decorated body, on the other hand, dressed (if even only in a belt), tattooed, or mutilated, publicly exhibits humanity and membership in an established group. As Theophile Gautier said, "The ideal disturbs even the roughest nature, and the taste for ornamentation distinguishes the intelligent being from the beast more exactly than anything else. Indeed, dogs have never dreamed of putting on earrings."

categorical
absolute

11   So, it is by their categorical refusal of nakedness that human beings are distinguished from nature. The "mark makes unremarkable"—it creates an interval between what is biologically and brutally given in the animal realm and what is won in the cultural realm. The body is tamed continuously; social custom demands, at any price—including pain, constraint or discomfort—that wildness be abandoned.

12   Each civilization chooses—through a network of elective relationships which are difficult to determine—which areas of the body deserve transformation. These areas are as difficult to define and as shifting as those of eroticism or modesty. An individual alone eludes bodily modifications; they are the expression of a homogeneous collectivity which, at a chosen moment, comes to a tacit agreement to attack one or another part of the anatomy.

13   Whatever the choices, options, or differences may be, that which remains constant is the transformation of appearance. In spite of our contemporary western belief that the body is perfect as it is, we are constantly changing it: clothing it in musculature, suntan, or makeup; dying its head hair or pulling out its bodily hair. The seemingly most innocent gestures for taking care of the body very often hide a persistent and disguised tendency to make it adhere to the strictest of norms, reclothing it in a veil of civilization. The total nudity offered at birth does not exist in any region of the world. Man puts his stamp on man. The body is not a product of nature, but of culture.

adhere
to stick fast, as if glued

Notes

1. Of course, there are also many different sexual mutilations, including excisions and circumcisions, which we will not go into at this time as they constitute a whole study in themselves.
2. C. Lévi-Strauss, *Tristes Tropiques* (Paris: Plon, 1955), p. 214.
3. J. Cuvelier, *Relations sur le Congo du Père Laurent de Lucques* (Brussels: Institut royal colonial belge, 1953), p. 144.

Source: Parabola, Fall 1994.

REVIEWING THE READING

DIRECTIONS   Write the letter of the choice that best completes each statement in the space provided.

Checking Your Comprehension

_____ 1. The author believes that bodily decoration is

     a. unpleasant.
     b. inevitable.
     c. not done by all cultures.
     d. humorous.

_____ 2. The main point of this selection is that body decoration is decided by

     a. culture.
     b. mothers.
     c. committee.
     d. nature.

_____ 3. Paragraph 11's main idea is that people are different from animals because people

     a. are able to think.
     b. celebrate rituals.
     c. can communicate.
     d. do not remain naked.

_____ 4. The feet of young Chinese girls were often

     a. scarred.
     b. bound.
     c. elevated.
     d. painted.

_____ 5. In paragraphs 5 through 7, the main ideas are explained using

     a. definitions.
     b. time sequence.
     c. research.
     d. examples.

Checking Your Vocabulary

_____ 6. _Anatomy_ (paragraph 2) is a person's

     a. jewelry.
     b. unique personality.
     c. relative.
     d. physical body.

_____ 7. Something that is *unornamented* (paragraph 5) is

    a. not decorated.
    b. related to a winter holiday.
    c. rough textured.
    d. not feminine.

_____ 8. A substance that is *malleable* (paragraph 9) is

    a. difficult.
    b. made of clay.
    c. beautiful.
    d. easily changed.

_____ 9. An *inscription* (paragraph 9) is a(n)

    a. invisible line.
    b. kind of writing.
    c. type of skin.
    d. kind of nudity.

_____ 10. *Brutish* (paragraph 10) means

    a. like an animal.
    b. similar to a leader.
    c. soft.
    d. intelligent.

MAKING CONNECTIONS

1. Define the term *body adornment.* Does the term have the same meaning for each author? Give examples to support your answer.
2. Each author offers reasons why people adorn their bodies. First, write a list of reasons. Then decide whether the authors are in agreement on the purposes of body adornment.
3. What types of body adornment do humans use? Make a list of the types discussed in each reading. Are there types of adornment not discussed by any of the authors?
4. Compare the tone used in each of the readings. Which is more serious? Which is more academic?
5. What further information would you need in order to write a paper or make a speech on body adornment?

WORLD WIDE WEB ACTIVITY

Key Word Searches

Experiment to see how much information you can find on the topic of body adornment by completing the following activities:

1. Reread one of the articles on body adornment and list five possible key words or phrases that you might use to find related information on the Web. For example, from the first article, the phrases "body adorn-

ment," "head coverings and customs," or "Middle Eastern veils" might be used.

2. Select a search engine such as Lycos, Yahoo!, AltaVista, or Google. Use only one search engine as you try the following steps:

   a. Examine the Help page to learn the method for doing a key word search using the search engine you selected. Follow the directions for how to enter key word phrases.

   b. In the Search box, enter one of your possible key word phrases. When the list of resources appears on your search page, scroll down through the list, skimming the titles of articles and names of Web sites to see what kinds of sites you have found. Make notes on what kinds of sites and how many of them the key word phrase led you to. Follow the same steps for each key word phrase.

3. Share your key word phrases and search results with your classmates. Which key word phrases uncovered which kinds of sources? Were any of the key word phrases particularly useful?

THEME MEN'S AND WOMEN'S COMMUNICATION

Communication

B–1 Textbook Excerpt: Communication Between Women and Men

Alex Thio

1 In the world of women, connection and intimacy are the primary goals of life, and individuals cultivate friendship, minimize differences, seek consensus, and avoid the appearance of superiority. On the other hand, status and independence are the primary goals of life in men's world, so individuals seek status by telling others what to do, attain freedom from others' control, avoid taking orders, and resist asking for help. Thus, when the two sexes communicate with each other, women tend to use the language of connection and intimacy, and men the language of status and independence. Both may use the same English language, but in effect they speak and hear different dialects called genderlects, **linguistic** styles that reflect the different worlds of women and men (Tannen, 1994a; 1990).

linguistic
relating to language

Speaking Different Genderlects

2 Failure to understand each other's genderlects can spell trouble for **intergender** communication. Consider a married couple, Linda and Josh. One day Josh's old high school buddy from another city called to announce that he would be in town the following month. Josh invited him to stay for the weekend. When he told Linda that they were going to have a houseguest, she was upset. Often away on business, she had planned to spend that weekend with Josh alone. But what upset her the most was that Josh had extended the invitation without first discussing it with her. Linda would never make plans without first checking with Josh. "Why can't you do the same with me?" Linda asked, But Josh responded, "I can't say to my friend, 'I have to ask my wife for permission!'" To Josh, who lives in the men's world of status, checking with his wife means seeking permission, giving up his independence, or having to act like a kid asking his mom if it's okay to play with a friend. In Linda's female world of connection, checking with her husband has nothing to do with permission. In fact, Linda likes to tell others, "I have to check with Josh," because it makes her feel good to reaffirm that she is involved with someone, that her life is bound up with someone else's (Tannen, 1990). In short, Linda and Josh speak and hear different genderlects, one having to do with connection and intimacy, the other with status and independence.

intergender
between the sexes

3 There are other ways the different genderlects can throw a monkey wrench into the communication between women and men. Accustomed to speaking for the purpose of giving *information* only, men tend to misunderstand women by taking literally what women say. On the other hand, women, more **habituated** to talking for the

habituated
conditioned, accustomed to

An Example of Proxemics at Work

purpose of expressing *feelings,* tend to misunderstand men by reading emotional meanings into what men say.

4   Thus women and men tend to communicate at cross-purposes. If a woman says to her husband, "We never go out," he may upset her by responding, "That's not true. We went out last week." The husband fails to grasp the feeling the wife is trying to convey. In saying "we never go out," she in effect says something like "I feel like going out and doing something together. We always have such a fun time, and I enjoy being with you. It has been a few days since we went out." If on another occasion the woman asks her husband, "What's the matter?" and gets the answer, "I'm okay," she may respond by saying, "I know something's wrong. What is it? Why aren't you willing to share your problem with me? Let me help you." The wife fails to understand that, by saying "I'm okay," her husband means "I am okay; I can deal with my problem. I don't need any help, thank you" (Gray, 1992). In his male world, dealing with one's own problem is a hallmark of independence, which he tries to assert, and getting help from others is a sign of weakness, which he tries to avoid.

5   Genderlects are not confined to communication between intimates. They also influence communication in public. Sitting alone in a dining room where bank officers had lunch, sociolinguist Alice Deakins listened to what they were talking about at adjacent tables. When no woman was present, the men talked mostly about business and rarely about people. The next most popular topics were food, sports, and recreation. When women talked alone, their most frequent topic was people, especially friends, children, and partners in personal relationships. Business was next, and then health, including weight control. Together, women and men tended to avoid the topic that each group liked best and settle on topics of interest to both, *but they followed the style of the men-only conversations.* They talked about food the way men did, focusing on the food and restaurant rather than diet

and health. They talked about recreation the way men did, concentrating on sports figures and athletic events rather than on exercising. And they talked about housing the way men did, dealing mostly with location, property values, and commuting time, rather than whether the house is suitable for the family, how safe the neighborhood is for the children, and what kinds of people live next door. In other words, in public communication between the sexes, the male genderlect tends to dominate, mostly centering on things and activities, thus ignoring the female genderlect, which primarily concerns people and relationships (Tannen, 1994a; 1990).

Playing the Gendered Game of Proxemics

proxemics
the study of the distance individuals keep between each other in social interaction

6 In gender-mixed groups, men's proxemics differs from women's. Men usually sprawl with legs spread apart and hands stretched away from the body, taking up considerable space around them. Women are more likely to draw themselves in, using only little space with "ladylike" postures such as closing or crossing the legs and placing the hands near the body.

7 A more direct way for men to dominate women in proxemics involves invading their personal space. As has been suggested, men often let their hands rest on women's shoulders but women rarely do the same to men. A similar proxemic domination prevails in interactions of mutual affection. When an intimate couple walk down the street, the man may place his arm around the woman's shoulders, but the woman is far less likely to put her arm around the man's shoulders. Doesn't this merely reflect the fact that the man is usually taller so that it would be uncomfortable for the sexes to reverse positions? No. The same ritual of man playing the powerful protector and woman the helpless protected is often observed when both are of about the same height or even when the man is slightly shorter. If the man is too short to stretch his arm around the woman's shoulders, they still will not reverse positions but will instead settle for holding hands. If a tall woman does put her arm around a shorter man's shoulders, chances are that she is a mother and he is her child (Tannen, 1994a; 1990). In the world of gender inequality, a man is likely to cringe if his girlfriend or wife treats him like a child by putting her arms around his shoulders.

8 Even in the most intimate moments between a man and a woman, male domination reigns. When both lie down in bed, he typically lies on his back, flat and straight, but she lies on her side, her body nestled against his. She further places her head on his shoulder, and he his arm around her. It is a picture of an unequal relationship, with the man appearing strong and protective and the woman weak and protected (Tannen, 1994a; 1990).

Questions for Discussion and Review

1. What are genderlects, and how do they affect the communication between women and men?
2. How do men and women play the gendered game of proxemics?

Source: Sociology, pp.121–131.

REVIEWING THE READING

DIRECTIONS   Write the letter of the choice that best completes each statement in the space provided.

Checking Your Comprehension

_____ 1. The author's purpose in this selection is to show

   a. how gender affects communication between men and women.
   b. why men are superior to women in modern society.
   c. how to communicate in business meetings.
   d. different kinds of body language used by women.

_____ 2. The central point of this selection is that

   a. women allow men to dominate them in social relationships.
   b. communication would be easier if everyone spoke the same language.
   c. men and women perfectly complement each other in the ways they communicate.
   d. communication differences affect relationships between men and women.

_____ 3. Paragraph 8's main idea is that

   a. lack of communication is a problem in our society.
   b. talking too much can ruin a relationship.
   c. body language often makes men appear dominant.
   d. women are afraid to express themselves.

_____ 4. When men and women talk to each other in groups, they

   a. use male conversation styles.
   b. argue over words.
   c. take turns choosing topics.
   d. talk only about food.

_____ 5. The communication between Josh and Linda in paragraph 2 is organized using

   a. time sequence.
   b. definition.
   c. enumeration.
   d. comparison–contrast.

Checking Your Vocabulary

_____ 6. _Genderlects_ (paragraph 1) are

   a. ways of achieving status.
   b. female ways of asserting independence.
   c. men's and women's styles of speech.
   d. words used to show emotions.

_____ 7. If you *misunderstand* (paragraph 3) someone you

    a. make a mistake about his or her meaning.
    b. ignore him or her.
    c. tell him or her a lie.
    d. are unable to convince him or her.

_____ 8. To *dominate* (paragraphs 5 and 7) something means to

    a. hide it.
    b. laugh about it.
    c. argue about it.
    d. control it.

_____ 9. *Proxemics* (paragraph 6) is

    a. an individual's use of space.
    b. aerobic exercise.
    c. public communication.
    d. shared activities.

_____ 10. *Interactions* (paragraph 7) occur

    a. under supervision.
    b. between opposites.
    c. between people.
    d. alone.

B–2   The Talk of the Sandbox: How Johnny and Suzy's Playground Chatter Prepares Them for Life at the Office

Deborah Tannen

1 Bob Hoover of the Pittsburgh Post-Gazette was interviewing me when he remarked that after years of coaching boys' softball teams, he was now coaching girls and they were very different. I immediately whipped out my yellow pad and began interviewing him—and discovered that his observations about how girls and boys play softball parallel mine about how women and men talk at work.

2 Hoover told me that boys' teams always had one or two stars whom the other boys treated with deference. So when he started coaching a girls' team he began by looking for the leader. He couldn't find one. "The girls who are better athletes don't lord it over the others," he said. "You get the feeling that everyone's the same." When a girl got the ball, she didn't try to throw it all the way home as a strong-armed boy would; instead, she'd throw it to another team member, so they all became better catchers and throwers. He went on, "If a girl makes an error, she's not in the doghouse for a long time, as a boy would be."

3 "But wait," I interrupted. "I've heard that when girls make a mistake at sports, they often say 'I'm sorry,' whereas boys don't."

in the doghouse
idiom meaning to be in disfavor or disgrace

A Workplace Scene

4   That's true, he said, but then the girl forgets it—and so do her teammates. "For boys, sports is a performance art. They're concerned with how they look." When they make an error, they sulk because they've let their teammates down. Girls want to win, but if they lose, they're still all in it together—so the mistake isn't as dreadful for the individual or the team.

5   What Hoover described in these youngsters were the seeds of behavior I have observed among women and men at work.

6   The girls who are the best athletes don't "lord it over" the others—just the ethic I found among women in positions of authority. Women managers frequently told me they were good managers because they did not act in an authoritarian manner. They said they did not flaunt their power, or behave as though they were better than their subordinates. Similarly, linguist Elisabeth Kuhn found that women professors in her study informed students of course requirements as if they had magically appeared on the syllabus ("There are two papers. The first paper, ah, let's see, is due . . . It's back here [referring to the syllabus] at the beginning"), whereas the men professors made it clear that they had set requirements ("I have two midterms and a final").

7   A woman manager might say to her secretary, "Could you do me a favor and type this letter right away?" knowing that her secretary is going to type the letter. But her male boss, on hearing this, might conclude she doesn't feel she deserves the authority she has, just as a boys' coach might think the star athlete doesn't realize how good he is if he doesn't expect his teammates to treat him with deference.

authoritarian
expecting obedience

8   I was especially delighted by Hoover's observation that, although girls are more likely to say, "I'm sorry," they are actually far less sorry when they make a mistake than boys who don't say it, but are "in the doghouse" for a long time. This dramatizes the ritual nature of many women's apologies. How often is a woman who is "always apologizing" seen as weak and lacking in confidence? In fact, for many women, saying "I'm sorry" often doesn't mean "I apologize." It means "I'm sorry that happened."

9   Like many of the rituals common among women, it's a way of speaking that takes into account the other person's point of view. It can even be an automatic conversational smoother. For example, you left your pad in someone's office; you knock on the door and say, "Excuse me, I left my pad on your desk," and the person whose office it is might reply, "Oh, I'm sorry. Here it is." She knows it is not her fault that you left your pad on her desk; she's just letting you know it's okay.

intrigued
had interest in or curiosity about

10   Finally, I was intrigued by Hoover's remark that boys regard sports as "a performance art" and worry about "how they look." There, perhaps, is the rub, the key to why so many women feel they don't get credit for what they do. From childhood, many boys learn something that is very adaptive to the workplace: Raises and promotions are based on "performance" evaluations and these depend, in large measure, on how you appear in other people's eyes. In other words, you have to worry not only about getting your job done but also about getting credit for what you do.

11   Getting credit often depends on the way you talk. For example, a woman told me she was given a poor evaluation because her supervisor felt she knew less than her male peers. Her boss, it turned out, reached this conclusion because the woman asked more questions: She was seeking information without regard to how her queries would make her look.

12   The same principle applies to apologizing. Whereas some women seem to be taking undeserved blame by saying "I'm sorry," some men seem to evade deserved blame. I observed this when a man disconnected a conference call by accidentally elbowing the speaker-phone. When his secretary re-connected the call, I expected him to say, "I'm sorry; I knocked the phone by mistake." Instead he said, "Hey, what happened?! One minute you were there, the next minute you were gone!" Annoying as this might be, there are certainly instances in which people improve their fortunes by covering up mistakes.

13   If Hoover's observations about girls' and boys' athletic styles are fascinating, it is even more revealing to see actual transcripts of children at play and how they mirror the adult workplace. Amy Sheldon, a linguist at the University of Minnesota who studies children talking at play in a day care center, compared the conflicts of pre-school girls and boys. She found that boys who fought with one another tended to pursue their own goals. Girls tended to balance their own interests with those of the other girls through complex verbal negotiations.

14   Look how different the negotiations were:

15   Two boys fought over a toy telephone: Tony had it; Charlie wanted it. Tony was sitting on a foam chair with the base of the phone in his lap and the receiver lying beside him. Charlie picked up the receiver, and Tony protested, "No, that's my phone!" He grabbed the telephone cord and tried to pull the receiver away from Charlie, saying, "No, that—uh, it's on MY couch. It's on MY couch, Charlie. It's on MY couch. It's on MY couch." It seems he had only one point to make, so he made it repeatedly as he used physical force to get the phone back.

16   Charlie ignored Tony and held onto the receiver. Tony then got off the couch, set the phone base on the floor and tried to keep possession of it by overturning the chair on top of it. Charlie managed to push the chair off, get the telephone and win the fight.

17   This might seem like a typical kids' fight until you compare it with a fight Sheldon videotaped among girls. Here the contested objects were toy medical instruments: Elaine had them; Arlene wanted them. But she didn't just grab for them; she argued her case. Elaine, in turn, balanced her own desire to keep them with Arlene's desire to get them. Elaine lost ground gradually, by compromising.

18   Arlene began not by grabbing but by asking and giving a reason: "Can I have that, that thing? I'm going to take my baby's temperature." Elaine was agreeable, but cautious: "You can use it—you can use my temperature. Just make sure you can't use anything else unless you can ask." Arlene did just that; she asked for the toy syringe: "May I?" Elaine at first resisted, but gave a reason: "No, I'm gonna need to use the shot in a couple of minutes." Arlene reached for the syringe anyway, explaining in a "beseeching" tone, "But I—I need this though."

capitulated
surrendered, gave in

19   Elaine capitulated, but again tried to set limits: "Okay, just use it once." She even gave Arlene permission to give "just a couple of shots."

20   Arlene then pressed her advantage, and became possessive of her property: "Now don't touch the baby until I get back, because it is MY BABY! I'll check her ears, okay?" (Even when being demanding, she asked for agreement: "okay?")

21   Elaine tried to regain some rights through compromise: "Well, let's pretend it's another day, that we have to look in her ears together." Elaine also tried another approach that would give Arlene something she wanted: "I'll have to shot her after, after, after you listen—after you look in her ears," suggested Elaine. Arlene, however, was adamant: "Now don't shot her at all!"

adamant
stubbornly unyielding

22   What happened next will sound familiar to anyone who has ever been a little girl or overheard one. Elaine could no longer abide Arlene's selfish behavior and applied the ultimate sanction: "Well, then, you can't come to my birthday!" Arlene uttered the predictable retort: "I don't want to come to your birthday!"

23   The boys and girls followed different rituals for fighting. Each boy went after what he wanted; they slugged it out; one won. But the girls enacted a complex negotiation, trying to get what they wanted while taking into account what the other wanted.

24   Here is an example of how women and men at work used comparable strategies.

25   Maureen and Harold, two managers at a medium-size company, were assigned to hire a human-resources coordinator for their division. Each favored a different candidate, and both felt strongly about their preferences. They traded arguments for some time, neither convincing the other. Then Harold said that hiring the candidate Maureen wanted would make him so uncomfortable that he would have to consider resigning. Maureen respected Harold. What's more, she liked him and considered him a friend. So she said what seemed to her the only thing she could say under the circumstances: "Well, I certainly don't want you to feel uncomfortable here. You're one of the pillars of the place." Harold's choice was hired.

26   What was crucial was not Maureen's and Harold's individual styles in isolation but how they played in concert with each other's style. Harold's threat to quit ensured his triumph—when used with someone for whom it was a trump card. If he had been arguing with someone who regarded this threat as simply another move in the negotiation rather than a non-negotiable expression of deep feelings, the result might have been different. For example, had she said, "That's ridiculous; of course you're not going to quit!" or matched it ("Well, I'd be tempted to quit if we hired your guy"), the decision might well have gone the other way.

27   Like the girls at play, Maureen was balancing her perspective with those of her colleague and expected him to do the same. Harold was simply going for what he wanted and trusted Maureen to do likewise.

28   This is not to say that all women and all men, or all boys and girls, behave any one way. Many factors influence our styles, including regional and ethnic backgrounds, family experience and individual personality. But gender is a key factor, and understanding its influence can help clarify what happens when we talk.

29   Understanding the ritual nature of communication gives you the flexibility to consider different approaches if you're not happy with the reaction you're getting. Someone who tends to avoid expressing disagreement might learn to play "devil's advocate" without taking it as a personal attack. Someone who tends to avoid admitting fault might find it is effective to say "I'm sorry"—that the loss of face is outweighed by a gain in credibility.

30   There is no one way of talking that will always work best. But understanding how conversational rituals work allows individuals to have more control over their own lives.

Source: The Washington Post, December 11, 1994.

REVIEWING THE READING

DIRECTIONS   Write the letter of the choice that best completes each statement in the space provided.

Checking Your Comprehension

_____ 1. Tannen wrote the essay to

    a. argue that negotiation does not achieve good results in business communication.

    b. explore the causes of children's communication styles.

    c. explain differences in men's and women's communication styles.

    d. present evidence that sports has a negative impact on the way people communicate.

_____ 2. This selection's central point is that men and women

    a. communicate differently both as children and as adults.

    b. communicate similarly as children.

    c. use body language in similar ways.

    d. develop similar communication skills as they age.

_____ 3. The main idea of paragraph 10 is that, from childhood, boys learn the importance of

    a. getting credit for what they do.

    b. taking into account another person's point of view.

    c. looking good while they play a sport.

    d. acting as though they are authorities.

_____ 4. The study of conflicts among preschool boys and girls revealed that

    a. boys who fought with one another were unable to get what they wanted.

    b. both boys and girls tried to balance their own interests with those of others.

    c. girls tended to rely on physical force to get what they wanted.

    d. girls use complex verbal negotiations to get what they want.

_____ 5. The overall organizational pattern used in this selection is

    a. comparison–contrast.

    b. time sequence.

    c. enumeration.

    d. sequential administration.

Checking Your Vocabulary

_____ 6. _Deference_ (paragraph 2) means

    a. respect.

    b. fear.

    c. disappointment.

    d. equality.

_____ 7. A *syllabus* (paragraph 6) is a(n)

   a. exam.
   b. course outline.
   c. group of notes.
   d. speech.

_____ 8. To *conclude* (paragraph 7) something is to

   a. wait until later to finish it.
   b. decide or come to realize.
   c. run out of choices.
   d. let someone else help you.

_____ 9. If two things are *disconnected* (paragraph 12), they

   a. are on fire.
   b. do not look alike.
   c. are broken.
   d. are no longer joined together.

_____ 10. A *perspective* (paragraph 27) is a

   a. hidden meaning.
   b. manner of speaking.
   c. negotiation strategy.
   d. way of looking at things.

B–3   Communication Between Sexes: A War of the Words?

Barbara Ash

1   Dave Davis draws a blank when asked if he notices any differences in the way women and men communicate on the job. "I don't find any," says Davis, a researcher for Florida TaxWatch. "I think that's a stereotype that died, or should have died, years ago. In my experience working with state government, the women I see in meetings communicate just as well as males, are just as persuasive and as appreciated as males. I don't think it's an issue anymore."

2   Jayne Hoffman doesn't know Davis, but his response doesn't surprise her. "I'd imagine a man would say that," says Hoffman with a laugh. "Men have been running things, setting the pace and communication style from the beginning. When women started encroaching on their territory, men didn't have to change their style. We had to adjust ours to fit in," says the budget director at the Department of Highway Safety and Motor Vehicles. "Of course, it's not an issue for men."

3   But conversational style should be an issue for everyone, particularly women, because even the simplest exchanges at work can be, in a sense, a test, says Deborah Tannen, author of the best-seller *You Just Don't Understand: Men and Women in Conversation.* "What we say as we do our work can become the evidence on which we are judged, and

A Workplace Scene

the judgments may surface in the form of raises (or denials of raises), promotions (or lack of them), and favorable (or unfavorable) work assignments," Tannen says.

4   The hardest part about communication style is that everyone assumes they're communicating the same way, says Micki Kacmar, a Florida State University business professor and organizational communications consultant. "But people interpret the same message differently, and that causes problems. Unless the person you're communicating with understands your style, you won't be successful." That's why it's hard to grin and bear it when:

- You say something at a meeting and it's ignored, but then a man says the same thing and it's embraced as a wonderful idea.
- You speak up at the conference table and you're constantly interrupted by the men on your team, whose voices are louder, deeper, and more authoritative.
- You've worked overtime on a project, but don't get the credit.
- You give what you think are clear instructions, but the job doesn't get done.

5   People in positions of authority are judged by how they use that authority. That can pose a special challenge for women managers because the ways women are expected to talk are at odds with our traditional images of authority, Tannen says. In fact, the way women communicate, issue orders, and make decisions are often misinterpreted as a lack of confidence or even competence. "Women tend to be more polite and congenial. They want everything to be pleasant, and that doesn't always work because not everyone is playing by the same rules," says Darlene Long, a data-processing manager with the Agency for Health Care Reform.

6   A main difference between men and women's styles, Tannen says and many Tallahassee working women agree, is that men are more goal-oriented, while women are more people-oriented. "I'm more likely to take into consideration an employee's family situation and if the deadline is an important one before I make them work overtime to get a job done," says Hoffman, who supervises both men and women.

"If a man takes personal issues into consideration, it doesn't show. He's going to want to get the job done no matter what," Hoffman said.

7 Denise Rains, a public-affairs officer for the U.S. Forest Service, recalls that in a previous job she and other women on her leadership team would get a man to present suggestions. "We felt there was a better chance that people would listen to him," Rains admitted. "More than once, a woman would say something and the people at the meeting would say, 'OK,' ignore it, and go on. Then a man would say the exact same thing in a different way, and everyone would act like it's a new, great idea." Examples like this leave women feeling invisible.

8 "Women have told me they often come away from meetings feeling empty, feeling they haven't gotten across what they want to get across," says Tallahassee marriage and family therapist Kristen Overman, who counsels men and women on communication. Women tend to personalize experiences, thinking this is happening only to them, Overman said. "When they understand this is a general **dynamic**, they can use their good minds to develop methods of communicating their ideas in a way that will be heard," Overman says.

dynamic
process, way of interacting

9 Like Tannen, Overman and Kacmar don't consider men's communication style superior to women's, just different. In fact, adopting men's style for the most part doesn't work for women. Men tend to be more direct, more goal-oriented. They also tend to speak louder, longer, interrupt more, and speak more authoritatively at meetings. Men are more likely to start sentences with, "It's obvious that . . . ," "The facts show . . . ," "This will work if we . . ." Women, on the other hand, are more likely to speak less at meetings, apologize for taking up time, try to draw everyone into the decision-making process, ask opinions, and thank co-workers for listening to them. "We shouldn't be forced into a style or thought process that we're not comfortable with," Rains says.

10 Some women say you're damned if you act businesslike, and damned if you don't. Realtor Joan Raley says that if she approaches peers in a professional manner and is direct, like men tend to be, or if she displays annoyance or anger, she's viewed as "grumpy, grouchy, or bitchy." "People react to men's anger or irritability differently," she says. "They accept that as a part of their role as an assertive executive." "I'm just trying to get work done in a businesslike manner, which is how a top-flight male executive would approach his business. It's okay for a male to do that, but not a woman. Both men and women expect women to communicate and behave a certain way—to be quieter, not as direct, not as assertive. They expect us to be **nurturing**."

nurturing
helping to grow and develop

11 Overman and Kacmar agree that women and men don't have to change their communication styles. Instead, they need to be mindful of other conversational styles, and develop flexibility. "You must have a large **repertoire** of tactics to communicate effectively," she says. "You can keep your style as long as you know you're making your point." One tactic Long, the data-processing manager, has adopted is to continue talking when someone interrupts her. "When you're talking and men cut you off, I've learned to do what they do," she

repertoire
range or number of skills

says. "I'll continue talking until they realize what they're doing. I've had to be more assertive because if you're not, you'll end up being ignored."

subordinate
one who has a lower position job

12   Overman says she sees a lot of women who are frustrated and depressed because they feel their talents are devalued, and they're not listened to at work or at home." At work a woman's communication may be misinterpreted by a male subordinate because she's been raised to give directives in a polite, respectful manner," Overman says. "For instance, the female boss may say, 'You might want to consider making these changes in this report.' Her intention is to communicate that she wants something done." But the man may interpret that as a suggestion, rather than a directive, and may not follow it. The woman interprets his inaction as insubordination, and with good reason, Overman says. But he's unaware he was given a directive, and is perplexed at her anger. Men need to be spoken to directly, with specific requests.

13   "The frustration at work carries over to home," Overman says. "Home should be a place where the people who love you listen to you, but many women express frustration that their partners don't listen well either. "What frustrates men and women is when they misinterpret each other. They need to become familiar with each other's styles."

Source: Knight-Ridder Tribune News Service, February 13, 1996.

REVIEWING THE READING

DIRECTIONS   Write the letter of the choice that best completes each statement in the space provided.

Checking Your Comprehension

_____   1. In this selection, the author's purpose is to

   a. argue that men have the most effective communication methods.
   b. present strategies for improving communication.
   c. explain differences in how men and women communicate.
   d. convince men and women of the need to improve communication at home.

_____   2. The thesis of this selection is that

   a. communication differences cause miscommunication between men and women at work.
   b. men do not believe they misunderstand what women are saying.
   c. communication can be improved at home if men learn to speak like women.
   d. women do not get raises or promotions because they concentrate on their emotions.

_____ 3. The main idea in paragraph 3 is that conversational style is important because it

    a. shows if a person is goal-oriented.
    b. hides men's true weaknesses.
    c. affects how women are judged at work.
    d. requires flexibility at work.

_____ 4. Instead of changing how they speak, people should

    a. be more pleasant and congenial in the way they communicate.
    b. express their frustration about communication mix-ups.
    c. be more aware of the ways other people communicate.
    d. learn to be more direct and goal-oriented.

_____ 5. The overall pattern used to organize this selection is

    a. cause–effect.
    b. comparison–contrast.
    c. time sequence.
    d. enumeration.

Checking Your Vocabulary

_____ 6. A person who is *congenial* (paragraph 5) is

    a. louder.
    b. rushed.
    c. goal-oriented.
    d. friendly.

_____ 7. Behaving *authoritatively* (paragraph 9) shows you are

    a. in charge.
    b. apologetic.
    c. pleasant.
    d. uncomfortable.

_____ 8. A talent that is *devalued* (paragraph 12) is

    a. reduced in worth or importance.
    b. contradicted by others.
    c. confused about the facts.
    d. shown to be valuable.

_____ 9. Something that is *misinterpreted* (paragraph 12) is

    a. given a raise.
    b. ignored by others.
    c. understood incorrectly.
    d. translated into another language.

_____ 10. A *directive* (paragraph 12) is a(n)

    a. emotion.

    b. promotion.

    c. order.

    d. excuse.

MAKING CONNECTIONS

1. All three authors agree that men and women communicate differently. Specifically, what differences does each author identify?
2. Think of an example from your own experience that illustrates one of the differences discussed by one or more of the authors.
3. Which reading did you find most enjoyable and interesting? Why?
4. Which article seems most detailed and most carefully researched? Support your answer by referring to the readings.
5. Two of the readings appeared in newspapers. How do these two readings differ from the third, which was taken from a college textbook?

WORLD WIDE WEB ACTIVITY

A Researcher's Home Page

In the first reading about communication between women and men, two research studies by Tannen are cited in the first paragraph: Tannen, 1994a, 1990. The second reading, "The Talk of the Sandbox," is by Deborah Tannen. The third reading refers to a best-selling book that Tannen wrote called *You Just Don't Understand: Men and Women in Conversation.* From this group of readings, you can reason that Deborah Tannen is a well-known researcher in the area of men's and women's communication.

    Suppose you are writing a paper on this topic, and you'd like to know more about Tannen's research. Do a Web search using "Deborah Tannen" as your key word phrase to find the official Web site of Deborah Tannen. When you find it, answer the following questions:

1. How many books has Tannen written? How many of them seem to be on the topic of men's and women's communication? Where did you find this information?
2. Where does the link to her book *Talking from 9 to 5* take you? Where does the link to her Ph.D. degree take you? Are these related or remote links? How do you know?
3. In the list of "General Audience Publications" Tannen has written, which articles seem to be most relevant to the topic of women's communication at work? How do you know?

Biology and Environmental Science

C–1 Environment: Increased Hurricane Activity Tied to Global Warming

Stephen Leahy

1 As many as 12 more Atlantic tropical storms, four of them major hurricanes, are expected this year, according to the U.S. National Oceanographic and Atmospheric Administration (NOAA). "This may well be one of the most active Atlantic hurricane seasons on record, and will be the ninth above-normal Atlantic hurricane season in the last 11 years," Brig. Gen. David L. Johnson, director of the NOAA National Weather Service, said in a statement. NOAA forecasts a whopping 21 tropical storms—double the norm—before the end of hurricane season on Nov. 30. That means the U.S., Mexico and Caribbean region could still be pounded by another 10 to 12 storms, including a major hurricane on the scale of Katrina. Fortunately, not all of these are likely to make landfall.

2 Warm water in the Atlantic Ocean is being blamed. Seawater at 27 degrees Celsius or higher (81 degrees Fahrenheit) puts enough moisture in the air to prime hurricane or **cyclone** formation. Once started, a hurricane needs only warm water and the right wind conditions to build and maintain its strength and intensity. When Hurricane Katrina first hit southern Florida last week, it was just Category One on the Saffir-Simpson scale, which rates hurricanes from one to five according to wind speeds and destructive potential. Less than 24 hours after it entered the warm waters of the Gulf of Mexico, it quickly gained strength, becoming a Category Five with winds blowing continuously above 250 kilometers an hour.

3 While Katrina lost strength to a Category Four when it hit the U.S. Gulf Coast, it was extremely large in size, cutting a broad swath of destruction. The city of New Orleans is evacuated because of severe flooding. "There's no question that the warm waters of the Gulf provided the heat that turned Katrina into a major storm," said Ross Gelbspan, a Pulitzer Prize–winning reporter and author of two books on global warming. The ultimate cause, however, is global warming, Gelbspan told IPS.

4 That's a controversial view in a country with many officials who vigorously deny the existence of global warming or climate change. But scientific evidence—and the numerous record-breaking storms, droughts, floods and forest fires—suggest that the climate is indeed changing. Climatologist David Easterling of NOAA's National Climatic Data Center has found that rainfall intensity in the U.S. has increased significantly, which he **attributes** to climate change. However, whether the currently warmer mid-Atlantic is the result of global warming or a natural cycle "is pretty hard to say," he said.

cyclone
violent tropical storm originating in Pacific Ocean

attributes
relates to

A Survivor of Hurricane Katrina Amid the Debris.

5   On a global scale, there is clear evidence of human-produced warming of the world's oceans, said Tim Barnett, a marine physicist at Scripps Institution of Oceanography in California. "The amount of heat that has gone into the oceans is truly remarkable," Barnett said in a statement. Over the last 40 years, the top 300 meters of the world's oceans have warmed about a half-degree Celsius on average. Although that's not a new finding, Barnett is the first to say he has proved it is the result of emissions of greenhouse gases from burning fossil fuels. Using a combination of computer models and real-world "observed" data, scientists say they measured for the first time the impact of global warming in the oceans. "This is perhaps the most compelling evidence yet that global warming is happening right now," Barnett said.

6   And according to another landmark study the warmer ocean is pumping up the destructive power of hurricanes and typhoons. The global increase in ocean temperature has resulted in a doubling of the destructive power of North Atlantic hurricanes, Kerry Emanuel of the Massachusetts Institute of Technology wrote in July in the journal *Nature*. In the other region Emanuel studied, storms in the northwest Pacific Ocean are 75 percent more powerful than they were 30 years ago. Emanuel measured the wind speed of storms and their duration to produce an analysis of the destructive potential of each storm. Actual destruction was not measured because most storms do not make landfall. He found no evidence for an increase in the number of storms.

7   Other studies have shown that global warming is creating conditions that are more favorable for hurricanes to develop and be more severe. Predictions made about climate change 10 years ago are coming true: sea level and temperature rises, increased air temperatures, and now increased storm intensity.

8   It is well past time for the U.S. to take action on climate change and follow the lead of Britain and Germany with dramatic cuts in emissions

emissions
gases and particles released
into the air by burning
fossil fuels

of 60 percent, says Gelbspan. "We don't need to wait for another 10 years of studies before reducing emissions as the (George W.) Bush administration suggests," says Michael Mastrandrea, an environmental science and policy researcher at Stanford University. "Waiting to start making major reductions in emissions runs the risk of triggering irreversible impacts," Mastrandrea told IPS. Because there is a long lag in the climate system, the full effects of past greenhouse gas emissions are yet to come, he said. Adding ever higher levels of emissions puts future generations at risk. "We should hedge our bets and act now," Mastrandrea said.

Source: Global Information Network, September 1, 2005

REVIEWING THE READING

DIRECTIONS   Write the letter of the choice that best completes each statement in the space provided.

Checking Your Comprehension

_____ 1. The main purpose of this selection is to

   a. demonstrate the positive effects of reducing emissions of greenhouse gases.
   b. discuss climate changes that may be causing increased hurricane activity.
   c. predict the number of hurricanes that will form during the remainder of this hurricane season.
   d. persuade U.S. policymakers to take immediate action on climate change.

_____ 2. The thesis of this selection is that the increase in hurricane activity

   a. is definitely caused by global warming.
   b. is actually the result of a natural cycle.
   c. may be linked to climate change.
   d. is completely unrelated to changes in the climate.

_____ 3. The Saffir-Simpson scale rates hurricanes according to

   a. geographic location.
   b. wind speeds and destructive potential.
   c. actual destruction after landfall.
   d. sea level and temperature rise.

_____ 4. One important finding of the landmark study by Kerry Emanuel was that

   a. rainfall intensity in the United States has increased significantly.
   b. the world's oceans have warmed a half-degree over the last 40 years.

     c. storms in the northwest Pacific Ocean cause more actual destruction than North Atlantic storms.

     d. warmer oceans have caused the destructive power of North Atlantic hurricanes to double.

_____ 5. The main point of paragraph 8 is that

     a. it is urgent that the United States act now to reduce emissions.

     b. past predictions about climate change are coming true.

     c. Britain and Germany must make major cuts in emissions.

     d. there should be further studies before reducing emissions.

Checking Your Vocabulary

_____ 6. To *prime* (paragraph 2) means to

     a. prepare or make ready.

     b. care for.

     c. bring to an end.

     d. search out.

_____ 7. A *swath* (paragraph 3) is a

     a. storm.

     b. path.

     c. tool.

     d. fire.

_____ 8. To do something *vigorously* (paragraph 4) is to do it

     a. weakly.

     b. without help.

     c. with force and energy.

     d. carelessly.

_____ 9. Evidence that is *compelling* (paragraph 5) is

     a. mistaken.

     b. persuasive.

     c. confusing.

     d. upsetting.

_____ 10. A *lag* (paragraph 8) in a system means there has been a

     a. sudden change.

     b. disagreement.

     c. problem.

     d. delay.

C–2　Have We Exceeded Earth's Carrying Capacity?

dwindling
getting less

1　In Cote d'Ivoire (Ivory Coast), a small country in West Africa, the government is waging a battle to protect some of its rapidly dwindling tropical rain forest from thousands of illegal hunters, farmers, and loggers. Officials burn the homes of the squatters, who immediately return and rebuild. One illegal resident is Sep Djekoule. "I have 10 children and we must eat," he explains. "The forest is where I can provide for my family, and everybody has that right." His words illustrate the conflict between population growth and environmental protection, between the desire to have many children and the ability to provide for them using Earth's finite resources. The middle level United Nations projection is that the human population will reach 8.9 billon by the year 2050, and will still be increasing. How many people can Earth support?

2　Humans have already increased carrying capacity by the use of technology. We have the potential to increase it further while reducing our destructive impact, for example by developing higher-yield crops, reducing erosion, conserving energy and water, reducing manufacturing wastes, and recycling far more paper and plastic, and the metals that we currently mine and discard. However, our ability to reproduce far exceeds our ability to increase Earth's carrying capacity.

prestigious
highly esteemed

ecosystems
communities of organisms living together in their environment as a unit

3　Recently, a group of 11 scientists from around the world published a paper in the prestigious *Proceedings of the National Academy of Sciences* in this rigorous assessment of humanity's impact on global ecosystems, the researchers compared the resource needs of the global human population with the ability of global ecosystems to provide them. They identify six types of human activities that place demands on Earth's biological resources: growing crops, grazing livestock, fishing, harvesting timber, occupying space (for housing, roads, and

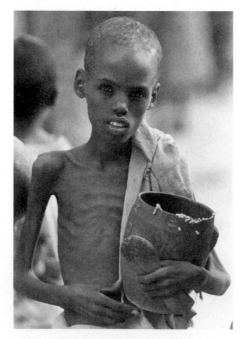

A Child Suffering from Malnutrition

biosphere
the portion of Earth and its atmosphere that support life

industry), and burning fossil fuels (which places demands on the biosphere to absorb CO_2). The authors calculated the amount of biologically productive space needed to supply the demands of an average person at current levels of technology, an area they call an **ecological footprint**. They provide compelling evidence that the collective ecological footprint of Earth's 6.3 billion people already exceeds the available biologically productive space (4.7 acres per person) by about 20%. In other words, these calculations suggest that Earth's carrying capacity has already been considerably exceeded by the human population. Unfortunately, these estimates are conservative; they do not take into account the depletion of nonrenewable fossil fuels and underground freshwater stores, or the need to leave significant portions of the biosphere untouched to provide habitat for species other than people. Currently, only 3% of land has been set aside in such preserves, and ecologists estimate that we may need 10 times that much to adequately protect other species. When carrying capacity is exceeded, the biosphere is damaged and its ability to sustain the population (in this case, people) is reduced. There is compelling evidence that this is already occurring.

4   Stanford University biologist Peter Vitousek estimates that human activities have already reduced the productivity of Earth's forests and grasslands by 12%. Each year, overgrazing and deforestation futher decreases the productivity of land, especially in developing countries. In a world where nearly 780 million people are chronically undernourished, two-thirds of the world's agricultural land is suffering moderate to servere erosion. The quest for more agricultural land is leading to deforestation and attempts to farm land that is poorly suited for agriculture. These actions contribute to the destruction of tens of millions of acres of rain forest annually. As a result, some ecologists estimate that we are driving 50 to 150 undescribed species to extinction each day. Each year, the U.S. loses nearly half a million acres of productive farmland to development for homes, shopping malls, and roads. Already, most countries must import the grain they need for countries such as the U.S. As our growing population spreads onto our farmland, our future ability to export grain to help sustain other nations will diminish, while their needs increase. Worldwide, the amount of cropland per person has declined by half in the past 50 years.

5   In many developing countries, water supplies are badly polluted and underground water supplies, called *aquifers,* are depleted and not replaced. Both India and China are rapidly depleting aquifers to supply the needs of their growing cities and to irrigate their cropland. Currently, about 1.5 billion people lack access to safe drinking water, and this number is expected to double in the next 25 years.

6   The demand for wood in developing countries causes large areas to be deforested annually. This leads to erosion of precious topsoil, runoff of much-needed fresh water, and a decline in the ability of the land to regrow forests or support crops. The total world fish harvest peaked in the late 1980s and has been gradually declining since then, despite increased investments in fishing equipment, improved technology for

finding fish, and increased harvests of smaller and less-desirable fish species. Almost 70% of commercial ocean fish populations have been fully exploited or overfished, and many formerly abundant fish populations, such as cod harvested off New England, Canada, and the North Sea, have collapsed because of overfishing. Our present population, at its present level of technology, is clearly "overgrazing" the world ecosystem. As the 5 billion people of less-developed countries strive to increase their standard of living, the damage to Earth's ecosystems accelerates.

7   In estimating how many people Earth can—or should—support, it is important to recognize that people desire more from life than a minimum number of food calories daily. The standard of living in developed countries is already an unattainable luxury for most of Earth's inhabitants. Inevitably, the human population must stop growing. Either we must voluntarily reduce our birth rates, or various forces of environmental resistance, including disease and starvation, will eventually dramatically increase human death rates; the choice is ours. Hope for the future lies reduce our population before we decimate our biodiversity and irrevocably damage the biosphere.

Source: Biology, pp. 812–813.

REVIEWING THE READING

DIRECTIONS   Write the letter of the choice that best completes each statement in the space provided.

Checking Your Comprehension

_____   1. The main purpose of this selection is to

   a. describe the conflict between population growth and environmental protection.
   b. explain the reasons for the rapid growth of the population of the United States.
   c. present detailed strategies for increasing Earth's carrying capacity.
   d. argue for the right of humans to have as many children as they want.

_____   2. The thesis of this selection is that

   a. Earth's carrying capacity is in no danger of being exceeded because it is unlimited.
   b. technology has the potential to increase Earth's carrying capacity far beyond human needs.
   c. human activities and our growing population threaten the future of life on Earth.
   d. land that has been set aside to provide habitat for other species should be used for humans.

_____ 3. The main point of paragraph 6 is that

a. developing countries' demand for wood has caused large areas of deforestation.
b. human activities have been causing damage to the world ecosystem.
c. the total world fish harvest has been declining since the late 1980s.
d. people in developing countries are striving to increase their standard of living.

_____ 4. The amount of biologically productive space needed to supply the demands of an average person at current levels of technology is called

a. a biosphere.
b. an ecological footprint.
c. an aquifer.
d. a global ecosystem.

_____ 5. The fundamental course of action called for in this selection is for humans to

a. reduce water pollution in developing countries.
b. use technology to increase the carrying capacity of Earth.
c. improve the productivity of the world's agricultural land.
d. stop population growth by reducing birth rates.

Checking Your Vocabulary

_____ 6. If something is _finite_ (paragraph 1) it is

a. limited.
b. powerful.
c. plentiful.
d. desirable.

_____ 7. A _rigorous_ (paragraph 3) assessment is one that is extremely

a. repetitive.
b. negative.
c. thorough.
d. rapid.

_____ 8. _Depletion_ (paragraph 3) means

a. production.
b. improvement.
c. reduction.
d. contribution.

_____ 9. When something *accelerates* (paragraph 6) it

    a. becomes smaller.

    b. speeds up.

    c. changes shape.

    d. gradually decreases.

_____ 10. Another word for *decimate* (paragraph 7) is

    a. discover.

    b. benefit.

    c. choose.

    d. destroy.

C–3   Stem-cell Therapy: Promise and Reality

1 The potential of stem cells to treat devastating diseases has been hailed as one of the greatest medical breakthroughs of all time. But the rapidly unfolding ability of scientists to manipulate those undifferentiated cells into any type of specialized cell, including the pulsing cells of the heart, the insulin-producing cells of the pancreas, and the nerve cells in the spinal cord and brain, has also aroused controversy.

undifferentiated cells cells that have not yet formed into specific or specialized types of cells

2   While President Bush has said there's great promise in this research, in August 2001 he announced that federal funding for embryonic stem-cell research would be limited. He cited "profound ethical questions" as the reason for restricting government-funded studies to some 60 embryonic stem-cell lines that were in use when the executive order was signed. Research on adult and animal stem cells was not limited.

3   The combination of high hopes and contention has left many people confused about where those potential treatments stand today, seven years after human embryonic stem cells were isolated and grown in the laboratory. This report separates the hype from the hope and reports on the current state of stem-cell treatments for a wide variety of chronic diseases and disabilities.

Basis of Therapy

4 All of the 200 specialized cell types in the human body derive from the undifferentiated cells that begin to divide when an egg is fertilized by a sperm. If the ability of those early dividing cells to change into any type of cell could be harnessed, the theory goes, it might someday be possible to replace diseased or defective cells that cause degenerative diseases and disabilities. One day, researchers may even be able to use stem cells to grow entire hearts, livers, or kidneys.

5 Stem cells are found in embryos and in the umbilical-cord blood of newborns. They have also been identified in adults. Adult stem cells have been found in blood, bone marrow, brain, liver, skeletal muscle, skin, and even fat cells. Unlike embryonic stem cells, the ability of adult stem cells to morph into specialized cells and grow appears to be limited.

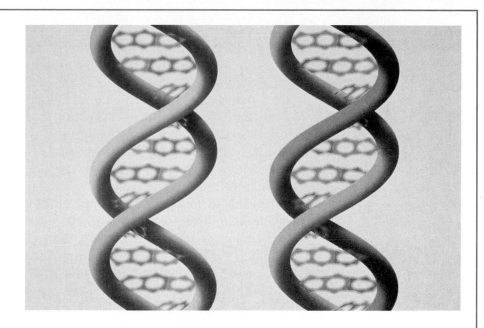

Strands of DNA

Sources of Cells Used in Research

6 Federally funded embryonic stem-cell research uses stem-cell lines derived before Aug. 9, 2001, from fertilized eggs donated by infertile couples who underwent in-vitro fertilization procedures. Some people object to such research on fertilized eggs because extracting the stem cells destroys the potential for life.

7   When the fertilized eggs are smaller than a grain of sand, stem cells lining the inner surface of a hollow ball of cells called a blastocyst are taken out. Some researchers customize unfertilized eggs by removing their genetic material and replacing it with DNA from the stem-cell recipient. This experimental technique creates an embryonic stem-cell line that is almost genetically identical to the DNA donor, reducing the chance that stem cells transplanted back into the donor would trigger an immune response and cause rejection of the transplanted stem cells.

Treatments Available Today

8 Blood-forming stem cells found in adult bone marrow and the circulatory system develop into the red blood cells that fight infection, white blood cells that carry oxygen, and platelets that help the blood to clot. They are commonly collected from a matched donor and given to cancer patients to replace the bone-marrow cells destroyed by chemotherapy or radiation.

9   Some 45,000 to 50,000 bone-marrow transplants are performed worldwide each year for patients with life-threatening diseases who urgently needed stem cells to regenerate their bone marrow.

10   About 4.5 million Americans have registered as volunteer bone-marrow donors. In addition, doctors have begun to collect cancer patients' own stem cells, returning them as autologous transplants after treatments have ended and the drugs have washed out of patient's systems. When patients get back their own stem cells, there is

in-vitro fertiliztion
a procedure in which an egg is fertilized in an artificial environment, such as a test tube

autologous transplants
transplants using the patient's own blood, bone marrow, or tissue

graft-vs.-host disease
the body's rejection of transplanted material as foreign

no chance of immune mismatch or potentially fatal graft-vs-host disease. An additional problem is that not all patients who need transplants can find suitably matched donors, and not all diseases can be treated with adult stem cells.

11   Stem-cell treatment is also being used for blood disorders including aplastic anemia, sickle-cell anemia, and amyloidosis, a rare disease that can damage major organ systems. Some insurance companies will pay for all or part of stem-cell transplants. The federal government announced in March that Medicare is considering covering stem-cell transplants from amyloidosis.

12   Private and public banks are now available for freezing and storing blood left over in the umbilical cord after a child is born. This blood is rich in the stem cells used in the treatment of certain cancers and blood disorders. Private banking of the cord blood for person use is considered an option for families with a child who has a disease that could someday require a stem-cell transplant. Public cord–blood banks accept donations of umbilical cord blood and make them available to patients who need a transplant, if a close match can be found.

Scientific Barriers to Stem-cell Therapies

13 Many scientific hurdles to stem-cell transplants remain. To use adult stem cells more widely, researchers need to find ways to identify them in the body and grow them in sufficient numbers. For both embryonic and adult stem-cell lines, methods need to be found to enable the cells to differentiate into the desired cell types. Then techniques are needed to transplant the stem cells so that they integrate and survive in the surrounding tissue and function as desired.

14   Investigators would need to somehow modify these cells and the recipient's immune system to help prevent rejection of the stem cells as foreign material. Another concern is the possible risk that transplanted stem cells could turn cancerous if cell division went out of control. However, encouraging results are beginning to be reported in human clinical studies involving patients with congestive heart failure, and from lab and animal research into other major diseases and disorders.

State Initiatives

15 Last fiscal year, the National Institutes of Health awarded $24 million for embryonic stem-cell research. That's not enough to advance research, say some experts. They worry that this may lead to a brain drain as scientists leave for labs outside the U.S., where there are fewer restrictions and more money for research. California and New Jersey are currently the only states that expressly permit embryonic-stem-cell research, according to the National Conference on State Legislatures. Ten other states are considering such legislation. Last year California voters approved a statewide referendum that earmarks $3 billion in state funding over the next 10 years for studies on embryonic stem cells and, secondarily, umbilical-cord blood and adult stem cells. In New Jersey, a state-funded stem-cell research center will be constructed

at Rutgers University. In Massachusetts, seven teaching hospitals have collaborated to form the Harvard Stem Cell Institute to develop therapies from embryonic and adult stem cells.

Source: www.ConsumerReportsHealth.org, June 2005.

REVIEWING THE READING

DIRECTIONS   Write the letter of the choice that best completes each statement in the space provided.

Checking Your Comprehension

_____   1. The main purpose of this selection is to

    a. explain the need for restrictions on adult and animal stem-cell research.
    b. encourage international collaboration among scientists conducting stem-cell research.
    c. criticize the president's policy limiting the use of federal funds for embryonic stem-cell research.
    d. describe the current state of stem-cell treatments for a variety of diseases and disabilities.

_____   2. The central thought of this selection is that

    a. there is too much controversy surrounding the use of stem cells to allow any real progress to be made.
    b. federal restrictions and a lack of funding in the United States will force stem-cell researchers to seek labs in other countries.
    c. the development of stem-cell therapies has met with some success although many challenges remain.
    d. ethical questions about the use of human embryonic stem cells must be resolved before further research is conducted.

_____   3. According to the selection, stem cells have been used successfully in treating all of the following disorders *except*

    a. cancer.
    b. diabetes.
    c. sickle-cell anemia.
    d. amyloidosis.

_____   4. In paragraph 12, the author compares

    a. embryonic and adult stem-cell lines.
    b. bone-marrow transplants and stem-cell therapy.
    c. private and public cord-blood banks.
    d. potential stem-cell treatments currently in use.

_____   5. Paragraph 15 uses the enumeration pattern to present

    a. state initiatives on stem cell research.
    b. chronic diseases treated by stem cells.

      c. scientific barriers to stem-cell treatments.

      d. experimental techniques for creating stem-cell lines.

Checking Your Vocabulary

_____ 6. To *manipulate* (paragraph 1) something is to

    a. change it.

    b. remove it.

    c. destroy it.

    d. replace it.

_____ 7. An issue that leads to *contention* (paragraph 3) is one that involves

    a. great expense.

    b. optimism.

    c. disagreement or debate.

    d. illegal goods.

_____ 8. To *derive* (paragraph 4) means to

    a. donate.

    b. originate.

    c. divide.

    d. mock.

_____ 9. Cells that can *morph* (paragraph 5) are able to

    a. disappear completely.

    b. harm other cells.

    c. grow uncontrollably.

    d. change into something else.

_____ 10. For something to *integrate* (paragraph 13), it must

    a. remain separate.

    b. prevent progress.

    c. become part of something else.

    d. be defective.

MAKING CONNECTIONS

1. For one of the issues discussed in this section, identify what types of further information you would need to understand the issue more fully.

2. In your opinion, which of the issues addressed in this section is the most serious? Justify your answer.

3. Which issue could have the greatest impact on the largest number of people?

4. For which, if any, of the issues addressed in this section is government intervention needed or appropriate? If it is needed or appropriate, indicate what actions government could or should take.
5. What other topics could have been included in this section titled "Controversies in Science"?

WORLD WIDE WEB ACTIVITY

Ecological Footprint

Calculate your impact on the Earth with this tool from Earthday Network:

http://www.earthday.org/footprint/index.asp#

Compare yourself to your classmates. What are some ways in which you can reduce your harmful impact on the planet?

THEME **D** CIVIL LIBERTIES

Political Science and Government

D–1   Textbook Excerpt: Civil Liberties and the Constitution

Edward S. Greenberg and Benjamin I. Page

Civil Liberties in the Constitution

1 Civil liberties are freedoms protected by constitutional provisions, laws, and practices from certain types of government interference. The framers of the Constitution were particularly concerned about establishing a society in which liberty might flourish. As embodied in the Bill of Rights, civil liberties are protected by prohibitions against government actions that threaten the enjoyment of freedom.

preamble
introduction to

2   In the Preamble to the Constitution, the framers wrote that they aimed to "secure the Blessings of Liberty to ourselves and our Posterity." But in the original Constitution, they protected few liberties from the national government they were creating and almost none from state governments. Rather than listing specific prohibitions against certain kinds of actions, they believed that liberty was best protected by a constitutional design that fragmented government power, a design that included separation of powers, checks and balances, and federalism. Still, the framers singled out certain freedoms as too crucial to be left unmentioned. The Constitution prohibits Congress and the states from suspending the writ of habeas corpus, except when public safety demands it because of rebellion or invasion, and from passing bills of attainder or ex post facto laws (see Table 13.1 for an enumeration).

habeas corpus
legal doctrine that arrested person must have timely hearing before a judge

bills of attainder
governmental decree that a person is guilty of crime punishable by death, without trial

ex post facto
after the fact, a law that retroactively says an action is illegal

3   Many citizens found the proposed Constitution too stingy in its listing of liberties, so the Federalists were led to promise a *"bill of rights"* as a condition for passing the Constitution. The Bill of Rights was passed by the 1st Congress in 1789 and was ratified by the required number of states by 1791. Passage of the Bill of Rights made the Constitution more democratic by specifying protections of political liberty and by guaranteeing a context of free political expression that makes popular sovereignty possible.

4   Looking at the liberties specified by the text of the Constitution and its amendments, however, emphasizes how few of our most cherished liberties are to be found in a reading of the bare words of the Constitution. Decisions by government officials and changes brought about by political leaders, interest groups, social movements, and individuals remade the Constitution in the long run, so many of the freedoms we expect today are not specifically mentioned there. Some extensions of protected liberties were introduced by judges and other officials. Others have evolved as the culture has grown to accept novel

TABLE 13.1   CIVIL LIBERTIES IN THE U.S. CONSTITUTION

The exact meaning and extent of civil liberties in the Constitution are matters of debate, but here are some freedoms from government spelled out in the text of the Constitution and its amendments or clarified by early court decisions.

CONSTITUTION

Article I, Section 9
Congress may not suspend a writ of habeas corpus.
Congress may not pass bills of attainder or ex post facto laws.

Article I, Section 10
States may not pass bills of attainder or ex post facto laws.
States may not impair obligation of contracts.

Article III, Section 2
Criminal trials in national courts must be jury trials in the state in which the defendant is alleged to have committed the crime.

Article III, Section 3
No one may be convicted of treason unless there is a confession in open court or testimony of two witnesses to the same overt act.

Article IV, Section 2
Citizens of each state are entitled to all privileges and immunities of citizens in the several states.

THE BILL OF RIGHTS

Amendment 1
Congress may not make any law with respect to the establishment of religion.
Congress may not abridge the free exercise of religion.
Congress may not abridge freedom of speech or of the press.
Congress may not abridge the right to assemble or to petition the government.

Amendment 2
Congress may not infringe the right to keep and bear arms.

Amendment 3
Congress may not station soldiers in houses against the owners' will, except in times of war.

Amendment 4
Citizens are to be free from unreasonable searches and seizures.
Federal courts may issue search warrants based only on probable cause and specifically describing the objects of search.

Amendment 5
Citizens are protected against double jeopardy and self-incrimination.
Citizens are guaranteed against deprivation of life, liberty, or property without due process of law.
Citizens are guaranteed just compensation for public use of their private property.

Amendment 6
Citizens have the right to a speedy and public trial before an impartial jury.
Citizens have the right to face their accuser and to cross-examine witnesses.

Amendment 8
Excessive bail and fines are prohibited.
Cruel and unusual punishments are prohibited.

Americans are often shocked when they learn that activists in other parts of the world have been jailed without a public trial. In the United States, the Constitution, its amendments, and Supreme Court decisions protect citizens against violations to their basic human rights.

and even once threatening ideas. Still other liberties have secured a place in the Republic through partisan and ideological combat. The key to understanding civil liberties in the United States is to follow their evolution during the course of our history. Let us consider first the right to privacy issue.

The Right to Privacy

5   The freedom to be left alone in our private lives—what is usually referred to as the *right to privacy*—is nowhere mentioned in the Bill of Rights. Nevertheless, most Americans consider the right to privacy one of our most precious freedoms; most believe we ought to be spared wiretapping, e-mail snooping, and the regulation of consensual sexual activities in our own homes, for instance. Many (though not all) constitutional scholars believe, moreover, that a right to privacy is *inherent* (not explicitly stated) in the Bill of Rights; note the prohibitions against illegal searches and seizures and against the quartering of troops in our homes, as well as the right to free expression and conscience. Such scholars also point to the Ninth Amendment as evidence that the framers believed in the existence of liberties not specifically mentioned in the Bill of Rights: "The enumeration in the Constitution of certain rights, shall not be construed to deny or disparage others retained by the people." The Supreme Court agreed with this position in *Griswold v. Connecticut* (1965), in which it ruled that a constitutional right to privacy exists when it struck down laws making birth control illegal.

construed
interpreted

6   Some advocates of the right to privacy see a growing peril in the ability of the new information technology to collect and make accessible a vast amount of data about each and every American. Under a new law designed to root out "deadbeat dads"—fathers who owe child support payments—the federal government, for example, has begun to

operate a computerized directory showing every person newly hired by every employer in the country. Federal officials say it will be one of the largest, most up-to-date, and most detailed files of personal information kept by the government.

7   So far the Supreme Court has refused to endorse the existence of a privacy-based "right to die." Indeed, in *Vacco v. Quill* (1997), it threw out two federal circuit court decisions that had overturned two state laws banning doctor-assisted suicide (Washington and New York) as unconstitutional. The Court majority ruled that states were free to ban doctor-assisted suicide. Their ruling did not prohibit states from passing laws establishing such a right, however. Indeed, five of the justices suggested in their written opinions that they might support a claim for the existence of such a right in the future.

8   Whether there is or ought to be a constitutionally protected right to privacy, and other rights (such as the right to die) associated with privacy, remains an issue of intense debate.

Source: Adapted from *The Struggle for Democracy, Brief Version,* pp. 336–348

REVIEWING THE READING

DIRECTION   Write the letter of the choice that best completes each statement in the space provided.

Checking Your Comprehension

_____ 1. The purpose of this selection is to

   a. explain why the Bill of Rights was written.
   b. discuss how the Constitution was ratified.
   c. argue that the Constitution is vague and abstract.
   d. explain the legal and historical bases of American civil liberties.

_____ 2. This selection's main point is that

   a. the right to privacy is part of the Constitution itself.
   b. all rights were clearly set out by the Constitution.
   c. civil liberties are still being debated and interpreted.
   d. the Bill of Rights is misunderstood.

_____ 3. The main idea of paragraph 5 is that

   a. the right to privacy exists, although not specifically mentioned in the Constitution.
   b. rights exist only when they are specifically enumerated in the Constitution.
   c. the right to privacy is a dangerous concept.
   d. our basic liberties are being threatened by new technology.

_____ 4. The Bill of Rights was

    a. part of the original Constitution.
    b. added to the Constitution.
    c. given to the United States by England.
    d. added to the Constitution recently.

_____ 5. In paragraph 6, the deadbeat dads law is used as a(n)

    a. contrast.
    b. definition.
    c. example.
    d. cause.

Checking Your Vocabulary

_____ 6. The word _crucial_ (paragraph 2) means

    a. legalistic.
    b. obvious.
    c. important.
    d. detailed.

_____ 7. _Unmentioned_ (paragraph 2) means

    a. private.
    b. revealed.
    c. unconstitutional.
    d. not discussed.

_____ 8. _Retroactively_ (paragraph 2 margin note) means

    a. applying to things that have happened in the past.
    b. occurring over and over again.
    c. following a major event.
    d. appearing before something happens.

_____ 9. If something is _inherent_ (paragraph 5) in a law, it is included in it but is not

    a. enforceable by the people.
    b. explicitly stated.
    c. meant to be used.
    d. added until later.

_____ 10. A _deadbeat dad_ (paragraph 6) is a father who

    a. has the right to die.
    b. owes child support.
    c. has no privacy.
    d. uses birth control.

D–2   Your Appearance, Good or Bad, Can Affect Size of Your Paycheck

Stephanie Armour

Jazzercise
an incorporated fitness program that combines dance, music, and aerobic exercise

franchisee
one who purchases a license to operate a business outlet

1   When Jennifer Portnick wanted to be a Jazzercise franchisee, she says, she was denied. The reason: The company had a policy that required exercise instructors to appear fit. Portnick, who weighed 240 pounds, didn't pass. So she filed a civil complaint under a San Francisco ordinance that bans discrimination based on weight and height. The company changed its policy, and she dropped her complaint. Portnick's story is just one example of how physical appearance can affect employment. A growing body of research supports what many suspect: In the workplace, an employee's physical appearance is a powerful symbol that affects job success.

2   "The issue was my image. I never thought I'd be complaining about discrimination," says 41-year-old Portnick, who now is a personal trainer and teaches intermediate aerobics classes every other Saturday for people of all sizes at World Gym. "We talk so much in workplaces about diversity. Do we want everyone to fit into one mold? I don't think that helps any company." Jazzercise officials say they don't believe they discriminated against Portnick.

3   The new research, as well as high-profile lawsuits alleging appearance-based discrimination, is raising new awareness about how looks hurt— or help—careers. It also has some organizations such as the International Size Acceptance Association calling for legal protections based on appearance.

4   In some cases, they're getting it. Michigan bans discrimination based on height and weight. Santa Cruz, Calif., bars discrimination based on height, weight or physical characteristics. Washington, D.C.,

Two Job Applicants

outlaws employment discrimination based on personal appearance. In San Francisco, it's illegal to discriminate against employees because of their weight and height.

5   But, for the most part, employees have no protection from appearance-based discrimination unless policies also single out workers based on their race, gender or age. Some employers, such as the Borgata Hotel Casino & Spa in Atlantic City, say it's not discriminatory to require that employees conform to appearance standards.

6   "Employers are free to be unfair," says Bill O'Brien, a Minneapolis-based employment lawyer. "Other than some protected classes, there isn't a great deal employees can do about it. We saw it first on the playground, when the popular people who were the leaders chose other people like them as friends."

7   But what began on the playground can have a profound impact on paychecks. In a recent analysis, the Federal Reserve Bank of St. Louis reviewed various economic studies to find possible links between looks and wages. The study's conclusion: A worker with below-average looks tended to earn significantly less—on average 9% less—per hour than an above-average-looking employee. And those with above-average looks tended to earn 5% more than their average-looking colleagues. "If someone looks like Brad Pitt or Julia Roberts, and society values that, that attribute is built into wages," says Michael Owyang, an economist who worked on the analysis.

An Intangible Asset

8   Looking good on the job is an intangible asset that can be important, just as sharp technology skills or the ability to be a team player can give certain workers an edge. It's important enough that Patti Pao, 40, vice president of brand management at David's Bridal in Conshohocken, Pa., never goes to a meeting without putting on lipstick. Says Pao: "You're a personification of who you work for."

9   It's the reason Matt Kennedy, 24, a public relations account executive in Orlando, no longer wears his hair to work in a fashion that looks like a modified mohawk. Instead, he wears glasses and sweeps his hair to the side in a style he describes as a bit like Clark Kent. "Before, I was struggling to get a job. Then I got three job offers in one week," Kennedy says. "On the weekends, I wear my trendy clothes and jeans that are bleached out."

10   It's the reason Brian Chernicky, 30, owner of the newly founded San Diego–based Real Online Marketing, wears a pair of fake glasses when wooing clients. He thinks it makes him look smarter. "Marketing is perception," he says.

11   Looking good on the job is one reason that mortgage broker Bill Schneider, 34, underwent hair transplant surgery. "I manage 60 guys in my office, a lot of younger guys," says Schneider, of Boca Raton, Fla. "They used to look at me as different from them. I used to look 40. Now guys come up and talk to me more comfortably, as a friend."

12   Some employers also agree that looks matter. Intranet software firm Mindbridge Software in Norristown, Pa., requires formal business

attire on the job. Men must wear ties, can't have beards and can't wear their hair past shoulder length. Also, employees can't have visible body piercings or tattoos. "Clients like to see a workforce that looks real conservative," says Scott Testa, chief operating officer. "We have people complain about it and people who like it." The approach is different from that of other software firms, which generally have laid-back dress codes, because the firm wanted to differentiate itself and present a businesslike image to clients.

Height and Weight Factors

13   It's not just a pretty face that helps boost wages. An employee's height and weight also play a role. For the book *Blink* by Malcolm Gladwell, half of the companies on the Fortune 500 were polled about the height of their CEOs. On average, male CEOs were just under 6 feet tall, or 3 inches taller than the average man.

14   It's a bias that some struggle with. Dan Okenfuss, public relations vice president at Little People of America, a group that represents people of short stature, says employees who don't fit societal norms can feel singled out. "People with dwarfism are capable of doing anything in the workplace," he says. "Some members feel they have been slighted, that they didn't get the promotion they wanted, and size may have been a factor. Companies need leaders to be tall and broad-shouldered."

15   Another area where employees feel an impact is their weight. A study done in part by New York University sociologist Dalton Conley found that an increase in a woman's body mass results in a decrease in her family income and her job prestige. Men, however, experience no such negative effect. For women, a 1% increase in body mass as measured by the body mass index results in a 0.6 percentage point decrease in family income. The work, sponsored by the National Bureau of Economic Research, was based on 3,335 men and women.

16   As health care costs climb and national attention turns to the problem of obesity in the USA, overweight workers are feeling pressure to slim down. The latest data from the National Center for Health Statistics show that 30% of U.S. adults age 20 and older (more than 60 million people) are obese. In a case that has attracted widespread attention, the Borgata Hotel Casino & Spa bans bartenders and cocktail waitresses (known as Borgata Babes) from gaining more than 7% of their body weight from the time they begin weigh-ins. That means a 125-pound woman couldn't gain more than 8.75 pounds. Those who do gain more receive a 90-day unpaid suspension, and after that, may be fired. Some employees upset by the policy filed a lawsuit and civil-rights complaints, which are pending. Employees have claimed the policy amounts to discrimination based on sex and disability.

17   The question of whether weight is a disability under the federal Americans with Disabilities Act is still being decided in the courts, but in many cases courts have determined that being obese is not a disability protected by the law.

18   Richard Chaifetz, president of ComPsych, a Chicago-based employee assistance provider, says overweight employees may not be as produc-

tive. More than 20% of very overweight employees have low morale, almost twice that of employees of healthy weights, according to a June survey by ComPsych. The survey was based on a poll of more than 1,000 client organizations.

19   Allen Steadham of the International Size Acceptance Association disagrees. He says he believes heavier employees are just as productive. Overweight employees "are more likely to be as productive, or more productive," Steadham says. "People are standing up for themselves with lawsuits. High-profile cases are bringing attention to the issue, and that brings change."

20   When employees sue, they tend to argue that appearance standards or hiring based on looks have evolved into racism or other illegal discrimination. Abercrombie & Fitch agreed last year to pay $50 million to settle a lawsuit with the government after a class-action lawsuit claimed employees were discriminated against. The lawsuit claimed the retailer hired white, attractive-looking men for sales and put minority workers in stockroom positions.

No Powder, No Blush

21 In another case, Darlene Jespersen, a former casino bartender at Harrah's Entertainment, sued her Reno-based employer after she was fired for not wearing makeup. She had worked there for 20 years and had not regularly worn makeup. The firm requires that women wear makeup, defined as powder or foundation, blush, lipstick and mascara. The 9th U.S. Circuit Court of Appeals heard arguments in the case last month after a lower court ruled in favor of Harrah's.

22   The company's policy has since been revised, says spokesman David Stow, and makeup is no longer mandatory. That change is not a result of the lawsuit but because of concerns from employees, Stow says. Stow also said Harrah's offered Jespersen her job back and agreed to **waive** their appearance standard for her. "Our main goal is to ensure all our employees have a professional and well-groomed appearance when they come into contact with the public," Stow says.

waive
to give up the right to

22   Jennifer Pizer, Jespersen's lawyer, says the conditions of her re-employment were not suitable and that other women at work would resent her if she got special exemption not to wear makeup. She is not going back to work at this time. "She felt it was a humiliation to have to wear the makeup," Pizer says. "There is a particular impact on women in our economy, especially in businesses catering to the public: 'All the women should be 16 and look like the girl next door.' Well, society isn't like that."

Source: USA Today, July 20, 2005.

REVIEWING THE READING

DIRECTIONS Write the letter of the choice that best completes each statement in the space provided.

Checking Your Comprehension

_____ 1. The main purpose of this selection is to discuss

a. why attractive people typically earn more money.
b. how a person's appearance can affect his or her career.
c. how overweight people are discriminated against.
d. what employees can do about discrimination in the workplace.

_____ 2. The thesis of this selection is that

a. being obese should be considered a disability protected by the law.
b. employers should be barred from practicing appearance-based discrimination.
c. standards of appearance vary widely depending on the industry.
d. an employee's physical appearance affects job success in the workplace.

_____ 3. The main idea of paragraph 7 is that

a. workers with above-average looks earn more than those with average or below-average looks.
b. the Federal Reserve Bank of St. Louis paid workers with below-average looks less money.
c. the Federal Reserve Bank of St. Louis preferred to hire workers with above average looks.
d. appearance-based discrimination has its beginnings on the playground.

_____ 4. The class-action lawsuit against Abercrombie & Fitch was based on a claim that

a female employees were suspended if they gained more than 7% of their body weight after beginning weigh-ins.
b. male employees were required to be clean-shaven and could not have visible body piercings or tattoos.
c. attractive-looking white males were hired for sales while minority workers were placed in stockroom positions.
d. female employees were required to wear makeup, defined as powder or foundation, blush, lipstick, and mascara.

_____ 5. The author supports her thesis with all of the following types of evidence _except_

a. statistics.
b. examples.
c. facts.
d. personal experience.

Checking Your Vocabulary

_____ 6. The word *alleging* (paragraph 3) means

    a. claiming.

    b. proving.

    c. lying.

    d. denying.

_____ 7. To *conform* (paragraph 5) is to

    a. disregard or ignore.

    b. talk together.

    c. act in agreement with.

    d. keep secret.

_____ 8. If something is *intangible* (paragraph 8), it is

    a. mistaken.

    b. hard to identify or define.

    c. of equal value.

    d. not efficient.

_____ 9. Another word for *stature* (paragraph 14) is

    a. weight.

    b. attractiveness.

    c. duty.

    d. height.

_____ 10. Something that is *mandatory* (paragraph 22) is

    a. optional.

    b. impossible.

    c. required.

    d. difficult.

D–3   Move Over, Big Brother

1 LIVING without privacy, even in his bedroom, was no problem for Louis XIV. In fact, it was a way for the French king to demonstrate his absolute authority over even the most powerful members of the aristocracy. Each morning, they gathered to see the Sun King get up, pray, perform his bodily functions, choose his wig and so on. One reported in 1667 that there "is no finer sight in the world than the court at the **lever** of the King. When I attended it yesterday, there were three rooms full of people of quality, such a crowd that you would not believe how difficult it was to get into His Majesty's bedchamber."

2   Will this past—life without privacy—be our future? Many futurists, science-fiction writers and privacy advocates believe so. **Big Brother**, they have long warned, is watching. Closed-circuit television cameras, which are proliferating around the world, often track your moves; your mobile phone reveals your location; your transit

lever
getting up in the morning, rising

Big Brother
reference to George Orwell's novel *1984*, in which the leader of a totalitarian society censors people's thoughts and actions

Surveillance Cameras at Work

pass and credit cards leave digital trails. "Light is going to shine into nearly every corner of our lives," wrote David Brin in his 1998 book "The Transparent Society." The issue, he argued, is no longer how to prevent the spread of surveillance technology, but how to live in a world in which there is always the possibility that citizens are being watched.

surveillance
close observation of a person or group

3   But in the past few years, something strange has happened. Thanks to the spread of mobile phones, digital cameras and the Internet, surveillance technology that was once mostly the province of the state has become far more widely available. "A lot has been written about the dangers of increased government surveillance, but we also need to be aware of the potential for more pedestrian forms of surveillance," notes Bruce Schneier, a security guru. He argues that a combination of forces—the miniaturisation of surveillance technologies, the falling price of digital storage and ever more sophisticated systems able to sort through large amounts of information—means that "surveillance abilities that used to be limited to governments are now, or soon will be, in the hands of everyone."

pedestrian
ordinary

4   Digital technologies, such as camera phones and the Internet, are very different from their analogue counterparts. A digital image, unlike a conventional photograph, can be quickly and easily copied and distributed around the world. (Indeed, it is easier to e-mail a digital image than it is to print one.) Another important difference is that digital devices are far more widespread. Few people carry film cameras with them at all times. But it is now quite difficult to buy a mobile phone without a built-in camera—and most people take their phones with them everywhere. According to IDC, a market research firm, 186 million camera-phones will be sold this year, far more than film-based

analogue
similar

cameras (47 million units) or digital cameras (69 million units) combined.

5   The speed and ubiquity of digital cameras lets them do things that film-based cameras could not. In October, for example, the victim of a robbery in Nashville, Tennessee, used his camera-phone to take pictures of the thief and his getaway vehicle. The images were shown to the police, who broadcast descriptions of the man and his truck, leading to his arrest ten minutes later. Other similar stories abound: in Italy, a shopkeeper sent a picture of two men who were acting suspiciously to the police, who identified them as wanted men and arrested them soon afterwards, while in Sweden, a teenager was photographed while holding up a corner shop, and was apprehended within an hour.

Watching Your Every Move

6   The democratisation of surveillance is a mixed blessing, however. Camera-phones have led to voyeurism—and new legislation to strengthen people's rights to their own image. In September, America's Congress passed the "Video Voyeurism Prevention Act," which prohibits the photography of various parts of people's unclothed bodies or undergarments without their consent. The legislation was prompted both by the spread of camera-phones and the growing incidence of hidden cameras in bedrooms, public showers, toilets and locker rooms. Similarly, Germany's parliament has passed a bill that outlaws unauthorised photos within buildings. In Saudi Arabia, the import and sale of camera-phones has been banned, and religious authorities have denounced them for "spreading obscenity." A wedding in the country in July turned into a brawl when one guest started taking pictures with her phone. South Korea's government has ordered manufacturers to design new phones so that they beep when taking a picture.

voyeurism
act of secretly watching unsuspecting people, usually strangers

7   There are also concerns about the use of digital cameras and camera-phones for industrial espionage. Sprint, an American mobile operator, is now offering one of its bestselling phones without a camera in response to demands from its corporate customers, many of which have banned cameras in their workplaces. Some firms make visitors and staff leave camera-phones at the entrance of research and manufacturing facilities—including Samsung, the South Korean company that pioneered the camera-phone.

industrial espionage
spying on one's competitors to gain an advantage for industrial purposes

8   Cheap surveillance technology facilitates other sorts of crime. Two employees at a petrol station in British Columbia, for example, installed a hidden camera in the ceiling above a card reader, and recorded the personal identification numbers of thousands of people. They also installed a device to "skim" account details from users as they swiped their plastic cards. The two men gathered the account details of over 6,000 people and forged 1,000 bank cards before being caught.

9   In another case, a man installed keystroke-logging software, which monitors every key pressed on a computer's keyboard, on PCs in several Kinko's copy shops in New York City. (Keystroke-logging software is sold for use by businesses to monitor their employees, or by parents who wish to monitor their children's activities online.) This enabled

him to remotely capture account numbers and passwords from over 450 people who rented the terminals, and to siphon money out of their bank accounts.

Surveillance Is a Two-way Street

10   But the spread of surveillance technology also has its benefits. In particular, it can enhance transparency and accountability. More and more video cameras can be found in schools, for example. Web-based services such as ParentWatch.com and KinderCam.com link to cameras in hundreds of American child-care centres, so that parents can see what their offspring (and those looking after them) are up to. Schools are also putting webcams in their classrooms: one American school district has plans to install 15,000 such devices for use by security personnel (and, perhaps one day, parents). And tech firms such as Google have put webcams in their staff restaurants, so employees can delay going to lunch if they see a long queue.

11   Steve Mann, a professor at the University of Toronto, calls the spread of citizen surveillance "sousveillance"—because most cameras no longer watch from above, but from eye level. Instead of being on top of buildings and attached to room ceilings, cameras are now carried by ordinary people. The video images of Rodney King being assaulted by police officers and the horrific pictures of prisoner abuse from the Abu Ghraib jail in Iraq are the best known examples. But as Mr. Mann and his colleagues organized the first "International Workshop on Inverse Surveillance" in April, there was no shortage of reports on other cases: in Kuwait, a worker took photos of coffins of American soldiers being loaded onto a plane; in New Jersey, a teenager scared off a kidnapper by taking his picture; in Strasbourg, a member of the European Parliament filmed colleagues making use of generous perks.

12   Camera-phones could have a profound effect on the news media. Technologies such as newsgroups, weblogs and "wikis" (in essence, web pages which anybody can edit) let people distribute images themselves, bypassing the traditional media, notes Dan Gillmor, a journalist, in his recent book "We the Media." Camera-phones make everyone a potential news photographer. Unsurprisingly, old media is starting to embrace the trend. The San Diego Union-Tribune recently launched a website to gather camera-phone images of news events taken by their readers, and the BBC also encourages users of its website to send in pictures of news events.

13   Companies and governments will have to assume that there could be a camera or a microphone everywhere, all the time, argues Paul Saffo of the Institute for the Future. Unsafe conditions in a factory or pollution at a chemical plant are harder to deny if they are not just described, but shown in photos and videos. Animal-rights activists, for instance, operate online multimedia archives where people can store and view graphic images from chicken farms, slaughterhouses and fur factories. Such material can cause outrage among consumers, as was the case with videos of dolphins caught in tuna nets.

14   Last year, a German member of parliament was caught photographing a confidential document of which only a few copies were handed out (and later collected) at a background meeting on health-care reform. Some Berlin politicians are said to let reporters eavesdrop on fellow parliamentarians by calling them right before an important meeting—and then failing to hang up, in effect turning their phones into bugs.

15   In November 1996, Senegal's interior minister was caught out when he admitted that there had been fraud in a local election, but failed to notice that a bystander was holding a mobile phone with an open line. The election was annulled. In the same country's presidential election in 2000, radio stations sent reporters to polling stations and equipped them with mobile phones. The reporters called in the results as they were announced in each district, and they were immediately broadcast on air. This reduced the scope for electoral fraud and led to a smooth transfer of power, as the outgoing president quickly conceded defeat.

16   The social consequences of the spread of surveillance technology remain unclear. Mr Brin suggests that it could turn out to be self-regulating: after all, Peeping Toms are not very popular. In a restaurant it is generally more embarrassing to be caught staring than to be observed with crumbs in your beard. "A photographically 'armed' society could turn out to be more polite," he suggests, referring to an American aphorism that holds "an armed society is a polite society." Alternatively, the omnipresence of cameras and other surveillance technologies might end up making individuals more conformist, says Mr. Brin, as they suppress their individuality to avoid drawing too much attention to themselves.

17   The surveillance society is on its way, just as privacy advocates have long warned. But it has not taken quite the form they imagined. Increasingly, it is not just Big Brother who is watching—but lots of little brothers, too.

Source: Economist, December 4, 2004.

REVIEWING THE READING

DIRECTIONS   Write the letter of the choice that best completes each statement in the space provided.

Checking Your Comprehension

_____   1. The main purpose of this selection is to describe

a. the widespread availability of surveillance technology.
b. how digital technologies differ from their analogue counterparts.
c. the reaction of traditional news media to digital technologies.
d. how surveillance technology has contributed to crime in the workplace.

_____ 2. The thesis of this selection is that surveillance technology

      a. should be restricted by law.
      b. should be available only for security purposes.
      c. has led to both positive and negative consequences.
      d. is becoming less available to ordinary people.

_____ 3. Paragraph 6 uses enumeration to present

      a. different situations showing the benefits of camera-phones.
      b. examples of legislation around the world regulating camera-phone use.
      c. reasons why film-based cameras are superior to digital cameras.
      d. ways in which camera-phones can help prevent crime.

_____ 4. The term _sousveillance_ refers to the fact that

      a. most mobile phones now come with a built-in camera.
      b. most cameras now watch from eye level rather than from above.
      c. many corporations have banned camera-phones in the workplace.
      d. video cameras and camera-phones are often used to break the law.

_____ 5. According to the selection, an important benefit of surveillance technology is that it can

      a. let people bypass the traditional media and distribute images themselves through newsgroups and Weblogs.
      b. allow businesses to become more competitive by using cameras to learn what others in the same industry are doing.
      c. lead to new legislation strengthening people's rights to their own photographic image.
      d. enhance transparency and accountability in schools, businesses, and governments.

Checking Your Vocabulary

_____ 6. If something is _proliferating_ (paragraph 2), it is

      a. spreading rapidly.
      b. becoming smaller.
      c. changing shape.
      d. losing power.

_____ 7. A _guru_ (paragraph 3) is a person who

      a. is considered unreliable.
      b. has radical ideas.
      c. is well-known in his or her field.
      d. follows others.

_____ 8. *Ubiquity* (paragraph 5) means

    a. unheard of.
    b. seeming to be everywhere.
    c. difficult to understand.
    d. slowness.

_____ 9. If technology *facilitates* (paragraph 8) something, it makes it

    a. easier.
    b. impossible.
    c. more complicated.
    d. illegal.

_____ 10. An *aphorism* (paragraph 16) is a

    a. type of technology.
    b. person who promotes something.
    c. necessity.
    d. saying or truism.

MAKING CONNECTIONS

1. How does each author feel about personal freedom and discrimination? Explain their similarities and differences.
2. Have you felt that our personal freedom has been more restricted in the past few years? Do you think more restriction is necessary in the modern world? Why or why not?
3. Have you ever felt discriminated against because of your appearance? How does discrimination relate to privacy?
4. Which selection presents the most compelling argument? Explain your answer.
5. What important issues in the areas of privacy and discrimination are missing from these readings? Which do you think is the most important?

WORLD WIDE WEB ACTIVITY

A Government Web Site

Visit the Federal Trade Commission's web site on privacy initiatives: http://www.ftc.gov/privacy/index.html Create a concept map linking the various agencies, laws and programs outlined on the site in order to visually illustrate the FTC's consumer protection mission.

Culture and Interpersonal Communication 9

Culture and Intercultural Communication

Cultural Differences

Improving Intercultural Communication

This sample textbook chapter is taken from *Messages: Building Interpersonal Communication Skills,* Sixth Edition, by Joseph A. DeVito, Chapter 9, "Cultural and Interpersonal Communication."

▶ Nacirema culture is characterized by a highly developed market economy which has evolved in a rich natural habitat. While much of the people's time is devoted to economic pursuits, a large part of the fruits of these labors and a considerable portion of the day are spent in ritual activity. The focus of this activity is the human body, the appearance and health of which loom as a dominant concern in the ethos of the people. While such a concern is certainly not unusual, its ceremonial aspects and associated philosophy are unique.

The fundamental belief underlying the whole system appears to be that the human body is ugly and that its natural tendency is to debility and disease. Incarcerated in such a body, man's only hope is to avert these characteristics through the use of the powerful influences of ritual and ceremony. Every household has one or more shrines devoted to this purpose. The more powerful individuals in the society have several shrines in their houses and, in fact, the opulence of a house is often referred to in terms of the number of such ritual centers it possesses. Most houses are of wattle and daub construction, but the shrine rooms of the more wealthy are walled with stone. Poorer families imitate the rich by applying pottery plaques to their shrine walls.

While each family has at least one such shrine, the rituals associated with it are not family ceremonies but are private and secret. The rites are normally only discussed with children, and then only during the period when they are being initiated into these mysteries. I was able, however, to establish sufficient rapport with the natives to examine these shrines and to have the rituals described to me.

The focal point of the shrine is a box or chest which is built into the wall. In this chest are kept the many charms and magical potions without which no native believes he could live. These preparations are secured from a variety of specialized practitioners. The most powerful of these are the medicine men, whose assistance must be rewarded with substantial gifts. However, the medicine men do not provide the curative potions for their clients, but decide what the ingredients should be and then write them down in an ancient and secret language. This writing is understood only by the medicine men and by the herbalists who, for another gift, provide the required charm. . . .

There remains one other kind of practitioner, known as a "listener." This witch-doctor has the power to exorcise the devils that lodge in the heads of people who have been bewitched. The Nacirema believe that parents bewitch their own children. Mothers are particularly suspected of putting a curse on children while teaching them the secret body rituals. The counter-magic of the witch-doctor is unusual in its lack of ritual. The patient simply tells the "listener" all his troubles and fears, beginning with the earliest difficulties he can remember. The memory displayed by the Nacirema in these exorcism sessions is truly remarkable. It is not uncommon for the patient to bemoan the rejection he felt upon being weaned as a babe, and a few individuals even see their troubles going back to the traumatic effects of their own birth.

From these observations of anthropologist Horace Miner (1956, pp. 503–504) you might conclude that the Nacirema are a truly strange people. Look more carefully, however, and you will see that we are the Nacirema and the rituals are our own: *Nacirema* is *American* spelled backwards. In the passage quoted, Miner describes the bathroom, the doctor writing prescriptions for the druggist, and the psychiatrist.

This excerpt brings into focus the fact that cultural customs (our own and those of others) are not necessarily logical or natural. Rather, they are better viewed as useful or not useful to the members of that particular culture. This passage is an appropriate reminder against ethnocentrism—the tendency to think that your culture's customs are right and the customs of others are wrong. It also awakens our consciousness, our mindful state, to our own customs and values.

Culture and Intercultural Communication

A good way to start the exploration of culture and intercultural communication is to define exactly what is meant by *culture* and to look at significant cultural processes and the nature of intercultural communication.

Culture and Cultural Processes

The word *culture,* you'll recall from Chapter 1, refers to the lifestyle of a group of people: their values, beliefs, artifacts, ways of behaving, and ways of communicating. Culture includes everything that members of a social group have produced and developed—their language, ways of thinking, art, laws, and religion—and that is transmitted from one generation to another through communication rather than genes. You learn the values and **cultural rules** of your culture through the teachings of your parents, peer groups, schools, religious institutions, government agencies, and media; this process is known as **enculturation.** Through enculturation you develop an ethnic identity, a commitment to the beliefs and philosophy of your culture (Chung & Ting-Toomey, 1999). The degree to which you identify with your cultural group can be measured by your responses to such questions as these (from Ting-Toomey, 1981). Using a five-point scale from 1 (strongly disagree) to 5 (strongly agree), indicate how true of you the following statements are:

- *I am increasing my involvement in activities with my ethnic group.*
- *I involve myself in causes that will help members of my ethnic group.*
- *It feels natural being part of my ethnic group.*
- *I have spent time trying to find out more about my own ethnic group.*
- *I am happy to be a member of my ethnic group.*
- *I have a strong sense of belonging to my ethnic group.*
- *I often talk to other members of my group to learn more about my ethnic culture.*

High scores (say, 5s and 4s) indicate a strong commitment to your culture's values and beliefs; low numbers (1s and 2s) indicate a relatively weak commitment.

Acculturation refers to the processes by which a person's culture is modified through direct contact with or exposure to (say, through the mass media) another culture (Kim, 1988). For example, when immigrants settle in the United States (the host culture), their own culture becomes influenced by the host culture. Gradually the values, ways of behaving, and beliefs of the host culture become more and more a part of the immigrants' culture. At the same time, of course, the host culture changes too. Generally, however, the culture of the immigrants changes more. As Young Yun Kim (1988) puts it, "a reason for the essentially unidirectional change in the immigrant is the difference between the number of individuals in the new environment sharing the immigrant's original culture and the size of the host society."

The acceptance of the new culture depends on several factors (Kim, 1988). Immigrants who come from cultures similar to the host culture will become accultur-

> " From the moment of his birth the customs into which [a person] is born shape his experience and behavior. By the time he can talk, he is the little creature of his culture. "
>
> —Ruth Benedict

> " If you see in any given situation only what everybody else can see, you can be said to be so much a representative of your culture that you are a victim of it. "
>
> —S. I. Hayakawa

Figure 9.1

A Model of Intercultural Communication
This model of intercultural communication illustrates that culture is a part of every communication act. More specifically, it illustrates that the messages you send and the messages you receive will be influenced by your cultural beliefs, values, and attitudes.

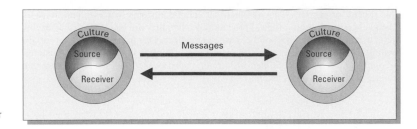

ated more easily. Similarly, those who are younger and better educated become acculturated more quickly than do older and less educated persons. Personality factors are also relevant. Persons who are risk takers and open-minded, for example, have a greater acculturation potential. Also, persons who are familiar with the host culture before immigration—whether through interpersonal contact or through mass media—will be acculturated more readily.

Intercultural Communication

Intercultural communication is communication between persons who have different cultural beliefs, values, or ways of behaving. The model in Figure 9.1 illustrates this concept. The larger circles represent the cultures of the individual communicators. The inner circles identify the communicators (the sources–receivers). In this model each communicator is a member of a different culture. In some instances the cultural differences are relatively slight—say, between persons from Toronto and New York. In other instances the cultural differences are great—say, between persons from Borneo and Germany, or between persons from rural Nigeria and industrialized England.

All messages originate from a specific and unique cultural context, and that context influences their content and form. You communicate as you do largely as a result of your culture. Culture (along with the processes of enculturation and acculturation) influences every aspect of your communication experience. And, of course, you receive messages through the filters imposed by a unique culture. Cultural filters, like filters on a camera, color the messages you receive. They influence what you receive and how you receive it. For example, some cultures rely heavily on television or newspapers for their news and trust them implicitly. Others rely on face-to-face interpersonal interactions, distrusting any of the mass communication systems. Some look to religious leaders as guides to behavior; others generally ignore them.

The term *intercultural* is used broadly to refer to all forms of communication among persons from different groups as well as to the more narrowly defined area of communication between different cultures. The model of intercultural communication presented in Figure 9.1 applies equally to communication between a smaller culture and the dominant or majority culture, communication between different smaller cultures, and communication between a variety of other groups. The following types of communication may all be considered "intercultural" and, more important, subject to the same barriers and gateways to effective communication identified in this chapter:

- Communication between cultures—for example, between Chinese and Portuguese, or between French and Norwegian.

? SKILLS VIEWPOINT

How many intercultural differences can you identify in this photo? How many might be hidden to visual inspection? What one interpersonal communication skill would you think would be most important to the woman speaking in this particular situation?

- Communication between races (sometimes called *interracial communication*)—for example, between African Americans and Asian Americans.
- Communication between ethnic groups (sometimes called *interethnic communication*)—for example, between Italian Americans and German Americans.
- Communication between people of different religions—for example, between Roman Catholics and Episcopalians, or between Muslims and Jews.
- Communication between nations (sometimes called *international communication*)—for example, between the United States and Argentina, or between China and Italy.
- Communication between smaller cultures existing within the larger culture—for example, between doctors and patients, or between research scientists and the general public.
- Communication between a smaller culture and the dominant culture—for example, between homosexuals and heterosexuals, or between older people and the younger majority.
- Communication between genders—between men and women. Some researchers would consider intergender communication as a separate area—as a form of intercultural communication only when the two people are also from different races or nationalities. But gender roles are largely learned through culture, so it seems useful to consider male–female communication as intercultural (Tannen, 1994a, b). That is, even though gender itself is transmitted genetically and not by communication, it is cultures that teach boys and girls different attitudes, beliefs, values, and ways of communicating and relating to one another (Payne, 2001). You act like a man or a woman partly because of what your culture has taught you about how men and women should act. Further, you can view male–female communication as cross-cultural because of the numerous differences in the way

Message Skills

Cultural Influences: Communicate with an understanding that culture influences communication in all its forms.

Culture and Ethics

Throughout history there have been numerous cultural practices that would be judged unethical and even illegal in much of today's world. Sacrificing virgins to the gods, burning people who held different religious beliefs, and sending children to fight religious wars are obvious examples. But even today there are practices woven deep into the fabric of different cultures that many people would find unethical. Consider just a few of these:

- Some cultures support bronco-riding events at which the bull's testicles are tied so that it will experience pain and will buck and try to throw off the rider.
- Some cultures support clitoridectomy, the practice of cutting a young girl's genitals so that she can never experience sexual intercourse without pain; the goal is to keep the girl a virgin until marriage.
- Some cultures support and enforce the belief that a woman must be subservient to her husband's will.
- Some cultures support the practice of wearing fur. In some cases this means catching wild animals in extremely painful traps; in others, raising captive animals so they can be killed when their pelts are worth the most money.

What Would You Do?

Imagine that you're on a television talk show dealing with the topic of cultural differences and diversity. During the discussion different members of the panel speak in support of each of the practices mentioned above, arguing that each culture is entitled to its own practices and beliefs and that no outsider has the right to object. Given your own beliefs about these issues and about cultural diversity in general, what ethical obligations do you have as a member of this panel?

"Because my genetic programming *prevents* me from stopping to ask directions—*that's* why!"

men and women speak and listen (Eckstein & Goldman, 2001). This does not deny that biological differences also play a role. In fact, research continues to uncover biological roots of behaviors once thought to be entirely learned, such as happiness and shyness (McCroskey, 1997).

Regardless of your own cultural background, you will surely come into close contact with people from a variety of other cultures—people who speak different languages, eat different foods, practice different religions, and approach work and relationships in very different ways. It doesn't matter whether you're a longtime resident or a newly arrived immigrant: You are or soon will be living, going to school, working, and forming relationships with people who are from very different cultures. Your day-to-day experiences are sure to become increasingly intercultural.

Cultural Differences

Cultures differ in terms of their (1) orientation (whether individualistic or collectivist), (2) context (whether high or low), and (3) masculinity–femininity; and each of these dimensions of difference has a significant impact on interpersonal communication (Hofstede, 1997; Hall & Hall, 1987; Gudykunst, 1991). Cultures also differ in their characteristic attitudes toward uncertainty, a topic discussed in Chapter 3.

Individualist and Collectivist Cultures

The distinction between **individualist** and **collectivist cultures** revolves around the extent to which the individual's goals or the group's goals are given greater importance. Individualist and collectivist tendencies are not mutually exclusive; this is not an all-or-none orientation but rather one of emphasis. Thus, you may, for example, compete with other members of your basketball team for most baskets or most valuable player award. In a game, however, you will act in a way that will benefit the group. In actual practice both individualist and collectivist tendencies will help you and your team each achieve your goals. Even so, at times these tendencies may conflict; for example, do you shoot for the basket and try to raise your own individual score, or do you pass the ball to another player who is better positioned to score the basket and thus benefit your team?

In an individualist culture you're responsible for yourself and perhaps your immediate family; in a collectivist culture you're responsible for the entire group. In an individualist culture success is measured by the extent to which you surpass other members of your group; you will take pride in standing out from the crowd. And your heroes—in the media, for example—are likely to be those who are unique and who stand apart. In a collectivist culture success is measured by your contribution to the achievements of the group as a whole; you will take pride in your similarity to other members of your group. Your heroes are more likely to be team players who do not stand out from the rest of the group's members.

In an individualist culture you're responsible to your own conscience, and responsibility is largely an individual matter. In a collectivist culture you're responsible to the rules of the social group, and responsibility for an accomplishment or a failure is shared by all members. In individualist cultures competition is promoted; in collectivist cultures cooperation is promoted.

Distinctions between in-group members and out-group members are extremely important in collectivist cultures. In individualistic cultures, which prize a person's individuality, these distinctions are likely to be less important.

Message Skills

Individualist and Collectivist Cultures: Adjust your messages and your listening with an awareness of differences between individualist and collectivist cultures.

High- and Low-Context Cultures

In a **high-context culture** much of the information in communication is in the context or in the person—for example, information shared through previous communications, through assumptions about each other, and through shared experiences. The information is not explicitly stated in the verbal message. In a **low-context culture** most information is explicitly stated in verbal messages or, in formal transactions, in written (contract) form.

To appreciate the distinction between high and low context, consider giving directions ("Where's the voter registration center?") to someone who knows the neighborhood and to a newcomer to your city. With someone who knows the neighborhood (a high-context situation), you can assume the person knows the local landmarks. So you can give directions such as "next to the laundromat on Main Street" or "the corner of Albany and Elm." With the newcomer (a low-context situation), you cannot assume the person shares any information with you. So you have to use directions that a stranger will understand; for example, "Make a left at the next stop sign" or "Go two blocks and then turn right."

High-context cultures are also collectivist cultures. These cultures (Japanese, Arabic, Latin American, Thai, Korean, Apache, and Mexican are examples) place great emphasis on personal relationships and oral agreements (Victor, 1992). Low-context cultures, on the other hand, are individualistic cultures. These cultures (German, Swedish, Norwegian, and American are examples) place less emphasis on personal relationships; they tend to emphasize explicit explanations and, for example, written contracts in business transactions.

Members of high-context cultures spend lots of time getting to know each other before engaging in any important transactions. Because of this prior personal knowledge, a great deal of information is shared and therefore does not have to be explicitly stated. High-context societies, for example, rely more on nonverbal cues in reducing uncertainty (Sanders, Wiseman, & Matz, 1991). Members of low-context cultures spend less time getting to know each other and therefore do not have that shared knowledge. As a result everything has to be stated explicitly.

When this simple difference is not taken into account, misunderstandings can easily result. For example, the directness and explicitness characteristic of the low-context culture may prove insulting, insensitive, or unnecessary to members of a high-context culture. Conversely, to members of a low-context culture, someone from a high-context culture may appear vague, underhanded, even dishonest in his or her reluctance to be explicit or to engage in communication that a low-context culture would consider open and direct.

Another frequent difference and source of misunderstanding between high- and low-context cultures is face-saving (Hall & Hall, 1987). People in high-context cultures place a great deal more emphasis on face-saving. For example, they are more likely to avoid argument for fear of causing others to lose face, whereas people in low-context cultures (with their individualistic orientation) will use argument to win a point. Similarly, in high-context cultures criticism should take place only in private so the person can save face. Low-context cultures may not make this public–private distinction.

Members of high-context cultures are reluctant to say no for fear of offending and causing a person to lose face. So, for example, it's necessary to understand when a Japanese executive's yes means yes and when it means no. The difference is not in the words but in the way they are used. It's easy to see how a low-context individual may interpret this reluctance to be direct—to say no when you mean no—as a weakness or as an unwillingness to confront reality.

Members of high-context cultures also are reluctant to question the judgments of their superiors. So, for example, if a product were being manufactured with a defect, workers might be reluctant to communicate this back to management (Gross, Turner, & Cederholm, 1987). Similarly, workers might detect problems in proce-

Message Skills

High- and Low-Context Cultures: Adjust your messages and your listening in light of the differences between high- and low-context cultures.

dures proposed by management but never communicate their concerns back to management. In an intercultural organization knowledge of this tendency would alert a low-context management to look more deeply into the absence of communication.

Masculine and Feminine Cultures

Cultures differ in the extent to which gender roles are distinct or overlap (Hofstede, 1997). A **masculine culture** typically views men as assertive, oriented to material success, and strong; people in such a culture tend to see women as modest, focused on the quality of life, and tender. In a **feminine culture** both men and women are supposed to be modest, oriented to maintaining the quality of life, and tender. On the basis of Hofstede's research on 53 countries, the 10 countries with the highest masculinity scores (starting from the top) are Japan, Austria, Venezuela, Italy, Switzerland, Mexico, Ireland, Jamaica, Great Britain, and Germany. The 10 countries with the highest femininity scores (starting from the top) are Sweden, Norway, the Netherlands, Denmark, Costa Rica, Yugoslavia, Finland, Chile, Portugal, and Thailand. Of the 53 countries ranked, the United States ranks 15th most masculine.

A study of babies raised in Japan and the United States illustrates the ways in which masculine and feminine cultures teach boys and girls differently (Otaki et al., 1986). Boys raised in Japan are significantly noisier than girls; girls raised in the United States are significantly noisier than boys. This difference is most likely due to the ways in which mothers and (to a somewhat lesser extent) fathers react to the babies. Both of these cultures are relatively high on masculinity and so, not surprisingly, teach girls and boys differently. In the dominant cultures of the United States, Japan, and Germany, for example, the emphasis on material success is seen in the importance that students place on grades. Students in such cultures are conditioned to strive to be the best, and school failure is shameful and extremely significant. Students from more feminine cultures place greater emphasis on the quality of life and give much less importance to such issues as grades. Students in these cultures are content to be average, and failing in school is unpleasant but nothing serious (Hofstede, 1997).

The masculine culture socializes its children to be assertive, ambitious, and competitive. A masculine organization emphasizes the bottom line and rewards its workers on the basis of their contribution to the organization. The feminine culture socializes its children to be modest and to emphasize close interpersonal relationships. A feminine organization is more likely to emphasize worker satisfaction and

Skill building *exercise*

Facilitating Intercultural Communication

Here are three scenarios involving people from different cultural orientations. For each situation *(a)* identify at least one difference between the two extremes that might cause communication difficulties, and *(b)* identify at least one thing the individuals can do so as not to let this difference obstruct effective communication.

1. An associate at work (high masculine) tells a colleague (high feminine) of a history of chronic fatigue syndrome and is now awaiting results of new blood tests.
2. A group of new advertising executives (three are from high-context cultures and three from low-context cultures) prepare to interact for the first time.
3. A couple (one from an individualist and one from a collectivist culture) see two children fighting in the street; no other adults are around, and the passersby worry that the children may get hurt.

Cultural teachings and orientations exert powerful (but often unconscious) influences on the way people communicate. A knowledge of such influences will often help suggest remedies for misperceptions and misunderstandings.

to reward its workers on the basis of need; an employee with a large family, for example, may get raises that a single person would not get even if the single person contributed more to the organization.

Masculine cultures are more likely to confront conflicts directly and to competitively fight out any differences; they are more likely to emphasize win–lose conflict strategies. Feminine cultures are more likely to emphasize compromise and negotiation; they are more likely to emphasize win–win solutions to conflicts.

Message Skills

Masculine and Feminine Cultures: Adjust your messages and your listening to allow for differences in cultural masculinity and femininity.

Improving Intercultural Communication

Murphy's law ("If anything can go wrong, it will") is especially applicable to intercultural communication. Intercultural communication is, of course, subject to all the same barriers and problems as are the other forms of communication discussed throughout this text. Here, however, are some suggestions designed to counteract the barriers that are unique to intercultural communication (Barna, 1997; Ruben, 1985; Spitzberg, 1991).

Prepare Yourself

There's no better preparation for intercultural communication than learning about the other culture. Fortunately, there are numerous sources to draw on. View a video or film that presents a realistic view of the culture. Read what members of the culture as well as "outsiders" write about the culture. Scan magazines and websites from the culture. Talk with members of the culture. Chat on international IRC channels. Read materials addressed to people who need to communicate with those from other cultures. The easiest way to do this is to search the online bookstores (for example, Barnes and Noble at www.bn.com, Borders at www.borders.com, and

7 Ways to Effective Intercultural Communication

The skills and qualities of conversational effectiveness (Chapter 8) are especially useful in intercultural interactions. Of course, exercise caution, as there may be important differences in the ways various cultures regard these qualities. Generally, however:

1. Be open to differences among people; specifically, be open to different values, beliefs, and attitudes as well as to ways of behaving.
2. Empathize; put yourself in the position of the person from another culture. Try to see the world from this different perspective. Let the person know that you feel as he or she is feeling.
3. Communicate positiveness; it helps put the other person at ease. However, the appropriateness of positive statements about yourself varies greatly with the culture.
4. Use immediacy to unite yourself with others and to surmount differences; be aware, however, that members of some cultures prefer to maintain greater interpersonal distance.
5. Engage in effective interaction management; be sensitive to differences in turn-taking. Be especially wary of interrupting; some cultures consider this extremely rude.
6. Communicate expressiveness and a genuine involvement in the interaction. Smile. Allow your facial muscles to express your interest and concern. At the same time, recognize that some cultures may frown on too much expressiveness.
7. Be other-oriented; focus your attention and the conversation on the other person. Listen actively, ask questions, and maintain eye contact. But go carefully—some cultures may find these messages too intrusive, so be guided by feedback from the listener.

Applying Interpersonal Skills/Then and Now
Recall a recent intercultural interaction that did not go as well as it might have. If you were having the same conversation today, what could you do to make it more effective?

> ❝ The highest result of education is tolerance. ❞
>
> —Helen Keller

Amazon at www.Amazon.com) for such keywords as *culture, international,* and *foreign travel.*

Another part of this preparation is to recognize and face fears that may stand in the way of effective intercultural communication (Gudykunst, 1991; Stephan & Stephan, 1985). For example, you may fear for your self-esteem. You may be anxious about your ability to control the intercultural situation, or you may worry about your own level of discomfort. You may fear saying something that will be considered politically incorrect or culturally insensitive and thereby losing face.

You may fear that you'll be taken advantage of by a member of the other culture. Depending on your own stereotypes, you may fear being lied to, financially duped, or made fun of.

You may fear that members of this other group will react to you negatively. You may fear, for example, that they will not like you or will disapprove of your attitudes or beliefs or perhaps even reject you as a person. Conversely, you may fear negative reactions from members of your own group. They might, for example, disapprove of your socializing with culturally different people.

Some fears, of course, are reasonable. In many cases, however, fears are groundless. Either way, you need to assess your concerns logically and weigh their consequences carefully. Then you'll be able to make informed choices about your communications.

Reduce Your Ethnocentrism

Before reading about reducing ethnocentrism, examine your own cultural thinking by taking the self-test below.

 Test Yourself

How Ethnocentric Are You?

Here are 18 statements representing your beliefs about your culture. For each statement indicate how much you agree or disagree, using the following scale: strongly agree = 5, agree = 4, neither agree nor disagree = 3, disagree = 2, and strongly disagree = 1.

_____ ❶ Most cultures are backward compared to my culture.

_____ ❷ My culture should be the role model for other cultures.

_____ ❸ Lifestyles in other cultures are just as valid as those in my culture.

_____ ❹ Other cultures should try to be like my culture.

_____ ❺ I'm not interested in the values and customs of other cultures.

_____ ❻ People in my culture could learn a lot from people in other cultures.

_____ ❼ Most people from other cultures just don't know what's good for them.

_____ ❽ I have little respect for the values and customs of other cultures.

_____ ❾ Most people would be happier if they lived like people in my culture.

_____ ❿ People in my culture have just about the best lifestyles of anywhere.

_____ ⓫ Lifestyles in other cultures are not as valid as those in my culture.

_____ ⓬ I'm very interested in the values and customs of other cultures.

_____ ⓭ I respect the values and customs of other cultures.

_____ ⓮ I do not cooperate with people who are different.

_____ ⑮ I do not trust people who are different.

_____ ⑯ I dislike interacting with people from different cultures.

_____ ⑰ Other cultures are smart to look up to my culture.

_____ ⑱ People from other cultures act strange and unusual when they come into my culture.

HOW DID YOU DO? This test was presented to give you the opportunity to examine some of your own cultural beliefs, particularly those cultural beliefs that contribute to ethnocentrism. The person low in ethnocentrism would have high scores (4s and 5s) for items 3, 6, 12, and 13 and low scores (1s and 2s) for all the others. The person high in ethnocentrism would have low scores for items 3, 6, 12, and 13 and high scores for all the others.

WHAT WILL YOU DO? Use this test to bring your own cultural beliefs to consciousness so you can examine them logically and objectively. Ask yourself if your beliefs are productive and will help you achieve your professional and social goals, or if they're counterproductive and will actually hinder your achieving your goals.

Source: Adapted from James W. Neuliep & James C. McCroskey (1997). The development of a U.S. and generalized ethnocentrism scale, _Communication Research Reports, 14,_ 393.

As you've probably gathered from taking this test, **ethnocentrism** is the tendency to see others and their behaviors through your own cultural filters, often as distortions of your own behaviors. It's the tendency to evaluate the values, beliefs, and behaviors of your own culture as superior; as more positive, logical, and natural than those of other cultures. To achieve effective interpersonal communication, you need to see yourself and others as different but as neither inferior nor superior—not a very easily accomplished task.

Ethnocentrism exists on a continuum. People are not either ethnocentric or nonethnocentric; rather, most people are somewhere along the continuum (Table 9.1 on page 200), and we're all ethnocentric to at least some degree. Most important for our purposes is that your degree of ethnocentrism will influence your interpersonal (intercultural) communications.

Message Skills

Ethnocentric Thinking: Recognize your own ethnocentric thinking and be aware of how it influences your verbal and nonverbal messages.

? SKILLS VIEWPOINT

What do you say to someone who tries to appear totally without prejudice and yet talks in the most offensive stereotypes and uses all the offensive cultural labels?

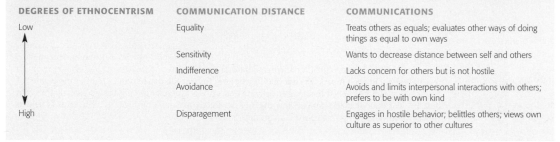

TABLE 9.1 **The Ethnocent rism Continuum**

Drawing from several researchers (Lukens, 1978; Gudykunst & Kim, 1992; Gudykunst, 1991), this table summarizes some interconnections between ethnocentrism and communication. The table identifies five levels of ethnocentrism; the general terms under "Communication Distances" characterize the major communication attitudes that dominate the various levels. Under "Communications" are some ways people might behave given their particular degree of ethnocentrism. How would you rate yourself on this scale?

DEGREES OF ETHNOCENTRISM	COMMUNICATION DISTANCE	COMMUNICATIONS
Low	Equality	Treats others as equals; evaluates other ways of doing things as equal to own ways
	Sensitivity	Wants to decrease distance between self and others
	Indifference	Lacks concern for others but is not hostile
	Avoidance	Avoids and limits interpersonal interactions with others; prefers to be with own kind
High	Disparagement	Engages in hostile behavior; belittles others; views own culture as superior to other cultures

Be Mindful

Being mindful rather than mindless (a distinction considered in Chapter 8), is especially helpful in intercultural communication (Hajek & Giles, 2003). When you're in a mindless state, you behave in accordance with assumptions that would not normally pass intellectual scrutiny. For example, you know that cancer is not contagious, and yet many people will avoid touching cancer patients. You know that people who cannot see do not have hearing problems, and yet many people use a louder voice when talking to persons without sight. When the discrepancies between available evidence and behaviors are pointed out and your mindful state is awakened, you quickly realize that these behaviors are not logical or realistic.

When you deal with people from other cultures, you're often in a mindless state and therefore may function nonrationally in many ways. When your mindful state is awakened, you may then shift to a more critical thinking mode—and recognize, for example, that other people and other cultural systems are different but not inferior or superior. Thus, these suggestions for increasing intercultural communication effectiveness may appear logical (even obvious) to your mindful state, even though they are probably frequently ignored in your mindless state.

Avoid Overattribution

You'll recall from Chapter 3 that overattribution is the tendency to attribute too much of a person's behavior or attitudes to one of that person's characteristics ("She thinks that way because she's a woman," "He believes that because he was raised a Catholic"). In intercultural communication situations, overattribution takes two forms. First, it's the tendency to see too much of what a person believes or does as caused by the person's cultural identification. Second, it's the tendency to see a person as a spokesperson for his or her particular culture—for example, to assume because a man is African American (as in the accompanying cartoon) that he is therefore knowledgeable about the entire African American experience or that his thoughts are always focused on African American issues. As demonstrated in the discussion of perception in Chapter 3, people's ways of thinking and ways of behaving are influenced by a wide variety of factors; culture is only one factor of many.

Listening without Bias

Just as racist, sexist, heterosexist, and ageist attitudes influence your language, they also influence your listening. In biased listening you hear what the speaker says through your preconceptions. You assume that what the speaker is saying merely reflects, for example, the speaker's gender, race, affectional orientation, or age.

Such biased listening occurs in a wide variety of situations. For example, when you dismiss a valid argument or give credence to an invalid argument, when you refuse to give someone a fair hearing, or when you attribute less credibility (or more credibility) to a speaker *because* the speaker is of a particular gender, race, affectional orientation, or age—and when these characteristics have nothing to do with the position or argument advanced—you're listening with bias.

To be sure, there are many instances in which speakers' characteristics are relevant and pertinent to your evaluation of the message. For example, the gender of a speaker who is discussing pregnancy, fathering a child, birth control, or surrogate motherhood is, most would agree, probably relevant to the message. On such topics it is not biased listening to hear the discussion in light of the gender of the speaker. But it is sexist listening to assume that only one gender has anything to say that's worth hearing—or that what one gender says can be discounted without a fair hearing. The same is true in regard to a person's race, age, or affectional orientation.

Applying Listening Skills

Chloe, a good friend of yours, has been assigned to train under the supervision of someone of a different race. Chloe confides in you that she just can't get herself to work with this person; she admits she is just too prejudiced to appreciate anything her supervisor says or does. What listening advice would you give Chloe?

Reduce Uncertainty

All communication interactions involve uncertainty and ambiguity. Not surprisingly, this uncertainty and ambiguity is greater when there are wide cultural differences (Berger & Bradac, 1982; Gudykunst, 1989, 1993). Because of this, in intercultural communication it takes more time and effort to reduce uncertainty and thus to communicate meaningfully. Reducing your uncertainty about another person is worth the effort, however; it not only will make your communication more effective but also will increase your liking for the person (Douglas, 1994).

Techniques such as active listening (Chapter 4) and perception checking (Chapter 3) help you check on the accuracy of your perceptions and allow you to revise

<table>
<tr><td>

Skill building exercise

</td><td>

Confronting Intercultural Differences

Here are a few cases of obvious intercultural differences. Select any one of them and indicate how you might communicate. For example: (1) What attitude would you approach the situation with? (2) What specific purpose would you hope to achieve? (3) What subordinate purposes might you hope to achieve? And (4) what would you say, and how would you say it?

1. You're in an interracial, interreligious relationship. Your partner's family ignores your "couplehood." For example, you and your partner are never invited to dinner as a couple or included in any family affairs. You decide to confront your partner's family.
2. Your parents persist in holding and verbalizing stereotypes about other religious, racial, and ethnic groups. You feel you must tell your parents how incorrect you think these stereotypes are.
3. Lenny, a colleague at work, recently underwent a religious conversion. He now persists in trying to get you and everyone else to undergo this same conversion. You decide to tell him that you find this behavior offensive.

Confronting intercultural insensitivity is extremely difficult, especially because most people will deny it. So approach these situations carefully, relying heavily on the skills of interpersonal communication identified throughout this text.

</td></tr>
</table>

and amend any incorrect perceptions. Also, being specific reduces ambiguity and the chances of misunderstandings; misunderstanding is a lot more likely if you talk about "neglect" (a highly abstract concept) than if you refer to "forgetting my last birthday" (a specific event).

Finally, seeking feedback helps you correct any possible misconceptions almost immediately. Seek feedback on whether you're making yourself clear ("Does that make sense?" "Do you see where to put the widget?"). Similarly, seek feedback to make sure you understand what the other person is saying ("Do you mean that you'll never speak with them again? Do you mean that literally?").

Recognize Differences

To communicate interculturally you need to recognize the differences between yourself and people who are culturally different, the differences within the culturally different group, and the numerous differences in meaning that arise from cultural differences.

Differences between Yourself and Culturally Different People   A common barrier to intercultural communication is the assumption that similarities exist but that differences do not. For example, although you may easily accept different hairstyles, clothing, and foods, you may assume that in basic values and beliefs, everyone is really alike. But that's not necessarily true. When you assume similarities and ignore differences, you'll fail to notice important distinctions. As a result, you'll risk communicating to others that your ways are the right ways and that their ways are not important to you. Consider: An American invites a Filipino coworker to dinner. The Filipino politely refuses. The American is hurt, feels that the Filipino does not want to be friendly, and does not repeat the invitation. The Filipino is hurt and concludes that the invitation was not extended sincerely. Here, it seems, both the American and the Filipino assume that their customs for inviting people to dinner are the same—when, in fact, they aren't. A Filipino expects to be invited several times before accepting a dinner invitation. In the Philippines, an invitation given only once is viewed as insincere.

> " I was raised to believe that excellence is the best deterrent to racism or sexism. And that's how I operate my life. "
>
> —Oprah Winfrey

Or consider age. If you were raised in the United States, you probably grew up with a youth bias (young is good, old is not so good—an attitude the U.S. media reinforce daily) and may well have assumed that this reverence for youth was universal across all cultures. But it isn't; and if you assume it is, you may be in line for inter-cultural difficulties. A good example is the case of the American journalist in China who remarked to a government official that the official was probably too young to remember a particular event. The comment would have been taken as a compliment by most youth-oriented Americans. But the official perceived it as an insult—as a suggestion that he was too young to deserve respect (Smith, 2002).

Differences within the Culturally Different Group   Within every cultural group there are wide and important differences. Just as all Americans are not alike, neither are all Indonesians, Greeks, Mexicans, and so on. When you ignore these dif-ferences—when you assume that all persons covered by the same label (in this case a national or racial label) are the same—you're guilty of stereotyping. A good example of this is the use of the term "African American." The term stresses the unity of Africa and those who are of African descent and is analogous to "Asian American" or "European American." At the same time, if the term is used in the same sense as "German American" or "Japanese American," it ignores the great diversity within the African continent. More analogous terms would be "Nigerian American" or "Ethiopian American." Within each culture there are smaller cultures that differ greatly from one another and from the larger culture as well as from other large cultures.

Differences in Meaning   Meanings exist not in words but in people (Chapter 5). Consider, for example, the different meanings of the word *woman* to an American and a Muslim, of *religion* to a born-again Christian and an atheist, or of *lunch* to a Chinese rice farmer and a Madison Avenue advertising executive. Even though dif-ferent groups may use the same word, its meanings will vary greatly depending on the listeners' cultural definitions.

Similarly, nonverbal messages have different meanings in different cultures. For example, a left-handed American who eats with the left hand may be seen by a Mus-lim as obscene. Muslims do not use the left hand for eating or for shaking hands but to solely clean themselves after excretory functions. So using the left hand to eat or to shake hands is considered insulting and obscene.

Message Skills

Intercultural Communication:
Become mindful of (1) differences between yourself and people who are culturally different, (2) differences within the other cultural groups, and (3) cultural differences in meanings.

Adjust Your Communication

Intercultural communication (in fact, all interpersonal communication) takes place only to the extent that you and the person you're trying to communicate with share the same system of symbols. Your interaction will be hindered to the extent that your language and nonverbal systems differ. There-fore, it's important to adjust your communication to compensate for cultural differences.

This principle takes on particular relevance when you realize that even within a given culture, no two persons share identical symbol systems. Parents and children, for example, not only have different vocabularies but also, even more important, associate dif-ferent meanings with some of the terms they both use. People in close relationships—either as intimate friends or as romantic part-ners—realize that learning the other person's signals takes a long time and, often, great patience. If you want to understand what an-other person means—by smiling, by saying "I love you," by arguing about trivial matters, by self-deprecating comments—you have to learn the person's system of signals.

In the same way, part of the art of intercultural communication is learning the other culture's signals, how they're used, and what they mean. Furthermore, you have to share your own system of sig-nals with others so that they can better understand you. Although some people may know what you mean by your silence or by your

? SKILLS VIEWPOINT

Of all the interpersonal communication skills considered so far, which would you identify as the most significant in effective intercultural communication?

avoidance of eye contact, others may not. You cannot expect others to decode your behaviors accurately without help.

Adjusting your communication is especially important in intercultural situations, largely because people from different cultures use different signals—or sometimes use the same signals to signify quite different things. For example, focused eye contact means honesty and openness in much of the United States. But in Japan and in many Hispanic cultures, that same behavior may signify arrogance or disrespect, particularly engaged in by a youngster with someone significantly older.

Communication accommodation theory, as explained in Chapter 1, holds that speakers will adjust or accommodate to the communication style of their listeners in order to interact more pleasantly and efficiently (Giles, Mulac, Bradac, & Johnson, 1987). As you adjust your messages, recognize that each culture has its own rules and customs for communication (Barna, 1997; Ruben, 1985; Spitzberg, 1991). These rules identify what is appropriate and what is inappropriate. Thus, for example, in U.S. culture you would call a person you wished to date three or four days in advance. In certain Asian cultures you might call the person's parents weeks or even months in advance. In U.S. culture you say, as a general friendly gesture and not as a specific invitation, "come over and pay us a visit sometime." To members of other cultures, this comment is sufficient to prompt the listeners actually to visit at their convenience. Table 9.2 presents a good example of a set of cultural rules—guidelines for communicating with an extremely large and important culture that many people don't know.

Recognize Culture Shock

Culture shock is the psychological reaction you experience when you encounter a culture very different from your own (Furnham & Bochner, 1986). Culture shock is normal; most people experience it when entering a new and different culture. Going away to college, moving in together, or joining the military, for example, can also result in culture shock. Nevertheless, it can be unpleasant and frustrating. Entering a new culture often engenders feelings of alienation, conspicuousness, and difference from everyone else. When you lack knowledge of the rules and customs of the new society, you cannot communicate effectively. You're apt to blunder frequently and seriously. In your culture shock you may not know basic things:

- how to ask someone for a favor or pay someone a compliment
- how to extend or accept an invitation
- how early or how late to arrive for an appointment, or how long to stay
- how to distinguish seriousness from playfulness and politeness from indifference

? SKILLS VIEWPOINT

You're assigned to help a group of students at your school prepare for the inevitable culture shock that they'll experience when they take their senior year at a foreign university. What do you say?

TABLE 9.2	*Interpersonal Communication Tips*

BETWEEN PEOPLE WITH AND WITHOUT DISABILITIES

Consider communication between people with general disabilities—such as people in wheelchairs or people with cerebral palsy—and those who have no such disability. Note that the suggestions offered here are considered appropriate in the United States but not necessarily in other cultures. For example, although most people in the United States accept the phrase "person with mental retardation," it's considered offensive to many in the United Kingdom (Fernald, 1995).

If you're the one without a general disability:

1. Avoid negative terms and terms that define the person in terms of the disability, such as "the disabled" or "the handicapped." Instead, say "person with a disability," putting the person, not the disability, first. Similarly, say "seizure" instead of "fit," "person with cerebral palsy," instead of "cerebral palsy victim," and "wheelchair user" instead of "wheelchair bound."

2. Treat assistive devices such as wheelchairs, canes, walkers, or crutches as the personal property of the user; be careful not to move these out of your way, as they're needed by the person with a disability.

3. If you shake hands with others in a group, also shake hands with the person with a disability. Don't avoid shaking hands, say, because the individual's hand is crippled.

4. Avoid talking about the person with a disability in the third person. For example, don't make remarks like "Doesn't he get around beautifully with the new crutches." Always direct your comments directly to the individual.

5. Don't assume that people who have a disability (such as slurred speech, as may occur with people who have cerebral palsy or cleft palate) are intellectually impaired. This definitely may not be the case, so be especially careful not to talk down to such people as, research shows, many people do (Unger, 2001).

6. If you're not sure how to act—for example, whether or not to offer walking assistance—ask: "Would you like me to help you into the dining room?"

7. If the person is in a wheelchair, it may be helpful for you to sit down or kneel down to get on the same eye level.

If you're the one with a disability:

1. Let the other person know if he or she can do anything to assist you in communicating. For example, if you want someone to speak louder, ask. If you want to relax and have someone push your wheelchair, say so.

2. Be patient and understanding with those who may not know how to act or what to say. Put them at ease as best you can.

3. If you detect discomfort in the other person, you might talk a bit about your disability to show that you're not uncomfortable and that you understand that others may not know how you feel. But, of course, you are under no obligation to educate the public—so don't feel this is something you ought to or have to do. If it makes you more comfortable, then do it; otherwise, don't.

Sources: These suggestions are based on a wide variety of sources; for example, http://www.empowermentzone.com/etiquet.txt (the website for the National Center for Access Unlimited), U.S. Department of Labor, http://www.dol.gov, http://www.dissvcs.uga.edu/com-peodis.html, and United Cerebral Palsy National, http://www.ucpa.org, all accessed April 5, 2002.

- how to dress for an informal, formal, or business function
- how to order a meal in a restaurant or how to summon a waiter

Culture shock occurs in four general stages, which apply to a wide variety of encounters with the new and the different (Oberg, 1960).

Stage One: The Honeymoon   At first you experience fascination, even enchantment, with the new culture and its people. You finally have your own apartment. You're your own boss. Finally, on your own! Among people who are culturally different, the early (and superficial) relationships of this stage are characterized by cordiality and friendship. Many tourists remain at this stage, because their stays in foreign countries are so brief.

Stage Two: The Crisis   In the crisis stage the differences between your own culture and the new one create problems. For example, students no longer find dinner ready or their clothes washed or ironed unless they do them themselves. Feelings of

> 66 Prejudice is a raft onto which the shipwrecked mind clambers and paddles to safety. 99
>
> —Ben Hecht

frustration and inadequacy come to the fore. This is the stage at which you experience the actual shock of the new culture. For example, in a study of students from more than 100 countries who were studying in 11 foreign countries, 25 percent of the students experienced depression (Klineberg & Hull, 1979).

Stage Three: The Recovery During the recovery period you gain the skills necessary to function effectively in the new culture. You learn how to shop, cook, and plan a meal. You find a local laundry and figure you'll learn how to iron later. You learn the language and ways of the society. Your feelings of inadequacy subside.

Stage Four: The Adjustment At the final stage you adjust to and come to enjoy the new culture and the new experiences. You may still experience periodic difficulties and strains, but on a whole, the experience is pleasant. Actually, you're now a pretty decent cook. You're even coming to enjoy it. And you're making a good salary, so why learn to iron?

People also may experience a kind of reverse culture shock when they return to their original culture after living in a foreign culture (Jandt, 2000). Consider, for example, Peace Corps volunteers who work in economically deprived rural areas around the world. On returning to Las Vegas or Beverly Hills, they too may experience culture shock. Sailors who serve long periods aboard ship and then return to, for example, isolated farming communities may also experience culture shock. In these cases, however, the recovery period is shorter and the sense of inadequacy and frustration is less.

Message Skills

Appreciating Cultural Differences: Look at cultural differences not as deviations or deficiencies but as the differences they are. Recognizing different ways of doing things, however, does not necessarily mean accepting them.

Summary of Concepts

This chapter explored culture and intercultural communication, the ways in which cultures differ, and ways to improve intercultural communication.

1. A culture is the specialized lifestyle of a group of people—their values, beliefs, artifacts, ways of behaving, and ways of communicating. Each generation transmits its culture to the next generation through the process of enculturation. In acculturation, one culture is modified through direct contact with or exposure to another culture.
2. Intercultural communication encompasses a broad range of interactions. Among them are communication between cultures, between races, between genders, between socioeconomic and ethnic groups, between age groups, between religions, and between nations.
3. Cultures differ in the degree to which they teach an individualist orientation (the individual is the most im-

portant consideration) or a collectivist orientation (the group is the most important consideration).
4. In high-context cultures much information is in the context or in the person's nonverbals; in low-context cultures most of the information is explicitly stated in the message.
5. Cultures differ in the degree to which gender roles are distinct or overlap. Highly "masculine" cultures view men as assertive, oriented to material success, and strong and view women as modest, focused on the quality of life, and tender.
6. Many tactics can help make intercultural communication more effective. For example, prepare yourself by learning about the culture, reduce ethnocentrism, communicate mindfully, avoid overattribution, reduce uncertainty, recognize differences, adjust your communication on the basis of cultural differences, and recognize culture shock.

Vocabulary Quiz: The Language of Intercultural Communication

Match the terms of intercultural communication with their definitions. Record the number of the definition next to the appropriate term.

_____ high-context culture

_____ acculturation

_____ intercultural communication

_____ low-context culture

_____ ethnocentrism

_____ culture

_____ mindfulness

_____ enculturation

_____ individualist cultures

_____ collectivist cultures

1. A culture in which most information is explicitly encoded in the verbal message.
2. The values, beliefs, artifacts, and ways of communicating of a group of people.
3. The process by which culture is transmitted from one generation to another.
4. Communication that takes place between persons of different cultures or persons who have different cultural beliefs, values, or ways of behaving.
5. The process through which a person's culture is modified through contact with another culture.
6. The tendency to evaluate other cultures negatively and our own culture positively.
7. A mental state in which we are aware of the logic that governs your behaviors.
8. Cultures that emphasize competition and individual success, and in which your responsibility is largely to yourself.
9. A culture in which much information is in the context or the person and is not made explicit in the verbal message.
10. Cultures that emphasize the member's responsibility to the group.

Four for Discussion

1. In this age of multiculturalism, how do you feel about Article II, Section 1 of the U.S. Constitution? The relevant section reads: "No person except a natural born citizen, or citizen of the United States at the time of the adoption of this Constitution, shall be eligible to the office of President."

2. Social Darwinism holds that much as the human species evolved from lower life forms to homo sapiens, cultures also evolve. Consequently, some cultures may be considered "advanced" and others "primitive." Cultural relativism, on the other hand, holds that although all cultures are different, that no culture is either superior or inferior to any other (Berry, Poortinga, Segall, & Dasen, 1992). What arguments can you advance in support of or against each position?

3. Men and women from different cultures were asked the following question: "If a man (woman) had all the other qualities you desired, would you marry this person if you were not in love with him (her)?" (LeVine, Sato, Hashimoto, & Verma, 1994). Fifty percent of the respondents from Pakistan, 49 percent from India, and 19 percent from Thailand said yes. At the other extreme were respondents from Japan (only 2 percent said yes), the United States (3.5 percent), and Brazil (4 percent). How would you answer this question? How is your answer influenced by your culture?

4. Some cultures frown on sexual relationships outside of marriage; others consider sex a normal part of intimacy. Intercultural researchers (Hatfield & Rapson, 1996) recall a discussion between colleagues from Sweden and the United States on ways of preventing AIDS. When researchers from the United States suggested promoting abstinence, their Swedish counterparts asked, "How will teenagers ever learn to become loving, considerate sexual partners if they don't practice?" "The silence that greeted the question," note Hatfield and Rapson (1996, p. 36), "was the sound of two cultures clashing." How have your cultural beliefs and values influenced what you consider appropriate relationship behavior?

Web Explorations

Explore our text website at
www.ablongman.com/devito
to find:

Exercises and Self-Tests

Exercises on culture and intercultural communication include (1) Random Pairs, (2) Cultural Beliefs, (3) From Culture to Gender, (4) Cultural Identities, and (5) The Sources of Your Cultural Beliefs. Two relevant self-tests are (6) How Open Are You Interculturally? and (7) Can You Distinguish Universal from Culture-Specific Icons?

Writing Resources and Assignments

Suggestions are available for writing papers of personal experience (for example, your experiences with intercultural communication), concept or principle explanation (for example, culture shock or ethnocentrism), review (the role of intercultural relationships in TV situation comedies), or research on culture and intercultural communication (for example, ethnocentrism of college students).

Explore our research resources at
www.researchnavigator.com
and

Read an article.

Read a popular or scholarly article on the nature of culture, cultural differences, or intercultural communication. On the basis of this article, what can you add to the discussion presented here?

Investigate key terms.

Investigate one of the key terms discussed in this chapter (for example, culture, masculine and feminine cultures, individualist and collectivist orientations, high- and low-context cultures, uncertainty reduction, culture shock, intercultural communication). What additional insights can you provide?

Find answers.

Try finding answers to one of the following questions, or design a research study to answer it.

1. How do cultures differ in their ways of communicating?
2. What are some of the culturally influenced communication differences between men and women?
3. What is the current status of interracial romantic relationships in the United States?

CREDITS

PHOTO CREDITS

Page 4: Frank Pedrick/The Image Works; **p. 5,** clockwise from top left: John B. Moore Jr./The Image Works; Ellen Senisi/The Image Works; CORBIS; **p. 8, top to bottom:** Elizabeth Crews/The Image Works; ImageState/Alamy; **p. 11:** Judy Gelles/Stock Boston; **p. 14,** clockwise from top left: Jean-Claude Lejeune/Stock Boston; Lawrence Migdale/Stock Boston; Lori Adamski Peek/Getty Images; **p. 16:** Bob Mahoney/The Image Works; **p. 21:** Barbara Stitzer/PhotoEdit Inc.; **p. 40:** USAF/Getty Images; **p. 189:** Topps Company; **p. 207:** © 2002 Thaves. Reprinted with Permission; **p. 209,** top to bottom: AP/Wide World Photos; Jason Lee/CORBIS; **p. 219:** Vahan Shirvanian/cartoonbank.com; **p. 220:** Donald Reilly/cartoonbank.com; **p. 243:** Robert E. Daemmrich/Stock Boston; **p. 451:** Hubertus Kanus/Photo Researchers; **p. 456:** Jupiter Images/Alamy; **p. 461:** Jeremy Horner/CORBIS; **p. 467:** View Stock/Alamy; **p. 471:** Mel Svenson/Getty Images; **p. 477:** Manchan/Getty Images; **p. 483:** Liz Hafalia/San Francisco Chronicle/CORBIS; **p. 486:** Reuters/CORBIS; **p. 491:** Paul Morrell/Getty Images; **p. 498:** Eugene Hoshiko/AP/Wide World Photos; **p. 501:** Dennis MacDonald/Alamy; **p. 507:** Reuters/CORBIS; **p. 513:** Chuck Savage/CORBIS; **p. 516:** BAVARIA/Getty Images; **p. 518:** Donald Reilly/cartoonbank.com; **p. 523:** James D. Wilson/Woodfin Camp; **p. 525:** Tom Cheney/cartoonbank.com; **p. 527:** Ilene Perlman/Stock Boston; **p. 528:** Bob Daemmrich/The Image Works

TEXT CREDITS

Success Workshops

p. 4: Edwards III, Wattenberg, and Lineberry, from *Government in America: People, Politics, and Policy*, 12/e, pp. 150–151. Copyright © 2006 by Pearson Education, Inc. Reprinted by permission.

p. 18: DeVito, Joseph A., from *Messages: Building Interpersonal Communication Skills*, 6/e, p. 155. Published by Allyn and Bacon, Boston, MA. Copyright © 2005 by Pearson Education. Reprinted by permission of the publisher.

Chapter 2

p. 54: Bloom, Benjamin, *Taxonomy of Educational Objectives: Cognitive Domain.* New York: McKay, 1956.

p. 56: Gronbeck, Bruce E., et al., from *Principles of Speech Communication*, Eleventh Brief Instructor's Edition, pp. 217–218. Copyright © 1992 by HarperCollins Publishers. Reprinted by permission of Addison-Wesley Educational Publishers, Inc.

Chapter 3

p. 62: Katz, Jane, *Swimming for Total Fitness: A Progressive Aerobic Program*, p. 99. Garden City, NY: Dolphin Books/Doubleday & Company, Inc., 1981

Chapter 5

p. 104: Henslin, James M., from *Sociology: A Down-to-Earth Approach, Core Concepts*, 1/e, pp. 40–43. Published by Allyn and Bacon, Boston, MA. Copyright © 2006 by Pearson Education. Reprinted by permission of the publisher.

p. 106: Zinn, Maxine, and Stanley D. Eitzen, from *Diversity in Families*, Fourth Edition, p. 205. Copyright © 1996 byHarperCollins College Publishers. Reprinted by permission of Addison-Wesley Educational Publishers, Inc.

p. 114: Thompson, William E., and Joseph V. Hickey, *Society in Focus: An Introduction to Sociology*, 5/e, p. 320. Boston: Allyn and Bacon, 2005.

p. 117: Gronbeck, Bruce, et al., from *Principles of Speech Communication*, 12/e, p. 53. Copyright © 1995 HarperCollins College Publishers. Reprinted by permission of Pearson Education, Inc.

p. 117: Harris, C. Leon, from *Concepts in Zoology*, 2/e, p. 573. Copyright © 1996 HarperCollins College Publishers. Reprinted by permission of Pearson Education, Inc.

p. 121: Wilson, R. Jackson, et al., from *The Pursuit of Liberty: A History of the American People*, 3/e, Vol. 2, p. 422. Copyright © 1996 HarperCollins College Publishers. Reprinted by permission of Pearson Education, Inc.

p. 122: Kinnear, Thomas C., Kenneth L. Bernhardt, and Kathleen A. Krentler, from *Principles of Marketing*, 4/e, p. Copyright © 1995 by HarperCollins College Publishers. Reprinted by permission of Pearson Education, Inc.

p. 122: Harris, *Concepts in Zoology*, 2/e, p. 130.

Chapter 6

p. 129: Agee, Warren K., Phillip H. Ault, and Edwin Emery, from *Introduction to Mass Communications*, 12/e. Copyright © 1997 by Addison Wesley Educational Publishers, Inc. Reprinted by permission of Pearson Education, Inc.

p. 129: Miller, Roger LeRoy, *Economics Today, 2001–2002 Edition*, p. 122. Boston, MA: Addison Wesley Longman, Inc., 2001.

p. 130: Thio, Alex, from *Sociology*, 5/e, p. 155. Copyright © 1998 by Addison-Wesley Educational Publishers. Reprinted by permission.

p. 130: Hicks, David, and Margaret A. Gwynne, from *Cultural Anthropology*, 2/e, p. 270. Copyright © 1996 by HarperCollins College Publishers. Reprinted by permission of Pearson Education, Inc.

p. 130: Wallace, Robert A., from *Biology: The World of Life*, 6/e, pp. 31–32. Copyright © 1992 by HarperCollins College Publishers. Reprinted by permission of Pearson Education, Inc.

p. 130: Ross, David A., from *Introduction to Oceanography*, p. 48. Copyright © 1995 David A. Ross. Reprinted by permission of Pearson Education, Inc.

p. 130: Preble, Duane, et al., par. "Texture" from *Art Forms: An Introduction to Visual Arts*, 6/e, p. 71. Copyright © 1999 by Addison-Wesley Educational Publishers. Reprinted by permission of Pearson Education, Inc.

p. 130: Nickerson, Robert C., from *Business and Information Systems*, p. 30. Copyright © 1998 by Addison-Wesley Educational Publishers. Reprinted by permission of Pearson Education.

p. 130: Newcombe, Nora, from *Child Development: Change Over Time*, 8/e, p. 223. Copyright © 1996 HarperCollins College Publishers. Reprinted by permission of Pearson Education, Inc.

p. 130: Gerow, Josh R., from *Essentials of Psychology: Concepts and Applications*, 2/e, p. 138. Copyright © 1996 by HarperCollins College Publishers. Reprinted by permission of Pearson Education, Inc.

p. 130: Marieb, Elaine N., *Essentials of Human Anatomy and Physiology*, 5/e, p. 119. Menlo Park, CA: The Benjamin/Cummings Publishing Co., Inc., 1997.

p. 131: Miller, Roger LeRoy, from *Economics Today*, 8/e, p. 98. Copyright © 1994 by HarperCollins College Publishers. Reprinted by permission of Pearson Education, Inc.

p. 132: Greenberg, Edward S., and Benjamin I. Page, from *The Struggle for Democracy*, Brief Version, 1/e, p. 291. Copyright © 1996 by HarperCollins College Publishers. Reprinted by permission of Pearson Education, Inc.

p. 132: Ross, *Introduction to Oceanography*, p. 62.

p. 132: Kinnear, Thomas C., Kenneth L. Bernhardt, and Kathleen A. Krentler, from *Principles of Marketing*, 4/e, pp. 79–81. Copyright © 1995 by HarperCollins College Publishers. Reprinted by permission of Pearson Education, Inc.

p. 132: Capron, H. L., *Computers: Tools for an Information Age*, Brief Edition, p. 82. New York: Addison Wesley Longman Publishing Company, 1998.

p. 133: Uba, Laura, and Karen Huang, *Psychology*, p. 148. New York: Addison-Wesley Educational Publishers, Inc., 1999.

p. 133: Mosley, Donald C., et al., from *Management: Leadership in Action*, 5/e, p. 317. Copyright © 1996 by HarperCollins College Publishers. Reprinted by permission of Pearson Education, Inc.

p. 133: Gronbeck, Bruce, et al., from *Principles of Speech Communication*, 12/e, Brief Edition, p. 302. Copyright © 1995 HarperCollins College Publishers. Reprinted by permission of Pearson Education, Inc.

p. 133: Thio, Alex, from *Sociology*, 4/e, p. 181. Copyright © 1996 by HarperCollins College Publishers. Reprinted by permission of Pearson Education, Inc.

p. 134: Agee, Ault, and Emery, *Introduction to Mass Communications*, 12/e, p. 225.

p. 136: Gerow, *Essentials of Psychology: Concepts and Applications*, 2/e, p. 289.

p. 136: Kinnear, Bernhardt, and Krentler, *Principles of Marketing*, 4/e, p. 191.

p. 137: Thio, *Sociology*, 4/e, p. 180.

p. 137: Nickerson, *Business and Information Systems*, p. 249.

p. 137: DeVito, Joseph A., *Human Communication: The Basic Course*, 7/e, p. 110. New York: Longman, 1997.

p. 137: Hewitt, Paul G., *Conceptual Physics*, 8/e, p. 279. Reading, MA: Addison Wesley Longman, 1998.

p. 137: Miller, *Economics Today*, 8/e, p. 213.

p. 138: Weaver II, Richard, *Understanding Interpersonal Communication*, 7/e, p. 220. New York: HarperCollins College Publishers, 1996.

p. 138: Preble, par. "Texture" from *Art Forms: An Introduction to Visual Arts*, 6/e, p. 64.

p. 138: Wallace, Robert A., *Biology: The World of Life*, 7/e, p. 167. Menlo Park, CA: Benjamin/Cummings, 1997.

p. 139: Hicks and Gwynne, *Cultural Anthropology*, 2/e, p. 258.

p. 143: Harris, C. Leon., from *Concepts in Zoology*, 2/e, p. 240. Copyright ©1996 HarperCollins College Publishers. Reprinted by permission of Pearson Education, Inc.

p. 143: Miller, *Economics Today*, 8/e, p. 84.

p. 143: Wallace, *Biology: The World of Life*, 6/e, p. 28.

p. 143: Newcombe, *Child Development: Change Over Time*, 8/e, p. 152.

p. 143: Anson, Chris M., and Robert A. Schwegler, *The Longman Handbook for Writers and Readers*, p. 78. New York: Longman, 1997.

p. 144: *The Struggle for Democracy*, Brief Version, 2/e, p. 190. New York: Longman, 1999.

p. 145: Greenberg and Page, *The Struggle for Democracy*, Brief Version, 1/e, pp. 107–108. Education, Inc.

p. 145: Audesirk, Gerald, Teresa Audesirk, and Bruce E. Byers, from *Biology: Life on Earth*, 7/e, pp. 4–5. Copyright © 2005. Reprinted by permission of Pearson Education, Inc., Upper Saddle River, NJ.

p. 145: Glynn, James, et al., from *Global Social Problems*, p. 222. Copyright © 1996 by HarperCollins College Publishers. Reprinted by permission of Pearson Education, Inc.

p. 146: Gronbeck, Bruce, et al., from *Principles of Speech Communication*, Edition, 12/e, pp. 32–33.

p. 147: Hicks and Gwynne, *Cultural Anthropology*, 2/e, p. 144.

p. 147: Miller, *Economics Today*, 8/e, p. 185.

p. 148: Harris, Marvin, *Cultural Anthropology*, 4/e, pp. 3–4. New York: HarperCollins College Publishers, 1995.

p. 148: Wallbank, T. Walter, and Alastair Taylor, et al., from *Civilization Past and Present*, 8/e, p. 831. Copyright © 1996 by HarperCollins College Publishers. Reprinted by permission of Pearson Education, Inc.

p. 148: Thompson, William E., and Joseph Hickey, from *Society in Focus: An Introduction to Sociology*, 2/e, p. 162. Copyright © 1996 William E. Thompson and Joseph V. Hickey. Reprinted by permission of Pearson Education, Inc.

p. 149: Newcombe, *Child Development: Change Over Time*, 8/e, p. 354.

p. 149: Coleman, James William, and Donald R. Cressey, *Social Problems*, 6/e, p. 130. New York: HarperCollins College Publishers, 1996.

p. 149: DeVito, Joseph A., *Elements of Public Speaking*, 7/e, pp. 132-133. New York: Longman, 2000.

p. 149: DeVito, Joseph A., from *Messages: Building Interpersonal Communication Skills*, 3/e, p. 153. Copyright © 1996 HarperCollins College Publishers. Reprinted by permission of Pearson Education, Inc.

p. 150: Audesirk, Audesirk, and Byers, *Biology: Life on Earth*, 7/e, p. 12.

Chapter 7

p. 158: Mix, Michael C., Paul Farber, and Keith I. King, from *Biology: The Network of Life*, 2/e. Copyright © 1996 by Michael C. Mix, Paul Farber, and Keith I. King. Reprinted by permission of Pearson Education, Inc.

p. 160: Audesirk, Theresa, Gerald Audesirk, and Bruce E. Byers, from *Life on Earth*, 3/e, pp. 51, 64. Copyright © 2003 by Pearson Education, Inc. Reprinted by permission of Pearson Education, Inc., Upper Saddle River, NJ.

p. 161: Kinnear, Thomas C., Kenneth L. Bernhardt, and Kathleen A. Krentler, from *Principles of Marketing*, 4/e p. Copyright © 1995 by HarperCollins College Publishers. Reprinted by permission of Pearson Education, Inc.

p. 161: Brennan, Scott, and Jay Withgott, from *Environment: The Science Behind the Stories*, p. 546. Copyright © 2005 Pearson Education, Inc., publishing as Benjamin Cummings. Reprinted by permission.

p. 162: Preble, Duane, et al., par. "Texture" from *Art Forms: An Introduction to Visual Arts*, 6/e, p. 60. Copyright © 1999 by Addison-Wesley Educational Publishers. Reprinted by permission of Pearson Education, Inc.

p. 162: Solomon, Michael R., from *Consumer Behavior: Buying, Having, and Being*, 6/e, p. 503. Copyright © 2004. Reprinted by permission of Pearson Education, Inc., Upper Saddle River, NJ.

p. 162: Wood, Samuel E., Ellen Green Wood, and Denise Boyd, *Mastering the World of Psychology*, 2/e, p. 210. Boston: Allyn and Bacon, 2006.

p. 163: Preble, et al., par. "Texture" from *Art Forms: An Introduction to Visual Arts*, 6/e, pp. 98, 99.

p. 164: Edwards III, Wattenberg, and Lineberry, from *Government in America: People, Politics, and Policy*, 12/e, pp. 179–180. Copyright © 2006 by Pearson Education, Inc. Reprinted by permission.

p. 164: Edwards III, Wattenberg, and Lineberry, from *Government in America: People, Politics, and Policy*, 12/e, p. 156 Copyright © 2006 by Pearson Education, Inc. Reprinted by permission.

p. 164: Thompson, William E., and Joseph Hickey, from *Society in Focus: An Introduction to Sociology*, 2/e, pp. 135–136. Copyright © 1996 William E. Thompson and Joseph V. Hickey. Reprinted by permission of Pearson Education, Inc.

p. 165: Brennan and Withgott, *Environment: The Science Behind the Stories*, pp. 591–592.

p. 165: Solomon, Michael R., Greg Marshall, and Elnora Stuart, *Marketing: Real People, Real Choices*, 4/e, p. 202. Upper Saddle River, NJ: Pearson Prentice Hall, 2006.

p. 165: Kinnear, Bernhardt, and Krentler, from *Principles of Marketing*, 4/e, p. 180.

p. 166: Edwards III, George C., et al., from *Government in America: People, Politics, and Policy*, 7/e, p. 230. Copyright © 1996 HarperCollins College Publishers. Reprinted by permission of Pearson Education, Inc.

p. 166: Miller, Roger LeRoy, from *Economics Today*, 8/e, p. 147. Copyright © 1994 by HarperCollins College Publishers. Reprinted by permission of Pearson Education, Inc.

p. 166: Applebaum, Richard, and William J. Chambliss, from *Sociology*, p. 55. Copyright © 1995 HarperCollins College Publishers. Reprinted by permission of Pearson Education, Inc.

p. 166: Mosley, Donald C., Paul H. Pietri, and Leon C. Megginson, from *Management: Leadership in Action*, 5/e, pp. 333–336. Copyright © 1996 by HarperCollins College Publishers. Reprinted by permission of Pearson Education, Inc.

p. 167: London, Barbara, and John Upton, *Photography*, 6/e, p. 134. New York: Longman, 1998.

p. 172: Laetsch, Watson M., *Plants: Basic Concepts in Botany*, p. 393. Boston: Little, Brown, 1982.

p. 175: Kinnear, Bernhardt, and Krentler, *Principles of Marketing*, 4/e, p. 290.

p. 177: Tortora, Gerard J., *Introduction to the Human Body: The Essentials of Anatomy and Physiology*, 2/e, p. 56. New York: HarperCollins College Publishers, 1991.

p. 179: Miller and LeRoy, *Economics Today*, 8/e, p. 335.

p. 180: Harris, C. Leon, from *Concepts in Zoology*, 2/e, p. 402. Copyright © 1996 HarperCollins College Publishers. Reprinted by permission of Pearson Education, Inc.

p. 180: Ferl, Robert J., Robert A. Wallace, and Gerald P. Sanders, from *Biology: The Realm of Life*, 3/e, pp. 252–253. Copyright © 1996 by HarperCollins College Publishers. Reprinted by permission of Pearson Education, Inc.

p. 180: Glynn, James, et al., from *Global Social Problems*, p. 154. Copyright © 1996 by HarperCollins College Publishers. Reprinted by permission of Pearson Education, Inc.

p. 180: Wallbank, T. Walter, and Alastair Taylor, et al., from *Civilization Past and Present*, 8/e, p. 671. Copyright © 1996 by HarperCollins College Publishers. Reprinted by permission of Pearson Education, Inc.

p. 180: Hicks, David, and Margaret A. Gwynne, from *Cultural Anthropology*, 2/e, p. 304. Copyright © 1996 by HarperCollins College Publishers. Reprinted by permission of Pearson Education, Inc.

p. 180: Zimbardo, Philip G., and Richard J. Gerrig, *Psychology and Life*, 14/e, p. 337. New York: HarperCollins College Publishers, 1996.

p. 181: Edwards III, et al., from *Government in America: People, Politics, and Policy*, 12/e, p. 593.

p. 183: Tortora, *Introduction to the Human Body: The Essentials of Anatomy and Physiology*, 2/e, p. 30.

p. 184: Thompson and Hickey, *Society in Focus: An Introduction to Sociology*, 2/e, p. 65.

p. 184: Kinnear, Bernhardt, and Krentler, *Principles of Marketing*, 4/e, pp. 475–476.

p. 185: Wade, Carole, and Carol Tavris, *Psychology*, 3/e, p. 77. New York: HarperCollins College Publishers, 1993.

Chapter 8

p. 191: Brennan, Scott, and Jay Withgott, from *Environment: The Science Behind the Stories*, p. 461. Copyright © 2005 Pearson.

p. 193: Mix, Michael C., Paul Farber, and Keith I. King, from *Biology: The Network of Life*, 1/e, p. 165. Copyright © 1992 by Michael C. Mix, Paul Farber, and Keith I. King. Reprinted by permission of Pearson Education, Inc.

p. 193: Edwards III, Wattenberg, and Lineberry, from *Government in America: People, Politics, and Policy*, 9/e, p. 210, Table 6.5. Copyright

p. 193: Kaufman, Donald G., and Franz, Cecilia M., from *Biosphere 2000: Protecting Our Global Environment*, p. 143. Copyright © 1993 HarperCollins College Publishers. Reprinted by permission of Pearson Education, Inc.

p. 193: Pride, William, and O. C. Ferrel, from *Marketing: Concepts and Strategies*, 9/e, p. 329; originally appeared in "Preference for Private Brands of Food Products by Age and Sex," *Yankelovich MONITOR*, 1989. Reprinted by permission of Yankelovich.

p. 193: Skolnick, Arlene S., from *The Intimate Environment: Exploring Marriage and the Family*, 5/e, p. 443. Copyright © 1992 by Arlene S. Skolnick. Reprinted by permission of Pearson Education, Inc.

p. 193: Edwards III, Wattenberg, and Lineberry, from *Government in America: People, Politics, and Policy*, 12/e, p. 180. Copyright © 2006 by Pearson Education, Inc. Reprinted by permission.

p. 193: Edwards III, Wattenberg, and Lineberry, graph from *Government in America: People, Politics, and Policy*, 12/e, p. 256. Graph data excerpted from Pew Research Center, "Party Identification Trend, by Demographic Groups," 2004, http://people-press.org. Reprinted by permission of The Pew Research Center for the People and the Press.

p. 199: Wright, Richard T., from *Environmental Science: Toward a Sustainable Future*, 9/e, p. 139. Copyright © 2005. Adapted by permission of Pearson Education, Inc., Upper Saddle River, NJ.

p. 200: Rollins, Boyd C., and Harold Feldman, graph from "Marital Satisfaction over the Family Life Cycle," *Journal of Marriage and the Family*, February 1970, 32:1, 26. Reprinted by permission of Blackwell Publishing Ltd.

p. 201: Donatelle, Rebecca J., from *Health: The Basics*, 4/e, p. 288, Fig. 2.12. Copyright © 2001 by Allyn and Bacon. Reprinted by permission of Pearson Education, Inc.

p. 201: Hitt, Michael, Stewart Black, Lyman W. Porter, from *Management*, 1/e, p. 241. Copyright © 2005. Reprinted by permission of Pearson Education, Inc., Upper Saddle River, NJ.

p. 202: Nickerson, Robert C., from *Business and Information Systems*, p. 309. Copyright © 1998 by Addison-Wesley Educational Publishers. Reprinted by permission of Pearson Education.

p. 202: Donatelle, *Health: The Basics*, 4/e, p. 386, Fig. 15.3.

p. 203: Edwards III, Wattenberg, and Lineberry, from *Government in America: People, Politics, and Policy*, 9/e, p. 474, Fig. 14.5.

p. 204: Solomon, Michael R., from *Consumer Behavior: Buying, Having, and Being*, 6/e, p. 293. Copyright © 2004. Reprinted by permission of Pearson Education, Inc., Upper Saddle River, NJ.

p. 205: Wallace, Robert A., from *Biology: The World of Life*, 5/e, p. 321. Copyright © 1987 by Scott, Foresman. Reprinted by permission of Pearson Education, Inc.

p. 206: Edwards III, George C., et al., from *Government in America: People, Politics, and Policy*, 7/e, p. 47. Copyright © 1996 HarperCollins College Publishers. Reprinted by permission of Pearson Education, Inc.

p. 207: Applebaum, Richard, and William J. Chambliss, from *Sociology*, p. 427. Copyright © 1995 HarperCollins College Publishers. Reprinted by permission of Pearson Education, Inc.

p. 210: Jewett, Sarah O., "A White Heron," 1886.

p. 210: Hardy, Thomas, "The Darkling Thrush," 1900.

p. 210: Compton's Interactive Encyclopedia, "Thrush" in Electronic Resources on Ornithology. Copyright © 1994, 1995, 1996, 1997, 1998, 1999 by the Learning Company, Inc. and its licensors. All rights reserved. Used by permission.

p. 213: Wallace, *Biology: The World of Life*, 5/e, pp. 237–238.

Chapter 9

p. 228: National Oceanic and Atmospheric Administration's National Weather Service page, http://www.nws.noaa.gov/.

p. 231: Site Map of *Literature, Arts, and Medicine Database*, http://endeavor.med.nyu.edu/lit-med/lit-med-db/. © New York University 1993–2006. Database is produced at New York University School of Medicine. Reprinted by permission

p. 231: Site Map of ARTSEDGE, http://artsedge.kennedy-center.org/aboutus/sitemap.cfm. Copyright © The Kennedy Center. Reprinted by permission.

p. 236: Curry, Tim, et al., *Sociology for the Twenty-First Century*, 2/e, p. 207. Upper Saddle River, NJ: Prentice-Hall, Inc., 1999.

Chapter 10

p. 241: Thio, Alex, from *Sociology*, 5/e, pp. 00–00. Copyright © 1998 by Addison-Wesley Educational Publishers. Reprinted by permission.

p. 244: Courlander, Harold, "The Lion's Share." From *The King's Drum and Other African Stories* by Harold Courlander. Copyright © 1962, 1960 by Harold Courlander. Reprinted by permission of Michael Courlander.

p. 244: Conniff, Dorothy, from "What's Best for the Child," *The Progressive*, November 1988. By permission of The Progressive Magazine.

p. 244: McMiller, "Stiff Laws Nab Deadbeats," *USA TODAY*, August 16, 1995. Copyright © 1995 USA TODAY. Reprinted with permission.

p. 244: Skolnick, Arlene S., from *The Intimate Environment: Exploring Marriage and the Family*, 6/e, p. 95. Copyright © 1996 by HarperCollins College Publishers. Reprinted by permission of Pearson Education, Inc.

p. 249: Greenberg, Edward S., and Benjamin I. Page, from *The Struggle for Democracy*, Brief Version, 1/e, p. 186. Copyright © 1996 by HarperCollins College Publishers. Reprinted by permission of Pearson Education, Inc.

p. 251: Agee, Warren K., Phillip H. Ault, and Edwin Emery, from *Introduction to Mass Communications*, 12/e, p. 466. Copyright © 1997 by Addison Wesley Educational Publishers, Inc. Reprinted by permission of Pearson Education, Inc.

p. 251: Clarke, Kevin, "Growing Hunger," *Salt*, March 1993.

p. 251: Oliveria, "Burning Will Go: That's Not All That Good," *Spokesman Review* (July 24, 2002).

p. 251: Cook, Roy A., Laura Yale, Joseph J. Marqua, *Tourism: The Business of Travel*, 2/e, p. 245. Upper Saddle River, NJ: Prentice Hall, 2002.

p. 252: Jones, Edwin, and Richard Childers, *Contemporary College Physics*, 2/e, p. 188. New York: Addison Wesley Publishing Co., 1993.

p. 252: Bayles, Martha. 2 par. (approx 287 words) "People used to tap their feet . . . " from "Rock 'n Roll has Lost Its Soul," *Wilson Quarterly*, Summer 1993.

p. 254: Waltrip, "Calling Dr. Phil: NASCAR Needs Black-and-White Penalties," *FOXSports.com* (September 2005).

p. 254: Bolte, Bill, "Jerry's Got to Be Kidding" from *In These Times*, September 16, 1992. Reprinted by permission.

p. 254: Mander, Jerry, from *In the Absence of the Sacred: The Failure of Technology and the Rise of the Indian Nations*. San Francisco: Sierra Club Books, 1991.

p. 255: Swardson, Roger, "Greetings the Electronic Plantation," *City Pages*, October 21, 1992.

p. 255: Durst, Will, from "We Don't Know Squat" as appeared in *Utne Reader*, March/April 1995, originally from *The Nose*. Reprinted by permission of Will Durst.

p. 256: Otto, Whitney, *How to Make an American Quilt*, p. 183. New York: Villard, 1991.

p. 261: "Misstep on Video Violence," *USA TODAY*, June 6, 2005. Copyright © 2005 USA TODAY. Reprinted by permission.

p. 262: "Death Penalty Debate Finally Produces Results," *USA TODAY*, June 22, 2005. Copyright © 2005 USA TODAY. Reprinted by permission.

Chapter 11

p. 270: Bennett, Jeffrey, Seth Shostak, and Bruce Jakosky, *Life in the Universe*, p. 2. San Francisco: Addison Wesley, 2003.

p. 271: Kennedy, X. J., and Dana Gioia, *Literature: An Introduction to Fiction, Poetry, and Drama*, 3/e, p. 454. New York: Longman, 2003.

p. 271: Margolis, Mac, "A Plot of Their Own," *Newsweek*, January 21, 2002.

Chapter 12

p. 284: [1]**Newell**, Sydney B., *Chemistry*, p. 17. Boston: Little, Brown, 1977.

p. 285: [2]**Campbell**, Bernard G., and James D. Loy, from *Humankind Emerging*, 7/e, p. 38. Copyright © 1996 by HarperCollins College Publishers. Reprinted by permission of Pearson Education, Inc.

p. 285: [3]**Wasserman**, Gary, *The Basics of American Politics*, p. 25. Boston: Little, Brown, 1985.

p. 285: [4]**Wasserman**, *The Basics of American Politics*, p. 8.

p. 285: [5]**Newell**, *Chemistry*, p. 43.

p. 285: [6]**Pillitteri**, Adele, *Nursing Care of the Growing Family*, p. 280. Boston: Little, Brown, 1976.

p. 285: [7]**Newell**, *Chemistry*, p. 45.

p. 285: [8]**Campbell**, Bernard G., and James D. Loy, from *Humankind Emerging*, 7/e, p. 21. Copyright © 1996 by HarperCollins College Publishers. Reprinted by permission of Pearson Education, Inc.

p. 285: [9]**Gannon**, Martin J., *Management: An Organizational Perspective*, p. 20. Boston: Little, Brown, 1977.

p. 287: [10]**MacMillan**, Donald L., *Mental Retardation in the School and Society*, p. 5. Boston: Little, Brown, 1982.

p. 288: [11]**Campbell** and Loy, *Humankind Emerging*, 7/e, p. 189.

p. 288: [12]**Wasserman**, *The Basics of American Politics*, p. 33.

p. 288: [13]**Newell**, *Chemistry*, p. 388.

p. 288: Harris, C. Leon., from *Concepts in Zoology*, 2/e, p. 417. Copyright © 1996 HarperCollins College Publishers. Reprinted by permission of Pearson Education, Inc.

p. 288: Thio, Alex, from *Sociology*, 5/e, p. 235. Copyright © 1998 by Addison-Wesley Educational Publishers. Reprinted by permission.

p. 289: [14]**Campbell** and Loy, *Humankind Emerging*, 7/e, p. 16.

p. 289: [15]**Wasserman**, *The Basics of American Politics*, p. 87.

p. 289: [16]**MacMillan**, *Mental Retardation in the School and Society*, p. 11.

p. 289: Wade, Carole, and Carol Tavris, *Psychology*, 6/e, p. 337. Upper Saddle River, NJ: Prentice-Hall, 2000.

p. 290: Harris, *Concepts in Zoology*, 2/e, pp. 408–409.

Chapter 13

p. 307: Roget, from *Roget's International Thesaurus*, 4/e. ed. by Robert L. Chapman. Copyright © 1997 by Robert Chapman. Reprinted by permission of HarperCollins Publishers.

Chapter 14

p. 319: Tortora, Gerard, from *Introduction to the Human Body*, 3/e, p. 221, Fig. 00. Copyright © 1994 Biological Science Textbooks, Inc. and A & P Textbooks, Inc. Reprinted by permission of Pearson Education, Inc.

p. 321: Thio, Alex, from *Sociology*, 4/e, p. 100. Copyright © 1996 by HarperCollins College Publishers. Reprinted by permission of Pearson Education, Inc.

p. 321: DeVito, Joseph A., *The Interpersonal Communication Book*, 9/e, p. 191. New York: Longman, 2001.

p. 321: Wallbank, T. Walter, and Alastair Taylor, et al., from *Civilization Past and Present*, 8/e, pp. 1012–1013. Copyright © 1996 by HarperCollins College Publishers. Reprinted by permission of Pearson Education, Inc.

p. 321: Gronbeck, Bruce E., et al., from *Principles of Speech Communication*, 11/e, Brief Instructor's Edition, p. 25. Copyright © 1992 HarperCollins College Publishers. Reprinted by permission of Pearson Education, Inc.

p. 321: Campbell, Bernard G. and James D. Loy, from *Humankind Emerging*, 7/e, pp. 22–23. Copyright © 1996 by HarperCollins College Publishers. Reprinted by permission of Pearson Education, Inc.

p. 321: Kinnear, Thomas C., Kenneth L. Bernhardt, and Kathleen A. Krentler, from *Principles of Marketing*, 4/e, p. 537. Copyright © 1995 by HarperCollins College Publishers. Reprinted by permission of Pearson Education, Inc.

p. 321: McCarty, Marilu Hurt, from *Dollars and Sense: An Introduction to Economics*, 8/e, pp. 272–273. Copyright © 1997 by Addison-Wesley Educational Publishers, Inc. Reprinted by permission of Pearson Education, Inc.

p. 323: Wade, Carole, and Carol Tavris, *Invitation to Psychology*, p. 182. New York: Longman, 1999.

p. 325: Thompson, William E., and Joseph Hickey, from *Society in Focus: An Introduction to Sociology*, 2/e, p. 65. Copyright © 1996 William E. Thompson and Joseph V. Hickey. Reprinted by permission of Pearson Education, Inc.

p. 328: McCarty, *Dollars and Sense: An Introduction to Economics*, 8/e, pp. 213–214.

p. 329: DeVito, Joseph A., from *Messages: Building Interpersonal Communication Skills*, 3/e, pp. 161–162. Copyright © 1996 HarperCollins College Publishers. Reprinted by permission of Pearson Education, Inc.

p. 331: Thio, Alex, from *Deviant Behavior*, 4/e, pp. 311–312. Copyright © 1995 by HarperCollins College Publishers. Reprinted by permission of Pearson Education, Inc.

p. 333: Campbell, Bernard G., and James D. Loy, from *Humankind Emerging*, 7/e, pp. 127–128. Copyright © 1996 by HarperCollins College Publishers. Reprinted by permission of Pearson Education, Inc.

Chapter 15

p. 338: DeVito, Joseph A., from *The Interpersonal Communication Book*, 8/e, pp. 266, 268. Copyright © 1998 Joseph A. DeVito. Reprinted by permission of Pearson Education, Inc.

p. 342: Donatelle, Rebecca J., from *Health: The Basics*, 4/e, p. 346. Copyright © 2001 by Allyn and Bacon. Reprinted by permission of Pearson Education, Inc.

p. 342: Solomon, Michael R., and Elnora W. Stuart, from *Marketing: Real People, Real Choices*, 2/e, p. 135. Copyright © 2000 Prentice-Hall, Inc. Reprinted by permission of Pearson Education, Inc., Upper Saddle River, NJ.

p. 342: Macionis, John J., from *Society: The Basics*, 5/e, Annotated Instructor's Edition, p. 308. Copyright © 2000 by Prentice-Hall, Inc. Reprinted by permission of Pearson Education, Inc., Upper Saddle River, NJ.

p. 342: Griffin, Ricky W., and Ronald J. Ebert, from *Business*, 8/e, p. 471. Copyright © 2006. Reprinted by permission of Pearson Education, Inc., Upper Saddle River, NJ.

p. 349: Barlow, Hugh D., *Criminal Justice in America*, p. 327. Upper Saddle River, NJ: Prentice-Hall, Inc., 2000.

p. 350: Macionis, *Society: The Basics*, 5/e, Annotated Instructor's Edition, pp. 253–254.

p. 350: Bennett, Jeffrey, from *The Cosmic Perspective*, Brief Edition, p. 57.Copyright © 2000 by Addison Wesley Longman. Reprinted by permission of Pearson Education, Inc.

p. 350: Christopherson, Robert W., *Geosystems: An Introduction to Physical Geography*, 4/e, p. 470. Upper Saddle River, NJ: Prentice-Hall, Inc., 2000.

p. 351: Donatelle, *Health: The Basics*, 4/e, p. 282.

p. 352: Barlow, *Criminal Justice in America*, p. 439.

p. 352: Solomon and Stuart, from *Marketing: Real People, Real Choices*, 2/e, p. 135.

p. 353: Donatelle, *Health: The Basics*, 4/e, p. 338.

p. 353: Macionis, *Society: The Basics*, 5/e, Annotated Instructor's Edition, p. 77.

p. 353: Solomon and Stuart, from *Marketing: Real People, Real Choices*, 2/e, p. 427.

p. 359: Berman, Lois, and J. C., *Exploring the Cosmos*, p. 145. Boston: Little, Brown, 1986.

Chapter 16

p. 367: Wallace, Robert A., from *Biology: The World of Life*, 5/e, p. 434. Copyright © 1987 by Scott, Foresman. Reprinted by permission of Pearson Education, Inc.

p. 367: von Eschenback, Wolfram, from *Parzival*, translated and with an introduction by Helen M. Mustard and Charles E. Passage. Copyright © 1961 by Helen M. Mustard and Charles E. Passage. Reprinted by permission of Vintage Books, a division of Random House, Inc.

p. 367: Ross, David A., from *Introduction to Oceanography*, p. 239. Copyright © 1995 David A. Ross. Reprinted by permission of Pearson Education, Inc.

p. 368: Wade, Carole, and Carol Tavris, *Psychology*, 4/e, pp. 124–125. New York: HarperCollins College Publishers, 1996.

p. 370: Wallace, *Biology: The World of Life*, 5/e, p. 443.

p. 370: United States Constitution, Section 7.

Chapter 17

p. 387: Lial, Margaret, et al., *Basic College Mathematics*, 5/e, p. 689. Reading, MA: Addison-Wesley Longman, Inc., 1998.

Chapter 18

p. 421: Multiple Choice Questions from DeVito, Joseph A., Accompanying Website of *Messages: Building Interpersonal Skills*, 6/e, http://wps.ablongman.com/ab_devito_messages_6/0,9329,1434159-content,00.utf8html. Published by Allyn and Bacon, Boston, MA. Copyright © 2005 by Pearson Education. Reprinted by permission of the publisher.

Chapter 19

p. 427: Kinnear, Thomas C., Kenneth L. Bernhardt, and Kathleen A. Krentler, from *Principles of Marketing*, 4/e, p. 311. Copyright © 1995 by HarperCollins College Publishers. Reprinted by permission of Pearson Education, Inc.

p. 430: Kinnear, Bernhardt, and Krentler, *Principles of Marketing*, 4/e, p. 654.

p. 436: Denesha, Timothy, "From a Vegetarian: Looking at Hunting from Both Sides Now," *The Buffalo News*, November 24, 1996. Reprinted by permission of the author.

p. 438: Kinnear, Bernhardt, and Krentler, from *Principles of Marketing*, 4/e, p. 61.

p. 438: "Aromatherapy: The Nose Knows" from *Berkeley Wellness Letter*, May 1995, Vol. 11, No. 8, p. 4 (I). Reprinted by permission of University of California at Berkeley Health Letter Associates.

p. 440: Donatelle, Rebecca J., from *Access to Health*, 7/e, pp. 40–41. Copyright © 2002 Pearson Education, Inc., publishing as Benjamin Cummings. Reprinted by permission of Pearson Education, Inc.

p. 440: Wallbank, T. Walter, et al., *Civilization Past and Present*, 6/e, Vol. 2, p. 533. Glenview, IL: Scott, Foresman, 1987.

p. 440: *The Intimate Environment: Exploring Marriage and the Family*, 6/e, p. 107. Copyright © 1996 by HarperCollins College Publishers. Reprinted by permission of Pearson Education, Inc.

p. 443: Kinnear, Bernhardt, and Krentler, from *Principles of Marketing*, 4/e, p. 495.

p. 443: Wallbank, T. Walter, et al., *Civilization Past and Present*, 6/e, Vol. 2, p. 781. Glenview, IL: Scott, Foresman, 1987.

Part Eight: Thematic Readings

p. 450: Hicks, David, and Margaret A. Gwynne, "Body Adornment" from *Cultural Anthropology*, 2/e, pp. 373–376. Copyright © 1996 by HarperCollins College Publishers. Reprinted by permission of Pearson Education, Inc.

p. 455: Clifford, Catherine, "From Bear Teeth to 'Pearls: Why We Adorn Ourselves,'"*Health*, August 1990, V. 2, No. 8, p. 74. Reprinted by permission of Time Health Media, Inc.

p. 460: Borel, France, "The Decorated Body" from *Le Vetement Incarne—Les Metamorphoses du Corps*. Copyright © Calmann Levy, 1992. Reprinted by permission of Calmann-Levy, Paris. English translation copyright © by Ellen Dooling Draper, as appeared in *Parabola*, Fall 1994, V. 19, No. 3, P. 74+. By permission of Ellen Dooling Draper.

p. 466: Thio, Alex, "Communication Between Men and Women" from *Sociology*, 5/e, pp. 129–131. Copyright © 1998 by Addison-Wesley Educational Publishers. Reprinted by permission

p. 470: Tannen, Deborah, "The Talk of the Sandbox," *The Washington Post*, December 11, 1994. Copyright Deborah Tannen. Adapted in part from *Talking from 9 to 5: Women and Men at Work* (Quill, 1994). Reprinted by permission of the author.

p. 476: Ash, Barbara, "Communication Between the Sexes: A War of the Words," *Hartford Courant*, 2/13/96. Copyright 1996, Knight Ridder/Tribune. Reprinted with permission.

p. 482: Leahy, Stephen, "Environment: Increased Hurricane Activity Tied to Global Warming" from *Inter Press Service / Global Information Network*, August 31, 2005. globalinfo.org. © 2005. Reprinted by permission.

p. 486: Audesirk, Gerald, Teresa Audesirk, and Bruce E. Byers, from *Biology: Life on Earth*, 7/e, pp. 00–00. Copyright © 2005. Reprinted by permission of Pearson Education, Inc., Upper Saddle River, NJ.

p. 490: "Stem-Cell Therapy: Promise and Reality." Copyright 2005 by Consumers Union of U.S., Inc. Yonkers, NY 10703-1057, a non-profit organization. Reprinted with permission from the June 2005 issue of *Consumer Reports on Health* ® for educational purposes only. No commercial use or reproduction permitted. http://www.consumerreportsonhealth.org/www.ConsumerReportsonHealth.org; http://www.consumerreports.org/www.ConsumerReports.org®.

p. 496: Greenberg, Edward S., and Benjamin Page, excerpts from "Civil Liberties in the Constitution" from *The Struggle for Democracy*, Brief Version, 2/e, pp. 336–339, 347–348. Copyright © 1999 by Addison-Wesley Educational Publishers, Inc. Reprinted by permission of Pearson Education, Inc.

p. 501: Armour, Stephanie, "Your Appearance, Good or Bad, Can Affect the Size of Your Paycheck," *USA TODAY*, 7/20/05. Copyright © 2005 USA TODAY. Reprinted with permission.

p. 506: "Move Over Big Brother," *The Economist*, December 4, 2004. © 2004 The Economist Newspaper Ltd. All rights reserved. Reprinted with permission. Further reproduction prohibited. http://www.economist.com.

Sample Textbook Chapter

p. 513: DeVito, Joseph A., from *Messages: Building Interpersonal Communication Skills*, 6/e, Chapter 9, pp. 189–208. Published by Allyn and Bacon, Boston, MA. Copyright © 2005 by Pearson Education. Reprinted by permission of the publisher.

p. 514: Passage on Nacirema culture is excerpted from Horace Miner, "Body Rituals among the Nicirema, *American Anthropologist* 58:3, June 1956, 503–507.

p. 515: Statements within "Culture and Cultural Processes" are from Stella Ting-Toomey, "Ethnic Identity and Close Friendship in Chinese-American College Students," *International Journal of Intercultural Relations*, 1981, Vol. 5, 383–406.

LINK TO ANSWER KEY

A complete Answer Key is provided in the Instructor's Manual. Instructors are granted automatic permission to reprint it.

INDEX